Late Ottoman Origins of Modern Islamic Thought

In this major contribution to Muslim intellectual history, Andrew Hammond offers a vital reappraisal of the role of Late Ottoman Turkish scholars in shaping modern Islamic thought. Focusing on a poet, a sheikh, and his deputy, Hammond re-evaluates the lives and legacies of three key figures who chose exile in Egypt as radical secular forces seized power in republican Turkey: Mehmed Akif, Mustafa Sabri, and Zahid Kevseri. Examining a period when these scholars faced the dual challenge of non-conformist trends in Islam and Western science and philosophy, Hammond argues that these men, alongside Said Nursi who remained in Turkey, were the last bearers of the Ottoman Islamic tradition. Utilising both Arabic and Turkish sources, he transcends disciplinary conventions that divide histories along ethnic, linguistic, and national lines, highlighting continuities across geographies and eras. Through this lens, Hammond observes the long-neglected but lasting impact these Late Ottoman thinkers had upon Turkish and Arab Islamist ideology.

Andrew Hammond is a tutor in Turkish history at the University of Oxford. He formerly worked as a journalist covering the Arab Spring and as a political analyst on Middle East Affairs. His previous books include *What the Arabs Think of America* (2007), *The Islamic Utopia: The Illusion of Reform in Saudi Arabia* (2012), and *Popular Culture in North Africa and the Middle East* (2017).

Cambridge Studies in Islamic Civilization

Editorial Board
Chase F. Robinson, *National Museum of Asian Art, Smithsonian Institution* (general editor)
Anne Broadbridge, *University of Massachusetts Amherst*
Michael Cook, *Princeton University*
Maribel Fierro, *Spanish National Research Council*
Alan Mikhail, *Yale University*
Intisar Rabb, *Harvard University*
Muhammad Qasim Zaman, *Princeton University*

Other titles in the series are listed at the back of the book.

Late Ottoman Origins of Modern Islamic Thought

Turkish and Egyptian Thinkers on the Disruption of Islamic Knowledge

ANDREW HAMMOND
University of Oxford

CAMBRIDGE
UNIVERSITY PRESS

CAMBRIDGE
UNIVERSITY PRESS

Shaftesbury Road, Cambridge CB2 8EA, United Kingdom

One Liberty Plaza, 20th Floor, New York, NY 10006, USA

477 Williamstown Road, Port Melbourne, VIC 3207, Australia

314–321, 3rd Floor, Plot 3, Splendor Forum, Jasola District Centre, New Delhi – 110025, India

103 Penang Road, #05–06/07, Visioncrest Commercial, Singapore 238467

Cambridge University Press is part of Cambridge University Press & Assessment, a department of the University of Cambridge.

We share the University's mission to contribute to society through the pursuit of education, learning and research at the highest international levels of excellence.

www.cambridge.org
Information on this title: www.cambridge.org/9781009199506

DOI: 10.1017/9781009199544

First published 2023

A catalogue record for this publication is available from the British Library.

Library of Congress Cataloging-in-Publication Data
Names: Hammond, Andrew, 1970– author.
Title: Late Ottoman origins of modern Islamic thought : Turkish and Egyptian thinkers on the disruption of Islamic knowledge / Andrew Hammond.
Description: New York : Cambridge University Press, 2022. | Series: Cambridge studies in Islamic civilization | Includes bibliographical references and index.
Identifiers: LCCN 2022030504 (print) | LCCN 2022030505 (ebook) | ISBN 9781009199506 (hardback) | ISBN 9781009199537 (paperback) | ISBN 9781009199544 (epub)
Subjects: LCSH: Islam–Turkey–19th century. | Islam–Egypt–19th century. | Muslim scholars–19th century–Bio-bibliography. | Muslim scholars–20th century–Bio-bibliography. | Mehmet Âkif, 1873-1936. | Ṣabrī, Muṣṭafá, 1869-1954. | Kawtharī, Muḥammad Zāhid ibn al-Ḥasan.
Classification: LCC BP161 .H26 2022 (print) | LCC BP161 (ebook) | DDC 297.09561/09034–dc23/eng/20220711
LC record available at https://lccn.loc.gov/2022030504
LC ebook record available at https://lccn.loc.gov/2022030505

ISBN 978-1-009-19950-6 Hardback

Contents

List of Figures — *page* ix
Preface — xi
Note on Style — xii

1 The Late Ottoman Intellectual Tradition: A Historiographical Review — 1
Introduction — 1
The Construction of Islam as a World Religion — 4
The Modernist View of Decline — 9
The Salafi View of Decline — 14
Late Ottoman Debate over Islam — 19

2 Ottoman Exiles: From Constantinople to Cairo — 26
Mehmed Akif: A Biography — 27
Mustafa Sabri: A Biography — 38
Zahid Kevseri: A Biography — 48
The State of Scholarship — 57
Cairo: Intellectual Centre of the Islamic West — 64
Language and Resistance — 69

3 The Ottoman Scholars and Their Reception of Muḥammad ʿAbduh — 77
Literature Regarding Egypt's Liberal Age — 77
Sabri's Early Attitude towards ʿAbduh — 81
Sabri and the Faraḥ Anṭūn Debate: 'The Imam of Modern Egypt Was a Sceptic' — 94
Akif and the Gabriel Hanotaux Debate: Defending ʿAbduh — 106
Akif and the Anglican Church Affair — 111
Der Wille zur Macht: Akif, Muḥammad Iqbāl, and Muslim Progress — 118

4 The Salafi Revolution: Kevseri's Defence of Sunni Traditionalism 131
Kevseri's Views on ʿAbduh 131
Kevseri's Defence of Ḥanafī-Māturīdism 145
Salafism: Origins and Definitions 155
Salafism, Saudi Arabia, and Nāṣir al-Dīn al-Albānī 162
Salafism and Modern Scholarship 173

5 Nation-State, Islamic State: The Egypt Exiles and New Political Imaginaries 189
Akif's Compromise with *Türkçülük* 189
Sabri's View of the National Struggle 200
Sabri's Radical Discourse in Egypt 204
Kevseri's Understanding of the Islamic Tradition 212
Sabri and Sayyid Quṭb: A Meeting of Minds 216
Abū al-Aʿlā Mawdūdī's Ideas in Quṭb's Conceptual Framework 222
Quṭb's Final Works 228
Who Influenced Quṭb? 232

6 The Late Ottomans' Impact on Modern Islamic Thought 240
Summary of Akif, Sabri, and Kevseri's Work 240
Turkish Republican Islam and Said Nursi 246
Turkish Islamism from 1950 253
Concluding Remarks 264

Appendices 270
Appendix 1: Sabri's Letter to the Vatican, 1925 271
Appendix 2: Chronological List of Kevseri's Articles (by Original Publication Date) 274
Appendix 3: Ottoman Letter Written by Kevseri, 1952, to His Brother in Düzce 277
Appendix 4: Ottoman Letter Written by Akif, 1932, Discussing Plans to Print Gölgeler 278
Bibliography 280
Index 314

Figures

1.1 The Turkish government organised celebrations throughout 2021 marking 100 years since Akif's national anthem was adopted. *page* 179

1.2 Akif's tomb at the Edirnekapı cemetery in Istanbul. 180

1.3 Akif at the Pyramids of Giza with his benefactor Abbas Halim. 181

2.1 Portrait of Zahid Kevseri. 182

2.2 Kevseri in Cairo in his final years. 183

2.3 Kevseri's tomb at the Shāfiʿī cemetery in Cairo. 184

2.4 Street plaque marking Kevseri's tomb in Cairo. 185

3.1 Portrait of Mustafa Sabri. 186

3.2 Sabri's tomb at the Ghafīr cemetery in Cairo. 187

3.3 Grave of Sabri's son İbrahim at the Brookwood cemetery in Woking, UK. 188

A1.1 Sabri's letter to the Vatican, 1925. 271

A3.1 Ottoman letter written by Kevseri, 1952, to his brother in Düzce. 277

A4.1 Ottoman letter written by Akif, 1932, discussing plans to print *Gölgeler*. 278

Preface

The current study began life as a doctoral thesis at the University of Oxford, and its initial question was, what happened to Late Ottoman Islamic thought, beyond its known and extensively researched political, intellectual, and institutional extensions inside modern Turkey? What happens to a centuries-old religious tradition when an elite that believes it has the power to transform, banish, or wish it away in an instant of historical time seizes control of the state to implement a project of radical transformation? The realisation that the major minds of that tradition's final era had in fact decamped to Cairo during the early republican period prompted further questions about their writing, their interactions with intellectuals and religious scholars in Egypt, and their engagement with events back in Turkey. Having co-opted, marginalised, and crushed opposition, Turkey's new leaders had set off on a revolutionary path to discard what they regarded as a corrosive pre-modern tradition in terms of religious belief and practice and embrace a draconian vision of what it means to be 'modern', 'national', and 'rational' that was in equal measure thrilling and horrifying to audiences both regional and global. The study in hand is the result of those investigations, and I would like to thank the various examiners and commentators for helping it wind its way to conclusion. They include Şükrü Hanioğlu, Rosalind O'Hanlon, Christopher Melchert, Laurent Mignon, Ronald Nettler, and Eugene Rogan, as well as the Cambridge Studies in Islamic Civilizations editor Chase Robinson and three anonymous readers. I would also like to thank Gerald Hawting with whom I studied early Islam and Owen Wright with whom I studied Arabic, in addition to Oxford's wonderful Turkish teacher Emine Çakır.

Note on Style

Since the religious scholars in question wrote mainly in Arabic, I have used Arabic as the default language for technical terminology, but when discussing Turkish texts or the Turkish public sphere I use Turkish. In footnotes, the *International Journal of Middle East Studies* is abbreviated to *IJMES* and the journals *Sırat-I Müstakim*, *Sebilürreşad*, and *Beyanülhak* to *SM*, *SR*, and *BH*, respectively. Translations of the various languages cited are by the author, except where otherwise indicated, and I have striven to cite from books from the original language in which they were written, in line with the study's key mission to trace the genealogy and trajectory of ideas. Translations of book and poem titles in Arabic and Turkish are given in the main text on first mention, but not in the notes; however, the list of dated articles by Kevseri in the Appendices includes a full translation. This list is intended to help in understanding how Kevseri's thought developed, since the collection of his articles published posthumously in 1953 lacks the original dates of publication. I have followed the *IJMES* system regarding transliteration of Arabic, Ottoman Turkish, and Persian (used also for Urdu), and other questions of style. Most names and titles from languages using the Arabic script today are transliterated in full, while certain commonly cited names and terms are given in the main text according to the *IJMES* recommendation in terms of italics and diacritics (hajj, hadith, shariʿa, ʿulamaʾ, *ʿālim*, ulema, mufti, Wahhabi, Qurʾan, etc.). Names such as Egyptian president Nasser are written with their common English spelling. Dates are usually rendered in the common era (ce) format, but ce dates are given in brackets when the Ottoman Rumi and Hijri calendar is cited. Dates after the 1 January 1918 alignment of the

Rumi with the Gregorian calendar are usually stated directly in ce format. I have only given diacritics with Ottoman-era Turkish terms that are not in use today, according to the *IJMES* style guide, but I use the Turkish Language Institute (Türk Dil Kurumu)'s guidance on use of the hatted diacritical mark (*şapka*); Turkish book titles and author names published in Latin script with the *şapka* and other transliteration marks are left intact. Ottoman-era words such as *taassub* and Mehmed are given their modern spellings only if a modern work prints them that way.

1

The Late Ottoman Intellectual Tradition

A Historiographical Review

INTRODUCTION

This book is a study of religious thought in an age of radical thinking. It looks specifically at three Late Ottoman thinkers – two of them ulema (Ar. ʿulamaʾ),[1] or scholars of the established forms of Muslim knowledge, and one a poet among the class of devout Muslim intellectuals[2] of the era – whose active period of work was marked by two political events in the countries they moved between, namely the rise to power of the Young Turk movement in Istanbul in 1908 and of the Free Officers in Egypt in 1952.[3] These three figures are Mustafa Sabri Efendi (1869–1954), the last major sheikh ül-Islam (Ar. shaykh al-Islam; chief mufti) of the Ottoman state; Mehmed Zahid Kevseri (1879–1952), Sabri's deputy for education (*ders vekili*) in the Ottoman religious bureaucracy known as the İlmiye; and Mehmed Akif Ersoy (1873–1936),[4] public intellectual and the poet who wrote the words to Turkey's national anthem. Disaffected with the

[1] I use ulema when discussing the Ottoman Turkish texts but ʿulamaʾ when the language is Arabic.

[2] I have used thinkers as a term, while imperfect, to encompass both the ulema and devout Muslim intellectuals. They are separate categories in that ulema are trained as the recognised interpreters of a specific body of sacred knowledge. On the use of 'devout intellectual' see Brett Wilson, *Translating the Qurʾan in an Age of Nationalism: Print Culture and Modern Islam in Turkey* (Oxford: Oxford University Press, 2014), *passim*.

[3] I use the name Istanbul although Turkey only changed its official name from Constantinople in 1930.

[4] Turkey's surname law of 1934 obliged citizens to adopt Turkish surnames. Akif's family adopted Ersoy, but on second reference I use Akif since it is the convention in most of the literature.

republic and its adoption of radical European positivist and materialist philosophies,[5] they each found themselves drawn to Egypt as a place of refuge from the nationalist movement of Mustafa Kemal Atatürk (1881–1938).

Although in exile, they were able to engage with their Egyptian counterparts regarding the iconoclastic ideas of the era impacting Islamic political, legal, and theological culture. Nationalist historiography, through ordering knowledge as variously Egyptian, Arab, or Turkish, has served to conceal this kind of transnational collaboration in the post-Ottoman intellectual world by which thinkers could still operate across national-linguistic lines. For example, a pervasive theme in scholarship regarding republican Turkey has been that Said Nursi (1877–1960), the celebrated *ʿālim* (religious scholar) who remained in Turkey during the early republic, single-handedly carried the torch of Ottoman Islam through his writing while enduring persecution at the hands of the Kemalist state. Yet this misses the role of the Cairo exiles in formulating the first systematic response to secular Turkey and establishing a blueprint for an Islamic Turkish nationalism that in the fullness of time was to win out against its rivals. It was easy to focus attention on Nursi because he shifted from using the Arabic of the ulema class to Turkish at a critical point in the trajectory of the modern state, while Sabri and Kevseri were equally deliberate in choosing to stick with Arabic. Turkish in its Late Ottoman form was essential to Akif's art and message, and his reception in Turkey and the Islamic world was impacted in turn by that fact. These were thinkers then who presented different challenges to the political and cultural categories that dominated following the demise of the Ottoman milieu.

The study examines a corpus of printed materials, including books, articles, and letters, written in Arabic, Ottoman, and Turkish by the three Muslim thinkers in question, tracing the transformation of concepts and terminologies across linguistic and discursive fields, from the Late Ottoman period to their post-Ottoman years in Cairo. Key works include Sabri's *Mawqif al-ʿAql wa-l-ʿIlm wa-l-ʿĀlam min Rabb al-ʿĀlamīn wa-Rusulihi* (The Position of Reason, Knowledge, and the World on

[5] The Young Turk movement was influenced by the French positivism of Auguste Comte and its notion of religion as an impediment to societal progress and the German materialism of Ludwig Büchner and its belief in natural forces as the organising principle of the universe. See M. Şükrü Hanioğlu, *Atatürk: An Intellectual Biography* (Princeton: Princeton University Press, 2017), 48–67; also, Banu Turnaoğlu, 'The Positivist Universalism and Republicanism of the Young Turks,' *Modern Intellectual History*, 14/3 (2017): 777–805.

God and His Messengers, 1949), the collection of Kevseri's writings published as *Maqālāt al-Kawtharī* (Kevseri's Articles, 1953), Akif's poetry collection *Safahat* (Ṣafaḥāt, meaning phases or pages), and the journals *Sırat-ı Müstakim/Sebilürreşad*[6] and *Beyanülhak* (Statement of Truth/God). The research takes in many other Ottoman and Arabic works by intellectuals who contributed to the modernist and Salafi discourse (which I take as distinct categories) of the period and who engaged, often directly, with Akif, Sabri, and Kevseri, including Muḥammad ʿAbduh (1849–1905), Mūsā Jārullāh Bigiev (1874–1949), Muḥammad Iqbāl (1877–1938), Sayyid Quṭb (1906–66), Abū al-Aʿlā Mawdūdī (1903–79), and Nāṣir al-Dīn al-Albānī (1914–99), as well as an array of Turkish-, Arabic-, and English-language secondary literature.

The introductory chapter (Chapter 1) looks at historiographical problems in both Islamic history and the intellectual history of the Late Ottoman period.[7] Chapter 2 gives in-depth profiles of Akif, Sabri, and Kevseri and considers how they have been treated in different fields of scholarship. Chapter 3 examines Sabri's response to the liberal Islamic trend he found dominating public space in the Egypt of the 1930s and 1940s, which had imbibed Europe's secular humanistic understanding of religion, and contrasts this with Akif's work in centering Late Ottoman Islamism around the ideas of ʿAbduh, the leading figure of this school of self-described reformist Islam. Chapter 4 looks at Zahid Kevseri's problematisation of the concept of the terms *salafī* and *salafiyya*, his attempt to withhold the legitimating potential inherent in the 'Salafi' label from the trend (distinct from that of ʿAbduh) that framed its iconoclastic approach to the Islamic legal and theological tradition in those terms. Chapter 5 looks at the three thinkers' views on the modern state as a universal model received from Europe, specifically, Akif's compromise with Turkish nationalism and Sabri's theorising on faith in a post-shariʿa society. The concluding chapter (Chapter 6) considers their impact on the ideological

[6] Both are Qurʾanic terms meaning the right/righteous path.

[7] Turkish nationalist historiography for long excluded the voices of ethno-religious minorities. On the Ottoman Jewish intellectual Avram Galanti (1873–1961) and his engagement with the republic, see Kerem Tınaz, *An Imperial Ideology and Its Legacy: Ottomanism in a Comparative Perspective, 1894–1928* (DPhil thesis, University of Oxford, 2018). On Late Ottoman literature see Laurent Mignon, 'Lost in Transliteration: A Few Remarks on the Armeno-Turkish Novel and Turkish Literary Historiography,' in *Between Religion and Language: Turkish-speaking Christians, Jews and Greek-Speaking Muslims and Catholics in the Ottoman Empire*, ed. Evangelia Balta and Mehmet Sönmez (Istanbul: Eren 2011), 111–23.

trend created by the conditions of modernity known as 'political Islam' (*al-islām al-siyāsī*), making use of interviews with Islamist figures active in the early period of transnational collaboration.

THE CONSTRUCTION OF ISLAM AS A WORLD RELIGION

Enlightenment ideas and their universalisation through European colonial expansion engendered new ways of thinking about religion, rooted in Europe's experience of religious institutions as an oppressive force in political and social life. European scholars and politicians came to objectify Islam as a category of world religion, as historian Wilfred Cantwell Smith theorised in his book *The Meaning and End of Religion* (1962). In the Islamic case this process of what Smith called reification entailed the production of the term Islam itself by Europeans, and then through apologetic osmosis by Muslims themselves, in unfamiliar contexts and senses. This approach to the Islamic tradition located in the conceptual framework of European thought I term modernist. One line of Muslim modernism – defined by its highly political and activist nature – would subsequently develop a theory of Islam as a complete system of life, which had implications for not only the individual but the state, expressed through innovative use of words such as *niẓām*,[8] while another strand within Muslim modernism – mimicking secular humanism – would be comfortable with the Enlightenment's individualist notion of religion as, in anthropologist Talal Asad's description, 'anchored in personal experience, expressible as belief-statements, dependent on private institutions, and practised in one's spare-time', on which basis various versions of secularism would develop.[9] In *Orientalism* (1978) Edward Said would re-frame this Islam-made-in-Europe through the prism of his discursive framework of 'Orientalism', which for him was a term that not only described scholars who studied 'the East' but the paradigm of thought made possible by European power and by which Europeans conceived of outside cultural groupings in a manner that stressed difference and need for reform.

[8] Wilfred Cantwell Smith, *The Meaning and End of Religion* (Minneapolis: Fortress Press, 1991), 115–17.

[9] Talal Asad, *Genealogies of Religion: Discipline and Reasons of Power in Christianity and Islam* (Baltimore: Johns Hopkins University Press, 1993), 207. For German philosopher Immanuel Kant (d. 1804) the key point of the Enlightenment was attaining untutored freedom of thought, first and foremost in religious affairs; see 'Was ist Aufklärung?' (1784); www.projekt-gutenberg.org/kant/aufklae/aufkl001.html.

Scholars across numerous fields of the humanities have examined how Muslim intellectual, cultural, historical, and moral understandings of the world were systematically described, deconstructed, and denigrated as unfit for what European intellectuals considered to be a new stage of social organisation.[10] The German philosopher Hegel (1770–1831) was one of the first prominent voices to present a systematic theory of Islam ('Mohametanism') as a civilisation that had run out of steam. In his series of lectures on the philosophy of history, first delivered in 1822, Hegel said Islam reflected an Arab obsession with the abstract that made for poetry good enough to fire the imagination of Goethe and science and philosophy useful to medieval Europe. But now that the north Europeans were marching to glory through the 'all-enlightening sun' (*die Alles verklärende Sonne*) of the Reformation, Islam had 'vanished from the stage of history' and 'retreated into Oriental ease and repose', he declared.[11] French historian and politician Francois Guizot's *Histoire générale de la civilisation en Europe* (General History of Civilisation in Europe, 1828) also posited the Reformation as the great event that unleashed Europe's creative powers and facilitated its civilisational advance ('une insurrection de l'esprit humain contre le pouvoir absolu dans l'ordre spirituel'),[12] while Arab-Islamic civilisation was in a state of stagnation (*état stationnaire*) because of its 'confusion of moral and material authority'[13] – a theme of modernist reform discourse that was to echo throughout the century as European entanglement with Muslim societies increased.

In *Islam in Liberalism* Joseph Massad identifies a second impulse for negative depictions of Islam. He examines the manner with which nineteenth-century European liberalism projected anxiety over the injustices of Europe's incomplete project of progress – the mass violence of colonialism, the dark Satanic mills of industrialisation, political and economic marginalisation of subaltern groups – onto an Oriental exterior.

[10] Recent studies of note include Joseph Massad, *Islam in Liberalism* (Chicago: University of Chicago Press, 2015); Shahab Ahmed, *What Is Islam?: The Importance of Being Islamic* (Princeton: Princeton University Press, 2016); Khaled El-Rouayheb, *Islamic Intellectual History in the Seventeenth Century: Scholarly Currents in the Ottoman Empire and the Maghreb* (Cambridge: Cambridge University Press, 2015); Muḥammad Qasim Zaman, *Modern Islamic Thought in a Radical Age: Religious Authority and Internal Criticism* (Cambridge: Cambridge University Press, 2012).

[11] G. W. F. Hegel, *The Philosophy of History* (Mineola, NY: Dover Publications, 1956), 355–60.

[12] François Guizot, *Histoire générale de la civilisation en Europe* (Paris: Victor Masson Libraire, 1851), 295.

[13] Ibid., 71.

This procedure allowed for a proliferation of phenomena understood as Islamic, including history, peoples, philosophy, sexual practices, cuisine, sartorial standards, and culture,[14] while Christian traditions were the template for thinking of *kalām* (rationalist discussion of Islamic doctrine) and *ʿaqīda* (dogma, belief, tenet) as theology, shariʿa as law, or *ṣalāh* as prayer. The breadth of terms deployed in Ottoman Turkish texts for Islam – *İslam*, *İslamiyet*, *İslamlık*, *Müslümanlık*, *İslam dini* – gives some indication of how jarring this reductive, homogenising construction of Islam must have been. Turkish republican historiography tended to parallel British and French scholarship in presenting Islamic institutions and belief systems as an impediment to progress.[15]

A third motivation behind the production of this Europeanised Islam was, as Said established, the tying of its fortunes to the colonial project.[16] Progress in other societies would come through the civilising mission of their ideas, whether delivered through colonialism or otherwise, but Islam was viewed as a dangerous creedal force commanding fanatical impulses of potential resistance to European power in the many colonies where Britain and France ruled over Muslim-majority populations. It was in this context that the term pan-Islamism was produced in British and French policy debate.[17] In the late nineteenth century Britain was troubled by the Ottoman state's use of Islamic motifs because of a perceived potential to stoke resistance to British power in Egypt and India.[18] This fed a tendency to stress division between putative national Islams. Wilfred Scawen Blunt, a British diplomat then writer, outlined a blueprint for an Arab caliphate in the Hijaz with symbolic spiritual powers that would engender an Islamic

[14] Massad, *Islam in Liberalism*, 4–6.

[15] Bernard Lewis in *The Emergence of Modern Turkey* (London: Oxford University Press, 1961) refers to 'reactionaries', and reaction (*irtica*) is a theme in Feroz Ahmad, *The Turkish Experiment in Democracy 1950–1975* (London: Hurst, 1977). French histories such as Robert Mantran's *Histoire de la Turquie* (Paris: Presses Universitaires de France, 1952) followed in the footsteps of Pierre Loti (1850–1923) et al. who presented Islam as an oppressive force in Late Ottoman society.

[16] Edward Said, *Orientalism* (New York: Vintage Books, 1994), 1–3, 58–9, 113–22, 343.

[17] This term appears as early as 1883 in French journalist Gabriel Charmes' *L'avenir de la Turquie: Le panislamisme* (Paris: Calmann Lévy, 1883). See Cemil Aydın, *The Idea of the Muslim World: A Global Intellectual History* (Cambridge/London: Harvard University Press, 2017).

[18] On how this played out in the Arabian Peninsula see William Ochsenwald, *Religion, Society, and the State in Arabia: The Hijaz under Ottoman Control, 1840–1908* (Columbus: Ohio State University Press, 1984), and Frederick Anscombe, *The Ottoman Gulf: The Creation of Kuwait, Saudi Arabia, and Qatar* (New York: Columbia University Press, 1997).

reformation outside 'the incubus of Turkish scholasticism' and disabused of the 'dream of empire'.[19] Even those Muslim intellectuals who grasped instinctively that European knowledge could not be disassociated from the physical control Europe exerted over their societies – that this knowledge was tainted by its serving imperial interests – were susceptible to the notion that Islam as the Europeans had constructed it was fundamental to their failure to maintain a pace of civilisational advance that would have kept European interventions at bay. In other words, European criticisms of Islam, however much they were repudiated, succeeded in problematising aspects of belief and practice in the minds of thinkers across Muslim societies who operated within a paradigm of reform derived terminologically from the Arabic *tajdīd* (renewal).[20]

European modernity's view of religion as irrational and a bar to civilisational progress brought with it a specific compartmentalisation of pre-modern time. With Europe's self-awareness of itself in the eighteenth century as experiencing what was termed an age of Enlightenment (*die Aufklärung*; *le siècle des Lumières*), new thinking conceptualised history as a discipline demarcating time via a tripartite division of ancient, medieval, and modern.[21] From the 1980s post-colonial studies began to push back against this taxonomy as an inaccurate, colonial imposition and to experiment with the notion of the pre-modern, which would fit somewhere between the late medieval period and the industrial capitalism of the nineteenth century. The pre-modern also served the purpose of restoring agency to non-European cultural groups in the Western story of what

[19] Wilfrid Scawen Blunt, *The Future of Islam* (Richmond: Curzon, 2001); 130–1, 174–5. Sylvia Haim suspected that ʿAbd al-Raḥmān al-Kawākibī derived his idea of an Arab caliphate in *Umm al-Qurā* (1900) from Blunt; 'Blunt and Kawakibi,' *Oriente Moderno*, 35/3 (1955): 132–43. This thesis is not widely accepted.

[20] Many scholars in the early Islamic centuries were bestowed with the title *mujaddid* by their followers on the basis of the hadith in which the Prophet says that every hundred years God will send someone who renews (*yujaddid*) the *dīn* of the *umma*; see Abū Dāwūd, 'Kitāb al-Malāḥim,' in *Sunan Abī Dāwūd*, ed. Shuʿayb al-Arnāʾūṭ, 8 vols (Damascus: al-Risāla al-ʿĀlamiyya, 2009), 5/349, no. 4291. The concept of the millennial *mujaddid* likely began with Indian Naqshbandī Sufi shaykh Aḥmad Sirhindī (1564–1624), whose *mujaddid* fulfils some functions of prophecy after Muḥammad; see Yohanan Friedmann, *Shaykh Aḥmad Sirhindī: An Outline of His Thought and a Study of His Image in the Eyes of Posterity* (New Delhi/Oxford: Oxford University Press), 13–21. In the late nineteenth century *tajdīd* emerges in public discussion as a broad concept for meeting the European challenge, overtaking previous notions of the *mujaddid*.

[21] Alexander Woodside, *Lost Modernities: China, Vietnam, Korea, and the Hazards of World History* (Cambridge, MA: Harvard University Press, 2006), 35. Reinhart Koselleck, *Futures Past: On the Semantics of Historical Time* (Cambridge, MA: MIT Press, 1985), 235.

came in the late nineteenth century to be called modernity.[22] It has allowed scholars to develop the notion of multiple modernities,[23] or nineteenth-century global history in which non-European peoples are integrated into a comprehensive narrative of a world system in formation.[24] This new terminology opened space for efforts to uncover modern temporality in India in response to British colonial scholars who developed the trope of the 'Hindu mind' that lacked a concept of historical time[25] and to discover early modern practices in diverse contexts such as eighteenth-century Japan, thirteenth-century China, and eleventh-century Java.

The field has not been without its critics,[26] but it is striking how long disinterest in writing Muslims into the category of pre-modernity has persisted[27] – a consequence, it would appear, of the pervasive theory of decline among both Orientalist and Muslim scholars in the nineteenth century.[28] Indeed, the ancient/medieval/modern arrangement of historical time meshes remarkably well with their classificatory framework – of the classical period of the early Islamic era with its imperial expansion and

22 The term *modernité* was coined by French writer Charles Baudelaire in his essay on artistic expression and its ability to express fast-developing Parisian life in *Le Peintre de la vie moderne* (1863); Baudelaire (trans. Jonathan Mayne), *The Painter of Modern Life and Other Essays*, 2nd ed. (London: Phaidon, 1995), 12–15.

23 S. N. Eisenstadt, 'Multiple Modernities,' *Daedalus*, 129/1 (Winter 2000): 1–29. Sudipto Kaviraj emphasises the divergent paths within Europe, contrasting British and French models of industrialisation and democracy with Germany, Italy, and Russia; Kaviraj, 'An Outline of a Revisionist Theory of Modernity,' *European Journal of Sociology*, 46/3 (2005): 497–526.

24 Christopher Bayly, *The Birth of the Modern World, 1780–1914: Global Connections and Comparisons* (Oxford: Blackwell, 2004); Immanuel Wallerstein, 'The Rise and Future Demise of the World Capitalist System: Concepts for Comparative Analysis,' *Comparative Studies in Society and History*, 16/4 (1974): 387–415.

25 Velcheru Narayana Rao and David Shulman, *Textures of Time: Writing History in South India, 1600–1800* (Delhi: Permanent Black, 2001); and Rosalind O'Hanlon, 'Contested Conjunctures: Brahman Communities and "Early Modernity" in India,' *American Historical Review*, 118/3 (2013): 765–87.

26 See Sheldon Pollock, 'Pretextures of Time,' *History and Theory*, 46 (October 2007): 366–83; Dipesh Chakrabarty, 'The Muddle of Modernity,' *American Historical Review*, 116/3 (June 2011): 663–75; and Jack Goldstone, 'The Problem of the "Early Modern" World,' *Journal of Sociology* 46/3 (2005): 249–84. The Marxist analysis of the Subaltern Studies group of Ranajit Guha also disliked the notion of pre-modernity; see Christopher Chekuri, 'Writing Politics Back into History,' *History and Theory* 46 (October 2007): 384–95.

27 The alternative term 'early modern' has seen a profusion of scholarly output since the 2000s in relation to the Ottoman empire in particular.

28 In 2010 the American University of Beirut held a symposium entitled 'Inhitat: Its Influence and Persistence in the Writing of Arab Cultural History'; www.beirut.com/l/5486 (accessed 19 June 2016).

construction of a vast legal-theological edifice (posited as ending with the Mongol destruction of Baghdad in 1258 and/or the rise of the Ottomans), followed by a post-classical decline (*inḥiṭāṭ*) in Muslim political power and the vitality of the Islamic system of knowledge, before recovering through the paradigm shifts of renaissance (*nahḍa*) and revival (*tajdīd*) from the nineteenth century (for modernists) or from the Wahhabi movement in the eighteenth century (for Salafis).

THE MODERNIST VIEW OF DECLINE

Decline has been a powerful and persistent paradigm for understanding the trajectory of Islamic societies before the colonial encounter.[29] Halil İnalcık's *The Ottoman Empire: The Classical Age, 1300–1600*, which has gone through numerous imprints since its publication in 1973, claims to find the beginnings of failure to meet the nineteenth-century challenge of Europe in a sixteenth-century 'triumph of fanaticism',[30] by which he means the juridical culture of the shariʿa schools and the rise of the Kadızadelis (Ḳāżīzādelī), the puritan movement that took up the anti-Sufi ideas of theologian Birgivi Mehmed (d. 1573). Writing firmly within the discursive framework of European Orientalism and the Muslim modernists, İnalcık depicts the shariʿa tradition of compilation, annotation, and commentary of foundational legal texts as hindering later jurists' ability to innovate[31] and he sees the Janissaries' storming of the Galata observatory in 1580 after the Ottoman ulema condemned astronomy and astrology[32] as an example of the zealotry that came to dominate. A professor at Chicago University who published mainly in English, İnalcık was typical of a tradition of republican historiography that fell

[29] See Muhammad Iqbal, *The Reconstruction of Religious Thought in Islam* (London: Oxford University Press, 1934); Fazlur Rahman, *Islam and Modernity: Transformation of an Intellectual Tradition* (Chicago: University of Chicago Press, 1982); Ali Bulaç, *İslam Dünyasında Düşünce Sorunları* (Istanbul: Burhan Yayınları, 1983); Wilfred Cantwell Smith, *Islam in Modern History* (Princeton: Princeton University Press, 1957); Nabil Matar, 'Confronting Decline in Early Modern Arabic Thought,' *Journal of Early Modern History*, 9/1 (2005): 51–78.

[30] Halil İnalcık, *The Ottoman Empire: The Classical Age, 1300–1600* (London: Weidenfeld & Nicolson, 1973), 3–4. Another definitive text is Bernard Lewis, 'Some Reflections on the Decline of the Ottoman Empire,' *Studia Islamica*, 9 (1958): 111–27.

[31] İnalcık, *The Ottoman Empire*, 173.

[32] Ibid., 179.

under the influence of Orientalist problematisation of Islam.[33] There are few fields in Late Ottoman history that the discourse of decline has not touched. E. J. W. Gibb could describe the Turks in racialist terms in his *A History of Ottoman Poetry* (1900–9) as a people who, after the wholesale adoption of Persian culture, were unable to produce an original literature of their own since their true genius 'lies in action, not in speculation'.[34] Laurent Mignon argues that this rejection of the Ottoman past was internalised in two stages: via the writings of poet, playwright, and Ottoman bureaucrat Namık Kemal (1840–8), who derided the literature as nothing more than 'old wives tales' (*kocakarı masalı*), and the work of the theorist of Turkish nationalism Ziya Gökalp (1876–1924), who described the Ottoman ruling class and their literary output as foreign, even colonial, in that its overlay of Arabic and Persian language and multi-ethnic authorship did not reflect a Turkish aesthetic or interest.[35] Indeed, in the republican era the Late Ottoman novel was for long regarded as a failure because it did not conform to European conventions.[36]

ʿAbduh was also susceptible to the trope of decline as both an Arab and an Islamic phenomenon through the influence of European intellectuals he read such as Guizot, liberal Protestant theologian David Strauss, and positivists such as Herbert Spencer, whom he met during a trip to Britain.[37] Guizot was cited in *al-Radd ʿalā al-Dahriyyīn* (Refutation of the Materialists, 1886), the Arabic translation of Jamāl al-Dīn al-Afghānī's

33 Republican historians who took this approach include Fuat Köprülü, Şemsettin Günaltay, Yūsuf Akçura, İsmail Hakkı Uzunçarşılı, Ömer Lütfi Barkan. Like Balkan historians, they treated the Ottoman Empire as a foreign occupation. See Buşra Ersanlı, 'The Ottoman Empire in the Historiography of the Kemalist Era: A Theory of Fatal Decline,' in *The Ottomans and the Balkans: A Discussion of Historiography*, ed. Fikret Adanir and Suraiya Faroqhi (Leiden: Brill, 2002), 115–54.

34 E.J.W. Gibb (ed. Edward G. Browne), *A History of Ottoman Poetry*, 6 vols. (Warminister: The E.J.W. Gibb Memorial Trust, 2013), 1: 6–7. On Gibb, see Walter G. Andrews, 'Ottoman Lyrics: Introductory Essay,' in *Ottoman Lyric Poetry: An Anthology*, ed. Walter G. Andrews, Najaat Black, Mehmet Kalpaklı (Seattle: University of Washington Press, 2006), 3–24; and Victoria Holbrook, *The Unreadable Shores of Love: Turkish Modernity and Mystic Romance* (Austin: University of Texas Press, 2004), 16–31.

35 Laurent Mignon, 'Sömürge Sonrası Edebiyat ve Tanzimat Sonrası Edebiyat Üzerine Notlar,' in *Elifbâlar Sevdası*, Laurent Mignon (Ankara: Hece Yayınları, 2003), 77–89.

36 This view was challenged by the seminal study of Berna Moran, *Türk Romanına Eleştirel bir Bakış: Ahmet Mithat'tan, A. H. Tanpınar'a* (İstanbul: İletişim Yayınları, 1983).

37 Albert Hourani, *Arabic Thought in the Liberal Age 1798–1939* (Cambridge: Cambridge University Press, 1983), 135.

(1838–97) attack on Indian positivism, *Haqīqat-i Mazhab-i Naycharī*, which ʿAbduh translated with al-Afghānī's assistant ʿĀrif Efendi: al-Afghānī, ʿAbduh's early mentor, suggesting that Islam required the kind of Protestant revolution that Guizot had outlined in his history.[38] ʿAbduh gave lectures on Guizot's book to Azharīs at the Dār al-ʿUlūm teacher training school in Cairo,[39] and his biographer Mark Sedgwick surmises that his lost work *Falsafat al-Ijtimāʿ wa-l-Tārīkh* (Philosophy of Society and History) applied Guizot's model of rising and falling civilisations to Arab history as a typology.[40] But its influence can be felt in ʿAbduh's theological statement *Risālat al-Tawḥīd* (Treatise on Unicity, 1897), which unlike a typical work of the genre placed Islam within a wider framework of societal evolution in human history. In his lecture on 'Islam and Science' delivered at the Sorbonne in 1883, two years after France added Tunisia to its North African possessions, Ernest Renan expounded further on the theme of Islamic decline but with an important shift from the earlier era of Orientalism: Now it was because of the Arabs themselves that Islam remained hostile to science,[41] despite Napoleon's 1798 expedition to Egypt opening up new vistas for Islam's rationalism *manqué*.[42] The response of Ottoman statesman and man of letters Namık Kemal in his *Renan Müdafaanamesi* (Refutation of Renan, 1910) was one of the strongest of the time, assailing Renan's linguistic mistakes and projection of Europe's history of religious intolerance onto an exogenous tradition.[43] As Mignon points out, Kemal used Renan's lecture as the occasion for one of the earliest attacks on Orientalist scholarship's claims to expertise,[44] and with Kemal we can see an early articulation of Said's theory that Europe's

38 Jamāl al-Dīn al-Afghānī (trans. Muḥammad ʿAbduh and ʿĀrif Efendi), *al-Radd ʿalā al-Dahriyyīn* (Cairo: Maṭbaʿat al-Mawsūʿāt, 1903, 3rd ed.), 65–6.

39 Ibid., 132.

40 Mark Sedgwick, *Muhammad Abduh* (Oxford: Oneworld, 2009), 16–17.

41 Bernard Lewis argued the same: see 'The Mongols, the Turks and the Muslim Polity,' *Transactions of the Royal Historical Society*, 18 (1968): 49–68.

42 In his response in French, al-Afghānī conceded the notion of religion as hostile to science; see Ernest Renan, *L'Islam et la science; avec la réponse d'Afghâni* (Montpellier: Archange Minotaure, 2003).

43 Namık Kemal, *Renan Müdafaanamesi* (Istanbul: Mahmut Bey Matbaası, 1910); issued in modern Turkish as Abdurrahman Küçük (trans.), *Renan Müdâfaanâmesi* (Ankara: Kültür ve Turizm Bakanlığı, 1988).

44 Laurent Mignon, 'Of Moors, Jews and Gentiles,' *Journal of Turkish Studies*, 35/1 (June 2011): 65–83; includes a review of other early responses to Renan.

Islam was a discursive prop to its exercise of unprecedented political and economic power over Muslim peoples.[45]

This new European focus on racial themes accompanied Darwin's theories on evolution and served imperial interests in the late nineteenth-century scramble for colonies. Britain and France feared the rallying power of Islam as a religious system whose hold over the believer was in general unimpaired by enlightenment and scientism. The discursive fragmentation of the Islamicate into ethnic constituent parts functioned as one way of managing this perceived challenge to imperial power in India and Africa. Problematisation of 'the Arabs' and 'the Turks' engendered in the colonial subject a heightened sense of historic duty to meet the challenge of civilisational responsibility set by Europe through delinking. Turkish, Egyptian, and Levantine intellectuals were particularly influenced by Gustave Le Bon (1841–1931). Many of his works were translated into Arabic including *La psychologie des foules* (The Psychology of Crowds, 1885), *Les lois psychologiques de l'évolution des peuples* (Psychological Laws of the Evolution of Peoples, 1894), the third part of *Les premières civilisations* (The First Civilisations, 1889), and *La civilisation des Arabes* (The Civilisation of the Arabs, 1884), which concluded with the statement that 'peu de races se sont élevées plus haut, mais peu de races sont descendues plus bas' (few nations rose so high then fell so low).[46] Timothy Mitchell argues that Le Bon had the most impact of all among the European political writers on turn-of-the-century Egypt, effecting the 'steady penetration of Orientalist themes into the writings of the Middle East'.[47] Le Bon was also an important source for Jurjī Zaydān, a Lebanese Christian living in post-1882 Egypt who authored decline-themed histories and novels. The government commissioned him to produce two school textbooks, *Tāʾrīkh Miṣr al-Ḥadīth* (Modern History of Egypt, 1889) and *al-Tāʾrīkh al-ʿĀmm* (Universal History, 1890), and his five-volume *Tāʾrīkh al-Tamaddun al-Islāmī* (History of Islamic Civilisation, 1901–6) cites a number of European works including *La civilisation des Arabes* in advancing the

45 On Renan's influence among secular Arab political and intellectual elites see Stefan Wild, 'Islamic Enlightenment and the Paradox of Averroes,' *Die Welt des Islams*, 36/3 (November 1996): 379–90. On Late Ottoman criticism of Western claims to knowledge about Muslim countries, see Zeynep Çelik, *Europe Knows Nothing about the Orient: A Critical Discourse from the East, 1872–1932* (Istanbul: Koç University Press, 2021).

46 Gustave Le Bon, *La civilisation des Arabes* (Paris: Firmin-Didot, 1884), 677.

47 Timothy Mitchell, *Colonising Egypt* (Berkeley: University of California Press, 1991), 169.

paradigm of rise and fall.[48] Guizot's *état stationnaire* and Renan and Le Bon's *décadence* are reproduced in the language of ʿAbduh's generation as *jumūd* (stagnation)[49] and *inḥiṭāṭ* (decline).[50] By contrast it was the elitism of Le Bon's abhorrence of the masses, privileging of the military caste, and racial supremacism that appealed to Ottoman elites, including the Young Turks in opposition, their Committee for Union and Progress (İttihad ve Terakki Cemiyeti, or CUP) once in power, and Mustafa Kemal's early republic.[51]

During this period ʿAbduh shifted position to viewing colonial Britain as too strong a power to resist, becoming a confidante of first Blunt and later Britain's post-invasion colonial administrator Lord Cromer.[52] Indian thinker Sayyid Aḥmad Khān (1817–98), founder of the modernist Aligarh school, had already reached similar conclusions regarding how to manage European power following the crushing of the anti-British revolt of 1857.[53] In British India colonial interventions had already gone much further than abstract argument and polemics, engaging directly in remodelling Islamic juridical and education systems.[54] Reforms began in 1790 with the abolition of blood money for murder and the introduction of hard labour to replace extreme punishments such as cutting off of limbs; specification of crimes for which a judge could impose discretionary punishments in 1803; codification of lashes and jail as the punishment for adultery in 1817; the end of the universal applicability of Muslim criminal law to non-Muslims in 1832; and the introduction of English trial by jury and revival of Hindu institutions such as the village assembly (*panchayat*).

[48] Many intellectuals objected to Zaydān's approach; their writings were collected by Rashīd Riḍā in *Intiqād Kitāb Taʾrīkh al-Tamaddun al-Islāmī* (Cairo: al-Manār, 1912).

[49] ʿAbduh, *Al-Islām bayn al-ʿIlm wa-l-Madaniyya* (Cairo: Dār al-Hilāl, 1960), 122, 142, 160.

[50] Al-Afghānī and ʿAbduh, *al-ʿUrwa al-Wuthqā* (Cairo: Hindāwī, 2014), 38, 53, 61, 72, 87, 112, 119, 161, 162.

[51] His main Turkish translator was CUP intellectual Abdullah Cevdet, whose most influential translation was *Les lois psychologiques de l'évolution des peuples* as *Ruhü'l-Akvam* (Cairo: Matbaa-i İctihad, 1907). For a summary of his impact see M. Şükrü Hanioğlu, *The Young Turks in Opposition* (New York: Oxford University Press), 206–11, and Hanioğlu, *Atatürk*, 44–5.

[52] Cromer thought ʿAbduh was a secret agnostic, see Earl of Cromer, *Modern Egypt*, 2 vols. (London: Macmillan, 1908), 2: 179–80. The friendship was used to discredit ʿAbduh; see Sedgwick, 108–14.

[53] On the post-1857 Muslim schools in India see ʿAzīz Aḥmad, *Islamic Modernism in India and Pakistan, 1857–1964* (London: Oxford University Press, 1967) and Zaman, *Modern Islamic Thought*, 143–75.

[54] Aḥmad, *Islamic Modernism*, 17–26.

Khān sought justification within the Islamic tradition for positions that conformed with European norms. He defended eating non-halal meat in a treatise on eating with People of the Book,[55] presaging ʿAbduh's famous Transvaal fatwa in 1903 regarding consumption of meat slaughtered by Christians and the wearing of European hats.[56] Similar dynamics were at play in Muslim Central Asia: Kazan Tatars established themselves in the 1850s and 1860s as the pioneers of new modes of education that would integrate Muslims into liberalising Russian imperial culture and society.[57]

THE SALAFI VIEW OF DECLINE

Decline was central to the thinking of those engaged in an internal critique of the Islamic tradition, one that challenged systematic adherence to the methodologies of the four Sunni legal traditions (*taqlīd*) for reasons related to their communal contexts. Shāh Walīullāh (d. 1762) was a Ḥanafī hadith scholar from India who upheld the monistic theosophy of Ibn ʿArabī (d. 1240) as well as the theological positions – associated with the Abbasid-era hadith movement – of the Ḥanbalī qadi and theologian of Damascus Ibn Taymiyya (d. 1328). He was driven by a concern over syncretic approaches prevalent in Mughal India, where Muslim elites were politically dominant but Muslim practice co-existed with diverse non-Muslim traditions.[58] Yemeni Zaydī scholar Muḥammad al-Shawkānī (d. 1834), on the other hand, sought to stabilise the political underpinnings of the Zaydī imamate through denuding the Zaydī imam of his role as a *mujtahid* and forbidding rebellion against the imam.[59] Both Walīullāh and

55 Ibid., 36.

56 Sedgwick, *Abduh*, 97–9, 110–11.

57 Danielle Ross, 'Caught in the Middle: Reform and Youth Rebellion in Russia's Madrasas, 1900-10,' *Kritika: Explorations in Russian and Eurasian History*, 16/1 (2015): 60–1. See also Adeeb Khalid, *The Politics of Muslim Cultural Reform: Jadīdism in Central Asia* (Berkeley: University of California Press, 1998).

58 Gail Minault, 'Sayyid Aḥmad Dehlavi and the "Delhi Renaissance",' in *Delhi Through the Ages: Essays in Urban History, Culture, and Society*, ed. Robert E. Frykenberg (Delhi: Oxford University Press, 1986), 287–98.

59 See Brinkley Messick, *The Calligraphic State: Textual Domination and History in a Muslim Society* (Berkeley: University of California Press, 1993), 149–51, and Bernard Haykel, *Revival and Reform in Islam: The Legacy of Muḥammad al-Shawkānī* (Cambridge: Cambridge University Press, 2003). Al-Shawkānī said a Muslim should only rise against an imam who displays blatant *kufr* (unbelief), the imam need only be a member of the Prophet's tribe Quraysh rather than of the specific lineage of ʿAlī/Fāṭima, and the imam should be free to designate his successor.

al-Shawkānī attacked *taqlīd* and emphasised the study of hadith independently of the methodologies of the legal schools. Walīullāh inspired the Ahl-i Hadis movement in India, while al-Shawkānī was influential for nineteenth-century scholars in Ottoman Baghdad and Damascus who articulated similar ideas around the organising motif of a return to the ways of the *salaf* (the early Muslims) with as little mediation of the elite scholastic culture of the *madhāhib* as possible.[60]

Modernist ʿulamaʾ and intellectuals, on the other hand, deployed these ideas in the service of their rationalist project, which though couched in Islamic terminologies and historical references was impacted by the European categories of reformation and enlightenment. Rather than traditionist disdain for post-classical legal and theological output, reformers upholding the scriptural authority of the Qurʾan could have the Lutheran model in mind to engender European-style progress.[61] Indeed, historian Reinhard Schulze sees a calque on the West European classicism of the era in the discourse around the *salaf* developed by late nineteenth-century modernist reformers.[62] ʿAbduh reworked al-Shawkānī's ideas on *ijmāʿ* (consensus) among jurists and used *ijtihād* (legal reasoning that engages directly with basic sources of Qurʾan and hadith) freed of the requirement to follow the legal reasoning of authoritative jurisprudents to arrive at desired conclusions in which the methodology of *uṣūl al-fiqh* was a secondary concern.[63] In this manner shariʿa was adapted to fit an understanding of modernity which, through codification in British India, the Ottoman Mecelle, the Turkish republic's civil code of 1926, and the changes introduced in Egypt and Arab states from the time of ʿAbduh to the work of ʿAbd al-Razzāq al-Sanhūrī in drafting Egypt's 1948 civil code, 'closed the open text of shariʿa jurisprudence'.[64] In *Risālat al-Tawḥīd*

[60] See David Commins, *Islamic Reform: Politics and Social Change in Late Ottoman Syria* (New York: Oxford University Press, 1990) and Itzchak Weismann, *Taste of Modernity: Sufism, Salafiyya, and Arabism in Late Ottoman Damascus* (Leiden: Brill, 2001).

[61] Juan Cole, 'Printing in Urban Islam,' in *Modernity & Culture: From the Mediterranean to the Indian Ocean*, ed. Leila Fawaz, Christopher Bayly, Robert Ilbert (New York: Columbia University Press, 2002), 352.

[62] Reinhard Schulze, *A Modern History of the Islamic World* (London/New York: I. B. Tauris, 2000), 18. See also Schulze, 'Was ist die Islamische Aufklärung?' *Die Welt des Islams*, 36/3 (1996): 276–325.

[63] Sedgwick, *Abduh*, 122–8.

[64] Messick, *The Calligraphic State*, 56. See also Wael Hallaq, *Sharīʿa: Theory, Practice, Transformations* (Cambridge: Cambridge University Press, 2009).

ʿAbduh went even further in generalising *taqlīd* as the antithesis of human progress; in other words *taqlīd* represents decline itself.[65]

In his study of al-Shawkānī, Bernard Haykel argues that while the jurist was aware of Napoleon's occupation of Egypt in 1798, which played a foundational role in subsequent Arab nationalist, Muslim reformist, and Western scholarship of the region, he conveyed no sense that his writings on *ijtihād* and *taqlīd* could be considered a form of response to Europe. 'In formulating these ideas, Shawkānī was unaware of the European enlightenment and perceived no intellectual threat to the world of Islam from Europe . . . For him, the sources of Muslim weakness were intrinsic insofar as they were to be found in the erroneous beliefs and practices of Muslims themselves,' Haykel writes.[66] Similarly, ʿAzīz Aḥmad notes of Walīullāh's opposition to *taqlīd* that it was a breakthrough 'absolutely unconnected with any western influences', inspired by spiritual and historical forces specific to Islamic society in the early eighteenth century and centred on the idea of decline in Mughal and Ottoman intellectual traditions.[67] There have been few attempts to argue that the eighteenth-century religious movement founded by Muḥammad ibn ʿAbd al-Wahhāb (1703–1892) in central Arabia, commonly known as Wahhabism, was in any meaningful way inspired by Europe.[68] So there is reason to resist the tempting assertion that it was European expansion alone that stimulated the notion of Muslim decline and the search for inspiration in earliest Islam.[69]

In Arabic writing in the early twentieth century the term *salafiyya* (Salafism) was coined to describe these revivalist movements, despite the diametrically opposed motivations of these two broad groups subsumed under its umbrella. In time the divergence in intellectual genealogies would find semantic expression in the use of the term *salafiyya* for only the second group, while derivatives of *tajdīd* came more to denote the first in recognition of its Europe-facing nature. This definitional vagueness over *tajdīd* and *salafiyya* is a salient feature in the writing of Islamic

[65] Muḥammad ʿAbduh (ed. Muḥammad ʿImāra), *Risālat al-Tawḥīd* (Cairo: Dār al-Shurūq, 1994), 140–4.

[66] Haykel, *Revival and Reform*, 234.

[67] Aḥmad, *Islamic Modernism*, 41.

[68] Ḥasan Ḥanafī argues Wahhabism was a reaction to European encroachment; 'Al-Salafiyya wa-l-ʿAlmāniyya,' in *Tarihte ve Günümüzde Selefilik*, ed. Ahmet Kavas (Istanbul: Ensar Neşriyat, 2014), 137.

[69] For example, Roxanne Euben, *Princeton Readings in Islamist Thought: Texts and Contexts from al-Bannā to Bin Laden* (Princeton: Princeton University Press, 2009), 5.

intellectual history in the modern period. A third group who could be termed the conservatives, or traditionalists,[70] opposed the reform agenda of both parties. Mustafa Sabri and Zahid Kevseri belong to this set of defenders of the tradition, while Akif we can consider a modernist reformer in the mould of ʿAbduh. In Late Ottoman Istanbul the modernist reformers were by far the loudest voice among the ulema and devout intellectuals because they engaged more forcefully with the dominant ideological trend of the period, that of the nationalists who, deeply influenced by European positivist and materialist philosophy, harboured inimical views of religion's place in public life.

Challenging decline has been easier within historical geographies stripped of their Islamic framing, such as the 'Ottoman empire', 'Ottoman Egypt', or 'early modern Egypt'. Baki Tezcan has been able to argue that Ottoman absolutism was gradually diluted by the socio-political power of the military institution (the Janissaries) and the juridical powers of the ulema, creating what he calls a process of proto-democratisation among the Muslim element of the populace (*reaya*) – a system disrupted by the autocratic reformations of the Tanzimat era.[71] However, a growing body of work is pushing back against tropes of Islamic decline which for long influenced analysis across a variety of socio-historical fields within what Marshall Hodgson called Islamicate society.[72] In a study of seventeenth-century

[70] I use traditionalist as a category within modern Islamic thought, separate from the Ahl al-Ḥadīth, whom I will call traditionists. In the early Islamic field traditionalist is often used to refer to the Ahl al-Ḥadīth; see for example Ahmed El Shamsy, *The Canonization of Islamic Law: A Social and Intellectual History* (New York: Cambridge University Press, 2015), 50, footnotes 27 and 28.

[71] Baki Tezcan, *The Second Ottoman Empire: Political and Social Transformations in the Early Modern World* (Cambridge: Cambridge University Press, 2010), 227–43. The burgeoning literature challenging Ottoman decline include: Cemal Kafadar, 'The Question of Ottoman Decline,' *Harvard Middle Eastern and Islamic Review*, 4/1–2 (1997–8): 30–75; Suraiya Faroqhi, *Artisans of Empire: Crafts and Craftspeople under the Ottomans* (London/New York: I. B. Tauris, 2009); Nelly Hanna, *Artisan Entrepreneurs in Cairo and Early-Modern Capitalism (1600–1800)* (Syracuse, NY: Syracuse University Press, 2011); Rhoads Murphey, *Ottoman Warfare, 1500–1700* (London: UCL Press, 1999); M. Şükrü Hanioğlu, *A Brief History of the Late Ottoman Empire* (Princeton: Princeton University Press, 2008; Daniel Neep, '"What Have the Ottomans Ever Done for Us?" Why History Matters for Politics in the Arab Middle East,' *International Affairs*, 17 September 2021.

[72] Hodgson's three-volume *The Venture of Islam* (1974) created a framework for understanding Islam as a world civilisation transcending different societies through the term Islamicate. It also challenged notions of European exceptionalism in the writing of what he termed world history before the genre solidified. An early pushback also came in Roger Owen, 'The Middle East in the Eighteenth Century – An "Islamic" Society in Decline:

intellectual currents in the Ottoman empire and non-Ottoman North Africa Khaled El-Rouayheb has questioned decline theory as the product of a legalistic outlook shared by both Orientalist scholars and different wings of Muslim reformism in its broadest sense. A default position took hold in twentieth-century Islamic and Western scholarship that placed law rather than the practice of theological reasoning at the heart of Islam,[73] imagining *kalām* as an apologetic practice that since its late Umayyad beginnings placed loyalty to Greek intellectual paradigms above the requirements of Islamic revelation.[74] El-Rouayheb points to two basic problems: this approach ignores other fields of knowledge such as philosophy, logic, astronomy, grammar, and theosophical Sufi thought, and it fails to explain what is inherently irrational or inflexible in a legal system that obliges jurists to consider its precedents, which is what the term *taqlīd*, often misleadingly translated as 'imitation', expresses.[75] *Kalām* was a practice that developed skills in logic and disputation, and it was this process of *taḥqīq* (verification of truth) that early modern Ottoman and North African scholars contrasted with *taqlīd*, not *ijtihād*.[76] Although *kalām* and its associated disciplines evolved and retained its vitality, the post-classical pre-modern period became a 'forgotten chapter in Islamic religious history',[77] El-Rouayheb says, partly because Ottomanists tend to look past ulema material since it was mainly written in Arabic, while Arabic-centred historical fields tend to consider Ottoman history in turn as a discipline unto itself.[78] Both El-Rouayheb and Madeline Zilfi reject the idea of the Kadızadeli movement as emblematic of an Ottoman decay rooted in religion.[79]

A Critique of Gibb and Bowen's *Islamic Society and the West*,' *Review of Middle East Studies*, 1 (1975): 101–12.

73 El-Rouayheb, *Islamic Intellectual History*, 234.

74 Josef van Ess, 'The Logical Structure of Islamic Theology,' in *Logic in Classical Islamic Culture*, ed. Gustave Grunebaum (Wiesbaden: O. Harrassowitz, 1970), 21–50.

75 Precedents in terms of the legal corpus of a school as interpreted by its muftis, not case law established by court judges. On this difference between Muslim and common law see Hallaq, *Sharīʿa*, 178; and also El-Rouayheb, *Islamic Intellectual History*, 358.

76 El-Rouayheb, *Islamic Intellectual History*, 358.

77 Ibid., 200.

78 Ibid., 128. Cole also notes that Ottoman legal texts were in Arabic; 'Printing in Urban Islam,' 357.

79 Madeline Zilfi, *The Politics of Piety: The Ottoman Ulema in the Post-Classical Age (1600–1800)* (Minneapolis: Bibliotheca Islamica, 1988). Yahya Michot links them to Ibn Taymiyya: *Against Smoking: An Ottoman Manifesto* (Oxford: Interface Publications, 2010). Mustapha Sheikh rejects this: *Qadizadeli Revivalism Reconsidered in Light of Aḥmad al-Rūmī al-Āqḥiṣārī's 'Majālis al-Abrār'* (DPhil thesis, University of Oxford, 2011).

LATE OTTOMAN DEBATE OVER ISLAM

Ottoman ulema became the subject of heightened contestation in the decades following the Tanzimat reforms of 1839. Although they continued with their Arabic-language output, the main theatre of their public engagement became the emerging Ottoman Turkish press.[80] The rule of Abdülhamid (from 1876 to 1909, but effectively ending in 1908) served ultimately to diminish their status through their implication in the retrenchment of sultanic absolutism. The Hamidian regime began with the promulgation of the first Ottoman constitution in 1876 but two years later it suspended parliament as territorial losses mounted and proceeded to deploy the İlmiye and Sufi orders in extending the writ of the state and fending off the Western missionary challenge, particularly in the domain of education in the empire's Arab and Kurdish peripheries.[81] This increased the Young Turk opposition movement in its conviction that the ulema and religion in general were an obstacle to the political, economic, juridical, and educational transformations required by scientific modernity. Public discourse objectified the scholars of the pre-modern order and their knowledge as a problem to a greater degree than in Egypt, but this only became consequential following the revolution of 1908 that brought back the constitutional order and freed public space for discussion of previously suppressed questions of religion and state.[82]

With the rise to power of the CUP, the İlmiye institution came under pressure to promote a reformist Islam, which for the CUP meant loosening the hold of the Meşihat (sheikh ül-Islam's office) over education and

[80] Benjamin Fortna, *Learning to Read in the Late Ottoman Empire and the Early Turkish Republic* (Basingstoke: Palgrave Macmillan, 2011); Johann Strauss, 'Who Read What in the Ottoman Empire,' *Middle Eastern Literatures*, 6/1 (2003): 39–76; Elisabeth Kendall, 'Between Politics and Literature: Journals in Alexandria and Istanbul at the end of the Nineteenth Century,' in Fawaz, Bayly, Ilbert, *Modernity & Culture*, 330–43.

[81] Selim Deringil, *The Well-Protected Domains: Ideology and the Legitimation of Power in the Ottoman Empire, 1876–1909* (London: I. B. Tauris, 1998), *passim*.

[82] On the complex situation the ulema found themselves in under Abdülhamid and in the post-1908 order see İsmail Kara, 'Turban and Fez: Ulema as Opposition,' in *Late Ottoman Society: The Intellectual Legacy*, ed. E. Özdalga (London: RoutledgeCurzon, 2005), 162–200; David Kushner, 'The Place of the Ulema in the Ottoman Empire During the Age of Reform (1839–1918),' *Turcica*, 19 (1987): 51–74; Butrus Abu-Manneh, 'Two Concepts of State in the Tanzimat Period: The Hatt-ı Şerif of Gülhane and the Hatt-ı Hümayun,' *Turkish Historical Review*, 6 (2015): 117–37; Amit Bein, *Ottoman Ulema, Turkish Republic: Agents of Change and Guardians of Tradition* (Stanford: Stanford University Press, 2011).

the judiciary.[83] This, one of the biggest questions in Ottoman public life of the time, was debated through the lively publications scene that arose from 1908: mainly, the Muslim modernist journal *Sırat-ı Müstakim* (1908–25, published as *Sebilürreşad* from March 1912), co-edited by Akif; the conservative religious newspaper *Beyanülhak* (1908–12), edited by Sabri; and journals that reframed Islam in fashionable Turkist terms such as the CUP-funded *İslam Mecmuası* (1914–18) and *Türk Yurdu* which were major outlets for nationalist ideologue Ziya Gökalp. In one of the earliest scholarly examinations of this debate, Ahmed Muhiddin used German social science theory to define the modernists as advocates of Islamic Reformation, dubbing them a 'Reformation trend' (*Reformasyon akımı*) whose positions reflected a European view of the path to modernity: access to scripture without priestly mediation, secular approaches to law that dilute the writ of shariʿa courts, creed that stresses human agency and rejects fatalism.[84] In this *Kulturbewegung* they stood in opposition to what Muhiddin called the 'historical Islam' (*tarihî İslam*) of the conservatives who upheld the juridical and theological framework of the Muslim polity in which they were the key functionaries.[85] The Arab reform trend taking Ibn Taymiyya as its cultic hero and intersecting with the Turkish modernists in its critique of Sufism and some aspects of received creed had only limited currency in Istanbul because of its association with the anti-Ottoman Wahhabi movement, its objection to the Ḥanafī-Māturīdī legal-theological system of the Turkish seminaries, and its chauvinistic Arabist undertones.[86] Devout intellectual İsmail Hakkı (1869–1946) was one of the first to integrate the new Arabic usages of *salaf* in his *Yeni İlm-i Kelam* (New Theology, 1920). In describing the Ahl al-Ḥadīth scholars who asserted the primacy of hadith in legal and doctrinal questions, Hakkı used the established term *eseriyye* (Ar. *athariyya*, in reference to *athar*, a report), but he was also innovative in referring to them in Turkish as *Selefiyye* (the spelling given in recent Latin script versions).[87]

[83] Akif's biographer Midhat Cemal Kuntay reports that reformist sheikh ül-Islam Musa Kazım was interested in Spiritism, as many modernists were; *Mehmet Akif: Hayatı-Seciyesi-Sanatı* (Istanbul: Oğlak, 2015), 42–3. See Marwa Elshakry, *Reading Darwin in Arabic, 1860–1950* (Chicago: University of Chicago Press, 2013).

[84] Ahmed Muhiddin, *Modern Türklükte Kültür Hareketi* (Istanbul: Küre, 2004), 128–41. In 1921 Muhiddin completed his doctoral thesis in Leipzig.

[85] Ibid., 114.

[86] Abdulaziz Al-Fahad, 'From Exclusivism to Accommodation: Doctrinal and Legal Evolution of Wahhabism,' *New York University Law Review*, 79 (2004): 500-1.

[87] İsmail Hakkı İzmirli, *Yeni İlmi Kelam* (Ankara: Ankara Okulu, 2013), 91–8; İzmirli İsmail Hakkı, *Yeni İlm-i Kelam* (Istanbul: Evkaf-i İslamiye Matbaası, 1920), 98–106.

It is in this intellectual milieu that the term 'Islamist' first appears. In 1904 Tatar intellectual Yūsuf Akçura (1876–1935) published an article in the Cairo-based journal *Türk* that outlined the three ideological schools competing to define the direction of a reformed Ottoman state: multi-ethnic, multi-confessional Ottomanism (*Osmanlılık*, *Osmanlı milliyeti*); ethnic Turkish unity (*Türklük*, *Türk milliyeti*, *Türk birliği*); pan-Islamic unity (*Müslümanlık*, *İslam birliği*, *İslamiyet politikası*). He concluded with the question: which will be the most beneficial and viable for the Ottoman state, *Müslümanlık* or *Türklük*?[88] As public debate expanded from 1908 these positions began to harden into opposed ideological camps.[89] In a series of eight articles published in *Türk Yurdu* in 1913, titled collectively 'Üç Cereyan' and the basis of his book *Türkleşmek, İslamlaşmak, Muasırlaşmak* (To Become Turkish, To Become Pan-Islamic, To Become Modern, 1918), Ziya Gökalp used the neologism *İslamcılık* alongside *İslamlık*, intending them as parallels to *Türkçülük* and *Türklük* in his discussion of the question of pan-Islamic action and identity.[90] Gökalp never used the term *İslamcı*, which would equate to the English Islamist in modern Turkish, but he did invent the terms *İslam ümmetçisi* and *İslam milliyetçisi*: only the former is acceptable, he said, because it understands an Islamic identity without the state project overtones of Islamic union in the latter.[91] In other words, a Turkist could feel at home talking in abstract terms of the international *ümmet* but *milliyet* should be reserved for ethnic nationalism alone.

The response of Akif's colleague Ahmed Naim (1872–1934) was a series of articles published in 1914 and as a book under the same name, *İslam'da Dava-ı Kavmiyet* (The Question of Nationalism in Islam), in which he argued that the Turkists were reviving the partisan tribalism that the Islamic revolution explicitly rejected in its earliest period. Naim took

[88] Yūsuf Akçura, *Üç Tarz-ı Siyaset* (Ankara: Türk Tarih Kurumu Basımevi, 1976), 36.

[89] Abdullah Gündoğdu, *Ümmetten Millete: Ahmet Ağaoğlu'nun Sırat-ı Müstakim ve Sebilürreşad Dergilerindeki Yazıları Üzerine bir İnceleme* (Istanbul: IQ Kültür Sanat Yayıncılık, 2007), 56.

[90] Ziya Gökalp, *Türkleşmek, İslamlaşmak, Muasırlaşmak* (Istanbul: Yeni Mecmua, 1918). *İslamlık* first appears on p. 9, *İslamcılık* on p. 33. *İslamlık* was already attested in public debate, paralleling *Hristiyanlık* (Christianity).

[91] Ibid., 34. It would be wrong to think of Gökalp at this stage in later Kemalist terms of pushing back against public religion and religiosity at all costs: see Markus Dressler, 'Rereading Ziya Gökalp: Secularism and Reform of the Islamic State in the Late Young Turk Period,' *IJMES*, 47/3 (2015): 511–31.

up the terms *Türkçü* and *İslamcı*, without apparently realising that Gökalp had talked only of Islamism (*İslamcılık*), not Islamists.[92]

How inappropriate this affixing of 'ci' to the words Turk and Islam is! I smell a contrived meaning here. In my view those describing themselves in this manner have chosen the wrong name because it doesn't make sense to call any Turk or Arab *Türkçü* and *Arabcı*. They are, in a word, Turk or Arab. Those with a minimum of expertise in the Turkish language know that '*İslamcı*' too cannot mean Muslim.[93]

Naim sensed that this terminology was intended as a polemical device to preserve the Turkists as believing Muslims in the face of ulema and devout intellectuals who openly charged them with atheism through use of the word *dinsiz* ('without religion').[94] Gökalp never recognised himself in these terms; indeed, their atheistic implication explains the republic's preference for the neologisms *laiklik* and *sekülarizm*.[95] He did use the Arabic-origin word *lā-dīnī* ('non-religious') but as a translation of the French *laïque* when advocating stripping the Ottoman religious establishment of its juridical powers to leave them authority only in matters of personal piety.[96]

By *islamlaşmak* Gökalp had meant an identitarian understanding of the state as a transnational representative of Muslims, with obligations beyond

92 Ahmed Naim, 'İslam'da Dava-ı Kavmiyet,' *Sebilürreşad* (henceforth *SR*), 10 Nisan 1330 (23 April 1914), 12/293: 114–28, and *İslam'da Dava-ı Kavmiyet* (Darülhilaafe: Sebilürreşad Kütüphanesi, 1914), 17.

93 Naim, *İslam'da*, 16, footnote 1.

94 Devout intellectuals wrote in the press from 1908 about the concepts of *dindarlık* and *dinsizlik*, which they used as analogues of the theological concepts of *iman* (faith) and *küfür* (absence of faith); see Mustafa Asım, 'Dindarlık ve Dinsizlik,' *Beyanülhak* (henceforth *BH*), 15 Şubat 1325 (28 February 1909), 2/49: 1038–40.

95 The Arabic *ʿilmāniyya* (separation of knowledge from religion)/*ʿalmāniyya* (separation of politics from religion) only imply atheism by association. Moroccan devout intellectual ʿAbd al-Raḥmān Ṭāhā calls these erasures of religion collectively *dunyāniyya*, his term for secularism, within which he perceives a third arm called *dahrāniyya* (separation of morals from religion); Ṭāhā, *Buʾs al-Dahrāniyya: al-Naqd al-Iʿtimānī li-Faṣl al-Akhlāq ʿan al-Dīn* (Beirut: Arab Network for Research and Publishing, 2014), 11–13. Secularism was coined by English socialist George Holyoake in 1851 to express separation of church and state and a non-theological approach to political, economic, and social affairs; see Holyoake, *English Secularism: A Confession of Belief* (Chicago: The Open Court Publishing Company, 1896).

96 Gökalp did this in two stages: First, in two articles titled 'İslamiyet ve Asri Medeniyet' in *İslam Mecmuası*, 26 Kanunusani 1332 (8 February 1917), 5/51 and 1 Mart 1333 (1 March 1917), 5/52, and translated in Charles Kurzman, ed., *Modernist Islam, 1840–1940: A Sourcebook* (New York: Oxford University Press, 2002), 192–7 (published unsigned, there is debate over their attribution, but Gökalp was likely the author). And second in his *Türkçülüğün Esasları* (Istanbul: Kültür Bakanlığı, 1976 [1923]), 168–9.

its borders that transcended race and language. In another work published first as a series of articles in *Sebilürreşad* and then as a book in 1918 under the title of *İslamlaşmak*,[97] former prime minister Said Halim Paşa (1865–1921) took the debate in a new direction, appropriating Gökalp's term for a theory of Islam as a total system governing the life of the individual and determining the shape of the modern state. 'Islam [*İslamiyet*] is the most perfect human religion [*din*] in that it possesses its own beliefs, ethics based on those beliefs, social values arising from those ethics, and politics springing from its social values,' he wrote. 'The totality of these basic factors is such that they manage the lives of men and though separate they act together to create a homogenous, perfect and indivisible whole [*bir küll*] which encompasses the idealist and positivist schools, like the moral individual who has religion [*dini bulunduğu şahs-ı manevide olduğu gibi*].'[98] This was one of the earliest articulations of the notion of Islam as a comprehensive personal, social, legal, and political system and expressed by the term 'Islamism', taking the reified religion identified by Smith beyond the realm of law and theology and into that of ideology, or the political, in a process of ideologisation.[99] Writing just after his exit from the Ottoman war cabinet, Said Halim also wrote that the current era was characterised by a 'distancing from Islam' (*İslam'dan uzaklaşma*) due to educational and legal innovations of French origin which had led in his view to moral chaos. The implication was that society could not *become* truly Muslim (*islamlaşmak*) if its citizens did not lead the life of believers, thus a process of re-Islamisation is in order. Said Halim's thesis received less attention in republican Turkey than Gökalp's writing, since the devout intellectuals lost out in the early reckoning with nationalism,[100] but

97 İsmail Kara suggests the title may have been Akif's suggestion; *Türkiye'de İslâmcılık Düşüncesi*, 3 vols. (Istanbul: Risale, 1986), 1: xxxvi. It was composed in French but never published in that language.

98 Said Halim Paşa, *İslamlaşmak* (Istanbul: Dār ül-Hilafe, 1918), 4.

99 I use Michael Freeden's definition of ideology as a 'distinct, reified, systems of ideas that exist as quasi-autonomous features of our world and can be studied independently'; Freeden, *Ideology: A Very Short Introduction* (Oxford: Oxford University Press, 2003), 101–2. Freeden's suggestion that political Islam does not fit the definition of ideology in my view contains the erroneous implication that ideology itself is a European category that cannot apply elsewhere.

100 There is one study of Said Halim in English, Ahmet Şeyhun, *Said Halim Pasha: Ottoman Statesman and Islamist Thinker (1865–1921)* (Istanbul: Isis Press, 2003) but also Ḥasan Kayalı, 'Islam in the Thought and Politics of Two Late Ottoman Intellectuals: Mehmed Akif and Said Halim,' *Archivum Ottomanicum*, 19 (2001): 307–33; and Michelangelo Guida, 'The Life and Political Ideas of Grand Vezir Said Halim Pasha,' *İslâm Araştırmaları Dergisi*, 18 (2007): 101–18. On Said Halim's discursive shift re the concept of

ideologised religion would become a major feature of twentieth-century Islamic thought in the hands of figures such as Ḥasan al-Bannā, Abū al-Aʿlā Mawdūdī, and Sayyid Quṭb.[101]

The intense ideological conflict unleashed by the 1908 revolution came to a head in the period 1918–22 as two separate political authorities developed in the context of post-war occupation – the sultanate based in Istanbul which co-operated with the British authorities and the Turkish national parliament (*Türkiye büyük millet meclisi*) established in Ankara in 1920. The ulema and devout intellectuals were faced with tough choices. Akif, Nursi, and a number of other religious figures moved to Ankara in 1920 in the belief that Ankara's victory over invading Greek forces and the political plans of the European Allied powers would lead to a harmonisation of nationalist and religious doctrine in whatever political arrangement emerged in the end. When Britain acquiesced to Ankara's forces taking control of government in Istanbul following the defeat of the Greek armies, Sabri and Kevseri fled abroad, not only because their support of the sultan's government meant likely prosecution and even death, but because they understood it as the final victory of a broadly secular nationalist worldview underpinned by positivism after years of bitter contestation. For Akif and Nursi the choice became co-option in the new educational and religious structures of the Turkish republic, declared in November 1923, or retreat from public life in the face of revolutionary tribunals and harassment of journalists. The death of Ali Kemal Bey, a writer and minister in one of the sultan's cabinets, at the hands of a mob in November 1922 was an indication of what was to come. Sabri, Kevseri, and Akif chose Egypt; Said Nursi remained.

Akif is a figure of enormous controversy. The leading advocate of ʿAbduh's ideas in Turkish-language debate and a gifted poet, Akif agreed to produce a Turkish translation of the Qurʾan for the religious affairs administration known as Diyanet established in 1924.[102] Though he

islamlaşmak, see Kara, *Türkiye'de İslâmcılık Düşüncesi*, 1: xxxiv–xxxvi. For a bibliography of Turkish material on Said Halim see M. Hanefi Bostan, 'Said Halim Paşa ve Fikirleri,' *21. Yüzyılda Eğitim ve Toplum*, 8/22 (2019): 53–90.

[101] Mawdūdī discussed the need to understand Islam as a political system in *Islām kā Naẓariyya-i Siyāsī* (1939), which first appeared in Arabic in 1946; Islam as a comprehensive system for life came in *Qurʾān kī Chār Bunyādī Iṣṭilāḥain* (1941), translated in 1955; see Mawdūdī (trans. Muḥammad Kāẓim Sabbāq), *al-Muṣṭalaḥāt al-Arbaʿa fī al-Qurʾān: al-Ilāh, al-Rabb, al-ʿIbāda, al-Dīn* (Kuwait: Dār al-Qalam, 1971 [1955]), 126, 129–30.

[102] On Diyanet, İstar B. Gözaydın, 'Diyanet and Politics,' *The Muslim World*, 98/2–3 (April/July 2008): 216–27.

returned to Istanbul to die in 1936, Akif never delivered the text out of concern that it would be misused by Kemalist radicals at the height of their influence in the 1930s to institutionalise a Turkish Islam severed from its Arabic base after their success in imposing the call to prayer in Turkish.[103] It has emerged in recent studies that Akif had completed his Turkish Qurʾan in several copies, at least two of which he entrusted to Mehmed İhsan Efendi (1902–61), a religious scholar who also left for Egypt and father to historian and former head of the Organisation of the Islamic Conference Ekmeleddin İhsanoğlu. İhsan Efendi revealed the existence of these copies to Ekmeleddin, Sabri's son Ibrahim, and three others when they were gathered around his deathbed in Cairo in June 1961. Published accounts of the incident say it was at İbrahim Sabri's insistence that Akif's wish for the text to be destroyed was honoured – burned in a laundry basin on a balcony in the district of ʿAbbāsiyya – for fear that the previous year's military coup signalled a return to the radical project of Turkicising Islam.[104]

Sabri and Kevseri never returned to Turkey, preferring the extant internationalism of Arabic Islamic culture in Cairo, where they became celebrated figures as rejectionists of the Salafi and liberal modernist trends. Operating across rapidly and radically reconstituted ethnic and linguistic lines, Sabri and Kevseri were bearers of a tradition that ideological and technological transformations had conspired to render obsolete. This realisation led them to engage in the polemical interventions of the new class of public intellectuals, of which Akif was an exemplar. In Egypt they became agents in the process of rethinking Islam as a belief system, juridical tradition, and political ideology, a process in which Turkey was to remain somewhat isolated for several decades.

[103] Proposals were considered for introducing pews, organs, and wearing shoes in mosques; see Wilson, *Translating the Qurʾan*, 281–3.

[104] The story was first recounted in İsmail Hakkı Şengüler, *Mehmed Akif Kulliyatı*, 10 vols. (Istanbul: Hikmet Neşriyat, 1992), 10: 230–5. Those present included Sabri, Ekmeleddin, Şengüler, Osman Saraç, Ali İhsan Okur. On the coup's impact: M. Ertuğrul Düzdağ (ed.), *Üstad Ali Ulvi Kurucu Hatıralar*, 5 vols. (Istanbul: Kaynak, 2007), 2: 153.

2

Ottoman Exiles

From Constantinople to Cairo

This chapter presents short biographies of Akif, Sabri, and Kevseri, describing the general lines of their thought, followed by sections looking at scholarship's changing approach to their work, the role of Egypt as a site for intellectual discourse, and the particular engagement these three thinkers had with Ottoman, Turkish, and Arabic as modes of expression. As Benjamin Fortna has argued, a low regard for biography among professional historians has done a disservice to Late Ottoman history as a discipline which tends to privilege the state over the individual.[1] On the other hand, biographical studies of religious figures have lacked an overarching analysis of their place in modern Islamic thought beyond Turkey. Regarding the three figures under study, in place of autobiography there exists a body of biographical sources in the form of their followers' memoirs as well as letters, sermons, and photographs.[2] Caveats apply when surveying this material: some of it is hagiographical,[3] mistakes regarding events and dates are common, and much is left unsaid, possibly as a form of self-censorship.[4] Still, there is a breadth of material to work with, and while there are likely more documents to be found among

[1] Benjamin Fortna, *The Circassian: A Life of Eşref Bey, Late Ottoman Insurgent and Special Agent* (London: Hurst, 2016), 10.

[2] We know Akif visited the Pyramids with his patron ʿAbbas Halim Paşa because of the photographs.

[3] Kevseri's students write against a backdrop of criticism from his Salafi detractors.

[4] Akif had to be wary of the Turkish government reading correspondence during his Egypt exile. Government documents on Akif's time in Egypt from the Turkish Republican Archive have been published; Muharrem Coşkun, *Kod Adı: İrtica - 906, Mehmed Akif Ersoy* (Istanbul: Gaziosmanpaşa Belediyesi, 2014).

government records in Istanbul, Ankara, and Cairo, as well as letter caches, these are not historical figures to be recovered from the archive.

MEHMED AKIF: A BIOGRAPHY

Mehmed Akif was born and grew up in the Sarıgüzel quarter of the Fatih district in central Istanbul to a Kosovo Albanian father and a mother from Tokat in northern Anatolia whose parents were Uzbeks from Bukhara. According to biographical notes Akif dictated in his final weeks of life, the family name of his father was Ragıyf, which was possibly derived from the Arabic *raghīf* (bread), but his parents registered him as Akif because it was what bureaucrats heard when they pronounced the Albanian name and *âkif* (Ar. *ʿākif*) denotes someone devoted to God.[5] On at least one occasion Akif visited his Kosovan relatives but he did not speak Albanian. Born three years before the aborted constitutional experiment of 1876, Akif had the education of a typical reform-minded if not Westernised Ottoman functionary. Following two years of religious education at the Emir Buhari school he moved to the state system of *iptidai* and *rüşdiye* schools. After three years at the civil service school known as the Mülkiye the tragedy of his father's death in 1889 and loss of the family home in a fire compelled Akif to enter the new veterinary boarding school (Mülkiye Baytar Mektebi) in the hope it would lead to a job. Upon graduation in 1883 he entered the ministry of agriculture's animal husbandry bureaucracy where he worked as an inspector for twenty years until 1913, affording him the opportunity to experience the empire from Rumelia to Damascus.

The religious knowledge Akif attained was largely informal. His father, a religious scholar from Şuşisa near İpek who taught at the Fatih *medrese* (Islamic school) in Istanbul, taught him Arabic, Qurʾan memorisation, and theology (*akide*).[6] 'Whatever I know I learned from him', Akif wrote in March 1913.[7] He studied Persian texts at the Fatih mosque seminary with the Sufi teacher Esad Dede (1843–1911) and Turkish at high school with

[5] Nevzad Ayas, 'Mehmed Akif, Zihniyeti ve Düşünce Hayatı,' in *Mehmed Âkif: Hayatı Eserleri ve Yetmiş Muharririn Yazıları*, Eşref Edib (Istanbul: Beyan, 2011), 494; Kuntay, *Mehmet Akif*, 162.

[6] Dücane Cundioğlu, *Bir Kur'an Şâiri: Mehmed Akif ve Kur'an Meâli* (Istanbul: Birun, 2000), 17.

[7] Mehmed Akif, 'Üç beyinsiz kafanın derdine, üç milyon halk,' from his *Hakkın Sesleri* collection; in Mehmed Akif (ed. M. Ertuğrul Düzdağ), *Safahat* [Arabic script] (Istanbul: Çağrı, 2015), 262, footnote 1. Citations will be from this edition unless otherwise indicated.

Kadri Nasıh (1855–1918), a Herzegovinian who later fled to Egypt where he established the *Kanun-i Esasi* newspaper in 1897. In his own words the early texts that impressed him and through which he improved his language skills were the pre-Islamic Arabic poems known as the *Muʿallaqāt*, the Abbasid grammarian al-Mubarrad's *al-Kāmil* (The Complete), *Gulistān* (Flower Garden) of Persian poet Saʿdī (d. 1291), the *Dīvān* of Persian poet Ḥafiẓ (d. 1390), the *Masnavī-i Maʿnavī* (Tr. *Mesnevi*) of Persian Sufi poet Jalāl al-Dīn al-Rūmī (d. 1273), the Azeri Turkish work *Dastan-ı Leyli vü Mecnun* by the Karbala-born poet Füzuli (d. 1556), and nineteenth-century French novelists and poets such as Hugo, Lamartine, Zola, and Daudet. He also read Ibn ʿArabī with fellow devout intellectual Ahmed Naim and the Sufi work *al-Wāridāt* (Mystical Inspirations) of Ottoman jurist Shaykh Badr al-Dīn (1358–1416)[8] with prominent religious scholar Musa Kazım (1858–1920).

From 1893 Akif began publishing poetry in journals including the influential *Servet-i Funun* and *Resimli Gazete*. His emergence as a leading poet and intellectual of the Muslim reform movement came suddenly with the publication of *Sırat-ı Müstakim* in August 1908 under the ownership of Akif's friend Eşref Edib and Ebü'l-Ula Mardin. With Akif as editor and lead writer, it became the leading outlet for devout intellectuals, advancing the vision of the Young Ottoman intellectuals Namık Kemal (1840–88) and Ziya Paşa (1825–80) of an Ottoman state in which Islam was the defining element.[9] Modelling itself on *al-Manār*, the journal was a vehicle for Akif to also promote the ideas of ʿAbduh and al-Afghānī, which famously coalesced in the anti-colonial journal they published from Paris in 1884, *al-ʿUrwa al-Wuthqā*. Describing ʿAbduh as al-Afghānī's 'greatest work',[10] Akif took up ʿAbduh's theme of mobilising the Muslim community to meet the challenge of Europe through rejecting juridical *taqlīd* and overcoming a putative cultural propensity for inaction (*atalet*, which functioned in place of the *jumūd* that ʿAbduh talked of) by advocating

[8] Ibid., 42–3.

[9] Kasuya Gen, 'The Influence of *Al-Manār* on Islamism in Turkey: The Case of Mehmed Akif,' in *Intellectuals in the Modern Islamic World: Transmission, Transformation, Communication*, ed. Stéphane Dudoignon, Komatsu Hisao, Kosugi Yasushi (London: Routledge, 2016), 80–1. See Şerif Mardin, *The Genesis of Young Ottoman Thought: A Study in the Modernization of Turkish Political Ideas* (Princeton: Princeton University Press, 1962).

[10] Akif, 'Cemaleddin Efgani,' *Sırat-ı Müstakim* (henceforth *SM*), 13 Mayıs 1326 (26 May 1910), 4/90: 208.

say ve amel (Ar. *al-saʿy wa-l-ʿamal*) i.e., forms of labour and action.[11] Akif appears to have articulated these ideas as early as 1895 in the journal *Maarif*, writing under the literary name Saʿdī, in reference to the Persian poet,[12] following in the footsteps of influential journalist Ahmed Midhat (1844–1912) who established *say ve amel* as a trope for national revival in *Sevda-yı Say ve Amel* (Passion for Labour and Action, 1880).[13] By 1912 Akif had published forty-five articles and three books of ʿAbduh in translation,[14] including the debate in 1900 between ʿAbduh and French diplomat Gabriel Hanotaux (1853–1944), his own thirty-five short works of *tafsīr* in the period 1912–1913, which were inspired by ʿAbduh's work published later as *Tafsīr al-Manār* (one is signed ʿAbduh and Akif, as if they had written it together),[15] and he also translated in article and book form the early works of ʿAbduh acolyte Muḥammad Farīd Wajdī (1875–1954).

Another Akif appears from 1912, influenced by the territorial losses to European powers in successive wars; an Akif whose concerns are markedly more political than before.[16] This is the period of Akif's great poetic collection *Safahat*. The first general observation one can make about Akif's intellectual output during this time concerns his view of Sufism, which was highly influential in Ottoman political and religious culture. Although he celebrated the hybrid nature of Ottoman Muslim identity and although his father had belonged to a Khālidī-Naqshbandī *tarikat* headed by Feyzullah Efendi (1805–76),[17] Akif had an ambiguous approach to Sufism typical of reform intellectuals. Like ʿAbduh and Arab reformers close to him, he saw in its complex network of saint figures a multivocality that weakened Muslims in their effort to meet the civilisational challenge of the Europeans and establish the rationalisation in religion that Enlightenment thought posited as a requirement of modernity.

[11] Akif, 'Mukallidliği de yapmıyoruz,' *SM*, 17 Eylül 1325 (30 September 1909), 3/56: 54–5.

[12] Saʿdī, 'Mebahis-i İlm-i Servet: Say ve Amel', *Maarif*, 27 June 1895, 7: 187, 261–3; and Saʿdī, 'Say ve Amelin Nazar-ı İslamdaki Mevkii', *Sırat-ı Müstakim*, 4 November 1908, 1: 11, 170–2.

[13] Ahmet Mithat, *Sevda-yı Sa'y ü Amel* (Istanbul: Kitap Dünyası, 2016), 4, 14, citing Qurʾān 21:94, 53:39–40.

[14] This included material from *Risālat al-Tawḥīd*, the journal *al-ʿUrwa al-Wuthqā*, and his *tafsīr* material as it appeared in *al-Manār*. Akif's articles, translations and poetry are collected in Latin script transliteration in Şengüler, *Mehmed Âkif Külliyatı*.

[15] Akif, 'Tefsir-i Şerif' (Qurʾan 103:3), *SR*, 12 Temmuz 1328 (25 July 1912), 8/1: 393–4.

[16] Emin Erişirgil says he becomes a 'political poet' (*politika şairliği*); *İslamcı bir Şairin Romanı Mehmet Âkif* (Istanbul: Atlas, 2017), 128.

[17] Ayas, 'Mehmed Akif,' 496. There is no entry on Feyzullah Efendi in the TDV İslâm Ansiklopedi but followers have set up this page: https://feyzullahefendi.wordpress.com/ (accessed 27 December 2017).

The literary output of Ottoman Sufi culture he considered to be aimless and indulgent. In Akif's first published poem in 1895, *Kur'ana Hitab* (Address to the Qur'an), he displayed a scripturalist attitude towards Islam as a European category of world religion that in typical modernist fashion configured the Qur'ān as the prime locus of Muslim faith, 'my companion of shared language in the world/My help and place of support in the next' (*Dünyada refik ü hemzebānım/'Uḳbāda muin ü müste'ānım*).[18] For Akif and other Ottoman reformers this signalled their rejection of the prevailing religious-cultural model. Yet Akif also embraced Sufism as a theosophical system whose monist elements he knew commanded respect in European intellectual circles, though he was irritated by the tendency among pro-West Ottomans to dismiss Ibn 'Arabī's thought as merely 'pantheism'.[19] Ottoman religious culture was heavily influenced by the Indian Naqshbandī shaykh Sirhindī, whose system sought to establish a clearer distinction between God and the created world, but the devout intellectuals remained drawn to the earlier system of Ibn 'Arabī (known popularly as *waḥdat al-wujūd*, Tr. *vahdet-i vücud*).[20] Akif's later poetry in particular is suffused with emanationist Sufi references and imagery, if shorn of the libertine elements that characterized the traditional canon.

Akif's poetics reflect a similar reforming, rationalising approach. Eschewing the elaborate language and *topoi* of the Ottoman tradition, Akif rejected prevailing notions of poetry as 'art for art's sake'. Emulating the French realist writers Hugo and Zola, he argued art had both to reflect society and offer new directions for its improvement. Thus when he first came to publish in book form (as *Safahat-ı Hayattan*) his series of poems issued in *Sırat-ı Müstakim* up to 1911, Akif wrote an introductory poem in which he positioned himself as the conscience of the nation revealing social truths rather than as a writer revelling in clever artifice: 'Ask me, dear reader, so that I may tell you/Of what nature my verses here are/A mass of words whose sole craft is sincerity/Since being not an artist, I know no artifice' (*Bana sor sevgili kari sana ben söyleyeyim/Ne hüviyette şu*

[18] Edib, *Mehmed Akif*, 621. Akif asserts the centrality of the Qur'an in his encounter with a Wahhabi qadi, likely in January 1916, cited in Cemal Kutay, *Necid Çöllerinde Mehmet Akif* (Istanbul: Posta Kutusu, 1978), 213.

[19] Akif, 'Hasbıhal', *SM*, 29 June 1911, 6:147, 257–9.

[20] Ibn 'Arabī did not in fact use this term in his work, which addressed the Neoplatonic question of the one and the many. See Su'ād al-Ḥakīm, *al-Mu'jam al-Ṣūfī: al-Ḥikma fī Ḥudūd al-Kalima* (Beirut: Dandara li-l-Ṭibā'a wa-l-Nashr, 1981), 1145–57. See also Alexander Knysh, *Ibn 'Arabī in the Later Islamic Tradition: The Making of a Polemical Image in Medieval Islam* (Albany: State University of New York Press).

karşında duran eş'ārım:/Bir yığın söz ki, samimiyeti ancak hüneri;/Ne tasannu bilirim, çünkü, ne sanatkârım).[21] The language deployed throughout this first collection displays a mastery of the *aruz* metre (Ar. *'arūḍ*) along with a sprinkling of vernacular in a simplified yet formal Ottoman Turkish to describe the lives of the subaltern classes of Istanbul, and in doing so it broke conventions and marked new directions. Ömer Rıza Doğrul (1893–1952), a Cairo-based Turkish writer who was to marry one of Akif's daughters, described Akif's *Fatih Kürsüsünde*, published in 1914 as the fourth volume of what Akif now marketed as the *Safahat* cycle, as flowing 'like scenes from a cinema reel' (*levhalar bir sinema şeridi gibi*) when he heard Akif read it aloud.[22] This populist approach was reminiscent of journalist Ahmed Midhat, who adopted a pioneering, direct style in his writings, as well as the poetics of Muallim Naci (1849–93). Although this style was a repudiation of the *hece* poetic metre being developed in Turkist circles, it was in conformity with the nationalist framework within which Akif's Islamic ideology was to express itself in subsequent years.

Akif joined the CUP in 1908 after its success in leading the Young Turk revolution, and as a concession to his religious principles he was allowed to avoid the declaration of 'unconditional obedience' to the party (*bilā ḳayd ü şart cem'iyetin emirlerine itaat*).[23] After taking a position as teacher of Ottoman literature at Istanbul's Darülfünun university,[24] in October 1908 he gave evening classes in Arabic translation at the CUP's Şehzadebaşı branch, teaching the *Mu'allaqāt*.[25] Akif published a section in the CUP book *Mevaiz-i Diniye* (Religious Sermons, 1912) under the title 'İttihad Yaşatır, Yükseltir Tefrika Yakar Öldürür' (Unity gives life and elevates, division destroys and kills) but he was forced out of his post at Darülfünun in late 1913 due to CUP irritation over his *Sebilürreşad*

[21] Akif, *Safahat*, 3. The introduction bears similarities to the Qur'an's opening verse. Its last two lines each begin with the imperative 'Oku', which retains the read/recite ambiguity in the Fātiḥa's 'Iqra'!'

[22] Ömer Rıza Doğrul, 'Mehmed Akif: Şahsi ve Aile Hayatı,' in Edib, *Mehmed Akif*, 437.

[23] Related by astronomer Mehmet Fatin Gökmen, who initiated Akif; in Edib, *Mehmed Âkif*, 248–9.

[24] Established in 1846, it was renamed Darülfünûn-u Şahâne (Imperial House of Multiple Sciences) in 1900 and Istanbul Darülfünûnu in 1912, before taking its current name Istanbul University in 1933.

[25] Recollections of Aksekili Ahmet Hamdi; 'Âkif'e ait Bazı Hâtirat,' in Edib, *Mehmed Âkif*, 547–8.

criticisms of how the Balkan wars were handled.[26] In February 1913 he gave three sermons, at the Bayezid, Fatih, and Süleymaniye mosques: his theme was that Muslims of different ethnic-linguistic backgrounds have a duty to overcome division to save the Ottoman state as 'Islam's last hope' (*Müslümanlığın son ümidi*).[27] The same themes inflect the rush of poetry he published in the period 1912–14: the second *Safahat*, which consists of one epic, titled *Süleymaniye Kürsüsünde* (At the Süleymaniye Mosque Pulpit), was serialised in *Sebilürreşad* in 1912 and issued in book form later that year, then a series of Qurʾanic *tafsīr* intended as poetic commentary on the Ottoman condition[28] and titled *Hakkın Sesleri* (Voices of God) was published in the same manner in 1913. In 1913–14 his second epic, *Fatih Kürsüsünde* (At the Fatih Mosque Pulpit), was serialised then published as the fourth volume of *Safahat*.

This commitment to the Ottoman idea deepened in a remarkable manner in 1914 when Akif began working as a government propagandist with the secret operations apparatus known as Teşkilat-ı Mahsusa. He was involved in two projects, a trip to Berlin in the period 1914–15 to help turn Muslim prisoners from French and British-held territories into Ottoman collaborators, and a second to Najd to secure the support of the Rashīdī and Saudi polities against the anticipated British effort to turn the Hijazis under Sharīf Ḥusayn against the Ottomans. Though the latter mission was top secret at the time, Akif gathered material to publish the poems *Berlin Hatıraları* (Berlin Memories, 1915–18) and *Necid Çöllerinden Medine'ye* (1918) in the subsequent *Safahat* collection *Hatıralar* (Memories), which also included material from a 1914 vacation he took in Egypt (*El-Uksur'da*, 1915). The origins of this organisation and its activities have been a topic of great controversy because of its role in the mass deportation and massacre of Armenians during the war. It appears to have been established by İsmail Enver Paşa (1881–1922), the minister of war from 1914 to October 1918, as a covert body under the ministry's supervision to conduct paramilitary, intelligence, propaganda, and other special operations. One of its most important leaders was Eşref Kuşçubaşı

26 M. Ertuğrul Düzdağ, 'Mehmed Âkif Ersoy: Hayatı ve Eserleri,' in Mehmet Âkif Ersoy, *Safahat* (Ankara: Kültür Bakanlığı, 1989), xx–xxi. The article was first published in *SM*, 11 Teşrinisani 1326 (24 November 1910), 5/116: 205–7.

27 Delivered on 2 February 1913, Bayezid mosque; in *SR*, 24 Kanunusani 1328 (6 February 1913), 9/2: 373–476.

28 An introductory article declares his intent to develop a *tafsīr* relevant to modern life, challenging trends that saw the Qurʾan as irrelevant; 'Tefsir-i Şerif,' *SR*, 24 Şubat 1327 (9 March 1912), 8/1: 5–6.

Sencer (1873–1964), son of a Circassian refugee who became the chief falconer at the sultan's court. Sencer lived the life of a brigand for some time in Izmir and then the Hijaz, before drawing the attention of Enver who gave him an assignment to lead a group smuggling junior officers from Egypt into Libya during the 1911–12 war with Italy.[29] The group included a Tunisian shaykh called Ṣāliḥ al-Sharīf, and it was al-Sharīf and Sencer who approached Akif to travel to Germany in 1914. How Akif first came into contact with them is not clear, but it is possible that Akif's Egypt trip was an official mission.[30] The Teşkilat-ı Mahsusa was tasked with spreading Ottoman propaganda to Muslim communities around the world to accompany the November 1914 jihad fatwa issued by the sheikh ül-Islam and declaration of holy war issued by the sultan. Pamphlets were prepared by al-Sharīf in Arabic and rendered in Turkish by Akif, including responses to speeches by British Prime Minister Lloyd George (in office 1916–22) and French Resident-General in Morocco Hubert Lyautey.[31] Between 1914 and 1923 Akif also translated a series of articles and books written by Egyptian *ʿālim* and pro-Ottoman anti-British agitator ʿAbd al-ʿAzīz Jāwīsh (1876–1929).[32]

Akif only spoke directly of his Berlin and Najd experiences through his poetry and further sermons he gave in 1920, but his words were also filtered through scattered recollections in the memoirs of his friends Eşref Edib and Midhat Cemal and, in considerably more detail, Sencer's recollections and private papers made available to journalist Cemal Kutay. Akif's second mission covered some five months from late 1915: a posse comprising Akif, al-Sharīf, Sencer, and Enver's aide-de-camp Mümtaz Bey took the Hijaz railway to Medina, then travelled through the desert with a twenty-five-man armed camel corps to Ḥāʾil. Gifts were delivered to Saʿūd

[29] Fortna, *The Circassian*, 51–81. The first major study in English was Philip Stoddard, *The Ottoman Government and the Arabs, 1911 to 1918: A Preliminary Study of the Teskilat-ı Mahsusa* (PhD thesis, Princeton University, 1963), for which Sencer spoke to the author. He also spoke to Kutay for his book *Necid Çöllerinde Mehmet Akif*. On the secret organisation, see Polat Safi, 'History in the Trench: The Ottoman Special Organization – Teşkilat-ı Mahsusa Literature,' *Middle Eastern Studies*, 48/1 (2012): 89–106.

[30] Kutay, *Necid Çöllerinde Mehmet Akif*, 13–14. Sencer says Enver was a fan of Akif's poetry.

[31] Cundioğlu, *Bir Kur'an Şâiri*, 64–5. For example, Ṣāliḥ al-Sharīf, 'Fisebillah Cihadın Hakikati, Gayesi, Hükmü, Mücahidinin Vezaifi,' *SR*, 13 Teşrinisani 1330 (26 November 1914), 13/315: 20–4. It may have been Akif who authored the French version, *La verité au sujet de la guerre sainte* (Bern: Wyss, 1916).

[32] *Kavmiyet ve Din* (1913), *İslam ve Medeniyet* (1913/1916), *Hilafet-i İslamiye* (1914), *Hastalıklar ve Çareleri* (1332–4), *Esrar-ı Kur'an* (1914–16), *İslam Din-i Fıtra* (1916–17), *Müslümanlık Fikir ve Ḥayāta Neler Bahsetti?* (1920–1), *Müslümanlıkta Kadının Hukuku* (1923), most of which were first published in Istanbul in Arabic.

ibn ʿAbd al-ʿAzīz, the Rashīdī emir of Ḥāʾil, and left with the emir of Burayda for the Saudi emir ʿAbd al-ʿAzīz who had apparently skipped town for al-Ahsa to avoid the risk of Britain discovering secret talks with an Ottoman delegation.[33] As they were returning via the Hijaz railway station at al-Muʿaẓẓam news came from Enver by telegraph of the Ottoman victory at Gallipoli (around 9 January), inducing a rapturous reaction in Akif.[34] Akif's friendship with Sencer was apparently warm and enduring, as Akif's exchange of letters from Egypt in 1930–1 demonstrates.[35]

How much store the Ottoman government set in these pan-Islamic policies is a question of debate, but the Sharīf of Mecca's revolt in 1916 confirmed to both the Ottoman and German governments their failure.[36] By 1917 the Turkist wing of the CUP led by Ziya Gökalp had prevailed; Said Halim Paşa, a friend of Akif who translated his French-language works on Islamic reform into Turkish, was replaced as prime minister by the interior minister Talat Paşa (1874–1921); and the government decided to remove religious schools from the purview of the sheikh ül-Islam and religious endowments (*evkaf*) ministry, placing them under the ministry of education. Stirred by the Ankara government's resistance to the Allied powers' plans to carve up the empire, Akif slipped out of British-occupied Istanbul in April 1920 for Ankara in an operation that Sencer appears to have organised, taking up a seat he was offered in the new parliament for a district as yet outside its control.[37] *Sebilürreşad* continued its operations from there, with brief sojourns in Kayseri and Kastamonu when Greek armies were close, until the journal was closed down following the Shaykh Said rebellion in 1925.

[33] Kutay, *Necid Çöllerinde*, 35. The gifts included gold, swords, daggers, watches, and leather horse saddle from Thessalonika; British intelligence reports valued the gold at 10,000 pounds; Fortna, *The Circassian*, 140, 169.

[34] Kutay, *Necid Çöllerinde*, 111–21.

[35] Sencer lists Akif and Jāwīsh among forty-nine Special Organisation agents cited in Stoddard, 'The Ottoman Government,' 173–9; al-Sharīf is among fifty-six names listed separately as the core *fedai żābıṭān* (self-sacrificing officers) working with Sencer. Al-Sharīf and Jāwīsh were also agents of the German Intelligence Office for the East, set up to organise German war propaganda. See Tilman Lüdke '(Not) Using Political Islam: The German Empire and Its Failed Propaganda Campaign in the Near and Middle East, 1914–1918 and Beyond,' in *Jihad and Islam in World War I*, ed. Eric Zürcher (Leiden: Leiden University Press, 2016), 84–5.

[36] Lüdke '(Not) Using Political Islam,' *passim*.

[37] Kutay, *Necid Çöllerinde*, 140–1. Sencer says Akif refused money from the organisation. Akif's son Emin confirms Sencer's role in the Ankara trip; Emin Âkif Ersoy, *Babam Mehmet Âkif: İstiklal Harbi Hatıraları* (Istanbul: Kurtuba, 2017), 44.

Akif was at the peak of his fame and his powers during this period. He gave a series of mosque sermons and addresses between February 1920 and February 1921 in Balıkesir, Konya, and Kastamonu which aimed to inform the population of the truth about the Treaty of Sèvres, the Western powers' original plan to carve up the empire, and rally support for the forces of Mustafa Kemal, who made a point of meeting Akif after his arrival in Ankara and arranging his seat in parliament.[38] The speeches were widely distributed by the government to provinces and war-fronts. His poem *Asım*, sixth in the *Safahat* cycle and published in *Sebilürreşad* between 1919 and 1924 (in book form in August 1928), met critical acclaim for its mix of metre, language, and message of hope for the coming generation. His poem *İstiklal Marşı* (Independence March) was chosen in 1921 as the national anthem and in 1919 the education ministry charged Akif and others with composing an Arabic dictionary that for unclear reasons did not go beyond the letter *alif*.[39] His entanglement with Ankara deepened when he was appointed in 1922 to the publications committee of the shariʿa and religious endowments ministry (şerʿiye ve evkaf vekaleti), established by Mustafa Kemal to shore up support among Islamic opinion in the ongoing conflict with Istanbul, Greece, and the Western powers. Headed by Jāwīsh, the committee published at least eight books before it was dissolved in March 1923, including two translations into Ottoman Turkish from Arabic texts by Jāwīsh: one responding to what was believed to be a request from the Anglican Church to explain Islam, published as *Anglikan Kilisesine Cevap* (Response to the Church of England, 1923),[40] and a second in praise of the trend towards prohibition in Western countries, *İçkinin Ḥayāt-ı Beşerde Açtığı Rahneler* (The Damage Alcohol Causes, 1923).[41]

Akif quit the national assembly in the aftermath of opposition leader Ali Şükrü Bey's assassination in March 1923 and *Sebilürreşad* moved

[38] The sermons are collected in Abdulkerim Abdulkadiroğlu and Nuran Abdulkadiroğlu, *Mehmed Akif'in Kur'an-ı Kerim'i Tefsiri Mev'iza ve Hutbeleri* (Ankara: Diyanet, 1992). For Konya see Edib, *Mehmed Âkif*, 113.

[39] Edib, *Mehmed Âkif*, 335. The dictionary is also cited in a letter Akif wrote on 25 February to Fuad Şemsi İnan; Yusuf Turan Günaydın, *Mehmet Akif Ersoy: Mektuplar* (Istanbul: Atlas, 2016), 109.

[40] Jāwīsh's Arabic original is *Ajwibatī fī al-Islām ʿan Asʾilat al-Kanīsa al-Anglīkāniyya*, but the only extant copy I have found, held at the Suleymaniye Library in Istanbul, is incomplete.

[41] Jāwīsh, *Āthār al-Khamr fī Naẓar Arqā al-Umam al-Masīḥiyya bi-Amīrqā wa-Ghayrihā* (1923).

operations back to Istanbul.[42] He was vacationing in Edirne in September 1923 as the British were preparing to withdraw following the Treaty of Lausanne when a telegram arrived from Said Halim Paşa's brother Abbas Halim (1866–1934), minister of public works in Said Halim's 1913 cabinet and at whose Heybeli estate Akif often spent time. Abbas Halim invited him to spend the winter at his residence in Ḥilwān just south of Cairo.[43] Akif returned to Istanbul in spring and left again to spend the winter in Egypt in late 1924. When he left a third time in October 1925, it was for what was to become a permanent stay that only ended in 1936 when his health deteriorated. A number of theories have been put forward for why he accepted Abbas Halim's offer, including government agents trailing him,[44] the closing of *Sebilürreşad* and trial of intellectuals including Eşref Edib in 1925,[45] and denunciations of Akif by Kemalist partisans,[46] all of which appear to have played a part in his thinking. Kemalist propagandists claimed he left out of objection to a 1925 law forcing men to wear European-style hats.[47]

Hagiographical writing about his Egypt years has revolved around certain themes – that he was desperately unhappy, broken by rejection in Turkey, incapable of matching his prodigious output since 1908, lacking money.[48] From his letters to family and friends, his poetry composed at

42 Düzdağ, 'Mehmed Âkif Ersoy: Hayatı ve Eserleri,' xxxiv–xxxv.

43 Ersoy, *Babam*, 183. Midhat Cemal found Akif's willingness to hobnob with aristocracy distasteful, considering it an anomaly of his character; Kuntay, *Mehmet Akif*, 40, 78. Erişirgil makes a similar observation, seeing naivety in Akif's views of his Egyptian patron; *İslamcı Bir Şairin Romanı*, 211.

44 Recollecton of Şefik Kolaylı who spoke with Akif the day before he left in 1925; Fahri Kutluay, 'Aydınlatılan iki mühim sır,' *SR*, 4/99 (April 1951): 375.

45 Erişirgil, *İslamcı Bir Şairin Romanı*, 345.

46 Akif was insulted at the March 1925 Gallipoli Victory Day as an 'irredeemable non-Turkish' poet (*çaresiz Türk olmayan bir adam*) whose paean to the dead – a section of *Asım* titled 'Çanakkale Şehitlerine', published 10 July 1924 in *Sebilürreşad* – was recited reluctantly since the speaker said no comparable work by a Turk could be found. The Republican People's Party official organ *Hakimiyet-i Milliye* also ran an article telling Akif to 'go play in the sand' (*hadi git artık, sen kumda oyna*), a line Akif used in his *Gölgeler* poem *Bir Ariza* (1929). The Gallipoli incident was related verbally from Ḥasan Basri Çantay to Osman Yüksel Serdengeçti, who published it in 'M. Akif,' *Yeni İstanbul*, 31 December 1967. See Cündioğlu, *Bir Ku'ran Şairi*, 133.

47 Şukufe Nihal, 'Bana Göre Mehmed Akif,' *Tan*, 31 December 1938; reproduced in Edib, *Mehmed Âkif*, 744–5. The law made hats compulsory for civil servants at work and all men in public places and banned the fez.

48 Admirers and detractors are prone to exaggerate his suffering: among the former see M. Ertuğrul Düzdağ, *Mehmed Âkif: Mısır Hayatı ve Kur'ân Meâli* (Istanbul: Şule, 2011) and among the latter see Fahir İz; 'Mehmet Akif: A Biography,' *Erdem*, 4/11 (May 1988): 316.

the time, and comments to visitors that appear in various memoirs, it appears that elements of this picture are inaccurate. Akif was happy to withdraw to Egypt, which he fetishised in his writing as 'the Great East' (*Koca Şark*).[49] The poetry of his Egypt years – his final *Safahat* collection was published in Cairo in 1933 under the title *Gölgeler* (Shadows), spanning material from 1919 to 1933 – includes his most lyrical and rapturous work. The life of seclusion he adopted in Ḥilwān was one he often celebrated in his letters. His wife and sons Emin and Tahir were with him throughout most of those years. What did cast a huge shadow over his life in Egypt was the commission he had reluctantly accepted before leaving: to produce a definitive Turkish version of the Qur'an to be published alongside a *tafsīr* written simultaneously by the *'ālim* Elmalılı Hamdi Efendi (1878–1942). It was not until 1931 that Akif had concluded he was being exploited to provide the Kemalists with what would be the jewel in the crown of the revolutionary project.[50] Yet even then he continued to engage in animated debate with friends over his translation work and retained hope of publishing his Qur'an independently of the Turkish government.[51]

After he became seriously ill from malaria in 1935 Akif returned to Turkey in the early summer of 1936. From his sickbed he held court for several months with a stream of visiting intellectuals and dignitaries, resisting financial temptations from Atatürk's emissaries to hand over his translation, until he finally succumbed to liver failure, passing away on 27 December 1936. Egyptian exile seemed strangely appropriate for a figure so in many ways unconventional and out of place. His early persona as the poet of the people was incongruous with the patronage of a pasha. Seniyüddin Başak, a lawyer from among his pre-1908 circle, once said that as a man who stuck to his ideals (*mefkûresinin adamı*) Akif had been lucky to find sanctuary with someone like Abbas Halim.[52] His patron saw it

[49] Emin Âkif Ersoy, *Babam*, 103. See *El-Uksur'da* (1915), in Akif, *Safahat*, 420.

[50] Cündioğlu suggests Akif first became uneasy in 1928, the year of the alphabet reform and removal of Islam as state religion from the constitution; *Bir Kur'an Şairi*, 146–53. Akif made final arrangements for Edib to break the contract in 1931; Günaydın, *Mektuplar*, 30. In a letter dated 18 May 1931, Akif describes the Ankara government as engaging in 'all forms of fearless excess' (*her türlü ifratı biperva kabul eden*) in the name of renewal; Günaydın, *Mektuplar*, 90. During a visit to Egypt in 1932 Edib says Akif denounced the regime as a 'Freemason cabal' (*farmason dolabı*) that wanted to exploit him; Edib, *Mehmed Âkif*, 172.

[51] Edib says Akif hoped to publish his work in London on silk paper with Arabic on one side, Turkish on the other, and notes of *tafsīr* below; Edib, *Mehmed Âkif*, 170.

[52] Edib, *Mehmed Âkif*, 282.

differently, once remarking: 'Akif can find an Abbas Halim any time, but I wouldn't find another Akif.'[53] His exile, his work in exile, his act of withholding work in exile – all seemed to further his standing in time rather than diminish it.[54] Akif's shift from themes of Islamic unity towards a form of Turkish nationalism pleased neither ulema nor nationalists,[55] but it did establish him as a Muslim-Turkish *ʿālim*-intellectual who could several decades later become emblematic of ascendant Turkish Islamism.[56]

MUSTAFA SABRI: A BIOGRAPHY

Operating unambiguously within the category of *ʿālim*, Sabri rejected modernist reform as an apologetic concession to secular nationalism that helped destroy the epistemic framework of the shariʿa state. Modernists like Akif would reject the notion that they were any less fierce than conservatives in their response to the challenge of European thought. Indeed, one of their major themes was the danger of 'blind imitation' of the West,[57] a charge they directed at Turkist intellectuals such as Gökalp and Tevfik Fikret (1867–1915), the latter of whom Akif attacked in poetry for his critique of Islam.[58] However, Sabri viewed their reworking of traditional theology as wholly unnecessary and noted a superficial

[53] Kuntay, *Mehmet Akif*, 130.

[54] He had no agriculture ministry pension, refused a reward for his national anthem, and returned money given him in the Qurʾan contract. 'Despite my famous Arabic, Persian, and French I can't find work in Cairo, Tehran, or Paris', he wrote in 1924; Günaydın, *Mektuplar*, 132. Yet he lived for free in homes provided by Abbas Halim.

[55] Diyanet head Ömer Nasuhi Bilmen seemed glad that Akif gave up the translation assignment, describing Elmalılı Hamdi as one of the 'real and capable ulema' (*hakiki ve kudretli ulema*); 'Mehmed Akif: Hayatı ve eserleri', in Edib, *Mehmed Âkif*, 817.

[56] He saw himself as above politics and ideology – thus his dismissive comment that Ziya Gökalp was a *nazariyatçı*, merely a 'theoretician'; Ayas, 'Mehmed Akif,' 540. Akif said in *Asım* he was neither *ʿālim*, *faqīh* (jurist) nor politician but a poet; Akif, *Safahat*, 483. Still, in one letter from April 1912, he called himself *müfessir* (expert in *tafsīr*) and *dai* (preacher); Günaydın, *Mektuplar*, 162.

[57] ʿAbduh, 'Taassub,' *SM*, 10 Eylül 1325 (23 September 1909), 3/55: 33–7. See Akif's discussion of *mukallidlik* (imitation), 'Hasbihâl,' *SM*, 30 Mayis 1329 (12 June 1913), 10/248: 221.

[58] Edib says Fikret is one of the few people Akif despised; *Mehmed Âkif*, 223. Fikret's poem *Tarih-i Kadim* (1905), in particular its description of the Qurʾan as an 'outdated book' (*kitab-ı köhne*) and the 'death of thought' (*maktel-i fikr*), provoked Akif to refer to Fikret with the line *hiç utanmaz Protestanlara zangoçluk eder* ('without shame he rings the bells for Protestants') in *Süleymaniye Kürsüsünde*; Akif, *Safahat*, 239. Fikret retorted by referring to Akif as Molla Sırat in an addendum to his poem, *Tarih-i Kadim'e Zeyl* (1914). See Kuntay, *Mehmet Akif*, 100–1; Erişirgil, *İslami bir Şairin Romanı*, 149.

semantic segue between their critique of imitation of Western knowledge and imitation as a principle of *fiqh*, through misuse of the term *taqlīd*. In Sabri's derisive rendering, most of their *tajdīd* (renewal) was in fact *taqlīd* (of the West) in itself.[59]

Sabri was born in the north central Anatolian town of Tokat in 1869 to parents of Turkic Anatolian origin.[60] His father, Aḥmad ibn Muḥammad al-Qāzābādī, or Ahmed Efendi, was devout though not a religious scholar. He actively encouraged the young Sabri, a child prodigy like Akif, to enter the ranks of the ulema, though he was concerned that the speed of his son's rise through the state bureaucracy could impact his independence of thought and action.[61] Sabri appears to have become a *ḥāfiẓ* of the Qurʾan by age ten[62] and pressed his parents to allow him to study in Kayseri, a centre of religious learning, although he had studied *fiqh*, Arabic, and logic with Zülbiyezade Ahmed Efendi in Tokat.[63] In Kayseri he studied disputation (*al-jadal wa-l-munāẓara*) with Mehmed Emin Efendi (1821–1908),[64] before moving to Istanbul where he did further studies in *ʿaqīda* and *fiqh* with a teacher called Shaykh Atif Bey, but more importantly was taken under the wing of the commissioner of medrese education (the *ders vekili*) at the office of the sheikh ül-Islam, Ahmed Asım Efendi (1836–1911).[65] After obtaining his *rüʾus-ı tedris* teaching qualification in 1890 he took a position as lecturer (*dersiam*) at the Fatih mosque seminary and married Ahmed Asım's daughter Ulviye.[66] His teaching covered *tafsīr*, hadith, *uṣūl al-fiqh*, and Arabic rhetoric, particularly *al-Muṭawwal* of the Ḥanafī-Māturīdī theologian Saʿd al-Dīn al-Taftāzānī (1322–89), one of Sabri's favourite scholars.

Sabri's acquaintance with Ahmed Asım was to open doors in that the latter had been responsible since 1875 for the *Huzur Dersleri* (Imperial Presence Lectures),[67] a practice established in 1758 whereby selected

[59] Sabri, *Mawqif al-Bashar Taḥta Sulṭān al-Qadar* (Cairo: al-Maktaba al-Salafiyya, 1933), 8.

[60] In his memoir Sabri's student Ali Özek claims a Georgian origin; Yıldırım, *Medrese'den Üniversite'ye*, 107.

[61] Sabri, *Mawqif al-ʿAql wa-l-ʿIlm wa-l-ʿĀlam min Rabb al-ʿĀlamīn wa-Rusulihi*, 4 vols. (Beirut: Dār Ihyāʾ al-Kutub al-ʿArabiyya, 1981), 1:1–2, 71. Sabri gives the Arabic form of his father's name.

[62] Sabri, *Masʾalat Tarjamat al-Qurʾān* (Cairo: al-Maktaba al-Salafiyya, 1932), 18.

[63] Ibid., footnote 2. He studied Quṭb al-Dīn al-Rāzī (d. 1364)'s *Sharḥ al-Shamsiyya*, a commentary on al-Kātibī (d. 1294)'s book on logic *al-Risāla al-Shamsiyya*.

[64] Sabri, *Mawqif al-ʿAql*, 1:1, footnote 2.

[65] The *ders vekili* was one of three deputies to the sheikh ül-Islam, responsible for education.

[66] Sabri, *Mawqif al-ʿAql*, 1:1. They had three children, Sabiha, Nezahet, and Ibrahim.

[67] Ebü'l-Ula Mardin, *Huzur Dersleri*, 3 vols. (Istanbul: Ismail Akgün, 1966).

religious scholars were invited to attend carefully scripted disquisitions on religious matters with the sultan during the fasting month of Ramaḍān.[68] Ahmed Asım invited Sabri to attend these lectures in 1897, a year after Sabri had become imam of the Beşiktaş Asariye Mosque, and Sabri drew the attention of Abdülhamid through a treatise he wrote correcting a point of *fiqh* raised in one discussion that he had been too timid to question at the time.[69] Impressed with the work, the sultan invited Sabri to serve as librarian (*hafız-ı kütüb*) at the Yıldiz Palace for four years, and in this same year, 1900, Sabri became secretary of the sultan's office. He had also taken on work during this period as a lecturer in *tafsīr* at both Darülfünun and the state's school for preachers (Medresetü'l-Vaizin).[70] In 1905 he was elected to the academic committee of scholarly publications and research for Islamic studies (Tedkikat ve Telifat-ı İslamiye Heyet-i İlmiyesi), which gave him the status to review and evaluate contemporary scholars' work.

Sabri followed an exemplary career path as a loyal and distinguished scholar within the İlmiye bureaucracy. But when political life was transformed with the revolution of 1908, he became one of the most political of the many ulema who entered the new arena of public discourse. Initially sympathetic to the CUP, Sabri wanted to preserve the Islamic features of the state, whether the state took the form of Hamidian autocracy or a constitutional system.[71] He plunged into the parliamentary arena with gusto, elected to the October 1908 assembly following the uprising and developing a particular view of what he would later call in Arabic 'Islamic democracy' (*al-dīmūqrāṭiyya al-islāmiyya*)[72] that would preserve the system of ulema-administered shari'a law and the sultan as ultimate arbiter

[68] See Zilfi, *Politics and Piety*, 227–35.

[69] The work was *Risālat al-Yamīn al-Ghamūs*, regarding the sin of false oath to attain property. The incident is related by Sabri's student in Egypt Muhammed Emin Saraç (1929–2021); interview in Mufarriḥ ibn Sulaymān al-Qawsī, *Muṣṭafā Ṣabrī: al-Mufakkir al-Islāmī wa-l-ʿĀlim al-ʿĀlamī wa-Shaykh al-Islām fī al-Dawla al-ʿUthmāniyya Sābiqan* (Damascus: Dār al-Qalam, 2006), 425–6.

[70] Abdülkadir Altunsu, *Osmanlı Şeyhülislamları* (Ankara: Ayyıldız, 1972), 254.

[71] His early writings included articles in the journals *Tarık* and *Malumat* in 1898, such as 'Cüretli Bir Dekadan,' *Malumat*, 1 Şaban 1316 (1 December 1898), 163: 863–5.

[72] Sabri, *Mawqif al-ʿAql*, 1:20. See also a speech Sabri gave extolling the restored constitutional order for guaranteeing equality and freedom of gathering, beliefs and rites for Muslims and Christians but excoriating the rich (*eşref*) for undefined unjust treatment of ordinary people; 'Taşrada İrad Olunmuş bir Nutuktan,' *BH*, 5 Nisan 1326 (18 April 1910), 2/56: 1150–3. 'We elected delegates; they made laws according to our wishes and passed them to government who implements them. So, government derives its power from delegates who as our representatives got their power from us'; 12 Nisan 1326 (25 April 1910), 2/57: 1164.

of the legislative process through his right to dissolve parliaments. Sabri's fear, ultimately realised, was of elected majorities altering the constitutional stipulations and basic laws that sustained the shariʿa state in accordance with the fashion of the times.[73] When over one hundred religious scholars formed the Society for Islamic Studies (Cemiyet-i İlmiye-i İslamiye) in August 1908, Sabri was elected a board member and editor of its journal *Beyanülhak* (1908–12). Sabri's opening editorial comment used the language of reform to address readers, stating that Islam was not against 'progress and civilisation', extolling 'freedom practised in a legitimate manner', 'love of [Islamic] sciences and modern knowledge', and eschewing absolutism and injustice.[74] In 1910 he was a founding member of a new party, the People (Ahali), which merged into an umbrella group formed in 1911, the Freedom and Accord Party (Hürriyet ve İtilaf Fırkası), or Liberal Entente. One of the key policy disputes of the time was the CUP's drive towards administrative centralisation, which Sabri saw as a tool for tightening the CUP's grip on the levers of power that was contrary to Ottoman political traditions. Sabri travelled the country in 1912 railing against the CUP in sermons as atheist traitors,[75] while in February 1913 Akif was still preaching for national unity during the Second Balkan War as a party member.

After its restoration to power via a *coup d'état* in January 1913, the CUP went after its political opponents, among them Sabri. He escaped from his home in the Çarşamba area of Fatih, climbing from a window onto the roof of the neighbour's carpentry workshop, then made his way to the house of a Greek Orthodox acquaintance in the Fanar district[76] before hopping on a boat to the Romanian Black Sea town of Köstence (Constanța).[77] It seems he headed for Paris via Bosnia-Herzegovina in order to attend the Arab National Congress held in June 1913 where the question of the status of Arab provinces of the Ottoman sultanate was discussed.[78] He settled in Bucharest where he had many acquaintances

[73] Sabri, *Mawqif al-ʿAql*, 4:333–4. On the sultan-caliph's role, see Sabri, *al-Nakīr ʿalā Munkirī al-Niʿma min al-Dīn wa-l-Khilāfa wa-l-Umma* (Beirut: Dār al-Qādirī, 1924), *passim*.

[74] 'Beyanülhak'ın Mesleği,' *BH*, 5 October 1908.

[75] Sadık Albayrak, *Şeriat Yolunda Yürüyenler ve Sürünenler* (Istanbul: Medrese, 1979), 24–5. Sabri refers to his sermons in *Mawqif al-ʿAql*, 4:340.

[76] Altunsu, *Osmanlı Şeyhülislamları*, 255.

[77] Ibid., 255.

[78] This is according to a biography of Sabri written by his son Ibrāhīm and published in al-Qawsī, *Muṣṭafā Ṣabrī*, 136, 396–7.

among the Muslim community[79] and made a living throughout the war by teaching Turkish; one report says he bought a house.[80] Arrested in 1918 when Bucharest came under German and Turkish occupation, Sabri was sent back to Istanbul and exile in the northwest Anatolian town of Bilecik for some two months.[81] Following the collapse of the CUP government he returned to Istanbul in January 1919 to help re-establish the Liberal Entente.

What followed was the most controversial chapter of his life: his turn as the sheikh ül-Islam who tried to put down Mustafa Kemal's National Forces (Kuva-yi Milliye). Sabri quickly came to dominate the religious hierarchy in the empire's twilight years, elected as the Tokat delegate to parliament in January 1919, appointed to the Darü'l-Hikmeti'l-İslamiye (Islamic House of Wisdom), an Islamic academy set up in 1918 as a sop to the religious establishment after the CUP had removed Islamic schools from İlmiye control,[82] and head of an elite body of ulema called the Cemiyet-i Müderrisin (later known as Teali-i İslam Cemiyeti), or Teachers' Association. It was then that he was appointed sheikh ül-Islam, serving four times in Liberal Entente cabinets under prime minister (*sadrazam*) Damad Ferid Paşa from 4 March 1919 until 25 September 1920, and deputising for him during the Versailles peace conference in June 1919.[83]

Sabri's actions should be understood according to his priority of reversing CUP efforts to de-Islamise public life and stopping the Turkists from reforming as a political force. He introduced Qurʾan recitations for the opening and closing of sessions in both houses of parliament, a request he had been making since 1908.[84] He failed to dissuade Sultan Vahideddin (Mehmed VI) from sending Mustafa Kemal to eastern Anatolia in May 1919 as general inspector of the army,[85] but spent hours convincing him

[79] Sabri mentions his time in Bucharest in *al-Nakīr*, 104.

[80] Recollection of his student Ali Yakub Cenkçiler, a Kosovan who left Turkey to study at al-Azhar in 1936; interview, in al-Qawsī, *Muṣṭafā Ṣabrī*, 413.

[81] Refik Halit Karay, who was banished to Bilecik with Sabri, mentions their imprisonment in *Minelbab İlelmihrab: 1918 Mütarekesi Devrinde Olan Biten İşlere ve Gelip Geçen İnsanlara Dair Bildiklerim* (Istanbul: İnkilâp, 1992), 42. Emin Saraç says the CUP wanted to execute Sabri but Talat Paşa, then prime minister, preferred banishment; interview, 428.

[82] Zekeriya Akman, *Osmanlı Devleti'nin Son Döneminde Bir Üst Kurul, Dâru'l-Hikmeti'l İslâmiye* (Ankara: DİB Yayınları, 2009).

[83] From 4 March 1919 to 18 May 1919, 19 May 1919 to 20 July 1919, 21 July 1919 to 1 October 1919, 31 July 1920 to 25 September 1920.

[84] Sadık Albayrak, *Son Devir Osmanlı Uleması: Ilmiye Ricalinin Teracim-i Ahvali*, 5 vols. (Istanbul: Medrese, 1981), 4:251.

[85] Ali Ulvi Kurucu, an al-Azhar student who left Turkey in 1939 and studied with Sabri for six years in Egypt, says Sabri had spies reporting on Kemal's movements in Istanbul before

to sign the cabinet decree ordering Mustafa Kemal to stand down on 9 July 1919.[86] British occupying authorities had relayed this request in June to Sabri, who suggested in his meetings with British officials that former CUP figures were bad faith actors who should be 'got rid of'.[87] By the time he was appointed sheikh ül-Islam for the last time in July 1920 Mustafa Kemal's nationalists had set up their own parliament in Ankara, and the Istanbul government had scrambled to form an army against it. As a member of the sultan's inner group of counsellors (Şura-ı Saltanat) Sabri supported accepting the Sèvres conditions at a meeting on 22 July 1920 (it was signed on 10 August 1920).[88] He removed muftis in Deniz, Isparta, Usak, Burhaniye, Antalya, and Sinop over suspected support for Ankara,[89] yet it was not Sabri but Dürrizade Abdullah Efendi who issued the fatwa as sheikh ül-Islam sanctioning the murder of Mustafa Kemal and others in his camp after a tribunal sentenced him to death in May 1920.[90] Sabri was party to at least the early statements of the Cemiyet-i Müderrisīn denouncing the National Forces,[91] though he was not a member from November 1919 when it changed its name.[92] His final resignation on 1 October 1920 stemmed from frustration that Damad

he left for the east and became convinced Kemal had an understanding with the British to end the caliphate; interview in al-Qawsī, *Muṣṭafā Ṣabrī*, 440–1.

[86] Sabri, *Mawqif al-ʿAql*, 1:473.

[87] The words of military attaché General Deedes describing Sabri's position to Vice-Admiral Sir A. Calthorpe in letter dated 8 June 1919; British Foreign Office archives, no. FO 371/4158/94640. Document is also in Bilal Şimşir, *İngiliz Belgelerinde Atatürk, 1919–1938*, 8 vols. (Ankara: Türk Tarih Kurumu Basımevi, 1973), 1:11–12.

[88] Altunsu, *Osmanlı Şeyhülislâmları*, 256–7. One report given by Altunsu has Sabri's wife asking him in tears how he could have consented to giving Izmir to the Greeks. Altunsu bases the report on interviews he did with Hatice Hanım, a cousin of his wife through her father Ahmed Asım, and her daughter Semiha Omay. Altunsu gives the location of the interview but not its date. He relates Ulviye Hanım's words as follows: 'Sen Allah'tan korkmadın mı, Peygamber'den utanmadın mı? İzmir'in Yunanlılara verilmesine nasıl razı oldun? İstifa edeydin, imza etmedeydin!' – to which he says Sabri said nothing.

[89] Sabahattin Selek, *Milli Mücadele*, 2 vols. (Istanbul: Burçak Yayınevi, 1966), 2:768–9.

[90] Sabri, 'Takrir al-Tadhkir,' *al-Muqattam*, 4 November 1923, 2. Cited in al-Qawsī, *Muṣṭafā Ṣabrī*, 142. Sabri was among Istanbul ministers condemned to death for treason by the Ankara High Court in July 1920.

[91] Its first statement was published in *İkdam*, 16 September 1919; in Ali Sarıkoyuncu, 'Şeyhülislam Mustafa Sabri'nin Milli Mücadele ve Atatürk İnkilapları Karşıtı Tutum ve Davranışları,' *Atatürk Araştırma Merkezi Dergisi*, no. 39 (1997): 795.

[92] Britain helped distribute its statements in northwestern Anatolia by air: see Kinross, *Atatürk*, 250; Ekmeleddin İhsanoğlu, 'Teâlî-i İslâm Cemiyeti,' *İslâm Ansiklopedisi* (Istanbul: Türkiye Diyanet Vakfı, 2001), 207–8; Tarık Zafer Tunaya's *Türkiye'de Siyasal Partiler*, 2 vols. (Istanbul: Hürriyet Vakfı Yayınları, 1986), 2:387–96.

Ferid was not more effective in challenging Ankara and possibly a failed intrigue to form his own cabinet.[93]

With Ankara's forces moving into Istanbul following the Convention of Mudanya in October 1922, Sabri fled once more.[94] Arriving in Alexandria, he was immediately met with hostile reaction because he had stood against those seen as fighting imperialism in the name of Islam, from vegetables thrown at him in the street,[95] to random telegrams warning him to leave Egypt,[96] to derisive articles in the press.[97] He accepted an invitation by Sharīf Ḥusayn to stay in Mecca, where he was joined by the deposed sultan, but returned to Egypt five months later.[98] After Turkey was formally declared a republic in October 1923, Sabri went to Lebanon in January 1924 to complete his book on republicanism and the caliphate, *al-Nakīr ʿalā Munkirī al-Niʿma min al-Dīn wa-l-Khilāfa wa-l-Umma* (Disavowal of Those who Reject the Blessings of Religion, Caliphate and Nation), which he completed on 24 March 1924, three weeks after the Ankara parliament abolished the caliphate as he had feared.[99] Sabri's next stop was Romania, from where he made a trip to the Vatican in 1925 to place a bold request for the papal authorities to work with 'patriotic Turks and eminent figures from the Muslim world' to restore the caliphate as a 'moderating force' (*puissance modératrice*) on the basis of their joint interest in combatting atheist nationalist destruction of the social-religious order (see Appendix 1).[100] In 1927 he took his family to Gümülcine (Komotini) in Greek Thrace, the hometown of his

93 Memoirs of senior civil servant Ali Fuat Türkgeldi, *Görüp İşittiklerim* (Ankara: Türk Tarih Kurumu, 1951), 243; and recollections of Ahmed Tevfik Paşa, who headed the last Ottoman government; Mahmud Kemal İnal, *Osmanlı Devrinde Son Sadrazamlar*, 4 vols. (Istanbul: Dergah Yayınları, 1982), 4:2071.

94 A cargo boat carrying his personal effects including his book *Dinî Müceddidler* was seized; al-Qawsī, *Muṣṭafā Ṣabrī*, 134.

95 Sabri, *al-Nakīr*, 232.

96 Two examples are published in al-Qawsī, *Muṣṭafā Ṣabrī*, 479–80.

97 Sabri defended himself in *al-Ahrām*; 'Shaykh al-Islām al-Sābiq Yabsuṭ Ārāʾahu wa-Yudāfiʿ ʿan Nafsihi wa-Yaḥmil ʿalā Khuṣūmihi,' *al-Ahrām*, 2 December 1922; cited in al-Qawsī, 517.

98 Sabri wrote that he left the Hijaz in order to preserve 'the independence of my ideas' (*Yarın*, 20 July 1928, p. 4, column 3) but Kurucu quotes him as saying he feared an 'English game' of having Sabri bless a Hijazi caliph; Düzdağ, *Hatıralar*, 2:56. Altunsu confuses the chronological order of Sabri's Greece, Hijaz and Cairo sojourns and states incorrectly that he taught at al-Azhar; *Osmanlı Şeyhülislamları*, 258.

99 The title is an allusion to the angels Munkar and Nakir who test the faith of the dead in Islamic eschatology.

100 'Espulsione del Califfo,' Turchia, Pos. 43–48, Fasc. 55, Archivio Storico, Segretaria di Stato, Vatican City; 6–7. The letter, dated Rome, 14 May 1925, was delivered in French

wife's father that retained a Turkish Muslim community. There he issued the newspaper *Yarın* (1927–30) with his son Ibrahim. The paper was officially banned in Turkey,[101] but it was not until Greek Prime Minister Eleftherios Venizelos visited Ankara in 1931 that Greece closed it down and Sabri was asked to move to Patra on the western side of Greece. Depressed after a few months in these new surrounds, Sabri was surprised to be offered a visa by the Egyptian ambassador in Athens, and on 20 January 1932 he and his family arrived back in Egypt where he would spend the last twenty-two years of his life.

Egypt was a second wind for Sabri. Shunned a decade before, he was now warmly welcomed by an elite of religious scholars and intellectuals, a circle that included the Shaykh of al-Azhar at the time Muṣṭafā al-Marāghī (1881–1945); Shaykh Maḥmūd Shaltūt (1893–1963), rector of al-Azhar, 1958–63; Shaykh Muḥammad al-Khiḍr Ḥusayn (1876–1958), shaykh of Al-Azhar from 1952–4;[102] the poet Maḥmūd Ḥasan Ismāʿīl (1910–77); Muḥammad Saʿīd al-ʿIryān (1915–64), who wrote school textbooks on Islamic issues after the 1952 revolution; the novelist Yaḥya Ḥaqqī (1905–92); and Maḥmūd Shākir (1909–97), a poet who held a weekly salon.[103] The ministry of religious endowments appointed him to its committee for improving the state of mosques for which he was given a salary of twelve Egyptian pounds a month, and out of respect for Sabri its members would often meet in his flat in the suburb of Heliopolis, which became a meeting point for intellectuals in its own right.[104] When his book *al-Qawl al-Faṣl bayn Alladhīna Yuʾminūn bi-l-Ghayb wa-Alladhīna Lā Yuʾminūn* (The Definitive Word on Those Who Believe in the Unseen and Those Who Don't) was published in 1943, a copy found its way to the chief regent, Muḥammad ʿAlī Tawfīq (1875–1955), who was so enamoured of it that he

to Cardinal Pietro Gasparri, the Cardinal Secretary of State. There is no Vatican record of a response to Sabri's initiative.

101 Al-Qawsī, *Muṣṭafā Ṣabrī*, 145. One of his first articles was a poem in response to news that the Turkish republic did not recognise him as a citizen, 'İstifa Ediyorum,' *Yarın*, 29 July 1927, pp. 1–2.

102 Shaykh Khiḍr, a Tunisian, was also drawn into the Ottoman-German propaganda scheme, sent by Enver in 1915 to engage with Muslim prisoners of war. See 'Sheikh Muḥammad Al-Khidr Ḥusayn, un Grand Imâm d'Al-Azhar,' islamophile.org, 16 May 2000, www.islamophile.org/spip/Sheikh-Muḥammad-Al-Khidr-Ḥusayn,376.html (accessed 4 March 2018).

103 Ali Ulvi Kurucu, *Gecelerin Gündüzü: Nurlu Belde Medine'den Yazılar* (Istanbul: Marifet, 1990), 225–31.

104 Al-Qawsī, *Muṣṭafā Ṣabrī*, 150. Sabri discusses his work on the committee in *Mawqif al-ʿAql*, 1:128–9. Sabri's salary is mentioned by Kurucu in his interview in al-Qawsī, *Muṣṭafā Ṣabrī*, 441.

invited Sabri to his Manyal palace and instituted a second monthly salary of the same amount.[105] When Sabri died on 12 March 1954 President Muḥammad Najīb sent a representative to attend the funeral procession from Taḥrīr Square in central Cairo to the ʿAbbāsiyya cemetery in Darrāsa. Sabri's son İbrahim became a professor of Near Eastern Languages at the University of Alexandria.

The lustre of republican Turkey's victories against the major European powers had clearly faded, creating space in Egypt for a renegade thinker like Sabri. The series of language reforms that began in 1928 and the experimentation in using Turkish instead of Arabic in prayer signalled an intent to engage not simply in a notional 'modernisation of Islam' but to sever Turkey from its Arab and Islamic environment. Sabri came to realise that modernist reform had grown deep roots in Egyptian political and intellectual life. Gradually Sabri's intellectual concerns shifted from their intense focus on the drama of Turkish politics to a second stage of more detached reflection on the epistemic violence of European ideas on Islamic state and society, but with an increasingly Egyptian flavour; in his words, his political jihad had given way to 'scholarly, religious jihad' (*jihād ʿilmī dīnī*).[106] His first Egypt-era book, *Masʾalat Tarjamat al-Quʾrān* (The Qurʾan Translation Question, 1932), surveyed a debate that traversed Egypt, Turkey, and India, and in which Akif had decisively intervened through refusing to play the role planned for him – Sabri addresses himself to the views of Shaykh al-Marāghī and Farīd Wajdī and makes no mention of Akif. His second, *Mawqif al-Bashar Taḥta Sulṭān al-Qadar* (Man's Subordination to Divine Decree, 1933), was his first to examine trends in Egypt regarding the theological questions of free will and predestination. His third, *Qawlī fī al-Marʾa* (My View Regarding the Women Issue, 1936) crystallised his views on a debate that had raged in both Egypt and Turkey since Qāsim Amīn published *Taḥrīr al-Marʾa* (Women's Emancipation) in 1899. In his next book, *al-Qawl al-Faṣl*, he discussed the genre of writing which became popular in Egypt in the 1930s and 1940s concerning the Prophet's 'genius' (*ʿabqariyya*), which he understood as an attempt to humanise the prophets to the extent of severing their link with the divine.[107]

105 Al-Qawsī, *Muṣṭafā Ṣabrī*, 150, 442. The regent spoke Turkish with Sabri. The 1943 publication date is given by Kurucu; Düzdağ, *Hatıralar*, 1:309.

106 Sabri, *Mawqif al-ʿAql*, 1:2.

107 On Enlightenment rethinking of the status of prophets see Talal Asad, *Formations of the Secular: Christianity, Islam, Modernity* (Stanford: Stanford University Press, 2003), 43–5.

This led Sabri to his final book, *Mawqif al-ʿAql wa-l-ʿIlm wa-l-ʿĀlam min Rabb al-Ālamīn wa-ʿIbādihi al-Mursalīn* (The Position of Reason, Knowledge, and the World Regards God and His Prophets), a four-volume work that he part-finished in May 1944 but did not fully publish until 1949. Bringing together all his ideas, including *al-Qawl al-Faṣl* which is incorporated in the fourth volume, Sabri surveyed what he called the 'new knowledge' (*al-ʿilm al-ḥadīth*) of contemporary Islamic and European theological and philosophical trends that he feared had brought the 'old knowledge' (*al-ʿilm al-qadīm*) of the Islamic system to the point of collapse.[108] Sabri defended the underpinnings in reason and abstract logic of Islamic theology, which he approached from an Ashʿarī perspective, and rejected the empirical and sceptical drift of European thought regarding concrete and abstract knowledge. In Sabri's view, the reformist intellectuals had accepted a notion of progress dependent upon adjustments to the ontological and epistemological bases of Muslim society and thought. Accepting the Orientalists' claim of fatalism in Islamic theology (viz. Ashʿarī occasionalism), they indulge pantheistic understandings of Sufism as a means of salvaging religion from science. There is no reason to jettison the classical system of *kalām* since it has not been proven inadequate in any way, he said; thus, the discourse of decline must be rejected. Separation of religion from state will lead to tyranny. These are some of his major themes.

Mawqif al-ʿAql's genesis lies in part in an ethic of political activism inspired by the Muslim Brotherhood.[109] At least three of Sabri's close acquaintances talk of his friendship with the group's founder Ḥasan al-Bannā, who would visit Sabri's home regularly.[110] Al-Bannā made use of Sabri as an informal advisor among non-Egyptian ʿulamaʾ he knew in Cairo.[111] Al-Bannā was a supporter of Sabri's project to write *al-Qawl al-Faṣl*, which evolved from an initiative among Azharī scholars to identify an influential voice to counter the ascendent liberalism of the era.[112]

[108] Sabri, *Mawqif al-ʿAql*, 1:97.

[109] The group is commonly known by this name although Society of Muslim Brethren is a better translation.

[110] Kurucu, interview, 442–3; Saraç, interview, 430; and Ali Yakub Cenkçiler, who moved in Brotherhood circles. See Cenkçiler, *Hatıra Kitabı* (Istanbul: Darulhadis, 2005), 25, 40–1, 91, 116, 118, 127.

[111] Ibrāhīm Munīr, deputy general guide of the Muslim Brotherhood; interview, London, 30 January 2019. Other advisors included Afghan ambassador Shaykh Ṣādiq Mujaddidī and Algerian shaykh al-Bashīr al-Ibrāhīmī.

[112] Kurucu, interview, 442.

The title is a reference to Qur᾽an 2:3's *'alladhīna yu᾽minūn bi-l-ghayb'*, but al-Bannā initially proposed *al-Qawl al-Faṣl bayn Īmānayn: Īmān Alladhīna Yu᾽minūn bi-l-Ghayb wa-Īmān Alladhīna Lā Yu᾽minūn* (The Definitive Word on the Faith of Those Who Believe in the Unseen and the Faith of Those Who Don't) and agreed to pay for a large batch of copies in advance to cover printing costs. Sabri was anguished over the implication in al-Bannā's title that it was still possible to talk of the modernists as possessing faith (*īmān*), convinced that their empirical turn placed them outside traditional boundaries, so he altered it accordingly[113] – an indication of a radicalism he developed in Egypt that will be examined in Chapter 5. Sabri became an admirer of Sayyid Quṭb (1906–66) even before the transformation in Quṭb's thinking in the late 1940s, and his discussion in *Mawqif al-ʿAql* of the fate of the Muslim's *īmān* in the post-shariʿa world is strikingly reminiscent of ideas that Quṭb was to elaborate.

ZAHID KEVSERI: A BIOGRAPHY

While Sabri's colleague Zahid Kevseri shared his concern about the infiltration of European positivist and materialist trends through the Islamic modernism movement, he was more specifically focussed on what he discerned as disruptive trends rippling within the Islamic tradition. Sabri committed himself to the political sphere from an early stage, but in Istanbul and in exile Kevseri devoted his energies to forming a counter-discourse to the movement staking a claim to the Salafi nomenclature and its assault on the predominant juridical and theological culture. Kevseri was perhaps better placed than Sabri to engage in this wider critique because of his thorough grounding in the Sufi tradition and Ḥanafī law, theology, and hadith method, since the main targets of the Salafis in their assault on what has been called late Sunni traditionalism were Sufism and Ḥanafism.[114]

Kevseri was born on 28 Shawwāl 1296 (16 September 1879) near the town of Düzce in northwest Anatolia in the village of Hacı Ḥasan.[115]

113 Ibid., 442–3. Kurucu wrote the text out in *riqāʿ* script for the typesetter because Sabri's handwriting was unclear and Cenkçiler wrote out *Mawqif al-ʿAql*; Düzdağ, *Hatıralar*, 1:309–10.

114 Jonathan Brown, *Hadith: Muḥammad's Legacy in the Medieval and Modern World* (Oxford: Oneworld, 2009), 262–4. See also Aḥmad Khan, 'Islamic Tradition in an Age of Print: Editing, Printing and Publishing the Classical Heritage,' in *Reclaiming Islamic Tradition: Modern Interpretations of the Classical Heritage*, ed. Elisabeth Kendall and Aḥmad Khan (Edinburgh: Edinburgh University Press, 2016), 52–99.

115 The republic renamed the village Çalıcuma.

The village was named after his father Hasan Hilmi Efendi (1831–1926) who established a school there after arriving as a refugee from the Ottoman sancak of Şapsığ in the Adyghe region of the northern Caucasus during the mass killings and expulsion of Russia's invasion in 1864.[116] Kevseri's family appear to have been speakers of West Circassian Adyghe, though the autobiographical and biographical information about him has little to say of his mother. His Circassian origin seems to have formed an important if underexamined part of his self-identity in that he spoke the language and went out of his way to help Circassians in Egypt.[117] Like Akif's father, Kevseri's was an *ʿālim* immersed in Sufism but he actively encouraged Kevseri in Sufi interests. Kevseri kept to traditional languages and knowledge systems (Arabic, Persian, Islamic sciences), contrary to Akif's embrace of French literature, leaving a detailed map of his educational profile through his books *Irghām al-Murīd* (Training the Sufi Disciple, 1910)[118] and *al-Taḥrīr al-Wajīz fīmā Yabtaghīhi al-Mustajīz* (Brief Description for Those Seeking an *Ijāza*, 1941). The latter was written as a prepared index of his education that would save him from writing out detailed teaching certificates (*ijāza*) by hand for the many students coming to study with him;[119] it would also prevent any false claims regarding those he taught or

[116] Kevseri told a student visiting Cairo around 1949 that the name Kevseri comes from a mispronunciation of the family's clan name Guser when written in the Ottoman Arabic script; see Muzaffer Özcanoğlu, 'M. Zâhid el-Kevserî İle Yaşadığım Kırık Anılarım,' in *Uluslararası Düzceli M. Zâhid Kevserî Sempozyumu Bildirileri* (Düzce/Sakarya: Sakarya Üniversitesi İlahiyat Fakültesi/Düzce Belediye Başkanlıgı, 2007), 756. Al-Kawtharī, by which he is known in Arabic, was an Arabisation he encouraged for its link to al-Kawthar, the Qurʾanic verse referring to a river in paradise. The name appears with the letter س instead of ث in his 1910 book *Irghām al-Murīd* (Cairo: al-Azhariyya, 2000), 79, 87. For this reason I have preferred Kevseri over the Arabised al-Kawtharī except when referencing his Arabic works in footnotes.

[117] His student Ali Ulvi Kurucu says Kevseri developed a relationship with Circassian royal chamberlain Ismāʿīl Taymūr Pāshā in order to help Circassians; Düzdağ, *Hatıralar*, 2: 181. His main biographer Aḥmad Khayrī says Kevseri spoke fluent Circassian; Aḥmad Khayrī, *al-Imām al-Kawtharī*, in al-Kawtharī, *Maqālāt al-Kawtharī* (Cairo: Al-Tawfikia Bookshop, 2000), 504. His knowledge was enough for him to suggest that the Mamluk dynasty in Egypt was named Burjī not in reference to Cairo's citadel towers but to their Circassian clan of origin; al-Kawtharī, *Muqaddimāt al-Imām al-Kawtharī* (Damascus: Dār al-Thurayyā, 1997), 534.

[118] One of Kevseri's few works translated into Turkish; Vehbi Şahinalp and M. Zahit Kalfagil, *Altun Silsile* (1983).

[119] ʿAbd al-Fattāḥ Abū Ghudda, preface to al-Kawtharī, *al-Taḥrīr al-Wajīz* (Aleppo: al-Matbūʿāt al-Islāmiyya, 1992), 1; cited in Muḥammad ibn ʿAbd Allāh Āl Rashīd, 'al-Imām al- Kawtharī wa-Ishāmātuhu fī ʿIlm al-Riwāya wa-l-Isnād,' in *Uluslararası Düzceli M. Zâhid Kevserî*, 121–2.

who taught him.[120] An invaluable source for understanding the alignment of Late Ottoman Sufism, *al-Taḥrīr al-Wajīz* lists twenty-four shaykhs with whom Kevseri studied before fleeing Istanbul and their biographies (*tarājim*), including eleven who gave him the *ijāza* certification and sixteen whom he knew in his émigré years (unusual for someone of Kevseri's stature), all but one of whom provided him with an *ijāza*. Among his main teachers in Düzce were his father Hasan Hilmi,[121] from whom he received hadith and *fiqh*, Düzce Mufti Hüseyin Vehij,[122] Şaban Fevzi Rizevi, with whom he studied Ottoman *mutakallim*, mathematician Gelenbevi İsmail Efendi (1730–91),[123] and Mehmed Nazım Efendi, a secondary school (*rüşdiye*) teacher with whom he studied Persian, geography, mathematics, and other subjects.[124] His father was first a disciple of the Khālidī Naqshbandī shaykh Şeyh Devlet (d. 1867/8) and Mūsā al-Istirkhānī al-Makkī (d. 1884/5), a Naqshbandī shaykh in the Hijaz whom he met during pilgrimage,[125] before his later well-known attachment to the Khālidī shaykh Ahmed Ziyaeddin Gümüşhanevi (1813–1893) which began in Istanbul in 1887.

Sufi teachers feature heavily among Kevseri's intellectual inspirations in Istanbul. He arrived in 1893 to study at the Kadiasker Ḥasan hadith school, then moved to the Fatih mosque seminary where his most influential shaykhs were Alasonyalı Ali Zeynelabidin (1852–1917) and Eğinli İbrahim Hakkı (d. 1900).[126] His certificate was awarded by a committee headed by the *ders vekili* Ahmed Asım Efendi, after which he began teaching at Fatih himself and was to remain there until 1914. By that time, when the CUP had seized full control of government, Kevseri had stirred their animosity through a successful move, as member of the committee examining the curriculum in the post-1908 reformed school system, to obstruct CUP plans to squeeze religious education through reducing Arabic classes. In Kevseri's view these were essential for Turkish-speakers in particular to access traditional fields of knowledge.[127]

120 Al-Kawtharī, *al-Taḥrīr al-Wajīz* (Cairo: al-Anwār, 1941), 4.
121 Al-Kawtharī, *Irghām al-Murīd*, 79–82; al-Kawtharī, *al-Taḥrīr al-Wajīz*, 42–4.
122 His name is sometimes prefaced Üsküplü for his family origins in Skopje; al-Kawtharī, *al-Taḥrīr al-Wajīz*, 28.
123 Al-Kawtharī, *Irghām al-Murīd*, 84; al-Kawtharī, *al-Taḥrīr al-Wajīz*, 43.
124 Al-Kawtharī, *al-Taḥrīr al-Wajīz*, 34.
125 Ibid., 43; Khayrī, *al-Imām al-Kawtharī*, 534; see Irfan Gündüz, *Osmanlılarda Devlet-Tekke Münasebetleri* (Ankara: Seha Neşriyat, 1984), 76.
126 Al-Kawtharī, *al-Taḥrīr al-Wajīz*, 33. Their biographies can be found in pp. 31–3 and 37–41.
127 Khayrī, *al-Imām al-Kawtharī*, 493–4. See Fortna, *Imperial Classroom*, 127.

He also opposed CUP efforts to loosen the İlmiye's bonds to Ḥanafism through a series of fatwas issued by the Meşihat allowing the use of other schools of law in the civil code (Mecelle-i Ahkam-ı Adliye), based on a decree issued in 1877.[128] When in 1914 professors at Darülfünun wanted to appoint him as lecturer in the history of *fiqh*, CUP administrators left the post vacant rather than give it to Kevseri.[129] Instead he took a job teaching Arabic in the new state (*nizami*) schools, but on the advice of friends in the CUP he quit the capital to avoid arrest and taught in a *nizami* school in Kastamonu, where he remained until the armistice in October 1918.

With the revival in fortune of religious conservatives following the collapse of the CUP government, Kevseri returned to Istanbul to a job teaching Arabic at a private religious school and a post in the prestigious Süleymaniye Schools, where Sabri also found work.[130] Then during Sabri's tenure as sheikh ül-Islam he was appointed *ders vekili* in August 1919.[131] With the departure of both Sabri and the protective environment of Damad Ferid's government in October 1920, Kevseri found himself again in conflict with forces determined to limit the power of the religious establishment. Damad Ferid's successor Ahmed Tevfik Paşa (1845–1936)[132] wanted to demolish the Laleli School, a waqf (*vakıf*) built in the period 1759–63 during the era of Sultan Mustafa III, but Kevseri exhausted legal avenues before claiming his prerogative as *ders vekili* to prevent it. He was forced out of office with the complaisance of the last sheikh ül-Islam, Medeni Mehmed Nuri Efendi (1859–1927).[133] As power in Istanbul shifted to the Kemalist nationalists in late 1922, Kevseri's days of freedom were numbered. When an acquaintance told him his arrest was imminent,

[128] Sadık Eraslan, *Meşihat-i İslâmiyye ve Ceride-i İlmiyye: Osmanlılarda Fetva Makamı ve Yayın Organı* (Ankara: DİB Yayınları, 2009), 89–111. The original decree of 1877 is reproduced in Ebü'l-Ula Mardin, *Medeni Hukuk Cephesinden Ahmet Cevdet Pasa* (Istanbul: Cumhuriyet, 1946), 66–7.

[129] Khayrī, *al-Imām al-Kawtharī*, 494.

[130] Khayrī relates that on the trip back he died when the boat he was on capsized in a storm, and he lost some manuscripts including a letter by the Egyptian Shāfiʿī *faqīh* Ibn Ḥajar al-Haytamī (d. 1566) praising Abū Ḥanīfa. Khayrī does not give its name but says it is not the known letter *al-Khayrāt al-Ḥisān*. Also lost was a copy of Egyptian Ḥanafī-Māturīdī *faqīh* al-Ṭaḥāwī's (d. 933) *ʿAqīda* by the hand of Aleppan historian Ibn al-ʿAdīm (d. 1262). Khayrī does not say if any of Kevseri's twenty-two works composed before he left for Egypt were among those lost at sea, but most of them are unaccounted for. Khayrī, *al-Imām al-Kawtharī*, 500.

[131] Albayrak, *Son Devir Osmanlı Uleması*, 4:128.

[132] Like Sultan Vahideddin he was sympathetic to Mustafa Kemal's nationalists, allowing the Ankara delegation to represent the empire at the Conference of London in 1921.

[133] Khayrī, *al-Imām al-Kawtharī*, 501–2.

Kevseri headed straight to the port and took the next boat to Alexandria without passing by his home, arriving 3 December 1922.[134] He was not to see his family for eight years when they finally came to join him. Kevseri's family life was beset by tragedy. After marrying in 1914 he had three daughters and a son; but his son and first daughter died before he left Istanbul in 1922, and in Egypt his daughter Seniha died of typhoid in 1934 and Meliha from complications related to diabetes in 1947. He was survived by his wife, however, who returned to Düzce after his death in 1952: his student and biographer Aḥmad Khayrī says of her only that she was an 'exemplary pious woman'.[135]

Kevseri blossomed in Egypt as a religious scholar. In contrast to Sabri's political activism, which ensured him a hostile reaction on his arrival in 1922, Kevseri quietly devoted himself to his own project: locating and preparing manuscripts across a range of Islamic sciences for publication with his annotation and preface, a format which became a key weapon in the polemical wars he waged from the late 1920s. Living an unstable life with little money during his early years in Egypt, Kevseri built up a deep knowledge of the manuscripts available in Cairo, mainly at Dār al-Kutub and the Ẓāhiriyya library in Damascus, which he could match with the knowledge he had acquired of Istanbul's manuscript collections. After a year of residing in cheap hotels and flats in the Cairo quarters of Ḥusayn, Shubra, and Heliopolis, he left for Damascus for a year, travelling via boat from Alexandria to Beirut. On his return Kevseri stayed at the Abū Dhahab Sufi lodge in Cairo where Turkish al-Azhar students usually resided (known as Ruwāq al-Atrāk).[136] He appears to have stayed there for three years (1925–7) since in 1928 he returned to Damascus for another year. Back in Egypt in 1929, his life settled into a pattern as he was employed to translate Ottoman documents into Arabic at the state archives (Dār al-Maḥfuẓāt), a modest post that afforded him enough of a salary to carry on his research unimpeded by the rigmarole and rivalry of higher office. He moved from flat to flat in several districts of Cairo before settling on a place in Heliopolis in 1939.[137]

134 Ibid., 502. See also ʿUmar Riḍā Kaḥḥāla, *Muʿjam al-Muʾallifīn: Tarājim Muṣannifī al-Kutub al-ʿArabiyya*, 15 vols. (Damascus: al-Taraqqi, 1961), 10:4; and Albayrak, *Son Devir Osmanlı Uleması*, 4:138. Kaḥḥāla says he was appointed to an institute specialising in collecting information on books and authors called Maʿhad al-Takhaṣṣus fī Maʿrifat Asmāʾ al-Kutub wa-Mawḍuʿātihā wa-Tarājim Muʾallifīhā; 10:4.

135 Khayrī, *al-Imām al-Kawtharī*, 496.

136 Ibid., 495–6.

137 During the Second World War he moved into Shaykh Yūsuf al-Dijwī's home in ʿIzbat al-Nakhl, after al-Dijwī suggested Heliopolis could be a target for German attacks. See Iyād

Kevseri preferred Cairo because of its access to materials and Azharī scholars after Turkey became a closed space for the dissident. During his first Damascus trips he obtained certificates from Sayyid Abū al-Khayr al-Ḥanafī, Muḥammad ibn Jaʿfar al-Kattānī, and Muḥammad ibn Saʿīd ibn Aḥmad al-Farrāʾ, and during the second trip Muḥammad Ṣāliḥ al-ʿĀmilī al-Ḥanafī, Muḥammad Tawfīq al-Ayyūbī, and the well-known hadith scholar Badr al-Dīn al-Ḥasanī (1850–1935).[138] Like Sabri, a close companion in Cairo, he became well connected among scholars and students at al-Azhar, establishing a weekly study circle at the Abū Dhahab mosque within the seminary's environs in Cairo.[139] His efforts to excavate manuscripts continued through his acquaintance with Muḥammad Amīn al-Khanjī (d. 1939), a bookseller from Aleppo who moved his business to the Egyptian capital,[140] Ismail Saip Sencer (1873–1940), manager of Bayezid library in Istanbul,[141] and Yūsuf Banūrī (1908–77), the Deobandi scholar who founded a school in post-Partition Karachi.[142] During his later Cairo years Ḥanafī jurist Muḥammad Abū Zahra (1898–1974) offered him work teaching in the shariʿa department of Fuʾād University[143] but Kevseri declined, citing age and his wife's health problems.[144] Around this time, when Turkey shifted to a multi-party system following the Second World War, he was asked by one of his former teachers, Ahmed Şakir, to teach in Istanbul, and while he made nice about

Aḥmad al-Ghūj, 'al-Imām al-Kawtharī wa-Sijillātuhu al-ʿIlmiyya fī al-Ṣuḥuf wa-l-Majallāt maʿ al-Kashf ʿammā Lam Yujmaʿ min Maqālātihi,' in *Uluslararası Düzceli M. Zâhid Kevserî*, 66, footnote 7.

138 Mehmet Emin Özafşar, 'Muhammed Zahid el-Kevseri Hayatı,' in *Muhammed Zâhid El-Kevserî: Hayatı-Eserleri-Tesirleri*, ed. Necdet Yılmaz (Istanbul: Seha, 1996), 48, footnote 36. On al-Ḥasanī, see Itzchak Weismann, 'The Invention of a Populist Islamic Leader: Badr al-Dīn al-Ḥasanī, the Religious Educational Movement and the Great Syrian Revolt,' *Arabica*, 52/1 (2005): 109–39.

139 Muḥammad Rajab Al-Bayyūmī, 'Muḥammad Zāhid al-Kawtharī, Rāwiyat al-ʿAṣr wa-Amīn al-Turāth al-Islāmī,' in al-Kawtharī, *Muqaddimāt al-Imām al-Kawtharī* (Damascus: Dār al-Thurayyā, 1997), 20.

140 See al-Kawtharī, 'Kalima ʿan Ḥayāt al-Sayyid Muḥammad Amīn al-Khanjī, Shaykh al-Kutubiyyīn,' *Maqālāt*, 437–9.

141 Ibid., 430–2.

142 After Banūrī visited Kevseri in 1938 during a trip to obtain material for the Majlis ʿIlmī established in 1931 by Shaykh Muḥammad ibn Mūsā Mayān Mayān (1905–63), the two established a correspondence lasting from 1939 to 1952; Kevseri's forty-five letters in the chain are published with annotation in Saʿūd Al-Sarḥān, *Rasāʾil al-Imām Muḥammad Zāhid al-Kawtharī ilā al-ʿAllāma Muḥammad Yūsuf al-Banūrī* (Amman: Dār al-Fatḥ, 2013).

143 The Egyptian University was renamed Fuʾād I in 1940 and Cairo University in 1952.

144 Muḥammad Abū Zahra, 'al-Imām al-Kawtharī,' in al-Kawtharī, *Maqālāt*, 18.

returning, health issues and familiarity with Egypt appear to have held him back.[145] He was also asked to take a post as professor of Turkish at the Oriental Languages Institute (Maʿhad al-Lughāt al-Sharqiyya) before it was incorporated in the Egyptian University's Arts Faculty in 1939, but turned the offer down because he had formed a bad opinion of European Orientalist scholars associated with the school.[146] Kevseri had the credentials to establish himself as a Sufi *murshid* had he so wished, particularly within the Khālidī Naqshbandiyya, but while he sometimes visited the Tijāniyya lodge of Shaykh Muḥammad Ḥāfiẓ Efendi with Sabri (who was a degree colder on Sufism) he chose not to follow that path.[147]

Kevseri's overarching concern was to prevent the mainstreaming of the nascent Salafi movement's hostile views of the *madhhab* culture of *fiqh* and *kalām*, a position he dubbed *lā-madhhabiyya*, which was 'the bridge to irreligion [secularism]' (*qanṭarat al-lādīniyya*), in an article published in 1937.[148] This he did via at least 106 articles in the weekly journal *al-Islām* from its inception in 1932 (some were published in *al-Sharq al-ʿArabī*)[149] and gathered on his death by Banūrī and Kevseri students into one book, *Maqālāt al-Kawtharī* (a partial list of their original publication dates is given in Appendix 2).[150] He also wrote fifty-seven prefaces to a range works on history, *fiqh*, hadith, *tafsīr*, and *kalām*, mostly from the classical tradition,[151] that he republished or published from manuscript for the first

145 ʿAmmār Jaydal, 'Mujmal Āthār wa-Ārāʾ Zāhid al-Kawtharī,' in *Uluslararası Düzceli M. Zâhid Kevserî*, 50. In a letter he wrote in 24 March 1951 to parliamentary delegate Gazioğlu Kazuk Kamil Bey, Kevseri expresses satisfaction about the Democrat Party win in the 1950 election, but adds, 'I await the day when people are free to wear what they want on their heads'; Özafşar, 'Muhammed Zahid el-Kevseri Hayatı,' 52. He would joke about his sense of being happily resigned to life in Egypt; see Özcanoğlu, 'M. Zâhid el-Kevserî ile,' 760.

146 Al-Bayyūmī, 'Muḥammad Zāhid al-Kawtharī,' 21.

147 Düzdağ, *Hatıralar*, 2:173.

148 Al-Kawtharī, 'al-Lāmadhhabiyya Qanṭarat al-Lādīniyya,' *Maqālāt*, 129–36.

149 Established in 1946 by *al-Islām* publisher Amīn ʿAbd al-Raḥmān as an alternative outlet. Many articles were republished by *Hudā al-Islām*, established by publisher Ḥasan Qasim whose family was tied to the Shadhilī Sufi order, and *al-Nadhīr*, established by Muslim Brotherhood breakaway group Shabab Sayyidna Muḥammad in 1940. See al-Ghūj, 'al-Imām al-Kawtharī', 69

150 Al-Ghūj says nine articles were not included in the collection and notes some omissions from the articles when first published, such as praise of King Fārūq; 'al-Imām al-Kawtharī,' 80, 83–4. A Turkish translation by theologian Ebubekir Sifil was published in 2014 with seven additional articles, likely given to Sifil by Abū Ghudda before his death in 1997; *Makalatu'l-Kevseri* (Istanbul: RıhleKitaap, 2014).

151 Some are contemporary, mainly students of his: ʿAbd Allāh al-Ghumārī's *Iqāmat al-Burhān ʿalā Nuzūl ʿĪsā fī Ākhir al-Zamān* (1945), Yūsuf Banūrī, *Bughyat al-Arīb fī*

time (and gathered in the collection *Muqaddimāt al-Kawtharī*, Kevseri's Forewords, 1997), twenty-three of which are among thirty-eight works he issued with annotation (most of them published).[152] This is in addition to thirty-five works he authored in his own right, five of which remain unpublished in manuscript form, including biographies of five early specialists in Ḥanafī law.[153]

While most of the twenty-one works he authored before his Egyptian exile are lost, two titles among them evidence an early concern with Ibn Taymiyya, *al-Buḥūth al-Wafiyya fī Mufradāt Ibn Taymiyya* (Investigations into Ibn Taymiyya's Peculiar Juridical Positions) and *al-Taʿaqqub al-Ḥathīth Limā Yanfīhi Ibn Taymiyya min al-Ḥadīth* (Investigations of Hadith Rejected by Ibn Taymiyya). One of his extant Istanbul books, *Irghām al-Murīd*, defends the concept of intercession (*tawassul*; Tr. *tevessül*), and in doing so Kevseri addresses the objections of Ibn Taymiyya in the first pages before detailing the chain of masters in the Khālidī Naqshbandī tradition with which he identifies.[154] At this early stage in his career (1910) Kevseri had established Ibn Taymiyya as the nodal point at which new trends seeking to reduce the Islamic tradition to an essential Arabness intersected. Kevseri's view was that Ibn Taymiyya's virulent objections to seeking the intercession of the dead, including the Prophet, and his understanding of God's power and attributes in terms rejected by the body of Ashʿarī-Māturīdī theologians as anthropomorphism (*tajsīm*) would be troubling to most of his modern admirers if they had detailed knowledge of his writings.

Kevseri's stances soon attracted attention after leaving for Cairo, where the assault on tradition from both the modernists and the self-styled Salafis had begun to overlap despite their different impulses and origins. In 1929 he engaged in one round of polemics with Muḥibb al-Dīn

Masāʾil al-Qibla wa-l-Maḥārīb (1939), Zakī Mujāhid, *al-Aʿlām al-Sharqiyya fī al-Miʾa al-Rābiʿa ʿAshara al-Hijriyya* (1949), Aḥmad Khayrī's *Izālat al-Shubuhāt ʿan Qawl al-Ustādh 'Kunnā Hurūfan ʿāliyāt'* (1950/51), Radwan Muḥammad Radwan, *Fahāris al-Bukhārī* (1949).

[152] Akif Coşkun, *İstanbul'dan Mısır'a Bir İslam Alimi: Zahidü'l-Kevseri* (Istanbul: Işık, 2013), 78–80, lists thirty-eight; *Muqaddimāt al-Kawtharī*, prepared by Muḥammad Abū Zahra, 645–7, 702, lists thirty-three.

[153] The total is listed in *Muqaddimāt al-Kawtharī*, 698–702. The jurists are Muḥammad al-Shaybānī (d. 805), Abū Yūsuf al-Qāḍī (d. 798), Imām Zufar (d. 775), Abū Jaʿfar al-Ṭaḥāwī (d. 933), al-Ḥasan ibn Ziyād (d. 819/820), Muḥammad ibn Shujāʿ (d. 880). Collected in Ḥamza al-Bakrī, ed., *Ḥusn al-Taqāḍī*, 2 vols. (Amman: Dār al-Fatḥ, 2017). See Bakrī's introduction, 5–79.

[154] Al-Kawtharī, *Irghām al-Murīd*, 5–6.

al-Khaṭīb (1886–1969), a colleague of ʿAbduh's disciple and collaborator Rashīd Riḍā (1865–1935), and a second with the Damascus *ʿālim* Muḥammad Bahjat al-Bayṭār (1894–1976) in 1938. In both cases Kevseri's opponents were prodded into action by the Jeddan notable Muḥammad Naṣīf (1885–1971), who was to spend several decades trying to persuade the Saudi-Wahhabi establishment to fashion their Islamic discourse as Salafism.[155] Al-Bayṭar's *al-Kawtharī wa-Taʿlīqātuhu* (Kevseri and His Commentaries, 1938) was first published under Naṣīf's name and Naṣīf appears to have edited and rewritten al-Bayṭār's text.[156] Kevseri responded with two books, *Taʾnīb al-Khaṭīb ʿalā Mā Sāqahu fī Tarjamat Abī Ḥanīfa min al-Akādhīb* (Rebuke of al-Khaṭīb over Lies in His Biography of Abū Ḥanīfa, 1941), a response to the publication in Cairo of anti-Ḥanafī elements in the hadith scholar al-Khaṭīb al-Baghdādī's (d. 1071) well-known *Tārīkh Baghdād* (History of Baghdad), and *al-Nukat al-Ṭarīfa fī al-Taḥadduth ʿan Rudūd Ibn al-Shayba ʿalā Abī Ḥanīfa* (Curious Anecdotes Regarding Ibn al-Shayba's Response to Abū Ḥanīfa, 1945). This spurned a third attack in the form of *Ṭalīʿat al-Tankīl Bimā fī Taʾnīb al-Kawtharī min al-Abāṭīl* (Precursor to Vituperation of the Nonsense in Kevseri's Taʾnīb, 1949), by the Yemeni shaykh ʿAbd al-Raḥmān al-Muʿallimī (1894–1966), and a fuller version of the same that was published by Naṣīf in Damascus after al-Muʿallimī's death with a preface and annotation by Nāṣir al-Dīn al-Albānī (possibly without al-Muʿallimī's blessing).[157]

These issues and their significance for the direction of Islamic thought in the twentieth century will be discussed more fully in Chapter 4. However, one more polemical dispute in which Kevseri actively engaged is worth noting here, that over predestination and free will with his fellow Ottoman exile Sabri. It is clear from Kevseri's letters to Banūrī that Sabri was among his close circle in Cairo, yet Kevseri regretted that Sabri's views had shifted from the generic Ottoman Māturīdī position that saw human action as more

155 David Commins, 'From Wahhabi to Salafi,' in *Saudi Arabia in Transition: Insights on Social, Political, Economic and Religious Change*, ed. Bernard Haykel, Thomas Hegghammer, Stéphane Lacroix (Cambridge: Cambridge University Press, 2015), 159–61.

156 Muḥammad ibn ʿAbd Allāh Āl Rashīd, 'Introduction,' in Al-Sarḥān, *Rasāʾil al-Imām*, 16–20. Al-Bayṭār told Kevseri's student Abū Ghudda he was the original author; Al-Sarḥān, *Rasāʾil al-Imām*, 16–17. Naṣīf/al-Bayṭār were responding to Kevseri's *al-Ishfāq ʿalā Aḥkām al-Ṭalāq* (1936), a response to hadith scholar Aḥmad Muḥammad Shākir's *Niẓām al-Ṭalāq*, and his annotated edition of Ibn ʿAsākir, *Tabyīn Kidhb al-Muftarī fīmā Nuṣiba ilā al-Imām Abī Ḥasan al-Ashʿarī* (1928).

157 Muḥammad ʿAwwāma, 'Manhaj al-Imām M. Zāhid al-Kawtharī fī Naqd al-Rijāl,' in *Uluslararası Düzceli M. Zâhid Kevserî*, 301–2.

independent of God's will than the Ashʿarī position allowed.[158] Kevseri, who very much held to the Māturīdī line, had hoped that his commentaries[159] would change Sabri's mind, but *Mawqif al-ʿAql* took aim at the Māturīdī understanding. Kevseri's rejoinder was his last book, *al-Istibṣār fī al-Taḥadduth ʿan al-Jabr wa-l-Ikhtiyār* (Insights Regarding the Debate on Predestination and Free Will, 1951). The debate brought into sharp focus the differing responses of these representatives of the Late Ottoman religious tradition to the fate of not only Ottoman thought but Islamic thought more generally in the face of revolutionary trends shaking the Islamic episteme. Kevseri said Sabri's views were the result of his low spirits during exile in Greece as Turkey went through radical secular change, which was no basis for re-examining a basic principle of theology and giving ground to fatalistic thought ('I told him once, "perhaps failure in your political endeavours made you believe in predestination, but why is your voluntary action [*ikhtiyār*] to blame for the countering actions of others?"').[160] Sabri had the last word, writing in an addendum to *Mawqif al-ʿAql* that Kevseri was apparently as afflicted as the modernist scholars by the 'propaganda of the foreigners' (*diʿāyat al-ajānib*) that predestination was to blame for Muslim backwardness.[161] The consequences of this debate for conceptualisations of Islam and the modern state will be examined in Chapter 5.

THE STATE OF SCHOLARSHIP

A vast amount has been written in Turkish about Akif. His death in 1936 provided an occasion for early debate about the Turkish republic

158 Fazlur Rahman considered Sabri's *Mawqif al-ʿAql* a defence of Ashʿarī predestination; see Rahman, *Islam and Modernity* (Chicago: University of Chicago Press, 1982), 70. See Sabri, see *Mawqif al-ʿAql*, 3:392, 419.

159 Kamāl al-Dīn al-Bayāḍī (d. 1686)'s *Ishārat al-Marām min ʿIbārat al-Imām* (1949), Ḥanafī jurist Ibrāhīm al-Ḥalabī's (d. 1549)'s *al-Lamʿa fī Taḥqīq Mabāḥith al-Wujūd wa-l-Ḥudūth wa-l-Qadar*, and al-Juwaynī (d. 1085)'s *al-ʿAqīda al-Niẓāmiyya*. The Sabri–Kevseri debate is discussed in Ramazan Altıntaş, 'Kevseri'nin Ta'lik Yöntemine bir Bakış: Cüveyni'nin El-Akidetü'n-Nizamiyye Adlı Eseri Örneği,' in *Uluslararası Düzceli M. Zâhid Kevserî*, 541–55; and Ömer Aydın, 'Mehmed Zahid Kevseri ile Mustafa Sabri Efendi'nin Kader Konusundaki Tartışması,' *Uluslararası Düzceli M. Zâhid Kevserî*, 637–47.

160 Al-Kawtharī, *al-Istibṣār fī al-Taḥadduth ʿan al-Jabr wa-l-Ikhtiyār* (Cairo: al-Azhariyya, 2005), 4.

161 Sabri, *Mawqif al-ʿAql*, 3:390. Sabri's student Kurucu writes that Sabri also railed in private against Kevseri for apparent acts of favouritism towards Circassians in Egypt; Düzdağ, *Hatıralar*, 2:181.

and the radical direction it had taken. His collaborator at *Sebilürreşad* Eşref Edib launched a cottage industry in Akif hagiography, which in time added to the general sense of alarm in Kemalist quarters over the revival of religious sentiment and its reconstruction as political ideology. Edib quickly published his biography of Akif with contributions from a host of intellectuals, and a conference was held in his honour at Istanbul University in 1938.[162] As early as February 1939 one writer could rue that nationalist icons Ziya Gökalp and Yūsuf Akçura were 'yet to find their Eşref Edib' who could eulogise them so effectively.[163] Since Akif was not on the 1924 blacklist of 150 enemies of the republic and he remained the author of the national anthem, his supporters saw their chance to frame him as an alternative, more authentic icon of the republic.[164] As Halim Sabit Şibay (1883–1946), an intellectual close to Gökalp, wrote, 'Akif lived as a great Muslim Turk. He thought in Turkish. He wrote in Turkish. He sang in Turkish.'[165] In the view of Kemalist writers, Akif's gift with language, and in particular his occasional use of colloquial registers, was a form of wizardry deployed to subvert the minds of ordinary Turks with his Islamic message. 'Akif worship' (*Akif-perestlik*) should be set aside so that Gökalp the intellectual and Tevfik Fikret the poet remain Turkey's national heroes, one writer said.[166]

Turkish historians who discussed Akif in English tended to present him as at one with their monochrome view of the Islamic reactionary (*mürteci*). In *The Development of Secularism in Turkey*, first published in 1964, Niyazi Berkes lumped together diverse Muslim thinkers and ulema as 'bigots' attached to the past.[167] Although he saw Akif as the most enlightened of the genre, Berkes could not forgive the decision to withhold his Qurʾan translation, which Berkes mistakenly attributes to a fear of being denounced as an apostate by Rashīd Riḍā.[168] It was not until the 1980s that historians came to a more nuanced, less politicised

[162] Edib, *Mehmed Âkif*, 723.

[163] *Cumhuriyet*, 14 Feb 1939; cited in Edib, *Mehmed Âkif*, 793–5.

[164] Kamil Erdeha, *Yüzellilikler yahut Milli Mücadelenin Muhasebesi* (Istanbul: Tekin, 1998).

[165] Halim Sabit, in Edib, *Mehmed Âkif*, 547.

[166] Ali Süha, 'Laik şair, din şairi,' *Tan*, 5 January 1939. Reproduced in Edib, *Mehmed Âkif*, 753–4.

[167] Niyazi Berkes, *The Development of Secularism in Turkey* (Montreal: McGill University Press, 1964), 338.

[168] Ibid., 338, 489. Riḍā began writing against Qurʾan translation in 1908 and condemned such enterprises in his book *Tarjamat al-Qurʾān* (1922). Riḍā's *al-Manār* series 'Muḥāwarāt al-Muṣliḥ wa-l-Muqallid' was published in *Sebilürreşad* in 1913. See Wilson, *Translating the Qurʾan*, 111–17.

understanding of Late Ottoman religious thought, starting with İsmail Kara's three-volume *Türkiye'de İslamcılık Düşüncesi* (Islamist Thought in Turkey, 1986) which published excerpts from key texts in simplified modern Turkish.[169] The industry in Akif writing found further impetus in the 1990s with the revelations of what had happened to Akif's Qur'an translation and subsequent discovery of extant parts of the text.[170] The ministry of culture and tourism issued a series of publications celebrating Akif in Turkish and English from 1986 on the occasion of the fiftieth anniversary of his death, though historian Fahir İz could still describe him in one article as 'unable to adjust his ideas to the new secular nationalist Turkey'.[171] Interest extended to the Turkish Left, drawn by Akif's sympathetic attention to the popular classes, particularly in his earlier work.[172]

Berkes' theory that Akif scuppered the Turkish Islam project at the behest of Arab radicals reappeared in 1999 in a speech by Professor Brigadier General Yalçın Işımer before the 1999–2000 cohort of the prestigious Gülhane Military Medical Academy in Ankara, titled 'Atatürk'üm ve Türkçem' (My Atatürk and My Turkish). Işımer embellished the story with more details, such as that Akif went to Egypt in order to consult with Riḍā at al-Azhar and plan a Turkish university in Akif's name (one opened in 2006) that would create 'Azhar-minded people' (*el-Ezher kafalı adamlar*).[173] After three years spent abroad to avoid wearing the state-mandated hat, Akif returned in 1926 to inform Atatürk formally that he would not translate the Qur'an, Işımer claimed.[174] Events in this retelling are clearly garbled; in fact, Akif's testimony in his dying months was that he was happy to complete the project, but on his own terms, not those of Ankara.[175] Işımer's statement, which provoked considerable media coverage at the time, came after the military had forced

[169] Kara discusses his work in a rare interview in English in 2017; www.themaydan.com/2017/10/islam-islamism-turkey-conversation-ismail-kara/ (accessed 26 January 2018).

[170] İhsan Efendi entrusted a third of the text to Mustafa Runyun, one of the Sabri–Kevseri circle of students.

[171] İz, 'Mehmet Akif: A Biography,' 315.

[172] A. Cerrahoğlu (aka Kerim Said), one of the few Marxist intellectuals in Turkey to engage critically with Islam, published *Bir İslam Reformatörü, Mehmet Akif* in 1964. See Arif Yılmaz, 'Mehmet Akif Ersoy'un Şiirlerinde Halk Dilinin Kullanımı,' *Mustafa Kemal University Journal of Social Sciences Institute*, 6/11 (2009): 189–210.

[173] Yalçın Işımer, 'Atatürküm ve Türkçem,' *Gülhane Tıp Akademisi 1999–2000 Eğitim-Öğretim Yılı Açılış Töreni* (Ankara: GATA, 27 September 1999), 65–72; reproduced in Cündioğlu, *Bir Kur'an Şâiri*, 536.

[174] Cündioğlu, *Bir Kur'an Şâiri*, 536.

[175] 'The spiritual bounty I feel is very great [*duyduğum manevi feyiz çok büyüktür*]', he said in 1936 of having completed the translation. In Edib, *Mehmed Âkif*, 166.

Necmettin Erbakan's Welfare Party (Refah Partisi) from office in 1997. Under the Justice and Development Party (Adalet ve Kalkınma Partisi, or AKP), which took office in 2002, interest in Akif continued unabated.[176] Akif became the resistance poet who successfully challenged secular radicalism through his 'resistance translation' (*direnen meal*), to quote the title of one recent volume analysing Akif's Qurʾan.[177] This new environment even opened the door to criticism of Akif from Islamic opinion over positions such as his denunciation of Sultan Abdülhamid.[178]

As for Akif in Arabic, his son-in-law Ömer Rıza Doğrul recounts that he had established a certain name in Egypt by the time he visited in early 1914. Doğrul was working in Cairo as translator with a pro-Ottoman newspaper called *al-Shaʿb*. Staff gathered to listen to Akif discussing his poetry, with Doğrul translating into Arabic (then he took him to meet Muḥammad Farīd Wajdī, who, to the surprise of both of them, spoke Turkish).[179] Akif's friend, the diplomat and poet ʿAbd al-Wahhāb ʿAzzām (1894–1959) published an obituary in *al-Risāla* upon his death and followed that with translations of his poetry to introduce his work to Arabic-speaking audiences.[180] It was Sabri's son İbrahim who first translated Akif's *Gölgeler* into Arabic as *al-Ẓilāl* in 1953.[181] Despite this Akif remains largely unknown in Arabic writing on modern Islamic thought.[182]

Sabri tends to feature in Turkish histories of Late Ottoman ulema in starkly polarised terms. For Feroz Ahmad, Sabri is typical of the Islamic movement *tout court*, with a mentality 'little different from that prevailing

176 A glossy culture and tourism ministry book lists 321 works in Turkish on Akif, most of them published since the 1980s. Mustafa İsmet Uzun, ed., *Mehmed Akif Ersoy* (Ankara: Kültür ve Turizm Bakanlığı, 2011).

177 Recep Şentürk, ed., *Direnen Meal: Akif'in Kur'an Meali'nin Tarihi ve Tahlili* (Istanbul: Mahya, 2016).

178 Television drama *Payitaht Abdülhamid* suggested Akif was part of a Masonic conspiracy against the sultan. '"PayitahtAbdülhamid" dizisinde Mehmet Akif Ersoy'a "Mason" göndermesi', T24, 13 October 2020; https://t24.com.tr/video/payitaht-abdulhamid-dizisinde-mehmet-akif-ersoy-a-mason-gondermesi,33217 (accesssed 31 March).

179 Doğrul, 'Şahsi ve Aile Hayatı,' in Edib, *Mehmed Âkif*, 430–1.

180 ʿAbd al-Wahhāb ʿAzzām, 'Shāʿir al-Islām Muḥammad ʿĀkif,' *al-Risāla*, 1 February 1937, 5/187: 181–2; a Turkish translation is provided in Edib, *Mehmed Âkif*, 200-3. Azzam's translation of the opening of *Safahat 1* and *Hüsran* from *Gölgeler* was published in *al-Risāla*, 22 March 1937, 5/194: 469–70.

181 İbrahim Sabri's critical writings on Akif, *Mısır Daneleri*, are held at IRCICA library in Istanbul.

182 There are two studies: ʿAbd al-Salām ʿAbd al-ʿAzīz Fahmī, *Shāʿir al-Islām Muḥammad ʿĀkif* (Mecca: al-Ṭālib al-Jāmiʿī, 1984) and Isa Mustafa Yucar, *Muḥammad ʿĀkif: ʿAṣruhu wa-Juhūduhu fī al-Daʿwā al-Islāmiyya* (PhD thesis, Umm al-Qurā University, Mecca 1990).

in Afghanistan today'.[183] Niyazi Berkes casts Sabri as the chief fanatic of the period and challenges Sabri's claim that Kemalist secularism should be described by the word 'non-religious' (*ladinî*).[184] On the other hand, Sadık Albayrak, a researcher who represented Erbakan's Welfare Party in parliament from 1991 to 1995, depicts Sabri as a hero in *Son Devir Osmanlı Uleması* (Late Ottoman Ulema, 1981), *Hilafet ve Kemalizm* (Kemalism and the Caliphate, 1992), and other books.[185] İsmail Kara's seminal work in the 1980s signalled a new trend in academic writing of impartial appraisal of Sabri and others. Although a series of articles about Sabri appeared in Turkish scholarly journals in the 1990s, a pejorative tone remained discernible.[186] The difficulty for writers was to engage dispassionate discussion of Sabri's contribution to modern Islamic thought without being impacted by his negative views of Turkish nationalism.[187] Although there was renewed interest in his legacy during AKP rule, including the publication in Turkish of *Mawqif al-ʿAql*, Sabri's memory remained a sensitive issue – nationalists vandalised a religious school established in his home town of Tokat in 2017, forcing it to change its name.[188]

The first major biography of Sabri was that of Saudi scholar Mufarriḥ ibn Sulaymān al-Qawsī, *al-Shaykh Muṣṭafā Ṣabrī wa-Mawqifuhu min al-Fikr al-Wāfid* (Shaykh Mustafa Sabri and His Position Regards Foreign Ideology, 1997), which followed a series of reprints of his major works in Cairo and Beirut from the 1980s. Al-Qawsī describes Sabri as a leading light of the era who challenged subordination (*tabaʿiyya*) to Western

[183] Feroz Ahmad, Review of *Muslims in Modern Turkey: Kemalism, Modernism and the Revolt of the Islamic Intellectuals* by Sena Karasipahi, *Journal of Islamic Studies*, 22/1 (2011): 89–91.

[184] Niyazi Berkes, *Türk Düsününde Batı Sorunu* (Ankara: Bilgi Yayınevi, 1975), 49–50, 81, 142.

[185] Albayrak's son Berat married a daughter of AKP founder Recep Tayyip Erdoğan. His book *Religious Struggle in Turkey* (1992) gives a succint summation of the Islamist view of the rise of the secular republic.

[186] Ahmet Akbulut, 'Şeyhulislam Mustafa Sabri ve Görüşleri (1869–1954),' *İslami Araştırmalar*, 6/1 (1992): 32–43; Ali Sarıkoyuncu, 'Şeyhülislam Mustafa Sabri'nin,' 787–812; Yusuf Şevki Yavuz, 'Mustafa Sabri Efendi,' *Islam Ansiklopedisi*, vol. 31 (2006): 350–3; Ramazan Boyacıoğlu, 'II. Meşrûtiyet Döneminde Beyânü'l-Hak Dergisindeki Bazı Görüş ve Düşünceler Üzerine,' *Cumhuriyet Üniversitesi İlahiyat Fakültesi Dergisi*, vol. 3, December 1999: 27–50.

[187] An AKP-backed Imam-Hatip religious school established in Sabri's name in his hometown of Tokat changed its name in 2017 after acts of vandalism.

[188] *Mawqif al-ʿAql* was published in 2005 as *Şeyhulislâm Mustafa Sabri Efendi'nin Mısır Ulemâsı ile İlmî Münâkaşaları* and *al-Qawl al-Faṣl* as *Gaybın Önünde: El-Kavlu'l-Fasl* in 2019. His Ottoman Turkish works were reproduced in modern Turkish earlier, starting with *Dinî Müceddidler* in 1977.

intellectual culture and its atheistic core.[189] He followed here in the footsteps of Palestinian academic Isḥāq Mūsā al-Ḥusaynī, who made a similar appraisal of Sabri before his death in 1954. In one of the first studies of the Muslim Brotherhood, al-Ḥusaynī named Sabri as the leading figure in one of three groups characterising contemporary Muslim debate: those content with the evolving separation between religion (*al-dīn*) and science (*al-ʿilm*), those like Farīd Wajdī attempting to reconcile the two, and those such as Sabri seeking to re-establish the traditional theological-philosophical credentials of religious belief.[190] Sabri's recent book, *Mawqif al-ʿAql*, al-Ḥusaynī noted, defended the rationalist underpinnings of faith and attacked those such as ʿAbduh who hold that reason cannot support some aspects of received creed. The only comparable works in the Turkish sphere are Mehmet Kadri Karabela's thesis *One of the Last Şeyhülislâms, Mustafa Sabri Effendi (1869–1954): His Life, Works and Intellectual Contributions* (2004) and Muhammed Beşir Beşir's *Farklı Yönleriyle Şeyhülislam Mustafa Sabri Efendi* (The Different Facets of Sheikh ül-Islam Mustafa Sabri, 2013). While Beşir's book is hagiographic, Karabela's, the most detailed in English available, examines most of Sabri's core ideas effectively but sidesteps his critique of the Turkish nation-state, stating only that certain of his opinions may be outdated.[191] Sabri's career in Istanbul is discussed in Amit Bein's article ''ulama' and Political Activism in the Late Ottoman Empire: The Political Career of Şeyhülislâm Mustafa Sabri Efendi' (2009) and his book *Ottoman Ulema, Turkish Republic: Agents of Change and Guardians of Tradition* (2011).[192]

Writing on Kevseri has been largely compartmentalised within Islamic Studies.[193] As a (Circassian) Turk writing within the traditional categories

[189] Al-Qawsī, *Muṣṭafā Ṣabrī*, 381.

[190] Isḥāq Mūsā al-Ḥusaynī, *al-Ikhwān al-Muslimūn: Kubrā al-Ḥarakāt al-Dīniyya al-Ḥadītha* (Beirut: Dār Beirut, 1952), 180–1; published as *The Moslem Brethren: The Greatest of Modern Islamic Movements* (Beirut: KḤayāt's College Book Cooperative, 1956). Sabri was also discussed in Muḥammad Ḥusayn, *al-Ittijāhāt al-Waṭaniyya fī al-Adab al-Muʿāṣir* (Cairo: al-Adab, 1954), 348.

[191] Mehmet Kadri Karabela, *One of the Last Ottoman Şeyhülislams, Mustafa Sabri Efendi (1869–1954): His Life, Works and Intellectual Contributions* (MA Thesis, McGill University, August 2003), 102.

[192] The article can be found in *Guardians of Faith in Modern Times: ʿulamaʾ in the Middle East*, ed. Meir Hatina (Leiden/Boston: Brill, 2009), 67–90. See also Ahmet Şeyhun, *Islamist Thinkers in the Late Ottoman Empire and Early Turkish Republic* (Leiden: Brill 2015), 44–52; and on Sabri's criticisms of Kant, see Halim Çalış, 'Mustafa Sabri Efendi ve Kant Felsefesine Yaptığı Eleştiriler,' *Yeni Ümit* 54 (2001): 58–62.

[193] See Stefan Wild, 'Muslim und Madhab: Ein Brief von Tokio nach Mekka und seine Folgen in Damaskus,' in *Die Islamische Welt zwischen Mittelalter und Neuzeit: Festschrift*

of *fiqh*, hadith, *kalām*, etc. – his foray into the public sphere through his journal articles notwithstanding – he has been largely invisible to Middle East Studies. Writing almost entirely in Arabic, Kevseri has only in recent years begun to attract attention among Turkish scholars, either through the lens of pre-modern Islamic sciences or contemporary Islamic thought and movements. İsmail Kara's compendium *Türkiye'de İslamcılık Düşüncesi* overlooked him, as did Amit Bein's *Ottoman Ulema, Turkish Republic* and Ahmet Şeyhun's *Islamist Thinkers in the Late Ottoman Empire and Early Turkish Republic* (2015). Kevseri acquired a comprehensive entry in the authoritative *İslam Ansiklopedisi* (published by Diyanet, Turkey's religious affairs administration) as late as 2013, whereas Sabri's entry first appeared in 2006 and Akif's in 1995. Two conferences bringing together Arab and Turkish researchers working on different aspects of Kevseri's thought went some way to rectify these lacunae in knowledge across scholarly boundaries.[194] Kevseri's Arabic works have been in publication since the 1950s, when his admirers published the collection *Maqālāt al-Kawtharī* the year after his death, and it is by this work – which provides a comprehensive overview of his thinking – that Kevseri is known to most scholars of Islamic history and modern thought. But even within Islamic Studies the focus on Ibn Taymiyya and his followers has obscured or even sought to diminish Kevseri's role leading the traditionalist pushback against the aggressive propagandisation of Ibn Taymiyya in the struggle over normativity and orthodoxy that played out in Islamic publishing.[195]

The partisan controversies of Kevseri's work have guided his posthumous publication trajectory. After fully embracing the term Salafi from the 1950s, Nāṣir al-Dīn al-Albānī made of Kevseri his Other against which the ideological category of Salafism with its radical reworking of the Sunni hermeneutical tradition defined itself. Al-Albānī wrote the preface to al-Muʿallimī's *al-Tankīl* when it was finally published in 1966 and, acquiring a status as the definitive anti-Kevseri text, it was reissued by the publications wing of the Saudi Council of Senior Religious Scholars

für Hans Robert Roemer zum 65. Geburtstag, ed. Hans Robert Roemer, Ulrich Haarmann, Peter Bachmann (Beirut: Wiesbaden, 1979), 674–89; and Aḥmad Khan, 'Islamic Tradition in an Age of Print,' *passim*.

194 Published as *Muhammed Zahid el-Kevserî: Hayatı-Eserleri-Tesirleri* (1996) and *Uluslararası Düzceli M. Zâhid Kevserî Sempozyumu Bildirileri* (2007).

195 See Ahmed El Shamsy's brief discussion of Kevseri, *Rediscovering the Islamic Classics: How Editors and Print Culture Transformed an Intellectual Tradition* (Princeton: Princeton University Press, 2020), 212–17.

(Hay᾿at Kibār al-ʿUlamā᾿ al-Saʿūdiyya) in 1983. In the late 1990s al-Azhar's publication house began reissuing Kevseri's books under the title 'Min Turāth al-Kawtharī' (From the Tradition of Kevseri). A first comprehensive biography in Turkish was published by Akif Coşkun in 2013, and Ebubekir Sifil finally published a Turkish translation of *Maqālāt* in 2014. Kevseri's anti-Salafi discourse, situated in the Ottoman legal-theological binary of Ḥanafī-Māturīdism, makes him today an attractive figure for both religious and secular nationalists seeking to prove the existence of an eternal, unique 'Turkish Islam'.[196] But the discovery, from texts in Arabic produced in Egypt, is a belated one and Kevseri's relative lack of interest in Turkey (from the priority he evidently gave to wider issues of the Islamicate) in subtle ways sours contemporary Turkish writing on him.[197]

CAIRO: INTELLECTUAL CENTRE OF THE ISLAMIC WEST

With the Turkish republic's radical turn, Cairo became a place of refuge for Ottoman exiles, although Turkish cultural life in Egypt was in its twilight years.[198] Before 1908 Egypt had been a place of refuge for Young Turk dissidents, which led to a blossoming of Turkish printing in Egypt that accorded with British imperial interests. Leading CUP intellectual Abdullah Cevdet (1869–1932) alone published eighteen works in Egypt between 1896 and 1909.[199] Anti-regime publishing was also centred in Cairo during the early republic.[200] Viewed as possessing the ability to rally Turkish and pan-Islamic opposition, Akif came under the surveillance of Turkish diplomats. The interior ministry's Internal Security

[196] For example Hilmi Demir and Muzaffer Tan, *Ehl-i Sünnetin Reislerinden İmam-ı Matüridi* (Istanbul: Büyük Resim, 2017). On the trope of Turkish Islam see Elisabeth Özdalga, 'The Hidden Arab: A Critical Reading of the Notion of "Turkish Islam",' *Middle Eastern Studies*, 42/4 (July 2006): 551–70.

[197] Note his student Muzaffer Özcanoğlu's effort to stress Kevseri's longing for the homeland in his presentation to the 2007 conference on Kevseri; in 'Kırık Anılarım,' 755–63.

[198] Ekmeleddin İhsanoğlu (trans. Humphrey Davies), *The Turks in Egypt and Their Cultural Legacy* (Cairo: American University in Cairo Press, 2012), 62–3. During the reign of King Fārūq (1936–52) Turkish was not spoken at the palace and actively discouraged by the king.

[199] On Turkish political publications in Egypt from 1895 to 1947, see İhsanoğlu, *The Turks in Egypt*, 219–33, 253–95.

[200] The main critical newspaper was *Müsavat*, established by Liberal Entente figure Hafiz İsmail in Cairo in 1927. *Muhadenet*, established in 1927 by Hüseyin Remzi Bey, published pro-Turkey material in Turkish and Arabic with articles by Egyptian writers including Wajdī and ʿAzzām. *Cephe*, published 1943–7, was pro-Turkey and pro-Allied powers. See İhsanoğlu, *The Turks in Egypt*, 288–95.

Directorate (Emniyet İşleri Umum Müdürlüğü) sent a troubled note to the consulate in Alexandria in July 1936 to find out why Akif had been granted a visa, declaring that Akif had engaged in pro-caliphate propaganda in Egypt and citing a trip he made in 1935 to Antakya in French mandate Syria (*inkılâp ve rejimimiz aleyinde çok kötü sözler sarfettiği ve hilâfet propagandası yaptığı*); the note also said Akif had been in close contact with dissidents on the list of 150.[201] Akif's letters throughout his thirteen years in Egypt are sparing in their political content, giving the impression that he was wary of their falling into the hands of censors and his being banned from ever returning home as a result. His biographer Ertuğrul Düzdağ argues that republican bureaucrats should be thanked for keeping Akif off the list of subversives, otherwise the *İstiklal Marşı* would have been replaced and 'it would be an issue even to talk about him today'.[202] Sabri, by contrast, was free to engage his intellectual pursuits in Egypt and maintained contact with Akif and Kevseri, but none of the biographical sources mention a relationship between Akif and Kevseri.

Akif was the kind of modernist intellectual whom Sabri relentlessly attacked in his work, but any rancour between them was focussed on the dramatic post-war period of occupation and the new republican order. Indeed, before their split in 1920 over Mustafa Kemal's rival authority in Ankara, the conservative and modernist Islamic thinkers drew closer together: from May to July 1919 *Sebilürreşad* serialised Sabri's *Dinî Müceddidler* (Religious Reformers, 1922) and the last section of *Yeni İslam Müctehidlerinin Kıymet-i İlmiyesi* (The Scholarly Value of Islam's New Mujtahids, 1919),[203] Sabri's two Ottoman Turkish works against the reformers. Sabri later suggested Akif had innocently rendered ʿAbduh and Wajdī a great service they did not deserve in translating their works.[204] Their major difference arose over how to respond to Mustafa Kemal's nationalist movement. Sabri's complaint to Akif and intellectuals in general was 'you left me alone' (*beni yalnız bıraktınız*)[205] in fighting the

201 No. 8056, dated 13/7/1936 and no. 8297, dated 20/7/1936; cited in Düzdağ, *Mehmed Âkif*, 20–1. The Cairo consulate responds that it had not heard of such activities but makes the comment that he opposed wearing the hat due to his 'religious extremism' (*dinî taassub*); undated document, Düzdağ, *Mehmed Âkif*, 22.

202 Ibid., 17–18.

203 This last was published as 'Terakki Edelim, fakat Müslüman Kalmak Şartıyla,' *SR*, 24 Temmuz 1335 (24 July 1919), 17/431: 113–15.

204 'Akif translated their works lovingly with that beautiful flowing style', Kurucu quotes Sabri as saying; Düzdağ, *Hatıralar*, 2:65.

205 Muhammed Beşir Beşir, *Farklı Yönleriyle Mustafa Sabri Efendi* (Istanbul: Tahlil, 2013), 69.

Kemalist regime. Why did Akif not come join Sabri in his *Yarın* project? 'In time we wrote what we could. We stayed and struggled so that the country would not come to this,' Akif replied when Sabri harangued him over the issue after Sabri's arrival in Cairo.[206] And why did Akif join Kemal's nationalists? There was no choice when the Greek army was occupying Anatolia, Akif protested (*tercih yapacak zaman olmadığı*).[207] On another occasion Sabri pressed him on whether he thought Atatürk was an exceptional figure, to which Akif replied that his only exceptional quality was an intimidating gaze (*korkutan bir bakış*).[208] Despite this frostiness Akif still visited Sabri in his home to console each other over the death of Ahmed Naim in 1934 and Sabri viewed Akif as something of a divinely inspired poet.[209] During the Naim visit Sabri's son İbrahim pressed Akif on why he had not deployed his skills to denounce the changes in Turkey and mobilise opposition, which İbrahim felt he was uniquely positioned to do.[210] Akif said he had been reduced to someone unable to pray or write, and had considered writing a play on the issue titled *Bize Neler Oldu* (What Happened to Us): 'I swear, I had no strength left, I could not pull myself together. These events impacted me greatly. Let me explain the extent of my misery: I could not pray without making mistakes. Even in prayer I was lost. That's how distracted I was.'[211] Akif spent more time with İhsan Efendi, whom he had met on the boat to Egypt in 1924, and Turkish students in his circle such as İsmail Ezherli Hoca (1906–76) and Bayramiçli Hafız Eşref.[212] After his death, it was widely suspected that Akif had entrusted his Qurʾan to İhsan Efendi. For many years Akif acquaintances from Istanbul and embassy officials in Cairo would come to him seeking the truth about what happened. As late as 1949 the Turkish embassy approached Kevseri. He is reported to have told them: 'If İhsan Efendi said he destroyed it then it's true. He's someone true to his word.'[213]

[206] Recollection from Sabri to his student Kurucu; Düzdağ, *Hatıralar*, 2:112.
[207] Ibid., 2:111–12.
[208] Ibid., 2:112.
[209] Ibid., 2:113–14.
[210] He expressed this view to Ali Özek, one of the Turkish students in Cairo during the 1950s; Ramazan Yıldırım *Medrese'den Üniversite'ye Ali Özek* (Istanbul: Düşün Yayıncılık, 2012), 102.
[211] 'Yeminim olsun ki mecalım kalmadı, kendimi toparlayamıyorum. Bu yapılanlar bana çok ağır geldi. Perişanlığımın derecesini size şöyle anlatayım: Secde-i sehivsiz namaz kılamaz oldum. Yahu namazda dalıp gidiyorum. Zihnim öyle perişan'; Düzdağ, *Hatıralar*, 2:114–16, 154. It's not clear if Ibrahim or his father told Kurucu this.
[212] Ibid., 1:331.
[213] Özcanoğlu, 'Kırık Anılarım,' 761–2.

Bar his encounters in Ḥilwān with its rector Shaykh al-Marāghī, Akif kept his distance from al-Azhar, but both Kevseri and Sabri were heavily engaged with Azharīs and the Egyptian intellectual scene. They brought with them from Ottoman Istanbul experience of the same debates on Westernisation, Islam, and reform, thus the knowledge and vehemence they injected into their polemical skirmishes in the Egyptian arena were effective enough to stir strong reactions and even efforts to limit their influence.[214] Sabri was not the only one with links to the Muslim Brotherhood: lines can also be drawn between Akif and Kevseri to Ḥasan al-Bannā. ʿAbd al-Fattāḥ Abū Ghudda (1917–97) was a student of Kevseri who made al-Bannā's acquaintance during the period 1944–50 when studying at al-Azhar and in Kevseri's circle and who went on to serve as Mufti of Aleppo and Supreme Guide of the Syrian Muslim Brotherhood (1973–6).[215] Akif met al-Bannā at least once in Ḥilwān at the home of ʿAbd al-Wahhāb ʿAzzām, where he was also introduced to al-Azhar's al-Marāghī.[216] However, the recollections of Turkish students and religious scholars in Cairo during the 1930s and 1940s describe Sabri as the main point of contact between the Turks in Egypt and the Brotherhood. The religious scholar Ali Yakub Cenkçiler (1913–88), one of the Turkish students of Sabri and Kevseri in Cairo, is an important source on this point. In his memoirs he explains that he went to Egypt with the specific intent of joining the circles of Akif and Sabri. After receiving news while en route of Akif's early death,[217] he arrived to discover that Sabri was the 'chief wrestler' of an Egyptian-Turkish Islamic intellectual scene (*bu münakaşa ve münazara meydanının başpehlivanı*) that included al-Bannā.[218] For Cenkçiler al-Bannā was the great activist of the era and Sabri was its theoretician.[219] With the deaths of Sabri, Kevseri, and al-Bannā, Egypt

[214] Sabri said sympathetic ʿulamaʾ and writers advised him to keep quiet for an easier life. Beşir, *Mustafa Sabri Efendi*, 44.

[215] On Abū Ghudda in Syria see Hashimi Muḥammad ʿAli, *al-Shaykh ʿAbd al-Fattāḥ Abū Ghudda Kamā ʿAraftuhu* (Beirut: al-Bashāʾir al-Islāmiyya, 2004); Raphaël Lefèvre, *Ashes of Hama: The Muslim Brotherhood in Syria* (London: Hurst, 2013); Thomas Pierret, *Religion and State in Syria: The Sunni ʿulamaʾ from Coup to Revolution* (Cambridge: Cambridge University Press, 2013). Abū Ghudda wrote a preface to Kevseri's *Fiqh Ahl al-ʿIrāq wa-Ḥadīthuhum* (Beirut: Maktab al-Matbūʿāt al-Islāmiyya, 1970) and *al-Taḥrīr al-Wajīz* (1993).

[216] Al-Bannā told Kurucu this in Medina in 1946. Akif, he said, was an 'honourable man' (*asil bir insan*); Düzdağ, *Hatıralar*, 2:263–4.

[217] Cenkçiler, *Hatıra Kitabı*, 22.

[218] Ibid., 116.

[219] Ibid., 25, 155.

had no more taste for him and he returned to Istanbul.[220] Ali Ulvi Kurucu (1922–2002), another student of the group, relates a meeting in 1945 between Amīn Ḥusaynī (1895–1974), Mufti of Jerusalem, and Sabri and his students in Cairo during which Sabri led the conversation to the topic of al-Bannā, asking al-Ḥusaynī if he had met him yet. Al-Ḥusaynī proceeds to lavish praise on al-Bannā for an integrity he says won him huge a following among youth inside and outside Egypt. 'My sons', he exhorts the group, 'live by me, live by Ḥasan al-Bannā – God-willing, you will become like shaykh al-Islam Mustafa Sabri or Zahid Kevseri.'[221]

Two other figures sought refuge in Cairo during this period, forming a coda to the period of republican exile in Egypt. At some point soon after Atatürk's death in 1938 Eşref Sencer moved to Alexandria, staying with relatives and avoiding political activity, until 1950 when he returned to Turkey following the electoral victory of the Democrat Party (Demokrat Parti).[222] Another visitor to Cairo was Mūsā Jārullāh Bigiev, Sabri's poster-child for modernist delusion in *Dinî Müceddidler* and *Yeni İslam Müctehidlerinin Kıymet-i İlmiyesi.* One of many Tatar activists in the Istanbul milieu, Bigiev published Ottoman works around modernist themes after five years in Egypt during which he followed ʿAbduh, Shaykh Muḥammad Bakhīt al-Muṭīʿī (d. 1935), who later served as chief mufti, and others. The work that first attracted the opprobrium of conservatives was *Rahmet-i İlahiye Burhanları* (Proofs of God's Mercy, 1911) which argued that God would save non-believers as well as Muslims. Bigiev was forced to flee the Soviet Union in 1930 and was jailed by the British authorities in India during the Second World War. In 1947 he settled in Egypt, where he died in October 1949 after Sabri and Khadīja ʿAbbās Ḥalīm, daughter of the former khedive Tawfīq (ruled 1879–92), helped him find medical treatment and a place to stay.[223]

220 Ibid., 118. Attendees at his funeral in 1988 included Necmettin Erbakan, İskenderpaşa Naqshbandī shaykh Esad Coşan, and Recep Tayyip Erdoğan; ibid., 93.

221 Düzdağ, *Hatıralar*, 2:234. The meeting took place after al-Ḥusaynī left France for Cairo in May 1945 when Britain sought his arrest. Al-Ḥusaynī talks in his memoirs of how he kept a low profile living in Cairo; ʿAbd al-Karīm al-ʿUmar, *Mudhakkirāt al-Ḥājj Muḥammad Amīn al-Ḥusaynī* (Damascus: Ahālī, 1999), 259.

222 Fortna, *The Circassian*, 268–70

223 Al-Sarḥān, *Rasāʾil al-Imām*, 108–14, footnote 1. On Bigiev, see Ahmet Kanlıdere, *Reform within Islam: The Tajdid Movement among the Kazan Tatars, 1809–1917* (Istanbul: Eren, 1997); Rotraud Wielandt, 'Main Trends of Islamic Theological Thought from the Late Nineteenth Century to Present Times,' in *The Oxford Handbook of Islamic Theology*, ed. Sabine Schmidtke (Oxford: Oxford University Press, 2016), 707–64; Wilson, *Translating the Qurʾan*, 117–47.

LANGUAGE AND RESISTANCE

Use of language was a critical element in these thinkers' engagement with the transformations of the age. All three were highly proficient in not only Arabic, but Persian. Indeed, Kevseri's first work was a Persian-language treatise on Arabic grammar, *Naẓm-i ʿAvāmil-i Iʿrāb*.[224] Akif taught Persian texts while he lived in Ankara during the post-war occupation. Kevseri wrote almost entirely in Arabic, with only one known work in Ottoman Turkish, a biography of Sirhindī composed while he was in Kastamonu.[225] Engaged more with the public sphere than Kevseri, Sabri shifted from Turkish to Arabic in the critical period 1922–4 when the Ottoman state was transformed from Islamic sultanate/caliphate to Turkish republic, publishing his first major Arabic work *al-Nakīr ʿalā Munkirī al-Niʿma*. In Cairo these two religious scholars published solely in Arabic-language media and with Arabic-language publishers. Akif, on the other hand, never published in Arabic. As his *Safahat* project evolved, Akif formulated a very particular lexical, semantic, and morphological style located in the interplay of Turkish, Arabic, and Persian in which he retained the use of *aruz* metre with its associations of transnational Islamic identity but directed himself to a Turkish audience. He could only have done this within the medium of Ottoman Turkish, and it is only Akif who would have broken the law had he continued his literary project inside the Turkish republic, since he published in the Ottoman Arabic script.[226] *Gölgeler* was published at the Shabāb printing press in Cairo in 1933 and when Akif sent a shipment of 2,175 copies to Istanbul to accompany his return in 1936 the ministry of interior had some destroyed and a batch sent back to Egypt due to their use of Arabic script, denouncing the collection as 'backward propaganda' (*irticai propagandalar*).[227]

The language law of 1928 should more accurately be described the alphabet law, since it mandated the use of a modified Latin script for

[224] Listed by Aḥmad Khayrī, but apparently lost; al-Kawtharī, *Maqālāt*, 517.

[225] Ibid., 517.

[226] Among the literati Refik Halit Karay (1888–1965) also continued publishing in Ottoman script, but the output of many dried up, even if they were public supporters; Laurent Mignon, 'The Literati and the Letters: A Few Words on the Turkish Alphabet Reform,' *Journal of the Royal Asiatic Society*, 20/1 (2010): 11–24.

[227] Murad Bardakçı, 'Mehmed Âkif devlet tarafından "İrtica-906" diye kodlanmış, ölüm döşeğinde yatarken bile izlenmiş ve Safahat'ı da imha edilmişti,' *Habertürk*, 19 November 2018; www.haberturk.com/yazarlar/murat-bardakci/2225662-mehmed-akif-devlet-tarafindan-irtica-906-diye-kodlanmis-olum-doseginde-yatarken-bile-izlenmis-ve-safahati-da-imha-edilmisti (accessed 12 August 2019).

Turkish, with municipalities given discretion to apply penalties for use of Arabic script after a two-month grace period. The law was the first step in a series of linguistic changes over the following decade which as a whole are termed the language revolution (*dil devrimi*), encompassing elimination of words of Arabic and Persian origin, invention of Turkish equivalents, removal of Arabic and Persian from the school curriculum in 1929, banning the Arabic call to prayer from 1932, and the obligatory use of Turkish surnames from 1934.[228] However, the use of the Ottoman Turkish continued in private, and letter writing is one sphere where the Arabic script survived into the 1960s.[229] For some this was an ideological issue, but for many it was a question of habit and confidence in expression. A mixture of both motives explains Akif's use of Ottoman in correspondence with family and friends in Turkey in the period from 1928.[230] We know too that Kevseri wrote at least one letter in Ottoman to his brother in 1952 (see Appendices 3 and 4).[231] Akif was a master of register in Turkish, shifting from colloquial in letters to his family to elaborate formality in letters to the composer Şerif Muhiddin Targan (1892–1967), whom he revered,[232] but he expressed regret on occasion over the reforms for having in his view simply replaced one foreign lexicon for another: 'With nothing remaining of what we took from the Persians, or to be precise that literary style's complete demise, we seem to have begun to steal from the Westerners and especially the French. I don't

[228] Geoffrey Lewis, *The Turkish Language Reform: A Catastrophic Success* (Oxford: Oxford University Press, 1999); Uriel Heyd, *Language Reform in Modern Turkey* (Jerusalem: Israel Oriental Society, 1954); Hüseyin Sadoğlu, *Türkiye'de Ulusçuluk ve Dil Politikaları* (Istanbul: Bilgi Üniversitesi Yayınları, 2003); Tuğrul Şavkay, *Dil Devrimi* (Istanbul: Gelenek, 2002).

[229] Emmanuel Szurek, 'The Linguist and the Politician. The Türk Dil Kurumu and the Field of Power in the Single-party Period,' in *Order and Compromise: Government Practices in Turkey from the Late Ottoman Empire to the Early 21st Century*, ed. Marc Aymes, Benjamin Gourisse and Élise Massicard (Leiden: Brill, 2015), 68–96; Hale Yılmaz, 'Learning to Read (Again): The Social Experiences of Turkey's 1928 Alphabet Reform,' *IJMES*, 43/4 (2011): 677–97.

[230] Akif's correspondence continued from 1928 with his daughter Suad and her husband Ahmed, Eşref Edib, Mahir İz, Eşref Sencer, Fuad Şemsi İnan, Şefik Kolaylık, Asım Şakir Gören, Princess Emine ʿAbbas Halim, Ömer Rıza Doğrul, and Abdulillah Bey. The letters Akif received have not been made public or found.

[231] Dated 8 Jumādā al-Ākhira 1371 (5 March 1952), Kevseri informs Necati in Düzce that he and his wife are ill and may not live much longer; www.facebook.com/arslan.hamdi2016/posts/10155424320453953 (accessed 5 February 2018).

[232] See four letters to Muhiddin, a celebrated oud player who moved to New York in 1924. Reproduced in Günaydın, *Mektuplar*, 76–82.

know when we'll attain a literature born of our own soul.'[233] As a criticism, this observation seems rather soft if we are to take Akif as a Muslim radical opposed to the republican project. Akif's commitment to Ottoman was considerable. Indeed, his career was given to developing a modern Ottoman that retained a core of Arabic and Persian features yet was functionally Turkish. In other words, Akif's Ottoman was a form of resistance to the more radical elements of Turkish nationalism, but not to its basic premises.

Mustafa Sabri's reaction to the language reforms, on the other hand, was more viscerally rejectionist. Ali Ulvi Kurucu recounts how Sabri would listen to state radio broadcasts from Ankara, noting down the newly minted words. Sabri realised that the aim was to create a new generation of Turks capable only of reading the new Turkish, unable to access that which came before. Sabri predicted that an impoverished, truncated, smaller language would emerge, cut off from its deep historical roots.

> Turkish was once one of the richest languages through the Turkicising of Persian and Arabic. But at this rate, not only 1,000-year-old works, but works only twenty or thirty years old will become incomprehensible. Turkish used to flow like water in sermons, speeches, and poetry. When you wrote or spoke you wouldn't repeat the same words, but with these repetitions what awaits us is an ugly, sterile, and incongruous Turkish and an ugly poetry of jarring words that don't rhyme.[234]

Kevseri made no clear reference to the language revolution, nor indeed to other aspects of the early Kemalist period in Turkey, but he surely agreed with Sabri's assessment. In Kevseri's view, Mustafa Kemal was the 'tyrant of atheism' (*ṭāghiyat al-ilḥād*) from whom no good could come.[235]

Both Sabri and Kevseri's mastery of written Arabic placed them at the end of a long tradition of Arabic-language material in Islamic sciences produced by Arabic-proficient ulema and men-of-letters. The republic would even refashion the ulema as professors of divinity (*ilahiyat*) in university faculties.[236] Sabri and Kevseri were able to adapt the form of expression with which they were familiar inside the disciplinary categories of *kalām*, hadith, and *fiqh* to the popular intellectual debate in the journals

[233] Letter to Princess Emine ʿAbbas Halim, 9 February 1936; in Günaydın, *Mektuplar*, 143.

[234] Beşir, *Mustafa Sabri Efendi*, 82–3. The comments were made at some point during the Second World War.

[235] Letter 11 (undated) from Kevseri to Yūsuf Banūrī; Al-Sarḥān, *Rasāʾil al-Imām*, 117.

[236] The Imam-Hatip schools from 1950 were an attempt to return ulema their status; see Iren Özgür, *Islamic Schools in Modern Turkey: Faith, Politics, and Education* (Cambridge: Cambridge University Press, 2012).

of the day. Rarely did weaknesses show through. In the view of Muḥammad Abū Zahra, Kevseri's writing betrayed no indication that Arabic was not his mother tongue.[237] Kevseri's facility with the language extended to the gentle turn of phrase,[238] the obscure,[239] the neologistic insult,[240] defence of Abū Ḥanīfa's Arabic,[241] the florid riposte,[242] and of course Qurʾanic hermeneutics.[243] Arabic was the medium of communication in Kevseri's dealings with Yūsuf Banūrī and other Indian-Pakistani scholars, and he appears to have been more familiar with colloquial Arabic in Egypt than either Sabri or Akif, which likely accounts for the impression one gets of his wider interaction with Egyptians. 'I don't understand their Arabic and they don't understand mine', Sabri once said,[244] and while Sabri would exchange views in writing with modernist intellectual Ṭāhā Ḥusayn (1889–1973),[245] Kevseri would receive Ḥusayn at his house.[246] Akif also

237 Abū Zahra, 'al-Imām al-Kawtharī,' in al-Kawtharī, *Maqālāt*, 15.

238 The Prophet's death as *zaman luḥūqihi bi-l-rafīq al-aʿlā*; Kevseri, 'Maṣāḥif al-Amṣār wa-ʿAẓīm ʿInāyat Hādhihi al-Umma bi-l-Qurʾān al-Karīm fī Jamīʿ al-Dawāʾir,' *Maqālāt*, 26.

239 The use of the verb *istaqʿad*; 'Hal li-Ghayr Allāh Ḥaqq fī al-Ījāb wa-l-Taḥrīm,' *Maqālāt*, 110. The verb is not cited in the classical dictionaries but appears in *Nahj al-Balāgha* and is used in some colloquial speech.

240 He derides his Salafi and modernist opponents as, variously, *mutamajhid*, *mustajhid*, and *mutasallif*; al-Kawtharī, *al-Ishfāq ʿalā Aḥkām al-Ṭalāq* (Cairo: al-Azhariyya li-l-Turāth, 1994), 8; and al-Kawtharī, *Taʾnīb al-Khaṭīb ʿalā Mā Sāqahu fī Tarjamat Abi Ḥanīfa min al-Akādhīb* (publisher unknown, 1990), 105.

241 His use of *bi-abā qubays*, which al-Khaṭīb al-Baghdādī claims is wrong; Kevseri, *Taʾnīb al-Khaṭīb*, 47. He argues Abū Ḥanīfa was the best grammarian of the four imams, noting mistakes in Ibn Ḥanbal's writing; ibid., 54. He accuses al-Khaṭīb of questioning Abū Ḥanīfa's Arabic on the basis of his non-Arab origin; ibid., 246–8.

242 To the suggestion in *Ṭalīʿat al-Tankīl* that Kevseri is a dog or a prostitute, Kevseri says al-Muʿallimī is a 'failed slanderer' (*al-bāhit al-mutahāfit*) and 'al-Kawtharī is not one to talk like a barking dog or a prattling prostitute'; al-Kawtharī, *al-Tarḥīb bi-Naqd al-Khaṭīb*, in al-Kawtharī, *Taʾnīb al-Khaṭīb*, 374. See also the wordplay of '*ishbāʿ ashʿabiyyataka*' in his response to Muḥibb al-Dīn al-Khaṭīb's accusation of anti-Arab *shuʿūbiyya* that al-Khaṭīb is an opportunist who only wants to 'satiate his greed'; al-Kawtharī, *Ṣafʿāt al-Burhān ʿalā Ṣafaḥāt al-ʿUdwān* (Cairo: al-Azhariyya li-l-Turāth, 2005), 40.

243 In the debate over literal understandings of the Qurʾanic text, he argued that *istawā ʿalā al-ʿarsh* in 57:4 could not be understood as God's occupying a position (*al-istiqrār al-makānī*) on a throne since the same verse also says God is *maʿakum aynamā kuntum*, which no one understands literally as a physical presence; Kevseri, 'Khuṭūrat al-Qawl bi-l-Jiha Faḍlan ʿan al-Qawl bi-l-Tajsīm al-Ṣarīḥ,' *Maqālāt*, 271.

244 Cited in Özcanoğlu, 'Kırık Anılarım,' 759. Sabri made the comment during a tram ride. Khayrī says Kevseri had only a slight accent, presumably in colloquial Arabic; Khayrī, *al-Imām al-Kawtharī*, 504.

245 Sabri, *Mawqif al-ʿAql*, 1:446–54 and 4:459–61, which includes correspondence between them.

246 Özcanoğlu, 'Kırık Anılarım,' 759. The visit occurred after Ḥusayn was appointed education minister in 1950.

made light of his abilities in Egyptian Arabic, telling his Turkish-language students at the Egyptian University where he began teaching in 1929, 'if you don't laugh at my Arabic I won't laugh at your Turkish'.[247] In Istanbul, however, it was Akif who was regarded as the prime Arabist of the era due to his knowledge of the literary tradition. Indeed, his confidante Midhat Cemal Kuntay writes that the intellectual elite were in awe of Akif's Arabic,[248] and the decision to give him the Qur'an translation project is testament to that.

The political implications of language were drawn out by Sabri most of all. For Sabri, as he wrote in his last Ottoman work *Dinî Müceddidler*, acquiring Arabic was more important than being Arab or Turkish (*zaten bence Türkün Arap veyahud Arabın Türk olmasının ehemiyeti yoktur. Yalnız lisan itibariyle Arapçanın tefevvükünü kabiliyet-i te'ammümünü itiraf etmek zaruridir*).[249] He qualified this statement with the proviso, 'let it not be thought that I want to gradually Arabise the Turks' (*Türkleri tedricen Araplaştırmak istediğim zannolunmasın*).[250] However, in Greece in 1930 he seemed to go further, writing that he would have favoured Turks switching to Arabic, though not for the purpose of claiming membership of any ethnic Arabness (*Arap milliyeti*) which would be no better than Turkish chauvinism.[251] Two decades later in Cairo he avoided phrasing his views in such a manner but was equally controversial:

If we are to speak about preferences among peoples, I preferred the Arabs over my people, the Turks, and I declared this before my present status as an emigré from Turkey. I declared it in the Ottoman parliament when I was a member and its Arab Syrian, Hijazi, Iraqi, and Yemeni members heard this. Today too I hold to my position of preferring the Arabs, because the Qur'an was revealed in their language, and it was memorised as it was revealed. So because of the Qur'an and the interest in it of the religious scholars of Islam from all nations, and who established Arabic grammar which has no peer among the world's languages, the language of the Arabs became the clearest (*afṣaḥ*) and the best (*afḍal*) of all languages.[252]

European occupation of Anatolia would have been better than Kemalist rule since the faith in an individual's heart can survive non-Muslim rule

247 Kuntay, *Mehmet Akif*, 133.
248 Ibid., 22.
249 Sabri, *Dinî Müceddidler, Yahud 'Türkiye İçin Necat ve İğtila Yolları'nda bir Rehber* (Istanbul: Âsitâne Kitabevi, nda), 260.
250 Ibid., 260.
251 Sabri, 'Din ve Milliyet - 1,' *Yarın*, 14 April 1930, p. 1.
252 Sabri, *Mawqif al-'Aql*, 1:92.

intact but not that of apostates,[253] but it was specifically his view that Turkish ethnicity is of secondary importance to knowledge of Arabic that was omitted from the 1994 translation of *Dinî Müceddidler* into modern Turkish.[254]

Akif shared this sense of Arabic's importance as the lingua franca of the Islamicate,[255] but was devoted to Ottoman Turkish with its heterogeneous Arabic, Persian, and Turkish lexicon. His biographer Emin Erişirgil contrasted Akif's methodology with that of Ziya Gökalp, whose view was that a core of Arabic and Persian-origin words was acceptable only if they operated according to Turkish language rules and were rendered in a Turkish (Istanbul) accent.[256] Akif could support this approach as a compromise with the Turkists, though his preference was to celebrate a word's Arabic or Persian source environment to the full. This can be seen at several points in his *Safahat* where Yakup Çelik, one of his editors in modern Turkish, has opted for familiar Ottoman understandings of Arabic terms over an alternative from Arabic and the *kalām* genre.[257] As the prime adaptor of modernist Islamic thought into Ottoman Turkish, Akif played an important role in the transfer and formulation of concepts, and Arabic was his first reference point for coining new terms.[258] At the same time, he deployed Persian to particular effect in his more lyrical and

253 Sabri cites a Ḥanafī legal ruling regarding the disputed custodianship of a child in which the child's non-Muslim parent is favoured over a Muslim who would take him as a slave. Sabri, *Mawqif al-ʿAql*, 4:340–1.

254 Sabri, *Dinî Müceddidler* (Istanbul: Sabil, 1994), 249; compare to p. 260 in the Ottoman version.

255 'For Islamic history it is imperative above all else to be familiar with Arabic-language', he wrote; Akif, 'Medeniyet-i İslamiye Tarihinin Hataları,' *SR*, 22 Mart 1328 (4 April 1912), 8/187: 92.

256 Erişirgil, *İslamcı bir Şairin Romanı*, 187.

257 The Latin script imprint of *Safahat* edited by Yakup Çelik – Mehmet Akif Ersoy, *Safahat* (Istanbul: Akçağ, 2013) – consistently defines *heyula* as *hayal* (apparition, spectre) in its footnotes, yet Akif intends its *kalām* sense of matter; see the phrase *uzaktan andırıyorken, dumanı heyulayı* and accompanying footnote in *Ezanlar* from Akif/Çelik, *Safahat*, 130. Akif uses the word five times in total: 130 (in the Düzdağ-edited Arabic script version, 128), 353 (Çelik)/447 (Düzdağ), 508/673, 523/693; only 527/698 is better understood as 'apparition'.

258 Akif translated *idéalisme* and *positivisme* in Said Halim Paşa's *İslamlaşmak* (1918) as *fikriye* and *is̱bātiye* (p. 4). Sabri followed Naim and Akif in using *ithbātiyya* in Arabic rather than *al-falsafa al-waḍʿiyya* preferred in Egypt; Sabri, *Mawqif al-ʿAql*, 1:147, footnote 3. Sabri used *ḥusbāniyya* for Scepticism, the theory of impossibility of arriving at absolute truth, from Ottoman *ḥisbāniye*, though *shukūkiyya* was the more common Arabic usage.

Sufi-inspired texts,[259] but was content to absorb elements of the *Türklük* vocabulary, not least since it afforded him a more varied palette with which to paint.[260] Akif possessed the lexical mastery of Arabic, Persian, and Turkish to deploy whichever word served the sentiment he sought to convey, as he explained in a theoretical essay on *ahenk* (harmony) written for his Darülfünun classes.[261] Words of different origins were fitted seamlessly into the array of *aruz* metric forms in which Akif had a grasp like few others.[262] Yet Akif's attempt to create what we might call a workable Turkist Ottoman Turkish pleased neither nationalists who resented his appeal to religious themes nor ulema who, however subtly revealed, resented his encroachment upon their territory.[263]

Akif, Sabri, and Kevseri were writers who preserved Arabic and Persian vocabulary and constructions at a time when language had become an intense field of contestation in Turkey and beyond. They fought to uphold a transnational linguistic aesthetic while their peers were content to separate into more clearly defined Turkish and Arabic discursive domains. As adherents of Arabic and Arabic script, they were champions of a form of textual expression embedded in what scholars of ancient writing systems call a sumptuous materiality, bearing all the prestige of a venerated historical tradition. Script was about more than text and meaning conveyed through words and grammar. As Moustapha and Sperl write in a recent study, in its harmony and geometry the Arabic calligraphical tradition expressed not only the language of God's revelation but the integrity

259 Note his use of Persian to soften his language and relay a sense of religious ecstasy in *Ezanlar* (1908), *Asım* (1919–24), and the *Gölgeler* collection, in particular *Secde* (1925) and *Gece* (1925).

260 See use of *İlahi*, *Tanrı* and *Yezdan* for God in *Hicran* (1925), from *Gölgeler*; Akif, *Safahat*, 666–7.

261 In Ömer Hakan Özalp, *Osmanlı Edebiyatı Ders Notları 1908–1909 Eğitim Dönemi* (Istanbul: Bağcılar Belediye Başkanlığı, 2014) and Yusuf Turan Günaydın, *Kavâid-i Edebiyye* (Istanbul: Büyüyenay Yayınları, 2016), 31–40.

262 In a letter to Mahir İz, Akif expresses fear that *aruz* could disappear if more *keder* (anguish) is brought to the nation; no. 13, dated 1 September 1928, in Günaydın, *Mektuplar*, 67. On Akif's use of *aruz* see İsmail Habib, 'Şahsiyeti, Evsaf-ı Mümeyyizesi,' in Edib, *Mehmed Âkif*, 379–85, and Mehmet Behcet Yazar, 'Mehmed Âkif: Lisanı, Nazmı, Şiiri, Sanatı,' in Edib, *Mehmed Âkif*, 484–8; Akif, *Safahat*, 27–47.

263 Elmalılı Hamdi questioned Akif's linking together of some Qur'anic verses in his translation; see Akif's letter to Mahir İz dated 1 March 1926, cited in Günaydın, *Mektuplar*, 43. İz mentions the issue in his biography *Yılların İzi* (Istanbul: Kitabevi, 1990), 358. Some critics said Akif's Qur'anic language was not Turkish enough; Cündioğlu, *Bir Kur'an Şairi*, 271.

and justice of the cosmic order.[264] However, the interwar period was what İlker Aytürk calls the 'heyday of an international romanization movement' when the drive to romanise scripts in the Soviet Union and European colonies was promoted even by the League of Nations.[265] Non-Western societies were drawn into Western modernity's refocusing of language towards its instrumental function of conveying meaning in a transparent fashion, which meant writing was expected to efface as much as possible of its own materiality.[266] Thus, Atatürk's language reforms reordered the spatial and visual elements of writing as a sacred practice: shorn of its magical aspects and redirected towards positivist ends, Ottoman became Turkish.

264 Ahmed Moustafa and Stefan Sperl, *The Cosmic Script: Sacred Geometry and the Science of Arabic Penmanship* (London: Thames & Hudson, 2014), 11. Also, J. R. Osborn, *Letters of Light: Arabic Script in Calligraphy, Print, and Digital Design* (Cambridge, MA: Harvard University Press, 2017).

265 İlker Aytürk, 'Script Charisma in Hebrew and Turkish: A Comparative Framework for Explaining Success and Failure of Romanization,' *Journal of World History*, 21/1 (2010): 97–130 (98, footnote 4).

266 Andréas Stauder, Lecture on Materiality and Reading (ancient/modern) of Ancient Egyptian Texts, Queen's College, University of Oxford, 31 May 2017. John Baines, 'Writing and its Multiple Disappearances,' in *The Disappearance of Writing Systems: Perspectives on Literacy and Communication*, ed. John Baines, John Bennet, Stephen Houston (London: Equinox, 2008), 347–62.

3

The Ottoman Scholars and Their Reception of Muḥammad ʿAbduh

This chapter looks in detail at the Turkish exiles' engagement with the modernist trend in Egypt and the ideas of Muḥammad ʿAbduh. It reviews the *Islāmiyyāt* literature of Egyptian intellectuals in the 1930s and 1940s, Sabri's response to this trend, his belief that Egypt had voluntarily adopted the radical ideas that Atatürk had forced on the Turkey he fled, and his conviction that ʿAbduh's reformism was responsible for this. It then looks at Mehmed Akif's work in Istanbul and Cairo in centring Late Ottoman Islamism around the ideas of ʿAbduh and considers comparisons between Akif and Indian thinker Muḥammad Iqbāl, whom Akif helped introduce to Arab audiences.

LITERATURE REGARDING EGYPT'S LIBERAL AGE

In his extensive study of the impact of Western philosophy on Islamic thought and defence of the Islamic tradition, Mustafa Sabri expresses shock at the inroads atheistic Western materialist trends had made in Egypt. Fleeing Turkey after what he called the collapse of the '*mujāhid* Turkish Muslim state' (*dawlat al-turk al-muslima al-mujāhida*), Sabri wrote: 'I found the cultural atmosphere in Egypt too poisoned by the Western trend [*masmūm min tayyār al-gharb*], and this shook me more than the position of the new Turkey regarding this trend, as did the realisation that my Arab brothers prefer this Turkey to the old Muslim one.'[1] In the early pages Sabri establishes his main targets – Muṣṭafā

[1] Sabri, *Mawqif al-ʿAql*, 1:23.

al-Marāghī, shaykh of al-Azhar in the periods 1928–1929 and 1935–45; ʿAbd Allāh al-Qaṣīmī (1907–96), a Najdi intellectual who studied at al-Azhar and reneged on Wahhabism to write the atheistic text *Hādhihi Hiya al-Aghlāl* (These are the Chains, 1946);[2] Muḥammad Ḥusayn Haykal (1888–1956), author of *Ḥayāt Muḥammad* (1935) and other works; Muḥammad Farīd Wajdī, the well-known intellectual who became editor of *Majallat al-Azhar*; Shaykh Shaltūt, who later as rector of al-Azhar under Nasser issued a fatwa recognising worship according to the various Shiʿi, Druze, and ʿAlawite rites as valid for any Muslim; the writers ʿAbbās al-ʿAqqād and Qāsim Amīn; and the father of the movement, ʿAbduh. Sabri will mention others in his assault on Egypt's liberal age, but these are the names he returns to again and again.

Sabri's central thesis was that the discourse of *tajdīd* had gradually acquired a position of dominance in public space, as represented in al-Azhar and print media. He noted that while ʿAlī ʿAbd al-Rāziq's *al-Islām wa-Uṣūl al-Ḥukm* (Islam and the Foundations of Governance) led to his dismissal from al-Azhar after its publication in 1925 for advancing Islamic justifications for a Kemalist political order, it was telling that he later became the minister of religious endowments in the 1940s. Similarly, Ṭāhā Ḥusayn became dean of Fuʾād University's faculty of arts years after his *Fī al-Shiʿr al-Jāhilī* (On Jāhiliyya Poetry, 1926) caused him to lose his teaching post. Sabri's contemporaries among Western scholars were also interested in the *tajdīd* movement. Hamilton Gibb used it in a series of four articles he published between 1928 and 1933, titled 'Studies in Contemporary Arabic Literature', in which he praised this new trend whose figurehead he considered to be ʿAbduh.[3]

Charles Adams elaborated further on the nature of the movement in *Islam and Modernism in Egypt: The Reform Movement Inaugurated by Muḥammad ʿAbduh*, defining it as 'an attempt to free the religion of Islam from the shackles of a too rigid orthodoxy, and to accomplish reforms which will render it adaptable to the complex demands of modern life'.[4]

[2] Al-Qaṣīmī was initially a Wahhabi critic of the Azharī modernist trend, publishing *al-Burūq al-Najdiyya fī Iktisāḥ al-Ẓulumāt al-Dijwiyya* (1931) in respond to Shaykh Yūsuf al-Dijwī's criticism of Wahhabism and its opposition to practices associated with intercession.

[3] Gibb informed his readers that some Egyptian writers consider Arabic inadequate for expressing modern ideas. H.A.R. Gibb, 'Studies in Contemporary Arabic Literature — III,' *Bulletin of the School of Oriental and African Studies*, 5/3 (1929): 465, 459, 451.

[4] Charles Adams, *Islam and Modernism in Egypt: A Study of the Modern Reform Movement Inaugurated by Muḥammad ʿAbduh* (London: Oxford University Press/H. Milford, 1933), vi.

Adams supported ʿAbduh's identification of Azharī education, the culture of Sufism, and *taqlīd* in the legal tradition as pre-modern phenomena hindering the achievement of modernity as well as his later rejection of al-Afghānī's pan-Islamic activism. Adams makes the telling comment that ʿAbduh considered that 'the religion of Islam as conceived by the doctors of the schools has become so vast and complex a system, that it is difficult for anyone, particularly if he be an uneducated person, to know just what Islam is'.[5] In other words, ʿAbduh had understood the European imperative that Islam should be knowable by a European standard. Adams also noted some of the theological shifts ʿAbduh was seen as having effected that diluted the notion of God as the immediate cause of all things and aligned the Qurʾan with empirical thinking, such as asserting free will over pre-determination,[6] taking the Qurʾanic phrase *sunnat Allāh* as an expression of the idea of natural law,[7] his discussion of the notion of prophethood and miracles, promotion of the doctrine of the created Qurʾan (which stirred opposition in al-Azhar despite reflecting the post-classical Ashʿarī-Māturīdī consensus),[8] and his attempt to match scientific knowledge with Qurʾanic knowledge.[9] Adams examined the different trends emanating from ʿAbduh, judging them by rubrics such as those who studied with him, supported his educational reforms, or furthered this theological innovations, and he noted their considerable divergence, from the activism of Rashīd Riḍā to the literary endeavours of Ṭāhā Ḥusayn.

These trends – the liberal humanist and the Islamically political – evolved during the two decades following Adams' work, but contemporary Western scholarship – seeing their links with the anti-colonialism of

[5] Ibid., 107.

[6] Al-Afghānī and ʿAbduh, 'al-Qaḍāʾ wa-l-Qadar,' *al-ʿUrwa al-Wuthqā*, 81–8.

[7] Adams, *Islam and Modernism*, 140.

[8] The first edition of *Risālat al-Tawḥīd* in 1897 (taken from lecture notes from 1885 to 1888) stated briefly that the word of God is an eternal, pre-existent (*qadīm*) attribute but went on to say that the pronounced word is by contrast created and not pre-existent. This second point was removed in subsequent editions after his colleague Shaykh al-Shinqiti convinced him it was provoking anger among Azharīs. The dispute likely stemmed from ʿAbduh's implication that Aḥmad ibn Ḥanbal only refused to acknowledge that the pronounced Qurʾan is a human creation because of political circumstance, but also a wider suspicion over the intent behind ʿAbduh's reformist theological programme. See Muḥammad ʿAbduh (ed. Maḥmūd Abū Rayya), *Risālat al-Tawḥīd*, 1st ed. (Cairo: Dār al-Maʿārif, 2003), 14, footnote 1; the pages removed in subsequent editions are 53–5.

[9] Microbes could be understood as a form of jinn and jinn could be responsible for epilepsy: ʿAbduh, 'Bāb Tafsīr al-Qurʾān al-Ḥakīm,' *al-Manār*, 23 June 1906, 9/5: 334–5. The article appears never to have been translated and published in Akif's journal. See Adams, *Islam and Modernism*, 137–8.

the period – tended to view them as failures.[10] Gibb was the harshest, writing that because the liberal modernists were intellectually incoherent and did not understand ʿAbduh's revolutionary ideas they had ceded ground to Islamic reactionaries and fallen back upon al-Afghānī's activism. Gibb appears to have had in mind Riḍā's attempt to merge Wahhabi Ḥanbalī themes into his thought.[11] Gibb makes some effort to rescue ʿAbduh from this framing, citing his inspiration in Ibn Khaldūn's theory of historical change,[12] but describes his modernists, whether they are intellectuals like Haykal and Wajdī or activists like Riḍā, as 'discarding almost the whole medieval apparatus of interpretation': 'The tradition as a whole . . . is treated by modernists with scant respect when it runs counter to their ideas, and European scholarship has itself furnished them with the means to discredit it.'[13] Alongside their rationalised Qurʾan, Gibb accused the modernists of having created a cult of the Prophet as a form of compensation for their systematic vilification of Sufism. Gibb's disappointment was reflected in other works that took issue with the writing of Wajdī, Haykal, and Ḥusayn and rise of movements such as the Muslim Brotherhood.[14]

Attitudes began to shift with Hourani's *Arabic Thought in the Liberal Age*. First published in 1962, this study framed the Egyptian intellectuals as the latter stage of a period of positive engagement with Western culture that began in the early nineteenth century, positive in that like Gibb, his teacher and mentor, Hourani understood it to have been an era of drawing on Western intellectual ideas without promoting forms of resistance. Taking their cue from Hourani, Western scholars began to analyse the intellectual lights of pre-republic Egypt as constructing a discourse that could be understood on its own terms in an Egyptian context and not through the lens of apologetics. Thus, Israel Gershoni describes the modernist intellectuals as a natural component of the Egyptian urban bourgeoisie (*efendiyya*) in a typical developing nation. Their project was to

[10] Israel Gershoni, 'The Theory of Crisis and the Crisis in a Theory: Intellectual History in Twentieth-Century Middle Eastern Studies,' in *Middle East Historiographies: Narrating the Twentieth Century*, ed. Israel Gershoni, Amy Singer, Hakan Erdem (Seattle: University of Washington Press, 2011), 138.

[11] His reference to 'Neo-Ḥanbalīte Manār modernists'; H.A.R. Gibb, *Modern Trends in Islam* (Chicago: The University of Chicago Press, 1947), 46.

[12] Ibid., 128.

[13] Ibid., 72–3.

[14] Gustave von Grunebaum, *Islam: Essays in the Nature and Growth of a Cultural Tradition* (London: Routledge and Kegan Paul, 1955); Smith's *Islam in Modern History*; P. J. Vatikiotis, *The Modern History of Egypt* (London: Weidenfeld and Nicolson, 1969).

'borrow selectively elements of European culture, especially scientific and technological products, but also the ideas of humanism and rationalism, and incorporate them into local (Islamic-Arab-Egyptian) cultural traditions'.[15] Against these variations on modernisation theory, in which religion is harmonised with European notions of progress,[16] Samira Haj argues that ʿAbduh's project should be seen as rooted firmly in the Islamic tradition, 'not a mere ideological weapon, a ruse, or a reaction to European power'.[17] ʿAbduh and the movement he inspired should not be understood through the Western lens of secular humanism since their central concerns were intrinsicly Islamic questions regarding the monist theoretical and experiential culture of Sufism, the conceptualisation of God, and the legal methodologies of *taqlīd* and *ijtihād*, she says. ʿAbduh wanted to preserve religion as the defining authority on morality, rejecting colonialism's claims to reorder society according to Enlightenment notions of progress and reason;[18] his new Muslim subject was rooted in the theologian al-Ghazālī's (d. 1111) personal ethics and Muʿtazilī reason-based knowledge rather than the West's individualism and tradition-free liberalism.[19] However, Haj stretches her taxonomy to the limit in considering ʿAbduh and the Najdi Wahhabi movement as partners in the creation of this modern Muslim subject, despite the extensive differences of political, social, educational, and geographical context in which they operated.[20]

SABRI'S EARLY ATTITUDE TOWARDS ʿABDUH

Sabri's attitude to ʿAbduh changes over time. In a way this is surprising for so well-known a figure as ʿAbduh, who became the touchstone of the Turkish modernists at the onset of the second constitutional era in 1908 through Akif and *Sırat-ı Müstakim*.[21] Ziya Gökalp appeared to

15 Gershoni, 'The Theory of Crisis,' 169.

16 See also Wielandt, 'Main Trends of Islamic Theological,' *passim*, for a similar positive approach.

17 Samira Haj, *Reconfiguring Islamic Tradition: Reform, Rationality, and Modernity* (Stanford: Stanford University Press, 2009), 28.

18 Ibid., 98–9.

19 Ibid., 113.

20 Ibid., 30–66.

21 Despite Lord Cromer's efforts to dissuade him, ʿAbduh visited Istanbul in 1901 with Shaykh ʿAlī Yūsuf, editor of *al-Muʾayyad*. He met Abdülhamid and the sheikh ül-Islam Mehmet Cemaleddin Efendi. According to Yūsuf, the mufti and ʿAbduh agreed that the body of ʿulamaʾ were to blame for the innovation of non-shariʿa courts in Egypt since they had been distant from ordinary people, failing to serve the public good. This led to a flurry

allude to ʿAbduh's theory of microbes-as-jinn in his 'Üç Cereyan' series, describing transnational pan-Islamism (*milliyetçilik*) as a microbe attacking both Islam and the Ottoman state.[22] However, ʿAbduh does not feature in any of Sabri's early writing, where the thrust of his views in a series of articles published from 1908 to 1911 was to uphold a conservative approach to *fiqh* clearly at odds with that of ʿAbduh on a range of issues such as polygamy, divorce, inheritance, and usurious loans (Ar. *riba*).[23] It is not until 1919 that Sabri takes a strong position publicly against usury – the topic of one of ʿAbduh's most well-known and controversial fatwas – when his book *Dinî Müceddidler* was serialised in *Sebilürreşad*, although interest on loans is cited in a list of conditions of Islamic shariʿa that Sabri outlines in the 1908 introduction to his series in *Beyanülhak* on contemporary 'issues of debate in Islam' (*din-i İslam'da hedef-i münakaşa olan mesail*).[24] His *Sebilürreşad* articles said interest was one of the iniquities of the European capitalist system that had provoked the communist counter-reaction in Russia.[25]

ʿAbduh is first directly referred to in *Yeni İslam Müctehidleri*, Sabri's response to the Tatar intellectual Bigiev. During his Romanian exile Bigiev's book *Rahmet-i İlahiye Burhanları* had been brought to Sabri's attention by the Bucharest mufti, introducing Sabri to Bigiev's other

of conservative criticism of ʿAbduh in the Egyptian press. See Riḍā, *Tārīkh al-Ustādh al-Imām al-Shaykh Muḥammad ʿAbduh*, 3 vols. (Cairo: Dār al-Faḍīla, 2006), 1:847–57.

22 Gökalp, *Türkleşmek*, 60. On the other hand, Gökalp often used medical terminology. Other Westernists such as Abdullah Cevdet also had a high opinion of ʿAbduh.

23 See his defence of the fez, 'Fes ve Kalpak,' *BH*, 3 Teşrinisani 1324 (16 November 1908), 1/7: 146–9; on polygamy, 'Teaddüd-ü Zevcāt,' *BH*, 1 Kanunuevvel 1324 (14 December 1908), 1/11: 226–31; on divorce, 'Din-i İslam'da hedef-i münakaşa olan mesailden: Talak,' *BH*, 16 Mart 1325 (29 March 1909), 1/26: 595–8; on Islamic inheritance, 'Din-i İslam'da hedef-i münakaşa olan mesailden: İrs, Zekve,' *BH*, 22 Şubat 1325 (7 March 1910), 2/50: 1060–2; he objected to photography (which ʿAbduh approved of), 'Din-i İslam'da hedef-i münakaşa olan mesailden: Suret,' *BH*, 26 Kanunusani 1324 (8 February 1909), 1/19: 426–8; on action and work ethic (without referencing ʿAbduh), 'Din-i İslam'da hedef-i münakaşa olan mesailden: Say ve Servet,' *BH*, 8 Şubat 1909 (21 February 1909), 2/48: 1020–3; on insurance, 'Din-i İslam'da hedef-i münakaşa olan mesailden: Sigorta, Kumar,' *BH*, 21 Şubat 1326 (6 March 1911), 4/100: 1858–61; and the limits of permissability in music, 'Din-i İslam'da hedef-i münakaşa olan mesailden: Musiki,' *BH*, 24 Mayıs 1326 (6 June 1910), 3/63: 1258–62.

24 'Din-i İslam'da hedef-i münakaşa olan mesailden: Mukaddime,' *BH*, 6 Teşrinievvel 1324 (19 October 1908), 1/3: 8. The Turkish term used is *faiz*. He mentions the issue again in 'Suret,' *BH*, 1/22, 492.

25 Sabri, *Dinî Müceddidler*, 62; *Sebilürreşad*, 'Dinî Müceddidler,' 12 Haziran 1335 (12 June 1919), 16/421: 35.

writings on the theme of reform in the context of Tatar Jadīdism.[26] Bigiev's writing provoked controversy in Tatar circles but also induced Sabri to engage his first major critique of the modernist movement. Bigiev had two objectives in his book: to question the belief in eternal punishment for non-Muslims (*hulūd meselesi*) and to challenge Islamic theology as a disciplinary practice. His was an intervention in an ongoing debate regarding hellfire, its duration and its subjects, in which pre-modern theological understandings of scripture, upheld by Sabri, were remodelled towards a moral theism that considered anyone who believes in God and does good deeds as a viable candidate for salvation.[27] Bigiev accused the *mutakallimūn* of misinterpreting Qurʾanic material to restrict divine mercy to believers (*muʾminūn*), adding that it was in Sufi writers that he found clear thinking on the issue.[28] Sabri saw in this an attempt by non-specialists to produce a European Islam in which Ibn ʿArabī's pantheistic themes were accentuated in accordance with liberal humanism's objectification of Christian mercy and *taqlīd* was problematised in the modernist effort to destabilise the Islamic tradition. Sabri accused Bigiev of misinterpreting Qurʾanic verses to impute a forgiveness for *kufr* and *shirk* that isn't there and lessen their admonitory impact, and he said Bigiev had attributed a clarity to Ibn ʿArabī's thinking on eternal damnation in *al-Futūḥāt al-Makkiyya* (The Meccan Revelations) that overlooked its contradictory statements.[29] Sabri also accused Bigiev of deriving an interpretation of Jesus in Qurʾan 5:116–18 as a figure interceding with God to forgive idolators from Ibn ʿArabī and his follower ʿAbd al-Karīm al-Jīlī (d. 1424) and their concept of the perfect man (*al-insān al-kāmil*).[30] Sabri cited Qurʾan 88:21–6 to argue that the Prophet can only guide and warn, while God makes clear that the suffering of the final reckoning is His affair

[26] Bigiev's book was first published in the Russian Muslim journal *Şura* in Orenburg in 1909. A modern Turkish edition was published along with Sabri's book; Ömer H. Özalp, *İlâhî Adale* (Istanbul: Pınar Yayınları, 1996). See also Wielandt, 'Main Trends of Islamic Theological Thought,' 732 and Wilson, *Translating the Qurʾan*, 39–44.

[27] Mohammad Hasan Khalil argues Rashīd Riḍā pioneered the modern debate, but Khalil does not discuss the Tatar contribution; see Khalil, *Islam and The Fate of Others: The Salvation Question* (Oxford: Oxford University Press, 2012), 110–45.

[28] Musa Jarullah Bigiev, *Rahmet-i İlahiye Bürhanları*, in *İlâhî Adalet*, ed. Ömer Özalp (Istanbul: Pınar Yayınevi, 1996), 263–71.

[29] Sabri, *Yeni İslam Müctehidlerinin Kıymet-i İlmiyesi* (Istanbul: Âsitâne Kitabevi, nda), 114-29. See Ibn ʿArabī, *al-Futūḥāt al-Makkiyya*, chapters 124, 297, 320, 558.

[30] Sabri, *Yeni İslam Müctehidleri*, 58–64. Bigiev, *Rahmet-i İlahiye*, 311–12. Sabri cites Ibn ʿArabī, *al-Futūḥāt al-Makkiyya*, chapter 358. On Ibn ʿArabī's understanding of Jesus in Qurʾan 5:116, see Maurice Gloton, *Jesus Son of Mary in the Qur'an and According to the Teachings of Ibn 'Arabi* (Louisville, Kentucky: Fons Vitae, 2016).

alone. He then added that ʿAbduh, 'one of the renewers of the last era' (*son asır müceddidlerinden*), had commented appropriately on the verse by saying simply that there was no escape from God's warning.[31] Sabri's use of *müceddid* here was intended polemically to dismiss modernist intellectuals as undeserving of the term, which had become common currency; indeed, it's clear from Sabri's visceral reaction to ʿAbduh in later years that he was not at this point aware of the nature of ʿAbduh's thinking at all.

After this praise, ʿAbduh only took Sabri's attention again in an article published in his *Yarın* newspaper in 1928 which attacked arguments made by reformers to justify neglecting the Ramaḍān fast. Sabri was provoked into writing by an article by Süleyman Nazif, an Ottoman governor, poet, and admirer of Akif, and another by Ubeydullah Efendi, which Sabri viewed as typifying the assault on religious belief and practice of the era. The fast was an issue that reformers had focussed on for some time. Bigiev published a book in 1911 arguing for laxer rules, *Uzun Günlerde Ruze* (Long Days Fasting), which Sabri referenced in his riposte. As sheikh ül-Islam, Sabri had taken up the issue, ordering demobilised soldiers to maintain the fast in public places following the armistice.[32] In his article, Sabri directly addressed ʿAbduh's view that not only the elderly and ill but coal workers and prisoners engaged in hard labour should all be absolved of fasting and allowed to feed the poor for every day missed rather than obliged to fast the missed days after Ramaḍān.[33] From this comment it would appear that Sabri had read at least some of ʿAbduh's *tafsīr* material, whether through its publication in *al-Manār* or in book form.

That Sabri's worldview was markedly different from ʿAbduh's is clear from his first statement of position in *Beyanülhak*. In its first issue Sabri wrote in an editorial comment that the CUP and army had found it necessary to take action against despotic rule (*devr-i istibdad*), which he equated with the shariʿa category of *munkar* (reprehensible act), in part because ulema including himself had failed in their duty

[31] Ibid., 68. Akif translated ʿAbduh's *tafsīr* of these verses; ʿAbduh, 'Tefsir-i Sure-i Gaşiye, 17–26,' *SR*, 24 Şubat 1327 (9 March 1911), 8/1: 183–4. The original is in Muḥammad ʿAbduh (ed. Muḥammad ʿImāra), *al-Aʿmāl al-Kāmila*, 5 vols. (Cairo: Dār al-Shurūq, 1993), 5:375–81.

[32] Sabri, 'Fetva-yı Meşihatpenahi,' 29 Mayıs 1335 (29 May 1919), in *SR*, 16/419: 21–2.

[33] Sabri, 'Savm-i Ramazan: Fidye ile Geçiştirilebilir mi?' *Yarın*, 13 April 1928, 1/19: 2–4. ʿAbduh's *tafsīr* of Qurʾan 2:286 ('rabbanā lā tuḥammilnā mā lā ṭāqa lanā bihi') is in *al-Aʿmāl al-Kāmila*, 4:739–43.

(*vaktiyle vazifemizi maatteessüf eda edemediğimiz*) as consultants to rulers,[34] but the ulema's role now was to preserve Islamic rites and national-religious morals (*şeʿāʾir-i islamiye ve adab-ı milliye*) through active participation in public life.[35] At pains to stress that his group of ulema supported the new order, Sabri seemed anxious to make sure that radical trends did not shut out conservative voices. He pressed his case in more detail from the third issue, inaugurating his series on contemporary issues in Islam. He started by saying there are some who object to Islamic shariʿa ordinances *in toto* or, no less incoherently, in part and it's not clear if they are criticising the ulema or religion itself, but it is through *ilm-i kelam* that the foundations of religion in 'the world of Islam' (*alem-i İslam*) must be defended from such attacks.[36] Rather than the decline of *taqlīd* in *fiqh*, Sabri championed the branches of knowledge associated with *kalām* such as logic, disputation, mathematics, and philosophy. However, there are trends now seeking to diminish this system of knowledge, he wrote. Empirical knowledge does not replace abstract logic, since it is only through logic that empirical knowledge can be appraised. Western thinkers involve themselves in an obsessive manner with 'the most unnecessary' (*en lüzumsuz*) empirical details,[37] but thus far Ottoman education has not been critically corrupted by this approach and Arabic remains the vehicle for learning the Islamic sciences. Efforts to demonstrate that prophetic hadiths affirm the notion of the Earth moving around a static sun are appreciated, he said, but one should not seek such indications of modern science in the Qurʾan since as a text guiding the individual and society its basic function lies elsewhere; this was to give solutions for afflictions of the spirit rather than of the body (*emraz-ı cismaniye ziyade emraz-ı ruhaniyeye çare-sāz olur*).[38] Some hadith may be useful relating to medical issues, for example, but the Prophet was a man of wisdom, not a specialist in medicine (*peygamber hakîmdi, tabip değildi*).[39] The ulema's task is to protect Islamic ordinances from mingling with European thinking and fortunately the methodology

[34] 'Beyanülhak'ın Mesleği,' *BH*, 22 Eylül 1324 (5 October 1908), 1/1: 2.

[35] Ibid., 3.

[36] Sabri, 'Din-i İslam'da hedef-i münakaşa olan mesailden: Mukaddime,' *BH*, 6 Teşrinievvel 1324 (19 October 1908), 1/3: 9.

[37] Sabri, 'Din-i İslam'da hedef-i münakaşa olan mesailden: Mukaddime 2,' *BH*, 20 Teşrinievvel 1324 (2 November 1908), 1/5: 90.

[38] Sabri, 'Din-i İslam'da hedef-i münakaşa olan mesailden: Mukaddime 3,' *BH*, 27 Teşrinievvel 1324 (9 November 1908), 1/6: 107.

[39] Ibid., 107.

of hadith narrators and jurists was so rigorous in the early period, more so than that of modern historians whose personal character is rarely adduced in evaluations of their work,[40] that the Islamic system of knowledge remains strong.

Without using the words *tecdid* or *müceddid*, Sabri expressed here an ethos that was plainly in contrast to that of ʿAbduh, in particular his rejection of the trend seeking Qurʾanic bases for European science. His mention of diseases of the body and spirit may have been another allusion to ʿAbduh's discussion of microbes, but the issue was not in his view serious enough to warrant calling ʿAbduh out. Sabri's focus was primarily on intellectuals with the intent to sabotage religion (*dini baltalamak*) who claimed interpretive authority in Islamic affairs, rather than ulema whose critique he viewed as manageable.[41] Why he did not take aim then at Akif and others in the *Sırat-ı Müstakim* group is not clear. One explanation is Gündoğdu's argument that the period from 1908 until the 1912 coup against the CUP was one of relative civility in public debate when nationalist intellectuals were still welcome in Islamic journals as well-intentioned advocates of Islamic modernism. Indeed, there was some overlap in the views of conservative ulema and reformist intellectuals. *Sırat-ı Müstakim* serialised Akif's translation of Muḥammad Farīd Wajdī's *al-Marʾa al-Muslima* (The Muslim Woman, 1901), which was a response to Qāsim Amīn's two works, *Taḥrīr al-Marʾa* and *al-Marʾa al-Jadīda* (The New Woman, 1900). Wajdī makes two points with which Sabri would hardly disagree: a defence of veiling (*ḥijāb* in the Arabic text, *mestūriyet* in Akif's Ottoman) as in conformity with the innate God-given characteristics (*fiṭra*/*fıtrat*) of women and theories of national development (*takmīl al-umma wa-taḥsīn ḥālihā al-ijtimāʿiyya*/*ümmetin terakkisini tekmil etmek [ve] heyet-i ictimāʿiyenin hâlini bir kat daha yükseltmek*), and a rejection of Western materialist values which have disfigured humanity (*shawwahat wajh al-insāniyya*/*insaniyetin yüzünü karartan*).[42] Wajdī's other works published in *Sırat-ı Müstakim* at this time, *Hadika-i Fikriye* (*al-Ḥadīqa al-Fikriyya*/The Garden of Thought, 1901) and *Müslümanlıkta Medeniyet* (*al-Madaniyya wa-l-Islām*/Civilisation and Islam, 1901), presented an anti-materialist, anti-colonial polemic behind which lay concessions to

[40] Sabri, 'Din-i İslam'da hedef-i münakaşa olan mesailden: Mukaddime 4,' *BH*, 10 Teşrinisani 1324 (23 November 1908), 1/8: 155–6.

[41] Ibid., 155.

[42] Muḥammad Farīd Wajdī, *al-Marʾa al-Muslima* (Cairo: al-Taraqqi, 1901), 5, 202; the Ottoman is *Müslüman Kadını* (Istanbul: Sırat-ı Müstakim, 1325 [1909]), 5, 163.

the Enlightenment's epistemological system that only became apparent to Sabri once he was in Egypt. Third, much of this material took time to flood into the Ottoman market following the collapse of Hamidian censorship – Wajdī's book was published in Egypt in 1901, serialised in Ottoman in 1908, then published in book form in 1909. Fourth, during his wartime exile Sabri's anxiety over *müceddid* intellectuals crystallised around the figures of Bigiev and Haşim Nahid (1880–1962), an employee of the finance ministry and public intellectual who wrote in nationalist publications.

Sabri's first significant discussion of ʿAbduh came in *Mawqif al-Bashar Taḥta Sulṭān al-Qadar*, published in 1933. His second book written in Egypt, it followed *Masʾalat Tarjamat al-Qurʾān* (1932) which took aim at Mustafa al-Marāghī and Muḥammad Farīd Wajdī over their support for translating the Qurʾan into national languages. Debate over the question of translation was intense during this period and focussed on Egypt as the nexus of intellectual authority in Islam. Al-Azhar's authoritative Arabic imprints of 1924 and 1936 enhanced Egypt's status, but leading figures began to see advantage in an English Qurʾan that would be propagated by al-Azhar. Al-Marāghī also saw a chance to push back against Christian missionary activity with a missionary drive of Islam's own and to check the propaganda efforts of the Lahore Aḥmadiyya who had led the way with a translation published in 1917, but Sabri's focus was the linguistic nationalism of the Kemalists. In his book Sabri pressed the point that his Egyptian interlocuters did not appear to appreciate the radical nature of the Turkish project and challenged the argument that Abū Ḥanīfa had approved the use of Persian in prayer regardless of one's knowledge of Arabic with the point that he is believed to have later reneged on that position.[43] However, with al-Marāghī reappointed to head al-Azhar in 1935 and Rashīd Riḍā's change of heart on the issue, Egypt began printing English Qurʾans in 1938.[44]

Mawqif al-Bashar took as its target Shaykh al-Muṭīʿī over an article in the journal *al-Hidāya* in which he expressed a Māturīdī view of extensive free will in human action and blamed Ashʿarīsm for what he called Muslim backwardness (*taʾakhkhur*).[45] This became the occasion for Sabri to take on the trend he had observed towards reformulating theological understandings on free will as the basis for bringing Muslim societies up to par with Europe in political, economic, and technological strength. Sabri saw

[43] Sabri, *Masʾalat Tarjamat al-Qurʾān*, 35–67.
[44] Wilson, *Translating the Qurʾan*, 186–209.
[45] Sabri, *Mawqif al-Bashar*, 20–2.

ʿAbduh's influence behind al-Muṭīʿī, who had succeeded him as chief mufti (though some question the degree to which he should be seen as a disciple).[46] Citing ʿAbduh's *Risālat al-Tawḥīd* and its section on men's actions (*afʿāl al-ʿibād*), Sabri revived the accusation of Muʿtazilism directed at ʿAbduh during his lifetime, a polemical charge which has been used to denounce any number of ʿAbduh's views, from his teaching of logic and *kalām*, to his rejection of adherence to the single legal school, to his Ashʿarī-Māturīdī view of the Qurʾan as God's speech.[47]

The complexities of any thinker's ideas are *ipso facto* hard to define, but in ʿAbduh's case the issue is complicated by his changing views, the unclear authorship of some works, and the attempts of later strands within Sunni Arab modernism to align his views with their thinking. The eighteen issues of *al-ʿUrwa al-Wuthqā* he published with al-Afghānī in 1884 are attributed variously to ʿAbduh, al-Afghānī or both.[48] Akif translated its well-known article on predestination and free will under ʿAbduh's name, yet Sabri considered it to be primarily al-Afghānī's work because of its divergence from ʿAbduh's argument in *Risālat al-Tawḥīd*.[49] The *Risālat al-Wāridāt* (Treatise on Mystical Inspirations), published in 1908 though apparently written in 1874, has been the topic of considerable debate: it expresses a pantheistic illuminationist theosophy absent in *Risālat al-Tawḥīd*, in which the theme of causality puts God at a certain remove from modern society. Adams considered it to be ʿAbduh's work, while editor Muḥammad ʿImāra left it out of his collected works of ʿAbduh first published in 1972. From personal papers he examined in Tehran, Iranian scholar Sayyid Hādī Khusraw Shāhī supported this view of al-Afghānī as

46 In *Ḥaqīqat al-Islām wa-Uṣūl al-Ḥukm* (1926) al-Muṭīʿī rejected ʿAlī ʿAbd al-Rāziq's claim that the Prophet had not mandated a political system; Adams, *Islam and Modernism*, 208; Hourani, *Arabic Thought*, 189–92.

47 ʿAbduh's early nemesis at al-Azhar was Shaykh ʿIllaysh (d. 1882), who questioned his teaching of Saʿd al-Dīn Taftāzānī's (d. 1390) commentary on Najm al-Dīn al-Nasafī (d. 1142)'s *ʿAqāʾid*, a standard Māturīdī work; see ʿAbduh, *al-Aʿmāl al-Kāmila*, 3:210. As Mālikī Mufti ʿIllaysh objected to ʿAbduh's stepping outside the Ashʿarī curriculum and misrepesented teaching al-Nasafī as an act of Muʿtazilism. It seems the underlying issue was ʿAbduh's broad, free-style, anti-*taqlīd* approach in questions of fiqh, *kalām* and logic; *Sunni Islam* (London: Tauris Academic Studies, 2010), 93–7; and El-Rouayheb, *Islamic Intellectual History*, 175, 360.

48 The ideas were said to be Afghānī's but the words ʿAbduh's. See Keddie, 'Al-Sayyid Jamal al-Din 'al-Afghani',' in *Pioneers of Islamic Revival*, ed. Ali Rahnema (London: Zed, 1994), 28; Riḍā, *Tarīkh*, 1:190.

49 ʿAbduh, 'Kaza ve Kader,' *SM*, 23 Nisan 1335 (6 May 1909), 2/35: 133–6; and 30 Nisan 1325 (13 May 1909), 2/36: 149–50.

the primary author, a view also upheld by Rotraud Wielandt.[50] ʿImāra and Riḍā implied al-Afghānī was responsible for ʿAbduh's interest in Sufi theosophy and Shiʿi *ʿirfān*,[51] while Riḍā tried to configure him as the inheritor of Ibn Taymiyya's mantle;[52] Arab Islamist circles have also asserted against considerable evidence that al-Afghānī was a Sunni.[53] The authorship of *al-Taʿlīqāt ʿalā Sharḥ al-ʿAqāʾid al-ʿAḍudiyya* (Comments on ʿAḍud al-Dīn's Creed), a commentary on the standard Ashʿarī theological text of Jalāl al-Dīn al-Dawānī (d. 1502) that itself explicates ʿAḍud al-Dīn al-Ījī's *Mawāqif*, is also disputed. Written in 1876 but published in' 1904 in the name of both al-Afghānī and ʿAbduh, it also contains passages favouring the notion of continuous material causality, or infinite regress, in the world. It is likely for that reason that ʿImāra attributed it primarily to al-Afghānī, bar footnotes that carry ʿAbduh's signature, but Robert Wisnovsky argues ʿAbduh was its prime author.[54] As for ʿAbduh's Qurʾan commentary, it was first published from 1900 in *al-Manār*, based on lecture notes taken by Riḍā, and then later published by Riḍā as *Tafsīr al-Manār* in 1927, but it only ran as far as 12:107 and ʿAbduh had only even then been closely involved in the text up to 4:125.[55]

The 1884 article that Sabri attributed approvingly to al-Afghānī alone set out to prove that European claims regarding divine predetermination of events (*al-qaḍāʾ wa-l-qadar*) in Islam, seen as the source of numerous forms of social, political, and economic malaise, had misunderstood and distorted the Ashʿarī compromise between free will and predestination as what in *kalām* terms would be considered *jabriyya*. *Al-qaḍāʾ wa-l-qadar*, it said, expresses the notion of human action that takes place within the context of a chain of events, the external features of which alone can be known to men but the totality of which only God (*mudabbir al-kawn al-aʿlā*) can know. Therefore, no one can conclude that their life term is

[50] See Wielandt, 'Main Trends of Islamic Theological Thought,' 716–19.

[51] Vincent J. Cornell, 'Muḥammad ʿAbduh: A Sufi-Inspired Modernist?' in *Tradition and Modernity: Christian and Muslim Perspectives*, ed. David Marshall (Washington: Georgetown University Press, 2013), 108–11.

[52] Riḍā even rebukes ʿAbduh for neglecting to mention Ibn Taymiyya in his edition of *Risālat al-Tawḥīd*; *Risālat al-Tawḥīd* (Cairo: al-Manār, 1942), 26, footnote 2.

[53] Keddie, 'Al-Sayyid Jamal al-Din,' 28.

[54] Robert Wisnovsky, 'Avicenna's Islamic reception,' in *Interpreting Avicenna: Critical Essays*, ed. Peter Adamson (Cambridge: Cambridge University Press, 2013), 191, footnote 4. See Alnoor Dhanani, '*Al-Mawāqif fī ʿilm al-kalām* by ʿAḍūd al-Dīn al-Ījī (d. 1355), and Its Commentaries,' in *The Oxford Handbook of Islamic Philosophy*, ed. Khaled El-Rouayheb and Sabine Schmidtke (New York: Oxford University Press, 2016), 375–98.

[55] Khalil, *Islam and The Fate of Others*, 111–12.

fixed, that their livelihood is assured, and that God will perpetually intervene in the direction of their affairs. Correct belief encourages movement and action not inertia and inaction, although they added, 'we do not deny that in the souls of some Muslims this belief has been spoiled by the belief in *al-jabr* [predestination], which could be the cause of some of the calamities they have suffered in recent times'.[56] Sabri seems to have overlooked not only that closing comment but the strident statement in *al-ʿUrwa al-Wuthqā*'s inaugural editorial that Muslims must rid themselves of the illusion of constant divine action in the smallest detail of human affairs, lest their societies become overwhelmed by the greater forces of the modern world (*ẓannū anna al-quwwa al-ālihiyya, wa-in qilla ʿimāluhā, yadūm lahā sulṭān ʿalā al-kathra al-ʿadadiyya*).[57]

What attracted Sabri to the article was that although it leaned towards the Māturīdī view in that man was the unambiguous source of his own action, it did not openly challenge Ashʿarī doctrine in the manner of ʿAbduh's *Risāla*.[58] In the latter's section on human actions, ʿAbduh states in the first line that man is fully aware of his existence through his reason and senses, without need for evidence or a teacher to guide him (*lā yaḥtāj fī dhālik ilā dalīl yuhdīhi wa-lā muʿallim yurshiduhu*), a position that diverges from the Ashʿarī belief in classical *kalām* debates in the need for a prophet who establishes the divine law.[59] Through his mental faculties man intuits that a higher power guides his actions, though in a manner he cannot comprehend (*quwwa asmā min an tuḥīṭ bihā qudratuhu/sulṭān lā taṣil ilayhi sulṭatuhu*); and he understands that all events in the universe are reliant upon (*mustanida ilā*) one necessitating entity for existence (*wājib wujūd wāḥid*) who makes possible the voluntary mental and physical actions of men.[60] ʿAbduh goes on to justify this position as the midway between early Muʿtazilī belief in the total independence of human action, which implies God has no power in worlds He has created, and supporters of predestination, including 'those who upheld it while disavowing it by name' (*man qāla bihi wa-tabarraʾa min ismihi*) – a reference to the Ashʿariyya[61] – who in effect negate the reason and responsibility inscribed in divine law (*hadm li-l-sharīʿa wa-maḥw li-l-takālīf wa-ibṭāl*

[56] Al-Afghānī and ʿAbduh, 'al-Qaḍāʾ wa-l-Qadar,' *al-ʿUrwa al-Wuthqā*, 87.
[57] Al-Afghānī and ʿAbduh, *al-ʿUrwa al-Wuthqā*, 33.
[58] Sabri, *Mawqif al-Bashar*, 46.
[59] ʿAbduh (ed. ʿImāra), *Risālat al-Tawḥīd*, 61. See Toshihiko Izutsu, *The Concept of Belief in Islamic Theology* (Kuala Lumpur: Islamic Book Trust, 2006), 108–19.
[60] ʿAbduh (ed. ʿImāra), *Risālat al-Tawḥīd*, 61–2.
[61] ʿImāra clarifies this intent to readers in a footnote; Riḍā makes no comment.

li-ḥukm al-ʿaql al-badīhī).[62] So man's happiness is dependent upon his will and his ability (*al-ʿabd yaksib bi-irādatihi wa-qudratihi mā huwa wasīla li-saʿādatihi*), which are powers bequeathed by God.[63]

Sabri was suspicious. ʿAbduh was taking aim at the Ashʿarīsm that European scholars had identified as the source of a malaise and inaction that was meant to explain why Muslim countries had failed to achieve the progress of Europe. ʿAbduh seemed to have allowed himself to become an unwitting accomplice to the 'falsification of one after the other of Islam's ideas and beliefs and their replacement with what Europe wants for us [*istibdāl mā tarḍāhu lanā urubbā makānahā*]'.[64] Since he did not read ʿAbduh as simply advancing Māturīdism, Sabri reached for the polemical charge of Muʿtazilism and he was helped in this by the fact that ʿAbduh did not use the language of particular and universal will (*al-irāda al-juzʾiyya/al-juzʾ al-ikhtiyārī* and *al-irāda al-kulliyya*), Māturīdī concepts of human agency that Philipp Bruckmayr has shown developed in Ottoman Naqshbandī discourse.[65] Sabri was well aware of this terminology since although he was not a Naqshbandī adept the language had influenced the general tenor of Ottoman *kalām*.[66] Sabri said ʿAbduh was exaggerating in his description of Muʿtazilism as a school in favour of free will in order to balance out his criticism of the Ashʿariyya and deflect the charge of Muʿtazilism.[67] Of course, ʿAbduh was positive elsewhere in the opening section of his *Risāla* about Ashʿarīsm as an effective compromise in early theology around questions of God's power and human responsibility.

62 Ibid., 63.

63 Ibid., 64.

64 Sabri, *Mawqif al-Bashar*, 45.

65 Philipp Bruckmayr, 'The Particular Will (*al-irādat al-juzʾiyya*): Excavations Regarding a Latecomer in Kalām Terminology on Human Agency and its Position in Naqshbandī Discourse,' *European Journal of Turkish Studies*, 13/2011: 1–23 The terminology was not widespread in Egypt, India and Hijaz, though used by Ḥasan al-ʿAṭṭār (1776–1835), al-Azhar rector from 1830–35. Peter Gran, 'Ḥasan al-ʿAṭṭār,' in *Essays in Arabic Literary Biography: 1350–1850*, ed. Roger Allen and Terri DeYoung (Wiesbaden: Harrassowitz, 2009), 56–68.

66 Sabri was a member of the the İslah-ı Medaris-i İslamiye Cemiyet-i Hayriyesi (Beneficial Society for the Reform of Islamic Schools), established by the Khālidī Naqshbandīs of Konya; Bruckmayr, 'The Particular Will,' 9. This school system became the model for the Daru'l-Hilafeti'l-Aliye established in Istanbul in 1914. See Ismail Bilgili, 'Bekir Sami Paşa Nakşbendî Halidî Zaviyesinin Konya Islah-i Medâris-i İslamiye Medresesine Dönüşümü Bağlamında Nakşbendîliğin İlmi Ḥayāta Tesiri,' *Uluslararası Bahaeddin Nakşibend ve Nakşibendilik Sempozyumu* (Istanbul: Hüdayi Vakfı, 2016), 312–40.

67 Sabri, *Mawqif al-Bashar*, 38. He was correct on this point in that Jahm ibn Ṣafwān (d. 746), one of the early figures of the Muʿtazila movement, favoured a strict determinism.

Sabri was particularly sensitive to these issues at this point since it was in *Mawqif al-Bashar* that he declared his switch from Māturīdism to Ashʿarī thinking on predestination. He talked of his exile and isolation in Thrace, where difficulties he said he had always faced in reconciling the Qurʾanic verses on divine will with the Māturīdī position on human responsibility (*masʾūliyyat al-ʿibād*) came to a head through reading the views of Egyptian ʿulamaʾ.[68] He described his new position as an Ashʿarī 'midway determinism' (*al-jabr al-mutawassiṭ*),[69] in that volition (*irāda/ikhtiyār*) is entirely God's but realised upon man's 'readiness for will' (*al-istiʿdād li-l-irāda*) via a divine *tafwīḍ* (authorisation) that empowers action – in other words an intersection of divine causation and human desire to act (*jabr wa-tafwīḍ maʿan*).[70] Sabri's defence of Ashʿarī occasionalism stood out for its framing in the language of Māturīdī partial will and unabashed embrace of the language of *jabriyya*. Māturīdism, he said, was a radical form of free will attracting attention among Egyptian liberal modernists for the wrong reasons:[71] if theology was an explanation of the state of nations then how to explain the strength of early Muslims, given the intense sectarian conflict over theological questions or the ascendance of modernists today who do not in effect believe in predestination at all?[72] Sabri's change of heart on human agency was not in itself prompted by his experience in Egypt, which at the time of writing *Mawqif al-Bashar* was not long, but by the collapse of the Ottoman state and rise of the radical republic, about which he provided an early analysis in his first major Arabic work *al-Nakīr* (1924). However, the book registered his sense of shock at the extent to which liberal modernist *apologia* had taken hold in Egypt and the first hints that he blamed ʿAbduh for this. Had he been aware of the 'collapse and dissolution' (*al-suqūṭ wa-l-inḥilāl*) that subsequently befell Islamic thought, ʿAbduh – still 'the genius shaykh' in Sabri's estimation[73] – would have regretted the loose manner with which he discussed these issues, he wrote.[74]

In his earlier Turkish works *Yeni İslam Müctehidleri* (1919) and *Dinî Müceddidler* (1922) Sabri assailed modernist intellectuals in the Ottoman sphere as fools in the service of the CUP/Kemalist enterprise by having

[68] Ibid., 93–4. This refers to Qurʾan 81:29 and 76:30, 'wa-mā tashāʾūn illā an yashāʾ Allāh'.
[69] Ibid., 56, 148.
[70] Ibid., 47, 72. This is a position he praises with regard to Gelenbevi in the latter's gloss to al-Dawānī's *Sharḥ al-ʿAqāʾid al-ʿAḍudiyya*.
[71] Ibid., 145, 160–3.
[72] Ibid., 219–20.
[73] Ibid., 33.
[74] Ibid., 45–6.

internalised Orientalist tropes of Islam as a fatalistic system of knowledge requiring a Protestant revolution to set it right. Among the 'the intellectuals of our country who imitate Europe' (*memleketimizin Avrupayı taklid eden münevverleri*) it was Bigiev Sabri had in mind.[75] Bigiev's early Turkish translation of the Qurʾan had been viewed by some in Ottoman circles as a 'Lutheran moment',[76] prompting Haşim Nahid to declare him 'Islam's Luther' (*İslamiyetin Luteri*), a *müceddid* and *mücahid* liberating Islamic thought and ethics. 'A Russian Muslim has taken the first step towards the truth of religion; let us too follow him [*Rusiyeli bir Müslüman dinin hakikatine doğru ilk adımını attı, biz de onu takib edelim*]', Nahid wrote in his book *Türkiye İçin Necat ve İğtila Yolları* (Means of Salvation and Progress for Turkey, 1912).[77] Building on Bigiev's ideas, Nahid elaborated on the nature of this Lutheran liberation as the end of the monopoly on scriptural interpretation enjoyed by the ulema.[78] The canon of books studied in Arabic grammar, logic, *kalām*, *fiqh*, and philosophy had emptied education of the true spirit of Islam, he wrote;[79] a 'social shariʿa' (*şeriat-i ictimāʿiye*) was required to spread the notion of love for people of the same country;[80] effort and initiative (*teşebbüs*) would result from freedom of thought (*hürriyet-i fikriye*) and human agency (*azim ve irade*).[81]

[75] Sabri, *Dinî Müceddidler*, 239.

[76] Doğan Gürpınar, *Ottoman/Turkish Visions of the Nation, 1860–1950* (Basingstoke: Palgrave Macmillan, 2013), 73. For a discussion of the Late Ottoman Luther debate see Suat Mertoğlu, 'Ahmed Muhiddin: Hayatı, Eserleri, Düşüncesi,' in Muhiddin, *Modern Türklükte Kültür Hareketi*, 36–9 and Wilson, *Translating the Qurʾan*, 23. The call for a Muslim Luther began with al-Afghānī and was made in Istanbul around 1892; Roman Loimeier, 'Is There Something Like Protestant Islam?' *Die Welt des Islams*, 45/2 (2005): 245.

[77] Haşim Nahid, *Türkiye İçin: Necat ve İğtila Yolları* (Istanbul: Ikbal Kitaphanesi, 1912), 214. Sabri's *Dinî Müceddidler* had a subheading that described it as a response to Nahid's book. Other writers attack the search for a Luther; see Mustafa Naim, 'Luterlik Yapmak Istiyorlar,' *Medrese İtikadları*, 2 Ağustos 1329 (15 August 1913), issue 13: 103–4. But CUP and republican intellectuals openly called for Islam to find its Luther: see Abdullah Cevdet, the appendix to his translation of of Dutch Orientalist Reinhart Dozy's *Essai sur l'histoire de l'Islamisme* (1879), 'Tekmile: Son Kırk Sene Zarfında İslamiyet,' in *Tarih-i İslamiyet*, 2 vols. (Istanbul: Matbaa-i İctihad, 1909), 2:720–1; and Celal Nuri, *Türk İnkılabı* (Istanbul: Sühulet Kütüphanesi, 1926), 368–82. Atatürk was compared to Luther by US ambassador Charles Sherrill in 1932–3 for promoting the Turkish Qurʾan and Turkish call to prayer; see *A Year's Embassy to Mustafa Kemal* (New York/London: Charles Scribner's Sons, 1934), 195.

[78] Nahid, *Türkiye İçin*, 132–3.

[79] Ibid., 230–1.

[80] Ibid., 242–3.

[81] Ibid., 240–1, 244. Namık Kemal also indulged the trope of Muslim inaction in an essay published posthumously in 1912; 'Say,' in *Kıraat-ı Edebiye*, 3 vols., ed. Celal Sahir Erozan and Mehmed Fuad Köprülü (Istanbul: Karabet Matbaası, 1912), 1:51–8.

SABRI AND THE FARAḤ ANṬŪN DEBATE: 'THE IMAM OF MODERN EGYPT WAS A SCEPTIC'

By the time Sabri came to write *Mawqif al-ʿAql* he had expanded his understanding of the elements of Islamic tradition under attack from the modernists and refined his opinion of ʿAbduh as the eponymous founder of the movement. Sabri's starting point was ʿAbduh's celebrated debate in 1901 with Faraḥ Anṭūn (1874–1922), a Lebanese Christian who left Tripoli for Egypt in 1897 to establish the journal *al-Jāmiʿa al-ʿUthmāniyya*.[82] Anṭūn stirred the ire of ʿAbduh and Riḍā, who emigrated to Egypt with him on the same boat, with a series of articles on the figure of Ibn Rushd (1126–98), the Andalusian philosopher who upheld Aristotle's model of a more distant creator in whose dominion natural laws were created through continuous divine agency but not individual human acts, i.e., God delegates his power through secondary causes.[83] Like Renan, Anṭūn viewed Ibn Rushd as a heroic figure who faced persecution for his effort to rationalise the Islamic version of the Semitic monotheistic system, in particular of prophecy. His experience thus became in their view emblematic of intolerance within religious systems and a need to separate the temporal and spiritual functions of the state. Anṭūn made clear his intent to address contemporary realities in the dedication to the book he published in 1903 gathering in one volume the main elements of his exchange with ʿAbduh. The new generation 'in the East', understanding the damage inherent in religion playing a role outside its sacred space (*makān muqaddas*), wishes to 'keep pace with the new trend of European civilisation' (*mujārāt tayyār al-tamaddun al-urubbī al-jadīd*).[84] I will look at this debate in some detail, then consider what some scholars have extracted from it alongside Sabri's analysis.

In his initial article Anṭūn argued that despite protestations to the contrary Ibn Rushd did in fact believe in the three positions that al-Ghazālī (d. 1111) famously held up as heretical among the philosophers – the eternity (*qidam*) of the world, denial of God's knowledge of secondary causes (*juzʾiyyāt*), and denial of bodily resurrection (*baʿth al-ajsād wa-ḥ*

[82] Hourani, *Arabic Thought*, 254.

[83] He wrote commentaries on Artistotle's works except *Politics*, which was not translated into Arabic until 1948. Majid Fakhry, *Averroës (Ibn Rushd): His Life, Works and Influence* (Oxford: Oneworld, 2001).

[84] Faraḥ Anṭūn, *Ibn Rushd wa-Falsafatuhu* (Alexandria: al-Jamiʿa, 1903), dedication (*Ihdāʾ al-Kitāb*). On this new Enlightenment conceptualisation of the sacred see Asad, *Formations of the Secular*, 30–7, 236–7.

ashruhā).[85] The key element that concerned Anṭūn was the second, the *kalām* orthodoxy that all matter is created by a God who has absolute powers of intervention in all matters of creation (*khāliq muṭlaq al-taṣarruf fī al-kawn*), which he was convinced Ibn Rushd's philosophy challenged.[86] Ibn Rushd did this by positing an Aristotelian theory that Anṭūn considered synomymous with that of modern materialists (*māddiyyūn*) in which subsequent creation is possible through the motion initiated by the God, the prime mover (*al-muḥarrik al-awwal alladhī huwa maṣdar al-quwwa wa-l-fiʿl*) whose originating action and existence, according to the Aristotelian language of Ibn Sīnā's (d. 1037) system, is alone necessary (that is, He is *wājib al-wujūd*, the necessary existent).[87] Man is independent with regards to his own actions but bound by external events affecting them, while it is through acquired knowledge or the ascetic practice of Sufism that one can achieve a form of direct contact (*ittiṣāl*) with God. As for death, Anṭūn acknowledged that Ibn Rushd's views were more complicated, or obtuse, than to say he did not believe in the afterlife (*al-ḥayāh al-thāniya*), as was long claimed in Christian European writing, but Ibn Rushd did not believe the individual intellect (*al-ʿaql al-khāṣṣ al-munfaʿil*) would survive physical death, Anṭūn wrote.[88]

ʿAbduh responded to this saying Anṭūn was oversimplifying classical debates over creed. The Muslim *mutakallimūn* had never claimed that all causes come from God, as if 'it's not eating that causes satisfaction, rather God creates satisfaction upon eating'.[89] At the same time Anṭūn had constructed an erroneous image of Ibn Rushd as a materialist in Greek philosophical terms – a non-deistic view of the world as nothing but matter – which is to misunderstand the Aristotelian tradition in Muslim philosophy to which Ibn Rushd belonged, ʿAbduh said.[90] Ibn Rushd, who lived after al-Ghazālī, did indeed hold to the orthodox conception of God

[85] Anṭūn, *Ibn Rushd*, 34; Abū Ḥāmid al-Ghazālī (ed. Ṣalāḥ al-Dīn al-Hawwārī), *Tahāfut al-Falāsifa* (Beirut: al-Maktaba al-ʿAṣriyya, 2005), 225. See Ibn Rushd, *Tahāfut al-Tahāfut* (Beirut: al-Maktaba al-ʿAṣriyya, 2005), 372–5.

[86] Anṭūn, *Ibn Rushd*, 34.

[87] Ibid., 34.

[88] Ibid., 36–7. On Ibn Rushd's concept of universal (active) and individual (habitual/material) intellect see R. Arnaldez, 'Ibn Rus̲h̲d,' in *Encyclopaedia of Islam, Second Edition*, ed. P. Bearman, Th. Bianquis, C. E. Bosworth, E. van Donzel, W. P. Heinrichs; http://dx.doi.org/10.1163/1573-3912_islam_COM_0340 (accessed 20 July 2019). Also, Richard C. Taylor, 'Averroes on the Ontology of the Human Soul,' *The Muslim World*, 102/3–4 (2012): 580–96.

[89] Anṭūn, *Ibn Rushd*, 90.

[90] Ibid., 93.

as the sole eternal (*azalī*) entity, who is judge of the soul in death and aware of all universals and particulars in creation.[91] ʿAbduh said Anṭūn was simply following in the tracks of European thinkers who, acknowledging his influence on the medieval church, liked to think of Ibn Rushd as a Sufi theorist in his thinking on spiritual and physical existence whose rationalism made him a stepping-stone to modern European thought.[92]

Anṭūn pressed on, accusing ʿAbduh of denying secondary causes[93] and ridiculing Muslim scholars as unaware of their own intellectual genealogy. Arabs only became aware of Ibn Rushd's works through Latin and Hebrew translations, and Ibn Rushd was reliant upon Arabic translations from the Greek, he wrote; Ernest Renan, on the other hand, could refer to the Greek originals in his writing on Ibn Rushd and engage in comparative study.[94] Anṭūn also noted ʿAbduh's use of the term *al-ʿaql al-faʿʿāl* for Ibn Rushd's theory of the one universal intellect, although Ibn Rushd called it *al-ʿaql al-fāʿil*, suggesting ʿAbduh had confused it with Ibn Sīnā and al-Fārābī's terminology.[95] Anṭūn's main point was that ʿAbduh could not admit the theologians had good reason to consider that Ibn Rushd did not belong to a 'creedal deist school' (*madhhab ilahī millī*)[96] – i.e., that he was indeed philosophically speaking a materialist – and that their most important objection to him was elaborated by al-Ghazālī when he declared allegorical interpretation (*taʾwīl*) of the Qurʾanic text with regard to the afterlife as out of bounds.[97] The Ibn Rushd controversy indicates the fundamental divide between religion and reason since the three Abrahamic monotheisms have similar conceptualisations of life after death, Anṭūn said. Thus, religion should be designated a new ontological category, the realm of the heart (*dāʾirat al-qalb*), leaving reason to grapple with the world of empirical knowledge (*al-mushāhada wa-l-tajriba wa-l-imtiḥān*).[98]

[91] Ibid., 96.

[92] Ibid., 96, 76–84; these sections contain Anṭūn's description of the 'victory of Ibn Rushd's philosophy' in Europe.

[93] Ibid., 98, 104.

[94] Ibid., 114–16. He is referring to Renan's book *Averroès et l'Averroïsme: Essai historique* (1852).

[95] Ibid., 117.

[96] Ibid.

[97] Ibid., 121; see al-Ghazālī, *Tahafut*, 215–16. On al-Ghazālī's notion of *taʾwīl* see Martin Whittingham, *Al-Ghazālī and the Qurʾān: One Book, Many Meanings* (London: Routledge, 2007). Also, Frank Griffel, *Al-Ghazālī's Philosophical Theology* (New York/ Oxford: Oxford University Press, 2009), 71, 118.

[98] Anṭūn, *Ibn Rushd*, 122. This thinking can be traced back to Descartes' *Meditationes de Prima Philosophia* (1641) and Blaise Pascal's *Pensées* (1669). See John Cottingham,

In his second response to Anṭūn ʿAbduh set aside this element of the disputation to take up Anṭūn's classic Enlightenment argument, which he had made in a separate article, that Christianity had helped birth modern civilisation (*al-tamaddun al-ḥadīth*) because it alone contained within it the capacity to separate itself from the state: ʿAbduh put himself in the position of defending Islam from the charge that Islam was intolerant and unmodern.[99] ʿAbduh reached first for the Qurʾan in response, citing its injunction that there should be no compulsion in religion. Many Muslims are satisfied to have their children study in Christian missionary schools today, while in Anṭūn's own country there are two Muslim sects (by which he meant Druze and ʿAlawite) living in peace with other communities despite the view of many Muslims that they are heretics. Internecine strife in Muslim societies has been political at heart rather than theological and in the early Islamic period many individuals from non-Muslim communities assumed high positions of state or importance in intellectual culture. Christianity, on the other hand, has been characterised by heavy dependence on miracles as signs of truth,[100] and a tendency towards extreme asceticism rather than reason as its disciplinary practice of choice for the strengthening of faith. Its religious authorities instituted regimes of thought control that continued throughout the recent centuries of technological progress, while persecution flowed from the Protestant reformers no less than their Catholic enemies. The claim that religion has been subjugated by temporal authority is false in that authority derives ultimately from God, ʿAbduh added.[101]

In his response to this[102] Anṭūn characterised ʿAbduh as having shifted to an unbecoming attack on his Christian brethren 'who placed a lot of hopes in him', an attack that gives materialism, the real enemy, the tools with which to attack all religious systems including Buddhism, Confucianism, and idolatry (*al-wathaniyya*).[103] He also suggested throughout that ʿAbduh should have deferred to Renan as an authority on Christian history, through translations of his work published in Anṭūn's journal.[104] Despite whatever

Philosophy of Religion: Towards a More Humane Approach (New York: Cambridge University Press, 2014), 13–17.

99 Anṭūn, *Ibn Rushd*, 124–5.

100 Ibid., 133.

101 Ibid., 140–1.

102 Ibid., 141–206. Anṭūn published a truncated version of ʿAbduh's 35-page article.

103 Ibid., 142.

104 Anṭūn refers to his 'history of Jesus and the apostles (*al-rusul*) book'. Renan published *Vie de Jésus* (1863), which was republished in 1882 as *Histoire des Origines du Christianisme* with a second chapter titled *Les Apôtres*. Anṭūn published a translation of *Vie de Jésus* in 1904, *Tārīkh al-Masīḥ*.

arguments can be made about religious persecution in Islamic and Christian history, knowledge and philosophy won out in Europe because religion was detached from governing power (*al-sulṭa al-madaniyya*), Anṭūn said.[105] The duty of modern government is to ensure freedom of the individual regardless of sect and belief within the frame of the constitution (*ḥurriyyat kull shakhṣ ḍimn dāʾirat al-dustūr*) and the wider public good (*maṣlaḥat al-jumhūr*).[106] National unity is possible but religious unity is not;[107] therefore what Europe has attained could be called *dīn al-insāniyya* (by which he meant humanism) that embraces all religions outside government functions.[108] 'The desire to restrict interpretation of religion and right of leadership to the Arabs alone and place the faith of other believing nations below them does not conform to the needs of the age', Anṭūn wrote.[109] It is useless to argue that Islam is the religion of reason and Christianity that of miracles because all religions are ultimately irrational;[110] religion can only attain the status of knowledge if it is rational (*ʿaqlī*), since religion is faith in an unseen creator, an afterlife, revelation, prophecy, and miracles.[111] To object to Christian miracles is to object to the Qurʾan where many of the same miracles, such as the immaculate conception, take place.[112]

After only brief descriptions of three more responses from ʿAbduh, Anṭūn pushed on. Christian Europe's separation of *dīn* and *dunyā* was what facilitated civilisation in the world (*mahhada subul al-madaniyya fī al-ʿālam*) which speaks to something in the essence of Christianity.[113] We can't say that Islamic civilisation was the model of human perfection, otherwise why did Muslim rulers and legal scholars not think to put limits on men's divorce rights and marriage rules that damage the family?[114] A final response to this from ʿAbduh was summarised in one page, in which ʿAbduh gave alternative reasons for the advances of European science that did not rely on the notion of Christianity's natural propensity for separation from the state but concluded with praise for the tolerance

[105] Ibid., 147.
[106] Ibid., 151–2.
[107] Ibid., 158–9.
[108] Ibid., 171.
[109] Ibid., 176.
[110] Ibid., 182.
[111] Ibid., 182–3.
[112] Ibid., 185.
[113] Ibid., 208.
[114] Ibid., 213.

of British colonial rule.[115] Anṭūn allowed himself one more reply, in which he welcomed ʿAbduh's comment on the British empire as 'the words of a rational man' (*qawl rajul ʿāqil*), while noting that the Irish might not agree.[116] In his final comments Anṭūn talked of the bad blood the debate had engendered, suggesting it was the work of Riḍā and *al-Manār*.[117] Indeed, ʿAbduh occupied the post of state mufti of Egypt throughout this period, and one is left with the impression he had been lured into a public tussle that he ought to have been above but through which Anṭūn found his foil for advancing an Enlightenment vision in Arabic of nationalism transcending religion.

The views of scholars who have studied the debate have been influenced by the source through which they received it. In *al-Islām wa-l-Naṣrāniyya* (Islam and Christianity, 1905), a collection of ʿAbduh's articles of response first published in *al-Manār* in 1902 and issued in book form after his death, Riḍā offers only a summation of Anṭūn's positions in the introduction. The text often diverges from the responses ʿAbduh sent to *al-Jāmiʿa*, and the early stage of the debate over the question of secondary causes is omitted in its entirety. Charles Adams relied upon Riḍā's collection, and so viewed the Anṭūn debate as an extension of ʿAbduh's other great debate with French diplomat Gabriel Hanotaux, published over the pages of *Le Journal de Paris* and *al-Muʾayyad* in 1900. The combined effect of both was that ʿAbduh became the foremost defender of Islam in the face of the European political and intellectual onslaught, Adams argued. In this view ʿAbduh responded effectively to the charge that Islam is less tolerant than other faiths, that Islam is hostile to learning and knowledge, and that European modernity is a universal model that emerged as a consequence of Christianity's tolerance and limited claims on the state.[118]

Hourani's view, based on his reading of Anṭūn's book, was quite different. He picked up on the confidence of Anṭūn's claims and their basis in Anṭūn's penchant for Renan, as well as Anṭūn's ulterior motive as a member of a minority confessional community in advocating for a supra-religious national order, 'a secular State in which Muslims and Christians can participate on a footing of complete equality'.[119] ʿAbduh, he argued,

[115] Ibid., 218. See Muḥammad ʿAbduh, *al-Islām wa-l-Naṣrāniyya fī al-ʿIlm wa-l-Madaniyya* (Beirut: Dār al-Ḥadātha, 1988), 196–8.
[116] Anṭūn, *Ibn Rushd*, 225.
[117] Ibid., 227.
[118] Adams, *Islam and Modernity*, 86, 89-90.
[119] Hourani, *Arabic Thought*, 255.

agreed with much of Anṭūn's vision of national freedom and equality, but his fundamental dispute was over the notion of a need to relegate Islam to the 'realm of the heart' since he believed that it was via a purified shariʿa that the Islamic political order would thrive, if in a modernised form. Hourani emphasises Anṭūn's argument that it was through a separation of religious and governmental jurisdictions that Europe had advanced in civics, science, and other fields, allowing for the development of a culture of tolerance. In his telling, ʿAbduh has been reduced to 'anger' through the brusque message from Anṭūn that, in Hourani's words, 'the world has changed ... modern States are no longer based on religion, but on two things – national unity and the techniques of modern science'.[120] Hourani's ʿAbduh is a Romantic, the classic *nahḍa*-era Muslim modernist who thinks Islam is to be restored to its civilisation-defining role through the return of its centre of gravity to the Arabs.

Relying on ʿAbduh's book (as reproduced in ʿImāra's *al-Aʿmāl al-Kāmila*) as well as Riḍā's discussion of the debate in his *Tārīkh al-Imām*,[121] Samira Haj understands ʿAbduh as mounting a challenge to the Eurocentric vision of historical development. The relegation of religion to the non-political sphere was the outcome of a trajectory particular to Europe in which religion was regarded as the site of unruly passions and tolerance was the outcome of conflict between papal authority and provincial monarchy. The involvement of early Abbasid caliphs in doctrinal disputes among scholars over the nature of the Qurʾan never rose to the level of violence of the Inquisition, the series of state campaigns to enforce Catholic orthodoxy which began in twelfth-century France and was abolished in the early nineteenth century, if it was comparable in any meaningful way at all. So ʿAbduh was not objecting to the Enlightenment notion of secular authority per se, but suggesting it was for Muslims to define the boundaries of civic power and the role of religious scholars, shariʿa law, and Islamic ethics.[122] In other words ʿAbduh rejected a priori the validity of Anṭūn's comparative approach. Mark Sedgwick has a similar view of ʿAbduh in his study: he was asserting that Islam does not merge civic and religious authority in the manner of Catholicism in that the Sunni caliph was a temporal figure, not an *ʿālim* from the class of theologians or jurisprudents.[123]

120 Ibid., 257.
121 Riḍā, *Tarīkh*, 1:805–16.
122 Haj, *Reconfiguring Islamic Tradition*, 98.
123 Sedgwick, Muhammad Abduh, 53–4. Also D. M. Reid, *The Odyssey of Farah Antun: A Syrian Christian's Quest for Secularism* (Minneapolis: Bibliotheca Islamica, 1975), 80–97.

Sabri bases his argument on both books. In this view, the second is an attempt to compensate for ʿAbduh's capitulation in the first, but it is to the first one should look to understand the apologetic nature of the modernist reformers.[124] In Sabri's analysis Anṭūn's most important claim was that religion conflicts with reason because it is not verifiable by the empirical standard of modern knowledge. Religion is 'faith in an unseen creator and unseen afterlife, and revelation, prophecy, miracles, gathering of the dead and their resurrection, reward, and punishment are all unperceivable and irrational [*ghayr maḥsūsa wa-ghayr maʿqūla*]', Anṭūn said.[125] ʿAbduh's great failure in the debate was to leave this central point unanswered, because, Sabri concludes, ʿAbduh was himself a sceptic (*raybī*) or even an atheist who shared this view.[126] In Sabri's view Anṭūn was correct in his appraisal of Ibn Rushd as a proto-materialist of the Enlightenment era because of his arguments in support of the causative powers of matter (*mādda/hayūlā*) and ʿAbduh was disingenuous in denying this of Ibn Rushd.[127] ʿAbduh also appeared weak in the debate because he broadly agreed with the Anṭūn–Renan thesis of civilisational stagnation for which Islam (as law, creed and socio-political structure) is responsible, Sabri said.[128]

The Anṭūn debate is the first of four broad arguments Sabri makes in his case against ʿAbduh. Second, Sabri argues that ʿAbduh's proofs for the existence of God and oneness of God as sole creator departed from the theories usually presented in the field of *kalām*. He points to some of the numerous statements in the commentary on al-Dawānī's *Sharḥ* rejecting the classical *kalām* argument (known as *buṭlān al-tasalsul*, or *burhān al-taṭbīq*) that aims to establish the impossibility of an infinite chain of causes (*al-tasalsul*). Sabri cites the commentary's statement that 'thus far no proof has been posited of finitude to any chain whose parts are in existence, let alone one that is indisputable' as evidence that ʿAbduh wanted to invalidate *wājib al-wujūd* as proof of the existence of God.[129] While there is no such mention of infinite regress in *Risālat al-Tawḥīd*, Sabri notes that ʿAbduh omitted *wājib al-wujūd* in establishing the oneness of God

124 Sabri, *Mawqif al-ʿAql*, 1:133.
125 Ibid., 1:23 and 4:17. Anṭūn, *Ibn Rushd*, 183.
126 Sabri, *Mawqif al-ʿAql*, 1:304–5, 4:18.
127 Ibid., 3:360.
128 Ibid., 1:14, 103 (footnote 1), 134, 143, 223 (footnote 1), 370, 4:345–6. Also, *Mawqif al-Bashar*, 23. ʿAbduh discusses stagnation at length; *al-Islām wa-l-Naṣrāniyya*, 133–67.
129 Sabri, *Mawqif al-ʿAql*, 1:230 and 3:365–89; and al-Afghānī and ʿAbduh, *al-Taʿlīqāt ʿalā Sharḥ al-ʿAqāʾid al-ʿAḍudiyya* (Cairo: Maktabat al-Shurūq al-Dawliyya, 2002), 217.

(*waḥdāniyyat Allāh*), relying alone on the logical argument known as *burhān al-tamānuʿ*, which Sabri claims he in any case misunderstands.[130] Sabri suggests ʿAbduh adopts these positions to avoid arguments located in abstract logic that would not pass the test of empirical knowledge (*shahādat al-ḥiss wa-l-tajriba*).[131] Third, ʿAbduh fails to defend unseen paranormal phenomena (*al-khawāriq*) such as belief in the existence of angels, the devil, and miracles, 'as if the shaykh agrees with his opponent [Anṭūn]'. ʿAbduh and the modernists create a new paradigm for the Muslim prophet that considers him as merely one of the 'great reformers' (*al-ʿuẓamāʾ al-muṣliḥūn*) among men in history.[132] Sabri takes ʿAbduh's views on prophethood again from the commentary on al-Dawānī, which defines a prophet (*nabī*) as someone 'born with an innate sense of what's right in knowledge and practice [*fuṭira ʿalā al-haqq ʿilman wa-ʿamalan*]',[133] though he was remiss in failing to note ʿAbduh's careful description of the prophets in his *Risāla* as possessed of an unbreakable spiritual bond with God.[134]

Sabri saw himself engaging the critique of Anṭūn's work that ʿAbduh failed to achieve. He described *Mawqif al-ʿAql* as an effort to resume the debate, as if he was articulating the arguments ʿAbduh could not and as if ʿAbduh's disciples among Sabri's Egyptian contemporaries were the voice of his antagonist Anṭūn.[135] If Anṭūn said religions are only rational when proven through experiential knowledge, Sabri responded that no, speculative reason has long been able to offer arguments to prove the existence of God.[136] Discussing in detail Descartes, Hume, Kant, and Hegel, Sabri argued that in questioning the ability of abstract logic (*al-manṭiq al-tajrīdī*) to establish truth and relying instead on the fideistic notion of naturally intuited religion, the modernists were taking cues from the Western philosophical tradition's response to the scientific revolution. ʿAbduh was under the influence of Hegel and Kant, he said, in particular Kant's *Critique of Pure Reason* (1781), which though it pushed back against the

130 ʿAbduh discusses the proof in terms of rival creative forces causing disorder in the universe, rather than to establish that no god could be God if he was obliged to negotiate creation with another entity. See Sabri, *Mawqif al-ʿAql*, 1:136–8, 2:83–4, footnote 1; and ʿAbduh (ed. ʿImāra), *Risālat al-Tawḥīd*, 46–8.
131 Sabri, *Mawqif al-ʿAql*, 1:141.
132 Ibid., 1:142–3.
133 Al-Afghānī and ʿAbduh, *al-Taʿlīqāt*, 152–3.
134 ʿAbduh (ed. ʿImāra), *Risālat al-Tawḥīd*, 81–2.
135 Sabri, *Mawqif al-ʿAql*, 4:18, footnote 1.
136 Ibid., 2:35–6.

scepticism (*ḥusbāniyya*) and inductive reasoning (*manṭiq istiqrāʾī*) of David Hume still imagined great limits to what reason could know of the world.[137] Thus, Western philosophers paid only lip service to Christian faith since they had given up on the idea of reason defending religion, based on the new consensus that the only demonstrative rationality that mattered was the empirical.[138] Sabri wrote: 'The conflict over denying and proving certainty [*al-yaqīn*] concerns me a lot. It is the central axis of this book in that Islam turns on proving certainty [regards the metaphysical]. Since we Muslims do not hesitate in acknowledging the existence of certainty in human knowledge, we do not consider this belief to be contrary to reason as the Christian West did.'[139] It is this divide that emerged in European philosophy between religion and reason that has led to Western moral and social chaos that now threatens their countries with destruction and collapse, Sabri said, in apparent reference to the recent world war and post-war conflict.[140] He also noted the apologetic nature of Anṭūn's description of the Christian Trinity and attempt to draw parallels to Islamic creed, that the Trinity can be understood in terms of Islamic attributes of God such as knowledge, will, and ability (*ʿilm*, *irāda*, *qudra*)[141] and that there is no substantive difference between the Christian terminology of men as 'sons of God' (*abnāʾ Allāh*) and the Qurʾan's 'servants of God' (*ʿibād Allāh*).[142] Like his hero Renan, Anṭūn did not believe in Jesus' divinity, yet still described himself as a Christian, Sabri said.[143] Anṭūn's intent then was to entice Muslims towards this vague religiosity in which good, virtue, and righteousness (*khayr, faḍīla, ṣalāḥ*) replace reason and knowledge (*ʿaql* and *ʿilm*), the pre-modern path to establishing God's existence and creation of the world.[144]

Central to Sabri's thesis was the argument that the Muslim *kalām* tradition had adapted the best of Greek philosophy, ditching its sceptical elements and rethinking its ideas on the distant creator and eternal nature of the

[137] Ibid. 1:305. Sabri relied to some degree upon Aḥmad Amīn and Zakī Najīb Maḥmūd's study of European philosophy, *Qiṣṣat al-Falsafa al-Ḥadītha* (Cairo, 1935) for his views of the European philosophers.

[138] Ibid., 2:149, 151. On Descartes, 2:211–28, and Kant, 2:228–33, 3:66–75.

[139] Ibid., 2:155.

[140] Ibid., 2:24–5.

[141] Ibid., 2:42–5. Modern scholarship has argued that the Muslim theology of attributes indeed developed as a polemical response to Christian writing in Arabic defending the Trinity and its Christology in the late Umayyad and early Abbasid period.

[142] Ibid., 2:52.

[143] Ibid., 2:51.

[144] Ibid., 2:62-3.

world (*qidam al-ʿālam*), to develop rational proofs of God, His nature, and His unique creative powers.[145] He rejects the arguments of the modernists, whether they are ʿulamaʾ like ʿAbduh or public intellectuals such as Bigiev, that Greek thought poisoned the purity of Islamic thought in the classical era of translation, producing a tradition of elitist *kalām* and associated disciplines that distanced Islam from its fundamentals and its public.[146] Sabri makes the observation that Muslim modernists (*alafranga zümresi*, 'the European group') are different from the trend associated with Ibn Taymiyya, despite their outwardly similar approach in rejecting juridical *taqlīd* for *ijtihād*, because there could be no suspicion over the latter's 'firmness in religion' (*salabet-i diniye*), by which he means the depth of their knowledge and sincerity of faith.[147] ʿAbduh has introduced theological scepticism (*al-ḥusbāniyya/al-raybiyya*) and relativistic thinking to disorient Muslim culture in its epistemological certitude.[148] He did this through compromising the theory of the necessary existent with the notion of an endless chain of causation, which builds bridges to the materialist understanding of a world without beginning or end. Therefore, ʿAbduh cannot prove the existence of God, and neither can Kant, despite the empirical-rationalist tradition's description of itself as positive knowledge.[149] They favour natural laws that have no need for a creator[150] and that reduce reason/rationality (*al-ʿaql*) to the phsyical and chemical actions of the brain and other parts of the body rather than a metaphysical power related to the divine (*quwwa makhṣūṣa rūḥāniyya*).[151] In Sabri's telling, such materialists are similar to thieves (*luṣūṣ*) in their failure to acknowledge that the discoveries of man are intentional disclosures from God, made at specific points in time, 'secrets of the cosmos, held by God in created things and revealed to those who discover them' (*al-asrār al-kawniyya allatī kanazahā Allāh fī al-kāʾināt wa-abāḥahā li-muktashifīhā*).[152]

[145] Ibid., 1:205, 219; 2:113.

[146] See Sabri's opening remarks on Bigiev and Nahid in *Dinî Müceddidler*, 3–22.

[147] Sabri, *Yeni Islam Müctehidleri*, 8. He calls Ibn Taymiyya's group independent (*istiklal takib eden*), reflecting his view (and Kevseri's) that it was not a mainstream trend.

[148] Sabri, *Mawqif al-ʿAql*, 1:304–5. He notes Cromer's comment that ʿAbduh seemed agnostic (*raybī*) about God's existence. Sabri does not draw out ʿAbduh's relativistic, historicist approaches in the *Risāla* and elsewhere in the same way that he does his theological shifts.

[149] Ibid., 2:307–8.

[150] Ibid., 2:308–9.

[151] Ibid., 2:313.

[152] Ibid., 2:353–4. This view of knowledge forms part of the secondary proof of God in the *kalām* tradition known as the theory of final causes (*al-ʿilla al-ghāʾiyya*); see 2:342–470.

Summarising various lines of argumentation in Egyptian modernist thinking, Sabri formed a conception of the ʿAbduh trend that: promoted the notion of faith in the unseen as faith in the unrealistic (*ghayr wāqiʿ*);[153] downgraded prophethood as a category of human experience to the field of human genius (*ʿabqariyya*);[154] reconceptualised the Qurʾan as Islam's single miraculous event whose most important element is the call to examine natural phenomena;[155] questioned the authenticity of prophetic hadith as a whole;[156] rejected belief in resurrection;[157] favoured discarding unclear Qurʾanic material (the *mutashābihāt* verses);[158] reconfigured the concept of the devil as 'evil in the world' and rejected the existence of angels as well as the ascent and return of Christ;[159] and introduced new vocabulary such as Wajdī's *iʿtiqādiyyūn* as an alternative to *muʾminūn*, a calque on the English/French *believer/croyant*.[160] The corollary of this wholesale rationalisation of the Islamic tradition was a spiritless cult of the Prophet ('through studying the life of the Prophet they tried to find the pleasure of faith and reassurance they had lost')[161] and a turn towards

[153] Ibid., 4:4. Muḥammad Farīd Wajdī, 'Muḥammad Ṣallā Allāh ʿalayhi wa-Sallam fī Taqdīr Quḍāt al-Raʾy fī Urubbā,' *Majallat al-Azhar*, 8/5 (1937): 358–61.

[154] Sabri, *Mawqif al-ʿAql*, 1:30, 4:5–16, 4:40–2. Among the contemporary texts Sabri discusses are: Zaki Mubarak, 'Asmaʿūnī Sīḥat al-Ḥaqq,' *al-Risāla*, 27 February 1939, 7/295: 387–9; Wajdī, 'al-Sīra al-Muḥammadiyya Taḥta Ḍawʾ al-ʿIlm wa-l-Falsafa,' *Majallat al-Azhar*, 11/7 (1940): 385–90; Wajdī, 'al-Sīra al-Muḥammadiyya Taḥta Ḍawʾ al-ʿIlm wa-l-Falsafa: Muqaddima,' *Majallat al-Azhar*, 10/1 (1939): 12–17; Wajdī, 'Mā Hiya al-Nubuwwa wa-Mā Hiya al-Risāla wa-l-Adilla al-ʿIlmiyya fī Imkān al-Waḥy,' *Majallat al-Azhar*, 10/2 (1939): 90–8; Wajdī, 'Mā Rabaḥahu al-Dīn min al-ʿIlm fī al-Zamān al-Ākhar,' *al-Risāla*, 6 January 1947, 15/705: 12–13; ʿAbbās al-ʿAqqād, *ʿAbqariyyat Muḥammad* (1942); Muḥammad Ḥusayn Haykal, *Ḥayāt Muḥammad* (1935); Shiblī Shumayyil, *Falsafat al-Nushūʾ wa-l-Irtiqāʾ* (1910).

[155] Ibid., 4:16.

[156] Ibid., 4:48–62. Haykal, *Ḥayāt Muḥammad* (Cairo: Dār al-Maʿārif, 2001), 46–50.

[157] Ibid., 4:209–17. Wajdī shifted position from rejecting both corporal and spiritual resurrection, which the *mutakallimūn* uphold, to accepting spiritual resurrection only, the position of Muslim philosophers.

[158] Ibid., 1:175. See Wajdī, 'Madhhab al-Qurʾān fī al-Āyāt al-Mutashābihāt,' *al-Ahrām*, 30 August 1933, in Sabri, 4:407–12; Wajdī, 'Madhhab al-Qurʾān fī al-Āyāt al-Mutashābihāt,' *al-Ahrām*, 10 September 1933, in Sabri 4:432–8; Wajdī, 'Tafṣīl Baʿd Mā Ajmalnāhu min al-Mutashābihāt,' *al-Ahrām*, in Sabri 4:450–3. See also Aḥmad Zakī, 'Ayna Wādī al-Naml al-Madhkūr fī al-Qurʾān?' *al-Ahrām*, 6 August 1933, in Sabri 4:391–6, Wajdī's response, 'Wādī al-Naml wa-Madhhab al-Qurʾān,' in Sabri 4:397–9, and Sabri's response to Wajdī and defence of Aḥmad Zakī, 'Wādī al-Zalal Baʿd Wādī al-Naml,' *al-Ahrām*, 26 August 1933, in Sabri: 4:400–6.

[159] Sabri, *Mawqif al-ʿAql*, 1:34, 360–2.

[160] Ibid., 1:52. See Wajdī, 'al-Dīn fī Muʿtarak al-Shukūk,' *al-Risāla*, 15 January 1945, 13/602: 57–60.

[161] Sabri, *Mawqif al-ʿAql*, 1:123.

naturalism under titles such as spiritism,[162] vitalism,[163] pantheism,[164] or Ibn ʿArabī's *waḥdat al-wujūd*.[165] In Sabri's analysis it was in no small part due to the Anṭūn–ʿAbduh debate that these heretical, atheistic beliefs had colonised the minds of the intelligentsia, for whom religion (*al-dīn*) had become 'a bothersome, unwanted tradition' (*turāth muzʿij lā yurghab fīhi*)[166] rather than a set of beliefs and practices rooted in affirmation of a creator whose existence is necessary (*wujūd mawjūd wājib al-wujūd*).[167] 'There is no difference between modern Egypt and Turkey in the victory of atheism [*ilḥād*] over religion, except that while in Turkey the secular revolution [*al-inqilāb al-lādīnī*] was established by force in the era of Mustafa Kemal, in Egypt it spread through the publishing and propaganda of writers and the support of a government itself supported by the West', Sabri wrote.[168]

AKIF AND THE GABRIEL HANOTAUX DEBATE: DEFENDING ʿABDUH

Although Qāsim Amīn and Muḥammad Farīd Wajdī were early champions of ʿAbduh's ideas in Egypt, the Istanbul ecumene was one of the first to witness the comprehensive packaging of ʿAbduh's thought, which happened through the work of Akif. Of ʿAbduh's two great debates, Akif ignored that of Faraḥ Anṭūn for Gabriel Hanotaux, a former foreign minister of France. Though Sabri had nothing to say about it, the Hanotaux debate had a wider impact outside Egypt, not least because ʿAbduh's interlocuter was a prominent European politician and it was conducted in French as well as Arabic.[169] It also gave ʿAbduh's supporters further material with which to draw him as a warrior against imperialism and thus burnish the credentials of reformist Islam. Akif was effective in framing both ʿAbduh and al-Afghānī in this manner, rebutting arguments

162 Ibid., 1:210, 2:235 re Wajdī.
163 Ibid., 2:304.
164 Ibid., 3:90.
165 Ibid., 3:85–315 (most of vol. 3). Typical of its critics, Sabri saw Sufi theosophy as dissolution of the difference between creator and created that spread from Late Antiquity into Islamic *kalām* and *falsafa*.
166 Ibid., 1:441–2.
167 Ibid., 1:433.
168 Ibid., 1:30.
169 It inspired playwright and novelist Tawfīq al-Ḥakīm (1898–1987) to write 'al-Difāʿ ʿan al-Islām' (*al-Risāla*, 15 April 1935, 3/93: 576–80) after reading Voltaire's *Le fanatisme, ou Mahomet le prophète* (1773). See Israel Gershoni and James P. Jankowski, *Redefining the Egyptian Nation, 1930–1945* (Cambridge: Cambridge University Press, 1995), 192.

that their political activism came at the expense of soundness in matters of creed or devotion (*zühd*). 'To fight against Monsieur Hanotaux and defend the rights of millions of Muslims in the Western Islamic world [*magribdeki*] I would say is more of a good deed than centuries of futile piety [*nevāfil*]', he wrote.[170] 'Today there is no Jamāl al-Dīn or Muḥammad ʿAbduh. The Islamic world is in a truly lonely and wretched state. We must remember such greats of the nation with mercy and respect, so that those who come after do not give up the struggle.'[171]

The debate initially raged over the pages of *al-Muʾayyad* in Cairo and *Le Journal* in Paris, then *al-Ahrām* when its editor Bishāra Taqlā conducted a long, adulatory interview with Hanotaux. The material was covered in numerous books: Egyptian entrepreneur Muḥammad Ṭalʿat Ḥarb (who later founded Bank Misr) published *L'Europe et l'Islam* (1905), a Tatar Turkish version of ʿAbduh's interventions by Zakir Kadiri (*Islam ve Hanoto*, 1909), Wajdī in Arabic (*al-Islām*, 1910), and the publisher Muḥammad Amīn al-Khanjī's *al-Islām wa-l-Radd ʿalā Muntaqidīhi*, issued in 1924 when veneration for ʿAbduh was gaining ground in Egypt's early constitutional period.[172] Hanotaux's original articles (published in two parts) began by applying the grand racialist judgements of Guizot and Renan to an analysis of France's Islamic problem.[173] Through its African colonies, Aryan, Christian, and egalitarian France has established itself 'in the centre of Islam', controlling the lives of Semitic Muslims of Asian origin whose religiosity is abnormally intense, he says. The bond of fraternity that unites those who turn to Mecca in prayer (*l'etroite confraternite religieuse de tout le monde islamique/rābiṭat al-akhāʾ al-jāmiʿa li-afrād al-ʿālam al-islāmī*) – the Islamic world – is now a threat to French empire.[174] Then he moved on to theology: the Trinity serves to bring mankind closer to God, as did the Greek gods, and this reflects the Aryan mentality, but Islam demands total submission to a distant and forbidding God who is at the same time interventionist in that He leaves man with no room for free will.

170 Akif, 'Hasbihâl,' *SM*, 20 Mayıs 1326 (2 June 1910), 3/91: 222–3. This is a modernist swipe at Sufi culture.
171 Ibid., 223.
172 Afaf Lutfi Al-Sayyid-Marsot, *Egypt's Liberal Experiment, 1922–1936* (Berkeley: University of California Press).
173 Published in *Le Journal de Paris* of 21 and 28 March 1900.
174 Gabriel Hanotaux, *L'Europe et l'Islam* (Cairo: J. Politis, 1905), 27; Muḥammad ʿAbduh and Gabriel Hanotaux, *al-Islām wa-l-Radd ʿalā Muntaqidīhi* (Cairo: Maṭbaʿat al-Tawfīq al-Adabiyya, 1924), 9.

This took Hanotaux to the two diametrically opposed views in France towards the question of how the French state should deal with its Muslim subjects. On the one hand, there are those who think of Islam as a mental pathology, a 'leprosy' (*lèpre,*[175] *judhām*[176]) in which adepts live by irrational regulations such as those forbidding wine and pork and acts of mass hysteria such as pilgrimage (*la folie mystique,*[177] *al-junūn al-rūḥānī*)[178]. He attributes these views to anti-Muslim essayist Daniel Kimon in his book *La pathologie de l'Islam et les moyens de le détruire* (The Pathology of Islam and the Means to Destroy It, 1897), who, Hanotaux explains, suggested the Prophet's tomb be moved from Mecca (where both Kimon and Hanotaux apparently thought it was located), to the Louvre. On the other hand, there are those lost souls in search of religion who see in Islam the strength of faith that Europe once had and wonder if France could pivot to acting as a champion of Islam in sub-Saharan Africa. Finally, Hanotaux turned to his own view. France should listen to the Arabist experts inside its colonial apparatus and organise a major research project to bring to politicians' attention the fact that a great transformation is taking place in Islamic societies thanks to France. Religious and political authority has been separated in Tunisia without fuss or fanfare, keeping mosques closed to Christians and changing only some laws as necessary; European ideas have been absorbed by the population, allowing for a synthesis of French and indigenous authority; Tunisia is relinquishing Mecca and its Asian past for a new beginning in which two religions co-exist in peace and harmony.

ʿAbduh's response came in three articles.[179] Hanotaux, he wrote, has produced an amalgam of misinformed tropes about Islam that he wants to pass off as expertise to the French public. First and foremost, he has confused the Muslim concept of God's transcendent non-anthropomorphic nature (*tanzīh*) with the issue of predetermination and human agency, a question on which Christian theology itself is divided. ʿAbduh then elaborated on a theme in decline discourse that appears in several of ʿAbduh's writings, that it was converts to Islam in the Umayyad and early Abbasid periods – he cites Persians and Byzantines, while in his response to Anṭūn he cited Persians and Turks – who corrupted the early faith that emerged from

[175] Hanotaux, *L'Europe*, 31.
[176] ʿAbduh and Hanotaux, *al-Islām*, 12.
[177] Hanotaux, *L'Europe et l'Islam*, 31.
[178] ʿAbduh and Hanotaux, *al-Islām*, 13.
[179] Published in *al-Muʾayyad* on 6, 13, and 20 May 1900.

the world of the uncivilised Bedouin. Accepting the charge that fatalism and inaction were Muslim features, ʿAbduh suggested that Sufism and its Iranian and Indian practitioners were to blame rather than the core Islamic belief system.[180] Muslim creed does not sever the relationship between man and God, it removes the notion of intermediaries between them. As for Kimon's views, ʿAbduh argued that Hanotaux was acting in bad faith in reproducing them in the course of his argument. It is not the fact that France rules over Muslims that causes resentment, but the lack of respect shown to them, since it is 'justice, rights, and respecting beliefs after understanding them that lighten the authority of the victor over the defeated'.[181]

In Hanotaux's responses, one in *al-Ahrām*'s French and Arabic editions in interview with its editor, followed by a shorter one in *Le Journal*, he was defensive. He only cited Kimon to indicate a broad base of opinion in France, Britain, and Germany, he explains. In separating religious and civil authority, we, France, made the advances that allowed us to expand into other territories, but now we want to help you advance too. Calls for Islamic union only serve to frighten Europe: Arab Muslims would be better to follow the example of Japan which managed to stave off colonial subjugation through adopting European science, technology, and the nation-state model. It is European powers who are helping protect and maintain the Ottoman empire. He holds up two Turkish intellectuals as exemplars: Young Turk intellectual Ahmed Rıza (1858–1930), who founded the CUP paper *Meşveret* in French and Turkish from Paris, and the journalist Ahmed Midhat. While he suggests that Rıza has an idealised view of tolerance – a reference to his French book *Tolérance musulmane* (1897) which was heavily critical of colonialism – Midhat is for Hanotaux 'the most justifiably famous of Turkish writers right now', citing his modernist views that Islam has no need of clergy, Muḥammad has no miraculous qualities as a prophet, and the Qurʾan should be Islam's sole source of authority – ideas that he seemed unaware were within ʿAbduh's frame of reference.[182] ʿAbduh's final word was to stress the successes of the reformist approach. Islam may contain some blind religious fanaticism (*al-taʿaṣṣub al-dīnī al-aʿmā*), but the many rational Muslims are engaged in a process of correcting misunderstandings over foundational texts.[183]

[180] ʿAbduh and Hanotaux, *al-Islām*, 32.
[181] Ibid., 43.
[182] Hanotaux, *L'Europe et l'Islam*, 68–9. He seems to mean Midhat's anti-materialist essay *Ben Neyim?* (1891).
[183] ʿAbduh and Hanotaux, *al-Islām*, 75. From *al-Muʾayyad*, 25 July 1900.

Both Istanbul and Cairo have established non-shariʿa courts in some jurisdictions, but Europeans should realise that the sultan/caliph does not exercise papal authority, he only guarantees the functioning of the shariʿa system. Had Hanotaux restricted his intervention to the political interests of Muslim states we would have welcomed his advice, but he insisted to pontificate vainly on Muslim theology.

The transfer into Arabic of French conceptualisations of Islam in this exchange gives a sense of the subtle crafting of Islam as an objective category of world religion in Arabic texts of the period. Prosaic inventions such as *la religion mahometane* are rendered without comment as simply *al-islām*,[184] or *le mahometisme* as *al-diyāna al-muḥammadiyya*,[185] or *la foi mohametane* as *al-īmān al-muḥammadī*;[186] while *le monde musulman* is translated via the calque *al-ʿālam al-islāmī*, which with its 'Arab world' counterpart came to attain a translingual hegemony that holds to this day.[187] The lexical intersection between the French *civilisation* and the notion of temporal (*contra* religious) powers in the term *civile* is reproduced in the Arabic and Ottoman terms *tamaddun/medeniyet* for civilisation and *madanī/medeni* for both civilised and temporal/non-religious.[188] This conflation is seen throughout the Hanotaux material in talking of *al-sulṭa al-madaniyya/saltanat-i medeniye* and *tamaddun/medeniyet*.[189] These modernist internalisations of European conceptions of religion and its role vis-à-vis the state can be contrasted with the fact that Akif had no compunction in censoring jarring passages such as Kimon's proposal to steal the Prophet's tomb text or Hanotaux's concluding statement that Tunisia is home to a diverse historical heritage 'under the sponsorship of France and its humanity' by excising them completely from his Ottoman text.[190]

184 Hanotaux, *L'Europe et l'Islam*, 29; Abduh and Hanotaux, *al-Islām*, 11.

185 Hanotaux, 31; ʿAbduh and Hanotaux, 12.

186 Hanotaux, 37; ʿAbduh and Hanotaux, 18.

187 Hanotaux, 25; ʿAbduh and Hanotaux, 7.

188 Kevin Reinhart, 'Civilization and its Discussants: Medeniyet and the Turkish Conversion to Modernism,' in *Converting Cultures: Religion, Ideology, and Transformations of Modernity*, ed. Dennis Washburn and A. Kevin Reinhart (Leiden: Brill, 2007), 267–79. The Arabic *madanī* later came to indicate civil society.

189 For example, for ʿAbduh see ʿAbduh and Hanotaux, *al-Islām*, 79–90; for Akif see his *Hanotonun Hücumuna Karşı Şeyh Muhammed Abdunun İslamı Müdafaası* (Istanbul: Tevsi-i Tıbaat Matbaası, 1913), 72–3.

190 ʿAbduh and Hanotaux, *al-Islām*, 15; Akif, *Hanotonun Hücumuna Karşı*, 13.

AKIF AND THE ANGLICAN CHURCH AFFAIR

The text Akif worked on with ʿAbd al-ʿAzīz Jāwīsh, published in 1923, was in many ways the pinnacle of the Ottoman modernist project. For both figures, it was the coda to a decade of anti-colonial activism. A graduate of both Dār al-ʿUlūm and al-Azhar where he studied under ʿAbduh, Jāwīsh was sent by the Egyptian education ministry for training in Britain and wrote manuals on English-Arabic translation. Through his acquaintance with historian David Margoliouth he was appointed as Arabic teacher to British officials heading for service in Egypt and Sudan at New College, Oxford from 1902 to 1906, but he understood the experience as colonialism's attempt to co-opt governing elites into the imperial enterprise.[191] During these classes Jāwīsh came to realise that students saw Islam as 'slavery, divorce, and polygamy' (*dīn al-istirqāq, wa-l-ṭalāq wa-taʿaddud al-zawjāt*) and understood Muḥammad's function in terms of Jesus in Christianity, and this prompted him to write *al-Islām Dīn al-Fiṭra wa-l-Ḥurriyya* (Islam is the Religion of Nature and Freedom, 1905).[192] Back in Egypt he veered towards journalism, establishing his own paper *al-Hidāya* in 1910, but after falling foul of the authorities for anti-British, pro-Ottoman agitation (causing a rift with Rashīd Riḍā who favoured an Arab caliph)[193] he was deported to Istanbul in 1912. Building on relationships established with leading CUP figures Enver and Talat Paşa during a trip in 1909,[194] Jāwīsh joined the CUP-backed Pan-Islamic Islamic Benevolent Society (al-Jamʿiyya al-Khayriyya al-Islāmiyya) established by Arab and Turkish dignatories in Istanbul in 1913[195] and worked with Akif on wartime propaganda. During these years he travelled frequently to Germany and other European states, attending conferences, and establishing newspapers as part of the Ottoman-German effort to win over Muslim subjects of the Allied powers.[196] With the fall of

191 Anwar al-Jundī, *ʿAbd al-ʿAzīz Jāwīsh min Ruwwād al-Tarbiya wa-l-Ṣiḥāfa wa-l-Ijtimāʿ* (Cairo: al-Muʾassasa al-Miṣriyya al-ʿĀmma, 1965), 50–2.

192 ʿAbd al-Azīz Jāwīsh, *al-Islām Dīn al-Fiṭra wa-l-Ḥurriyya* (Cairo: Dār al-Hilāl, 1905), 10. His son Nāṣir says the book was published in English as *Islam: Religion of Instinct and Freedom* but it appears never to have gone to print; Nāṣir Jāwīsh, 'Preface,' in Jāwīsh, *al-Islām*, 5–8.

193 Al-Jundī, *ʿAbd al-ʿAzīz Jāwīsh*, 113–15.

194 Ibid., 121.

195 Jacob M. Landau, *The Politics of Pan-Islam: Ideology and Organization* (Oxford: Clarendon Press, 1990), 109–11. Shakīb Arslān, *Sīra Dhātiyya* (al-Mukhtāra: al-Dār al-Taqaddumiyya, 2008), 87–8.

196 The papers included *al-Hilāl al-ʿUthmānī* and *al-Haqq Yaʿlū* in Cairo, *Die Islamische Welt* in Germany, *al-ʿalām al-Islāmī* in Istanbul, and *L'Égypte* in Switzerland.

the CUP he left Istanbul to work with the Egyptian delegation to Versailles, but returned to Turkey in 1922 at Atatürk's request to head his Islamic publications committee.[197]

The genesis of the Jāwīsh book is not as yet fully understood. A letter was delivered to the sheikh ül-Islam's office in Istanbul on 21 December 1918 in the name of Arthur Boutwood (1864–1924), a civil servant with the British government's Charity Commission and public intellectual who had written a number of books on questions of national identity, religion, and education.[198] No copy of the original letter has been found in the Müftülük archives in Istanbul, among Boutwood's private papers in Corpus Christi College, Cambridge, or in Church of England archives. However, an Ottoman translation of the text was published on two separate occasions by members of the Darü'l-Hikmeti'l-İslamiye which the Mufti Haydarizade Ibrahim had charged with providing a response, Ahmed Rasim Avni in the newspaper *Alemdar*,[199] and Eşref Efendizade Şevketi in his book *Say ve Sermaye Mücadelatının Dinen Suret-i Halli* (Religion's Solution to Conflicts of Labour and Capital, 1923). Şevketi recounts how he was present at the Meşihat when the document arrived and he translates a second letter he received personally from Boutwood dated 3 April 1921 in response to a request Şevketi had made for more information regarding Boutwood's key questions: what is the Prophet's religion, what is its contribution to thought and life, what is its solution to the troubles of our times (*zamanımızın mezahimi*), what does it have to say about the political and spiritual forces currently transforming the world?[200] In the translations of his letter, Boutwood neglects to spell out his work for the British government, saying only that the authoritative description of Islam, to be authored by a prominent personage, was for a small library being prepared by the Church of England's publications wing.

Boutwood's request was taken seriously by the Ottoman religious establishment for two reasons: it was misunderstood to have come from the head of the Anglican Church himself and it came at the onset of the British occupation of Istanbul. After long deliberations over who should

197 Jāwīsh, *al-Islām*, 8.

198 On his contribution to public debate in Britain see E.H.H. Green, *Ideologies of Conservatism: Conservative Political Ideas in the Twentieth Century* (Oxford: Oxford University Press, 2002), 46–56.

199 Ahmed Rasim Avni, 'Anglikan Encümen-i İlmiyesine Cevap,' *Alemdar*, 12 September 1919; cited in Nurettin Ceylan, *Gerçeğin Aynasında Bediüzzaman* (Istanbul: Nesil, 2016), 177.

200 Eşref Efendizade Şevketi, *Say ve Sermaye Mücadelatının Dinen Suret-i Halli* (Istanbul: Matbaa-ı Osmaniye, 1923), 5. Transliterated in Ceylan, *Gerçeğin Aynasında*, 174.

author the response, the Mufti chose İsmail Hakkı. Boutwood appears to have received one section of Hakkı's book sometime in 1920,[201] noting with amusement that its author addressed the package 'care of the Archbishop of Canterbury' and referring to it flippantly as 'a piece of Islamic propaganda'.[202] The comment seems discordant in that Boutwood had a genuine interest in languages and cultures of the non-Western world, nurturing a belief, post-war, that Islam was in a position to retain the spirituality he felt materialist Europe was losing. Indeed, his writings make clear his opposition to both materialist trends in Western philosophy and attempts to provide rational explanation for miracles in the narrative of early Christianity. His original letter to Istanbul expressed the hope to hear the East speak for itself (*kendi sesiyle*) rather than through Muslims whose minds are 'filled with the most modern culture' (*en asri bir harsla zihinleri doldurulmuş kimseler*).[203] His private papers show that he was in contact with British Muslim leader Sayyid Amīr ʿAlī (1849–1928) to write the preface to an English edition of the Hakkı version, and said he was planning Persian, Urdu, and Arabic editions.[204] He also talked of using the book to convince British Prime Minister Lloyd George, who was strongly pro-Greek in the divided British government during the Greco-Turkish War of 1919–22, that the caliph was not a pope with authority in matters of faith, that Turkey's retention of the caliphate as well as the vilayets of Smyrna and Eastern Thrace should not be considered problematic for Britain, which should act to preserve the Ottoman polity.[205] Boutwood often expressed the fear to his interlocuters, who included British and Indian Muslim leaders and Ottoman diplomats, that British government policy was putting the integrity of its empire at risk by stoking resentment among Muslims. He was an interlocuter with an array of Muslim figures in Britain, Turkey, the Ottoman Arab provinces, and India (including Lahore Aḥmadī leader Muḥammad ʿAli) regarding what was termed at the time 'Eastern policy'.

[201] The book is İsmail Hakkı, *El-Cevabü's-Sedid fî Beyan-ı Dinü'l-Tevhid* (Ankara: Tedkikat ve Telifat-ı İslamiye Heyeti, 1923).

[202] Arthur Boutwood Papers, Corpus Christi College Library, Cambridge, UK: see box 'Ignotus,' vol. 2, 337–8 (biography written by his wife) and 'Letters 1900–1924,' Letter to Chief Charity Commissioner H.P. Morris, 1 April 1920: 246–7.

[203] Şevketi, *Say ve Sermaye*, 5.

[204] Ibid., 338.

[205] Arthur Boutwood Papers, 'Letters,' Letter to Ahmed Vehbi, 21 May 1921: 305, and 'Letters,' Letter to Syed Ameer Ali, 29 January 1921: 305c.

It remains possible, then, that Boutwood was acting not out of purely intellectual interest in the service of a church project but as part of an intelligence operation. His effort to establish a channel to the Ottoman Islamic authorities came one month into the British occupation of Istanbul, which made the issue particularly suspect to some figures, most notably Said Nursi, as an effort to co-opt Muslim authorities.[206] Boutwood's letters are full of enigmatic references to ulterior motives.[207] Though his papers talk of his distress at not rising to the heights of the British bureaucracy, he was writing speeches for government ministers during the war and involved in drafting documents during Versailles. At the time there was no shortage of English-language materials explaining Islam, though perhaps of too apologetic a nature in Boutwood's view.[208] The specific source of British concern that seems to have prompted his letter to Istanbul is in fact revealed in the separate correspondence Boutwood conducted with Eşref Efendizade Şevketi in 1921: fear over the spread of communism following the Russian Revolution in 2017. With working-class consciousness rising in the West, 'Lenin has friends in every land' (*Lenin'in her memlekette dostları var*), he wrote in his explanation of the book request – which prompted Şevketi to write the first Turkish Muslim work responding to socialist critique of capitalism.[209] Boutwood was close to the British historian Arnold Toynbee, an intelligence operative during the war who Priya Satia has shown was anxious to prevent a meeting of what he called 'Islamic consciousness' and the 'European Labour Movement' and who also published pro-Ankara material after the war.[210] Boutwood's pen-name Hakluyt Egerton referred to English

206 Ceylan, *Gerçeğin Aynasında*, 171–86. Zekeriya Akman suggests the same in his discussion of the Anglican Church affair, writing 'it's possible they wanted to know Islam from Muslims to give direction to their activities in the Islamic geography, their target population'; Akman, 'Anglikan Kilisesi'nin Meşihat Kurumuna Soruları ve Bunlara Verilen Cevaplar,' *Hikmet Yurdu*, 6/11 (January–June 2013): 358.

207 The unsigned introduction to his letters collection – likely authored by his wife – refers to 'strangers' who destroyed many boxes of papers kept at his office after his sudden death, as well as a package marked confidential 'implicating many pillars of society' that it says his wife burned; Introduction, 'Letters,' 2.

208 Sayyid Amīr ʿAlī published *The Spirit of Islam* in 1902 and the Aḥmadīs of the Woking Mosque began publishing *The Islamic Review* journal in 1913 and a host of books by its writers.

209 Şevketi, *Say*, 5–6; the English original is in 'Ignotus,' 2:337–8. On his book see Mustafa Yıldız, *Bir İslamcıya Göre Kapitalizm ve Sosyalizm* (Istanbul: Çıra Publications, 2014).

210 For Boutwood's mention of Toynbee see 'Scribbling Diary 1905,' Boutwood Papers, 58b; and on Toynbee's espionage role see Priya Satia, *Spies in Arabia: The Great War and the Cultural Foundations of Britain's Covert Empire in the Middle East* (Oxford: Oxford

geographer and diplomat Richard Hakluyt (d. 1616) who championed Britain's early imperial expansion in North Americas.

Boutwood's interest flagged as political realities shifted and British fear of Turkish communism receded.[211] The Anglican Church affair was now to acquire new life on the Turkish side just at the point in 1922 when Ankara's National Forces were poised to make their final victory against the Greek occupation, wrest control of Istanbul from the rival government of the sultan, and enter the Lausanne peace talks with Britain, France, and Italy. Mustafa Kemal's government seized on the idea of publishing a new 'response to the Anglican Church' as a prestigious state project that would bolster its Muslim credentials before domestic and international audiences. It was among the first matters passed to the publications committee of Ankara's shariʿa and religious ministry in August 1922 and in parliament a delegate accused Istanbul of having failed to provide appropriate answers to the Church of England.[212] Rather than choose someone from within the İlmiye to write it, prime minister and formerly the navy's chief-of-staff Hüseyin Rauf Orbay turned to Jāwīsh, a familiar figure to the wartime CUP government. Jāwīsh was brought from Munich to not only write the book but head the publications committee itself, while Akif was commissioned to translate Jāwīsh's Arabic text into Turkish.[213] *Sebilürreşad* praised the choice of Jāwīsh, describing him as a *müceddid* in the line of great renewers such as ʿAbduh.[214] Declaring the project a 'great duty' (*büyük vazife*) with the first instalment of Jāwīsh's work in its issue of 5 July 1923, *Sebilürreşad* said it augured well for the Turkish parliament and would raise its status around the Islamic world.[215] Atatürk praised the publications committee in a speech in March 1923, declaring its role to be 'comparing Islamic philosophy with Western scientific and philosophical theories, researching the Islamic peoples' beliefs and scientific, social, and economic life, and publishing the results', and for this

University Press, 2008), 211, footnote 21. Toynbee's journalistic dispatches were published as *The Western Question in Turkey and Greece* (1923). Corpus Christi college, where Boutwood's papers are held, hosts a lecture in Boutwood's name every two years.

211 Boutwood worked with Canon John Douglas, a reader of Turkish who translated letters for him, on a project to reconcile the Christian churches and bring together representatives of the Eastern Orthodox churches for a commemoration of Council of Nicaea, which was held in Westminster Abbey in 1925.

212 Müfid Efendi (deputy for Kırşehir); *TBMM Zabıt Ceridesi*, 24 August 1922, 3/22: 354–5.

213 TBMM document no. 030_18_01_01_6_48_15, Türkiye Cumhuriyeti Devlet Arşivleri, Sadabad, Istanbul.

214 'Anglikan Kilisesine Verilen Cevaplar Hakkında,' *SR*, 17 January 1924, 23/584: 188.

215 'Anglikan Kilisesine Cevap - 1,' *SR*, 5 July 1923, 21/542–3: 170.

purpose books from Europe, Egypt, and Istanbul were being collected for display in a grand library, he said.[216] *Sebilürreşad* hailed the Jāwīsh–Akif book as a manifesto for modern Islam, consonant with the progress of the era (*bugünkü harikulade terakkiyatı*) and capable of providing solutions to modern problems.[217]

Both the Jāwīsh and final Hakkı books appear never to have been sent to Britain, but in Jāwīsh's case that was not the point. His published Ottoman text is the *apologia* that Boutwood hoped to avoid, a quintessential modernist narration of Islam as Europe's idea of a world religion. Christian missionaries have depicted Islam as blind submission to God without independent thought or agency (*fikirsiz, iradesiz*),[218] but Islamic faith is predicated upon reason (*akla istinad*), it says.[219] The Qurʾan is Islam's only miracle (*Kur'andan başka harika olamayacağını bildiriyor*) and Islam does not oblige reason to accept impossible beliefs or rules which defy proof (*muhal olan bir akidenin yahud hilaf-ı burhan ile sabit bir hükmün kabuluna aklı Ilzām etmek müstaḥīldir*).[220] This form of rationality is compatible with individual freedom of conscience (*ferdî hürriyet-i vicdan*), which means equality of responsibility for actions among sexes, classes, and states, while the obligation to perform certain duties such as prayer and fasting is an individual responsibility indicating that men are free of inherited sin[221] and that no individual can atone for the sins of others – a rejection of Christian and Muslim intercession. Jāwīsh reviews early Church debates on Christ's divinity[222] and considers that God brings recompense for some good and bad deeds in this life rather than leave that for the next.[223] Echoing Said Halim's *İslamlaşmak*, he says Islam is comprehensive in its view of history and approach to modern life, from its prescriptions for eating, drinking, attire, health, work, marriage, happiness, and sadness,[224] to an integrationist understanding of the pre-Islamic prophets and the Enlightenment philosophers.[225] Muslims are called to labour and effort

[216] Mustafa Kemal, 'Birinci Dönem, Dördüncü Toplanma Yılını Açarken,' 1 March 1923, in *Gazi M. Kemal Atatürk, Eğitim Politikası Üzerine Konuşmalar*, Kemal Aytaç (Ankara: Türk İnkilap Tarihi Enstitüsü, 1984), 44.
[217] 'Anglikan Kilisesine Cevap - 1,' *SR*, 5 July 1923, 21/542–3: 170.
[218] Abdülaziz Çaviş, 'Anglikan Kilisesine Cevap - IV,' *SR*, 2 August 1923, 22/547–8: 3.
[219] Çaviş, *SR*, 9 August 1923, 22/549–50: 17.
[220] Ibid., 18.
[221] Çaviş, *SR*, 13 August 1923, 22/553–4: 51.
[222] Çaviş, *SR*, 20 September 1923, 22/561–2: 113–15.
[223] Çaviş, *SR*, 9 August 1923, 22/549–50: 20.
[224] Çaviş, *SR*, 23 August 1923, 22/553–4, 23: 52.
[225] Çaviş, *SR*, 20 September 1923, 22/561–2: 113.

(*say, mücahede*), and not to fall into despair or entertain notions of divine predetermination of human affairs, which he says Sufism has encouraged.[226]

But the text also sought to present Islam with a distinct modern religious identity of its own, building on the ideas of Akif, Hakkı, Ahmed Naim, Namık Kemal, and Said Halim. Islam partakes of a unique transational, egalitarian identity and is comprehensive in its prescriptions for all aspects of modern life: the Muḥammadan nation (*ümmet-i Muhammedî*) possesses a religious nationalism (*kavmiyet-i diniye*) that encompasses language, thought, architecture, lifestyle, family, and ethics.[227] European democracy is often dysfunctional, since political and financial interests managing to control parliaments, he said,[228] and Ḥanafī law on the rights and duties of women is superior to the mixed pattern seen across Western societies.[229] And Jāwīsh explicitly linked European discourse on the Orient to imperatives of empire. 'In addition to desires on Africa and a policy of appropriation in its northern part that prevent showing Islam in its true form, European countries began to misrepresent and besmirch Islam in seeking to obtain its territories', he writes.[230]

So they began to revive anti-Islamic works from the Middle Ages and spread propaganda against Islamic rules and the Qur'an, and after publishing books to that effect, judgements were made that Islam was incompatible with civilisation [*İslam'ın medeniyeti kabule müsaid olmadığı*] and that because of Islam Muslim peoples were incapable of reaching the level of European nations. Whenever there was something they wanted in the Islamic world, they arrived at their colonial aims through this form of attack.[231]

In acting in this manner, the Europeans were exploiting the decline that Muslim states had experienced in terms of political organisation and

226 Çaviş, *SR*, 27 September 1923, 22/563–4: 129–32.

227 Çaviş, *SR*, 4 October 1923, 22/565–6: 147–8. This represented a reworking of the rejection of *kavmiyet* in Ahmed Naim's *İslam'da Dava-yı Kavmiyet* (1914).

228 Çaviş, *SR*, 13 December 1923, 23/579: 98.

229 Çaviş, *SR*, 20 December 1923, 23/580: 114–16; *SR*, 3 January 1924, 23/582: 146–9; *SR*, 10 January 1924, 23/583: 161–3; *SR*, 17 January 1924, 23/584: 178–80; *SR*, 31 January 1924, 23/586: 209–10; *SR*, 7 February 1924, 23/587: 226–7; *SR*, 14 February 1924, 23/588: 241–2.

230 Abdülaziz Çaviş (trans. Akif), *Anglikan Kilisesine Cevap* (Istanbul: Evkaf-i İslamiye Matbaası, 1339 [1923]), 197. It is not clear why this section was not published in *Sebilürreşad*.

231 Ibid., 197–8.

knowledge production, though a few good Orientalists had been perceptive and honest enough to acknowledge the Islamic impulse to know, he said.[232]

Despite Jāwīsh and Akif's best efforts, the mood against any role for Islamic institutions in Turkish public affairs had turned and the Muslim intellectuals' hope that the Ottoman state could reemerge as a revitalized Islamic polity quickly dissipated. Jāwīsh first suspected the government's intent to create a completely new political, legal, and social order after two long discussions, one with Mustafa Kemal in December 1922 and a second with his inner circle in January 1923, during which he was pressed on the viability of rendering the caliphate a purely spiritual office and parliament assuming some of its functions.[233] Mustafa Kemal had also surprised a British journalist in late 1922 with a denunciation of Turkish society as a 'priest-ridden' nation.[234] Jāwīsh left for Egypt in November 1923 after the publications committee was disbanded and Turkey declared a republic. In the following months nationalist historian Fuat Köprülü (1890–1966), who had just published his *Türkiye Tarihi* (The History of Turkey, 1923), would smear both the Hakkı and Jāwīsh books on modern Islam as 'rather primitive' (*pek iptidai*),[235] the caliphate would be abolished, and the Diyanet administration formed, taking on the functions of the now defunct shariʿa and religious endowments ministry which itself had subsumed the office of sheikh ül-Islam. Islam as the religion of state was removed from the constitution in 1928.[236]

DER WILLE ZUR MACHT: AKIF, MUḤAMMAD IQBĀL, AND MUSLIM PROGRESS

During his early years in Cairo when he was busy on his Qurʾan work and the main body of his *Gölgeler* collection there is no record of Akif maintaining contact with Jāwīsh, who died in 1929. However, Akif's network expands from that year through the friendship he established

[232] He cites positively French thinker Jules La Beaume's *Le Koran analysé* (1878); Çaviş, *Anglikan Kilisesine Cevap*, 202.

[233] Al-Jundī, *ʿAbd al-ʿAzīz Jāwīsh*, 139–43.

[234] Grace Ellison, *Turkey To-Day* (London: Hutchinson, 1928), 23–4; the comments were recorded in English through an interpreter.

[235] 'Anglikan Kilisesine Verilen Cevaplar Hakkında,' *SR*, 17 January 1924, 23/584: 188.

[236] The French terminological framing of *laïcité* was not adopted (as *laiklik*) until the Republican People's Party programme of 1931 and the constitution of 1937, though the model differed in critical ways (state management and honouring of religion through the Diyanet administration).

with ʿAbd al-Wahhāb ʿAzzām. Born in 1894 to a well-known family of religious scholars, ʿAzzām had an Azharī education, studied to become a judge, then spent three years studying philosophy and literature at the Egyptian University. He served as the imam of the Egyptian embassy in London while doing his masters on Persian Sufi poet Farīd al-Dīn ʿAttār (d. 1220) at the School of Oriental Studies where he graduated in 1928. On his return he took a university post teaching Persian while he completed his doctorate on Ferdowsi's *Shahname*.[237] He only came to know about Akif's presence in Ḥilwān during a trip to Istanbul when accompanying his uncle ʿAbd al-Raḥmān ʿAzzām (first secretary general of the Arab League)[238] to a meeting with Akif's son-in-law Ömer Rıza Doğrul.

Doğrul described their friendship as an intellectual match that drew Akif out of his seclusion, in that ʿAzzām arranged for Akif's teaching job and drew him into his Ḥilwān circle.[239] They shared a passion for Arabic and Persian literature, on the one hand, and French literature, on the other, but were troubled by European representation of Muslim culture. During his German sojourn Akif met the professor of Islamic Studies Martin Hartmann (1851–1918), concluding he was 'of superficial knowledge' (*sathî bilgili*) on Persian literature.[240] On his return he made three complaints of the Germans: the empty vanity (*kuru bir gösteriş*) of their Orientalists, foreign policy too mindful of the United States, and their cuisine with its boiled cabbage.[241] Akif documented attitudes that might today be described as Islamophobic. The German government warned them during their wartime mission in Berlin that due to anti-Muslim sentiment there was a deep scepticism in parliament over their collaboration. 'The country's ideas had become so poisoned against us over centuries by journalists, novelists, and those so-called Orientalists, who claimed to understand Eastern languages, Eastern sciences and arts,

237 For a summary of his life see Aḥmad Tammām, 'ʿAbd al-Wahhāb ʿAzzām, al-Diblūmāsī al-Adīb (fī Dhikrā Wafātihi),' Islam Online, https://archive.islamonline.net/?p=9053 (accessed 5 May 2018). From 1947–56 he was Egypt's ambassador to Saudi Arabia, Pakistan, and Yemen, then established Riyadh University.

238 He also worked with the Ottomans in Libya during the First World War; see Ralph Coury, *The Making of an Egyptian Arab Nationalist: The Early Years of Azzam Pasha, 1893–1936* (Reading, UK: Ithaca Press, 1998). Stoddard lists Dr Abdürrahman Bey among the Fedai Zabıtan; *The Ottoman Government and the Arabs*, 173.

239 Edib, *Mehmed Akif*, 451.

240 Ömer Rıza Doğrul, 'Mehmed Akif,' 439.

241 Ibid., 439. See also Akif, 'Köy Hocası,' *SR*, 12 December 1918, 15/382: 331–2. Hartmann shared the Orientalist view of Islam as fatally crippled by fatalism; see Cundioğlu, *Bir Kur'an Şairi*, 67.

Eastern morals and customs, that there was no possibility of an understanding or peace between us', Akif said.[242] He relates his shock at the Austrian government lighting the streets in celebration when Jerusalem fell to the British because of its liberation from Muslim hands.[243]

Given these interests it was fortuitous that Akif and ʿAzzām should develop a mutual admiration for Indian poet and intellectual Muḥammad Iqbāl. ʿAzzām explains in his obituary his debt to Akif for introducing him to Iqbāl, specifically his Persian-language poetry collection *Payām-i Mashriq* (Message of the East, 1923), after which ʿAzzām obtained *Asrār-i Khūdī* (Secrets of the Self, 1915) and *Rumūz-i Bīkhūdī* (Mysterics of Selflessness, 1917)[244] from Indian acquaintances in Cairo, and they would read all three works together.[245] ʿAzzām later translated these works into Arabic, publishing *Payām-i Mashriq* in Pakistan during his time as Egypt's ambassador and the others in Egypt.[246] In the introduction to his *Payām-i Mashriq* translation ʿAzzām says he first heard of Iqbāl as a 'Sufi poet' from Indian students during his time at London University, which didn't encourage him to know more.[247] However, it was ʿAzzām rather than Akif who had the chance to meet Iqbāl when Iqbāl was hosted by the Muslim Youth Association in Cairo on his way to the attend the Islamic conference held in Jerusalem in December 1931. Iqbāl was feted in Egypt over five intense days during which he met with intellectuals on several occasions, and though ʿAzzām even gave an address in his honour there is no record of Akif's having attended.[248] It is possible that Akif drew no attention from the Egyptian journalists, but he never made any subsequent mention of the event. Why Akif would not have gone is something of a mystery. He may have been too shy to insert himself into the mix, since he did not know English and was not confident of his spoken Arabic; he also knew that

242 Akif, 'Nasrullah Kürsüsünde,' *SR*, 25 November 1920, 18/464: 251.

243 Ibid., 251. In Midhat Cemal's telling, Akif was in Germany or Austria at the time. Given Jerusalem fell to British forces between 17 November and 30 December 1917, this would place Akif in Europe later than is normally assumed.

244 These titles are usually rendered in modern Turkish as *Peyam-i Maşrik*, *Esrar-i Hodi*, and *Rumuz-i Bihodi*.

245 ʿAbd al-Wahhāb ʿAzzām, 'İslam Şairi Mehmed Âkif,' in Edib, *Mehmed Âkif*, 200–3.

246 *Payām-i Mashriq: Risālat al-Mashriq* (1951); *Dīwān al-Asrār wa-l-Rumūz* (1956), combining *Asrār-i Khūdī* and *Rumūz-i Bīkhūdī*; his Urdu collection *Żarb-i Kalim* (1936) as *Ḍarb al-Kalim: Iʿlān al-Ḥarb ʿalā al-ʿAṣr al-Ḥāḍir* (1952).

247 ʿAzzām, 'Muqaddimat al-Mutarjim,' in *Payām-i Mashriq: Risālat al-Mashriq*, Muḥammad Iqbāl (Lahore: Iqbāl Academy Pakistan, 1981), 2. ʿAzzām says he retained the copy Akif gave him.

248 The visit is detailed in Ḥāfiẓ Maḥfūẓ and Nabīla Isḥāq, *Iqbāl wa-l-Azhar* (Cairo: Dār al-Bayān, 1999), 25–7.

Iqbāl did not read Turkish and may not have had a chance to become familiar with his work. It seems highly unlikely that ʿAzzām would not have informed him in advance.[249]

Parallels between Akif and Iqbāl have been noted by a number of scholars, notably in Turkish.[250] Annemarie Schimmel commented on the similarity during her five years teaching at Ankara University in the 1950s.[251] Schimmel recognised Akif as the one of the first Muslim intellectuals outside India to appreciate Iqbāl's importance and she also cited the impact of Ottoman Turkish thinkers (Akif, Said Halim, Gökalp) on Iqbāl. Iqbāl's poem *Tarāna-i Hind* (1904) became popular in Istanbul as an anti-colonial anthem and Iqbāl turned his attention to Ottoman losses in the Balkan wars and Libya, which inspiring several of his works.[252] The parallels go beyond age, life span, social background, and belief in art as the field where intellectuals should theorise construction of nation. The fate of their choices in language is also similar: Sahota notes that Iqbāl's Persian was reduced after his death to a national language belonging to neither India nor Pakistan, but Akif also laboured over a language whose form (alphabet reform) and much of its substance (language reform) was discarded in the transformation of Turkish begun in the early republican period.[253] They also shared a direct, if contrasting, experience of Germany: Iqbāl spent three years studying for his doctorate in Persian metaphysics under the guidance of British and German Orientalists and had as a result a more positive view of European claims to expertise in Islam than Akif. Iqbāl even managed the trip to Andalusia that Akif was

[249] ʿAzzām is silent about Akif in the Turkish section of his travelogue *Riḥlāt* (Cairo, 1939), 72–92.

[250] Yusuf Karaca, 'Akif ve İkbal,' *İslami Edebiyat*, Issue 3, January–March 1990: 28–30; İsa Çelik, 'Çagdaş İki İslam Şairi: Muhammed İkbal ve Mehmed Akif,' *Atatürk Üniversitesi İlahiyat Fakültesi Dergisi*, Issue 22 (Erzurum, 2004): 151–92; Faik Gözübüyük, 'Mehmed Akif ve Muhammed İkbal,' *Türk Yurdu*, 50/280, January 1960: 49–51; Münevver Ayaşlı, *İşittiklerim Gördüklerim Bildiklerim* (Istanbul: Güryay Mat., 1973), 154–64; Neşet Çağatay, 'Allama Muhammad İqbal and Mehmet Akif Ersoy,' *İslam İlimleri Enstitüsü Dergisi*, no. 4 (1980): 61–6; Beşir Ayvazoğlu, 'Mehmed Akif ve Muhammed İkbal,' *Muhammed İkbal Kitabı Uluslararası Muhammed İkbal Sempozyumu Bildirileri* (Istanbul: Istanbul Büyükşehir Belediyesi Kültür İşleri, 1997), 43–56.

[251] Annemarie Schimmel, 'Önsöz,' in *Cavidname*, Muhammed İkbal (Istanbul: Kırkambar, 2010 [1958]), 12.

[252] Nisar Ahmed Asrar, 'Muhammed İkbal'in Eserlerinde Türkiye ve Türkler,' *Muhammed İkbal Kitabı*, 76–9.

[253] G.S. Sahota, 'Uncanny Affinities: A Translation of Iqbal's Preface to Payam-e Mashriq,' *Postcolonial Studies*, 15:4 (2012): 437–52. Transliterated into Latin script Akif's work remains generally comprehensible.

planning in December 1925 in his early Egypt years before fatigue and illness struck him down.[254]

As Sahota points out, *Payām-i Mashriq* undercut the Western notion of civilisation's mono-directional flow from European metropolitan centre to Oriental satrapy.[255] It was heavily influenced by Johann Wolfgang von Goethe's *West-östlicher Divan* (1819), which was partly inspired by Ḥāfiẓ. Iqbāl talks of the 'Eastern influence' Goethe channelled from his professor Johann Gottfried Herder (1744–1803), who was interested in the poetry of Saʿdī, and Austrian diplomat Joseph von Hammer-Purgstall (1774–1856), who in 1812 published the first translation of Ḥāfiẓ's *Divan* in a Western language. Goethe in turn inspired a series of Persianists in German literature of the time, including August Platen (1796–1835), Friedrich Rückert (1788–1866), and Friedrich von Bodenstedt (1819–92). Iqbāl noted himself that Goethe borrowed from the poetic style and structure of Persian literature in particular without embracing its Sufi substance and monist theory, with the implication that he could do the same with both Sufi and German traditions.[256] The Islamic East must wake up from centuries of slumber – the 'ease and indolence' of Persian thought – to reassert both the individual and society and thus play its role at a critical juncture in world history in light of the moral decline of Europe as evidenced by the First World War and the new possibilities revealed in the physics of Albert Einstein (1879-1955) and the philosophy of Henri Bergson (1859–1941).[257]

So frank was Iqbāl's engagement with modern Western knowledge that he was accused of mimicking many of its elements, in particular the concepts of the *Übermensch* and the will to power (*der Wille zur Macht*) in German philosopher Friedrich Nietzsche's (1844–1900) system. The phrase 'der Wille zur Macht' appeared in *Also Sprach Zarathustra* (Thus Spake Zarathustra, 1883) and *Jenseits von Gut und Böse* (Beyond Good and Evil, 1886), and his notes on the concept were put together posthumously under the same title in 1901, thus it lacked a systematic explication. Nietzsche was inspired by Arthur Schopenhauer's (1788–1860)

254 Günaydın, *Mektuplar*, 135. Iqbāl's poem was 'Masjid-i Qurṭuba', published in the collection *Bāl-i Jibrīl* (1935) after a visit in 1931. It was one of Iqbāl's few works to focus on architecture, a major theme for Akif. Akif wanted to visit the Elhambra in Grenada for another poem taking Islamic architecture as his inspiration.

255 Ibid., 444–5.

256 See his later written introduction, translated from Urdu, in Iqbāl (trans. Syed Abbas Ali Jaffery), *The Moonbeams over the East: A Translation of Poems from Allama Iqbal's Payām-i-Mashriq* (Karachi: Royal Book Co., 1996), 53.

257 Ibid., 55–6.

theory of the will to live, as well as Darwinian evolutionary theory, and though subsequently interpreted by many admirers and detractors in political and/or racial terms, will to power was developed in the context of Nietzsche's critique of German culture and nationalism as outlined in essays he published in the 1870s, as well as his view of the Hegelian notion of progress and the diminished status of religion as a metaphysical system explaining creation. Hegel was Nietzsche's arch-villain in what he saw as an intellectual class with a naive understanding of modern Europe as the teleological apotheosis of human history, an understanding that masked a sense of unease over Germany as a late-comer to nationhood and high culture. Rather than engage in modernity's detached historicisation of knowledge, the creative and independent man of action should himself produce knowledge in the present through the arts.[258] Out of this thinking emerges Nietzsche's *Übermensch*, the ideal type developed in the godless landscape of *Also Sprach Zarathustra* who rejects Platonic and Christian ethics and metaphysics for a new understanding of man in the world. Iqbāl made no secret of his interest in Nietzsche. Both Nietzsche and Schopenhauer are addressed directly in *Payām-i Mashriq*,[259] Nietzsche is compared to the Sufi martyr Manṣūr Ḥallāj (d. 922) in his *Jāvīdnāma* (1932),[260] and Nietzsche is often brought up in Iqbāl's speeches and articles.[261] In his public comments Iqbāl also related his concept of self-hood to Freud's ego.[262]

So Iqbāl welcomed the broad similarity in Nietzsche's thinking and his own as far as this intersection could be described as identifying and exalting an innate inner driving force in humans, even if he understood that Nietzsche's use of these terms took place in a particular historical context regarding the trajectory of rational philosophy, national culture, and belief in God in nineteenth-century German society. Iqbāl's purpose,

[258] Friedrich Nietzsche, 'The Use and Abuse of History,' in Nietzsche (trans. Anthony M. Ludovici and Adrian Collins), *The Untimely Meditations (Thoughts Out of Season Parts I and II)* (Lawrence, Kansas: Digireads.com, 2009), 96–133.

[259] Muḥammad Iqbāl, *Payām-i Mashriq: Dār Javab-i Divan-i Sha'ir-i Almanavi Go'eṭe* (Lahore: Dr Javid Iqbāl, 1969), 117–18.

[260] 'There was a Ḥallāj who was a stranger in his own land' (*būd ḥallājī bih shahr-i khūd gharīb*); see Iqbāl's translation, in *Speeches, Writings and Statements of Iqbal*, ed. Latif Aḥmad Sherwani (Lahore: Iqbāl Academy Pakistan, 1995), 187. Ḥallāj is also 'the free man who knows good and evil' (*mard-i āzādī kih dānad khūb ve zisht*). See Iqbāl (trans. A. J. Arberry), *Javid-Nama* (Ajman, UAE: Islamic Books, 2000), 93, 112.

[261] Iqbal, 'Muslim Democracy,' The New Era, Lucknow, 28 July 1917, cited in Sherwani, *Speeches*, 161.

[262] Address to All-India Muslim Conference, 1932, in Sherwani, *Speeches*, 41; 'McTaggart's Philosophy,' Indian Arts and Letters, 6/1 (1932): 25–31, cited in Sherwani, *Speeches*, 183.

however, was to address the condition of contemporary Muslims, who had for the most part fallen under the yoke of European powers because, he believed, after ascending to the civilisational heights of socio-political organisation and intellectual achievement they had lost the way. He was blunt in the lectures which became the basis of his book *The Reconstruction of Religious Thought in Islam* (1930). Here he outlined the Muslim modernist understanding of, on the one hand, excessive intellectualisation within the Sufi tradition that had diverted attention from more pressing and worthy tasks of communal guidance and, on the other, rigid adherence to the established legal and theological traditions that had crushed the creative spirit of individual and community. As for Nietzsche's *Übermensch*, Iqbāl's concept of the *mard-i muʾmin* (the believing man) draws equally if not more on al-Jīlī's *al-insān al-kāmil*, on which Iqbāl wrote an essay in 1900.[263] Iqbāl was advocating neither post-God materialism nor absorption of the ego in the infinity of the divine, but the human personality's full embrace of God.[264]

Akif can also be located inside this cluster of ideas. How influenced was he by Iqbāl? Reading ʿAzzām offers some insight into Akif's understanding of Iqbāl, given their extensive discussions about *Payām-i Mashriq*. In the preface to his translation, ʿAzzām writes of the lesson he learned from Akif in what he calls instinctive translation (*bi-l-fars*), retaining the obscurity of meaning that Iqbāl often conveys as well as the metre, but altering phrases that would convey different meanings in Arabic.[265] ʿAzzām gives an explanation of Iqbāl's philosophy based on his reading of Iqbāl's first collection, *Asrār-i Khūdī* (1915), and then applies these ideas to *Payām-i Mashriq*. The key to Iqbāl's thinking, ʿAzzām says, is *khūdī* (Ar. *al-dhātiyya*), which is equivalent to selfhood, or, in Freudian terms, the concept of the ego.[266] Men must be true to their innate character in order to express this selfhood through independent thought and creativity; while imitation (*taqlīd*) weakens the self, the trials of life strengthen

[263] Iqbal, 'The Doctrine of Absolute Unity as Expounded by Abdul Karim al-Jilani,' in Sherwani, *Speeches*, 77–97.

[264] Annemarie Schimmel, *Gabriel's Wing: A Study into the Religious Ideas of Sir Muḥammad Iqbal* (Leiden: Brill, 1963), 118–21. For more on Iqbāl see Mir Mustansir, *Iqbal* (New Delhi: Oxford University Press, 2006), H. C. Hillier (ed.), *Muḥammad Iqbal: Essays on the Reconstruction of Modern Muslim Thought* (Edinburgh: Edinburgh University Press, 2015), M. Saeed Sheikh, *Studies in Iqbāl's Thought and Art: Select Articles from the Quarterly 'Iqbāl'* (Lahore: Bazm-i Iqbāl, 1972).

[265] ʿAzzām, 'Muqaddimat al-Mutarjim,' 11–12.

[266] Ibid., 14–16.

it,[267] and Iqbāl's descriptions of animals such as the self-reliant and independent hawk serve as examples in nature of the kind of free agent man should be.[268] Thus, Iqbāl believed men had free will but were under the illusion of divine order (*ḥurr mukhtār yatawahham annahu mujbar*).[269] ʿAzzām says Iqbāl also believed in the primacy of passion over reason (*ʿishq* over *ʿaql*) and the man of action who rejects the entrapments of Ashʿarīsm's anti-voluntarist tendencies.[270]

Second, Akif wrote to a friend on 8 March 1925 that he had received by post two works by Iqbāl, one of which was *Payām-i Mashriq*.[271] Akif adds he had seen a short work by Iqbāl while in Ankara and found him similar to himself (*sahibini kendime benzetmiştim*).[272] He talks of Iqbāl's familiarity with all the works of the Sufi masters while 'thorougly digesting Western philosophy through going to Germany' (*Almanya'ya giderek Garp felsefesini adamakallı hazmeden İkbal*) and notes approvingly that Iqbāl writes in Persian and has strong Arabic. It's not clear if *Asrār-i Khūdī* or *Rumūz-i Bīkhūdī* were among his Iqbāl readings in Ankara or the package he received in 1925.[273] Following his introduction to Iqbāl, Akif says he gave copies of the *Safahat* collection to Indian Muslims who visited him at *Sebilürreşad* offices in Istanbul for them to pass on to Iqbāl. Akif's friend Mahir İz talks in his memoirs of reading *Payām-i Mashriq* with Akif in his Istanbul home,[274] and in a letter dated 1 February 1927, Akif asked İz to send him a copy of *Payām-i Mashriq* that he had once left at İz's home.[275] Unsubstantiated claims have been made that Iqbāl and Akif engaged in direct correspondence from 1930. Researcher Mehmet Önder says Akif's son-in-law Ömer Rıza Doğrul read out a letter from Iqbāl to Akif at a conference he organised in Konya on

267 ʿAzzām cites the Arabic section 'Schopenhaeur wa-Nietzsche'; Iqbāl (trans. ʿAzzām), *Payām-i Mashriq*, 117.

268 Ibid., 'Naṣīḥat Ṣaqr li-Farkhihi,' 40–1.

269 Ibid., 'al-Ṭāʾira,' 76.

270 Ibid., 'Muḥāwarāt al-ʿIlm wa-l-ʿIshq,' 34–5; 'Naqsh al-Ifranj,' 110; 'Risālat Bergson,' 123. Iqbāl gave a clear exposition in English of his ideas in the preface to an English translation of *Asrār-i Khūdī* published in 1920; Muḥammad Iqbal (trans. Reynold Nicholson), *The Secrets of the Self (Asrár-i Khudí): A Philosophical Poem* (Lahore: Sh. Muhammed Ashraf, 1920), xvi–xxix.

271 Letter to Asım Şakir Gören, in Edib, *Mehmed Akif*, 203–4.

272 Ibid., 203.

273 Erişirgil thinks the first major work he read was *Payām-i Mashriq*; *İslamcı bir Şairin*, 363.

274 İz, *Yılların İzi*, 141.

275 Letter to Mahir Iz, 1 Şubat 1343 (1 February 1927), in Günaydın, *Mektuplar*, 56. Also Süleymaniye Library, Archive No. 2568, 'Mektuplar: Mehmet Akif Ersoy' (Letters to Mahir Iz), p. 19.

Iqbāl and Rūmī at some point during Ömer Rıza's time as a member of parliament in the 1950s. However, the text published by Önder, which is not cited elsewhere, talks only of love for modern Turkey and a desire to visit Rūmī's tomb in Konya, without any mention of Akif.[276] In his *Reconstruction of Religious Thought* (1930) and *Jāvīdnāma* (1932) Iqbāl mentions Atatürk, Gökalp, and his disciple Halim Sabit, and Akif's collaborator Said Halim Paşa – but not Akif himself.

So while it is possible that Akif's lyrical Sufi turn in the *Gölgeler* collection, including *Firavun ile Yüz Yüze* (Face to Face with Pharaoh, December 1924), *Gece* (Evening), *Hicran* (Separation), and *Secde* (Prostation in Prayer, all January 1925), was influenced by *Payām-i Mashriq*, as for Akif's earlier work containing his thinking on human agency, the good and bad of the Sufi tradition, art and the nation, he was writing along the same lines as Iqbāl independently. *Sanatkâr* (Artist), the very last poem of *Gölgeler*, and written August 1933, makes explicit reference to Iqbāl. The poem is an homage to composer Şerif Muhiddin Targan and dedicated to Archibald Roosevelt, son of the American president Theodore Roosevelt, in recognition of what Akif says in a footnote was the kindness he showed Muhiddin during his time in New York. In that spirit, Akif pieces together various tableaus of high cultural achievement from East and West to highlight crossflows between them. A traveller marvels at urban Americana observed from the window of the train he boards in Boston, then is surprised to see someone prostrating in prayer, which act is the apparent reason for describing him as an artist (*sanatkâr*). But Akif's Muhiddin is inside the carriage, where his lover praises him effusively for an oud performance he has given. Applying familiar figurative devices from Ottoman poetry, Muhiddin's playing is likened to the dove's longing cry and the burning heart of nightingales: 'Yes, the voice first heard by our civilised West/This breath bursting from the desert's burning heart/This speech of ages, like the call of God' (*Evet, bizim medeni Garb'ın ilk işittiği ses,/Çölün yanık yüreğinden kopup gelen bu nefes,/Nida-i Hak gibi edvarı haşreden bu hitab*).'[277] Even New York concert pianist Leopold Godowsky (1870–1938) makes an appearance in the text to praise the oud player, whose artistry springs from the blood

[276] Mehmet Önder, 'Mehmet Akif ve Muhammed İkbal,' *Milli Kültür*, 57 (May 1987), 51–3. Önder makes reference in a footnote to another article of his that contains in fact no mention of Akif at all; Mehmet Önder, 'İkbal'in Yaşamı ve Mevlana Hayranlığı,' *Pakistan Postası*, 24/1, January 1976: 5–6, 14. Önder cites a visit he made in 1976 to Iqbāl's home where he found a copy of *Safahat* but not apparently any correspondence.

[277] Akif, *Safahat*, 698.

of the prophets as the pinnacle of Eastern sensitivity (*O kanda bir galeyan: Şark'a en temiz heyecan*).[278] Yet this East is today suffering 'the despair of an afflicted nation' (*hāsir bir ümmetin ye'si*),[279] and to express this despair Akif's narrator quotes 'the poet of India, that philosopher Iqbāl': '*Heyecana verdi gönülleri,/Heyecanlı sesleri gönlümün;/Ben o nağmeden müteheyyicim:/Ki yok ihtimali terennümün*' (Their hearts were ecstatic/ The ecstatic sounds of my heart/So ecstatic am I from that music/That I cannot sing).[280] The poem ends on a note of ambiguous optimism, blind hope for a bright future.

Payām-i Mashriq's interest in European thought and questioning of Sufism was hardly new territory for Akif.[281] His ideas evolve in a clear progression. In *Süleymaniye Kürsüsünde*, touring the mosque, which was completed by the architect Sinan in 1558 under Suleyman the Magnificent, Akif describes it as a superlative human achievement that transcends nations and ideologies. 'One day courts and temples would be destroyed/ The purest of places soiled by the filthiest feet/Mankind would know a new religion, atheism/God's name erased from man's memory [*Yıkılır bir gün olur mahkemeler, ma'bedler/En temiz yerleri en kirli ayaklar çiğner/ Beşeriyet yeni bir din tanıyıp ilḥādı/Beşerin Ḥāfiẓasından silinir Hakk'ın adı*]', he writes, but 'not one stone from this home of God will fall' (*Yine tek bir taşı düşmez şu Hüda lānesinin*) since it is destined to remain 'the only home of truth on earth' (*doğruluğun yerdeki tek yurdu*).[282] In *Fatih Kürsüsünde* the focus shifts: two friends marvelling over another high-point of Ottoman architecture, the Fatih mosque, muse over the deterioration seen in contemporary standards, the state of disrepair of schools, mosques, and coffee-houses, and the innovations of intellectuals.[283] In *Berlin Hatıraları* German urban planning is commended for its functionality: 'What of the streets they talk of? Space without end/No chance of wandering on crooked bends [*Sokak dediler neymiş? Feza-i bī-pāyān/Ki tayyedilmesinin yoktur ihtimali yayan*].'[284] European achievement came

278 Ibid., 701.
279 Ibid., 702.
280 Ibid., 703. The quatrain is from verse twenty-five of the section 'May-i Bāqī' from *Payām-i Mashriq*; 'dil-i yārān az navāhā-yi perishānam sūkht/man az ān naghmih tepīdam kih surūdan natavān'. See Ali Nihat Tarlan, *İkbal'den Şiirler: Şarktan Haber ve Zebur-u Acem* (Istanbul: Türkiye İş Bankası Kültür Yayınları, 1971), 107.
281 On Akif's spiritual despair in Egypt see Çelik, 'Çagdaş İki İslam Şairi,' 158–60.
282 Akif, *Safahat*, 198.
283 Ibid., 306–7.
284 Ibid., 430.

with wars, Akif notes; but while Germany was able to recover from its Napoleonic defeats, the Ottomans could not benefit from the positive sciences as Europe has done – an argument that Iqbāl and Akif each made in their work.[285] Akif's subsequent *Asım* is his most forthright in outlining a theory of applying European knowledge in the construction of the modern nation, but with memorialisation of Gallipoli as the nation's foundational event. Akif intends the figure of Asım as representative of the new generation that will emerge stronger for the failures of its forebears, Akif's generation.[286] Asım transforms religious and nationalist zeal in war into a quest to attain the positive sciences (*müsbet ulum*) from Europe so that he can return for the nation-building project;[287] because of the sacrifice and success of Gallipoli he can engage Europeans now on an equal footing. Towards the end of the poem, viewed by admirers as Akif's most significant, a fictional conversation takes place between al-Afghānī and ʿAbduh over the nature of the revolutionary action they seek. The character who represents Akif agrees with ʿAbduh's gradualist approach focussed on education rather than political violence.[288] In the final lines Asım's father too counsels a revolution (*inkılab*), but one that bridges Islamic and European knowledge.[289]

The theme of the call to action also runs throughout Akif's work.[290] In *Fatih Kürsüsünde* his preacher gives an extended exposition on creation which appears to draw on the ideas and language of the Sufi, philosophical, and *kalām* traditions, in particular the emanationist *fayḍ* of Ibn Sīnā, al-Ghazālī, and Ibn Rushd, as well as ʿAbduh and the German philosophers. 'The sea of [divine] power's lasting work has no beginning/The call of bounteous eternity is manifest in every drop [*Beliğ sayidir umman-i kudretin ezeli/Hurūş-i feyz-i ezel her ḳuṭeyresinde celi*]', the preacher says.[291] 'Will, if considered, is always its eternal striving/But whose? That of the pure divine power, of the veiled secret/It neither rests nor remains idle for even a second/From stirring the affairs of creation [*İrade*

285 Iqbal, 'Islam and Aḥmadism,' *Islam*, January 1936, cited in Sherwani, *Speeches*, 225.
286 Erişirgil argues Akif modelled the poem on Namık Kemal's play *Vatan Yahud Silistre* (1872); *İslamcı bır Şairin Romanı*, 256.
287 Akif, *Safahat*, 610.
288 Ibid., 605–6. Ḥasan Kayalı argues that this refers to the CUP coup of 1913; 'Islam,' 328.
289 Akif, *Safahat*, 609–10.
290 Discussed in Turkish in Ertan Erol, 'Safahat'ta Emek ve Gayret Kavramları Üzerine,' *Uluslararası Sosyal Araştırmalar Dergisi*, 5/21 (Spring 2012): 106–16.
291 Akif, *Safahat*, 318. Feyz refers to the Neoplatonic emanation that entered Arabic as *fayḍ* in the philosophic and Sufi tradition.

hep ezelî sayidir, bakılsa, onun/Kimin? O kudret-i mahzın, o sırr-ı meknūnun/Ne dinlenir, ne de atıl kalır, velev bir an/Şuun-ı hilkati kesif edip yaratmaktan].'[292] He goes on to say that the creative power in the world could be articulated in terms of material (*madde*) that takes on different forms through *say*,[293] but he also uses the more familiar *kalām* term *zerre*, the smallest forms of matter which exhibit the same life force as the harmony of the seas and skies.[294] Akif then elaborates on the ecological system of the natural world as an 'endless chain' (*bir bī-nihāye silsile*) of dynamic energy, the same *kalām* innovation that Sabri saw in ʿAbduh and viewed as a surrender to the new European epistemology.[295] Akif's preacher continually returns to his refrain: 'Those who survive know that striving is a duty/Keep working to deserve survival through your effort' (*Bekayı hak tanıyan, sayi bir vazife bilir/Çalış çalış, ki beka say olursa hakkedilir*).[296]

The sermon uses this discussion of divine power and causes, in which the Ashʿarī-Māturīdī terminology of human acquisition of divine authority to act (*kasb/tafwīḍ*) have in a sense been replaced by his concept of *say*, as a device for Akif's polemical point regarding 'the West that is active' (*mücahid olan Garb*) and 'the East that is stagnant' (*atıl olan Şark*).[297] The reason for this is to be found in the nexus of beliefs which express the lethargy of the times: *kader* and *tevekkül* (Ar. *qadar* and *tawakkul*). Popular understandings of God's decree have deviated from the intention as outlined in *kalām*: there are possible existences that exist as archetypes (*Kader: Şeraiti mevcud olup da meydanda/Zuhura gelmesidir mümkinātın aʿyānda*), but their realisation requires the effort of responsible men (*Niçin nasıl geliyormuş ... O büsbütün mechūl/Biz ihtiyarımızın suretindeniz mesul*).[298] Through placing faith in the guiding hand of God, Muslim *tevekkül* has become *tahakküm*, a form of arrogant prejudging of God's will that renders Him effectively subservient to man (*Hüdayı kendine kul yaptı, kendi oldu Hüda*).[299] These passages recall Ibn ʿArabī's *Fuṣūṣ al-Ḥikam* (Gems of Wisdom) and its section on God's act of

[292] Ibid., 319.
[293] Ibid.
[294] Ibid., 328.
[295] Ibid., 328–9.
[296] Ibid., 318, 320, 325, 328, 329, 331.
[297] Ibid., 332. Akif is playing to the modernist trope of the West being more truly Islamic than the Muslim East.
[298] Ibid., 341.
[299] Ibid., 340.

enabling the existence of all things (their as yet non-existent prototypes, or *aʿyān*) that display the desire for existence, regardless of their function or intent in the world – a text Akif was almost certain to have read.[300]

Despite their considerable points of intersection, Iqbāl and Akif are only cited together by Turkish scholars. Through his English and German connections, Iqbāl had a voice in the West that Akif did not, and this is likely one reason why he acquired a status in Arabic that Akif did not. Akif's audience was purely his own community, something that could not be said of Iqbāl. Despite his columns in *Sebilürreşad* and sermons in time of national crisis, Akif did not engage in theory or politics outside his poetry: he never endeavoured a reconstruction of religious thought and exile prevented him from playing a role in the national project during his lifetime. On the other hand, Iqbāl's renunciation of the Aḥmadiyya movement in 1935 over its failure to affirm the finality of Muḥammad's prophethood meant that the early institutionalisation of his memory in Pakistan was not impaired once ostracization of the Aḥmadiyya began.[301] Ultimately Akif's poetry operates within intellectual boundaries a degree narrower than those of Iqbāl, less flamboyantly damning of the Sufi tradition, less dialectically engaged with European thinkers.[302] Yet a tension permeates the work of both in that they elaborate a metaphysics of existence situated in the very tradition they seek to reformulate. What both Akif and Iqbāl represent is a final effort by modernist intellectuals to preserve something of the edifice of Sufism from the purificatory wave of Islamic rationalisation of which they were an integral part.

[300] Abū al-ʿAlāʾ ʿAfīfī (ed.), *Fuṣūṣ al-Ḥikam li-Muḥyī al-Dīn Ibn ʿArabī* (Beirut: Dār al-Kitāb al-ʿArabī, 1980), 177–80.

[301] A series of articles and comments on the topic are published in Sherwani, *Speeches*, 197–241.

[302] Viewing these events from a distance, Iqbāl supported ending the caliphate and other elements of the Kemalist revolution. Ibid., 232–5.

4

The Salafi Revolution

Kevseri's Defence of Sunni Traditionalism

This chapter looks at Kevseri's conflicts with the emerging Salafi trend. It looks first at his approach to ʿAbduh and the modernists, and how it differed from Sabri's, then reviews the polemical debates between Kevseri and his Salafi opponents as they evolved from the 1920s to the early 1950s. While like Sabri he saw the *tajdīd* reformers as attempting to transform Islam into a calque on post-Enlightenment religion, Kevseri identified what would become the Salafi movement as more destabilising to the Islamic tradition, since it was speaking more authentically from within it with the aim of radically altering its multi-vocal, heterogenous disposition. It considers that Kevseri was able to delay the final semantic stabilisation of the term Salafi around the ideas that characterise the ideological movement of that name today, but that Syrian *ʿālim* Nāṣir al-Dīn al-Albānī used the work of Kevseri as a foil against which he was able to construct 'Salafism' following Kevseri's death.

KEVSERI'S VIEWS ON ʿABDUH

Kevseri was no less concerned about the intellectual direction of the modernist movement than Sabri. Like Sabri he initially had a positive opinion of ʿAbduh but came to adopt a view of him as a disruptor, though in questions of *fiqh* rather than creed. Having developed closer ties to al-Azhar than Sabri, Kevseri was more deferential to his Egyptian hosts in choosing not to express his thoughts in too frank a manner. ʿAbduh came up in Kevseri's first polemical scuffle with the Salafi group in the late 1920s. Kevseri's contribution to an annotated collection of three well-known commentaries on the hadith scholar al-Dhahabī's (d. 1348) *Tadhkirat al-Ḥuffāẓ* (Memorial of the Hadith Scholars) provoked Riḍā's colleague Muḥibb al-Dīn al-Khaṭīb to accuse Kevseri of anti-Arab bias in his assessment of *tajsīm* (anthropomorphism in the sense of corporeal understandings of God) in the writings of Ibn Taymiyya.

In a review of the book when it was first published al-Khaṭīb had thanked Kevseri for his comments in a work that he initially thought had done a service to al-Dhahabī, an important figure in the traditionist canon due to theological views that aligned with those of Ibn Taymiyya.[1] This prompted the Jeddan publisher Muḥammad Naṣīf to write to al-Khaṭīb chiding him for having overlooked what Kevseri had written in his commentary and footnotes.[2] Kevseri had evidently begun to draw attention with his early critical editions of theological works associated with the traditionists.[3] In 1926 he had published in Cairo an annotated edition of Ibn al-Jawzi's (d. 1201) *Daf' Shubhat al-Tashbīh* (Refutation of the Suspicion of Anthropomorphism), a Ḥanbalī work rejecting the accusation of *tashbīh* (anthropomorphism in the sense of likening God to his creation).[4] In 1928 Kevseri was the first to publish from manuscript an annotated print of al-Dhahabī's *Bayān Zaghl al-'Ilm* (Explication of the Debasement of Knowledge) in which al-Dhahabī agreed with Ibn Taymiyya on general points of theology – the nature of *īmān*, the uncreatedness of the Qur'an, the attributes of God, and the idea that these represent the position of earlier Muslims[5] – but admonished him for having drawn accusations from his Syrian and Egyptian peers of arrogance and desire for office.[6] Al-Dhahabī suggested Ibn Taymiyya's attacks on practitioners of logic and philosophy made him as guilty as those he

[1] Muḥibb al-Dīn al-Khaṭīb (unsigned), 'Ḥarakat al-Nashr wa-l-Ta'līf: Dhuyūl Tadhkirat al-Ḥuffāẓ li-l-Dhahabī,' *al-Zahrā'*, Dhū al-Qa'da 1347 (May 1928), 5/5: 364. The book, titled *Dhayl Tadhkirat al-Ḥuffāẓ li-l-Dhahabī*, was published by the Damascus publisher Ḥuṣām al-Dīn al-Qudsī in 1928.

[2] Al-Khaṭīb, ''Udwān 'alā 'Ulamā' al-Islām Yajib An Yakūn Lahu Ḥadd Yaqif 'Indahu,' in al-Kawtharī, *Ṣaf'āt al-Burhān*, 57.

[3] Āl Rashīd, 'Introduction,' in Al-Sarḥān, *Rasā'il al-Imām*, 12. Kevseri's initial article is published in *Ṣaf'āt al-Burhān*, 52–6, titled 'Ta'līqunā 'alā Ibn Fahd fī Dhuyūl Tadhkirat al-Ḥuffāẓ' (undated).

[4] A previous book, his first in Egypt, was a response to Ibn Quṭayba (d. 889)'s *Ta'wīl Mukhtalif al-Ḥadīth* titled *Raf' al-Rayba 'an Takhabbuṭāt Ibn Quṭayba* but the manuscript has never been published. Cited in al-Bayyūmī, *al-Muqaddimāt*, 699. Better known is Kevseri's annotated edition of Ibn Quṭayba's *al-Ikhtilāf fī al-Lafẓ wa-l-Radd 'alā al-Jahmiyya wa-l-Mushabbiha*, published in 1930.

[5] Al-Kawtharī, *Bayān Zaghl al-'Ilm wa-l-Ṭalab* (Cairo: al-Azhariyya li-l-Turāth, 2010), 23.

[6] Ibid., 17.

accused,[7] and even questioned one aspect of Ibn Taymiyya's theological system, the idea that God can be conceived of as occupying any spatial location (*al-jihāt*) He so wishes.[8] Kevseri also appended a controversial letter of advice known as *al-Naṣīḥa al-Dhahabiyya*, in which al-Dhahabī repeated those charges directly to his former master.[9] Kevseri disagreed with most of al-Dhahabī's opinions but what attracted him to the material was the fact that Ibn Taymiyya was excoriated by one of his own, even on points of theology.

Naṣīf was right in his assumption that al-Khaṭīb had not looked closely at what Kevseri said in the book of al-Dhahabī commentaries.[10] In it Kevseri faulted the al-Dhahabī commentator Taqī al-Dīn Muḥammad ibn Fahd al-Makkī (d. 1466/7)[11] for his description of Damascus *muḥaddith* al-Jamāl ʿAbd Allāh ibn Ibrāhīm al-Sharāʾiḥī (d. 1417/8) as a great hadith scholar despite his being *ummī*, or not having learned to read or write in his youth.[12] Kevseri used this example to argue that there exists a generalised problem of hadith narrators (*ruwāh*) who when at school in their early years moved straight from learning the basic skills of reading and writing to hadith narration without immersion in other Islamic sciences. This meant they had a tendency to absorb the opinions of teachers who had wayward views on theological questions. Thus, the trope of the stellar *ummī* scholar was not the issue, what mattered was whether they remained *ʿāmmī*, i.e., without the proper training to be considered among the elite of ʿulamaʾ who are of sound knowledge, commoners not experts. Kevseri implied that Ibn Taymiyya and his Damascus followers including al-Dhahabī[13] were the former for their position on *al-jihāt* – that God's omnipotence means it is

[7] Ibid., 24.

[8] Ibid., 16.

[9] Ibid., 35–6. Caterina Bori considers the *Naṣīḥa* to be authentic; see Bori, 'al-Dhahabī,' in *Encyclopaedia of Islam 3*, ed. Kate Fleet, Gudrun Krämer, Denis Matringe, John Nawas and Everett Rowson (Leiden/Boston: Brill, 2016) [henceforth EI3]; http://dx.doi.org/10.1163/1573-3912_ei3_COM_25995 (accessed 21 July 2018).

[10] Al-Khaṭīb also missed that the catalogue of al-Qudsī's publications contained several Kevseri-edited pro-Ḥanafī works slanted against the theology of Ibn Taymiyya. See the back-cover list in Aḥmad Rāfiʿ al-Ṭahṭāwī, *al-Tanbīh wa-l-Īqāẓ li-Mā fī Dhuyūl Tadhkirat al-Ḥuffāẓ* (Damascus: al-Qudsī, 1929).

[11] John Lash Meloy, 'Ibn Fahd', in *EI3*; http://dx.doi.org/10.1163/1573-3912_ei3_COM_30441 (accessed 21 July 2018).

[12] Kevseri, *Ṣafʿāt al-Burhān*, 52–6. Kevseri's section in the *Dhayl* that provoked al-Khaṭīb is reprinted here.

[13] He mentions al-Dhahabī, Ibn al-Qayyim, and Aḥmad ibn Abī Qāsim ibn Badrān al-Dashtī (d. 1313). Regards al-Dashtī, see al-Dhahabī, *Muʿjam al-Shuyukh al-Kabīr*, 2 vols. (Ṭāʾif: Maktabat al-Ṣiddīq, 1987), 1:101–2.

logical to conceive of his possessing a limitless ability of movement that opponents would consider anthropomorphic – that were largely drawn from the writings of ʿUthmān ibn Saʿīd al-Dārimī (815–93/5), a student of Aḥmad ibn Ḥanbal.[14] He suggested they had absorbed these ideas from the non-Muslim communities in which they grew up or converted or were socialised as Muslims. Kevseri's final point was an appeal to readers not to be duped by anti-Ashʿarī and anti-Māturīdī propaganda in the name of the *salaf*, an appeal that contained the essence of the idea that came to dominate Kevseri's thought: that marginal theology is making a comeback through the legitimating language of Salafism.[15]

Kevseri's intervention was something of a *coup de théâtre*, surprising his opponents in several ways. He had attacked not only their ideas but struck at the underlying assumption that ethnic Arab origin implied privileged knowledge, particularly in the grasp of hadith. He had done so, moreover, as a non-Arab Circassian from an Ottoman intellectual environment viewed in some Arab circles as deficient in hadith scholarship.[16] This sense of initial disarray comes across in al-Khaṭīb's response to Kevseri, which began by accusing him of 'sharp-tongued impudence' (*salāṭa wa-ṭūl lisān*).[17] Al-Khaṭīb's line of attack was to bring up a passage from ʿAbduh's response to Faraḥ Anṭūn in which he argued that Islam as an 'Arab religion' (*al-islām kāna dīnan ʿarabiyyan*) had been corrupted (*ustuʿjima*) in the Abbasid era by the caliph al-Muʿtaṣim (ruled 833–42) bringing into his army non-Muslim Turks and Persians who proceeded to take control of key arms of the state while secretly holding to other religions and their practice.[18] Though this argument was apologetic in the context of Anṭūn

14 Binyamin Abrahamov, 'al-Dārimī, Abū Saʿīd,' in *EI3*; http://dx.doi.org/10.1163/1573-3912_ei3_COM_23880 (accessed on 21 July 2018).

15 He refers to a Cairo-era book he wrote, *Taḥdhīr al-Khalaf min Makhāzī Adʿiyāʾ al-Salaf*, apparently lost. Al-Bayyūmī refers to it as a manuscript in *Muqaddimāt* (p. 700) but does not say anything more.

16 I owe this point to Dr Ḥamza al-Bakrī of Fatih Sultan Mehmet University. Aḥmad Khayrī mentions hadith lessons Kevseri took in Damascus in 1928 with renowned hadith scholar Badr al-Dīn al-Ḥasanī (1850–1935); *al-Imām al-Kawtharī*, 9. Kevseri also studied hadith intensively during his early years (see Özafşar, 'Muhammed Zahid el-Kevseri 'Hadis Yönü',' *Muhammed Zahid el-Kevserî*, 92–3), as was in fact typical of the Khālidī Naqshbandī line of Gümüşhanevi to which Kevseri's father belonged; see Butrus Abu-Manneh, 'Shaykh Ahmed Ziyāʾüddīn el-Gümüşhanevi and the Ziyāʾī-Khālidī suborder,' in *Shiʿa Islam, Sects and Sufism*, ed. Frederick De Jong (Utrecht: M.Th. Houtsma Stichting, 1992): 105–17. Kevseri discusses Gümüşhanevi's role in Ottoman hadith dissemination in *Irghām al-Murīd*, 69–76; and *al-Taḥrīr al-Wajīz*, 26–7.

17 Al-Khaṭīb, 'ʿUdwān ʿalā ʿUlamāʾ al-Islām,' 57.

18 ʿAbduh, *al-Islām wa-l-Naṣrāniyya*, 134.

and Ernest Renan's accusation of Islamic stagnation (*jumūd*), Rashīd Riḍā's editing magnified it further with annotations that framed ʿAbduh's words in an exclusively anti-Turk context ('what evil he [al-Muʿtaṣim] did in enabling the Turks to seize control of the nation').[19] Al-Khaṭīb presented the text in the same manner to argue that Kevseri as a Circassian Turk was motivated by anti-Arab animus to assail revered hadith scholars from Arab lands (*fī al-aqṭār al-ʿarabiyya*).[20] While on the one hand al-Khaṭīb made a false assumption that ʿAbduh identified with the theological views in question, on the other he rejected the charge of *tajsīm* by claiming there was no such manuscript attributed to Ibn Taymiyya in Damascus's Ẓāhiriyya library where his father was custodian.[21] Reinforcing the Arabist othering of Kevseri as a Turk, he concluded with the dig that the Kemalists were wasting their time in trying to sow dissent in 'countries that still know the value of the *salaf*' (*bilād lā tazāl taʿrif li-l-salaf aqdārahum wa-faḍlahum*).[22]

Kevseri's fifty-page response, *Ṣafʿāt al-Burhān ʿalā Ṣafaḥāt al-ʿUdwān* (Evidence That Strikes Down Hostile Writing), written and published in Damascus in 1929 just before his return to Cairo, established the lines of argumentation that were to mark the next two decades of his engagement with the main currents in twentieth-century Islamic thought. It is also clear from this work that Kevseri had more than a passing knowledge of ʿAbduh. First, he praised ʿAbduh as an honest scholar whose ideas had been exploited outside their context. ʿAbduh was 'the uncontested imam of the Egyptian renaissance, who has been of enormous service to Egypt, the East, and all of us' and left a 'beautiful memory', but, Kevseri added, 'not all of his opinions and comments are beyond criticism, not least after his trips to the West; indeed, some of his ideas and views indicate extremism [*taṭarruf*]'.[23] He politely rejected ʿAbduh's comment that some Turkic-origin officials dissimulated their beliefs, noting Ibn Khaldūn's praise of the faith and fighting prowess of the Turkish contingent in his

[19] Ibid., 134, footnote 1; 'biʾsamā ṣanaʿa fī tamkīn al-Turk min salb mulk al-umma'.

[20] Al-Khaṭīb, 'ʿUdwān ʿalā ʿUlamāʾ al-Islām,' 59.

[21] Ibid., 61. Kevseri did not mention such a manuscript in his article, but al-Khaṭīb said the publisher al-Qudsī told him he was convinced to publish after Kevseri said he had found one. Traditionists habitually rejected the *tajsīm* charge; al-Albānī, 'Preface to *al-Tankīl*,' in Muḥammad Bahjat al-Bayṭār et al., *al-Kawtharī wa-Taʿaddīhi ʿalā al-Turāth wa-Bayān Ḥālihi fī Muʾallafātihi wa-Muʿallaqātihi* (Cairo: Dār al-Ḥaramayn, 1999), 141.

[22] Al-Khaṭīb, 'ʿUdwān ʿalā ʿUlamāʾ al-Islām,' 62.

[23] Al-Kawtharī, *Ṣafʿāt al-Burhān*, 19.

Muqaddima.[24] As for the suggestion that Kevseri wanted to avenge himself of ʿAbduh's words against Turks, he wrote: 'Knocking on the doors of odious nationalism [*al-qawmiyyāt al-mamqūta*] is a trap set by the West for the East, and the peoples who fall into this abyss are those for whom God wishes destruction. It is not at all in the interests of Islam, Arabism (*ʿurūba*), or peoples to knock on these doors.'[25]

In *Ṣafʿāt al-Burhān* Kevseri mounted a major assault on the emerging discourse of Salafism for its opposition to the juridical and intellectual culture of the schools, on the one hand, and its resurrection of marginal theology, on the other. The Salafiyya championed by al-Khaṭīb and the group elevating Ibn Taymiyya expresses a racially charged Arabism, he said;[26] they promote un-Islamic national identity and radical theology through rejection of the established *madhāhib* and claims to an *ijtihād* that bypasses that of the Sunni imams; they display a violent streak through extensive use of *takfīr* regarding their opponents;[27] and they exploit the prestige of the first generations of Muslims who have links to the Prophet (*al-salaf al-ṣāliḥ*) to market this theology through modern publishing culture, the battleground on which defenders of tradition against these efforts at destabilisation must fight.[28] It is in this context that Kevseri coined the phrase *lā-madhhabiyya* (anti-madhhabism), here in the heat of this polemical skirmish in 1929, and not in the better-known article of 1937 which addressed this issue specifically and employed the word in its title. The *madhhab* loyalty Kevseri wants to preserve is to the four Sunni schools of law and their interpretive traditions, based in the principle of precedent (*taqlīd*) and the specific role accorded to *ijtihād*.[29] Kevseri wrote:

Those who are trying to remove the sanctity [of the imams] in the hearts of the nation are the *lā-madhhabiyya* group, and their continuous efforts to divert

[24] Ibid., 21–2. He points out that ʿAbduh was of Turcoman origin on his father's side; 17.

[25] Ibid., 18.

[26] 'So, who cares if I didn't follow this kind of *salafiyya*, your current *salafiyya*, and if *salafiyya* meant Arabism and noble Arab tribes, then what branch of Rabīʿa or Muḍar is this Ḥarrānī Shaykh [Ibn Taymiyya]?'; ibid., 41.

[27] Ibid., 15. He cites, for example, the Ḥanbalī preacher al-Ḥasan ibn ʿAlī al-Barbahārī (d. 941), who is said to have caused rioting in defence of Ḥanbalī-defined orthodoxy against Ashʿarī, Muʿtazilī, and Shiʿi opponents. See Christopher Melchert, 'al-Barbahārī,' *EI3*; http://dx.doi.org/10.1163/1573-3912_ei3_COM_22944 (accessed on 22 July 2018).

[28] Ibid., 41.

[29] On *taqlīd* see Ahmed Fekry Ibrahim, 'Rethinking the Taqlīd-Ijtihād Dichotomy: A Conceptual-Historical Approach,' *Journal of American Oriental Society*, 136/2 (2016): 285–303; El Shamsy, *Canonization*, 185–9.

people's attention through claiming their own *ijtihād*, to denounce this or that imam by obsessively separating rulings from their evidence . . ., and to publish books by these abnormal figures [*kutub al-shudhdhādh*] has been a notable reality in many countries for quite some time. In this manner they have cleared the road to secularism [*lā-dīniyya*] and built a bridge [*qanṭara*] towards it. Thus, it has become clear to the thinking public that '*lā-madhhabiyya* is the bridge to secularism [*sic*]. I don't know if the two parties have been cooperating in this aim since the beginning, or if the first leads to the second only out of ignorance, but what I do know is that the *lā-madhhabiyya* are among those most connected to this bloated voice [*lā-dīniyya*].[30]

Who did Kevseri mean by the *lā-dīniyya* party? It seems unlikely that he intended ʿAbduh and modernist reformers acting in his name since he had already praised ʿAbduh as a positive if sometimes misguided leader of renaissance. It seems more plausible that he had in mind the positivist-materialist political and intellectual class who had been dominant in Ottoman and Turkish affairs since 1908 and to whom the ulema and devout intellectuals applied the term *dinsizlik* that Gökalp studiously tried to avoid. His comment in the later article that the consequence of *lā-madhhabiyya* would be 'the *lā-dīniyya* dominant in other countries whose fate has been atheism [*ilḥād*] and misfortune [*taʿāsa*]' reinforces this view.[31] In other words, Kevseri was drawing a connection between two iconoclasms: Salafi subversion of the Islamic tradition and secular nationalism. After his skirmish with al-Khaṭīb Kevseri rarely acknowledged the term *salafiyya*.[32] He saw claims to represent the belief and practice of the first Muslims as a 'false Salafism' (*salafiyya zāʾifa*)[33] seeking to 'enter the pure hearts of ordinary Muslims'[34] of today through the legitimacy conferred by the term.

Kevseri spoke directly to the question of ʿAbduh on three occasions during his period of public commentary in Egypt. Directing harsh if polite

[30] Ibid.

[31] Al-Kawtharī, 'Al-Lāmadhhabiyya Qanṭarat al-Lādīniyya,' *Maqālāt*, 137. In another article he expanded *lā-madhhabiyya* to include Ibn Taymiyya anthropomorphists, proponents of *ijtihād*, Sufi libertines, and revivers of Ismaʿili Shiʿism; 'Khuṭūrat al-Tasarruʿ fī al-Iftāʾ,' *Maqālāt*, 142.

[32] He calls Naṣīf 'that Salafi notable'; 'Ḥawla Kalima Tuʿzā ilā al-Suyūṭī Ghalaṭan,' *Maqālāt*, 307.

[33] Al-Kawtharī, *Ṣafʿāt al-Burhān*, 40.

[34] Al-Kawtharī, 'Taḥdhīr al-Umma min Duʿāt al-Wathaniyya,' *Maqālāt*, 278; first published June 1939.

criticism, he clearly viewed ʿAbduh as of a different genus from his Salafi interlocutors. In the first, he took up a letter ʿAbduh sent to the Ottoman sheikh ül-Islam Uryanizade Esad Efendi (1814–89) in 1887 and published posthumously by *al-Manār* in 1906, which highlighted what Kevseri considered to be ʿAbduh's once exceptional character. In it ʿAbduh praised the Ottoman state as a pillar of Islam, with a mission more lofty than modern ideas such as 'name of nation and interest of country' (*ism al-waṭan wa-maṣlaḥat al-bilād*), and rued European success in weakening Muslim identity through the network of missionary schools to which even the children of senior officials were sent, rendering them Muslim in name only (*kuffār taḥta ḥijāb ism al-islām*) and agents of the foreigners once they took up government careers.[35]

In a second article, Kevseri rejected efforts to align ʿAbduh alongside Muḥammad ibn ʿAbd al-Wahhāb as reformers opposed to Sufi intercession.[36] He began by pointing to ʿAbduh's early interest in Sufi metaphysics as evidenced by his *Risālat al-Wāridāt* and the commentary on al-Dawānī's *Sharḥ*, in which he saw evidence of the doctrine of *waḥdat al-wujūd* (Kevseri says this despite his favouring Sirhindī's less monistic *waḥdat al-shuhūd*). As outlined in Chapter 3, ʿAbduh's authorship of both has been the subject of debate, but at the least they were written under the influence of al-Afghānī.[37] Kevseri noted ʿAbduh's debt to al-Afghānī's teachings in philosophy and rued that ʿAbduh subsequently spent time in the West where he 'sipped from its muddy waters' (*karaʿa min yanābīʿihi al-ʿākira*), but he rejected Rashīd Riḍā's claim that ʿAbduh later repudiated Sufi metaphysics.[38] Kevseri's wider point was that there is only a superficial congruence between ʿAbduh's ideas and those of Ibn ʿAbd al-Wahhāb: the Najdi shaykh's intellectual inspiration was Ibn Taymiyya, his theology,

[35] Al-Kawtharī, 'Raʾy Shaykh Muḥammad ʿAbduh fī Baʿd al-Masāʾil,' *Maqālāt*, 469–70.

[36] He was responding to two articles by liberal intellectual Aḥmad Amīn (1886–1954); 'Muḥammad ibn ʿAbd al-Wahhāb - 1,' *al-Thaqāfa*, 30 November 1943, no. 257: 5–8; and 'Muḥammad ibn ʿAbd al-Wahhāb - 2,' *al-Thaqāfa*, 7 December 1943, no. 258: 5–8.

[37] Oliver Scharbrodt, 'The Salafiyya and Sufism: Muḥammad ʿAbduh and His *Risālat al-Wāridāt* (Treatise on Mystical Inspirations),' *Bulletin of the School of Oriental and African Studies*, 70/1 (2007): 89–115 and Vincent Cornell, 'Muḥammad ʿAbduh. A Sufi-Inspired Modernist?' 109–11.

[38] Al-Kawtharī, 'Ibn ʿAbd al-Wahhāb wa-Muḥammad ʿAbduh fī Naẓar Ṣāḥib *al-Thaqāfa*,' *Maqālāt*, 335. He sees evidence of ʿAbduh retaining his Sufism in his commentary on Qurʾan 2:186, 'wa-idhā saʾalaka ʿibādī ʿannī fa-innī qarīb'. In his *Tafsīr* ʿAbduh said it meant there was no 'veil or saint or intercessor' between the believer and God; ʿAbduh, *al-Aʿmāl al-Kāmila*, 4:452. Riḍā also wrote a footnote into *al-Wāridāt* to say ʿAbduh supported *waḥdat al-shuhūd* not *waḥdat al-wujūd*; ʿAbduh (ed. Rashīd Riḍā), *Risālat al-Wāridāt* (Cairo: al-Manār, 1925), 31.

jurisprudence, and opposition to *kalām* and *falsafa* as disciplines. ʿAbduh's views he saw as more consonant with the totality of the Islamic tradition.

In a third article, published in June 1942, Kevseri was critical of the grand mufti, Shaykh ʿAbd al-Majīd Salīm, over an opinion (originally issued in November 1928) regarding the wearing of hats that concurred with the well-known Transvaal fatwa issued by ʿAbduh in 1903. ʿAbduh had responded to South African Muslims that wearing a *burnayṭa* – by which was understood at the time to mean European fedoras and top hats – did not contradict the legal principle of avoiding imitation (*tashabbuh*) of non-Muslims as long as it was for a purpose such as avoiding the sun.[39] Kevseri noted that ʿAbduh's fatwa had provoked a great reaction at the time, but the current mufti was going further in his legal reasoning that ignored the views of the four imams as if he were an absolute *mujtahid*. Kevseri concluded with a denunciation of modernist ʿulamaʾ (*ʿālim 'mūdirn'*) as 'imposters in knowledge' (*adʿiyāʾ al-ʿilm*).[40] He hoped that the authorities would keep those who 'break the bonds of *fiqh* one by one' (*yanquḍūn ʿurā al-fiqh al-islāmī ʿurwatan ʿurwatan*) away from positions of leadership in religion and purify society of those who think their mission is to 'disturb the order and challenge the *fiqh* tradition' (*taʿkīr al-nabʿ wa-l-tajarruʾ ʿalā al-fiqh al-mutawārith*).[41] The use of *ʿurwa* most likely signals this was a reference to ʿAbduh.[42]

ʿAbduh looms unnamed in two other issues Kevseri tackled in his writings, one concerning practice according to the *madhāhib* and the other concerning modernist theology. Regarding the first, in an article published in May 1947 Kevseri noted a trend in Egyptian *lā-madhhabiyya* circles to lead prayer while wearing sandals. Like the wearing of hats, this was an issue in which the views of the reformers and the self-styled Salafis intersected. ʿAbduh applied the principles of custom (*ʿurf*), public good (*maṣlaḥa*), and use of different schools of Sunni law (*talfīq*) during his time as mufti,[43] but the question of wearing sandals indicated the radical direction towards a notion of applied pre-*madhhab fiqh*. The sandals issue was taken up by Riḍā in 1903[44] and later by al-Albānī in his

39 ʿAbduh, *al-Aʿmāl al-Kāmila*, 2:508–9.
40 Al-Kawtharī, 'Manshaʾ Ilzām Ahl al-Dhimma bi-Shuʿār Khāṣṣ wa-Ḥukm Talabbus al-Muslim bihi ʿInd al-Fuqahāʾ,' *Maqālāt*, 227.
41 Ibid., 227.
42 The journal took the name *al-ʿUrwa al-Wuthqā* from the phrase in Qurʾan 2:256 and 31:22.
43 Sedgwick, *Muhammad Abduh*, 80, 119, 216–17.
44 Rashīd Riḍā, 'Bāb al-Suʾāl wa-l-Fatwā,' *al-Manār*, 6/17, 20 November 1903: 827–8.

1961 book *Ṣifāt Ṣalāt al-Nabī*, which tries to provide the bare, established hadiths without the distortion of *madhhab* framing to enable readers to act on the prophet's injunction to 'pray as you saw me pray'.[45] There are uncorroborated reports that ʿAbduh had also advocated prayer in sandals, though they are not recorded by Riḍā in his *Tārīkh* or the complete works compiled by Muḥammad ʿImāra.[46] If true, ʿAbduh biographer Mark Sedgwick suggests his motive was to align Muslim practice with that of Europe.[47] This was certainly the logic behind proposals in Turkish government circles from at least 1928 to introduce church-like pews inside mosques and a public call for sandals in Turkish mosques. Ubeydullah Efendi (1858–1937), a pro-government propagandist during the CUP years and the early republic, gave a sermon advocating the latter in 1925, the period when the state began its push for delivery of the Friday prayer sermon in Turkish.[48]

For Kevseri the issue of praying in sandals or leading prayer in sandals was a red line: if some imams insist on this they should be obliged to use specific places of worship (*maʿbad khāṣṣ*) that separate them from those practicing normative Islam and built through funds other than those dispensed by the waqf for mosque building: in other words it is a non-Muslim practice and should be treated as such.[49] The prophet may well have led prayer in this manner since the streets of Medina were clean at that time and foot coverings could be easily cleaned, he said.[50] Ḥanafī jurists argued that the toes must touch the ground during prostration,[51] but today the streets of towns and cities are soiled with alcohol and other substances, making it impossible to clean them quickly, plus there would nothing in this that sets Muslims apart from Christians and Jews, Kevseri argued.[52]

45 Nāṣir al-Dīn al-Albānī, *Ṣifāt Ṣalāt al-Nabī min al-Takbīr ilā al-Taslīm Ka-annaka Tarāhu* (Riyadh: Maktabat al-Maʿārif li-l-Nashr wa-l-Tawzīʿ, 1996), 80–1.

46 See Sedgwick, *Muhammad Abduh*, 101. See the incident recounted in Jacques Jomier, *Le Commentaire Coranique du Manar: Tendances Modernes d'Exégèse Coranique en Égypte* (Paris: G. P. Maisaneuve, 1954), 100–1, footnote 2.

47 Muhammad Abduh Blog, 18 April 2012, http://Abduhinfo.blogspot.com/2012/04/solution-to-problem-of-why-Muhammad.html (accessed 2 August 2018).

48 Mehmed Ubeydullah, 'Camilere Ayyakabıyla Girmek,' *Vatan*, 15 Mayıs 1341 (15 May 1925). The article is published in Dücane Cundioğlu, *Türkçe İbadet 1* (Istanbul: Kitabevi, 1999), 191–4.

49 Al-Kawtharī, 'Kashf al-Ruʾūs wa-Libs al-Naʿāl fī al-Ṣalāh,' *Maqālāt*, 178–80.

50 Ibid., 169.

51 Ibid., 172–3. His Ḥanafī jurists are al-Karkhī (d. 951/2), *al-Uṣūl* and Najm al-Dīn al-Zāhidī (d. 1259/60), *Qunyat al-Munya li-Tatmīm al-Ghunya*.

52 Discussed in M. J. Kister, '"Do Not Assimilate Yourselves ..." Lā tashabbahū ... [*sic*],' *Jerusalem Studies in Arabic and Islam 12* (1989): 321–70.

Regarding the second issue, Kevseri took aim at the trope of Jesus' resurrection as a miraculous event unfit for the modern age, an issue taken up by ʿAbduh acolytes including Shaykh Shaltūt and part of Sabri's case against ʿAbduh.[53] For Kevseri this question highlighted not only the dangers of relying solely on experiential knowledge in the pursuit of truth, which puts humans at the level of animals (*al-iqtiṣār ʿalā al-maḥsūs shaʾn al-bahīm*), but the long established debate in the field of *uṣūl al-fiqh* over the role of hadith in establishing epistemological certainty.[54] In 1942 Shaltūt, later rector of al-Azhar, issued a religious opinion in response to a question from an Aḥmadī Indian officer deployed with the British occupying forces in Egypt asking if Jesus was dead or alive in the view of Qurʾan and sunna, what the judgement is of a Muslim who denies he is alive, and what the judgement on someone who did not believe in him would be if he returned.[55] Shaltūt argued that Jesus had died, was not alive, and would not come back, that holding such views did not constitute apostasy (*ridda*), and that hadith explaining the Qurʾan on these points were single-transmitter, or *āḥād*, and thus inadmissible in questions of creed.[56] This reflected a position popular in modernist circles that the Qurʾan alone establishes such truth: indeed, ʿAbduh had written in his *Risāla* that no believer was obliged to accept *āḥād* hadiths.[57] Since the

[53] Sabri, *Mawqif al-ʿAql*, 4:241.

[54] Al-Kawtharī, 'Kalimat Faḍīlat al-Ustādh al-Kabīr,' *Maqālāt*, 258. On certitude and hadith, Aron Zysow, *The Economy of Certainty: An Introduction to the Typology of Islamic Legal Theory* (Atlanta: Lockwood Press, 2013); Hüseyin Hansu, 'Notes on the Term Mutawātir and Its Reception in Ḥadīth Criticism,' *Islamic Law and Society*, 16/3–4 (2009): 383–408; and Jonathan Brown, 'Did the Prophet Say It or Not? The Literal, Historical, and Effective Truth of Ḥadīths in Early Sunnism,' *Journal of the American Oriental Society*, 129/2 (2009): 259–85.

[55] The question was put to al-Azhar rector al-Marāghī who passed it on to Shaltūt to answer. Shaltūt published his fatwa in 'Rafʿ ʿĪsā,' *al-Risāla*, 11 May 1942, 10/462: 515–17 and later issues 516–19. They were republished in 1960 in *al-Fatāwā: Dirāsa li-Mushkilat al-Muslim al-Muʿāṣir fī Ḥayātihi al-Yawmiyya al-ʿĀmma* when Shaltūt was rector of al-Azhar. The first fatwa is reproduced in al-Kawtharī, *Naẓra ʿĀbira fī Mazāʿim man Yunkir Nuzūl ʿĪsā ʿalayhi al-Salām Qabla al-Ākhira* (Cairo: Dār al-Khalīl, 1987), 23–31.

[56] Shaltūt argues that the Qurʾanic verses including the phrases *innī mutawaffīka wa-rāfiʿuka ilayya* (3:55) and *bal rafaʿahu Allāh ilayhi* (4:158) meant God had raised Jesus' station in honouring him and saving him from death at the hands of his enemies to end his days according to God's plan, not that God had physically taken him to His side. Re his return in the end days, Shaltūt said al-Ṭabarī's interpretation in his *Tafsīr* of 4:159 and 43:61 has been privileged by jurists over alternative readings found in *tafsīr* literature (al-Kawtharī, *Naẓra ʿĀbira*, 38–46). Shaltūt said the *fiqh* consensus is illogical since it concerns a future event that cannot be known, and 'there is no place for *ijtihād* regards the future' (*al-ḥissī al-mustaqbil lā madkhala li-l-ijtihād fīhi*); ibid., 49.

[57] ʿAbduh (ed. ʿImāra), *Risāla*, 177.

classical period hadith scholars have preferred terminology around the notion of sound/weak (*ṣaḥīḥ/ḍaʿīf*) to that of single/multi-sourced (*āḥād/ mutawātir*) because of arguments that prophetic hadith cannot be considered *āḥād* at all.[58] Kevseri made two points: that the hadiths regarding Jesus' return were in fact multi-sourced and that to reject *āḥād* hadiths on principle would be to deny the faith of most Muslims (*ikfār dahmāʾ al-umma*), a typical Kevseri argument.[59] Kevseri's responses in three articles[60] and a book, *Naẓra ʿĀbira fī Mazāʿim man Yunkir Nuzūl ʿĪsā ʿalayhi al-Salām Qabla al-Ākhira* (Brief Review of the Claims of Those Who Deny Jesus' Return Before the Hereafter, 1943) also presented the issue in terms of a threat from the Aḥmadiyya in India. For Kevseri the Aḥmadiyya was another dangerous movement challenging the inherited tradition, reworking elements in the concepts of final prophecy and revelation and making use of print media to propagate a disruptive message.[61] In May 1942 Kevseri wrote that Aḥmadīs were trying to place a foot in al-Azhar,[62] and expressed his concerns in letters to Indian shaykh Yūsuf Banūrī, who became a leading campaigner against Aḥmadī legal status as Muslims following Pakistan's independence.[63]

One further point also suggests it would be wrong to think of Kevseri as roundly opposed to ʿAbduh. Kevseri's Māturīdism overlaps with ʿAbduh's liberal thinking on questions of faith, human responsibility for created actions in the world, and the nature of the Qurʾan. As scholars have noted, the caliph Maʾmūn (ruled 813–33) appealed not only to Muʿtazilī thinking on the created nature of the Qurʾan, over which he famously instituted an inquisition (*miḥna*), but to nascent Ḥanafī thinking that was later developed in the Māturīdī tradition. While early Muʿtazilīs theorised that the Qurʾan could not be eternal (*qadīm*) because this would put it alongside God and thus violate the notion of His absolute unity, the Ḥanafī argument was that all things by definition are created by God.[64]

58 Hansu, 'Notes on the Term Mutawātir,' 394–400.
59 Al-Kawtharī, 'Kalima,' 260.
60 Al-Kawtharī, 'Kalima,' *Maqālāt*, 257–60; 'Inkār Nuzūl ʿĪsā wa-Iqrār ʿAqīdat al-Tajsīm,' *Maqālāt*, 261–2, '*Al-Risāla* wa-l-Azhar,' *Maqālāt*, 317–21.
61 Al-Kawtharī, 'ʿInd Juhaynat al-Khabar al-Yaqīn: Murūq al-Qadyāniyya,' *Maqālāt*, 321–3.
62 Al-Kawtharī, 'Al-Risāla wa-l-Azhar,' 320. He cites Aḥmadī students who had been ejected from al-Azhar.
63 Letter 11 (undated), Al-Sarḥān, *Rasāʾil*, 115–16. Kevseri dismissed both Mīrza Ghulām and Musa Jarullah Bigiev as 'fake scholars' (*mutaʿālim*) meddling with received knowledge.
64 Wilferd Madelung, 'The Origins of the Controversy Concerning the Creation of the Koran,' in *Orientalia Hispanica sive studia F. M. Pareja octogenario dicata*, ed. J. M. Barral (Leiden: E. J. Brill, 1974), 504–25, esp. 509–11. Also, John Nawas, 'A

Reports on Abū Ḥanīfa's views listed in al-Khaṭīb al-Baghdādī's *Tārīkh Baghdād* were typical of the traditionist accusation that the Ḥanafīs professed a created Qurʾan.[65] Kevseri's comments on these reports appealed to post-*miḥna* understandings of the issue. For example, regarding one that states Abū Ḥanīfa was the first to assert the createdness of the Qurʾan, Kevseri dismissed it for including a fabricator in its chain of transmission (*isnād*) and added that Abū Ḥanīfa said in response to the teaching of Khurasan-based theologian Jahm ibn Ṣafwān (d. 746) regarding God's attributes that on the contrary God's speech (*kalām Allāh*) is an eternal attribute subsisting in Him (*qiyāmihi billāh*). Kevseri went on: 'But as for what is on the tongue of reciters, in the minds of memorisers, and on pages in terms of vocalisation, mental images and textual writing, it is created like those bearing them, and the majority of ʿulamaʾ settled on that view.'[66] This argumentation is essentially the same as that of ʿAbduh in the first version of *Risālat al-Tawḥīd* that he was pressed to alter for alleged Muʿtazilism, despite the fact that what he wrote – that the Qurʾan is God's pre-existent eternal speech but its pronunciation is not – was standard Ash'arī-Māturīdī doctrine.[67] Although the first part of ʿAbduh's statement runs counter to Muʿtazilī rejection of the notion of God engaging in the human act of speech,[68] it is around the theme of Muʿtazilism that debate over ʿAbduh's ideas has centred.[69] Even Ibn

Reexamination of Three Current Explanations for al-Maʾmun's Introduction of the *Miḥna*,' *IJMES*, 26/4 (1994): 615–29.

65 Christopher Melchert, 'The Adversaries of Aḥmad Ibn Ḥanbal,' *Arabica*, 44/2 (April 1997): 239.

66 Al-Kawtharī, *Taʾnīb al-Khaṭīb*, 107–8. The thrust of Kevseri's defence is that as the earliest of the four Sunni imams Abū Ḥanīfa was a frontline defender of an assumed Islamic orthodoxy against the first wave of over-rationalist Muʿtazilī thinking (p. 119). See also the lengthy footnote in his edition of Ibn Quṭayba's *al-Ikhtilāf fī al-Lafẓ* (Cairo: al-Maktaba al-Azhariyya, 2001 [1930]), 40–3, footnote 1.

67 ʿAbduh (ed. Abū Rayya), *Risālat al-Tawḥīd*, 14, footnote 1; 53–5.

68 Madelung, 'The Origins of the Controversy,' 506–7.

69 Those discussing ʿAbduh as a neo-Muʿtazilī include: Elie Kedourie, *Afghani and ʿAbduh An Essay on Religious Unbelief and Political Activism in Modern Islam* (London: Cass, 1966), 13–14; Detlev Khalid, 'Some Aspects of Neo-Muʿtazilism,' *Islamic Studies* 8/4 (1969): 320–1; Robert Caspar, 'Un aspect de la pensee musulmane moderne: le renouveau du moʿtazilisme,' *Melanges de l'Institut Dominicain d'Etudes Orientales du Caire* 4 (1957): 141–202; Louis Gardet, 'Signification du 'renouveau Muʿtazilite' dans la pensée musulmane contemporaine,' *Islamic Philosophy and the Classical Tradition*, ed. S. M. Stern, A. Hourani, V. Brown (Oxford: Cassirer, 1972), 63–75. Gardet accepts ʿAbduh's thought could also be considered an 'Ashʿarisme rénové'.

Taymiyya tried to moderate Ḥanbalī absolutism on the question through arguing that there are occasions in which God's speech is created and not eternal.[70]

ʿAbduh certainly did not subscribe openly to one specific theological school. Rather than be led by the texts of one tradition, he would pick and choose among the views of the theologians he cited, including al-Ashʿarī, Abū Manṣūr al-Māturīdī, and the Muʿtazilī Abū al-Ḥusayn al-Baṣrī (d. 1044), in the service of his wider aim of creating a rationalised, accessible Islam for a new religious public. But ʿAbduh also outlined a Māturīdī notion of faith as affirmation of a certitude of belief in God, His prophets, and the day of judgement that has been attained through reason,[71] the same reason that is aware of the voluntary nature of human actions,[72] but needful of the guidance of shariʿa to know which of them bring rewards and which of them bring punishments.[73] This was a compromise between faith and reason that ʿAbduh clearly felt was compatible with modernity (he may have had in mind the First Vatican Council of 1869–70's statement that God could still be known through reason, despite the damage wrought by modern thought),[74] and while on its own it would not be enough to satisfy Sabri, it may have spoken to Kevseri.[75] Through al-Afghānī, ʿAbduh had been schooled in Ibn Sīnā,

[70] Madelung, 'The Origins,' 524–5. Ibn Taymiyya says that although it was God's voice heard by Moses, His speech at that point was a non-eternal act in time; see Ibn Taymiyya (ed. Rashīd Riḍā), *Majmūʿat al-Rasāʾil wa-l-Masāʾil* (Beirut: Dār Iḥyāʾ al-Turāth al-ʿArabī, 1972), 149–50. Kevseri also held that the voice Moses heard was 'a created happening, not subsisting in God' (*ḥādith makhlūq lā yaqūm billāh*); al-Kawtharī, ed., *al-Asmāʾ wa-l-Ṣifāt li-l-Imām al-Bayhaqī* (Cairo: al-Maktaba al-Azhariyya li-l-Turāth, 2000 [1939]), 191, footnote 1.

[71] ʿAbduh (ed. ʿImāra), *Risālat al-Tawḥīd*, 178.

[72] Ibid., 61 (63 on Ashʿarī-Māturīdī *kasb al-afʿāl*).

[73] Ibid., 78–9, 175; 'the law came to clarify that which exists, it is not the creator of good' (*muḥdith al-ḥusn*). Caspar ('Un aspect,' 169) considers ʿAbduh's comments in *Tafsīr al-Manār* regarding Qurʾan 4:14 on grave sins committed knowingly as exiting the Muslim from faith and ensuring hellfire to be evidence of Muʿtazilism. ʿAbduh certainly said that he was giving his view in the context of disputes between the Sunnis and Muʿtazilism on the question; ʿAbduh, *al-Aʿmāl al-Kāmila*, 5:176–7. But his *Tafsīr* was begun during his period under the influence of Riḍā, who would see this view as conforming to Ibn Taymiyya's ethics of faith and action.

[74] Cottingham, *Philosophy of Religion*, 30.

[75] On ʿAbduh and Māturīdism see Malcolm Kerr, *Islamic Reform: The Political and Legal Theories of Muḥammad ʿAbduh and Rashīd Riḍā* (Berkeley: University of California Press, 1966), 127. Duncan B. Macdonald, 'Al-Māturīdī,' in *Shorter Encyclopaedia of Islam*, ed. H. A. R. Gibb (Leiden: E. J. Brill, 1953), 363. Hourani, *Arabic Thought*, 142.

Māturīdī, and Sufi texts,[76] and in his later period under Riḍā's influence his ideas appear to align more with Ibn Taymiyya (viz. his comments disparaging the miracles of saints).[77] There is every likelihood that Kevseri would have been aware of the *Risāla*, not least because it was published in Kazan Turkish in 1911 and serialised in Ottoman Turkish in 1919, including the controversial section on the created Qur'an.[78] So it remains very possible that Kevseri was forgiving in his criticism of ʿAbduh because he saw Māturīdism in his theological and ethical positions.

KEVSERI'S DEFENCE OF ḤANAFĪ-MĀTURĪDISM

Kevseri perceived an assault on the Ottoman Ḥanafī-Māturīdī system stemming largely from Egypt where he observed the power of print culture and the determination of Ibn Taymiyya's followers to make use of it. In the introduction to his annotated edition of Egyptian jurist Taqī al-Dīn al-Subkī's *al-Sayf al-Ṣaqīl fī al-Radd ʿalā Ibn Zufayl* (The Polished Sword Refuting Ibn Zufayl, 1937), a manuscript responding to Ibn al-Qayyim al-Jawziyya (d. 1350) that Kevseri claimed to have found in the Khālidiyya library in Jerusalem, Kevseri said there would have been no need to respond to them were it not for the low-price imprints of their books on the streets.[79] Publishing is in a state of chaos, he said, because of the nonchalance of commercial publishing as regards the fate of the Islamic tradition.[80] He pointed to Faraj Allāh al-Kurdī (d. 1940), a Kurdish émigré in Cairo, who established the Kurdistan al-ʿIlmiyya printing press and began publishing works by Ibn Taymiyya and his disciples[81] (al-Kurdī later embraced Bahāʾism, for which he was

[76] Thomas Hildebrandt, 'Waren Ǧamāl ad-Dīn al-Afgānī und Muḥammad ʿAbduh Neo-Muʿtazilīten?' *Welt des Islams* 42 (2), 2002: 210–11, 215. Hourani, *Arabic Thought*, 142.

[77] ʿAbduh (ed. ʿImāra), *Risālat al-Tawḥīd*, 181–3: he said there was no need to accept *karāmāt al-awliyāʾ*.

[78] ʿAbduh (trans. Abdullah Bubi), *Tevhid* (Kazan: Örnek, 1911); ʿAbduh (trans. Hüseyin Mazhar), 'Tevhide Dair,' *SR*, eleven issues between 23 January 1919 (15/388) and 17 April 1919 (16/406).

[79] Al-Kawtharī, Introduction, *al-Sayf al-Ṣaqīl fī al-Radd ʿalā Ibn Zufayl*, Taqī al-Dīn al-Subkī (Cairo: al-Azhariyya li-l-Turāth, 2003), 18–19.

[80] Ibid., 28. 'What's it got to do with me [*mālī anā*]?' they say in their Cairene Arabic.

[81] They included Ibn Taymiyya's well-known anti-Mongol fatwas, the Mardin fatwa and fatwas against the Levantine Nuṣayrīs (ʿAlawīs). These justified fighting the Mongols as rebels against Mamluk rule, justified Muslims' remaining under Mongol rule in Mardin, as

denounced by Rashīd Riḍā).[82] This was followed by Muḥibb al-Dīn al-Khaṭīb's Salafiyya publication network, launched in Egypt in 1909, and a third enterprise of concern to Kevseri in Egypt, that of the Anṣār al-Sunna al-Muḥammadiyya organisation of Muḥammad Ḥāmid al-Fiqī (1892–1959), a prominent Ḥanbalī admirer of Ibn Taymiyya.[83]

Modern scholarship has faced a taxonomic challenge in thinking about Māturīdism. Rudoph Ulrich has argued that it was only with the work of Wilferd Madelung and his article 'The Spread of Māturīdism and the Turks' (1971) that the close association of Māturīdī theology with Ḥanafī *fiqh* and the movement of Māturīdism westwards from Central Asia via Turkic tribes began to find appreciation.[84] The Māturīdīs of Transoxania had from an early stage identified themselves as followers of Abū Ḥanīfa, who predated Māturīdī, but from the seventeenth-century Ottoman scholars became interested in harmonising Māturīdī theology with Ashʿarīsm, which accounts for the conflation between the two found in much of the modern literature.[85] Māturīdism remained little known west of Transoxiana until the eleventh century and only known in Baghdad in the late Seljuq period before the Mongol conquest.[86] The task of defining these theological traditions must contend with problems such as seemingly contradictory views in works attributed to their eponymous founders, questions over authenticity of texts, and later views which speak in the name of the broadly defined school.

The main division between the Ashʿarīs and Māturīdīs was on the theory of faith (*īmān*). They broadly agreed that faith did not rise or fall to the extent of exiting a Muslim from the community of believers and so was fixed, although divergent views are found in the writings of al-Ashʿarī

long as they could practise Islam unimpeded, and considered esoteric sects as apostate (*murtadd*).

82 Juan Cole, 'Rashid Rida on the Bahaʾi Faith: A Utilitarian Theory of the Spread of Religions,' *Arab Studies Quarterly*, 5/3 (1983): 276–91.

83 See Khan, 'Islamic Tradition in an Age of Print,' 63 and 93, note 49. On the impact of 'Salafi' approaches to *tafsīr* in the early twentieth century see Walid Saleh, 'Preliminary Remarks on the Historiography of *tafsīr* in Arabic: A History of the Book Approach,' *Journal of Qur'anic Studies* 12 (2010): 6–40 (21–31).

84 Wilferd Madelung, 'The Spread of Māturīdism and the Turks,' in *Actas IV: Congresso de Estudos Arabes e Islamicos, Coimbra-Lisboa 1968* (Leiden: Brill, 1971), 109–68. See Izutsu, *Concept of Belief*, 105; and Ulrich Rudolph (trans. Rodrigo Adem), *Al-Māturīdī and the Development of Sunnī Theology in Samarqand* (Leiden: Brill, 2015), 1–17.

85 Rudolph, *Al-Māturīdī*, 1–17.

86 Madelung, 'Spread of Māturīdism,' 112–17. Judges from Merv and Khwārazm who upheld the Muʿtazila's thesis of the Qurʾan were appointed in Egypt from 820; El Shamsy, *Canonization*, 122, 130.

himself.[87] But the Ḥanafī Māturīdīs said knowledge of God is attained through reason whereas Ashʿarīs said it required the sending of a prophet and establishment of divine law;[88] the Ashʿarīs qualified the statement 'I am a believer' with 'if God wills';[89] and they differed over the creation of *īmān* and *kufr* in that the Ḥanafī-Māturīdī view was that both were created acts of human responsibility, even if God was ultimately aware of what choice men would make.[90] These differences were in part reflections of the geographical location of Māturīdīs in Samarqand and Bukhara and Ashʿarīsm's integration of the Ḥanbalī critique of rationalist theology and hadith methodology in the intense sectarian milieu of Abbasid Baghdad, but the political choices of dynasties cementing their rule through imposing one rite over another also played a role.[91] The Ashʿarī school of thought put forward forms of semi-rationalist compromise with the traditionists on a range of issues provoked by early dialectical speculation such as faith and its relationship to performing acts of worship (*ʿibādāt*), free will and causality, the Qurʾan as God's speech, and the certainty of metaphysical knowledge through hadith, a compromise that was to become expressive of a broad Muslim mainstream.[92] The continuing main line of attack against the speculative theology of *kalām* was that it placed restrictions on God's will and power and subverted Qurʾanic meaning through exposing its language to allegorical interpretation (*taʾwīl*),[93] in effect filtering the Qurʾanic God through the semantic prism of Aristotelian and Neoplatonic thought. So although Muʿtazilism was rejected by the emerging Sunni consensus, elements of rationalism

[87] In *Kitāb al-Ibāna* it rises and falls, but not in *Kitāb al-Lumaʿ fī al-Radd ʿalā Ahl al-Zaygh wa-l-Bidaʿ*; see Izutsu, *Concept of Belief*, 141.

[88] Izutsu, *Concept of Belief*, 108–19.

[89] Ibid., 194–203.

[90] Definitions of *īmān* varied widely in different Ashʿarī, Māturīdī, and traditionist texts from faith as a personal event in one's life to faith as an essential, idealist category, and the debate over faith in this latter sense was often framed along the lines of Qurʾanic debate in terms of faith as created or uncreated, Izutsu writes; ibid., 207–8, 221–4. On *kufr*'s original meaning of ingratitude for God's benevolence see Izutsu, *Ethico-Religious Concepts in the Qurʾān* (Montreal: McGill-Queen's University Press, 2002), 25–6.

[91] Seljuq rulers ruthlessly crushed the Shāfiʿī-Ashʿarī ʿulamaʾ of Khurasan, accusing them of theorising that the common people were en masse in a state of *kufr*; see Madelung, 'Spread of Māturīdism,' 129, footnote 52.

[92] Melchert, 'Adversaries of Aḥmad Ibn Ḥanbal,' 253.

[93] For example, *istawā ʿalā al-ʿarsh* in Qurʾan 7:54, 10:3, 13:2, 25:59, 32:4, 57:4; and *ʿalā al-ʿarsh istawā*, 20:5.

survived through the theological and jurisprudential traditions that coalesced to survive the tumultuous classical period as schools of thought.[94]

Ibn Taymiyya and his followers mounted the first major counter-attack of the Ḥanbalī traditionists against this consensus.[95] Among the works they championed that were issued in the twentieth century, al-Dārimī's *Radd ʿalā Bishr al-Marīsī* (Refutation of Bishr al-Marīsī, 1939), which an al-Azhar committee had censured but not prevented from publication, particularly exercised Kevseri.[96] One of the earliest Ḥanbalī theorists, al-Dārimī expounded the theology of *al-jihāt*, or God's positionality, which was formulated as a rejection of the arguments first attributed to Jahm ibn Ṣafwān that to understand God as possessing limit, boundary, or end would be to conceive of Him in human terms and flout the fundamental principle of God's transcendence (*tanzīh*). Kevseri attacked al-Dārimī's stance by applying the polemical term *ḥulūl al-ḥawādith*, the notion that God 'incarnates actions' or 'resides in events', which he considered a form of *tajsīm*,[97] and arguing that to revive this theology was a form of destabilisation of the established system.[98]

[94] See A. J. Wensinck, *The Muslim Creed: Its Genesis and Historical Development* (Cambridge: University Press, 1932); and Joseph Schacht, 'New Sources for the History of Muḥammadan Theology,' *Studia Islamica*, 1 (1953): 23–42, which argues for Muʿtazilī rationalism's survival among the Māturīdīs in particular.

[95] Nabil Mouline, *The Clerics of Islam: Religious Authority and Political Power in Saudi Arabia* (New Haven: Yale University Press, 2014), 11–45.

[96] Western scholarship has been unclear on his influence. Some argue that his legal and creedal positions dislodged Ashʿarīsm from its predominance before the modern period; see George Makdisi, 'Law and Traditionalism in the Institutions of Learning of Medieval Islam,' in *Theology and Law in Islam*, ed. Gustave Grunebaum (Wiesbaden: Harrassowitz, 1971), 75–88, and Josef Van Ess, 'The Logical Structure of Islamic Theology,' in *Logic in Classical Islamic Culture*, ed. Gustave Grunebaum (Wiesbaden: O. Harrassowitz, 1970), 21–50. El-Rouayheb's work is refutation of this approach; see *Islamic Intellectual History*, 173–234.

[97] On al-Dārimī's theology see *Maqālāt*, 'Namādhij Mimmā fī Naqd al-Dārimī Alladhī Ubīḥa Nashruhu', 262; 'Inkār Nuzūl ʿĪsā wa-Iqrār ʿAqīdat al-Tajsīm,' 260–2; 'ʿAqīdat al-Tanzīh,' 312–15; 'Taḥdhīr al-Umma min Duʿāt al-Wathaniyya,' 277–82; 'Fitan al-Mujassima wa-Ṣunūf Makhāzihim,' 288–95; 'Kitāb Yusammā Kitāb al-Sunna wa-Huwa Kitāb al-Zaygh,' 296–302; 'Al-Ṣirāʿ al-Akhīr bayn al-Islām wa-l-Wathaniyya,' 304–7. Kevseri suggested Ibn Taymiyya's ideas on *ḥulūl al-ḥawādith* were influenced by philosopher Ibn Malkā's (d. 1164/5) critique of Aristotelian philosophy, *Kitāb al-Muʿtabar*; in al-Kawtharī, *Muqaddimāt*, 143. He also published an edition of Muḥammad al-Tabrīzī's commentary on Mūsā ibn Maymun (aka Maimonides, d. 1204)'s anti-*tajsīm* premises in *Dalālat al-Ḥāʾirīn*; al-Kawtharī, *al-Muqaddimāt al-Khams wa-l-ʿIshrūn* (Cairo: al-Saʿāda, 1949). He accused Ibn Taymiyya of using Maimonides's text in framing his arguments against *tajsīm*; *Muqaddimat*, 141–5.

[98] On destabilising the tradition, see al-Kawtharī, *al-Ishfāq*, 75–6 and 'Manshaʾ Ilzām,' *Maqālāt*, 227.

The second creedal issue that took Kevseri's attention was that of deferred judgement on faith (*irjāʾ*) and demotion of circumstantial action and acts of worship to a secondary status in its evaluation. Later Abbasid writers on sects and heresies referred to the different groups elaborating variations on these basic points in the Umayyad period as the Murjiʾa, or 'those who delay'.[99] Their thinking fared better than that of their contemporaries the Muʿtazila among the early dialecticians, being largely adapted into the Ashʿarī and Māturīdī systems. However, *irjāʾ/murjiʾ/jahmī* (after Ibn Ṣafwān) became terms of abuse in the later writing of their main opponents, the Ḥanbalī traditionists who claimed to have views more soundly located in Qurʾan and hadith. They in turn were dubbed the Ḥashwiyya, a label suggesting they had 'stuffed' their hadiths with unreliable narrators and claims to justify their literal understandings of Qurʾanic anthropomorphisms and rejection of the *kalām* enterprise.[100] Ibn Taymiyya ordered traditionist thinking in a schema of *islām-īmān-iḥsān* by which a Muslim attained stages of faith through actions at constant risk of relapse.[101] As the most prominent of early juridical figures elaborating rationalist theological views, Abū Ḥanīfa became a target for the traditionists. One of the most well-known attacks was a biographical entry written by al-Baghdādī in his massive compendium *Tārīkh Baghdād*.[102] Kevseri recounts that his publisher friend Muḥammad Amīn al-Khanjī, one of the group preparing the book, had complained to him about the anti-Ḥanafī material in volume thirteen, which was based on a manuscript in Dār al-Kutub in Cairo.[103] A rushed commentary written by Kevseri for inclusion was edited against his wishes by al-Fiqī, who was also involved in the project, and although eventually al-Azhar intervened, the book was still distributed in India with the funding of Muḥammad Naṣīf. Kevseri's response was his *Taʾnīb al-Khaṭīb* (1941) in which he goes through 150 hadith reports concerning Abū Ḥanīfa in meticulous detail, following

[99] In *Maqālat al-Islāmiyyīn*, Ashʿarī divided the Murjiʾa into twelve groups; see Izutsu, *Concept of Belief*, 83–92.

[100] Jon Hoover, 'Ḥashwiyya,' in *EI3*; http://dx.doi.org/10.1163/1573-3912_ei3_COM_30377 (accessed 24 April 2019).

[101] Izutsu, *Concept of Belief*, 57–60. The actions Ibn Taymiyya had in mind for preferring faith were shariʿa prescriptions regarding acts of worship. See Ibn Taymiyya, *Kitāb al-Īmān* (Beirut: al-Maktab al-Islāmī, 1996), 7–8, 15–16, 129–30, 162–4, 204–8, 242–5.

[102] Fedwa Malti Douglas, 'Controversy and Its Effects in the Biographical Tradition of Al-Khaṭīb Al-Baghdādī,' *Studia Islamica*, 46 (1977): 115–31.

[103] Al-Kawtharī, *Taʾnīb al-Khaṭīb*, 28–30. Al-Khanjī issued a revised edition of vol. 13 the same year with a commentary by al-Dhahabī defending Abū Ḥanīfa, placed after the biography of Abū Ḥanīfa.

an introduction that restated his defence of the schools, impugned the character and scholarship of al-Baghdādī, and listed classical works refuting him.[104]

One clear theme in the reports against Abū Ḥanīfa is that he was a supporter of the Jahmiyya and Murjiʾa, a feature that afforded Kevseri the opportunity to offer a modern appraisal of these theological debates.[105] Jahm ibn Ṣafwān was at one extreme of the *murjiʾ* spectrum, reported as holding that faith was an inner conviction alone that no act could call into question.[106] Al-Baghdādī cites reports that seek to highlight the absurdity of these views if taken to the extreme. For example, in one report Abū Ḥanīfa passes by a drunk man standing urinating in the street; when he reprimands him, saying could he could at least do it while sitting down, the man insults him with 'just be on your way, you *murjiʾ*' (*a-lā tamurr yā murjiʾ?*).[107] In another, Abū Ḥanīfa is asked if a man who kills his father, drinks from his skull, and fornicates with his mother is still to be considered a believer (*muʾmin*), and he says yes.[108] Kevseri rejects the report as a partisan fabrication, but his response takes two approaches. First, he tackles it on methodological grounds, citing in its transmission chain three unreliable figures, one unknown name, and a colleague of Abū Ḥanīfa whose good character means he cannot possibly have related such a report. Second, he turns to theology, asserting that despite the extremity of the case the basic principle holds that the established faith of Muslims is not invalidated by actions – 'the believer does not exit faith, no matter how great his sin, unless scholars judge a shortcoming to have appeared in his creed' (*al-muʾmin la yakhruj min al-īmān mahmā kabura dhanbuhu illā bi-ṭurūʾ khalal fī ʿaqīdatihi ʿind ahl al-ḥaqq*).[109]

Kevseri's view in *Taʾnīb* is that Ḥanafī-Māturīdism is the most consistent defender of this principle, which was shared across the spectrum of early theological schools but, he believed, was under threat in the modern period. Kevseri draws on the Māturīdī and Sufi thinking on shades of *īmān* in men's hearts that may be more, or less, illuminated than others, which allows for some notion of levels and degrees of a faith that is still basically

[104] Ibid., 7–28.
[105] Ibid, 83–103, 131–4, 319–20.
[106] This is the presentation in Andalusian theologian Ibn Ḥazm's *Kitāb al-Fiṣāl fī al-Milal wa-l-Ahwāʾ wa-l-Niḥal* and Ibn Taymiyya's *Kitāb al-Īmān*; see Izutsu, *Concept of Belief*, 151–4.
[107] Al-Kawtharī, *Taʾnīb al-Khaṭīb*, 83.
[108] Ibid., 85–7.
[109] Ibid., 87.

fixed.[110] He also articulates the Ashʿarī-Māturīdī charge that faith judged through action risks condemning the common people to unbelief during their lifetimes, thus their statement of faith through following the recommendations of their religious leaders must be accepted (*īmān bi-l-taqlīd*).[111] Kevseri writes that the endurance of faith differs among the prophets, the ʿulamaʾ, and the masses and is dependent upon the means by which one first arrived at conviction (*jazm*). The faith of prophets cannot change since it is based on their experience of revelation and the faith of the ʿulamaʾ is based on reflection (*naẓar*), but that of the ordinary people (*ʿawāmm*) is vulnerable since it was acquired through community.[112] The ʿulamaʾ must then be attendant to the beliefs of the masses since they are susceptible to the arguments of those in positions of authority, he says. So while the roster of minor to major sins will certainly impact the Muslim's level of faith, the Sunni consensus has been that ultimate judgement upon faith is delayed for God to make, and were it not for Abū Ḥanīfa and his followers it would have been possible 'to declare the mass of fallible Muslims unbelievers through shortcomings in one action or another at one point in time, which would be the greatest calamity' (*ikfār jamāhīr al-muslimīn ghayr al-maʿsumīn li-ikhlālihim bi-ʿamal min al-aʿmāl fī waqt min al-awqāt wa-fī dhālik al-ṭāma al-kubrā*).[113] Kevseri had in mind here popular practices related to intercession that cut across a range of Sunni and Shiʿa communities threatened by Ibn Taymiyya and his followers' reinvigoration of *takfīr*.[114] In other words, Kevseri perceived self-described Salafi theology as a social danger.

Alongside *Taʾnīb*, Kevseri's other main work defending Abū Ḥanīfa was *al-Nukat al-Ṭarīfa* (1946). Here he took issue with a section in the *Muṣannaf* (Compilation) of hadith scholar Ibn Abī Shayba (d. 849) which said Abū Ḥanīfa had wrongly questioned 125 cases of authenticated prophetic hadith.[115] Kevseri said he had decided to respond to this because his opponents had published the section as a separate book in

[110] Ibn Taymiyya makes this connection to Sufi *aḥwāl* and *maqāmāt* in *Kitāb al-Īmān*, 152; see Izutsu, *Concept of Belief*, 174, 192.

[111] Izutsu, *Concept of Belief*, 119–30.

[112] Al-Kawtharī, *Taʾnīb al-Khaṭīb*, 134.

[113] Ibid., 91.

[114] Kevseri singled out the Yemeni scholar al-Shawkānī for declaring grave visits and following the schools as acts of *kufr*; see 'Al-Hijra al-Nabawiyya,' in *Maqālāt*, 385, and al-Kawtharī, *al-Ishfāq*, 70.

[115] Scott C. Lucas, 'Where Are the Legal Ḥadīth? A Study of the Muṣannaf of Ibn Abī Shayba,' *Islamic Law and Society*, 25/3 (2008): 283–314.

India,[116] the number of issues questioned was miniscule among the tens of thousands of reports Abū Ḥanīfa addressed,[117] many of the reports have broken (*mursal*) chains of transmission,[118] there is no other evidence he held the views cited,[119] none of them concerned cases reflecting the general principles of Abū Ḥanīfa's *fiqh*,[120] and Abū Ḥanīfa would have used independent reasoning (*ijtihād*) in rejecting an *āḥād* hadiths rather than reject them in principle.[121] The book and the cases in question illustrate Kevseri the *muḥaddith* as much as the *mutakallim*.[122] Kevseri rejected the accusation that Ḥanafī methodology was little interested in hadith, opposed outright to single-source reports, indifferent to the weak *isnād*, and over-focussed on analysis of content (*matn*).[123] These became common charges in the classical period following the widespread acceptance of jurist Muḥammad ibn Idrīs al-Shāfiʿī's (d. 820) revolutionary methodology that rejected Ḥanafī *raʾy* (dialectical reasoning),[124] Mālikī communal practice, and Muʿtazilī theories of certitude-through-consensus in favour of utilising Qurʿan and hadith (understood as specifically prophetic) as the sources of a generalised Islamic law.[125]

Kevseri's approach was that narrators who were considered unreliable in their memorisation were not always wrong and those considered reliable were not always right, so that well-known collections of both good and bad hadith could be subjected to close reading and both companions

[116] Al-Kawtharī, *al-Nukat al-Ṭarīfa fī al-Taḥadduth ʿan Rudūd Ibn Abī al-Shayba ʿalā Abī Ḥanīfa* (Cairo: al-Maktaba al-Azhariyya li-l-Turāth, 2000), 6.

[117] Ibid., 4.

[118] Ibid.

[119] Ibid.

[120] Ibid., 5.

[121] Ibid., 246.

[122] Hadith studies were the subject of a ten-point report Kevseri was asked to prepare by al-Azhar rector Muṣṭafā ʿAbd al-Rāziq during his period of office (1945–7) but never presented due to the latter's death. He imagined a comprehensive programme examining chains of transmission, character of narrators, and content material to understand the narrator's thinking, and this would allow for part rather than wholesale acceptance or rejection of hadiths; al-Kawtharī, 'Iḥyāʾ ʿUlūm al-Sunna fī al-Azhar,' *Maqālāt*, 481–90.

[123] See introduction to *Taʾnīb al-Khaṭīb*, 7–22, and al-Kawtharī (ed. ʿAbd al-Fattāḥ Abū Ghudda), *Fiqh Ahl al-ʿIrāq wa-Ḥadīthuhum* (Cairo: al-Maktaba al-Azhariyya li-l-Turāth, 2002), originally published as the introduction to his edition of Ḥanafī jurist ʿUthmān ibn ʿAlī al-Zaylaʿī's (d. 1342) *Naṣb al-Rāya li-Takhrīj Aḥādīth al-Hidāya*.

[124] This was a form of legal reasoning dominant before the primacy of hadith was established in the Islamic legal tradition.

[125] El Shamsy, *Canonization*, 44–68.

and imams could be considered fallible.[126] However, the status of the four imams as absolute *mujtahid* was justified since they were the earliest juridical and theological thinkers to have considered in the most comprehensive manner the earliest material, passed down from the prophet through only a few narrators. Therefore, they lived among generations with a historical memory of the earliest period, they better understood the language of that period before it was subject to semantic transformation, and they were better placed to make a judgement about the character of transmitters (Abū Ḥanīfa, d. 767; Mālik ibn Anas, d. 796). Kevseri relates the turn against Abū Ḥanīfa – his use of *ra'y* in *fiqh* and deferred judgement of faith in *'aqīda* – to an atmosphere of sectarian retribution following the caliph al-Mutawakkil's lifting of the inquisition in 848, since a preponderance of the *miḥna* judges had been followers of Abū Ḥanīfa in *fiqh*.[127]

Kevseri's opponents took his knowledge of hadith seriously, to the point of making the polemical charge that he considered himself a *mujtahid muṭlaq* in the discipline.[128] In 1961 al-Albānī edited a commentary attributed to a Damascus scholar called 'Alī Ibn Abī al-'Izz (d. 1390) on the tenth-century creedal work of the Ḥanafī jurist Abū Ja'far al-Ṭaḥāwī (d. 933) known as *al-'Aqīda al-Ṭaḥāwiyya*.[129] Al-Albānī's choice of Ibn Abī al-'Izz's commentary was political in that the work was conciliatory towards Ḥanbalī theology and their sensitivities regarding hadith-based *fiqh*, making it acceptable to twentieth-century Ḥanbalīs.[130] In the 1971 imprint of the book, al-Albānī added a long introduction attacking Kevseri as an irredeemably fanatical Ḥanafī (*ḥanafī hālik fī al-ta'aṣṣub*)

[126] Özafshar, 'Muhammed Zahid el-Kevseri,' 97. See his criticism of Ibn 'Adī (d. 976)'s collection of weak hadith narrators, *al-Kāmil fī Ḍu'afā' al-Rijāl* and that of Abū Ja'far al-'Uqaylī (d. 934), *Kitāb al-Ḍu'afā' al-Kabīr* in 'Kalima fī Kutub al-Jarḥ wa-l-Ta'dīl,' dated 3 Jumādā al-Ākhira 1357 (31 July 1938), in *Fiqh Ahl al-'Irāq*, 84–93.

[127] Al-Kawtharī, *Ta'nīb al-Khaṭīb*, 15.

[128] Al-Albānī, Introduction to al-Mu'allimī, *al-Tankīl*, in al-Bayṭār, *al-Kawtharī wa-Ta'addīhi*, 143. Al-Albānī wrote a longer introduction in 1967 to the second edition: *al-Tankīl* (Beirut: al-Maktab al-Islāmī, 1986), 171–5.

[129] Kevseri published a biography of al-Ṭaḥāwī in 1949 that dismissed Ibn Abī al-'Izz as an anthropomorphist; *al-Ḥāwī fī Sīrat al-Imām Abī Ja'far al-Ṭaḥāwī* (Cairo: al-Azhariyya li-l-Turāth, 1999), 39. Khan gives the impression Kevseri wrote in response to al-Albānī, whose polemics came later; Khan, 'Islamic Tradition,' 61–2.

[130] Christopher Melchert, *The Formation of the Sunni Schools of Law, 9th–10th centuries C.E.* (Leiden: Brill, 1997), 116–23. The book was first published by the Salafiyya Press in Mecca in 1930/1931, then in Cairo, edited by Aḥmad Muḥammad Shākir, in 1954; see Shakir (ed.), *Sharḥ al-Ṭaḥāwiyya fī al-'Aqīda al-Salafiyya* (Cairo: Dār al-Turāth, 1954), 5–8.

who denies God's attributes (*jahmī mu'aṭṭil*).[131] Its genesis was a report that Kevseri's student Abū Ghudda had presented to religious authorities in Saudi Arabia where he was lecturing at Riyadh University.[132] Al-Albānī defended himself from charges of sloppy scholarship, but then shifted to taunting Abū Ghudda, a fellow Syrian, for choosing loyalty to Kevseri over what al-Albānī called the Salafi school of Ibn Taymiyya and Ibn ʿAbd al-Wahhāb.[133] Like al-Khaṭīb four decades before, al-Albānī seemed outraged at Kevseri's gall in assailing traditionist theology and at the esteem Abū Ghudda bestowed on him in his own writing.[134] Al-Albānī was also outraged by Kevseri's willingness to question *ṣaḥīḥ* hadith in the collections of al-Bukhārī and Muslim because they run counter to the logic of reports elsewhere. For al-Albānī this was evidence of a juridical mind looking to justify preordained outcomes with a Ḥanafī bias.[135] However, the same charge could equally well be directed al-Albānī in his drive to excavate a pre-school legal tradition from the Qurʾan, prophetic hadith, and example of the companions of the Prophet. Setting himself the task of identifying weak hadith in the canonical collections in his thirteen-volume *Silsilat al-Aḥādīth al-Ḍaʿīfa wa-l-Mawḍūʿa wa-Atharuhā al-Sayyiʾ fī al-Umma* (The Chain of Weak and Fabricated Hadiths and their Negative Impact on the Umma, 1959),[136] al-Albānī would on occasion discard hadiths in the six canonical collections, rely on the views of later scholars in assessing the reliability of narrators, judge authenticity through comparing lines of transmission in variant reports on the same topic, and

131 Nāṣir al-Dīn al-Albānī (ed.), *Sharḥ al-ʿAqīda al-Ṭaḥāwiyya* (Beirut: al-Maktab al-Islāmī, 1971), 44–5. Al-Albānī also describes Kevseri as 'known for extreme hostility [*ʿadāʾ shadīd*] to the people of sunna and hadith' in his 1972 introduction to al-Dhahabī, *Mukhtaṣar al-ʿUluww li-l-ʿAliyy al-Ghaffār* (Beirut: al-Maktab al-Islāmī, 1981), 15. Al-Albānī's earliest criticism of Kevseri was in 'Silsilat al-Aḥādīth al-Ḍaʿīfa: 3,' *al-Tamaddun al-Islāmī*, 21 (1954): 657–64. A fuller attack followed in al-Albānī's 1965 edition of al-Muʿallimī's *al-Tankīl*.

132 ʿAbd al-Fattāḥ Abū Ghudda, ed., *al-Rafʿ wa-l-Takmīl fī al-Jarḥ wa-l-Taʿdīl li-l-Imām Abī al-Ḥasanāt Muḥammad ʿAbd al-Ḥayy al-Laknawī al-Hindī* (Aleppo: Maktabat al-Matbūʿāt al-Islāmiyya, 1963).

133 Al-Albānī, *al-Ṭaḥāwiyya*, 47.

134 Ibid., 46.

135 Ibid., 32–3. He cites Kevseri's rejection of two hadiths from companions in *Ṣaḥīḥ Muslim* (no. 969, 970) against building and decorating graves through other reports that counter the inference from the hadiths alone that destroying graves is legitimate and through noting the many centuries during which the two hadiths had not been activated for that purpose; 'Bināʾ al-Masājid ʿalā al-Qubūr wa-l-Ṣalāh ʿalayhā,' *Maqālāt*, 153–6.

136 Jonathan Brown, *The Canonization of al-Bukhārī and Muslim: The Formation and Function of the Sunnī Ḥadīth Canon* (Leiden: Brill, 2007), 321–34.

resort to analogy to arrive at desired conclusions.[137] The two scholars were not as diametrically opposed to each other as sometimes assumed. Kevseri was not al-Albānī's warrior against *āḥād* hadith, and they both objected to the Qurʾanist approach of contemporaries like Shaltūt.[138] But while Kevseri saw the ʿulamaʾ as inheritors of the Prophet, guiding the community to divine truth, al-Albānī saw them as obstacles, and they each established methodological approaches to divine sources through which they could defend their favoured theologies.

SALAFISM: ORIGINS AND DEFINITIONS

Two problems attend to the historical evolution of *salafiyya*, one lexical and the second semantic. From the term *salaf* as a referent for the first generations of Muslims, the discursive landscape of early twentieth-century Islamic thought witnessed the production of *salafī* as a noun describing someone whose views, whether in *fiqh* or *ʿaqīda* or other questions, were considered to reflect those of the *salaf* and/or the structure of early Islam as a religious community that did not yet know the complex of sects and ideas that were to develop. These Salafis could then be considered representatives of a modern ideology of Salafism. I will now outline some instances of *salafī/salafiyya* to demonstrate the fluidity of meaning these words carried, then examine their debut in public discourse as terms embracing movements as diverse as ʿAbduh modernism and the Wahhabi Ḥanbalīs.

The word itself is rare in the earliest source material. It appears once in the Qurʾan (43:56) to refer to Pharaoh's people who in being drowned were made a *salaf*, a thing of the past, and an example to those who came later (*al-ākhirīn*).[139] Of the six canonical hadith collections it comes once in the *Ṣaḥīḥ* of al-Bukhārī with the apparent meaning of companions of the Prophet, elsewhere referring to cash loans and advance payment for goods.[140] In modern usage these two basic senses remain in the verbal

[137] Christopher Melchert, 'Muhammad Nasir al-Din al-Albānī and Traditional Hadith Criticism,' in Kendall and Khan, *Reclaiming Islamic Tradition*, 43–5; and Kamaruddin Amin, 'Nāṣiruddīn al-Albānī on Muslim's Ṣaḥīḥ: A Critical Study of His Method,' *Islamic Law and Society*, 11/2 (2004): 149–76.

[138] Nāṣir al-Dīn al-Albānī, *Wujūb al-Akhdh bi-Ḥadīth al-Āḥād fī al-ʿAqīda wa-l-Radd ʿalā Shibh al-Mukhālifīn* (Damascus: al-Maktab al-Islāmī, 1974), 34–5.

[139] Melchert, 'Muḥammad Nāṣir al-Dīn al-Albānī,' 34.

[140] Al-Bukhārī, *Ṣaḥīḥ al-Bukhārī* (Beirut: al-Maktaba al-ʿAṣriyya, 2010), 995; no. 5423, titled 'food, meat and other items the *salaf* would store in their houses and on journeys'.

derivatives of *s-l-f*: passage of time/time past and lend/borrow. In his *Iljām al-ʿAwāmm ʿan ʿIlm al-Kalām* (Restraining the Populace from Creedal Discussion), al-Ghazālī said he was writing to refute the claim that literal understandings of Qurʾanic text represented *madhhab al-salaf*, by which he appears to have meant the views of the companions; indeed, the book also circulated under the title *Risāla fī Madhāhib Ahl al-Salaf* (Treatise on the Teachings of the Companions).[141] Another two centuries ahead, Ibn Taymiyya asserted once more that it was the traditionist programme – which he considered to be untouched by Aristotelian logic, Neoplatonic philosophy, and popular practices rooted in the notion of post-Prophet divine charisma – that truly reflected the position of the *salaf* in matters of creed.[142] Ibn Taymiyya became a somewhat marginal figure within Ḥanbalism,[143] until the Wahhabi movement's adoption of his ideas in the mid-eighteenth century and his rediscovery by Arab scholars in the metropolitan centres of Damascus and Baghdad, launching a new struggle over normativity, this time in the context of Western modernity.[144]

The term *madhhab al-salaf* was deployed by various scholars from different backgrounds with different motives and agendas throughout the nineteenth century, sometimes with reference to theology, sometimes to rejection of *taqlīd* in law. The Yemeni jurist al-Shawkānī emphasised juridical *ijtihād* based on Qurʾan and hadith as a means of overcoming periods of weakness in the imamate system in which the Zaydi imam was considered an absolute *mujtahid*. Abū Thanāʾ Shihāb al-Dīn Maḥmūd al-Ālūsī (d. 1854), Ḥanafī mufti in Baghdad and a follower of the Khālidī Naqshbandiyya, developed his ideas of a theology of the *salaf*

[141] Al-Ghazālī, *Iljām al-ʿAwāmm ʿan ʿIlm al-Kalām* (Istanbul: Siraç Yayınevi, 2017), 21–2. On this work, see Ovamir Anjum, 'Cultural Memory of the Pious Ancestors (*Salaf*) in al-Ghazālī,' *Numen*, 58/2–3 (2011): 344–74 and Frank Griffel, *Al-Ghazālī's Philosophical Theology* (New York/Oxford: Oxford University Press, 2009), 266–74.

[142] Ibn Taymiyya, *al-Fatāwā al-Kubrā*, 5 vols. (Cairo: Dār al-Kutub al-Ḥadītha, 1966), 5:141, 147, 152 (section 141– 66); Ibn Taymiyya, *Majmūʿat al-Rasāʾil wa-l-Masāʾil*, 25; Ibn Taymiyya, *Majmūʿ Fatāwā Ibn Taymiyya*, 35 vols. (Medina: Majmaʿ al-Malik Fahd, 1995), 33:170.

[143] Christopher Melchert, 'The Relation of Ibn Taymiyya and Ibn Qayyim al-Jawziyya to the Ḥanbalī School of Law,' in *Islamic Theology, Philosophy and Law: Debating Ibn Taymiyya and Ibn Qayyim al-Jawziyya*, ed. Alina Kokoschka, Birgit Krawietz, Georges Tamer (Berlin: De Gruyter, 2013), 146–61.

[144] For a review of recent literature on Ottoman knowledge of Ibn Taymiyya, see Derin Terzioğlu, 'Ibn Taymiyya, *al-Siyāsa al-Sharʿiyya*, and the Early Modern Ottomans,' in *Historicizing Sunni Islam in the Ottoman Empire, c. 1450–c. 1750*, ed. T. Krstić and D. Terzioğlu (Boston: Brill, 2020), 101–54.

against a backdrop of Ottoman political intrigues.[145] In his multi-volume *tafsīr*, *Rūh al-Maʿānī* (The Spirit of Meanings), al-Ālūsī rejected the fundamentals of Ashʿarī doctrine on God's attributes, causation, and predestination, and attacked the Sufi networks as institutions of state power.[146] In his book *Gharāʾib al-Ightirāb* (Curiosities of Travelling Afar), part travelogue and part theological discussion, al-Ālūsī recounted his defence of Ibn Taymiyya's views to the Ottoman sheikh ül-Islam Arif Hikmet (in office 1846–54). He ascribes to *madhhab al-salaf* the view that the meaning of obscure Qurʾanic passages is known only to God and can be neither taken literally nor stated with conviction to mean something else but uses the term *salafiyyūn* to describe the mass of prominent scholars of the classical period.[147]

Al-Ālūsī's son Nuʿmān Khayr al-Dīn (d. 1899) developed these ideas in his book *Jalāʾ al-ʿAynayn fī Muḥākamat al-Aḥmadayn* (Clarity in Judging the Two Aḥmads), published in Cairo in 1881. Khayr al-Dīn took a refutation of Ibn Taymiyya by the Egyptian Shāfiʿī scholar Ibn Ḥajar al-Haytamī (d. 1566) as the point from which to launch his effort to rehabilitate the Damascene shaykh. Al-Haytamī had issued a fatwa condemning Ibn Taymiyya's creedal positions and his objection to popular practices of intercession. Appearing at the cusp of modern print culture's first great flush, Khayr al-Dīn's book had a considerable impact, on his nephew Maḥmūd Shukrī al-Ālūsī (1857–1924), on the Damascus *ʿālim* Jamāl al-Dīn al-Qāsimī (1866–1914), and on Rashīd Riḍā.[148] Maḥmūd Shukrī al-Ālūsī took over the mantle from his uncle after Khayr al-Dīn's death in 1899, maintaining correspondence with scholars in not only Damascus, but Kuwait, Jeddah, Najd, Qatar, and Istanbul.[149]

ʿAbduh uses the term *salafī* in his debate with Faraḥ Anṭūn. In his *al-Islām wa-l-Naṣrāniyya* articles from 1902 ʿAbduh described three sects

[145] Basheer Nafi, 'Abu al-Thanaʾ al-Alusi: An ʿAlim, Ottoman Mufti, and Exegete of the Qurʾan,' *IJMES*, 34/3 (2002): 465–94.

[146] Ibid., 485–6.

[147] Shihāb al-Dīn al-Ālūsī, *Gharāʾib al-Ightirāb wa-Nuzhat al-Albāb* (Baghdad: Shahbandar Press, 1909/10), 387–9, 394. See El-Rouayheb, 'From Ibn Hajar al-Haytami (d. 1566) to Khayr al-Dīn al-Ālūsī (d. 1899): Changing Views of Ibn Taymiyya among non- Ḥanbalī Sunni Scholars,' in *Ibn Taymiyya and His Times*, ed. Yossef Rapoport and Shahab Ahmed (Karachi: Oxford University Press, 2010), 307–8. Also, Edouard Méténier, 'al-Ālūsī family,' in *EI3*; http://dx.doi.org/10.1163/1573-3912_ei3_COM_22713 (accessed 8 August 2018).

[148] Commins, *Islamic Reform*, 25.

[149] Detailed in Muḥammad Bahjat al-Atharī, *Maḥmūd Shukrī al-Ālūsī wa-Ārāʾuhu al-Lughawiyya* (Cairo: al-Kamāliyya Press, 1958), 44. Discussed in Commins, *Islamic Reform*, 25.

in creed, the Salafis, the Ashʿarīs, and the Muʿtazila, but he considered the Salafis and Ashʿarīs as two branches of Sunni Islam, closer to each other than the Muʿtazila.[150] Both Riḍā and ʿImāra consider the term worthy of a footnote in their editions of ʿAbduh: Riḍā (writing circa 1905) says only that the *salafiyya* are 'those adopting the creed of the *salaf*' (*al-ākhidhīn bi-ʿaqīdat al-salaf*)[151] but ʿImāra (writing circa 1972) says ʿAbduh means Ḥanbalīs and Ẓāhirīs who reject Qurʾanic *taʾwīl* and take Qurʾan and hadith as the sole acceptable sources in law.[152] Three points can be inferred from the passage: ʿAbduh is either coining a new term or using one that had been in circulation for some time; he is applying it to a theological group within *kalām* disputation; and he is conceding the appellation to a group of which he does not consider himself a part. In the same book he regrets a lack of awareness of 'the works of the *salaf*' (*āthār al-salaf*) among ordinary Muslims of the era, citing specifically the texts of al-Ashʿarī and al-Māturīdī.[153] This reflects ʿAbduh's usage in *Risālat al-Tawḥīd* in which the *salaf* are the eminent figures of the first four Muslim centuries, disregarding the traditional taxonomy that defines them as the first three generations.[154]

The next notable point in the development of Salafi as an identity marker came in correspondence between Maḥmūd Shukrī al-Ālūsī and Jamāl al-Dīn al-Qāsimī between 1908 and 1913. Here *salafī* is used to refer to individuals among the first generation of the *salaf*, as well as Ibn Taymiyya and followers; it is also an adjective describing the latter group's theology,[155] and in one letter included in the collection it describes Ibn Taymiyya's purported non-*madhhab* allegiance, despite his Ḥanbalī affiliation.[156] Still, the usage as a self-identifier remains timid in letters between the two scholars, and it is notable that al-Qāsimī's group in Damascus had

[150] ʿAbduh, 'al-Ittihād fī al-Naṣrāniyya wa-l-Islām,' *al-Manār*, 5/15, 4 September 1902: 405 (*al-Aʿmāl al-Kāmila*, 3:267); 'shiddat al-tabāyun bayna ʿaqāʾid ahl al-iʿtizāl wa-ʿaqāʾid ahl al-sunna salafiyyīn wa-ashāʿira'.

[151] ʿAbduh, *al-Islām wa-l-Naṣrāniyya*, 17.

[152] ʿAbduh, *al-Aʿmāl al-Kāmila*, 3:267.

[153] Ibid., 359.

[154] ʿAbduh (ed. ʿImāra), *Risālat al-Tawḥīd*, 27–8. Al-Kawākibī wrote in 1900 that residents of the Arabian Peninsula were *salafī* for Sunni concensus positions that eschew severity and Sufi excess; *Umm al-Qurā*, 5, 42, 88.

[155] Muḥammad ibn Nāṣir al-ʿAjmī, *al-Rasāʾil al-Mutabādila bayn Jamāl al-Dīn al-Qāsimī wa-Maḥmūd Shukrī al-Ālūsī* (Beirut: al-Bashāʾir, 2001), 47, 60, 74, 190.

[156] Ibid., 104; 'wa-in kāna ḥanbaliyyan fī al-furūʿ, fa-huwa fī uṣūl al-dīn jāmiʿ li-madhāhib al-arbaʿa al-āʾimma'. The letter is from Muḥammad al-Makkī ibn ʿAzzūz al-Tūnisī in Istanbul, dated Dhū al-Ḥijja 1327 (December 1909/January 1910) and was sent to ʿAbd al-Razzāq al-Bayṭār.

for some time used the phrase *jamʿiyyat al-mujtahidīn* to describe themselves, eschewing any *salafī* label,[157] while their detractors referred to them as followers of *al-madhhab al-jamālī* after al-Qāsimī's name.[158] Al-Qāsimī was a scholar like ʿAbduh whose critique of the ʿulamaʾ and *madhhab* culture stemmed from his awareness of European advances; indeed, he was leery of some of the creedal positions associated with Ibn Taymiyya and his followers.[159]

The challenge to Sunni traditionalism from scholars in Baghdad and Damascus was intimately tied to the Ottoman Arab provinces' relationship with the political centre in Istanbul, from the Tanzimat reforms launched in 1839, to the attempt to consolidate state power under Abdülhamid. A particularly significant figure in this regard was the scholar Abū al-Hudā al-Ṣayyādī (1850–1909), whose career was closely associated with Abdülhamid and his rule.[160] From a prominent Aleppan family of Sufi *ashrāf*,[161] al-Ṣayyādī became an adviser to the young sultan in 1879 and expanded the Rifāʿiyya *ṭarīqa* in Baghdad in the hope of better integrating Shiʿa into the empire.[162] He was similar to Naqshbandī shaykhs such as Gümüşhanevi in preaching obedience to authority.[163] Selim Deringil has outlined how Ḥanafism was propagated as state orthodoxy in unprecedented ways during the Hamidian period, particularly in Arab provinces where it was seen as providing a surer footing for the Ottoman dynasty because of the Ḥanafī view that the caliph did not have to be a Qurayshī Arab.[164] Abu Manneh argued that these policies consciously aimed to check Arabist and Syrian nationalist identity (new ideas in themselves, however), such that few books on what would be considered Arab history or literature were printed in Syrian cities in this period, contributing to the

[157] Commins, *Islamic Reform*, 50–5.

[158] Mun'im Sirry, 'Jamāl al-Dīn al-Qāsimī and the Salafi Approach to Sufism,' *Die Welt des Islams*, 51/1 (2011): 81.

[159] Ibid., *passim.*

[160] Deringil, *The Well-Protected Domains*, 65.

[161] On how Riḍā's animus for Abdülhamid and Abū al-Hudā drove him to flee Tripoli for Egypt in January 1898, see Ibrāhīm Aḥmad al-ʿAdawī, *Rashīd Riḍā, al-Imām al-Mujtahid* (Cairo: al-Muʾassasa al-Miṣriyya al-ʿĀmma, 1964), 108–28.

[162] Thomas Eich, 'Abū l-Hudā al-Ṣayyādī', in *EI3*; http://dx.doi.org/10.1163/1573-3912_ei3_SIM_0028 (accessed on 12 August 2018); Itzchak Weismann, 'Abū l-Hudā l-Ṣayyādī and the Rise of Islamic Fundamentalism,' *Arabica*, 54/4 (October 2007): 586–92; and Butrus Abu Manneh, 'Sultan Abdülhamid II and Shaikh Abulhuda Al-Sayyadi,' *Middle Eastern Studies*, 15/2 (May 1979): 131–53.

[163] Abu Manneh, 'Shaykh Ahmed Ziyaʾuddin,' 105–17.

[164] Deringil, *The Well-Protected Domains*, 43–69.

exodus of intellectuals to Cairo.[165] Yūsuf al-Nabhānī (1849–1932), a jurist from Haifa, was another important figure who upheld the Islamic institutional order of the Ottoman state.[166] In a number of works he condemned attempts to undermine the *madhhab* tradition, the theology of *al-jihāt*, and the polemics against shrine visits and intercession; he took aim at a range of iconoclastic contemporaries including Khayr al-Dīn al-Ālūsī, al-Afghānī, ʿAbduh, al-Qāsimī, and the Wahhabi movement, which was in the process of making a comeback after the Saudi family established the third Najdi state in 1899; and he condemned the use of new media to advance these ideas.[167] His writings appear to presage Kevseri, who had apparently read *Ḥujjat Allāh ʿalā al-ʿAlāmīn fī Muʿjizāt Sayyid al-Mursalīn* (God's Proof to Men Regarding the Miracles of God's Chief Messenger, 1898) since he makes reference to the work in his 1910 book *Irghām al-Murīd*.[168] While al-Nabhānī conflated various figures and trends into one, he did not call any of them Salafism.

As can be seen, *salafī* had become a descriptor shifting between a wide spectrum of meanings, from simply early Muslim, to modern follower of the theological tradition associated with the Ḥanbalīs, to modern critic of affiliation to established schools of law and their hierarchy of authoritative voices. Salafism as an abstract noun emerges in the public sphere with the bookstore and printing press established in Cairo under the name Dār al-Maṭbaʿa al-Salafiyya by Rashīd Riḍā's colleague Muḥibb al-Dīn al-Khaṭīb. Al-Khaṭīb later wrote that he got the idea of the name from his mentor, the Algerian-origin Syrian teacher Ṭāhir al-Jazāʾirī (1852–1920) who was part of a Syrian circle of ʿulamaʾ and intellectuals interested in broad themes of Islamic reform and Arabism, including Jamāl al-Dīn al-Qāsimī, ʿAbd al-Razzāq al-Bayṭār (1837–1916, grandfather of Kevseri's nemesis Muḥammad Bahjat), Muḥammad Kurd ʿAlī (1876–1953), and others.[169] In 1905 al-Jazāʾirī moved to Cairo where he became part of Riḍā's circle, which began to think of ʿAbduh and Ibn Taymiyya as iconic heroes of

[165] Abu Manneh, 'Sultan Abdülhamid II,' 147–8.

[166] Amal Ghazal, 'Sufism, *Ijtihād* and Modernity: Yūsuf al-Nabhānī in the Age of Abd al-Ḥamīd II,' *Archivum Ottomanicum*, vol. 19 (2001): 239–71.

[167] His main works were: *Ḥujjat Allāh ʿalā al-ʿAlāmīn fī Muʿjizāt Sayyid al-Mursalīn* (1898), *Shawāhid al-Ḥaqq* (1905), and *Rafʿ al-Ishtibāh fī Istiḥālat al-Jiha ʿan Allāh* (nda). Al-Ālūsī responded with *Ghāyat al-Amānī fī al-Radd ʿalā al-Nabhānī* (1909).

[168] Al-Kawtharī, *Irghām al-Murīd*, 21.

[169] Muḥibb al-Dīn al-Khaṭīb (unsigned), 'al-Wahhābiyya,' *al-Zahrāʾ*, Ṣafar 1345 (February 1926) 2/2: 87, footnote 1.

Salafism,[170] despite the fact that ʿAbduh did not consider himself to be a *salafī* and did not accord Ibn Taymiyya any particular esteem. The abstract noun was further propagated through a journal by the name of *al-Majalla al-Salafiyya* (1917–18) on which al-Jazāʾirī served as editing consultant and which attracted the interest of French Orientalist Louis Massignon.[171] The term was subsequently discussed in various French and English works in the 1920s as a reference to the reform movement of ʿAbduh and al-Afghānī, and in 1932 Henri Laoust rendered it in French as *le salafisme*.[172] Salafiyya bookstores opened in Multān in today's Pakistan, in Damascus, and one was established in Mecca with funding from Naṣīf to serve the propaganda interests of the expanding Saudi state.[173]

In 1930 *salafiyya* was attacked in a booklet written by a supporter of Kevseri, the Egyptian shaykh Yūsuf al-Dijwī, and issued in Damascus by Kevseri's publisher and one-time student Ḥusām al-Dīn al-Qudsī.[174] The text was a letter of support to Kevseri from al-Dijwī, a member of al-Azhar's committee of senior ʿulamaʾ, in which he condemned Ibn Taymiyya for arrogating himself the right of *ijtihād* above other ʿulamaʾ and his followers for their use of *takfīr* against other Muslims. Al-Dijwī also criticised ʿAbduh for blindly following the Europeans (*yasīr warāʾ kull nāʿiq min al-urubbiyyīn*).[175] The Salafi label was adopted to only a limited degree by al-Fiqī's Anṣār al-Sunna al-Muḥammadiyya, whose programme excoriated Sufism, Ashʿarī-Māturīdī theology, and the *taqlīd* of the schools.[176] Al-Fiqī moved into the Saudi orbit, taking a position as head of publishing in Mecca and funding from King ʿAbd al-ʿAzīz to build the group's Cairo headquarters.[177] Saudi researcher Aḥmad Muḥammad al-Ṭāhir makes heavy use of the Salafi label in his 2004 history of the

170 J. H. Escovitz, 'He was the Muḥammad ʿAbduh of Syria: A Study of Ṭāhir Al-Jazāʾirī and his Influence,' *IJMES*, 18/3 (1986): 293–310.

171 Henri Lauzière, 'The Construction of Salafiyya: Reconsidering Salafism from the Perspective of Conceptual History,' *IJMES*, 42/3 (2010): 374–7.

172 Ibid., 378–81. Henri Laoust, 'Le réformisme orthodoxe des 'Salafiya' et les caractères généraux de son orientation actuelle,' *Revue des études islamiques* 2 (1932), 175–224.

173 Ibid., 383. See al-Khaṭīb's memoir: Ḥasan al-Samāḥī Suwaydān, ed., *Min Siyar al-Khālidīn bi-Aqlāmihim: Aḥmad Shawqī, Muḥammad al-Bashīr al-Ibrāhīmī, Muḥibb al-Dīn al-Khaṭīb* (Damascus: Dār al-Qādirī, 1998).

174 Yūsuf al-Dijwī, *Kalima fī al-Salafiyya al-Ḥāḍira*, in Aḥmad al-Ghumārī, *Qatʿ al-ʿUrūq al-Wardiyya min Ṣāḥib 'al-Burūq al-Najdiyya'* (Leiden: Dār al-Muṣṭafā, 2007), 25–33. It is dated 1 December 1929.

175 Ibid., 32.

176 Aḥmad Muḥammad al-Ṭāhir, *Jamāʿat Anṣār al-Sunna al-Muḥammadiyya* (Riyadh: Dār al-Faḍīla, 2004), 57, 66–7.

177 Ibid., 91.

organisation.[178] Anṣār al-Sunna is often associated with an earlier charity group, al-Jamʿiyya al-Sharʿiyya, established in 1912, since the two were forcibly merged by the Egyptian government in 1969 for three years. Al-Jamʿiyya al-Sharʿiyya never made claims to represent anything *salafī* but did embody an anti-Sufi agenda. Both organisations are part of a phenomenon of Islamic charities in modern Egypt which often mixed pious works with political activities – the Muslim Brotherhood being the most well-known example.[179] Sensing the currency it had acquired, Ḥasan al-Bannā added *salafī* to a list of terms defining the group in a statement of purpose he issued at the Brotherhood's Fifth Conference in 1939. The Brotherhood was a Salafi calling, a Sunni *ṭarīqa* and a Sufi truth, he said, deploying a mixture of terminologies to present the group as all things to all men and above the sectarian fray. Al-Bannā added that Salafi calling (*daʿwā salafiyya*) indicated the Brotherhood's desire for Islam to return to its roots in Qurʾan and sunna – on its own, nebulous language that no one could dispute, without any agreement on what it meant.[180]

SALAFISM, SAUDI ARABIA, AND NĀṢIR AL-DĪN AL-ALBĀNĪ

In the 1920s concerted efforts were made by Rashīd Riḍā and Muḥibb al-Dīn al-Khaṭīb to bring the Saudi-Wahhabi movement within the purview of their *salafiyya*. Wahhabism's aggressive claim to represent the ideas of Ibn Taymiyya had ensured its frequent citation in polemics against the modernist reformers and had obliged nineteenth-century ʿulamaʾ who were interested in framing elements of his thought in the language of *madhhab al-salaf* to give some consideration in their writings to what they thought of the Najdis.[181] Due to their work on *al-Manār*, particularly Riḍā's criticism of Sufism, 'Wahhabi' became a slur directed against both

[178] Al-Albānī visited the group's headquarters in Cairo in 1960; ibid., 89.

[179] On Islamic charities in Egypt see Aḥmad Muḥammad al-Ṭāhir, *Jamāʿat Anṣār al-Sunna al-Muḥammadiyya* (Riyadh: Dār al-Hady al-Nabawī, 2004); Saba Mahmood, *Politics of Piety: The Islamic Revival and the Feminist Subject* (Princeton: Princeton University Press, 2005); Denis Joseph Sullivan and Sana Abed-Kotob, *Islam in Contemporary Egypt: Civil Society vs. the State* (Boulder/London: Lynne Rienner, 1999); Alaa Al-Din Arafat, *The Rise of Islamism in Egypt* (London: Palgrave Macmillan, 2017).

[180] 'Risālat al-Muʾtamar al-Khāmis,' in *Majmūʿat Rasāʾil al-Imām al-Shahīd Ḥasan al-Bannā*, Ḥasan al-Bannā (Beirut: Dār al-Andalus, 1965), 248.

[181] For a review of responses to Ibn ʿAbd al-Wahhāb see Hamidi Redissi, 'The Refutation of Wahhabism in Arabic Sources, 1745–1932,' in *Kingdom Without Borders: Saudi Arabia's Political, Religious and Media Frontiers*, ed. Madawi Al-Rasheed (London: Hurst, 2008), 157–81.

ʿAbduh and Riḍā, and in ʿAbduh's period of deteriorating relations with Khedive ʿAbbās Ḥilmī the Egyptian ruler had encouraged people to smear him with the epithet.[182] During a trip to Tunisia in 1903 ʿAbduh was denounced by Shaykh Ṣāliḥ al-Sharīf,[183] the same Ottoman agent during the First World War who worked with Akif. Riḍā was also harangued during a lecture in October 1908 at the Umayyad mosque in Damascus by a man Riḍā described as a North African called Shaykh Ṣāliḥ who had been sent from Istanbul by Abū al-Hudā al-Ṣayyādī to denounce him as a Wahhabi opposed to intercession and the schools.[184] This appears to have been the same Shaykh Ṣāliḥ.[185] After the incident Jamāl al-Dīn al-Qāsimī and his followers maintained a low profile for several months,[186] but during the same tour Riḍā was physically attacked in Tripoli.[187] Riḍā's activities and the opening of the Salafiyya bookstore and printing press in Mecca in 1927 offered the Saudi state a path to normalising a fringe religious movement that had been in an antagonistic relationship with Istanbul and other regional centres for over a century.[188] In a speech delivered in 1929 ʿAbd al-ʿAzīz explicitly rejected use of the term Wahhabi to describe adherents of Ibn ʿAbd al-Wahhāb's mission, arguing that the Najdi shaykh was not the founder of a new school but preaching for a return to the belief and practice of the *al-salaf al-ṣāliḥ*, a *mujaddid* not an innovator. This was probably an attempt to link Wahhabiyya with the Salafi wave, yet even then it was only tangentially done in that he avoided mention of the *salafī/salafiyya* formulations as alternative

[182] Aḥmad Shafīq Bāshā, *Mudhakkirātī fī Niṣf Qarn*, 2 vols. (Cairo: Maṭbaʿat Miṣr, 1934), 2:34–9. Cited in Ghazal, 'Sufism, Ijtihad and Modernity,' 269. Riḍā first drew attention with his anti-Sufi tract *al-Ḥikma al-Sharʿiyya fī Muḥākamat al-Qādiriyya wa-l-Rifāʿiyya*, which was first published in *al-Manār*, 1/28, 7 October 1898: 524–34.

[183] Commins, *Islamic Reform*, 130–1.

[184] Rashīd Riḍā, 'Riḥlat Ṣāḥib *al-Manār* fī Sūriyya - 3,' *al-Manār*, 11/12, 22 January 1909: 936–53.

[185] Commins, *Islamic Reform*, 130–3; Ghazal, 'Sufism, Ijtihad and Modernity,' 270, footnote 164. In 1906 he had moved to Istanbul to work with the Ottomans, who Riḍā opposed; see Peter Heine, 'Sâlih ash-Sharîf at-Tûnisî, a North African Nationalist in Berlin during the First World War,' *Revue de l'Occident musulman et de la Méditerranée*, 33/1 (1982): 89–95. Also, Jacob M. Landau, *The Politics of Pan-Islam*, 114–15.

[186] Commins, *Islamic Reform*, 130–1.

[187] Yūsuf Ibīsh, *Riḥlat al-Imām Muḥammad Rashīd Riḍā* (Beirut: al-Muʾassasa al-ʿArabiyya Li-l-Dirāsāt wa-l-Nashr, 1971), 13. Discussed in Ghazal, 'Sufism, Ijtihad and Modernity,' 270.

[188] Redissi, 'The Refutation of Wahhabism,' 175–6.

identity markers.[189] One reason for this was likely his wider aim of reassuring the Ḥanafī Hijazis about their fate now that they had been incorporated in the Saudi realm, but it speaks to a deeper problem Wahhabiyya had and continues to have with the conceptual innovation of Salafism.

Salafism as a recognisable ideological trademark in modern Islamic thought begins to take shape in 1960s Saudi Arabia in the context of the government's nascent projection of an Islamic foreign policy and the activism of Nāṣir al-Dīn al-Albānī.[190] Al-Albānī's influence was felt institutionally through the Islamic University of Medina where he taught briefly from its inception from 1961 to 1963 and the al-Jamāʿa al-Salafiyya al-Muḥtasiba (the Salafi Ḥisba Group, or Salafi Group for Promoting Virtue and Preventing Vice), an informal circle established by his disciples in 1966. It was al-Albānī who heavily propagated the term in the Saudi sphere with motivations and implications beyond Riḍā's usage, arguing that it was necessary for a Muslim, freed from the constraints of the diverting tradition of *fiqh* schools, to declare his method (*manhaj*) as *salafī*, and even suggesting that Ibn ʿAbd al-Wahhāb wasn't fully *salafī* because while his theological positions were sound, he still followed Ḥanbalī law.[191] Al-Albānī's thinking had three main elements to it: the theology of Ibn Taymiyya; a critique of *madhhab fiqh* that brought together the ideas of Ibn Taymiyya, al-Shawkānī, and the Riḍā network; and rejection of the participation in political systems favoured by movements such as the Muslim Brotherhood.[192] Al-Albānī constructs

[189] 'Fī al-Maʿdaba al-Kubrā,' *Umm al-Qurā*, 16 May 1929, no. 229, pp. 1 and 3. Mouline notes that ʿAbd al-ʿAzīz was following his Syrian and Egyptian advisors in trying to tap into contemporary currents, to the extent that Muḥammad Bahjat al-Bayṭār was brought over to head an Islamic Institute (*al-Maʿhad al-Islāmī*) in Mecca, but it closed after a year for lack of interest among elite Wahhabi families; *The Clerics of Islam*, 9, 111.

[190] On his activities in Saudi Arabia in the 1960s see Stephane Lacroix, 'Between Revolution and Apoliticism: Nasir al-Din al-Albani and his Impact on the Shaping of Contemporary Salafism,' in *Global Salafism: Islam's New Religious Movement*, ed. Roel Meijer (New York: Columbia University Press, 2009), 59–82.

[191] ʿIṣām Mūsā Hādī, *al-Daʿwa al-Salafiyya: Ahdāfuhā wa-Mawqifuhā min al-Mukhālifīn Lahā* (Amman: npa, 2013) collects al-Albānī's comments from cassettes regarding his concept of *salafiyya*. Hadi gives no dates for the various al-Albānī sources he uses.

[192] On al-Albānī's rejection of political action, see Hādī, *al-Daʿwa al-Salafiyya*, 48–9; and Stephane Lacroix, 'Between Revolution and Apoliticism,' 58–80. Al-Albānī's position on violence against Muslim rulers was ambiguous in that he hovered on the margins of insurrectionary groups. He argued that allegiance should not be given to Al Saud since they are not members of Quraysh but cautioned the Salafi Ḥisba Group against *takfīrī* thinking, advising them to read Ibn Taymiyya's *Kitāb al-Īmān*; see Nāṣir al-Ḥuzaymī, *Ayyām maʿa Juhaymān: Kuntu maʿ al-Jamāʿa al-Salafiyya al-Muḥtasiba* (Beirut: Arab

something new, which he gives an appropriately new label, and in that regard his Salafism moves into the territory of ideology in the terms drawn out by Wilfred Cantwell Smith and Michael Freeden[193] since it is a transformation touched by the conditions of modernity. Yet his *manhaj* remains located in internal critique of the Islamic tradition in a way that Riḍā's, with his concern for the fate of Islam vis-à-vis the West, was not.

Al-Albānī's methodology, his innovative propagation of Salafism, and his casting of Kevseri as its organising Other all came together to coalesce as one package in the 1960s after his initial period of teaching in Syria from 1945.[194] His first book was written in 1952, *Ḥijāb al-Marʾa al-Muslima fī al-Kitāb wa-l-Sunna* (The Muslim Woman's Head-covering in Qurʾan and Sunna; republished in 1991 as *Jilbāb al-Marʾa al-Muslima*, The Muslim Woman's Robe), looked beyond the school tradition to direct analysis of hadith material, but without framing his approach as Salafism.[195] During a lecture in 1960 at the Anṣār al-Sunna al-Muḥammadiyya offices in Cairo he was introduced as *al-shaykh al-salafī* known for his *salafiyya*, his main ideas were summarised as emulating (*yuqallid*) the Prophet alone and rejecting accusations of *tajsīm*, and his talk, which defended God's positionality and denounced intercession, referred to right-minded Muslims as *salafiyyūn*, with the clarifying moniker *muḥammadiyyūn*.[196] In his account of membership in the Salafi Ḥisba Group, a faction of which under Juhaymān al-ʿUtaybī

Network for Research and Publishing, 2011), 48. Al-Albānī was attacked by some Wahhabi scholars for reticence in the question of faith and action; thus, Muslims could not be denounced for visiting shrines if they were unaware of their error (Hādī, *al-Daʿwa al-Salafiyya*, 79) and neglect of proscribed prayer was not enough to establish *kufr*, as he wrote in in *Ḥukm Tārik al-Salāh* (Riyadh: Dār al-Jalālayn, 1992). These positions were within the scope of Ibn Taymiyya's *Kitāb al-Īmān*.

193 Freeden, *Ideology: A Very Short Introduction*, 101–2. See Chapter 1 in this volume, footnote 99.

194 Olidort has a similar view of al-Albānī's focus on Kevseri in the construction of his discourse, though he does not critically examine the genealogy of the term Salafism; Jacob Olidort, *In Defense of Tradition: Muḥammad Nāṣir al-Dīn al-Albānī and the Salafī Method* (PhD thesis, Princeton University, 2015), 193–9. The genealogy is discussed by Yasir Qadhi, 'On Salafi Islam,' Muslim Matters.org, 28 April 2014; http://muslimmatters.org/2014/04/22/on-salafi-islam-dr-yasir-qadhi/5/ (accessed 28 April 2019).

195 Discussed in Melchert, 'Muhammad Nasir al-Din al-Albani,' 33–51. Al-Albānī alters the date of completion from 7 to 9 Jumādā al-Awwal 1371 (5 February 1952). *Salafiyya* as an abstract noun also does not appear in *Ṣifāt Ṣalāt al-Nabī*.

196 Al-Albānī's lecture on 27 August 1960 can be heard at: www.4shared.com/file/75693629/8f9c2cdd/albani-1960.html?dirPwdVerified=4f3514e1 (accessed on 26 April 2019). This contradicts Olidort's claim that he became interested in Ḥanbalī theology from 1961 when he moved to Saudi Arabia; Olidort, *In Defense of Tradition*, 169. Olidort cites

launched the failed Mecca insurrection in 1979, Naṣir al-Ḥuzaymī recounts how al-Albānī Salafism was the touchstone of the movement: as a new entrant al-Ḥuzaymī was made familiar with the work of al-Albānī, visited the Salafi community in Kuwait, learned that being Salafi meant rejecting the intellectual tradition of the schools in creed and *fiqh* methodology, and discovered that Kevseri was their bête noire.[197] Numerous anti-Kawtharī works have been published by figures in the Salafi–Wahhabi orbit over the years, the most prominent of which include writings by judge Bakr Abū Zayd (1944–2008), who was a member of the Council of Senior Religious Scholars and its permanent *fatwa* committee, such as *Barāʾat Ahl al-Sunna min al-Waqīʿa fī ʿUlamāʾ al-Islām* (Absolving Sunnis of Guilt Over the Slandering of Islam's ʿUlamaʾ, 1987). Published by the Saudi Ministry of Information, this book included a preface from the head of the government religious publications condemning Kevseri as 'the sinful criminal' (*al-mujrim al-āthim*) and Abū Ghudda for his attachment to him.[198] Al-Albānī inspired many students who passed through Saudi Arabia and who knew him during his later years in Jordan,[199] but his renown was also fed by his closeness to the influential Saudi *ʿālim* ʿAbd al-ʿAzīz ibn Bāz (1910–99), who served as Grand Mufti from 1993 to 1999, as well as his opposition to the Muslim Brotherhood. These Saudi associations were despite the fact that he was forced out of the kingdom in 1963 and only able to visit intermittently over the following two decades.[200]

his influences as Rashīd Riḍā, Jamāl al-Dīn al-Qāsimī, and Muḥammad Bahjat al-Bayṭār, though he only had direct contact with the latter, attending some of his classes.

197 Al-Ḥuzaymī, *Ayyām maʿa Juhaymān*, 14–15, 169.

198 Bakr Abū Zayd, *Barāʾat Ahl al-Sunna min al-Waqīʿa fī ʿUlamāʾ al-Islām* (Riyadh: Ministry of Information, 1987), 3. The other major books in this tradition are Ṣādiq ibn Salim ibn Ṣādiq, *Takḥīl al-ʿAyn bi-Jawāz al-Suʾāl ʿan ʾAllāh Ayn?'* (2007), a Saudi critique of Kevseri's Māturīdism and anti-Salafi polemics; Moroccan shaykh Aḥmad al-Ghumāri (d. 1960)'s *Bayān Talbīs al-Muftarī Muḥammad Zāhid al-Kawtharī* (1993), accusing him of Ḥanafī bias and printed through the efforts of Bakr Abū Zayd; and *Tanbīh al-Bāḥith al-Sirrī ilā Mā fī Rasāʾil wa-Taʿālīq al-Kawtharī* (1948) by Muḥammad al-ʿArabī ibn al-Tabbānī (d. 1970), an Algerian who taught at the mosque schools of Mecca and Medina.

199 Al-Albānī student Muqbil al-Wādiʿī (1933–2001) took the Salafi banner with him to Yemen where he is considered the father of the movement; ʿAbd al-Raḥmān ʿAbd al-Khāliq (b. 1939) did the same in Kuwait.

200 On al-Albānī's influence in Saudi Arabia see Lacroix, 'Between Revolution and Apoliticism,' 58–80; also, Olidort, 'In Defense of Tradition,' 169–202. Al-Albānī's disdain for the Brotherhood was not as ideological as it seemed. His position evolved over time and may have had a personal element to it with regards to Abū Ghudda. The difficult environment for Brotherhood activists in the 1960s confirmed his view that political activity was best left alone; Pierret, *Religion and State in Syria*, 107.

The disconnect between al-Albānī's views and Wahhabism's commitment to Ḥanbalism produced a tension that has put enduring limits on the Saudi state and its scholars' use of *salafiyya* as a label of self-definition.[201] Senior scholars came to accept the term but within a limited scope that avoided association with al-Albānī's rigid rejection of school affiliation.[202] The Mecca-based World Muslim League's Islamic Fiqh Council issued a resolution in 1987, and republished in its journal in 2005, that condemned both 'school fanaticism' (*al-taʿaṣṣub al-madhhabī*) and *lā-madhhabiyya*, the latter of which it described as a 'hateful method' (*uslūb baghīḍ*).[203] However, Salafism retained some efficacy in repackaging Wahhabism as a tool of Saudi foreign policy and improving the kingdom's image in Western eyes.[204] After King Faysal assumed power in 1964 US administrations began to work closely with Saudi Arabia as a vanguard of anti-Soviet and anti-Arab nationalist mobilisation in the Middle East. As Rosie Bsheer has shown, this US–Saudi relationship was lodged not so much in petro-imperialism as in the use of Islam to crush the secular Left.[205] The promotion of Islamic themes took on a new urgency due to a confluence of challenges in the period 1979–80: the Wahhabi insurrection in Mecca, the Iranian Revolution, and the Soviet invasion of Afghanistan. During the reign of King Fahd Saudi Arabia adopted a new approach: it published a new edition of the Qurʾan for global distribution

201 See his accusation of Ḥanbalī partisanship against Shaykh Ḥammūd ibn ʿAbd Allāh al-Tuwayjirī in *Ṣifāt Ṣalāt al-Nabī*, 30.

202 Under Ibn Bāz the permanent fatwa council issued a fatwa describing *salafiyya* as a plural term for the *salaf* (the first three generations), but adding it is become a generic term for Sunni Muslims who follow the way of the *salaf*; Aḥmad ibn ʿAbd al-Rāziq al-Dawīsh, *Fatāwā al-Lajna al-Dāʾima li-l-Buḥūth al-ʿIlmiyya -wa-l-Daʿwā wa-l-Irshād*, 23 vols. (Riyadh: Dār al-Muʾayyad, 2003), 2: 165–6 (no. 1361).

203 'Bi-Shaʾn al-Khilāf al-Fiqhī bayn al-Madhāhib wa-l-Taʿaṣṣub al-Madhhabī,' *Majallat al-Majmaʿ al-Fiqhī al-Islāmī*, Year 4, 2nd edn (Mecca: World Muslim League, 2005), 383–6. The first resolution emerged from its tenth session; Mecca, 17–21 October 1987. Nabil Mouline suggests Wahhabism was more interested in establishing itself as the heir of classical Ḥanbalism than appropriating the term Salafism. Between 1960 and 2000, more than 300 classic Ḥanbalī works were edited and published. See Mouline, *The Clerics of Islam*, 45.

204 Aḥmad Maḥmūd Ṣubḥī, *Hal Yuʿadd al-Madhhab al-Wahhābī Salafiyyan?* (Alexandria: Dār al-Wafāʾ, 2004).

205 Rosie Bsheer, 'A Counter-Revolutionary State: Popular Movements and the Making of Saudi Arabia,' *Past and Present*, 239/1 (2018): 233–77. See also Toby Matthiesen, 'Saudi Arabia and the Cold War,' in *Salman's Legacy: The Dilemmas of a New Era in Saudi Arabia*, ed. Madawi Al-Rasheed (London: Hurst, 2018), 217–33. On the earlier, oil-based element of the relationship, see Robert Vitalis, *America's Kingdom: Mythmaking on the Saudi Oil Frontier* (Stanford: Stanford University Press, 2007).

through the King Fahd Complex for Printing the Holy Qur'an, the first such undertaking since al-Azhar published its version in 1926 following the dissolution of the Ottoman caliphate;[206] government funding for its coercive morality enforcement apparatus (Hay'at al-Amr bi-l-Ma'rūf wa-l-Nahy 'an al-Munkar) rose from 85.7 million riyals in 1979 to more than 203 million riyals in 1985, and in 1994 this body launched the journal *Majallat al-Ḥisba*, reasserting the state's monopoly in the policing of public morality in the face of Salafism's individualist empowerment;[207] and the Saudi government worked with its American counterpart to fund the Afghan mujahidin fighting the Soviets.

Salafiyya with the specific meaning al-Albānī had given it began to attain widespread currency from the 1980s. Abū Muḥammad al-Maqdisī, an associate of the Juhaymān group and acolyte of al-Albānī, deployed the terminology in a systematic manner in *Millat Ibrāhīm* (The Religion of Ibrahim, 1983).[208] In 1989 Egyptian *'ālim* Muḥammad al-Ghazālī (1917–96) condemned the 'alleged Salafism' (*salafiyya maz'ūma*)[209] challenging the traditional methodology of *fiqh*, provoking a vigorous response from al-Albānī and his Saudi followers.[210] Kevseri's torch of rejection was most notably taken up by the Syrian scholar Sa'īd Ramaḍān al-Būṭī (1929–2013), who published two notable refutations of the al-Albānī school, *Al-Lāmadhhabiyya: Akhṭar Bid'a Tuhaddid al-Sharī'a al-Islāmiyya* (Al-Lāmadhhabiyya: The Most Serious Innovation Threatening Islamic Shari'a, 1969) and *Al-Salafiyya: Marḥala Zamaniyya Mubāraka Lā Madhhab Islāmī* (Salafism: A Blessed Historical Phase, Not an Islamic School, 1988).[211] In the latter, despite the title, al-Būṭī effectively conceded

[206] Walid Saleh, 'The politics of Qur'anic hermeneutics: royalties on interpretation,' public lecture, www.international.ucla.edu/cnes/article/110233 (accessed 26 April 2019). Also, interview with Khaled Abou El Fadl: Franklin Foer, 'Moral Hazard,' *New Republic*, 18 November 2002.

[207] Mouline, *The Clerics of Islam*, 213.

[208] Abū Muḥammad al-Maqdisī, *Millat Ibrāhīm wa-Da'wā al-Anbiyā' wa-l-Mursalīn* (c.1984), 33, footnote 10; idem, *al-Kawāshif al-Jaliyya fī Kufr al-Dawla al-Sa'ūdiyya* (Amman: Minbar al-Tawḥīd wa-l-Jihād, 1989), 132.

[209] Muḥammad al-Ghazālī, *al-Sunna al-Nabawiyya bayn Ahl al-Fiqh wa-Ahl al-Ḥadīth* (Cairo: Dār al-Shurūq, 1989), 14–15.

[210] See the responses of al-Albānī, al-Wādi'ī and Rabī' al-Madkhalī in Abū 'Abd Allāh Shakīb al-Salafī, ed., *Aqwāl Ahl al-'Ilm fī Muḥammad al-Ghazālī al-Saqqā* (Riyadh: Saḥāb al-Salafiyya, nda). Also, Khaled Abou El Fadl, *The Great Theft: Wrestling Islam from the Extremists* (New York: Harper San Francisco, 2005), 93.

[211] See Andreas Christmann, 'Islamic Scholar and Religious Leader: A Portrait of Shaykh Muḥammad Sa'īd Ramaḍān al-Būṭī,' *Islam and Christian–Muslim Relations*, 9/2 (1998): 149–69.

that the *lā-madhhabiyya* resisted by Kevseri had successfully transformed itself into a school called *salafiyya*. At this time the term began to appear in the Western public arena. In his 1992 study *L'echec de l'Islam politique* (The Failure of Political Islam) Olivier Roy discussed Salafiyya solely in the context of the early century reform movement.[212] In examining what he called the 're-Islamization' of the 1980s and 1990s, he avoided the term Salafi for 'neo-fundamentalism', by which he intended the tradition of disengagement from political processes that was fostered by ʿulamaʾ in the Saudi orbit. However, in *Globalized Islam: The Search for a New Ummah*, published twelve years later, this neo-fundamentalism had become Salafism. Similarly, the original 2003 edition of Raymond Hinnebusch's study *The International Politics of the Middle East*, a standard work in the field, contains almost no discussion of Saudi deployment of Islam internationally,[213] while the 2015 imprint notes the Islamisation of its foreign policy, citing Saudi state support for Salafi networks in Egypt and Syria.[214]

If al-Albānī found a receptive audience in Saudi Arabia, this was far less the case in his native Syria, where, as in Turkey, Sufi networks and metaphysics retained much of the power they had enjoyed throughout the Ottoman period. The Baʿth government took an inimical position towards al-Albānī and his Salafi movement because, Thomas Pierret argues in a study of Syrian ʿulamaʾ, the state ceded control of the field of religious education to the existing body of traditionalist ʿulamaʾ, who upheld Ashʿarī-Māturīdī theology, Sufi practice, and *madhhab* adherence, and the ʿulamaʾ in turn used their position to further orient the state towards their views.[215] To popularise his ideas, al-Albānī promoted the work of a Tajik shaykh named Muḥammad Sulṭān al-Maʿṣūmī (1880–1960) who attained status in Saudi Arabia where he took up residence after studies in Cairo and Damascus. Al-Maʿṣūmī authored a fatwa in 1939, and printed in Cairo as a book in 1949, which responded to a request from Japanese converts in Tokyo regarding the obligation to choose a *madhhab*, since while Indians there favoured Ḥanafism Indonesians preferred the

212 Roy, *Globalized Islam*, 11–12, 31–5.

213 Raymond Hinnebusch, *The International Politics of the Middle East* (Manchester: Manchester University Press, 2003), 122.

214 Ibid., 84 (2015, 2nd edn).

215 Pierret, *Religion and State*, 23–63, 102. See also Annabelle Böttcher, 'Official Islam, Transnational Islamic Networks, and Regional Politics: The Case of Syria,' in *The Middle East and Palestine: Global Politics and Regional Conflict*, ed. Dietrich Jung (New York: Palgrave Macmillan, 2004), 125–50.

Shāfiʿī rite.[216] Al-Maʿṣumi's fatwa said not only that it was not necessary or recommended (*laysa bi-wājib wa-lā mandūb*) for the non-specialised Muslim to follow one school exclusively[217] but that any believer could circumvent the schools and ʿulamaʾ entirely through direct access to the Qurʾan and hadith collections.[218] Al-Maʿṣūmī gave al-Albānī a copy of his book when they met during the hajj pilgrimage in 1949.[219]

Al-Maʿṣūmī's book began to stir responses in Syria after al-Albānī reissued it under the title *Hal al-Muslim Mulzām bi-Ittibāʿ Madhhab Muʿayyan min al-Madhāhib al-Arbaʿa?* (Is the Muslim Required to Follow One of the Four Schools?).[220] Among several works written in response was al-Būṭī's *Lā-Madhhabiyya.*[221] This led to a personal encounter between al-Būṭī and al-Albānī in 1970 after the publication of al-Būṭī's first edition. In al-Būṭī's telling, al-Albānī came to him to complain that al-Būṭī had misunderstood the intent of al-Maʿṣūmī's book, which was simply that following

216 The question was relayed to al-Maʿṣūmī via two Central Asian Muslims in Tokyo, Muḥammad ʿAbd al-Ḥayy Qūr Bi-l-ʿAlī and Muhsin Çabakoğlu; al-Maʿṣūmī (ed. Salīm ibn ʿĪd al-Hilālī), *Hal al-Muslim Mulzām bi-Ittibāʿ Madhhab Muʿayyan min al-Madhāhib al-Arbaʿa?* (Riyadh: Markaz al-Dirāsāt al-Manhajiyya al-Salafiyya, 1984), 47. Al-Maʿṣūmī escaped Soviet persecution and made his way back to Mecca where he taught Turkish pilgrims at Dār al-Ḥadīth and wrote some works in Ottoman Turkish; al-Hilālī, 'Introduction,' in al-Maʿṣūmī, *Hal al-Muslim*, 14–15.

217 Al-Maʿṣūmī, *Hal al-Muslim*, 55. He comments: 'This path is easy to follow, it requires no more than [the six canonical hadith collections]. These books are well-known, you can obtain them in no time; you should know this if you didn't already.'

218 Ibid., 115–16. It is not clear why Japanese Muslims would not have consulted Abdürreşid Ibrāhīm, the Russian-Tatar who became the first imam of the Tokyo Mosque in 1938. Ibrāhīm has inspired a large literature in modern scholarship as an early figure of transnational Islam and Pan-Asianism. See Noriko Yamazaki, 'Abdürreşid İbrahim's Journey to China: Muslim Communities in the Late Qing as Seen by a Russian-Tatar Intellectual,' *Central Asian Survey*, 33:3 (2014): 414; Ulrich Brandenburg, 'The Multiple Publics of a Transnational Activist: Abdürreşid İbrahim, Pan-Asianism, and the Creation of Islam in Japan,' *Die Welt des Islams*, 58 (2018): 143–72; Komatsu Hisao, 'Muslim Intellectuals and Japan: A Pan-Islamist mediator, Abdurreshid Ibrahim,' in Dudoignon, Hisao and Yasushi, *Intellectuals in the Modern Islamic World*, 273–88.

219 It was among books mandated by the Saudi directorate for scientific research, fatwas, preaching and guidance after it was set up in 1971 for use in proselytization abroad; Ayman al-Yassini, *Religion and State in the Kingdom of Saudi Arabia* (Boulder, CO: Westview Press, 1985), 71. Saudi publications since the 1980s have framed al-Maʿṣūmī as a Salafi, though his texts do not use this language at all. Stefan Wild's claim that al-Maʿṣūmī described himself as a *salafī* seems unfounded; Wild, 'Muslim und Madhhab,' 679.

220 Al-Hilālī, 'Introduction,' 16–17.

221 Saʿīd Ramaḍān al-Būṭī, *Al-Lāmadhhabiyya: Akhṭar Bidʿa Tuḥaddid al-Sharīʿa al-Islāmiyya* (Damascus: 1970, 2nd edn), 15–26 (preface to 2nd edn). See Muḥammad al-Ḥāmid, *Luzūm Ittibāʿ Madhāhib al-Āʾimma Ḥasman li-l-Fawḍā al-Dīniyya* (1970) and Aḥmad ʿIzz al-Dīn Bayānūnī, *Al-Ijtihād wa-l-Mujtahidūn* (1968).

the methodology of the schools is fine for those among the ʿulamaʾ who have not attained the status of absolute *mujtahid*.[222] Al-Būṭī defined *lā-madhhabiyya* as the thesis that neither laymen nor non-*mujtahid* ʿulamaʾ are required to follow any of the four schools, exclusively or through shifting freely among them.[223] Al-Albānī said this was to misunderstand al-Maʿṣūmī's intent, which his lack of native expression in Arabic may have muddied; he further asserted that there is no such thing as *lā-madhhabiyya* since a layman or *ʿālim* who has not reached the level of *ijtihād* is obliged to follow the imams of the schools.[224] Al-Būṭī was sceptical about al-Albānī's claim that both he and al-Maʿṣūmī advocated nothing more than expanded rights to *ijtihād* among ʿulamaʾ.[225] Muḥammad ʿĪd ʿAbbāsī (b. 1938), a disciple of al-Albānī, responded with another version of the meeting as well as an account of his own session with al-Būṭī.[226] Notably in this book ʿAbbasi made liberal use of the terms Salafi and Salafism to describe the al-Albānī circle as they tried to rebut the charge of *lā-madhhabiyya* that began with Kevseri.[227] Al-Albānī was forced to leave Syria for good in 1979, and the circle of ʿAbd al-Qādir al-Arnāʾūṭ (1928–2004), the main representative of the al-Albānī Salafis who remained in Syria, never gained much following or status in his absence,[228] though Salafism later became influential through the transnational networks established since the 1990s in the context of late twentieth-century globalisation and the communications revolution.[229]

An institution exerting hegemonic power over orthodoxy and orthopraxis, al-Azhar no more succumbed to the neo-Ḥanbalī assault on mainstream Ashʿarī theology than did Syrian seminaries.[230] But scepticism

222 Al-Būṭī, *Al-Lāmadhhabiyya*, 15.
223 Ibid., 16.
224 Ibid., 15, 22.
225 Al-Būṭī also notes that if al-Albānī is to be believed he is giving far more leeway to al-Maʿṣūmī than he did to Ibn ʿArabī when he declared him an infidel; ibid., 21.
226 Al-Būṭī records this discussion too; ibid., 133–48, where al-Būṭī relates a debate with an unnamed figure who appears to be Abbāsī. For Abbasi's account, see Muḥammad ʿĪd Abbāsī, *Bidʿat al-Taʿaṣṣub al-Madhhabī wa-Āthāruhā al-Khaṭīra fī Jumūd al-Fikr wa-Inḥiṭāṭ al-Muslimīn* (Amman: al-Maktaba al-Islāmiyya, 1986 [1970]), 273–5. Abbasī's version of the al-Būṭī/al-Albānī meeting can be found at 336–46.
227 Al-Būṭī, *Al-Lāmadhhabiyya*, 17, footnote 1 acknowledges that they claim to represent *salafiyya*. On al-Albānī's rejection of the term, see Emad Hamdeh, 'Qurʾān and Sunna or the Madhhabs?: A Salafi Polemic Against Islamic Legal Tradition,' *Islamic Law and Society*, 24 (2017): 211–53.
228 Pierret, *Religion and State*, 108.
229 Ibid., 115.
230 Al-Azhar held a conference in defence of Ashʿarism in 2010, attended by al-Būṭī and Ḥuṣām al-Dīn al-Farfūr; cited in Pierret, *Religion and State*, 127.

about Sufism and *madhhab* adherence found firm roots, First through the activities of modernists such as al-Afghānī, ʿAbduh, and Riḍā, then more rigorously through the activities of the Anṣār al-Sunna al-Muḥammadiyya.[231] Al-Albānī here becomes the bridge to *salafiyya*, the link between Anṣār al-Sunna and the establishment of an Egyptian Salafi movement from the 1970s. Al-Albānī took part in two meetings of a hadith committee established by the waqf ministry in 1960 to establish a methodology on authentic hadith; such a rationalising enterprise appealed to the Nasserist state and its Kemalist drive to harness and direct religion in the service of modernisation.[232] Among the figures he met during the trip al-Albānī cites four: Muḥammad al-Ghazālī, who would have opposed his ideas (and he describes as *ustādh* rather than shaykh), Muḥibb al-Dīn al-Khaṭīb, the early propagandist for modernist Salafism, Shaykh ʿAbd al-Razzāq ʿAfīfī (1905–94), a former leader of Anṣār al-Sunna al-Muḥammadiyya who had moved to Saudi Arabia where he was appointed to the Council of Senior Religious Scholars,[233] Shaykh ʿAbd al-ʿAzīz ibn Rashīd Āl Ḥusayn (d. 1982/3), a Najdi who studied at al-Azhar and rejected *madhhab* methodology,[234] and Shaykh al-Sayyid Sābiq, the head of the ministry's cultural division who had published a *madhhab*-critical manual on *fiqh* at Ḥasan al-Bannā's request in 1946 (republished by al-Albānī in 1987).[235] In 1976 the organisation called al-Daʿwā al-Salafiyya was established in Alexandria with a mandate uniting the

[231] Sedgwick, *Muhammad Abduh*, 119.

[232] On his return al-Albānī discussed the committee's work in an interview with a Syrian daily; 'Ṣawt al-ʿArab Tasʾal wa-l-Muḥaddith Nāṣir al-Dīn al-Albānī Yujīb,' *Ṣawt al-ʿArab*, 28 April 1960; www.ahlalhdeeth.com/vb/showthread.php?t=256132 (accessed 2 September 2018). He convinced the ministry to publish Shihāb al-Dīn al-Būṣīrī's (d. 1436) hadith collection *Zawāʾid Ibn Mājah*, containing authentic hadith related only by Ibn Mājah and not found in the other five canonical collections.

[233] On ʿAfīfī, see Muḥammad ibn Aḥmad Sayyid Aḥmad, *al-Shaykh al-ʿAllāma ʿAbd al-Razzāq ʿAfīfī: Ḥayātuhu al-ʿIlmiyya, wa-Juhūduhu al-Daʿwiyya, wa-Āthāruhu al-Ḥamīda* (Riyadh: Maktabat al-Sawādī, 1418 [1997–8]).

[234] See al-Ṭāhir, *Jamāʿat Anṣār al-Sunna al-Muḥammadiyya*, 229–33; and Muḥammad Khayr Yūsuf, *Tatimmat al-Aʿlām li-l-Ziriklī*, 2 vols. (Beirut: Dār Ibn Ḥazm, 1998), 1:298.

[235] Al-Sayyid Sābiq, *Fiqh al-Sunna* (Jeddah: Dār al-Qibla al-Thaqāfīyya al-Islāmiyya, 1945); and al-Albānī, *Tamām al-Minna fī Taʿlīq ʿalā Fiqh al-Sunna* (Amman: al-Maktaba al-Islāmiyya, 1987 [1953]). Sābiq writes in his introduction that he wants to challenge *madhhab* partisanship and the idea of the closed door of *ijtihād*, a notion he said Western Orientalists had propagated. Saʿīd Ramaḍān, who married al-Bannā's daughter Wafāʾ and established the Brotherhood's regional and international presence in the 1950s and 60s, advanced the same ideas in *Islamic Law: Its Scope and Equity* (1970). Salafi shaykhs such as Abū Isḥāq al-Ḥuwaynī say Sābiq based his book on al-Shawkānī's *Nayl al-*

key elements that defined the movement, namely, rejection of: Ashʿarī-Māturīdī theology, *madhhab* methodology, Sufi belief and practice,[236] and the political activism of the Muslim Brotherhood, which with its re-emergence after Nasserist repression was significantly influenced by the al-Albānī revolution.[237] Through the discourse of Salafism the creedal questions of *irjāʾ* and *takfīr* became defining issues of Islam in the public sphere in the later twentieth century, following the earlier stage in the construction of modern Islamic thought characterised by the work of figures like ʿAbduh and their political heirs like al-Bannā.[238]

SALAFISM AND MODERN SCHOLARSHIP

Scholarship on the Salafi phenomenon has demonstrated three tendencies: First, a conflation of the modernist and Salafi movements; second, backdating what would be recognisably Salafism today to earlier historical periods; third, feeding Salafism's self-image as the expression of an original essence of Islam. I have argued that *salafiyya* is the outcome of a discursive genealogy in three stages: a proto-*salafiyya* in the nineteenth century before the terminology takes full form, emergence in public discourse in the early twentieth century but with multiple meanings, and the arrival of al-Albānī Salafism in the 1960s through the possibilities for mobilisation and intellectual production in Saudi Arabia, marking the

Awṭār; see this archived chatroom www.ahlalhdeeth.com/vb/archive/index.php/t-44680.html (accessed 10 August 2019).

236 On the fate of Sufism in Egypt in the twentieth century, the major works are Michael Gilsenan, *Saint and Sufi in Modern Egypt: An Essay in the Sociology of Religion* (Oxford: Clarendon Press, 1973) and Valerie Hoffman, *Sufism, Mystics, and Saints in Modern Egypt* (Columbia, SC: University of South Carolina Press, 1995).

237 On Salafi influence on the Muslim Brotherhood see Ḥusām Tammām, *Tasalluf al-Ikhwān: Taʾākul al-Uṭrūḥa al-Ikhwāniyya wa-Ṣuʿūd al-Salafiyya fī Jamāʿat al-Ikhwān al-Muslimīn* (Alexandria, Egypt: Bibliotheca Alexandrina/Future Studies Unit, 2010). On today's Salafism in Egypt see A. Shalata, *al-Ḥāla al-Salafiyya al-Muʿāṣira fī Miṣr* (Cairo: Madbouly, 2013); Aḥmad Salim and ʿUmar Basyuni, *Mā Baʿd al-Salafiyya: Qirāʾa Naqdiyya fī al-Khiṭāb al-Salafī al-Muʿāṣir* (Cairo: Markaz Namā, 2015); and Richard Gauvain, *Salafi Ritual Purity: In the Presence of God* (London: Routledge, 2013). On Lebanon see Zoltan Pall, *Lebanese Salafis between the Gulf and Europe* (Amsterdam: Amsterdam University Press, 2013), and Robert Rabil, *Salafism in Lebanon from Apoliticism to Transnational Jihadism* (Washington, DC: Georgetown University Press, 2014).

238 Developing the ʿAbduh-Rida agenda questioning the schools and Sufi practices, Salafism remained a term for modernist Islam far longer in Morocco. See Malika Zeghal, *Islamism in Morocco: Religion, Authoritarianism, and Electoral Politics* (Princeton: Markus Wiener Publishers, 2008), *passim*; and Lauzière, *The Making of Salafism*, 60–95.

beginning of semantic clarity over who the Salafis are and what they represent. Frank Griffel has a similar view, noting the genesis of the term in the modern period, its elastic and jargonistic nature, and its broad application, from rationalist reformers to today's Salafis who see in ʿAbduh, al-Afghānī, and even Riḍā[239] the antithesis of almost everything they stand for.[240] Khaled El-Rouayheb also rejects the notion of what he calls a 'timeless Salafism' that appears across a variety of writing impacted by modern secular, Islamist, and nationalist readings of history.[241] This position tends to see modernism and Salafism as separate movements and both as recent historical developments.

Another general trend has been to think of them both as part of a broader historical process which could be understood through the Salafi concept. Pierret considers al-Albānī's circle as unsophisticated versions of the Brotherhood-leaning white-collar professionals he considers to be the true Salafis, united in their drive for purified belief and practice.[242] Itzchak Weismann sees the origins of Salafism in the modernist movement which favoured constitutional government against Hamidian authoritarianism and opposed an irrational, ecstatic, and esoteric Sufism.[243] Jonathan Brown takes a longer historical view situated in hadith studies. Following Lucas' suggestion that the post-Shāfiʿī scholars of the formative period who most rigorously focussed on producing substantive *fiqh* from purely Qurʾan and prophetic hadith could be term Salafis,[244] Brown proposed that Salafi could be used to describe the Ahl al-Ḥadīth movement itself since in his view it forms the heart of Sunnism. Further, he considers that their literalist creedal positions, particularly on God's spatial and positional attributes, represent the 'original Sunni theological school' – a statement that appears to concede the claims of its adherents.[245] From the eighteenth century this opposition to different strands of rationalist thinking (law, theology, hadith) transmogrifies into an effervescence of counter-culture reform movements, questioning the notion of

239 Khaled Abou El Fadl, *The Great Theft*, 92.

240 Frank Griffel, 'What Do We Mean By "Salafī"? Connecting Muḥammad ʿAbduh with Egypt's Nūr Party in Islam's Contemporary Intellectual History,' *Die Welt des Islams*, 55 (2015): 186–220.

241 El-Rouayheb, *Islamic Intellectual History*, 15, 191.

242 Pierret, *Religion and State*, 103–5, 141–2.

243 Weismann, 'Abū l-Hudā l-Ṣayyādī and the Rise of Islamic Fundamentalism,' 586–92.

244 Scott C. Lucas, 'The Legal Principles of Muḥammad b. Ismāʿīl Al-Bukhārī and their Relationship to Classical Salafi Islam,' *Islamic Law and Society*, 13/3 (2006): 289–324.

245 Brown, *Hadith*, 180–2. He describes Kevseri as an 'extreme Ashʿarī' (p. 181).

consensus in canonical hadith and the institutionalisation of Ashʿarī-Māturīdism, that Brown divides into Traditionalist Salafism and Modernist Salafism.[246] All of Ibn ʿAbd al-Wahhāb, ʿAbduh, and al-Albānī would be subsumed under the rubric of Salafism according to the logic of this schema.

Another position has been to think of the modernism and Salafism as separate trends, but the Salafi among them as more historically authentic. For Henri Lauzière, whose ideas develop the approach of Bernard Haykel, Salafism is an appropriate name for the theological position of Ibn Taymiyya and his supporters and on this basis he depicts the one-time expansion of the term to encompass modernists as an act of propagandistic malfeasance by Riḍā, al-Khaṭīb, and Louis Massignon. While he agrees there was no Salafism by that name before the early twentieth century, Lauzière suggests *salafī* was a recognisable epithet in the post-classical period for Ḥanbalī dogma. Thus, 'premodern Muslims recognized a distinct Salafi school of thought that informed not only theology but also law'.[247] Following an initial article on the question published in 2010, Lauzière doubled down on his argument that Ḥanbalī theologians are the rightful owners of *salafiyya*, first in response to an article by Griffel,[248] then in a book.[249] Basheer Nafi and Butrus Abu Manneh also think of Salafi as an appropriate term for Ḥanbalī creed but one that expresses a return of Islam to its Arab roots. Nafi talks of the 'irrepressible Salafi determination to delineate man's position and limits' which corrected a long period of Arab-Islamic decline caused by the culture of Sufism and Ashʿarī intellectualism.[250] Abu Manneh discusses Salafism as a complement to the Arab *nahḍa* and response to Ottoman policies of division in Arab provinces.[251]

246 Ibid., 251–61. Brown, *Canonization*, 333–4.

247 Lauzière, 'The Construction of Salafiyya,' 372.

248 Henri Lauzière, 'What We Mean Versus What They Meant by "Salafi": A Reply to Frank Griffel,' *Die Welt des Islams*, 56/1 (2016): 89–96.

249 Henri Lauzière, *The Making of Salafism: Islamic Reform in the Twentieth Century* (New York: Columbia University Press, 2016). Possibly unaware of Kevseri's battle over the Salafi label, Lauzière accuses the Egyptian shaykh Yūsuf al-Dijwi of wantonly describing ʿAbduh as a Salafi in his booklet *Kalima fī al-Salafiyya al-Ḥāḍira* (1930), but in fact al-Dijwī was writing in support of Kevseri; see 'The Construction of Salafiyya,' 381–2.

250 Nafi, 'Abu al-Thanaʾal-Alusi,' 485–6. See also Nafi, 'A Teacher of Ibn ʿAbd al-Wahhāb: Muḥammad Ḥayāt al-Sindī and the Revival of Aṣḥāb al-Ḥadīth's Methodology,' *Islamic Law and Society* 13 (2006): 208–41.

251 Butrus Abu Manneh, 'Salafiyya and the Rise of the Khalidiyya in Baghdad in the Early Nineteenth Century,' *Die Welt des Islams*, 43/3 (2003): 349–72; idem, 'The Sultan and the Bureaucracy: The Anti-Tanzimat Concepts of Grand Vizier Mahmud Nedim Paşa,' *IJMES*, 22/3 (1990): 257–74.

The theory of timeless Salafism has been argued most vigorously by Bernard Haykel. In an article that sets out to give 'the pre-modern history of this movement', Haykel cites usages of *salafī/salafiyya/madhhab al-salaf* in two texts to argue that Salafism is a legitimate designation for both a literalist approach to the Qurʾanic text and scripturalist approach to sources of law. Haykel offers examples of *salaf*, *salafiyya*, and *madhhab al-salaf* from Ibn Taymiyya[252] in particular to imply, without stating it directly, that Salafism was a recognised term denoting the Ḥanbalī school or a branch thereof, ignoring the fact that al-Ghazālī and others debated the question of whose views among the schools of Sufis, philosophers, jurists, and theologians could be said to represent the *salaf* and that when the terminology made its appearance in the twentieth century there was widespread disagreement about what it meant. However, Haykel seemed shy of his own bold theory. Roel Meijer, editor of the 2009 volume in which Haykel's article appeared, wrote in his preface outlining the contributions that Haykel had proven the Abbasid origins of Salafism. In his article published one year later Lauzière seemed to absolve Haykel of this claim, stating plainly that since the primary sources do not 'explicitly corroborate' it Meijer must have got ahead of himself in his summation of Haykel's ideas.[253] Indeed, it is difficult to envisage any scholar in previous decades advancing the Haykel–Lauzière thesis, with its specific framing and formulations, since the Salafism they sought to furnish with an illustrious historical pedigree, whether with the name (Haykel) or without it (Lauzière), had not yet been imagined. Their approach brings to mind Foucault's warning of the dangers of creating 'unities of discourse' in disciplines such as the history of science, philosophy, literature, or

[252] Bernard Haykel, 'On the Nature of Salafi Thought and Action,' in Meijer, *Global Salafism*, 38. He cites ʿAbd al-Karīm al-Samʿānī (d. 1166), a Shāfiʿī biographer of scholars, who in his *Kitāb al-Ansāb* described *al-salafī* as 'an attribution to *al-salaf* and following their *madhhab*'. Al-Samʿānī gives three examples of such people, but their names are missing or illegible in manuscripts; *Kitāb al-Ansab*, 13 vols. (Hayderabad: Dāʾirat al-Maʿārif al-ʿUthmāniyya, 1976), 7:168–9. His second example is from Ibn Taymiyya, who used terms such as *salafiyya* to refer to the companions and *madhhab al-salaf* to refer to their teachings, as previously discussed.

[253] Meijer writes, 'As Bernard Haykel shows in chapter 1, the name Salafism goes back to the Ahl al-Ḥadīth during the Abbasid caliphate'; 'Introduction,' *Global Salafism*, 4. Lauzière writes with reference to Meijer's statement, 'Although Haykel left *salafiyya* untranslated, his contribution has quickly been taken to mean that a single noun translatable as "Salafism" goes back to the medieval period. Primary sources, however, do not explicitly corroborate this claim.' Lauzière, 'Construction of Salafiyya,' 371, footnote 9.

thought, where there is in fact disruption and discontinuity.[254] We can also identify in the discourse of Salafism the aligning of texts to meet the needs of 'national classicism' examined by Hans Robert Jauss of the Konstanz school in his study of national literatures, whereby narratives of origin, with their absolute beginning, middle, and totalising end, are deployed in the production of intellectual history conforming to contemporary realities and understandings.[255]

The wider issue here is that of the organisation of Islamic knowledge, who organises it, when, and why. Since the nineteenth century there has been a convergence of approach among much Western scholarship and reform trends in centring narrations of the Islamic tradition around legalism and to that end the ideas of Ibn Taymiyya.[256] Despite different desired outcomes, they shared an interest in producing fixed knowledge from divine texts, in establishing the centrality of scripture, in imagining a fully-formed first religion 'after which the authenticity of the original article is progressively corrupted',[257] and in placing law, rather than the practice of theological reasoning, philosophy, logic, or the experiential phenomena of popular practices, at the heart of their Islam.[258] On the other hand, the approach of figures such as Kevseri and al-Būṭī aligns somewhat with recent directions in Western scholarship critical of this legalistic approach. In *Kubrā al-Yaqīniyyāt al-Kawniyya* (The Greatest of Universal Certainties, 1969), which addressed modern Western philosophies and ideologies using *Mawqif al-ʿAql* as its model, al-Būṭī argued that both *lā-madhhabiyya* and the reformers' embrace of empiricism were a product of British interference following the 1882 occupation of

254 Michel Foucault, *The Archaeology of Knowledge* (London: Routledge, 2002); 23–5, 173, 187.

255 Hans Robert Jauss (trans. Timothy Bahti), *Toward an Aesthetic of Reception* (Minneapolis: University of Minnesota Press, 1982), 51, 54, 110–12.

256 Leonard Binder, *Islamic Liberalism: A Critique of Development Ideologies* (Chicago: University of Chicago Press, 1988), 96; also Carool Kersten's comment on the critical thinkers Mohammed Arkoun and Muḥammad ʿĀbid al-Jābirī in Kersten, 'Critical Islam: Muslims and their Religion in a Post-Islamist World,' *Singapore Middle East Papers, Volume VI* (2015), 119.

257 Shahab Ahmed, *What Is Islam?*, 219.

258 On scholarship's sidelining of Sufism as central to Islamic faith and practice, see Bernd Radtke, 'Between Projection and Suppression: Some Considerations Concerning the Study of Sufism,' in Frederick De Jong, ed., *Shiʿa Islam, Sects and Sufism*, 70–82. Itzchak Weismann argues that Sufism has created its own equally hostile discourse of Salafi and modernist fundamentalism; 'Modernity from Within: Islamic Fundamentalism and Ṣufism,' in *Sufis and Salafis in the Contemporary Age*, ed. Lloyd Ridgeon (London: Bloomsbury, 2016), 30.

Egypt.[259] Turkish devout intellectual Hüseyin Hilmi Işık (1911–2001) denounced as 'Orientalist unbelievers' (*müsteşrik kafirler*) a broad range of forces he saw as disruptive to the Islamic tradition, including political ideologues of the twentieth century such as Abū al-Aʿlā Mawdūdī and Sayyid Quṭb – about whom more will be said in Chapter 5.[260]

Considered by some an appropriate designation for the modernist reformers and by others a blanket term embracing the gamut of change movements since the eighteenth century, Salafism eventually became the property of al-Albānī and his followers. Spurred by the Afghan jihad and the September 11 attacks in New York and Washington of 2001, Salafism metastasised in Western public fora into a burgeoning field traversing government policy circles, think tanks, and academia, some of it under the rubric of the equally neophyte Security Studies, and this has impacted how Islam is understood as a religion in the general culture, scholarly literature, and Muslim communities in terms of belief, law, practice, governance, economy, political ideology, and insurrectionary force.[261] It is a victory at the level of discourse that many Muslim scholars, foremost amongst them Kevseri, fought to avoid.

[259] Saʿīd Ramaḍān al-Būṭī, *Kubrā al-Yaqīniyyāt al-Kawniyya: Wujūd al-Khāliq wa-Waẓīfat al-Makhlūq* (Damascus: Dār al-Fikr, 1997), 222–8; idem, *al-Lamadhhabiyya*, 129–30.

[260] Hüseyin Hilmi Işık, *The Religion Reformers in Islam* (Istanbul: Ikhlas Publications, 1978), 133; *Dinde Reformcular* (Istanbul: Işık Kitabevi, 1976), 170. A chemist by training Işık became an adept of the Nakşibendi shaykh Abdülhakîm Arvasi (1865–1943), as did poet Necip Fazıl Kısakürek.

[261] See the widely used typology of jihadi Salafism (*jihādiyya*), political Salafism (*siyāsiyya*) and scholarly Salafism (*ʿilmiyya*) developed by Quintan Wiktorowicz; Wiktorowicz, 'Anatomy of the Salafi Movement,' *Studies in Conflict and Terrorism*, 29/3 (2006): 207–39. In this schema al-Albānī is a quietist figure from whom others deviate. A major text is Meijer's *Global Salafism*.

FIGURE 1.1 The Turkish government organised celebrations throughout 2021 marking 100 years since Akif's national anthem was adopted. President Erdoğan is seen speaking here at a ceremony on 11 March 2021.
Source: Halil Sagirkaya – Anadolu Agency via Getty Images

FIGURE 1.2 Akif was buried in the Edirnekapı cemetery in Istanbul next to his colleague Ahmed Naim and Süleyman Nazif, a Young Turk governor who published a hagiographical book about Akif in 1924. The inscription reads: 'The great poet of our *İstiklal Marşı*, Mehmet Akif Ersoy.'
Source: İsa Özdere – Alamy

FIGURE 1.3 Akif (back row, second from left) on a trip to the Pyramids with Abbas Halim to his right, probably in the early 1930s since Akif sent the photograph to his family with a letter referring to Egypt's Great Depression-related economic difficulties.
Source: Gamma-Keystone via Getty Images

FIGURE 2.1 A portrait of Zahid Kevseri likely taken in Cairo.
Source: Rıhle Kitap

FIGURE 2.2 Kevseri (right) in Cairo with his student ʿAbd al-Fattāḥ Abū Ghudda. Source: unknown

FIGURE 2.3 Kevseri's tomb near the Kaḥlāwī mosque in the al-Shāfiʿī cemetery in Cairo, next to the graves of his daughters Seniha and Meliha. The inscription contains Arabic verse he composed: 'Those who stand at the grave reflecting how the visitor one day is buried the next/Beware the sudden decree of death, pray for those who passed/Zāhid al-Kawtharī lies in his resting place, seeking mercy, begging forgiveness, waiting.'
Source: Patrick Werr

FIGURE 2.4 Plaque on the street marking the site of Kevseri's tomb.
Source: Patrick Werr

FIGURE 3.1 A portrait of Mustafa Sabri sometime during his early Cairo years. Source: unknown

FIGURE 3.2 Sabri's grave in the al-Ghafīr cemetery in Cairo. He is buried on the far right, behind Mehmed İhsan Efendi. The graves on the left are of other scholars buried inside the enclosure. The Ottoman inscription at the back on the right – a poem penned by his son İbrahim – reads:
'Visitor, here is buried a true hero who died a martyr/Seeking the beloved God to whom he was forever devoted. He sacrificed for the Merciful in a disloyal world/ He fought for the Islam with which he was captivated. His deep knowledge was inspired by God, as if he were filled with divine knowledge/Though he remained Turk, Muslims and Islam were indebted to him. Sheikh ül-islam Mustafa Sabri died willingly for his thought/Worthy it would be for a voice from the Unseen to tell the country: "This grief is more than all others".'
Source: Mustafa Öztürk – Anadolu Agency

FIGURE 3.3 İbrahim Sabri was buried in the Brookwood cemetery near London where he died on 28 July 1983 during a visit from Egypt for medical treatment. The Arabic inscription on the tombstone describes him as 'İbrahim Sabri, son of his excellence Shaykh Mustafa Sabri, former shaykh al-islam of the Ottoman state.' Source: Andrew Hammond

5

Nation-State, Islamic State

The Egypt Exiles and New Political Imaginaries

This chapter looks at Mehmed Akif's fundamental acceptance of the nation-state and reconciliation of Turkish and Islamic identity and sets that against Sabri and Kevseri's theoretical objections, which centre on the argument that the shariʿa system with its notion of a legal and moral core above the manipulations of politics and society was superior to man-made law. Noting that their work came (1) as Egypt finalised the process of codification and de-Islamisation of its courts and (2) as the era of military authoritarianism began its long reign in the Arab region, it goes on to examine Sabri's development of a radical view of Islamic faith and identity in the context of the modern state and how this may have impacted Sayyid Quṭb's thinking.

AKIF'S COMPROMISE WITH *TÜRKÇÜLÜK*

A modernist Islamic thinker like Mehmed Akif was far more comfortable with nationalist ideology and the nation-state than his peers in Turkish Islamic thought, Mustafa Sabri and Zahid Kevseri. While on the one hand, and not least in the Ottoman context, nationalism re-ordered borders, shunted – even annihilated – populations, changed language, re-framed history, and spawned new popular cultures, it also established politico-juridical arenas in which the Islamic, even if in a form radically different from the pre-modern and pre-colonial notion of what constituted Islam, would function within a new epistemic and ontological paradigm. Language played an important part in this process: through the nation-state, Arabic is propagated as official language across what comes to be called the Arab world and Turkish extends to all corners of the Turkish republic in media, education, literature, etc. In other words, two languages of Islamic high culture are set in stone as the medium through which generations of Muslims are socialised, and in time, as radical secular-nationalist polities such as Kemalist Turkey, Nasserist Egypt, Baʿthist Syria and Iraq, or Pahlavi Iran come into being, new renditions of the Islamic assert themselves hegemonically across all fields of life through reactions to and accommodations with the language, institutions, and ideologies of the twentieth-century nation-state.

Resistance to nationalist organisation was, however, stiff among the first generation of Ottoman-Turkish Islamists. Akif was of a generation that experienced nationalism as a means of dis-establishing Islam and propagating positivist reformulations of political and social structures, and *Safahat* wrestles with this development. Akif began to make concessions to Turkist vocabulary after the war ended and Istanbul fell under occupation, as seen in his *Asım*, published between 1919 and 1924, and texts of his 1920–1 sermons in favour of Ankara's challenge to the European powers who had been victorious in 1918. Akif had rejected ethnic chauvinism in the context of the severing of Albania from Istanbul as an independent state in November 1912. In a column published in *Sırat-ı Müstakim* in March 1910, Akif became one of many to take issue with Abdullah Cevdet's Ottoman translation of Dutch Orientalist Reinhart Dozy's (1820–83) *Essai sur l'histoire de l'Islamisme* (1879), published in Cairo in 1908 as *Tarih-i İslâmiyet*. The translation was something of a watershed as the first major Ottoman book publication openly critical of Islam,[1] including its suggestion that the Prophet suffered from epilepsy or a psychogenic muscular disorder, but with an introduction by Cevdet praising the work.[2] Akif focussed on Dozy's concluding discussion of whether Islam would lose its power in the manner of European Christianity for reasons of the ethnic and linguistic diversity of its adherents.[3] In his view the book 'took a blunt axe' (*bir kör baltayı eline alırdı*) to the Ottoman unity of Albanian, Turk, Arab, Laz, Kurd, and

[1] M. Şükrü Hanioğlu, 'Garbcılar: Their Attitudes toward Religion and Their Impact on the Official Ideology of the Turkish Republic,' *Studia Islamica*, 86 (1997): 137. The controversy over Cevdet's book is discussed in Sevda Ayluçtarhan, *Abdullah Cevdet's Translations (1908–1910): The Making of a Westernist Culture Repertoire in a Resistant Ottoman Context* (Saarbrücken: Lap Lambert Academic Publishing, 2017), 89–149.

[2] Reinhart Dozy, *Essai sur l'histoire de l'Islamisme* (Paris: Maisonneuve, 1879), 22–3. This was a translation of the 1863 Dutch original.

[3] Ibid., 534–6.

Circassian.[4] In Ottoman Māturīdī style, Akif stated that Islam does not permit inspection of an individual's belief, but, he added, in Cevdet's case it is legitimate to consider whether he is in fact an atheist. Akif took up the same theme following the Albanian loss in a hadith commentary dated to March 1913 that appeared in the third *Safahat* collection. He depicts both *kavmiyet* and *medeniyet* – which seem to stand here for secular nationalism – as concepts that will cause the disintegration of the Ottoman state and says his father would have been appalled at the failure to save Albania.[5] The final section of *Fatih Kürsüsünde*, the fourth *Safahat* published in 1914, was a paean to the Balkans as a lost Andalusia. More attention to Islamic education through establishing Qur'anic schools for children could have firmed the Albanians' commitment to Istanbul and prevented rebellion, he suggested.[6] The same point on preserving Islam's community of ethnic groups was repeated in his Bayezid mosque sermon of February 1913 and two of his Qur'anic commentaries published in the period 1912–13.[7]

In *Süleymaniye Kürsüsünde*, published in August 1912, Akif's mosque preacher rails against *kavmiyet* as a device for creating the division that enables colonial rule, 'the earthquake that will destroy Islam at its base' (*İslamı/Temelinden yıkacak zelzele*).[8] In contrast to *kavmiyet*, *milliyet* is held up as a concept of identity that embraces different ethnicities (*akvam*), a sort of Islamic nationalism, as Gökalp too understood *milliyet/milliyetçilik* in his writings at this time. But positivist intellectuals, who he implies are those associated with the CUP through his use of the word *terakki*, have gone too far in their attempts to craft nationalism as a set of characteristics for each people (*her millet için ancak o mahiyettır*),[9] with religion a secondary or regressive element that can have no role in progress. Akif's preacher, who is modelled on Abdürreşid İbrahim, the Tatar *ʿālim* who travelled in the Far East, concludes with the example of Japan. Akif/İbrahim argue that Japan has advanced – defeating China in 1895, Russia in 1905, and annexing Korea in 1910 – through staying true to its

4 Akif, 'Ebüzziya Tevfik Efendi'ye (Açık Mektup),' *SM*, 18 Şubat 1325 (3 March 1910), 3/78: 409.

5 Akif, *Hakkın Sesleri*, in *Safahat*, 261–7, dated 28 Rebiulevvel 1331 (7 March 1913).

6 Ibid., 359–60.

7 Akif, 'Hutbe ve Mevaiz: Bayezid Kürsüsünde,' *SR*, 20 Kanunısani 1328 (2 February 1913), 2/48 (9/230): 374; Akif, 'Tefsir-i Şerif,' *SR*, 7 Haziran 1328 (20 June 1912), 1/16 (8/198): 293–4; Akif, 'Tefsir-i Şerif,' *SR*, 27 Eylül 1328 (10 October 1912), 2/32 (9/214): 101–2.

8 Akif, *Safahat*, 230.

9 Ibid., 241.

own values while taking from the West only its technology ('To push through all stages of progress/Let your own "spiritual identity" be your guide/Since hope of salvation without it is futile').[10] Akif advances here a reasoning that is circular in that Japan's ethnic and linguistic homogeneity could equally well be cited as the cause of its success; it also omits Japan's Confucian, Buddhist, and shamanistic traditions. Ibrahim's book on Islam in Japan, *Alem-i İslam ve Japonya'da İntişar-ı İslamiyet* (The Islamic World and the Spread of Islam in Japan), printed in Istanbul in 1912 from material serialised since 1909 in Akif's journal, stressed Japan's patriarchal traditions. A more rigorous attempt to understand Japanese culture and its elements that could not easily be syncretised with Islamic belief and practice was undertaken by writer Samizade Süreyya (1869–1941) in *Büyük Japonya* (Great Japan, 1917). For Akif, however, there was no conundrum because his modernist approach, with its inspiration in ʿAbduh, saw the Japanese as Muslims in all but name: a conscientious, hard-working, moral people who in his telling only allowed in as much of Western method as necessary. 'Let me say this much: there the clear religion [Islam]/And its bounteous spirit have spread, only its form is Buddha [*Şu kadar söyleyeyim: Din-i mübīnin orada/Ruh-ı feyyazı yayılmış, yalnız şekli Buda*],' Akif's preacher declares.[11] Another important aim behind this Ottoman interest in Japan, which extended across the political spectrum, was, as Akif stated, to free Ottomans from dependency on Western scholarship in their knowledge of Asia.[12]

Akif again attacked nationalist sentiment, this time as *kavmiyetçilik*, in his first act of propaganda work against the Allied Powers and their plans to slice Anatolia into European territories and spheres of influence. Several months before those policies were formalised in the Treaty of Sèvres in August 1920, Akif took to the Zağnos Paşa mosque in Balıkesir province to rally against them. Two months after Akif delivered his sermon there in February 1920, Mustafa Kemal split with the sultan's government to set up a parliamentary assembly (*millet meclisi*) in Ankara and Akif quit Istanbul, where his sermon had caused friction with the

[10] Ibid., 245; *Bütün edvar-ı terakkiyi yarıp geçmek için/Kendi 'mahiyet-i ruhiyeniz' olsun kılavuz/Çünkü beyhudedir ümid-i selamet onsuz.*

[11] Ibid., 217–18.

[12] Akif, 'Gayet Mühim bir Eser,' *SM*, 1 Temmuz 1326 (14 July 1910), 4/97: 322–3. See Selcuk Esenbel, *Japan, Turkey and the World of Islam: The Writings of Selcuk Esenbel* (Folkestone: Global Oriental, 2011); Renée Worringer, *Ottomans Imagining Japan: East, Middle East, and Non-Western Modernity at the Turn of the Twentieth Century* (Basingstoke: Palgrave Macmillan, 2014).

authorities, for the nationalist stronghold. By *kavmiyetçilik* Akif intended a community so partisan that it could easily fall prey to internecine dispute, his example being the pagan Aws and Khazraj tribes that are said in Islamic tradition to have feuded before the Prophet established his system of government in Medina. Such a *kavmiyetçilik* he equates with *fırkacılık* (partisanship), but it is a term he appears to have used in order to accord *kavmiyet* an Islamic cast as a Turkish nationalism he could embrace.[13] The language of Akif's sermons always maintained this ambiguity regards nationalism: for example, he would tell his audience they faced 'a national task, a religious obligation' (*bir vazife-i vataniye, bir fariza-ı diniye*) in which there could be no dereliction of duty.[14]

This miasmic Turkish Islamic mix pervades a further four sermons that Akif delivered between November 1920 and February 1921 having fully staked his colours to the National Forces' cause – moving to Ankara, accepting a seat in its parliament – but now expressed in bellicose terms that seem at odds with Akif's humanist demeanour as a leading Muslim intellectual. Speaking at the Nasrullah mosque in Kastamonu on 21 November, Akif asked the question at the outset: Should we be compassionate with non-Muslims?[15] He proceeded to go through the experiences he had had with Europeans that would militate against such a position, focussing in particular on his months in Berlin during the war when he was on, as he put it, 'an important mission' (*mühim bir vazife*).[16] He states at the outset that he has come to his senses now that he has seen with his own eyes 'the injustice, treachery and contempt that the nations we call European see as appropriate for helpless people they took into bondage and ruled'.[17] Western culture may be irreligious as a general characteristic today, but that does not mean its education systems do not inculcate a deep anti-Muslim sentiment; they cannot consider as equal in humanity those who do not belong to their ethnic group, religion, or colour (*kendi cinslerinden, kendi dinlerinden, kendi renklerinden*),[18] and

[13] Akif, 'Mev'ize: Üstad-ı Muhterem Mehmed Akif Beyefendi'nin Karasi'de Zağnos Paşa Cami-i Şerifi'nde İrad Buyurdukları Mev'izenin Hulasası,' *SR*, 12 Şubat 1336 (12 February 1920), 18/458: 183–6.

[14] Ibid., 186.

[15] This sermon was also delivered in Diyarbakır at an unclear date; see Abdülkadiroğlu and Abdülkadiroğlu, *Mev'iza ve Hutbeler*, 144, asterisk footnote. Akif said in Kastamonu he had travelled to many parts of Anatolia.

[16] Akif, 'Nasrullah Kürsüsünde,' *SR*, 25 Teşrinisani 1336 (26 November 1920), 18/464: 250.

[17] Ibid., 250.

[18] Ibid., 251.

this shows in their art, poetry, novels, and newspapers, which 'continue to provoke these feelings' (*bu hislerini candlandırır dururlar*).[19] The technical achievements of their civilisation will be attainable by others through the same hard work the Europeans put in, Akif said, but Muslim nations must be internally united if they are to succeed. Stoking division is how the British managed an empire on minimal military resources, he added.

Referring to his audience as both 'Muslims' and 'Turks', Akif now turned to the threat at hand: that Greek forces are massing and the British, even though they would prefer to save Istanbul as a Muslim city in order to maintain calm in their Indian realm, could allow them into the capital. Expect Ottoman Greeks, Armenians, and Jews to be deployed among the small police force that Muslim Turks will be permitted to form but Greek and Armenian militias to attack Muslims nevertheless, Akif says, while financial structures will be established to impoverish them. Past experience in India and North Africa shows that neither British justice nor French civilisation are to be trusted,[20] so neither can we have faith in any post-war treaty.[21] The immediate task is thus to end infighting to better face the threat from the Greek army, which had occupied Izmir in May 1919 and began pushing inland towards Ankara after consolidating its hold of the Aegean coast. To this end, west Anatolia must do what east Anatolians had done and take the fight to the enemy: he cites the specific example of Kars, which Ankara's forces had re-taken from the Republic of Armenia the previous month. 'Let God grant success to our heroic fighters; may He inflict on this base enemy in Western Anatolia the fate the Armenians rightly suffered [*Cenab-ı Hak o kahraman mücahidlerimize tevfikler ihsan buyursun; Anadolumuzun garbındaki bu sefil düşmanı da Ermenilerin bihakkın uğradıkları akibete uğratsın*]', Akif says. 'Now the task of our coreligionists on this side of Anatolia is to rip up this filthy rag [Treaty of Sèvres] by throwing the enemies on other side of Anatolia into the sea.'[22]

Akif's intent here is ambiguous. Although in the immediately preceding sentences he used the phrase *Yunan ordusu* (Greek army) rather than *Rum*, which would refer to Greeks under Ottoman rule, and he contextualised his citation of the Armenian *akibet* with mention of the battle of Kars, his audience could well have understood his words as a call to evict Greek

19 Ibid.
20 Ibid., 258–9.
21 Ibid., 254–5.
22 Ibid., 259.

Ottomans just as the Armenian Ottomans were removed and murdered en masse during the war. The issue was hardly far from public awareness. A military court focussed largely on the treatment of Armenians was established by occupying British authorities in April 1919 with the co-operation of the Istanbul government, and in July 1919 it found the CUP and its wartime leaders guilty of intent to eliminate the Armenians through the Teşkilat-ı Mahsusa. A large number of administrators, officers, and intellectuals were exiled to Malta while the British tried to amass evidence against them from Ottoman documentary material. With the Ankara government staunchly opposed to the process, Britain released them in 1921 in exchange for British prisoners of war. Akif was among the Ottoman elite who moved to Kayseri in early 1921 for fear of a Greek siege of Ankara. Eviction was the eventual fate of not only the Greek army, but the Greek Orthodox population of Izmir, its surrounding towns, and the Anatolian interior, first through war when Izmir was taken by the National Forces in September 1922 and then through diplomacy, with the exchange of populations with Greece agreed in January 1923. Mustafa Kemal sent Akif a note of thanks for his work campaigning against Sèvres.[23]

In his later exchange of letters with Sencer, Akif commented on their shared fate of exile and repudiation, a 'public trial' (*imtihan-ı aleniye*) they had endured because of the revolutionary excesses (*inkılab namıyla her türlü ifrat*) of the ruling elite,[24] but the Armenian issue never comes up in the extant correspondence or anywhere else in Akif's writing. Questions over the extent of Sencer's knowledge of the Armenian deportations dogged him throughout his life.[25] The wartime prime minister Said Halim Paşa, whose works Akif translated and whose brother became Akif's patron, was among those sent to Malta on suspicion of having played a role, but Sencer spent the period from early 1917 to early 1920 there separately after falling into British hands in the Hijaz. However, Süleyman Nazif, a fellow poet and admiring acquaintance of Akif, wrote of his horror at signs of massacre in his native Diyarbakır region and possibly prevented atrocities in Baghdad province when serving as governor.[26] Akif was typical among the Ottoman

23 Düzdağ, 'Mehmed Âkif Ersoy: Hayatı ve Eserleri,' xxxi.

24 Letter 4 to Eşref Sencer, 18 May 1931, in Günaydın, *Mektuplar*, 90.

25 Fortna, *The Circassian*, 5 (note 8), 10–11, 166–8.

26 David Gaunt, *Massacres, Resistance, Protectors: Muslim-Christian Relations in Eastern Anatolia during World War I* (Piscataway, NJ: Gorgias, 2006), 306; Uğur Ümit Üngör, *The Making of Modern Turkey: Nation and State in Eastern Anatolia, 1913–1950* (Oxford: Oxford University Press, 2011), 93.

intelligentsia in moving in elite circles that were almost certainly aware of what was taking place.[27]

The further three published sermons Akif gave during this critical period of the Greek war pursue his themes of the need for unity to face the enemy and his notion of an Islamic nationalism, a readiness to 'defend the nation of Islam' (*vatan-ı İslamı müdafaa*) through attention to all obligations of faith including that of jihad.[28] For Akif these represent an opportunity to discuss the ideas of his poetry directly with ordinary people outside the parameters of poetic language, his theme of the Muslim nation that throws off its sloth to rise again after decline – a discourse that traverses the modernist and Salafi understanding of Islamic history as gradual corruption of an original purity. For example, he impressed upon his audience the argument that *tevekkül* should be understood as the belief that God will support the believer in realising the aims of his resolute action (*azim*),[29] which he developed from ʿAbduh and al-Afghānī's well-known article on the topic in *al-ʿUrwa al-Wuthqā*.[30] Akif had touched on this question before the war,[31] and returned to *tevekkül* in his poem in the *Gölgeler* collection 'Azimden Sonra Tevekkül' (After Resolve, Faith in God), written in November 1919. These arguments then made their way into the classic Late Ottoman text of Islamic modernism, *Anglikan Kilisesine Cevap*, authored by Jāwīsh and translated by Akif.[32] Most significant of all is the function of Akif's sermons. Their intent was to convince the Anatolian populace that Ankara's National Forces were not a reconstituted CUP movement, that their fight was not against religion and caliphate – indeed, that to join the fight was a religious duty incumbent on each person (*farz-ı ayn*) – and that if they were to lose, Muslim Turks would have nowhere else to go.[33]

[27] In mid to late 1918 he spent one month as a guest of the last Ottoman emir of Mecca ʿAlī Ḥaydar Pāshā in Beirut, where a large community of Armenian refugees had formed; Edib, *Mehmed Âkif*, 99.

[28] Akif, 'Tam Müslüman Olmadıkça Felah Yoktur,' *SR*, 13 Kanunevvel 1336 (13 December 1920), 18/466: 279.

[29] Akif, 'Ye'se Düşenler Müslüman Değildir,' *SR*, 3 Şubat 1337 (3 February 1921), 18/467: 294.

[30] Translated and published by Akif as 'Kaza ve Kader,' *SM*, 30 Nisan 1325 (13 May 1909), 2/36: 149–50. Note use of the word *azim* in the discussion of *tevekkül*.

[31] Akif, *Fatih Kürsüsünde*, in *Safahat*, 346; Akif, 'Tefsir-i Şerif,' *SR*, 8 Ağustos 1329 (21 August 1313), 10/258: 381.

[32] Jāwīsh, 'Anglikan Kilisesine Cevap,' *SR*, 27 Eylul 1339 (27 April 1923), 22/563: 129–32.

[33] Düzdağ says Akif made a speech to this effect when he first arrived in Ankara at the Hacı Bayram mosque, but it was never published in *Sebilürreşad*; 'Mehmed Âkif Ersoy: Hayatı ve Eserleri,' xxix.

Akif's use of language in this period provides further evidence that he was more accepting of Turkish nationalism than is often assumed, often using terms notably more ideological than the neutral, jurisdictional *vatan* or *memleket*.[34] Around 1921–2 he composed a poem for a military march that composer Ali Rifat set to music called 'Ordunun Duası' (Call of the Army), praising the institution in both ethnic and religious terms for fighting for the *millet*. 'We are Turkish men of heroic descent/Muslims who worship God [*Türk eriyiz, silsileyiz kahraman/Müslümanız, Hakk'a tapan Müslüman*]', it declares in one stanza.[35] In his letters from Egypt he displayed a strong sense of belonging with Turkish speakers, bewailing the kind of absent communal spirit that had caused Yūsuf Akçura and Ziya Gökalp to raise fears of Turkish assimilation.[36] He praised his son-in-law Ahmed's decision to vacation in the east of Turkey, since 'the nation is a unity that cannot be divided [*vatan bir külldür ki tecezzi kabul etmez*]: its east, west, north, south must be completely one in our thinking',[37] and he also praised Ahmed for carrying out his sacred national duty in performing military service (*vazife-i mukaddese-i vataniyeniz*).[38] He told his daughter not to complain about life in the east, where they had moved, noting that officials of the British empire did not hesitate to travel the world for the sake of nation (*vatanı uğrunda*): 'It seems we weren't born into the world, we were born to Istanbul [*bizler dünyaya gelmemişiz İstanbula gelmişiz*]', he joked.[39] In a letter of 29 April 1935, Akif wrote to his friend Şefik Kolaylık: 'May God give power and strength to you, so you can keep on working for the good of the nation [*vatanımızın hayrı için uğraş dur*].'[40] Then in a letter dated 19 July 1935 he recalled a recent trip to Antakya, his first visit to the republic in a decade, writing rapturously of 'a lush Turkish land [*yemyeşil bir Türk yurdu*] with trees, gardens, olive groves, vineyards staring upon the Taurus mountains, running down to the Orontes'.[41]

[34] For example, 'Mehmet Akif Ersoy nədən millətçiliyi deyil, ümmətçiliyi seçdi?' Modern.az, 10 February 2015; http://modern.az/articles/72035/1/#gsc.tab=0 (accessed 13 October 2018).

[35] In Akif, *Safahat*, 493.

[36] Letter to Asım Şakir Gören, dated 2 March 1925, in Günaydın, *Mektuplar*, 134. 'Even strong communities like Armenians, Greeks, Jews, Italians have difficulty finding work, so compare that to Turks who have no community [*hiçbir teşkilatı olmayan Türklerin maruz kalacağı sıkıntıyı artık bir kıyas edin*]', he wrote.

[37] Letter to Ahmed, 11 June 1932, in Ömer Hakan Özalp, *Firaklı Nâmeler Âkif'in Gurbet Mektupları* (Istanbul: Timaş Yayınları, 2011), 70.

[38] Letter to Ahmed, 31 December 1933, ibid., 106–7.

[39] Letter to Suad, 19 April 1934, ibid., 116–19.

[40] Letter to Şefik Kolaylı, 29 April 1935, in Günaydın, *Mektuplar*, 119–20.

[41] Letter to Emine Abbas Halim, 25 June 1935, in Günaydın, *Mektuplar*, 146–7.

Akif also used the phrase *Allah büyük* (in place of *Allāh kebir,* meaning 'let us rely on God') in some of his later letters,[42] *Tanrı* for God in his Kastamonu sermons (1920–1),[43] and *ırk* apparently meaning ethnic group in *Asım* (1919–24)[44] and in his national anthem. The latter example counters earlier usages of *ırk* that were clearly pejorative.[45] Akif would more often than not use the Ottoman Rumi calendar, sometimes both Rumi and Islamic, but rarely only Islamic. Akif's use of *millet* is more problematic. We have already seen how Gökalp attempted to claim the term for Turkish nationalism, and thus rejected any talk of Islamic *milliyetçilik* as suggestive of an Islamic unity of nations. This was consistent with the Young Turk usage of *millet* as a non-religious racial community or state, so the Germans or the Turks could be a such a nation.[46] Feroz Ahmad has noted, however, that the word retained its sense of religious community well into the republican period;[47] indeed, Erbakan's National Vision (Millî Görüş) movement – from which he formed his political parties – embraced the term *millî* with the implicit meaning of 'religious' and thus as a codeword for the lost religious unity of the caliphate, although the word had come to mean 'national'. Akif could then freely deploy *millet* with all its ambiguity, knowing it meant different things to different audiences. Ethnic and religious concepts are fused in the 'İstiklal Marşı' in which he talks of independence as the right of a God-worshipping nation (*Hakkıdır, Hakk'a tapan, milletimin istiklal*) and 'my hero people' (*kahraman ırkım*).[48] These shifts in language certainly did not put Akif in the category of ethnic nationalist. In a poem

[42] Letter to Eşref Sencer, 18 May 1931, ibid., 91. The more common Ottoman phrase was *Allah kerim.*

[43] Akif, 'Ye'se Düşenler Müslüman Değildir,' *SR*, 3 Şubat 1337 (3 February 1921), 18/467: 293–6.

[44] Akif, *Safahat*, 504; the use of *ırkın torunu* in reference to a feisty Turkish wrestler. The Arabic and Ottoman meaning was usually stock or kinfolk.

[45] See his reference to *ırk davaları* in his *tafsīr* of Qur'an 8:25; Akif, 'Tefsir-i Sure-i Enfal, 25,' *SR*, 20 Eylül 1328 (3 October 1912), 2/31 (9/213): 82. He noted that Germans considered the Asian race to be 'different' (*başka*) in *Berlin Hatıraları*, in Akif, *Safahat*, 441. Kayalı's suggestion that Akif was not aware of the new racialist implications of *ırk* seems unconvincing; it was a key concept in Turkist thinking of the time: 'Islam,' 328–9.

[46] On the late nineteenth-century debate on *millet* as a religious concept but given new nationalist meaning, see David Kushner, *The Rise of Turkish Nationalism, 1876–1908* (London: Cass, 1977), 23–5.

[47] Feroz Ahmad, 'Feroz Ahmad replies,' *The American Historical Review*, 102/4 (1997): 1302–3; reply to M. Şükrü Hanioğlu, 'To the Editor,' *American Historical Review*, 102/4 (1997): 1301–2.

[48] 'İstiklal Marşı,' Akif, *Safahat*, 709.

written in December 1918 after the CUP collapse he denounced pan-Turkic Turanism as a futile myth[49] and in an article of April 1919 he praised Said Halim's *İslamlaşmak* as sound ideology.[50] But they were noted by some of his contemporaries in the Turkist camp all the same.[51]

Several decades later, the journalist Cemal Kutay could even put a nationalist gloss on Akif's life in an account of his role working for the government in his wartime mission to Najd. Through the memory of Sencer, who Kutay interviewed as the basis for his book (first published in 1963), Akif is depicted as emerging from the arduous experience of the desert as a changed man, cured of delusions of Islamic unity and romantic notions of 'the East' with a more pragmatic nationalist focus for his Muslim faith. 'Now I know better what I want for my religion and my nation [*dinim ve milletim için*]', Akif is quoted saying by Sencer.[52] He also tells Sencer: 'Eşref, what is this scene, this poverty, this decline, this primitiveness [*bu inhitat, bu iptidailik*]? Its basic catastrophe, this spiritual collapse [*ruhi izmihlal*], what is it?'[53] The implication for the reader is that Akif has now understood that Turkey must detach itself from the Islamic East. Kutay even argues that the final section of Akif's 'Berlin Hatıraları' (dated 18 March 1915), in which an Englishman imagines a caliph in only name and separation of Arabs and Turks, was Akif's prediction of rising *Türkçülük*.[54] In Kutay's telling, Akif witnessed Arabian degeneracy first-hand when a Wahhabi judge in the Rashidi town of Ḥāʾil showed himself greedy for Ottoman money. In this incident, which probably took place in early January 1916, Sencer attended the meeting with Akif and Shaykh Ṣālih al-Sharīf. The judge began by praising the Turks for their great services to Islam except for allowing Muslims to seek intercession through visiting shrines, which leads to a theological discussion on actions that negate faith. After Sencer arranges for new annual payments of gold coins to the judge, who is only described as blind, they return to their creedal dispute. The narration of the debate fits standard tropes of Wahhabi disdain for Ottoman Islam but its details on the question of faith and action suggest a kernel of truth to the recollection. 'Among all peoples there are people incapable of understanding, but there should be no more

[49] 'Hala Mı Boğuşmak?' in *Gölgeler*; Akif, *Safahat*, 630. Discussed in Kayalı, 'Islam,' 322, footnote 54.

[50] Akif, 'İslamlaşmak,' *Sebilürreşad*, 10 April 1919, 16:404, 133.

[51] See Halim Sabit, in Edib, *Mehmed Âkif*, 546.

[52] Kutay, *Necid Çöllerinde Mehmet Akif*, 122.

[53] Ibid., 217.

[54] Ibid., 123. Akif, 'Berlin Hatıraları,' in *Safahat*, 453–4.

extremism [*taassup*]. Anyone who says, "there is no god but God" and means it in his heart is a Muslim. Everything else is between him and God', the Shaykh is reported as telling his Māturīdī guests in conciliatory words of farewell.[55]

SABRI'S VIEW OF THE NATIONAL STRUGGLE

Mustafa Sabri wrote at length about what Ankara termed the 'national struggle' (*millî mücadele*)[56] against occupation and partition in its immediate aftermath, in his first Arabic-language work *al-Nakīr* (1924). Sabri's first target in the book was the decision taken by the Ankara parliament in November 1922 to strip the caliph of any authority over government; his secondary aim was to question Ankara's conduct during the war, which for Sabri speaks to the nature of the secular-nationalist ideology guiding it. Sabri made here his first comments presaging the dark view on individual responsibility that he was to advance in *Mawqif al-ʿAql* some two decades later, in that he talked not only of the *lā-dīniyyīn*, meaning the secularists who formed the Ankara government, but questioned the Islam of Muslims under their rule. The first was a familiar theme in Late Ottoman religious debate, but the second was a new direction for someone within the Ḥanafī-Māturīdī Ottoman fold. 'Unfortunately, for some time the situation of Muslims is that more than ninety-five percent of them live under foreign rule, while the affairs of the rest who are less than five percent are in the hands of the secularists who are nominally Muslim', Sabri wrote.[57] He continued: 'The situation of this second group is worse than the first, in that the secularists are fiercer enemies to the Islamic religion than its other enemies and more cunning in sabotaging and misrepresenting it.'[58] Given the views expressed in his most recent book at the time, *Dinî Müceddidler* (1922), by *lā-dīniyyīn* Sabri intended not only the Kemalists of Ankara but modernist intellectuals. Though its members number fewer than 'the sincere Muslims' (*al-mukhliṣīn*), together they are in a position to wage war on Islam from the inside, he said, which began with

55 Kutay, *Necid*, 211–17.

56 This was the first term used to describe the post-1918 fighting that led to the republic. The republic later propagated *istiklal harbi* (war of independence) and *ulusal kurtuluş savaşı* (national war of liberation).

57 Sabri, *al-Nakīr*, 4. The Arabic is not clear: Sabri could also mean that the 5 per cent living under the rule of the irreligious are themselves nominal Muslims for that reason.

58 Ibid., 4. He cites a supporting view on this point from Rashīd Riḍā in his book *al-Khilāfa* (1921).

stripping the caliphate of its powers but will end with removing religion's role entirely from worldly affairs and politics (*shuʾūn al-dunyā wa-l-siyāsa*).[59] Sabri argued, however, that in his view Muslims living under the authority of a government that rejects the supervisory ordinances of shariʿa are liable to be considered apostates; in other words, their individual claims to belief are not enough to preclude the communal requirement to establish religious governance (*lā tanfaʿuhum diyānatuhum min ḥaythu afrāduhum mā lam yuqirrū bi-ḥukm al-dīn wa-ḥukūmatihi ʿalayhim*).[60] What risked facilitating the Kemalists in their task was that the pious (*al-mutadayyinūn min al-muslimīn*) attended to only their own religious observance, while the mass of ordinary believers (*ʿawāmm al-muʾminīn*) were oblivious and intellectuals and ʿulamaʾ too fearful for their lives to speak out.[61]

In Sabri's analysis it was Ankara's victory in Izmir that had enabled the Kemalists to move ahead with their plan for the caliphate, part realised at the time of his writing, and what he suspected was their undeclared plan to remove Islam from public policy altogether and restrict it to private space.[62] This ran counter to publicly stated positions and acts such as establishing the Ankara publications committee and commissioning the Jāwīsh-Akif book on modern Islam. The occupation of Anatolia by Greece and Istanbul by Britain and France was a result of both the CUP's fatal mistake of entering the war and their despotic rule, not the product of caliphal despotism (*istibdād*), Sabri said.[63] Sabri compared the orderly surrender of Bucharest to the Central Powers in May 1918, which he witnessed personally, to the destruction that befell Izmir after Ankara's forces took over.[64] He also condemned the Turco-Greek population exchange of 1923 as heaping more suffering upon Anatolians for a disingenuous narrative of Islamic solidarity (*ʿaṣabiyya islāmiyya*) whose ulterior motive was to bring Kemalist supporters from Rumelia into the Turkish state.[65] The ultimate aim was to create a

[59] Ibid., 5.
[60] Ibid., 83. Sabri refers to an article he published in 1923 on this topic in *al-Ahrām* and *al-Muqaṭṭam*.
[61] Ibid., 5–6.
[62] Ibid., 10–11. He says they plan to remove the shariʿa courts, following CUP changes to their status in 1917.
[63] Ibid., 24, footnote 40; 28, footnote 41.
[64] Ibid., 104.
[65] Ibid., 98. Sabri's attitude can be compared to the 1941 condemnation of persecution of Serbs, Jews, and Roma by the Nazi-allied Croatian regime during the Second World War; see Hikmet Karcic, Ferid Dautovic, Ermin Sinanovic, *The Muslim Resolutions: Bosniak Responses to World War Two Atrocities in Bosnia and Herzegovina* (Sarajevo/Shenandoah: Center for Islam in the Contemporary World, 2021).

'secular-national state' (*dawla lā-dīniyya qawmiyya*) that would be cut off from 'its Ottoman and Islamic past' (*māḍīhā al-ʿuthmānī wa-l-islāmī*) on the basis of 'ethnic chauvinism for the Turkish nation' (*al-ʿaṣabiyya al-jinsiyya li-ummat al-turk*), Sabri charged.[66] Sabri was very specific that *lā-dīnī* meant a political system in which legislation is devoid of explicit derivation in religious principles, the judiciary operates outside the structures of religious institutions, and the symbols of the state are ethnically nationalist rather than based on religion. As with Gökalp, he used this term as an equivalent to *laïque*, placing the French term in parentheses in citations from Arabic or Ottoman newspaper articles.[67] The grey wolf, which Kemalists had taken to placing on postage stamps, he ridiculed as a pre-Islamic symbol that ethnic Turks, including his own family, had never heard of.[68] Sabri said what he had forsaken was neither his *jins*, by which he meant ethnic group, nor his *qawm*, by which he meant religious community, but rather a clique that had wronged both people and caliph through placing secularism (*lā-dīniyya*) before faith and ethnicity (*jinsiyya*) before Islam.[69] We can add to this somewhat humanist face Sabri gives his anti-nationalism the further point he made that during his Ottoman years, contrary to some press reports, he never once issued the death penalty.[70]

The important element in Sabri's critique of nationalist ideology, and which sets him apart from modernist intellectuals such as Akif, is his analysis of the nature of the nation-state rather than his view of nationalism in the abstract. Sabri homes in on the fact that nation-state modernity has been received through war, militarisation of the state, and suppression of political life and free expression. In contrast, the shariʿa court system was not there to oppress society, rather its function was to check the power of the ruler and thus act as a protective structure for society; removing the institutional framework of shariʿa allows the military caste to do as it pleases. Thus, in Sabri's view a restricted role for religion, by his understanding of religion as an institutional state structure, is incompatible with the

66 Ibid., 105.

67 Ibid., 17–18, 93. He doesn't use the more neutral Arabic terms *ʿilmaniyya/ʿalmaniyya*.

68 Ibid., 58–60.

69 Ibid., 39. The Turkish translation uses *ırkçılık* for *jinsiyya* and *millet* for *qawm*; Sabri (ed. and trans. Oktay Yılmaz), *Hilafetin İlgasının Arka Planı* (Istanbul: Insan, 1998), 144.

70 Sabri, *al-Nakīr*, 18 (note 32). Sabri naming both the CUP as Freemasons (*bannāʾūn aḥrār*; ibid., 10) and the nationalist novelist Halide Edib as Jewish (ibid., 31, note 47) was intended as a slur. However, Yılmaz incorrectly translates Sabri as describing the CUP/Kemalists as *dönme* (Jewish converts to Islam); Sabri, *Hilafetin İlgasının*, 143, footnote 14.

notion of freedom (*kayfa yumkin al-tawfīq bayn al-ḥurriyya wa-l-dīn al-muqayyad?*).[71] Freedom should mean the freedom of nations to form their governments (*ḥurriyyat al-umam tujāh al-ḥukūmāt*), not freedom of governments to act independently of the Islamic system.[72] The foundation of both the CUP and the Kemalists' power was not the will of the people as expressed through election but acts of the army and outcomes of long drawn-out conflict between civilian and military wings of the CUP:[73] 'The military that we employed and prepared to protect us are those who attacked us with their weapons, although we had begged them to preserve our independence, our property, our freedom, our dignity, and our nation. But these sanctities became a plaything in their hands.'[74] It was an army outside civilian control that ran amok in Izmir and even provoked rebellion against itself in a number of Anatolian cities.[75]

Sabri outlines an ideal legislative framework, a static, conservative system in which laws are created and amended at a minimum. He sees three levels: a base of shariʿa laws, which he says is consonant to a degree with what physicists call natural laws, followed by constitutional law with protections against revision, and then circumstantial legislation.[76] His main example of arbitrary legislation enacted by the Kemalists is the Treason Law of 1920 (Hıyanet-i Vataniye Kanunu), which established the death penalty for questioning the legitimacy of the Ankara parliament and led to the creation of independence tribunals the same year. The law was amended in April 1923 to include opposition to the abolition of the sultanate and in February 1925 for establishing organisations using religion for political aims.[77] The period 1922–4 was critical in the victory of Kemalist republicanism over contesting visions of the post-war state which were not limited to the system of shariʿa and sovereign caliph advocated by the ʿulamaʾ and

[71] Sabri, *al-Nakīr*, 9.
[72] Ibid., 84.
[73] Ibid., 72. For modern scholarship on this question see: Hanioğlu, *A Brief History*, 164–5; Dankwart Rustow, 'The Army and the Founding of the Turkish Republic,' in *Men of Order: Authoritarian Modernization under Atatürk and Reza Shah*, ed. Touraj Atabaki and Eric Zürcher (London: I. B. Tauris, 2004), 164–208; Frank Tachau and Metin Heper, 'The State, Politics, and the Military in Turkey,' *Comparative Politics*, 16/1 (October 1983): 17–33; Feroz Ahmad, 'Military and Politics in Turkey,' in *Turkey's Engagement with Modernity: Conflict and Change in the Twentieth Century*, ed. Celia Kerslake, Kerem Öktem, Philip Robins (London: Palgrave Macmillan, 2010), 92–116.
[74] Sabri, *al-Nakīr*, 73.
[75] Ibid., 72.
[76] Ibid., 85.
[77] Ergün Aybars, *İstiklal Mahkemeleri* (Ankara: Bilgi Yayınevi, 1975), 43–54.

devout intellectuals.[78] Following the declaration of the republic in October 1923, three forms of republicanism were in conflict: Islamic, liberal, and radical, all centred around Mustafa Kemal as president.[79] Criticism of Kemalist authoritarianism led to trials of journalists from 1923 and a split in the Republican People's Party (Cumhuriyet Halk Partisi, or RPP), in 1924, after which the RPP consolidated its position in a single-party state. A series of laws followed targeting Ottoman Islamic institutions – the courts, the sheikh ül-Islam's office, the dervish orders, and Islam as religion of state. To Sabri, the pre-eminent voice among the disenfranchised religious class, there was nothing liberal about the secular republic at all.

SABRI'S RADICAL DISCOURSE IN EGYPT

Two decades later Sabri returned to these arguments. The final section of *Mawqif al-ʿAql* is an essay on modern legal and political systems titled, 'On the impermissibility of separating religion from politics in Islam'. Published in 1949, it was written after Sabri had observed close-up the theological transformations taking place in Egypt's public arena since the end of the caliphate and gradual erosion of the institutional system of Egyptian Islam. ʿAlī ʿAbd al-Rāziq's book *al-Islām wa-Uṣūl al-Ḥukm* (1925) advocated abandoning entirely the shariʿa court system, which under Ottoman inspiration and later British encouragement began to operate on twin civil and Islamic tracks from 1848, and in 1948 the revised Egyptian Civil Code was drafted by ʿAbd al-Razzāq al-Sanhūrī, merging shariʿa, French, and American law and becoming the basis for civil codes in a number of postcolonial Arab states.[80] Sabri notes other changes such as ending the requirement for the shaykh al-Islam, as head of the shariʿa courts and issuer of fatwas, to approve government contracts and agreements and relegation of the shaykh of al-Azhar's status in official protocol.[81]

[78] Banu Turnaoğlu, 'Ideological Struggle during the Formative Years of the Turkish Republic,' *Middle Eastern Studies*, 52/4 (2016): 677–93.

[79] Turnaoğlu's terminology; ibid., 686.

[80] Guy Bechor, *The Sanhuri Code and the Emergence of Modern Arab Civil Law (1932 to 1949)* (Leiden: Brill, 2007); Nathan Brown, *The Rule of Law in the Arab World: Courts in Egypt and the Gulf* (Cambridge, Cambridge University Press, 1997).

[81] Sabri, *Mawqif al-ʿAql*, 4:358. By shaykh al-Islam Sabri is apparently referring to the Dār al-Iftāʾ, formally established in 1895, which in fact never attained the control over shariʿa courts enjoyed by the Ottoman sheikh ül-Islam. See Jakob Skovgaard-Petersen, *Defining Islam for the Egyptian State: Muftis and Fatwas of the Dār al-Iftā* (Leiden: Brill, 1997), 100–6.

Sabri starts by arguing that separation of religion from state is a 'governmental revolution against the religion of the people',[82] which leads to the apostasy of not only those in government but ordinary Muslims under its control. Indeed, he states clearly: 'It entails the apostasy of individuals [*irtidād al-afrād*] too because of their acceptance of obedience to this apostate government, which claimed independence from the rule of Islam to which it had previously submitted.'[83] The result is that society, or the nation (he uses the word *umma*), becomes apostate itself, through obedience to such a government that claims to derive its authority from that same society. Thus, while it could be said there was no substantive difference between this government and foreign occupation, the latter would be more benign in that it would not interfere in the religious affairs of the people while deriving its authority from external forces in external locations.[84] This, Sabri says, is his view of the Kemalist government: if Izmir was for a time under Greek control, now all Turkey and its people have 'slipped from the hand of Islam' (*kharajat min yad al-islām*).[85] Such thinking might not appear shameful to those who consider 'the nation alone to be above all else' (*al-waṭan faqaṭ fawqa kull shay'*), but true Islam considers that the Muslim 'finds his nation through Islam' (*yatawaṭṭan ma'a al-islām*).[86]

Sabri is rejecting here the widely stated opinions of Shaykh al-Marāghī during his two stints as rector of al-Azhar (1927–9, 1935–45) regarding the Turkish republic as a model Muslim state whose secularism, which for Sabri meant *ḥukūma lā-dīniyya*, did not detract from the Islamic faith of its Muslim subjects. In comments published in 1936 al-Marāghī said it was unreasonable (*min ghayr al-ma'qūl*) for laws, texts, and principles of the early Islamic period to apply today.[87] Sabri says he has included this section on separation of religion and state, although his book is fundamentally concerned with creedal questions, because of the bitter experience of the Kemalist revolution (*al-inqilāb al-kamālī*) which many Muslims had not foreseen.[88] This now is the fate Sabri foresees for Egypt, and his key argument throughout the four volumes is that

82 Sabri, *Mawqif al-'Aql*, 4:281.
83 Ibid., 282.
84 Ibid., 284–5.
85 Ibid., 285.
86 Ibid.
87 Ibid., 285, 359; citing *al-Ahrām*, 28 February 1936.
88 Ibid., 286.

ʿAbduh's failure to refute the arguments for secularism put forward by Faraḥ Anṭūn was a foundational moment.[89]

In Sabri's understanding, modern governments want to free themselves from the Islamic juridical system in all its aspects – its law, its courts, its justices – in order to free themselves from 'Islam's supervision' (*riqābat al-islām*). He goes further than his previous analysis, which stressed the illiberal authoritarianism of a regime established by military officers, to draw a generalised picture of the post-colonial surveillance state, since not only religion but all aspects of social, economic, and political life are now under the purview of the government. Sabri writes:

> The politics which the government side appropriates and the religious side cedes, and which entails sovereignty and supervision over every person within the boundaries of the country [*al-siyāda wa-l-ishrāf ʿalā kull man yadkhul taḥta saqf al-bilād*], necessarily places religion and everything else in the country under the absolute authority of the government [*lā budd an taḍaʿ al-dīn taḥta amr al-ḥukūma wa-nahyihā maʿ kull mā yadkhul taḥta dhālik al-saqf*][.][90]

A state assuming such powers could choose not to oppress religion, as with Britain's protectorate in Egypt, or it could choose to oppress, as with Kemalist rule in Turkey. What Sabri expresses here is the idea that removal of the shariʿa structures opens the way to the full power of Foucault's Panopticon state to mould the modern subject at will. While the examples he cites are always Egypt and Turkey in their experiences of Western imperial power on the outside and Westernising forces on the inside, his concept of the totalitarian nature of the modern state was formed in the shadow of Europe's experience with fascist movements, and what he saw possibly saw as their emulation in the Middle East.[91] In other words, the advantage of shariʿa is the very *jumūd* that Europeans and reformist

[89] Sabri, *Mawqif al-ʿAql*, 1:162–3, where he summarises his view on the apostasy of modern state citizenry.

[90] Sabri, *Mawqif al-ʿAql*, 4:293.

[91] On Kemalism and fascist movements see Fikret Adanır, 'Kemalist Authoritarianism and Fascist Trends in Turkey during the Inter-war Period,' in *Fascism Outside Europe: The European Impulse against Domestic Conditions in the Diffusion of Global Fascism*, ed. Stein Larsen (Boulder: Social Science Monographs, 2001), 313–61; Vahram Ter-Matevosyan, 'Turkish Experience with Totalitarianism and Fascism: Tracing the Intellectual Origins,' *Iran and the Caucasus* 19/4 (2015): 387–401; and Hans-Lukas Kieser, 'Europe's Seminal Proto-Fascist? Historically Approaching Ziya Gökalp, Mentor of Turkish Nationalism,' *Die Welt des Islams*, 61/4 (2021): 1–37. As Kieser points out, Turkey's drive for ethnic homogeneity through the population exchange was praised by German critics of liberal democracy; see the preface to the second edition of Carl Schmitt's *Die geistesgeschichtliche Lage des heutigen Parlamentarismus* (1926), in

intellectuals identified as a backward non-modern characteristic. Divine law stands above man-made law, which is fashioned by men for their interests, and easily so in parliamentary systems in which just one seat is enough to allow majoritarian rule;[92] divine law prevents elites from gaming the system for their own ends. Thus, *jumūd* has been a factor for stability throughout the Islamic period when 'no Muslim state or nation from east to west complained of the stagnation of Islamic shariʿa and separating religion from state to end stagnation never crossed anyone's mind'.[93]

> In Europe there is a body of modernist scholars [*al-ʿulamāʾ al-mujaddidīn*] who consider the law a living entity that develops in the same way as social relations that are governed by law. Once law is written it becomes independent of those who wrote it, developing according to social circumstance. Thus, it should be interpreted in a manner that avoids stagnation and is commensurate with life, separated from the intent of the legislator[.][94]

It is the desire to create such a European-style juridical system that motivates the modernist ʿulamaʾ and intellectuals in their assault on the methodology of *taqlīd* and espousal of unconditional *ijtihād*.[95]

So Sabri's basic arguments are that Muslims in a secular state risk exiting Islam and that the secular state is the province of tyrannies of administration, surveillance, and coercion. These are positions that demonstrate the radicalism that a defender of 'old knowledge' and the premodern order was capable of, taking Sabri beyond the Ashʿarī-Māturīdī approach of the tradition he represented and its measured approach to questions of faith. Sabri's view on the function of the shariʿa state and the consequences of its demise presage the work in Western scholarship of Wael Hallaq. In a series of studies Hallaq has challenged the prevalent Western paradigm that imagines a vast unchanging corpus that was only shaken from its stagnation through the work of reformers like al-Afghānī and ʿAbduh and their 'reopening' of *ijtihād*. His is a conceptualisation of the ʿulamaʾ who from the Umayyad and early Abbasid period carved a socio-political role for themselves as a class defending society from the

Schmitt (trans. Ellen Kennedy), *The Crisis of Parliamentary Democracy* (Cambridge: MIT Press, 1985), 9.

92 Sabri, *Mawqif al-ʿAql*, 4:332–3.

93 Ibid., 345–6.

94 Ibid., 344. Compare the US originalist movement's text-based view of law and the constitution; see Scott Soames, 'Justice Scalia's Philosophy of Interpretation: From Textualism to Deferentialism,' in *Justice Scalia: Rhetoric and the Rule of Law*, ed. Brian G. Slocum and Francis J. Mootz III (Chicago: University of Chicago Press, 2019), 21–34.

95 Ibid., 349–52.

arbitrary power of rulers, which they succeeded in restricting to certain fields vis-à-vis the shariʿa system's extensive authority.[96] Sabri and Hallaq each use a distinctive lexical framework: while Sabri talks of separation of religion from politics, Hallaq talks of the politicisation of law as a legislative tool such that there can be no state sovereignty without state-manufactured law. They express essentially the same point: that the 1000-year-old pre-modern system in which law was a sacred domain based on principles emanating from outside the confines of the polity was abrogated by the notion of law as an instrument of state power.

Indeed, Hallaq argues that the pre-modern shariʿa state was not by modern definition a state at all, more of a an 'Islamic proto-state'.[97] The pre-modern connotation of the Arabic/Ottoman term used to describe the modern state, *dawla/devlet*, was of dynastic houses that came and went – over and above the shariʿa-sanctioned community – in a rotation (*tadāwul*) of power at the top of the social system.[98] Sabri's use of the term *siyāsa* expresses his focus on the ruler as the nodal point of the pre-modern *dawla*. Again echoing Sabri, Hallaq says the modern apparatus of coercion swept that system aside and surveillance replaced the obedience to God of the pre-modern shariʿa society. Hallaq writes: 'Where once God – or church – commanded loyalty and willing obedience, it is now the state and the ideological nation, nationhood and nationalism that demand such devotion. The world of the Shariʿa, by contrast, lived under the full shadow of an omniscient God who – by one of the most cardinal tenets of Islam – knew each and every particular of human conduct and misdemeanor.'[99] To what degree this was the outcome the reformers wanted is not clear. As we have seen, Samira Haj argues that ʿAbduh never intended the collapse of social and religious morality to occur in the new order, but the work of Late Ottoman and Egyptian liberal age intellectuals clearly points to the desire for a society in which God is decentred and the Enlightenment subject moves to the foreground. Hallaq has been criticised for a formulaic if not romantic paradigm of pre-modern Islamic governance that fails to account for the complex distribution of power outlined by Tezcan between Ottoman rulers who claimed extensive privilege to enact public law and the realm of shariʿa, which the Late Ottoman

[96] Also, Patricia Crone and Martin Hinds, *God's Caliph: Religious Authority in the First Centuries of Islam* (Cambridge: Cambridge University Press, 2003), 97–110.

[97] Hallaq, *Sharīʿa*, 549.

[98] Wael Hallaq, *The Impossible State: Islam, Politics and Modernity's Predicament* (New York: Columbia University Press, 2014), 62–3.

[99] Hallaq, *Sharīʿa*, 309.

constitutionalists, ulema included, fought to preserve.[100] Studying nineteenth-century Egypt, Khaled Fahmy sees Hallaq's vision of shariʿa as a 'non-state, community-based, bottom-up, jural order' centred on the *fuqahāʾ* and their courts as a reductive caricature that ignores the complementary *siyāsā* councils and the *qānūn* law enacted to maintain public order, both of which were in the hands of government.[101] For Sabri the key element was ʿulamaʾ oversight of the system, even if the state had eaten into the substance of their institutional prerogatives.

Sabri's analysis also bears comparison to the contemporaneous work of German political scientist Carl Schmitt on the notion of sovereign exception: juridical rule exercised by a state authority that does not need law to create law, that with the 'monopoly to decide' retains the power to suspend the law because it has placed itself outside it.[102] Sovereignty manifests itself in this capacity to suspend and restore the legal order while claiming to be part of that order; thus, sovereign power establishes spatial and juridical limits (*Ortnung* and *Ordnung*) to the polity. This is the problem of man-made law and the possibility of tyranny that Sabri believed the shariʿa solved. Sabri gives an example of Turkish elites gaming the system to their own ends in the Ottoman polity's twilight years: Sabri notes that he supported the CUP-led drive in 1908 to limit the sultan's freedom to dissolve parliament, but when Abdülhamid's successor Mehmed Reşad was under their thumb the Unionists tried to alter those constitutional stipulations to give power back to the sultan.[103] Schmitt is explicit that this absolute power claimed by the modern state once belonged to God, the omnipotent God became the omnipotent lawgiver, or in Hallaq's description of Schmitt's ideas, 'earthly political power was the new God'.[104] Schmitt was one of the first to make the systematic argument given in his *Politische Theologie* (Political Theology, 1922)

[100] The implication of Crone and Hinds' model of the Umayyad-Abbasid state that 'sat on the top of society' was also that it remained analytically applicable to subsequent Muslim states; *God's Caliph*, 109; for criticism of Hallaq see Said Salih Kaymakci, 'Wael Hallaq's *The Impossible State*,' *Maydan*, 18 December 2016; www.themaydan.com/2016/12/book-review-wael-hallaqs-impossible-state-said-salih-kaymakci/ (accessed 27 October 2018). Also, Tezcan, *Second Ottoman Empire*, 234–5.

[101] Khaled Fahmy, *In Quest of Justice: Islamic Law and Forensic Medicine in Modern Egypt* (Oakland: University of California Press, 2018), 27, which cites the quote from Hallaq, *Sharīʿa*, 549.

[102] Carl Schmitt, *Political Theology: Four Chapters on the Concept of Sovereignty* (Chicago: University of Chicago Press, 2005 [1922]), 5–15.

[103] Sabri, *Mawqif al-ʿAql*, vol. 4, 331, footnote 1.

[104] Hallaq, *Impossible State*, 89.

that the modern state, produced by the process of Reformation-to-Enlightenment, contained secularised reframings of Christian theological concepts and structures.[105] Schmitt developed his ideas further in *Der Begriff des Politischen* (The Concept of the Political, 1932), which outlined four frames of thought that dominated successive eras after the transformations in religious authority of the Reformation: the rational scientific thinking of the seventeenth century, the moral concerns of the Enlightenment in the eighteenth century, the economic focus of the nineteenth century, and finally the technology of the twentieth century, which threatens to bring the moral, cultural, and intellectual advancement of human society to an end.[106] Pondering the imminent collapse of the Weimar republic, Schmitt theorised that it represented a liberal archetype of harmonious space denuded of conflict and aspiration that was incapable of defending itself from radicals of the left and right who would use the order to upend the order. Only juridical theory that recognises the need for exceptional action can save such a state.

Some of Schmitt's ideas foreshadow the work of Hannah Arendt on twentieth-century totalitarianism and Foucault's notion of 'biopolitics'. In *The Human Condition* (1958) Arendt takes the launch of the first space satellite in 1957 as a starting point for considering questions of the liminality of human social and political activity,[107] and merges this with a critique of the recurrent theme in European political thought from Plato to Marx of the 'making' of societies through forms of political action in which ordinary people (*animal laborans*)[108] are viewed as merely raw material – thinking that helped produced the Nazi and Stalinist systems she discussed in *The Origins of Totalitarianism* (1951). Arendt traces these developments in Europe to economic changes instituted by the massive appropriations of church and peasant land during the Reformation,[109] which has parallels to the seizure of waqfs by the modernising Muslim polity and disruptive policies of agrarian reform and industrialisation. She describes a pre-modern private, familial space in which the apolitical 'good life' (*vita activa*/*bios politikos*) of contemplation bears a resemblance to the pre-modern insulated world of the believer in Sabri and

[105] Schmitt, *Political Theology*, 36–52.
[106] Schmitt, *Concept of the Political* (Chicago: University of Chicago, 2007), 89–96. This chapter, titled 'The Age of Neutralizations and Depoliticizations', was from a lecture in 1929 that was first published in 1930.
[107] Arendt, *The Human Condition*, 1–3.
[108] Ibid., 79–93.
[109] Ibid., 61–73.

Hallaq's shari'a state (but in which 'Abduh's breaking of the *jumūd* and Akif's *say ve amel* had no place).[110]

Foucault used the term biopolitics (first in 1976) to refer to the state's increasing hold over all aspects of human life throughout the nineteenth century and the problematisation of questions such as health, sanitation, birth-rate, longevity, race, and need for rationalising systems of surveillance, punishment, and registration.[111] Its unparalleled bureaucratic capacities produced a 'totalizing form of power',[112] which he examined in detail in *Surveiller et punir: Naissance de la prison* (1975) and *Histoire de la sexualité: La volonté de savoir* (1976). Giorgio Agamben synthesised the ideas of Schmitt, Foucault, and Arendt to argue that juridical exception and the biopolitical model intersect in the modern state through its placing biological life – or 'bare life', his rendering of *zoe* in Aristotle's *Politics* – at the centre of its calculations, so that it is possible to go further than all three of them to state that 'the production of a biopolitical body is the original activity of sovereign power'.[113] The Nazi concentration camp is posited as an archetypal site of this bio-state of normalised exception, a place for treatment of its surplus humanity. Agamben's influential thesis has been read into a range of contemporary political questions, often at his own instigation, from the extra-territorial incarceration of Guantanamo Bay to permanent states of emergency across Arab states.[114] Taking these writers as a whole, their extensive use of terminologies from ancient Greek political philosophy has been questioned, in particular the implication that twentieth-century Western politics carries an original genetic coding from ancient Greece with the work of Plato and Aristotle as foundational texts.[115] In his discussion of European philosophy Sabri makes no reference to contemporaries such as Schmitt or Arendt, and he has little direct comment on the rise of totalitarian movements in Europe,

110 Ibid., 22–58.

111 Michel Foucault, '*Society Must Be Defended': Lectures at the Collège de France, 1975–76* (New York: Picador, 2003), 239–64.

112 Michel Foucault, 'The Birth of Biopolitics,' in *Ethics: Subjectivity and Truth*, vol. 1, ed. Foucault and Paul Rabinow (New York: The New Press, 1997), 73; idem, 'Why Study Power? The Question of the Subject,' in *Michel Foucault: Beyond Structuralism and Hermeneutics*, ed. Hubert L. Dreyfus and Paul Rabinow (Chicago: University of Chicago Press, 1983), 213.

113 Giorgio Agamben, *Homo Sacer: Sovereign Power and Bare Life* (Stanford: Stanford University Press, 1998), 6.

114 Idem, *State of Exception* (Chicago/London: University of Chicago Press, 2005).

115 James Gordon Finlayson, 'Bare Life and Politics in Agamben's Reading of Aristotle,' *The Review of Politics*, 72 (2010): 97–126.

citing only the Turkish republican experience as an example of the tyranny of modernity unchecked by the moral edifice of shariʿa. His alarm about the modern condition that arose in the West but spread globally as a universal value is expressed independently.

KEVSERI'S UNDERSTANDING OF THE ISLAMIC TRADITION

Rather than Sabri's old knowledge, Kevseri talks of a living tradition across the Islamic sciences, and this difference in focus reflects the importance he attaches to the notion of a heterogenous social order with equal room for the prescriptions of the law, explorations in *kalām*, intellection of Sufi metaphysics, popular practices, etc. Sabri is first and foremost a *mutakallim* defending largely unchanging statements of belief; there were limits to his acceptance of Sufi metaphysics, whereas Kevseri, as his early work *Irghām al-Murīd* demonstrates, was very much a product of Ottoman Sufi intellectual culture. This highlights an important point about how Kevseri understood Islamic faith as a tradition transmitted through scholars as much as it was truth preserved in foundational texts: thus, his extensive interest in the biographical genre of *ṭabaqāt* literature and the deft intertextuality in his method of constant citation of previous writers' work.[116] In Kevseri's description of the threat at hand he continually talks of the Islamic legal and theological structure as a living tradition. This is what he appears to be expressing with his extensive use of the descriptor *mutawārith*, whether it be *al-fiqh al-mutawārith*, *al-ḥukm al-mutawārith*, *al-aḥkām al-mutawāritha*, *al-ʿaqīda al-mutawāritha*, etc.[117] Kevseri's use of this term precedes the spread of its cognate *turāth* amongst a later generation of Muslim intellectuals such as Ḥasan Ḥanafī (1935–2021), Muḥammad ʿĀbid al-Jābirī (1936–2010), Abdallah Laroui (al-ʿArawī, b. 1933), Mohammed Arkoun (Arkūn, 1928–2010), and Naṣr Abū Zayd (1943–2010) who applied the hermeneutics of the Western

[116] On this point see Norman Calder, 'The Limits of Islamic Orthodoxy,' in *Intellectual Traditions in Islam*, ed. Farhad Daftary (London: I. B. Tauris/Institute of Ismaili Studies, 2000), 78–9.

[117] See al-Kawtharī, 'Ḥadīth Ramaḍān: al-Tajdīd,' *Maqālāt*, 115; 'Ḥawla Fikrat al-Taqrīb bayn al-Madhāhib,' *Maqālāt*, 124; 'Ḥawla al-Taḍḥiya ʿan al-Awlād: Islāḥ wa-Īḍāḥ,' *Maqālāt*, 218; 'Manshaʾ Ahl al-Dhimma bi-Shuʿār Khāṣṣ wa-Ḥukm Talabbus al-Muslim bihi ʿInd al-Fuqahāʾ,' *Maqālāt*, 221, 223; 'Naẓar al-Marʾ ilā Sharʿ Allāh Miʿyāru Dīnihi,' *Maqālāt*, 234; ' al-ʿAqīda al-Mutawāritha wa-l-Fiqh al-Mutawārith,' *Maqālāt*, 247–49; 'Inkār Nuzūl ʿĪsā wa-Iqrār ʿAqīdat al-Tajsīm,' *Maqālāt*, 261; *al-Tarḥīb bi-Naqd al-Khaṭīb*, in al-Kawtharī, *Taʾnīb al-Khaṭīb*, 378.

academe to critique the objectified tradition from the outside, such that they came to be called the *turāthiyyūn*.[118] In Kevseri's occasional use of *turāth* he intends a corpus of what he understands to be orthodox beliefs and practices (sunna) under assault from an array of disruptive sects revived from the past or innovated in the present.[119] For Kevseri the basic principles of shariʿa stood as a regulating base-line for the governed and the governing.[120] He argued at length against the *maṣlaḥa* and *ʿurf* advocated by modernist reformers and for *fuqahāʾ* oversight of parliamentary legislators dealing in positive law (*qawānīn waḍʿiyya*).[121] But he was at pains to stress the fallibility of *mujtahids*[122] and the flexibility of legal reasoning within the shariʿa system. Kevseri outlined a social, moral, and political responsibility that the religious class have to the tradition they represent and that produced them, such that they should neither 'rigidly hold to the past nor renounce it to please the atheists' (*al-jumūd ʿalā kull qadīm wa-lā al-juhūd musāyaratan li-l-mulḥidīn*).[123] For Muḥammad Rajab Al-Bayyūmī (d. 2011), the editor of *Muqaddimāt al-Kawtharī*, this made Kevseri the true 'guardian of the Islamic tradition' (*amīn al-turāth al-islāmī*).[124] Kevseri feared not only that this tradition was losing its complexity but the truth claims of those who appeared to be winning in the battle to define it.[125]

It would be an exaggeration to understand Kevseri as the scholar who steps outside the tradition in the manner of al-Jābirī and Arkoun while remaining a member of its elite corps of interpreters. However, Kevseri's approach can be compared to the understanding of an Islamic discursive

118 See Armando Salvatore, *Islam and the Political Discourse of Modernity* (Reading: Ithaca Press, 1997), 219–41, and Carool Kersten, *Cosmopolitans and Heretics: New Muslim Intellectuals and the Study of Islam* (London: Hurst, 2011).

119 Al-Kawtharī, 'Al-Mawlid al-Nabawī wa-l-Daʿwā al-Nabawiyya,' *Maqālāt*, 368.

120 See his example of Aleppan Seljuq ruler Nūr al-Dīn Zengī's (d. 1174) insistence on adhering to judicial process in dealing with brigandage; al-Kawtharī, 'Naẓar al-Marʾ ilā Sharʿ Allāh Miʿyāru Dīnihi,' *Maqālāt*, 236.

121 Al-Kawtharī, 'Min Anbāʾ al-ʿIlm wa-l-ʿUlamāʾ,' *Maqālāt*, 456.

122 Al-Kawtharī, *Taʾnīb al-Khaṭīb*, 12; al-Kawtharī, *al-Tarḥīb bi-Naqd al-Taʾnīb*, 392; al-Kawtharī, *Ṣafʿāt al-Burhān*, 49; al-Kawtharī, 'Min Anbāʾ al-ʿIlm wa-l-ʿUlamāʾ,' *Maqālāt*, 462.

123 Al-Kawtharī, 'Min Anbāʾ al-ʿIlm wa-l-ʿUlamāʾ,' *Maqālāt*, 455.

124 Al-Bayyūmī, *Muqaddimāt al-Kawtharī*, 13.

125 See Pieter Coppens' discussion of modernity and the end of polyvalence in Islamic intellectual culture; Coppens, 'Did Modernity End Polyvalence? Some Observations on Tolerance for Ambiguity in Sunni Tafsīr,' *Journal of Qurʾanic Studies* 23/1 (2021): 36–70; and Thomas Bauer (trans. Tricia Tunstall), *A Culture of Ambiguity: An Alternative History of Islam* (New York: Columbia University Press, 2021).

tradition proposed by Talal Asad in his influential essay 'The Idea of an Anthropology of Islam' (1986). Asad challenges narrations of the Middle East as essentially Islamic and of Islam as uniquely political – paradigms which became dominant across a range of academic disciplines and media discourse from the 1970s with the collapse of modernisation theory and rise of Islamic political movements.[126] Asad says anthropologists have also had a tendency to present a diverse range of phenomena under the rubric 'Islamic' despite lacking any overarching centrifugal force, be it theological, institutional, political, or otherwise. His response is a rejection of both essentialist and nominalist approaches to advocate a 'discursive tradition' that relates itself to both lived experience as well as the theoretical framework of founding texts and thought systems, 'a tradition of Muslim discourse that addresses itself to conceptions of the Islamic past and future, with reference to a particular Islamic practice in the present'.[127] In Asad's view this interpretation undercuts the notion – that Sabri and Kevseri contemplate – of a stable pre-modern Islam destroyed by modernity, since by definition a complex and evolving tradition could not be overturned as if it were a unity of values.[128]

Influenced by Alasdair MacIntyre's discussion of tradition in *After Virtue* (1982), Asad was addressing a theoretical debate in anthropology over how to describe Islam. On the one hand, Abdul Hamid el-Zein had argued that the diversity of believers' lived experience in different contexts meant it was not possible to talk of a single analytical category called Islam; on the other, the work of Clifford Geertz and Ernest Gellner imagined rituals and social structures that were archetypically Islamic.[129] Asad's discursive tradition did not reject the notion of a scripture-based starting point, but aimed to avoid Orientalist essentialism and address anthropology's fear of totemistic unities. Thus, he offered a path for scholarship across a variety of disciplines to navigate questions of orthodoxy and unity vs diversity, with the inspiration of MacIntyre's proposal

[126] Asad, 'The Idea of an Anthropology of Islam,' *Qui Parle*, 17/2 (Spring/Summer 2009): 5–8.

[127] Ibid., 20.

[128] Ibid., 30. He has in mind Michael Gilsenan, *Saint and Sufi in Modern Egypt* (1973) and Ernest Gellner, *Muslim Society* (1981).

[129] Abdul Hamid el-Zein, 'Beyond Ideology and Theology: The Search for the Anthropology of Islam,' *Annual Review of Anthropology*, 6 (1977): 227–54. Discussed in Ovamir Anjum, 'Islamic as a Discursive Tradition: Talal Asad and His Interlocutors,' *Comparative Studies of South Asia, Africa and the Middle East*, 27/3 (2007): 658.

that a living tradition should be understood as a 'historically extended, socially embodied argument' about the goods that constitute the tradition.[130]

The diverging approaches of Sabri/Hallaq and Kevseri/Asad should be seen as differences of emphasis within the same broad paradigm rather than a question of incompatible analyses. Kevseri is no less attentive to the deconstruction of the shariʿa state; indeed, he is the sharpest critic of reforms to the waqf system. Ottoman efforts to bring waqfs under close state supervision had begun in the 1820s; following the Turkish republic's example in 1924, many countries enacted legislation to limit the freedom of waqf founders to establish foundations and limit their terms of life. In 1954 Egypt centralised the administration of public waqfs in one government ministry and abolished waqfs whose beneficiaries were deemed to be familial.[131] As inalienable tax-free land established by an individual to generate income and provide services for broadly defined charitable purposes, the institution of the waqf played a central role in the political, economic, and social history of Muslim societies from the early period. Kevseri cites French minister Edouard Engelhardt's *La Turquie et le tanzimat, ou Histoire des reformes dans l'Empire ottoman depuis 1826 jusqu'a nos jours* (1881) – published in 1912 in Turkish translation by the historian Ali Reşad Bey (1877–1929) – in which waqf was framed as a hindrance to free sale of real estate and revenue for the public treasury.[132] Engelhardt said France had given advice to this effect to the Ottoman government in 1867.[133] In 1942 Kevseri argued publicly against plans to seize control of the al-Azhar mosque waqf and spend it on state schools rather than the international body of Azharī students[134] and he rejected the Egyptian government's division of waqfs into 'charitable' (*khayrī*) and 'family'

[130] Alasdair MacIntyre, *After Virtue: A Study in Moral Theory* (London: Bloomsbury, 2018), 257.

[131] Wael Hallaq, *An Introduction to Islamic Law* (Cambridge: Cambridge University Press, 2009), 138. Pascale Ghazaleh, ed., *Held in Trust: Waqf in the Islamic World* (Cairo: American University in Cairo Press, 2011).

[132] Al-Kawtharī, 'Khuṭūrat al-Masās bi-l-Awqāf al-Islāmiyya,' *Maqālāt*, 197; Edouard Engelhardt, *La Turquie et le tanzimat, ou Histoire des reformes dans l'Empire ottoman depuis 1826 jusqu'a nos jours* (Paris: Cotillon, 1882), 208. Sabri also cites this book as evidence of the collaboration between European governments and local elites, finally revealed upon its Turkish translation, to remodel Islamic social, economic, legal, and political structures along what he calls Christian lines; *Mawqif al-ʿAql*, 4:348, footnote 1, and 1:80–1.

[133] Al-Kawtharī, 'Muḥādatha Qadīma Ḥawla al-Waqf al-Ahlī,' *Maqālāt*, 195; Engelhardt, *La Turquie*, 209.

[134] Al-Kawtharī, 'Dhikrā al-Hijra al-Nabawiyya wa-l-Azhar al-Sharīf,' *Maqālāt*, 398 and 'Al-Azhar Qubayla ʿĪdihi al-Alfī,' *Maqālāt*, 478–9.

(*ahlī*) categories as a false taxonomy to facilitate the process of state appropriation.[135] As *ders vekili* he had resisted government plans to seize the Laleli school through stressing its status as a *vakıf*. French intent was to 'facilitate foreigners' owning what they want and building what they want',[136] Kevseri said, thus integrating the Ottoman state into the capitalist system on Western Europe's terms. Hallaq has the same analysis: French politicians and scholars were instrumental in creating a discourse among elites of the Late Ottoman and successor states of economic malaise caused by family endowments and other aspects of Islamic social and legal culture holding up the free-market economy,[137] and these ideas persist in scholarship.[138]

SABRI AND SAYYID QUṬB: A MEETING OF MINDS

Sabri was an admirer of Sayyid Quṭb before his transformation into an Islamic writer. He mentions Quṭb three times in the first volume of *Mawqif al-ʿAql* when he was still merely a conservative light on the Egyptian literary scene. First, he praises Quṭb for his review of ʿAbd Allāh al-Qaṣīmī's *Hādhihi Hiya al-Aghlāl*, one of the numerous works of this period that were met with the charge of atheism.[139] Quṭb wrote that he had invited al-Qaṣīmī to his home to talk, but became alarmed when al-Qaṣīmī praised British colonialism and the materialism of the West despite what Quṭb terms the West's 'inhuman methods in war and beyond' (*wasāʾil ghayr insāniyya fī al-ḥurūb wa-ghayr al-ḥurūb*).[140] Still, he decided to give the book a chance for the sake of freedom of thought since there were calls in Saudi Arabia for al-Qaṣīmī's trial for apostasy, but he was shocked at al-Qaṣīmī's argument that only belief in individual human capacities would help Muslims face the challenge of the West.[141] Sabri was impressed by Quṭb's comments, especially his dismissal of al-Qaṣīmī as a 'Don Quixote', by which Quṭb meant that al-Qaṣīmī was a vacuous *poseur* defending Western secularism with no

[135] Al-Kawtharī, 'Muḥādatha Qadīma,' *Maqālāt*, 190–7.

[136] Ibid., 195.

[137] Hallaq, *Shariʿa*, 471. On the nineteenth-century reconstitution of the Ottoman legal system, see 401–20; on that of Egypt, see 420–5.

[138] Timur Kuran, *The Long Divergence: How Islamic Law Held Back the Middle East* (Princeton: Princeton University Press, 2010).

[139] Sabri, *Mawqif al-ʿAql*, 1:13, 92.

[140] *Al-Sawādī* journal, 11 November 1946; published in Muḥammad ʿAbd al-Razzāq Ḥamza, *al-Shawāhid wa-l-Nuṣūṣ min Kitāb al-Aghlāl* (Riyadh: Maṭbaʿat al-Imām, 1948), nn.

[141] ʿAbd Allāh al-Qaṣīmī, *Hādhihi Hiya al-Aghlāl* (Cologne: Al-Kamel Verlag, 2000), 16.

original thinking of his own.[142] Sabri also noted Quṭb's interventions in the public debate about the Qurʾan and modernist thinking about its metaphysical, supranatural aspects. Quṭb was part of a literary set traversing the Left and Islamism that accused the intellectual giants of the interwar period – Tawfīq al-Ḥakīm, ʿAbbās al-ʿAqqād, Ṭāhā Ḥusayn – of failing to develop a national culture independent of colonial power.

In 1947 the trope of demystification of the Qurʾan became the subject of intense public debate when Fuʾād University considered a thesis by student Muḥammad Aḥmad Khalaf Allāh in 1947 by the title *al-Fann al-Qiṣaṣī fī al-Qurʾān* (Narrative Art in the Qurʾan). After the ministry of education exonerated Khalaf Allāh and his supervisor Amīn al-Khūlī, an Arabic language professor, from the charge of arguing that Muḥammad had authored the Qurʾan, the thesis was published as a book in 1950. Sabri noted that defenders of the thesis saw the rejection of allegorical interpretation as an attack on ʿAbduh himself, which for Sabri only proved his point that ʿAbduh had acquired a hallowed position as the founder of Egyptian modernist Islam.[143] This brought Sabri to a discussion of Quṭb's commentary on the affair, which had some weight given Quṭb's work *al-Taṣwīr al-Fannī fī al-Qurʾān* (Artistic Representation in the Qurʾan, 1944). Over three articles in the journal *Al-Sawādī* Quṭb accused Khalaf Allāh and al-Khūlī of making sensationalist claims to advance their careers, echoing Sabri's view of ʿAlī ʿAbd al-Rāziq and Ṭāhā Ḥusayn's oscillating fortunes.[144] However, Sabri accused Quṭb of misjudging the seriousness of the issue because of faults in Quṭb's own theological understandings, since Quṭb revealed that he himself was ridden with doubt over some elements of the Qurʾan such as the resurrection.[145] Quṭb concluded by saying he was an intellectual (*rajul fikr*), not a religious scholar whose pure dogma would hinder free thought, so he would be open to anyone helping him find the truth. Sabri's response was that Quṭb only needed recourse to reason and logic since the free human mind would be a lantern lighting the path to certitude[146] and the only place for allegorical understanding in the Qurʾan is the human imagery used when talking of God.[147]

[142] Ḥamza, *al-Shawāhid*, ss.
[143] Sabri, *Mawqif al-ʿAql*, 1:320–4. The incident presaged the tribulations of Naṣr Abū Zayd in the 1990s, a point he made himself: Abū Zayd, 'The Dilemma of the Literary Approach to the Qurʾan,' *Alif: Journal of Comparative Poetics*, 23 (2003): 8–47.
[144] Cited in Sabri, *Mawqif al-ʿAql*, 1:325–6.
[145] Ibid., 327.
[146] Ibid., 328.
[147] Ibid., 329.

Sabri valued Quṭb, whom he regarded as 'the closest to the right path among those erring in evaluation of the Qur'an' (*aqrab al-ḍāllīn fī taqdīr al-qur'ān min al-hudā*), and gave him the excuse of being a layman unlettered in Islamic sciences.[148] Indeed, Sabri's text gives the impression of a certain familiarity between the two men, and Ali Ulvi Kurucu, a student of both Sabri and Kevseri in Cairo, confirms this in his memoirs. Quṭb would attend the same salons of writer Maḥmūd Shākir in which Sabri would take part with Kurucu.[149] Kurucu confirms that Sabri had begun reading Quṭb and appreciating him during this period when Quṭb began writing more on Islamic issues. Sabri prayed for him to find right guidance and admired his writing style, saying: 'His literary knowledge and fine style have helped him, and were he not such a litterateur his writings would not have this strength, appeal, and spirituality.'[150] Quṭb would have had at least two other opportunities to become familiar with Sabri's work: the publication of *al-Qawl al-Faṣl* in 1943 with the blessing of al-Bannā and the publication of *Mawqif al-ʿAql* in 1949, after al-Bannā's death in February 1949 and before Quṭb's return from the United States in August 1950. Quṭb would likely have been aware of the relationship between Sabri and al-Bannā and perhaps of their differences: Sabri altered al-Bannā's proposed title *al-Qawl al-Faṣl bayn Īmānayn* to remove the reference to two faiths, since he had moved to his radical position that the *īmān* of Muslim reformers was in doubt.[151]

The large literature on Quṭb has focussed heavily on the question of his transformation from liberal litterateur to Islamic ideologue:[152] his foreign travel from November 1948 (travelling to Britain, Switzerland, and Italy on his return), his acquaintance with the Indian Muslim *ʿālim* Abū al-Ḥasan Nadwī (1914–99) during hajj and through him with the ideas of Abū al-Aʿlā Mawdūdī, and his imprisonment from 1954. Many have noted not only his disdain for America's secular culture but also its racialist

[148] Ibid., 329, footnote 1.
[149] Düzdağ, *Hatıralar*, 2:301.
[150] Interview with Kurucu, in Al-Qawsī, *Muṣṭafā Ṣabrī*, 448.
[151] Ibid., 442–3.
[152] The many works on Quṭb include John Calvert, *Sayyid Qutb and the Origins of Radical Islamism* (London: Hurst, 2010); James Toth, *Sayyid Qutb: The Life and Legacy of a Radical Islamic Intellectual* (New York: Oxford University Press, 2013); Gilles Kepel (trans. Jon Rothschild), *Muslim Extremism in Egypt: The Prophet and the Pharaoh* (Berkeley: University of California Press, 1993); ʿAbd al-Fattāḥ al-Khālidī, *Sayyid Quṭb: Min al-Mīlād ilā al-Istishhād* (Damascus: Dār al-Qalam, 2007); Adnan Musallam, *From Secularism to Jihad: Sayyid Quṭb and the Foundations of Radical Islamism* (Westport, CT; Praeger, 2005).

hierarchies,[153] topics he often revisited in subsequent writings. Giedre Sabaseviciute, Omnia El Shakry, and others have argued that Quṭb's conversion to Islamism was more of a gradual transition than a sharp turn and one in harmony with a broader internal shift within Egypt's post-war intellectual scene.[154] Sabri's identification of Quṭb's religious leanings is consonant with that conclusion. Quṭb had a regular column in the journal *al-Risāla* but was involved in other projects such as *al-Fikr al-Jadīd* (1948) which brought together intellectuals of different backgrounds with a shared commitment to critique of the ruling elites. *Al-Fikr al-Jadīd*, which ran from January to March 1948, brought Quṭb further into contact with Brotherhood networks: it was owned by Muḥammad Ḥilmi al-Minyāwī, a member of the Brotherhood's consultative assembly, and published by Brotherhood-linked publishing house Dār al-Kitāb al-ʿArabī.[155] It was because of his sharp critical writing that the education ministry sent Quṭb abroad to avoid arrest by the palace.[156] After his return in August 1950, Quṭb began writing for the Brotherhood outlets *al-Daʿwā* and *al-Muslimūn*; in 1952 the Brotherhood printed his books *al-ʿAdāla al-Ijtimāʿiyya fī al-Islām* (Social Justice in Islam, 1949) and *Maʿrakat al-Islām wa-l-Raʾsmāliyya* (The Battle of Islam and Capitalism, 1951); and after he became formally a member in 1953 Quṭb was appointed editor of its official journal *Majallat al-Ikhwān al-Muslimīn* in 1954.

Al-ʿAdāla al-Ijtimāʿiyya is usually cited as the first work of Quṭb's Islamic phase. Written just before his American sojourn, it continued the themes of social justice, corruption, anti-colonialism, and Islamic solutions that had attracted attention in his *al-Fikr al-Jadīd* writing. The book's message was revolutionary: Muslim rulers who ape Western materialistic systems, be they capitalist or socialist, do not merit obedience because only

[153] Calvert, *Sayyid Qutb*, 148–9; the seventh edition adds African Americans to a list of Western injustices in chapter five that includes genocide of American Indians, racial laws in South Africa and Russian treatment of Muslims (p. 228). See Quṭb, *al-ʿAdāla al-Ijtimāʿiyya fī al-Islām* (Cairo: Dār Iḥyāʾ al-Kutub al-ʿArabiyya, 1954), 53. See Toth, *Sayyid Qutb*, 65 for a summary of other reasons posited by scholars.

[154] Giedre Sabaseviciute, 'Sayyid Qutb and the Crisis of Culture in Late 1940s Egypt,' *IJMES*, 50/1 (2018): 85–101. See also Yoav Di-Capua, 'The Intellectual Revolt of the 1950s and "The Fall of the Udaba,"' in *Commitment and Beyond: Reflections on/of the Political in Arabic Literature since the 1940s*, ed. Friederike Pannewick and Georges Khalil (Wiesbaden: Ludwig Reichert, 2015), 89–104; and Omnia El Shakry, 'The Vexed Archives of Decolonization in the Middle East,' *American Historical Review* 120 (2015): 920–34.

[155] Sabaseviciute, 'Sayyid Quṭb,' 92–3.

[156] Toth, *Sayyid Qutb*, 58.

the shariʿa system can ensure social justice and equality. Quṭb brings together various themes prevalent in modernist and Salafi thought of the period and expresses them in an ideological, anti-colonial vocabulary squarely outside the traditional genres of Islamic scholarship that Sabri, Kevseri, and some of their opponents would use. Islam is discussed in ideological terms as a political animal of the public sphere with the Qurʾan as its manifesto.[157] Behind the new language, Quṭb has adopted the theory of decline and rejection of the *kalām* and *falsafa* tradition as both futile and foreign,[158] and he downplays paranormal phenomena as a basis for belief (*dīn lam yaʿtamid ʿalā al-khawāriq wa-l-muʿjizāt*).[159] But he condemns positivist philosophy for allowing no place for morality,[160] which explains its colonial connections;[161] he denounces writers such as Haykal for attempting materialistic understandings of the motives of early Muslim leaders;[162] and he outlines a just economic system that forbids usury, pursues wealth redistribution through Islamic taxes, and views property as a trust from God.[163] Quṭb writes: 'Obedience to the ruler [*walī al-amr*] is derived from obedience to God and the Prophet, because the ruler in Islam is not obeyed for himself, but due to his establishing the shariʿa of God and His prophet; he derives the right of obedience from fulfilling this alone. If he deviates obedience lapses, and his order becomes non-binding [*idhā inḥarafa ʿanhā saqaṭat ṭāʿatuhu wa-lam yajib li-amrihi al-nafādh*].'[164] Egypt is no longer 'Islamic' (*islāmī*) because it has replaced the shariʿa system with French law, Quṭb says.[165] The contrast to Sabri's ideas, formed in light of the Turkish republic's policies, is subtle: where Sabri sees political oppression in the post-shariʿa state, Quṭb here sees economic oppression. Writing in the colonial context of a yet-to-become independent Egypt, Quṭb has still not drawn out Sabri's implication of an apostate society.

[157] On this point see Adnan Musallam, 'Sayyid Quṭb and Social Justice, 1945–1948,' *Journal of Islamic Studies*, 4/1 (1993): 62–3; Yvonne Haddad, 'The Qurʾanic Justification for an Islamic Revolution: The View of Sayyid Quṭb,' *Middle East Journal*, 37/1 (Winter 1983): 14–29; William Shepard, 'Islam as a "System" in the Later Writings of Sayyid Quṭb,' *Middle Eastern Studies*, 25/1 (January 1989): 31–50.

[158] Quṭb, *al-ʿAdāla al-Ijtimāʿiyya*, 22–3.

[159] Ibid., 17.

[160] Ibid., 252–6.

[161] Ibid., 176–7.

[162] Ibid., 132–5.

[163] Ibid., 105–45.

[164] Ibid., 97.

[165] Ibid., 225–7.

Al-ʿAdāla al-Ijtimāʿiyya went through numerous reprints which altered the text to reflect, first, Quṭb's changing relations with the Muslim Brotherhood and, second, his radical thinking in light of his prison experiences from 1954 to 1964.[166] These changes were observed in his other writings. His next major work was *Maʿrakat al-Islām wa-l-Raʾsmāliyya* (1951), which toughened his arguments against both imperialism and its local partners and moved closer to Sabri's vision of political oppression in a society denuded of its protective shield of shariʿa. Now he talked of exploitative *ṭughāh,* a Qurʾanic term in its alternative plural *ṭāghūn* and the singular *ṭāghiya*, signifying transgressive, oppressive peoples or rulers,[167] by which he intended elements among the ruling elites who prefer religious sentiment to remain restricted to superficial manifestations of faith and fear the consequences for their position of a shariʿa system.[168] On the contrary, 'Islam must rule' (*lā budd li-l-islām an yaḥkum*),[169] and the ruler who does not establish shariʿa justice loses his right to loyalty (*saqaṭat ṭāʿatuhu*).[170] Its replacement with a Western political system – parliamentary democracy – and the law that system enshrines – a melange of European codes – has failed to establish social justice and Egyptians have lost faith in the possibility. Democracy has meant not only capitalist exploitation of millions of impoverished and disenfranchised peasants but unchecked abuse by the state's coercive apparatus, of which he cites two graphic examples.[171] Torture is the story of every political detainee in the history of modern Egypt, Quṭb writes, posing the question, 'Was it constitutional parliamentary democracy that produced this, is responsible for it, and should be distanced from government since it is under its watch that these abominations are committed?'[172] Egypt's legal system brings together elements derived from different social, historical, theological, and customary contexts that do not reflect Egyptian realities, thus there is a conflict between 'the spirit of legislation and the spirit of the people for whom the legislation

[166] William Shepard, *Sayyid Quṭb and Islamic Activism: A Translation and Critical Analysis of Social Justice in Islam* (Leiden: Brill, 1996), ix–lix; Musallam, 'Sayyid Quṭb and Social Justice,' 61.
[167] See Qurʾan 37:30, 38:55, 51:53, 52:32, 68:31, 69:5, 78:22.
[168] Sayyid Quṭb, *Maʿrakat al-Islām wa-l-Raʾsmāliyya* (Cairo: Dār al-Shurūq, 1993), 6, 37, 103–6.
[169] Ibid., 56.
[170] Ibid., 74.
[171] Ibid., 77–9.
[172] Ibid., 79–80.

is prescribed'.[173] The solution is for Egyptians to take affairs into own hands – 'the toiling masses, deprived and duped, must deal with the issue by themselves; they must think of means of salvation and choose'.[174] This means of salvation is not to be found in political parties, communism, the United Nations, or the West, which based on his experience of American attitudes towards the Palestinian question (*ḥarb Filisṭīn*) he says feels 'violent animosity [*ʿadāʾ ʿanīf*]' towards Islam, the East, and coloured people generally,[175] but in 'Islam': 'O people, this is the path, this is the path!' (*ayyatuhā al-jamāhīr, hādhā huwa al-ṭarīq, hādhā huwa al-ṭarīq!*).[176] In Quṭb's evolving conceptualisation of Islam as a modern ideology, Islam is becoming a political order yet to be established (*ḥukm al-islām*).[177]

ABŪ AL-AʿLĀ MAWDŪDĪ'S IDEAS IN QUṬB'S CONCEPTUAL FRAMEWORK

Quṭb first met Abū al-Ḥasan Nadwī in Mecca in 1950, and it was through Nadwī that Quṭb became familiar with the work of Mawdūdī. Through them both Quṭb introduced terminologies that he elaborated into a unique framework of thought. During a subsequent visit to Quṭb's home in Cairo in January 1951 Nadwī asked Quṭb to write an introduction to the 1951 edition of Nadwī's book *Mādhā Khasira al-ʿĀlam bi-Inḥiṭāṭ al-Muslimīn* (What Did the World Lose Through the Collapse of the Muslims?, 1945) in which he made innovative use in Arabic of the term *jāhiliyya* in his argument that Islamic leadership can restore moral and spiritual order to the world.[178] Nadwī took the term beyond the literary trope of an unbalanced Arabian moral order set right by the mission of the Prophet,[179] by

[173] Ibid., 28.
[174] Ibid., 113.
[175] Ibid., 33.
[176] Ibid., 122.
[177] Ibid., 63. See Shepard, 'Islam as a "System,"' 31–50.
[178] On visiting Quṭb, Abū al-Ḥasan Nadwī, *Mādhā Khasira al-ʿĀlam bi-Inḥiṭāṭ al-Muslimīn* (Cairo: Maktabat al-Īmān, 1994), 27. Nadwī records a meeting with Kevseri in February 1951 during his Cairo trip but reprimands him for engaging in 'sectarian debates' (*munāqashāt madhhabiyya*); idem, *Mudhakkirāt Sāʾiḥ fī al-Sharq al-ʿArabī* (Beirut: Muʾassasat al-Risāla, 1975), 52.
[179] The term is usually translated as 'age of ignorance' as an antonym to knowledge (*ʿilm*), but its original meaning was the arrogant unbridled passion of tribal society, the opposite of the *ḥilm* of the Prophet, i.e., the moral reasonableness of civilised men; Izutsu, *Ethico-Religious Concepts in the Qurʾān*, 28–35 and Ignácz Goldziher, *Muslim Studies*, vol. 1 (London: Allen & Unwin, 1967), 201–8.

applying it polemically to the hegemonic global position of the European political, economic, and social order and the risk for Muslims of becoming 'allies of European *jāhiliyya*'.[180] He was developing here the use of the term in Urdu by Mawdūdī in the context of the political struggle over the shape of post-British India to describe a range of non-Islamic contemporary political and social phenomena, some stemming from materialist reification of the individual (*khāliṣ jāhiliyyat*) such as capitalism and socialism, and some of pre-modern origin such as pantheistic beliefs and ascetic practices.[181] In his preface Quṭb expanded on the key principle that *jāhiliyya* was a modern condition, stating it was 'not a period of limited time but a particular spiritual and mental characteristic'.[182] 'The Europeans have for long produced history for the world from their Western point of view, informed by their materialist culture and philosophy and by Western and religious chauvinism [*ʿaṣabiyya*]', he wrote.[183]

The major impact of these ideas was felt in Quṭb's vast work of *tafsīr*, *Fī Ẓilāl al-Qurʾān* (In the Shadow of the Qurʾan), whose long period of composition spanned the excitement of the monarchy's last days and the despair of post-colonial dungeons.[184] It began as a series of articles in the journal *al-Muslimūn* from January 1952 to March 1954,[185] followed by others written between 1954 and 1959 while in prison and then published together as a revised six-volume set in 1961 and revised and reissued again by his brother Muḥammad in 1978.[186] Tracing the development of Quṭb's thought is complicated by these various stages of publication, censorship, and editing. Like ʿAbduh and Akif before him, Quṭb set out to produce a *tafsīr* in unorthodox contemporary terms, relating the Qurʾanic text to the conditions of modernity that concerned him – in his case, the political

180 Nadwī, *Mādhā Khasira*, 229.

181 Abū al-Aʿlā Mawdūdī, *Islam aur Jahiliyyat* (Pathankot: Maktaba-i Jamāʿat-i Islāmī, 1941), *passim*. On the evolution of the concept of *jāhiliyya* in Mawdūdī's circle see M. A. Sherif, 'Review: A System of Life, Mawdudi and the Ideologisation of Islam,' *Salaam*; www.salaam.co.uk/a-system-of-life-mawdudi-and-the-ideologisation-of-islam (accessed 3 August 2021). On Mawdūdī's *jāhiliyya* see Jan-Peter Hartung, *A System of Life: Mawdudi and the Ideologisation of Islam* (London: Hurst, 2014), 62–72.

182 Quṭb, 'Preface,' in Nadwī, *Mādhā Khasira*, 12.

183 Ibid., 13.

184 Quṭb is said to have been particularly affected by the execution of twenty-one Brotherhood inmates in 1957.

185 'Fi Ẓilāl al-Qurʾān,' *al-Muslimūn*, 1/3 (28 January 1952), 237-40; 1/4 (March 1952), 331-9; 1/5 (27 March 1952), 434–42; 1/6 (November 1952), 534–42; 1/7 (June 1953), 749–54; 1/8 (July 1953), 752–62; 3/1 (February 1954), 357–64; 3/5 (March 1954), 453–60.

186 Toth, *Sayyid Qutb*, 81.

system in which Muslims lived. His final work, *Maʿālim fī al-Ṭarīq* (Signs on the Way, 1964), for which he was sentenced to death, was intended as an abridged version of some sections of *Fī Ẓilāl al-Qurʾan* for his growing number of followers,[187] and yet still written under the gaze of prison censors.[188] A number of other prison works were published in the following years, including *Hādhā al-Dīn* (This Religion, 1962), *Khaṣāʾiṣ al-Taṣawwur al-Islāmī wa-Muqawwimātuhu* (Characteristics and Bases of the Islamic Imaginary, 1962), *al-Islām wa-Mushkilat al-Ḥaḍāra* (Islam and the Problem of Civilisation, 1962), and *al-Mustaqbal li-Hādhā al-Dīn* (The Future Belongs to This Religion, 1965). Quṭb was feted by the military government in its early days as a Muslim anti-colonial writer of renown, invited in August 1952 to address the coup leaders including Nasser (Jamāl ʿAbd al-Nāṣir, 1918–70) on 'intellectual and spiritual liberation in Islam'. In an account of the evening given by Quṭb's colleague Aḥmad ʿAbd al-Ghaffūr ʿAṭṭār in 1967, Quṭb declared half-jokingly that although the revolution had come he still suspected he might end up in prison.[189] Quṭb acted as a liaison between the Brotherhood and the Free Officers, but the relationship soured in 1953 due to a number of factors: Quṭb turned down Nasser's offer of the post of minister of education, Brotherhood factions were drawn into the rivalry between Nasser and the first republican president Muḥammad Najīb, and, more broadly, the Brotherhood was unwilling to place its mass organisation in the service of the military regime on Nasser's terms.[190]

Fi Ẓilāl al-Qurʾān begins with a discussion of Quṭb's theory of the new *jāhiliyya* into which Muslims have regressed:[191] *jāhiliyya* 'surges on the earth' (*tamūj fī al-arḍ*),[192] mankind 'lives through the concepts of *jāhiliyya* in east and west, north and south',[193] Islam has been 'sidelined from

[187] Ibid., 72.

[188] Ibid., 80. Olivier Carré, *Mysticism and Politics: A Critical Reading of Fī Ẓilāl al-Qur'ān by Sayyid Quṭb (1906–1966)* (Leiden: Brill, 2003), 8.

[189] Al-Khalidi, *Sayyid Quṭb*, 302–4. Nasser is said to have stood up to say in reply, 'they will only get to you over our dead bodies, we promise you in the name of God.' The account is likely embellished.

[190] For a summary see Carré, *Mysticism and Politics*, 4–8.

[191] Sayyid Quṭb, *Fī Ẓilāl al-Qurʾān*, 6 vols. (Cairo: Dār al-Shurūq, 1992), 6:3549–50: Muslims must have 'honest intent to jihad to make his religion victorious among all religion, as God has desired, and not hesitate between word and action'. All citations are from the 1978 version edited by Muḥammad Quṭb. For guidance through the text, I have relied on Olivier Carré's *Mysticism and Politics*, but I will analyse Quṭb's arguments separately from the question of how they relate to the Qurʾanic verses in question.

[192] Quṭb, *Fī Ẓilāl*, 1:11.

[193] Ibid., 1:11.

leadership for *jāhiliyya* to take over once again' in the form of materialism (*al-māddiyya*).[194] However, since Islam is not only a set of theological doctrines but a 'general declaration to liberate men from their state of slavery' (*iʿlān ʿāmm li-taḥrīr al-insān min ʿubūdiyyat al-ʿibād*), it requires a mobilisational element, an offensive jihad of arms (*al-jihād bi-l-sayf*).[195] His model is the Medinans who prepared themselves in the utopian Islamic proto-state for an assault on the pagan cultic centre of Mecca, symbolising the liberation of all mankind.[196] So while within Muslim territory protection of the faith and functioning of the state are fundamental obligations, the ultimate aim is to take on that which lies outside the Islamic zone (*dār al-islām*),[197] contrary to the arguments of Orientalists who have tricked Muslims into believing that jihad has no universal aims.[198] Quṭb makes clear his inspiration on these points in Mawdūdī, citing extensively from *al-Jihād fī Sabīl Allāh*, the 1960 Arabic translation from Urdu of his first book *al-Jihād fī al-Islām* (Jihad in Islam, 1927).[199] Quṭb's ideological lexicon developed around this revolutionary view of Islam: he calls for a '*fiqh* of action' (*fiqh al-ḥaraka*) that reflects current realities,[200] in contrast to the '*fiqh* on paper' (*fiqh al-awrāq*) of previous eras.[201] Indeed, *ḥaraka/ḥarakī/yataḥarrak* are key concepts throughout *Fī Ẓilāl al-Qurʾān*, expressing the sense of revolutionary movement and dynamic community that Quṭb sought to convey.

There are several themes that overlap with Sabri's ideas. Quṭb accepts Ashʿarī causality without diluting divine intervention in human affairs in the manner of ʿAbduh, Akif, and other modernist thinkers.[202] In contrast to his earlier work, there is none of the modernist penchant for rationalising paranormal phenomena or devaluing the notion of *al-ghayb* (the unseen/unknown). To reject the unseen because we cannot comprehend it experientially is to 'relapse into the state of animals who live only in the

194 Ibid., 1:16–17.
195 Ibid. 3:1435.
196 Ibid., 3:1437, 4:2122.
197 Ibid., 3:1441.
198 Ibid., 3:1443.
199 Ibid., 3:1444–52.
200 Ibid., 4:2006. The term *fiqh al-wāqiʿ* is derived from this passage. He also uses *al-fiqh al-ḍarūrī* (necessary *fiqh*); 3:1619.
201 Ibid., 4:2006.
202 Ibid., 1:503: 'God organises causes and effects according to His will, then requires man to perform his duty, expend his effort, and fulfil his obligations.' See Daniel Gimaret, *La doctrine d'al-Ashʿarī* (Paris: Cerf, 1990).

realm of that which is sensed [*al-maḥsūs*]',[203] he says (echoing Kevseri), highlighting the Qur'anic phrase (2:3) *alladhīna yu'minūn bi-l-ghayb* which Sabri had used for the title of his book on political theory.[204] Secularism is a great prison sectioned off by the iron bars (*quḍbān ḥadīdiyya*) of empirical knowledge that block Islam's 'fountains of knowledge and light'.[205] Secular-materialism is advocated by 'agents' (*'umalā'*) in the guise of professors, philosophers, researchers, poets, artists, and journalists who 'bear only the names of Muslims'.[206] Unlike the positivists (*al-madhāhib al-waḍ'iyya*), those who believe in God regard unquestioned belief in the unseen as a measure of faith.[207]

Most notable of all, Quṭb's concept of *ḥākimiyya* expresses Sabri's concept of *ḥukm al-islām*, the divinely sanctified society in which no internal actor can manipulate the political and juridical system for his own ends. Tyrannical power (*ṭāghūt*) is that which does not recognise God's juridical authority (*ḥākimiyya*)[208] and juridical systems based on positive law turn their subjects into slaves (*'ubūdiyyat al-bashar li-l-bashar*) through conferring the sovereignty of men over men (*ḥākimiyyat al-bashar li-l-bashar*).[209] The claim that *ḥākimiyya* is a neologism invented to translate Mawdūdī's *ḥukūmat-i ilāhiya* (sovereignty of God) into Arabic from around 1946 onwards is inaccurate.[210] The term *hâkimiyet* was used in Ottoman Turkish and appears in Şemsettin Sami's Turkish-Arabic dictionary published in November 1899, with the French *souveraineté* given in explanation.[211] Said Nursi used it in an Ottoman article published in 1920 with the meaning of the absolute authority of the Qur'an in matters where there is no dispute in Sunni jurisprudence.[212] Sabri used *ḥākimiyya* in his Arabic book *Mawqif al-Bashar Taḥta Sulṭān*

[203] Quṭb, *Fī Ẓilāl*, 1:59.
[204] Ibid., 1:39–40, 2:1113–22. This encompasses belief in the existence of angels and jinn.
[205] Ibid., 6:3684.
[206] Ibid., 1:415.
[207] Ibid., 3:1338.
[208] Ibid., 2:926–7.
[209] Ibid., 4:1940.
[210] This claim is made by Stéphane Lacroix, 'Ḥākimiyya,' in *Encyclopaedia of Islam 3*, http://dx.doi.org/10.1163/1573-3912_ei3_COM_30217 (consulted 6 December 2018); also, Calvert, *Sayyid Quṭb*, 214. The Urdu phrase was used in the Jamā'at-i Islāmī's founding statement published in *Tarjuman* journal, May 1941; see Irfan Ahmad, 'Genealogy of the Islamic State: Reflections on Maududi's Political Thought and Islamism,' *Journal of the Royal Anthropological Institute*, 15/2009: 154.
[211] Şemsettin Sami, *Qamus-i Türki* (Istanbul: Çağrı Yayınları, 1996), 537.
[212] Said Nursi, 'Kur'an-ı Azimü'ş-Şa'nın Hakimiyet-i Mutlakası,' *SR*, 6 May 1920, 18/463: 242–3. It also appears in his *Lem'alar* (Istanbul: Sözler, 2012), thirtieth Lem'a, 368, as an

al-Qadar (1934), in which he first outlined his turn away from Māturīdī free will: Just as it was an act of God that brought each human into existence, God's intervention is no less in the continuing motions of life, and to assume otherwise would be to 'compare the ownership and sovereignty of God to any sovereignty or ownership' (*lā tushabbih mālikiyyat al-khāliq wa-ḥākimiyyatahu bi-ayyati ḥākimiyya aw mālikiyya*).[213]

Further, the term appeared in Urdu in a 1939 speech and pamphlet, *Islām kā Naẓariyya-i Siyāsī* (Islam's Political Theory), which was subsequently issued in Arabic as *Naẓariyyat al-Islām al-Siyāsiyya* in Lahore in 1946 and Cairo in 1950;[214] it also appeared in the 1955 translation into Arabic of *Qurʾān kī Chār Bunyādī Iṣṭilāḥain* (Four Concepts in the Qurʾan). It was from this second book that Quṭb likely became familiar with the term.[215] Written in 1941, Mawdūdī intended it as a statement of Jamāʿat-i Islāmī policy against the Muslim League's plan for a secular Muslim state in post-colonial India. It argued that Muslims had at an early stage forgotten the Qurʾanic understandings of Arabic terms which have implications for Islam as a total system impacting the individual and the state. Though not a central term in the work, *ḥākimiyya* was used in the Arabic edition to articulate Mawdūdī's central idea of a political order in which God is sovereign and *dīn* itself is identified with the modern state.[216] In this manner Mawdūdī hoped to create in Muslims an attitude that would prevent their dissolution in Hindu society. After Pakistan's founding Mawdūdī gave this practical form in an elected legislative body whose work was a form of *ijtihād*, usurping the traditional role of the

Arabic invocation used by the Turkish devout (*elhamdülillah ʿalā raḥmāniyetihi ve ʿalā ḥākimiyetihi*), though Arabic speakers did not say this.

213 Sabri, *Mawqif al-Bashar*, 230. Sabri, *Mawqif al-ʿAql*, 3:433–4.

214 It states: '*al-ḥākimiyya* (sovereignty) [*sic*] is God's alone and legislation [*tashrīʿ*] is in his hands.' Abū al-Aʿlā Mawdūdī (trans., Muḥammad ʿĀṣim al-Ḥaddād), *Naẓariyyat al-Islām al-Siyasiyya* (Damascus: Dār al-Fikr, 1967), 27, 33, 45.

215 The book, *al-Muṣṭalaḥāt al-Arbaʿa fī al-Qurʾān*, is cited in a footnote as a source for Quṭb's ideas in the Muḥammad Quṭb edition; 1/927. Calvert mistakes the translator as Nadwī; it was translated by Muḥammad Kāẓim Sabbāq in Lahore.

216 See Mawdūdī, *al-Muṣṭalaḥāt al-Arbaʿa*, 71: (*ḥākimiyya siyāsiyya*), 93 (defined as the English 'sovereignty', which is itself defined as *istikhdām al-quwwa al-qāhira*, 116), 120–1 (as the notion of God's authority expressed through the Qurʾanic term *dīn*). Mawdūdī's collaborator Khurshīd Aḥmad considers that *ḥākimiyya*'s significance in Mawdūdī's thought has been overstated; interview, Leicester, 23 February 2019. On the evolution of the concept in South Asian Islamist circles prior to Mawdūdī's usage see Muḥammad Qasim Zaman, 'The Sovereignty of God in Modern Islamic Thought,' *Journal of the Royal Asiatic Society*, 25/3 (July 2015), 389–418.

ʿulamaʾ (what Mawdūdī called theodemocracy).[217] Quṭb did not develop the term in any manner beyond Mawdūdī's framework.[218] Where Quṭb was innovative was in conceptualising *jāhiliyya* in sharper lines as a state of regression in human society in which modern Muslims were implicated[219] and setting it in a binary framework with *ḥākimiyya*.[220] Yet over *Fī Ẓilāl al-Qurʾān*'s 4000 pages he did not go so far as Sabri in declaring the apostate nature of the modern Muslim subject.

QUṬB'S FINAL WORKS

This takes us to Quṭb's more explicitly activist works of his final period of writing in the 1960s in which he draws closer to the outright denunciation of the modern state and its citizens. In his short book *Hādhā al-Dīn* Quṭb distils his arguments in a softer and more easily digestible manner, reasserting his concept of a divine politico-juridical framework that frees man from the self-serving interest of other men and Islam's calling to retake the emancipatory reins of global leadership. The same year, Quṭb published *Khaṣāʾiṣ al-Taṣawwur al-Islāmī*[221] in which he argued that the Qurʾan is no more a subject text for the deliberations of *tafsīr*, *kalām*, or *falsafa* than it is for the treatments of Hegelian rationalism or Comteian positivism, but a manifesto for action that Muslim society (*al-jamāʿa al-muslima*) must embrace.[222] This is the basis of what he describes as the 'Islamic thought' (*al-fikr al-islāmī*) that expresses the true 'Islamic

[217] Abū al-Aʿlā Mawdūdī (trans. Khurshīd Aḥmad), *The Islamic Law and Constitution* (Karachi: Jamaat-e-Islami Publications, 1955), 166. On Mawdūdī's Islamic state, see Vali Nasr, *Mawdudi and the Making of Islamic Revivalism* (New York: Oxford University Press, 1996), 80–106; Charles Adams, 'Mawdudi and the Islamic State,' in *Voices of Resurgent Islam*, ed. John Esposito (New York: Oxford University Press, 1983), 99–132; Haroon K. Ullah, *Vying for Allah's Vote: Understanding Islamic Parties, Political Violence, and Extremism in Pakistan* (Washington, DC: Georgetown University Press, 2014), 75–89.

[218] Both Mawdūdī and Quṭb link the term to the numerous uses of the lexical derivations of *ḥukm* in the Qurʾan, such as *al-ḥukm lillāh* (40:12).

[219] Quṭb, *Fī Ẓilal al-Qurʾan*, 2/891: 'the *jāhiliyya* is not a historical period but a state that comes into existence when its characteristics are found in a circumstance or order.'

[220] Shepard, 'Sayyid Quṭb's Doctrine of *jāhiliyya*,' *IJMES*, 35/4 (2003): 521–45.

[221] Its original title was *Fikrat al-Islām ʿan Allāh wa-l-Kawn wa-l-Ḥayāh wa-l-Insān*, which bears a resemblance to not only Mawdūdī's title *al-Muṣṭalaḥāt al-Arbaʿa fī al-Qurʾān* but also Sabri's *Mawqif al-ʿAql*.

[222] Sayyid Quṭb, *Khaṣāʾiṣ al-Taṣawwur al-Islāmī wa-Muqawwimātuhu* (Cairo: Dār al-Shurūq, 2002), 7.

concept' (*al-taṣawwur al-islāmī*) of revelation.[223] He faults, forgivingly, ʿAbduh for stressing reason (*ʿaql*) as if it were the antithesis of revelation (*waḥy*)[224] and Iqbāl for suggesting that the experience of the human soul transcends death as apologetic responses to Western materialism.[225] *Al-Mustaqbal li-Hādhā al-Dīn* (1964), written to reassure followers in the face of brutal repression, was a degree more political in its message. Quṭb now hailed the 'vanguards of the Islamic awakening' (*ṭalāʾiʿ al-baʿth al-islāmī*) around the Islamic nation (*al-waṭan al-islāmī*) who had survived attempts to smother Islam such as that of Atatürk's Turkey.[226] Political systems that do not establish Islamic rule are '*jāhiliyya* systems' (*nuẓum jāhiliyya*), he states bluntly,[227] before proceeding with an analysis of the soulless 'civilisation of the white man', a phrase he adapts from Bertrand Russell,[228] with heavy citations from French biologist-turned-eugenicist Alexis Carrel's *L'homme, cet inconnu* (1935) and its critique of industrial civilisation,[229] American Secretary of State John Dulles's *War or Peace* (1950) and its critique of Soviet communism, and Nadwī's *Mādhā Khasira*.

Quṭb began writing *Maʿālim fī al-Ṭarīq* in 1962, passing pages of the manuscript to the outside world through his visiting sisters. It begins with a stark statement of the state of humanity in light of the nuclear arms race, the surest proof of the bankruptcy of Western values: 'Humanity stands today on the edge of the precipice; not because of the threat of annihilation hanging over its head, which is a symptom of illness not the illness itself, but because of its bankruptcy in the world of values.'[230] Europe's democracy and communism are failed systems, despite the genius of their technology and material production, but mankind needs new leadership, one based on values (*qiyam*). Islam is not the name of an ethnic group on a specific territory, but a supranational *umma* that lost its sense of self (*wujūd*) and effective presence (*shuhūd*)[231] by breaking its links to God's shariʿa to join the body of post-colonial regimes referred to as the 'Islamic

[223] Ibid., 17.
[224] Ibid., 18–20.
[225] Ibid., 20–2.
[226] Sayyid Quṭb, *al-Mustaqbal li-Hādhā al-Dīn* (Cairo: Dār al-Shurūq, 1993), 7–8.
[227] Ibid., 10.
[228] Ibid., 47–8.
[229] Ibid., 59–67; translated as *al-Insān Dhālik al-Majhūl* (Beirut: Dār al-Maʿārif, nda). Quṭb discussed Carrel at length throughout *al-Islām wa-Mushkilat al-Ḥaḍāra* (Cairo: Dār al-Shurūq, 1992), esp. 9–23.
[230] Sayyid Quṭb, *Maʿālim fī al-Ṭarīq* (Cairo: Dār al-Shurūq, 1979), 3.
[231] Quṭb's use of *wujūd* and *shuhūd* appears intended to integrate the language of Sufism in his ideology. He also made extensive use of the Sufi concept of *dhawq*, on which see

world'. This world exists in a state of *jāhiliyya* because sovereignty has transferred from God to mankind. The Islamic rebirth requires a vanguard that will take the Qur'an as its guide to recognising the 'signs on the road' (*ma'ālim fī al-ṭarīq*) in order to change themselves before they move to the stage of saving humanity.[232] The Islamic movement's basic task (*manhaj al-ḥaraka al-Islāmiyya*) is thus to return to the Qur'an.[233]

The vanguard is called to take concrete measures. The Islamic movement must seek to remove the regimes and authorities supporting *jāhilī* belief systems through preaching and force,[234] since those with power over God's servants will not give up their authority through persuasion.[235] The new Muslim society must build up its organisational capacities in preparation for war against it.[236] Once the 'jihadist movement of Islam' (*ḥarakat al-islām al-jihādiyya*) has liberated men from their arbitrary politico-juridical systems they will be free to choose their beliefs away from political pressure.[237] The Muslim community will be honest with both those living in Islamic countries who claim they are Muslims (*yaz'umūn annahum muslimūn*) and those outside the Islamic nation in explaining that God wants to rescue them from the impure *jāhiliyya* in which they live.[238] Europeans have tricked Muslims into thinking there is a difference between civilised society and Muslim society.[239] In overcoming this challenge they should look to the first Muslims who held to their faith through much suffering.[240] They must also realise that the Prophet did not liberate peoples from despotic Persian and Byzantine rule for the sake of Arabism (*al-'urūba*) or an Arab despot (*ṭāghūt 'arabī*),[241] since what such ideologies miss is that it is Islam itself that is the target of colonialism and colonialism is the continuation of the Crusader wars in another guise.[242]

Denis Gril, *EI3*; http://dx.doi.org/10.1163/1573-3912_ei3_COM_26001 (consulted 2 December 2018).

232 This summarises Quṭb's introduction; 3–10.
233 Ibid., 18.
234 Ibid., 57. He cites from Ibn al-Qayyim's *Zād al-Ma'ād*.
235 Ibid., 60–1.
236 Ibid., 88.
237 Ibid., 63–4.
238 Ibid., 161–2.
239 Ibid., 106–7.
240 Ibid., 176–7.
241 Ibid., 23–4. This was a clear allusion to Nasser.
242 Ibid., 186.

Quṭb's lexical framework avoids the traditional matrix of Islamic theology. In place of *takfīr*, *irjāʾ*, *īmān*, *ridda*, *jahmiyya*, or *ḥashwiyya*, Quṭb develops his core concepts of *jāhiliyya/ḥākimiyya* with terms such as *ḥaraka*, *taṣawwur*, *qiyāda*, *ṭalīʿa*, *jamāʿa muslima*, etc. Quṭb borrowed from the ideas of the modernist and Salafi discourse of the period without adopting their language: he posited the Qurʾan as the sole basis of a purified faith but had little interest in the demystification of the text of ʿAbduh's followers or the war on Sufism of Ibn Taymiyya's adepts. Indeed, Carré sees him as a form of *derviche politique*[243] for whom the Sufi warrior was an exemplary modern Muslim.[244] What Quṭb did was to reconstitute the Islamic discursive tradition as an ideology of anti/post-colonial resistance located in Third World movements of the time. In that sense, among his contemporaries he could be compared to a thinker whose direct influence is not traceable at all: Frantz Fanon (1925–61). A psychiatrist from the French colony of Martinique who worked with French and Algerian patients during the Algerian war of independence, Fanon wrote three books, *Black Skin, White Masks* (1952), *A Dying Colonialism* (1959), and *The Wretched of the Earth* (1961) that resonated to only a limited degree with the Arab Left at the time. It is not known if Quṭb was aware of the contemporary translation of Fanon's last work as *Muʿadhdhabū al-Arḍ*, but it dealt with precisely the problem of decolonisation – the perpetuation of systemic iniquities by the elites who captured the post-colonial state – that Quṭb addressed. Quṭb critiqued what he saw as both collaborator national elites in the period before 1952 who championed European liberal democracy and the post-1952 regime of national liberation that adapted the methods of European totalitarianism for its own ends. One reason Quṭb was more radical during this second phase was his realisation that the oppressor was now indigenous and Muslim. For his part, Fanon could not sound more Quṭbian than when he writes, 'Let us not pay tribute to Europe by creating states, institutions and societies which draw their inspiration from her', or 'Humanity is waiting for something from us other than such an imitation, which would be almost an obscene caricature.'[245] Quṭb clearly went further than Fanon in rejecting European patterns of knowledge and advancing an alternative

[243] Olivier Carré, 'Eléments de la 'aqîda de Sayyid Quṭb dans "Fî zilâl al-qur'ân",' *Studia Islamica*, 91 (2000): 194.

[244] Carré, *Mysticism and Politics*, 173. On classes of faith in Medina, ibid., 166–8.

[245] Frantz Fanon (trans. Constance Farrington), *The Wretched of the Earth* (London: Penguin, 2001), 254.

which he saw as universal, and in this sense he was advocating a form of what Argentinian theorist Walter Mignolo has called 'decoloniality'.[246] But Omnia El Shakry and others are surely right to suggest that Quṭb and Fanon should be read alongside each other in the canon of literature on Arab decolonisation.[247]

WHO INFLUENCED QUṬB?

The question of influences, both experiential and ideological, has pressed heavily in the vast literature on Sayyid Quṭb. In terms of events these have included the Palestine war, his American sojourn, and Nasserist persecution and in terms of individuals Mawdūdī, Ibn Taymiyya, al-Bannā, Lenin, and Carl Schmitt. Some of these cases are clear. Quṭb mentions Mawdūdī often, even in his interrogation by prosecutors before trial;[248] he also cited regime violence as a reason for at least the idea of violence against the state,[249] an argument that became prominent in later Brotherhood writing about the period. Links to Lenin are hard to prove, but some have pointed to the idea of the vanguard that must mobilise the workers to create the revolution in his *What Is to Be Done?* (1902).[250] The arguments concerning Ibn Taymiyya appear to be based on the use to which Quṭb's followers put his ideas after his death. Emmanuel Sivan sees his influence in Quṭb's belief in the illegitimacy of Muslim rulers who do not rule through shariʿa[251] and

[246] On decoloniality v. decolonisation see Mignolo in Walter Mignolo and Catherine Walsh, *On Decoloniality* (Durham: Duke University Press, 2018), 136. Mignolo develops the term from Peruvian sociologist Aníbal Quijano's work on coloniality, the state of mind that persists once direct colonial political power is overthrown; see 'Coloniality and Modernity/Rationality,' *Cultural Studies*, 21/ 2–3 (2007): 168–78.

[247] Omnia El Shakry, '"History without Documents": The Vexed Archives of Decolonization in the Middle East,' *The American Historical Review*, 120/3 (2015): 920–4. See also Ibrahim Abu Rabiʿ, 'Sayyid Qutb: From Religious Realism to Radical Social Criticism,' *Islamic Quarterly*, 28/2 (1984): 112.

[248] Al-Khalidi, *Sayyid Quṭb*, 435. The text of the interrogation is reproduced in full.

[249] Sayyid Quṭb, *Limādhā Aʿdamūnī?* (London: Saudi Research and Publishing Company, 1980), 62; 'If we knew that detention would lead to a fair trial and legal penalties – even under the man-made laws in place – no one would have thought of responding to aggression with force.'

[250] Calvert, *Sayyid Qutb*, 16, 231; Glenn Robinson, 'Jihadi information strategy: sources, opportunities, and vulnerabilities,' in *Information Strategy and Warfare: A Guide to Theory and Practice*, ed. John Arquilla and Douglas A. Borer (London: Routledge, 2007), 92.

[251] Emmanuel Sivan, *Radical Islam: Medieval Theology and Modern Politics* (New Haven/ London: Yale University Press, 1990), 94, 102.

describes Quṭb as a neo-Ḥanbalī advocate of apostasy, but as we have seen Quṭb did not use such language. Ibn Taymiyya is a central figure in key texts of the radical movement usually classified as Jihadi Salafism in which Quṭb is sometimes also cited,[252] but Hüseyin Işık's writing makes clear why Quṭb's innovative eclectic approach would place limits on Salafi embrace of him.

The influence of fascist or totalitarian ideologies of the era has been claimed by many scholars, particularly Quṭb's interest in Alexis Carrel, who worked with the Vichy regime.[253] Though this interest can be traced to 1941, Quṭb only appears to have read Carrel closely after Nadwī and Iranian thinker ʿAlī Sharīʿatī (1933–77) cited him in their works.[254] Quṭb was attracted to Carrel's anti-materialist sentiments and his belief that religion is a universal system based on human nature but that religious truth is ultimately beyond the understanding of all men, including those of Western science. In the same book Carrel propounded the creation a new elite of the mentally and physical superior who would withdraw from society in preparation for its renewal through sterilisation and euthanasia of society's insane and criminal 'defectives',[255] ideas that bear striking similarities to Quṭb's notion of vanguard-led purification. His biological thinking regarding the role of women clearly appealed to Quṭb.[256]

[252] Quṭb was influential for revolutionary groups in Egypt and other countries. A group of Brotherhood prisoners led by Shukrī Muṣṭafā formed a group called Jamāʿat al-Muslimīn which took Quṭb's notion of separation from *jāhilī* society as its founding principle. The group had interactions with Juhaymān's Salafi Ḥisba Group; see al-Ḥuzaymī, *Ayyām*, 49–51. ʿAbd al-Salām Faraj, a member of the jihad group that assassinated Anwar Sadat (al-Sādāt) in 1981, cites Ibn Taymiyya at length but makes no mention of Quṭb in *Jihād, al-Farīḍa al-Ghāʾiba* (1982), and Jordanian *ʿālim* Abū Muḥammad al-Maqdisī's *Millat Ibrāhīm* (1984), a seminal text for today's jihadi Salafism, cites Ibn Taymiyya extensively and Quṭb occasionally. However, al-Qaʿida ideologue Ayman al-Ẓawāhirī's *Fursān fī Rāyat al-Nabī* (2001) makes extensive reference to Quṭb as the initiator of an Islamic revolution against internal and external enemies of Islam.

[253] Youssef Choueiri, *Islamic Fundamentalism: The Story of Islamist Movements* (London/New York: Continuum, 2010), 149–57; Aziz Al-Azmeh, *Islams and Modernities* (London: Verso, 1993), 77–101; Ibrahim Abu-Rabiʿ, *Intellectual Origins of Islamic Resurgence in the Modern Arab World* (Albany: State University of New York Press, 1996), 157–9.

[254] Nadwī, *Mādhā Khasira*, 193–4. ʿAlī Sharīʿatī, article (title unavailable) in *Nashriye-i Farhang-i Khurāsān*, 2/6 (1955): 1333–7; cited in David Hamilton, *The First Transplant Surgeon: The Flawed Genius of Nobel Prize Winner, Alexis Carrel* (Singapore: World Scientific, 2017), 557–8. Also, Calvert, *Sayyid Quṭb*, 91–2.

[255] Alexis Carrel (trans. Charles. E. Rosenberg), *Man, The Unknown* (New York/London: Harper, 1939), 17, 140–1, 153, 164.

[256] Ibid., 50–1. Quṭb quotes this in *al-Islām wa-Mushkilat al-Ḥaḍāra*, 134–5.

Quṭb translated none of Carrel's eugenics, but of all the texts in interwar Europe's wave of anti-Enlightenment writing it is striking he should choose this one. Carrel's status as Nobel Prize winner for chemistry in 1912 certainly accorded him an impeccable status that would attract him to Quṭb. Quṭb was not above criticising him, describing Carrel as a prisoner of Western reason in seeing more not less Western knowledge as the way out for modern man, but Quṭb did not go beyond the material that concerned him directly.[257] Choueiri suggests Quṭb's description of international capitalism as the work of an exploitative Jewish financier class was inspired by European anti-Semitism that he may have picked up from Carrel, though this theme was muted in *L'homme, cet inconnu*.[258] However, Quṭb had already entered that territory in an article titled 'Maʿrakatunā maʿa al-Yahūd' (Our Battle with The Jews, 1951) published after the 1948 war in Palestine.[259] Overall it seems more appropriate to think of Quṭb as finding validation in Carrel of an independently evolving worldview located in his own crisis of thought regarding modernity, decolonisation, and Islam.

Joseph-Simon Görlach reaches a similar conclusion, that while there were parallels between Islamic political thought and European totalitarian ideologies, in particular fascism, social and historical context was fundamental to the formation and characteristics of each of them.[260] Surface similarities to European fascism could be drawn too in the example of the Brotherhood's paramilitary activities, its mass organisation, and totalist programme for society (which Carré argues was a blueprint for Nasserism).[261] Quṭb built on the Brotherhood discourse formulated by

257 Quṭb, *al-Islām*, 167–72; Carrel, *Man*, 19–20.

258 Quṭb, *al-Islām*, 101.

259 This was one of a group of articles first published in *al-Daʿwā* in the period 1951–4 and as book by the same name in 1970; Sayyid Quṭb, *Maʿrakatunā maʿa al-Yahūd* (Cairo: Dār al-Shurūq, 1993), 20–38. Quṭb accuses Jews of responsibility for calamities including communism and the end of the Ottoman caliphate.

260 Joseph-Simon Görlach, 'Western Representations of Fascist Influences on Islamist Thought,' in *Cultural Transfers in Dispute: Representations in Asia, Europe and the Arab World since the Middle Ages*, ed. Jörg Feuchter, Friedhelm Hoffmann, Bee Yun (Frankfurt/New York: Campus Verlag, 2011), 149–68. Also, Israel Gershoni and James Jankowski, *Confronting Fascism in Egypt: Dictatorship Versus Democracy in the 1930s* (Stanford: Stanford University Press, 2010). Aḥmad Ḥusayn, leader of the Young Egypt (Miṣr al-Fatāh) party, attended a Nazi conference in Germany in 1936; Anouar Abdel-Malek (trans. Charles Lam Markmann), *Egypt: Military Society* (New York: Random House, 1968), 21, 392.

261 Carré, *Mysticism and Politics*, 197.

al-Bannā which used the concepts of the *ḥaraka islāmiyya*,[262] the *manhaj/minhāj*,[263] Islam as an all-encompassing system for life with the Qur'an at its centre,[264] the *mu'min* as a category apart among the mass of Muslims,[265] the attack on European positive law,[266] the condemnation of secular society as materialist.[267] His movement's aim was to propagate what it called correct Islam (*islām ṣaḥīḥ*) but al-Bannā made a point of rejecting *takfīr*.[268] Like Mawdūdī, al-Bannā discussed *jāhiliyya* without the implications drawn out by Quṭb.[269] Where al-Bannā was fundamentally different from Quṭb was in his belief in a mass movement that is engaged socially, economically, and politically with society at large, not hiding in the wings. This reflects the different circumstances in which they lived. In his final years Quṭb wanted to save a movement facing extinction, and it was in thanks for his efforts in that regard that the revived Brotherhood accepted Quṭb's work into its canon and separated Quṭb from those raising arms and openly excommunicating Muslims in his name.[270]

The claim of influence from Schmitt is made by Khaled Abou El Fadl, who writes that many of Quṭb's ideas and phrases in *Ma'ālim fī al-Ṭarīq* are adapted from the German political scientist. Abou El Fadl does not explain further except to say that it was through Western thinkers like Schmitt that Quṭb provided a detailed vision of the 'idealistic and utopian Islamic state'.[271] There are no translations of Schmitt's work, published in 1922 and 1932, for Quṭb to have become familiar with it.[272] Given that Quṭb was content to quote at length a lesser thinker such as Carrel it seems probable that he would have cited Schmitt by name. Abou El Fadl was

262 Ḥasan al-Bannā, *Mudhakkirāt al-Da'wā wa-l-Dā'iya* (Kuwait: Maktabat Āfāq, 2012), 167.

263 Ibid., 167.

264 Al-Bannā, *Majmū'at Rasā'il*, 247.

265 Al-Bannā, *Mudhakkirāt*, 159. See Mitchell, *Society*, 319.

266 Al-Bannā, *Majmū'at Rasā'il*, 118, 148, 276–9.

267 Ibid., 57–9, 123–5, 259. Al-Bannā, *Mudhakkirāt*, 66.

268 See *Risālat al-Ta'ālīm*, point 20, written in 1935; al-Bannā, *Majmū'at Rasā'il*, 20, 246.

269 Al-Bannā, *Majmū'at Rasā'il*, 8. Referring to Turkey's language reforms he said that ethnic nationalism had 'revived *jāhiliyya* customs'.

270 Barbara Zollner, 'Prison Talk: The Muslim Brotherhood's Internal Struggle during Gamal Abdel Nasser's Persecution, 1954 to 1971,' *IJMES*, 39/3 (2007): 427.

271 Khaled Abou El Fadl, *The Great Theft*, 82–3. Also, Abou El Fadl, *Reasoning with God: Reclaiming Shari'ah in the Modern Age* (Lanham: Rowman & Littlefield, 2014), 192.

272 *Political Theology* seems only to have been published in recent years in Arabic: Rāniyā al-Sāḥilī and Yāsir al-Ṣārūṭ, trans., *al-Lāhūt al-Siyāsī* (Beirut: Arab Center for Research and Policy Study, 2018) and Fāḍil Jatkar, trans. *Azmat al-Barlamānāt* (Beirut: Ma'had al-Dirāsāt al-Istrātījiyya, 2008).

most likely referring to Schmitt's observation that modern juridical formulations secularise what was once the absolute sovereignty of God, which, as argued earlier, bears similarities to Mustafa Sabri's concept of *ḥukm al-islām* and its usurpation in Kemalist Turkey and liberal Egypt. However, Quṭb did not need to receive these ideas from Schmitt or any other European thinker: they were propagated around Cairo over many years by Sabri, who attended the same salons as Quṭb, and set them forth in his book *al-Qawl al-Faṣl*, whose publication was curated by al-Bannā, and then in *Mawqif al-ʿAql*, where Sabri singled Quṭb out for praise among the Egyptian intellectuals of the period. Quṭb's concept of God's *ḥākimiyya* encompassed Sabri's *ḥukm al-islām* in politico-juridical terms and Sabri's *ḥākimiyya* in terms of creed. But in all Quṭb's extensive ideologising of the Islamic tradition he never went as far as Sabri's declaration of the apostasy of the modern Muslim.

Quṭb attempted to clear up his meaning regarding this last point in the months before he was executed. Under the eye of prison censors, he documented his view of the breakdown in the republic's relations with the Brotherhood and explained some elements of his ideas that led to his impending execution. Quṭb recounted how a fissure developed in Brotherhood ranks between Quṭb and his followers, on one side, and the Brotherhood leadership held in another prison, on the other, over his theory of the vanguard. By this he meant seclusion from society to focus on moral education since society was not yet ready for the Islamic system, and training in guerrilla activities to repel the state's security apparatus if it came calling. Quṭb rejected claims he was engaging in *takfīr*:

> We do not do *takfīr* – this has been relayed wrongly – but we say that people have become ignorant about the truth of faith, unable to conceptualise its true meaning, and far from the Islamic life; thus, they are in a condition similar to that of societies in the *jāhiliyya* [*fī ḥāl tushbih ḥāl mujtamaʿāt al-jāhiliyya*]. So, the starting point in the movement should not be establishing the Islamic system but replanting *ʿaqīda* and Islamic moral education. At issue is the method of the Islamic movement, not judgements about people.[273]

Quṭb said he was often asked, presumably by interrogators, why his group acted as if they were the only Muslims, to which he responded that Islam is about more than group prayers, hajj pilgrimage, and Islamic conferences, it is 'a complete system of life' (*niẓām ḥayāh kāmila*). Even in these

[273] Quṭb, *Limādhā Aʿdamūnī*, 23–4.

responses Quṭb avoided recourse to traditional terminologies and a clear statement on who is a believer and who is not.

The Brotherhood's leader Ḥasan al-Huḍaybī, alarmed by the radical turn Quṭb's followers were taking, wrote a book in 1969 that was widely understood as a response to the Quṭbist trend, *Duʿāh La Quḍāh* (Preachers, Not Judges).[274] Its publication in 1977 four years after al-Huḍaybī's death was specifically linked by the publisher to the appearance of Quṭb-inspired groups such as Shukrī Muṣṭafā's Jamāʿat al-Muslimīn, which had isolated itself from society according to Quṭb's model.[275] Al-Huḍaybī restated the Ashʿarī-Māturīdī view on faith and commission of grave sins (*al-kabīra*)[276] and tried to deflect blame for the controversy over *takfīr* from Quṭb to Mawdūdī. Simply uttering the testimony of faith (*shahāda*) is enough to be considered a Muslim and it is not for men to doubt its sincerity,[277] he said, but the followers of Mawdūdī have used his *Four Concepts in the Qurʾan* as an argument for questioning faith on the basis of actions.[278] Though Quṭb was not named, he was almost certainly on al-Huḍaybī's mind as much as Mawdūdī was when he said that 'ideologues, theorists and researchers' (*aṣḥāb al-fikr wa-l-naẓar wa-l-bāḥithīn*) had given the false impression that *ḥākimiyya* was a term in the Qurʾan or hadith.[279] 'It is incumbent upon us not to become attached to the terminologies of fallible men and to hold fast to the word of God and the infallible Prophet', al-Huḍaybī wrote.[280] Not only that, *ḥākimiyya* has been misunderstood as meaning that men have no call to formulate any legislation for themselves;[281] and it is all well and good to deal directly with the Qurʾan and hadith but authoritative knowledge matters.[282] Al-Huḍaybī rejected not only the claim that Muslims who obey a ruler defined as *ṭāghūt* can be deemed *kāfir*,[283] but that the absence of an Islamic government negates the faith of all subjects within that political space, the

[274] Barbara Zollner has argued that the book was a joint project of leading Brothers and al-Azhar scholars; *The Muslim Brotherhood: Hasan al-Hudaybi and Ideology* (London: Routledge, 2009).

[275] Ḥasan al-Huḍaybī, *Duʿāh La Quḍāh* (Cairo: Dār al-Ṭibāʿa wa-l-Nashr al-Islāmiyya, 1977), 12 (publisher's preface).

[276] Ibid., 45–57, 70–2, 180.

[277] Ibid., 20.

[278] Ibid., 25, 44–5.

[279] Ibid., 77.

[280] Ibid., 78.

[281] Ibid., 85.

[282] Ibid., 189.

[283] Ibid., 181–5.

claim that Sabri had advanced with more clarity than Quṭb.[284] The various elements of this critique indicate that al-Huḍaybī's book was intended as a rebuke to not only Mawdūdī but both Quṭb and his followers.[285]

It is in the context of this debate that the term *islāmī* emerges in Arabic as a term for adherents of the Brotherhood, its offshoots in Egypt, and similar religious movements in other countries. Since words with the adjectival ending *-ī* (properly *-iyy*) can also function as Arabic nouns, the potential for the application of *islāmī* to individuals of the movement flows from its use as a description of that movement. Both al-Bannā and Quṭb propagated the term *ḥaraka islāmiyya*, thus the word always had the potential to work as shorthand for adepts of the *ḥaraka*. However, the term appears to have emerged as a compromise to describe followers of different groups of the *ḥaraka islāmiyya* in light of the claim by some of Quṭb's followers that they alone were the true Muslims. This conflict was the source of a sharp divide in the prisons in the late 1960s, particularly in 1967 when the regime demanded that prisoners declare support for Nasser. Shukrī Muṣṭafā, who was released in 1971, went further in denouncing fellow inmates who did not agree with his Quṭbist group.[286] The transformation of meaning can be seen in the prison memoir of Aḥmad ʿAbd al-Majīd, who spent ten years behind bars over the case involving Quṭb. ʿAbd al-Majīd writes that if a ruler is negligent in applying Islamic ordinances then 'he is no longer an Islamic ruler' (*lam yaʿud ḥākiman islāmiyyan*), and any community of Muslims that accepts such a situation is also 'no longer *islāmī*, no matter what claims it makes'.[287] He goes on to say that the 'Muslim ruler' must not only avoid commission of major sins on a personal level but ensure application of Islamic laws. *Islāmī*/non-*islāmī* appear to function here as euphemisms for Muslim/no longer Muslim (or at the least, deficient in Islam) among the post-Nasser radical groups.[288]

284 Ibid., 172.

285 Zollner thinks it targets only Quṭb's followers; 'Prison Talk,' 425.

286 On Shukrī Muṣṭafā, see Aḥmad Rāʾif, *al-Bawwāba al-Sawdāʾ: Ṣafaḥāt min Tārīkh al-Ikhwān al-Muslimīn* (Cairo: al-Zahrāʾ li-l-Iʿlām al-ʿArabī, 1985), 398–401, 539, 573–5, 583–4. See Tariq Ramadan, *Aux Sources du Renouveau Musulman* (Paris: Bayard Editions/Centurion, 1998), 27–9.

287 Aḥmad ʿAbd al-Majīd, *al-Ikhwān wa-ʿAbd al-Nāṣir: al-Qiṣṣa al-Kāmila li-Tanẓīm 1965* (Cairo: al-Zahrāʾ li-l-Iʿlām al-ʿArabī, 1991), 229.

288 See the al-Jamāʿa al-Islāmiyya document, 'al-Ḥaraka al-Islāmiyya wa-l-ʿAmal al-Ḥizbī,' in *al-Nabī al-Musallaḥ 1: al-Rāfiḍūn*, Rifʿat Sayyid Aḥmad (London: Riad El-Rayyes, 1991), 219. Also, former al-Jamāʿa al-Islāmiyya member ʿAbd al-Munʿim Abū al-Futūḥ, *Shāhid ʿalā Tārīkh al-Ḥaraka al-Islāmiyya fī Miṣr 1970–1984* (Cairo: Dār al-Shurūq, 2012), 57, 116.

The word as a term for individuals is absent from official Brotherhood literature in the early years after the movement's revival from 1976 when it began to re-establish itself in public life – neither al-Huḍaybī's *Duʿāh La Quḍāh* nor his successor ʿUmar al-Tilmisānī's memoirs use it, nor does it appear in the official journal *al-Daʿwā*, most likely because of this genealogical relationship with *takfīr* and suspicion of claims to be the sole true Muslims.[289] On the other hand, in Syria Nāṣir al-Dīn al-Albānī used the term in 1972 in reference to 'preachers' and 'writers', including Quṭb, who talk of Islamic government (*ḥukm islāmī*) but without a rigorous approach to questions of creed and hadith methodology, i.e., lay expertise outside the domain of the ʿulamaʾ.[290] The Arabic Islamist emerges in Egypt, then, as a noun generated by the movement itself in a context of repression and regeneration,[291] but also in at least one case with reference to political actors who address Islamic issues in the public sphere, and this stands in contrast to the Ottoman-Turkish Islamist, which was a neologism coined by its opponents. The English term masks these semantic histories.

[289] Al-Tilmisānī wrote that the intent behind the Brotherhood's name was simply to suggest 'a group from among the Muslims'; *Dhikrāyāt Lā Mudhakkirāt* (Cairo: Dār al-Iʿtiṣām, 1985), 35.

[290] Al-Albānī, *Mukhtaṣar al-ʿUluww*, 56–60. He related this to his time at the Islamic University of Medina where many Muslim Brotherhood cadres were employed.

[291] To make the term pejorative, opponents have had to contort it to *islāmawī*.

6

The Late Ottomans' Impact on Modern Islamic Thought

SUMMARY OF AKIF, SABRI, AND KEVSERI'S WORK

This study has taken three Ottoman Turkish Muslim thinkers on the cusp of critical debates in Islamic thought in the early to mid-twentieth century and analysed them in terms of the changing functions of the *ʿālim* and the intellectual, the transformation from shariʿa state to nation-state, and the gathering of public activities – political, economic, intellectual, social, etc. – into national domains of operation. It traced their engagement with those questions from their experience of the Ottoman state's final years to their exile in Egypt during the Turkish republic's radical phase. These ʿulamaʾ-intellectuals wrestled with both external and internal challenges of destabilisation of the Islamic tradition and re-ordering of its institutions. Mehmed Akif seized the opportunity presented by the end of Hamidian restrictions on public debate to bring the modernist thought of Muḥammad ʿAbduh into the Ottoman Turkish sphere and, like Iqbāl, craft a contemporary Islamic discourse comparable to Enlightenment humanistic thought in an Ottoman Turkish language at once national and Islamic. Akif's national-linguistic focus limited his influence among Egyptian peers but helped establish him as the Late Ottoman intellectual of choice for the Islamic movement which gathered force in Turkish political and social life in the later twentieth century. Ahmed Muhiddin provided an early recognition of Akif's Turkish Islamism in his study of the Late Ottoman *Kulturbewegung*, describing his thought as 'a microcosm of the new Turkish world'[1] and noting the intersections between nationalist and religious

[1] Muhiddin, *Modern Türklükte*, 58.

reform thinking (return to Ur-Islam, simplified shariʿa, free *ijtihād*),[2] and biographer Mehmet Emin Erişirgil, who served as a government minister in the 1940s, was similarly prescient in noting social and educational parallels between Akif and Ziya Gökalp – their origins on the imperial periphery, losing fathers at a young age, a desire to merge Islamic and Western knowledge – that help explain the evolution of Akif as an alternative intellectual representative of modern Turkey.[3] Critical here was Akif's act of resistance – his exile in Egypt and refusal to hand over a superlative Turkish Qurʾan – which set him apart from most others in the Islamic reform fold, who were co-opted into working with the secular nationalist regime.[4]

The divergence in thinking between Akif and Gökalp is, however, instructive about the trajectory of the republic, even if some of its reforms would have been disconcerting to Gökalp too had he lived to see them.[5] While Akif read Ibn ʿArabī and his theory of divine archetypes in terms of encouraging human agency, Gökalp first tried to establish Sufi thought as an equal to European philosophical idealism (what he called *mefkûrecilik*), with the archetypes re-fashioned as the elements (ideals/*mefkûreler*) of reality that human perception can never grasp,[6] and then fashioned it as integral to Turkish nationalism in his major work *Türkçülüğün Esasları*

[2] Ibid., 114–17.

[3] There appears to have been a mutual respect – Gökalp said of Akif, 'don't compare him to this or that, he's something completely different' – but Akif apparently rejected an effort by Talat Paşa to effect a reconciliation between them, saying: 'This dispute didn't emerge from personal issues that we could quickly fix by meeting' (Erişirgil, *İslamcı bir Şairin Romanı*, 199–201). See Erişirgil's Gökalp biography, *Bir Fikir Adamının Romanı: Ziya Gökalp* (Istanbul: Remzi Kitabevi, 1984), 71–82.

[4] For example, Şemsettin Günaltay, a colleague of Akif who published *Zulmetten Nura* in 1913, worked on a commission formed in 1928 that recommended Turkicising prayer ritual; Şerif Mardin, *Religion and Social Change in Modern Turkey: The Case of Bediüzzaman Said Nursi* (Albany: State University of New York Press, 1989), 144. *Zulmetten Nura*, for which Akif wrote a preface of praise, extols *ijtihād* and condemns fatalism.

[5] On Gökalp as the prime influence on Kemalism: Taha Parla, *The Social and Political Thought of Ziya Gökalp, 1876–1924* (Leiden: Brill, 1985), and on Mustafa Kemal's influences Hanioğlu, *Atatürk*, 129–59. See also Alp Eren Topal, 'Against Influence: Ziya Gökalp in Context and Tradition,' *Journal of Islamic Studies* 28:3 (2017): 283–310; Markus Dressler, 'Rereading Ziya Gökalp: Secularism and Reform of the Islamic State in the Late Young Turk Period,' *IJMES*, 47/3 (2015): 511–31; and M. Sait Özervarlı, 'Reading Durkheim through Ottoman Lenses: Interpretations of Customary Law, Religion, and Society by the School of Gökalp,' *Modern Intellectual History*, 14/2 (2017): 393–419.

[6] Tevfik Sedat (pseudonym), 'Muhyiddin-i Arabî', *Genç Kalemler*, 2/4 (1912), 61–4, in *Makaleler II*, Ziya Gökalp (Ankara: Kültür Bakanlığı, 1981), 14–20.

(The Principles of Turkism, 1923). Religious practices were to be celebrated as part of Anatolian folk culture (*hars*, a neologism he coined from Arabic *ḥarth*), which was the central locus of Turkishness,[7] but the ulema class should be restricted to purely faith-based functions and the sultan-caliphate abolished since they were part of the defective civilization (*medeniyet*) of the non-national, un-Turkish urban elite. Akif believed it was only the mindset of the ulema that required re-configuring, not the institutions they controlled, but he tried to maintain a neutral posture during the first years of Kemalist power. In 1922 he could challenge both nationalist and Islamist circles by translating and publishing Said Halim's further ideas for an Islamic republic of elected president, elected legislature of ulema, and elected supervisory assembly;[8] but sitting in the Ankara parliament until May 1923, Akif never articulated such views himself. While he could accept republican nationalism, it was early republican nationalism that would not accept Akif.

Mustafa Sabri and Zahid Kevseri are of a different order. From among the ranks of those trained in the familiar fields of knowledge of the ʿulamaʾ class, they were defenders of an epistemic and ontological system that ʿAbduh, his peers, and his admirers felt required change in one way or another, but in their defence of 'old knowledge' (or Muhiddin's 'historical Islam') their approaches diverged. Reflecting his educational role in the Late Ottoman religious hierarchy, Kevseri operated by and large within the boundaries of pre-modern knowledge, writing on questions of *fiqh*, hadith, and *kalām* according to the accepted methodologies of those categories. He identified the central challenge to the tradition as the internal critique of the theological-juridical culture that had prevailed over some 1,000 years, particularly in al-Azhar and Ottoman institutions, a critique that unlike modernism had not developed as *apologia* vis-à-vis Europe. Kevseri feared that this destabilising critique was gaining legitimacy through its assumption of the powerful semantic framing of *salafiyya* with its implicit privileging of ethnic Arab understandings of Islamic faith and practice. This iconoclastic trend contained two dangerous elements in his view: it dusted off the shelves and brought into the mainstream a

[7] Gökalp, *Türkçülüğün Esasları*, 170–1.

[8] Said Halim Paşa, *Les institutions politiques dans la société musulmane* (Rome: Editrice Italia, 1921); published in *Sebilürreşad* from 26 February 1922 (19:493) to 13 May 1922 (20:501) as *İslam'da Teşkilat-ı Siyasiye*. It was published in British India as 'The Reform of Muslim Society,' *Islamic Culture: The Hyderabad Quarterly Review 1* (1927): 111–35, translated from French by Marmaduke Pickthall (mistakenly described as *İslamlaşmak*), and then translated into Urdu. It was likely read by both Iqbāl and Mawdūdī.

theology that had for centuries remained marginal for good reason, that is, its revitalising of the question of *irjāʾ* and *takfīr*, and it undermined the architecture of legal thinking constructed in the Abbasid period through an attempt to excavate an earlier tradition based solely on Qurʾan and prophetic hadith that Kevseri derided as *lā-madhhabiyya*. Kevseri was the first scholar to elaborate these counterarguments with such force, and for that reason he functions as a bête noire for the Salafi movement. Kevseri also upheld the experiential ontology of Sufism which complemented his Māturīdī resistance to questioning the faith of the believing masses.

Sabri directed his energies to the modernist Islamic theology that traded in some elements of the Salafi movement's programme – antipathy for the methodology of the dominant juridical culture, reservations about Sufi institutions and metaphysics, a purificatory drive towards rationalisation – but had entirely different motivations: rather than reconfigure the substance of the shariʿa state system, it aimed to break up its form. Sabri saw the Late Ottoman religious reformers as apologists for the vague notion of spirituality to which religion had been reduced by the ravages of Enlightenment thought[9] and enablers of the positivist and materialist trends that since the late nineteenth century had taken hold in influential quarters of the Ottoman elite. The social engineering of the early Turkish republic confirmed Sabri's worst fears regarding these trends; his final horror was to discover that the Egyptian intelligentsia, including many of its most prominent ʿulamaʾ, were advancing the same agenda despite the nominal independence Egypt had attained in 1922 and absence of Kemalist revolutionary nationalism. Sabri identified ʿAbduh as the notional founder of this trend, coming to a belated realisation of the nature of the ideas heavily propagated by Akif and his circle. Sabri considered the modernists to be engaged in a process of what Max Weber had called in the European context 'demagification' (*Entzauberung*),[10] a cleansing of religion of non-rational interpretations of reality, distilling from Islam's rich theological tradition whatever elements diminished divine intervention in man's affairs and augmented human agency.

Building on his political function as sheikh ül-Islam in the critical final years of the Ottoman empire, Sabri turned his attention to the question of

[9] See his numerous references to Kant's notion of innate morality as a sign of divine truth that is unknowable to the believer through reason alone. Sabri, *Mawqif al-ʿAql*, 1:232, 247; 2:24, 88, 206, 370–5; 3:71–5.

[10] Max Weber, 'Science as a Vocation,' in *From Max Weber: Essays in Sociology*, Max Weber, H.H. Gerth, and Wright Mills (London: Routledge, 2013), 139.

the nation-state. The Islamic system, at least in theory, would never require theories of the sovereign exception because internal manipulations threatening the integrity of the system were unimaginable in a juridical order whose ultimate arbiter was God. Internal challenges to the working of this system had come from historical Shiʿi movements such as the Ismaʿilis or contemporary movements such as the Aḥmadīs in British India with their re-opening of the closed door of revelation, or to a lesser degree the Salafis with their juridical methodology, but the modern European state, as it encroached on Muslim society in diverse ways, overturned the model entirely. This West European system, which he usually refers to as simply 'democracy' (*al-dīmūqrāṭiyya*), allows interest groups to manipulate the system for their own interests, through constitutional amendments and subsequent legislation that pay no heed to the ordering principles of shariʿa and its custodian ʿulamaʾ in the form of judges, fatwa givers, mosque preachers, teachers, and public intellectuals. Sabri wrote that the Muslim subject is thus exposed to both the arbitrary physical abuse of the secular ruler and the risk of apostasy if he does not take decisive action to alter this state of affairs.

Sabri's thought accords with a broad rejectionist tendency among Muslim intellectuals vis-à-vis European political systems that were received through varying forms of colonial coercion in different geographical and social contexts, a tendency that encompasses Said Halim in Late Ottoman Istanbul, Abū al-Aʿlā Mawdūdī in India/Pakistan, Ḥasan al-Bannā in liberal Egypt, and Sayyid Quṭb in Nasserist Egypt. Sabri's impact on Quṭb in particular cannot be discounted, concealed by the anti-Ottoman spirit of the times and the unwillingness of Arab writers to acknowledge the unfashionable influence of passé Turks. The influential Syrian traditionalist al-Būṭī was explicit about his debt to Sabri in *Kubrā al-Yaqīniyyāt* (1969), writing of *Mawqif al-ʿAql* that 'nothing like it has been written in this age [*lam yuktab mithluhu fī hādhā al-ʿaṣr*]', while saying nothing about Quṭb at all.[11] This rejection of European thought was framed in Islamic terms, despite sharing much with critiques of the West circulating within the West itself. Such was the level of disillusion with Western political, economic, technological, and philosophical advances that had produced liberal democracy, which was propagated through the colonial mission, fascism, which plunged Europe and the world into war, and socialism, whose atheistic element made it a non-starter for these thinkers.

[11] Al-Būṭī, *Kubrā al-Yaqīniyyāt*, 85, footnote 1. On ʿAbduh and his followers, see 185, 222–35, 327–37 and on Sabri, see 84–5, 94, 148–9, 185, 230, 233, 329.

The contrast between the iniquities of ascendant European civilisation and its injustices around the world, on the one hand, and the grand propaganda surrounding its universalist ideals, on the other, is a theme that runs throughout modern Islamic thought, from al-Afghānī, to Sabri, to Quṭb.[12]

The question of typology looms large. Sabri and Kevseri express a conservative traditionalism that in Sabri's case bleeds into an activist practice and ideological approach that merges elements of the modernist, the Salafi, the Sufi, the *faqīh*, and the *mutakallim* and eliding with Said Halim's proposition of 'Islamisation'. It would be wrong to see either of them as defenders of the old who would object *in toto* to such manifestations of the new as al-Bannā's organisation. Both are figures who can be observed on the edges of this ideologisation of the Islamic tradition – that is, the process of re-thinking, re-formulating, and rendering Islam in ideological terms – that flowed from the post-Enlightenment reification identified by Wilfred Cantwell Smith and Armando Salvatore: Kevseri's student Abū Ghudda became the leader of the Syrian Muslim Brotherhood, Sabri collaborated with al-Bannā, and their Cairo students considered Sabri, Kevseri, al-Bannā, and Quṭb collectively as the heroes of their era. Both understood that radical ruptures had taken place in the Islamic episteme that required radical solutions; their venturing into the arena of public debate and their considerable output during their Egyptian years are also testament to the fact that they appreciated a new approach was in order. The disruption of the times also put severe strains on their Māturīdism. Sabri strayed from his Māturīdī roots on the question of free will towards a *jabrī* Ashʿarīsm and developed an innovative position on apostasy that was outside the Ashʿarī-Māturīdī mainstream.[13] Despite his forceful rearticulation of Māturīdī rationalism on *īmān* and the (un) created Qurʾan, Kevseri could still suggest that, like Aḥmadī ideology, radical Salafi *lā-madhhabiyya* should be classified as non-Muslim belief and practice. Akif, too, typical of the discourse of *dinsizlik* deployed against the Ottoman positivists, could suggest that Dozy's Turkish translator had demonstrated by his writings that he was no longer a Muslim,

[12] The argument that Western modernity lacks an ethical base is taken up by ʿAbd al-Raḥmān Ṭāhā in *Suʾāl al-Akhlāq: Musāhama fī al-Naqd al-Akhlāqī li-l-Ḥadātha al-Gharbiyya* (Casablanca: al-Markaz al-Thaqāfī al-ʿArabī, 2000) and works following it. On his work, which is a retort to the modern Muslim philosopher-intellectuals (al-Jābirī, Arkoun, et al.), see Wael Hallaq, *Reforming Modernity: Ethics and the New Human in the Philosophy of Addurrahman Taha* (New York: Columbia University Press, 2019).

[13] Kurucu relates an occasion in 1944 when Sabri shocked his students in saying that even children should be ready to sacrifice their lives for God; Düzdağ, *Hatıralar*, 2:107–8.

while in *Dinî Müceddidler* Sabri beseeched his modernist adversaries to confess the same in the interests of fair public debate.[14]

The range of terminologies used by thinkers such as Akif, Sabri, and Kevseri in the construction of their thought was specific to them but not so discrete as to render comparison impossible, and the same can be said for the thought of Quṭb, Mawdūdī, Fanon, or Schmitt, in that the intent behind and context informing the specific idiom they chose is largely knowable. The literature on Salafism has exposed the risk of creating unsustainable historical narratives, but these writers, each with their own *Einbildungskraft*, or conceptual imagination with its own cluster of terms and phraseology,[15] display a mutual translatability across terminological, geographical, and political fields. Sabri and Kevseri could be classified as within the sphere of thought belonging to pre-industrial societies in the schema outlined by Patricia Crone, the closed system of world cultural blocs that had found durable solutions to the problems of pre-industrial organisation, as opposed to the aberrant European arena of constant contestation, with its perpetual shifts from what Schmitt called the conflictual to the neutral domain that becomes again an arena of struggle.[16] In a short period of historical time a great shuffling of functions had taken place among the various categories of *ʿālim*, Sufi, intellectual, preacher, activist. Islam became 'Islam', generating a range of definitions and connotations for both the Muslim and the European that constituted a radical break with the past. It is perfectly possible then to write the Ottoman exiles into a comprehensive history of modern Islamic thought that avoids the Arab-centric tendencies that characterise the field while still recognising the transformative nature of the period, since it was transformative in more than just the production of national identities and nationalist modes of knowledge and organisation.

TURKISH REPUBLICAN ISLAM AND SAID NURSI

This brings us to the trajectory of Islam as politics, theology, and law in Turkey following the loosening of the Kemalist guardrails from 1950, and its relation to the legacy of Akif, Sabri, and Kevseri. That in turn requires a

14 Sabri, *Dinî Müceddidler*, 5–6.

15 The term is Gadamer's; Joel Weinsheimer and Donald J. Marshall, 'Translator's note,' in *Truth and Method*, Hans-Georg Gadamer (London: Bloomsbury Academic, 2013), xii. See Gadamer, 410–17 and Izutsu, *Concept of Belief*, 228–32.

16 Patricia Crone, *Pre-Industrial Societies: Anatomy of the Pre-Modern World* (Oxford: Basil Blackwell, 1989), 147–75; Schmitt, *Concept of the Political*, 90.

reckoning with the work of a figure who has dominated discussion of Turkish Islam in the twentieth century: Said Nursi. Nursi was born in 1878 to a Kurdish family in the remote Eastern Anatolian village of Nurs, after which he was named, in the Taurus mountains south of Lake Van. He grew up in a Khālidī Naqshbandī environment but was also influenced by Shaykh ʿAbd al-Qādir Jīlānī (d. 1166), the founder of the Qādirī order, as well as al-Ghazālī and Illuminationist philosophers such as Suhrawardī (d. 1191).[17] It was because of Nursi's great capacity for text memorisation that he acquired the nickname Bediüzzaman ('wonder of the age') from his teacher Molla Fethullah Efendi.[18] Around 1899 he appears to have moved to Istanbul, staying at the family home of Eşref Sencer and spending time at the sultan's court, possibly to help with the state's Islamic propaganda efforts. Nursi did so on the recommendation of the governor of Dayr al-Zūr (in Syria) and palace advisor Nüzhet Paşa, who would have been familiar with Sencer's father, the court falconer,[19] and was impressed by Nursi's angry reaction to British anti-Muslim rhetoric following the anti-Armenian pogroms of 1895.[20] The obscure sojourn in Istanbul helps establish links between Nursi and the later Teşkilat-ı Mahsusa that remain unresolved in the sources.[21]

In late 1907 Nursi returned to the capital, establishing himself as an outspoken figure and presenting a petition to the palace for a revamped school system in the east where he said Kurds were disadvantaged by not knowing Turkish. He proposed that they offer a mixture of religious and modern knowledge (*ulum-i diniye ve fünūn-ı lazıme-i fenniye*) but under the name of *medrese* since it was more familiar to the local populace than the modern *mekteb*.[22] Remaining in Istanbul throughout the 1908

[17] Şükran Vahide, *Islam in Modern Turkey: An Intellectual Biography of Bediuzzaman Said Nursi* (Albany: State University of New York Press, 2005), 12; Mardin, *Religion and Social Change*, 71, 215.

[18] Vahide, *Islam in Modern Turkey*, 13.

[19] On Nursi staying at Sencer's home, see Fortna, *The Circassian*, 29–30; and Mardin, *Religion and Social Change*, 78.

[20] Necmeddin Şahiner, *Bilinmeyen Taraflarıyla Bediüzzaman Said Nursi* (Istanbul: Nesil, 1999), 80.

[21] Nursi's involvement was argued by the journalist Cemal Kutay, who interviewed Sencer before he died; Kutay, *Çağımızda bir Asr-ı Saadet Müslümanı Bediüzzaman Said Nursî* (Istanbul: Yeni Asya, 1980). But Stoddard's study, which was also based on access to Sencer, makes no mention of Nursi in its list of agents; Stoddard, 'The Ottoman Government', 173–9.

[22] The Ottoman text can be found in Şahiner, *Bilinmeyen Taraflarıyla*, 92. It was first published in *Şark ve Kürdistan Gazetesi*, 19 November 1908, issue 1. It's not clear if Nursi was given an audience with Abdülhamid himself, but the court sent him for

uprising, he was acquitted by a military court in 1909 for membership of the Muḥammadan Union after it was accused of fomenting the anti-CUP insurrection of that year. Kutay claims Nursi then embarked upon secret missions in eastern Anatolia in 1912, Edirne in 1913, and Libya in 1915, helping spread the Ottoman jihad proclamations. Şükran Vahide, author of a Nursi biography, says his known role fighting in the Great War supports the idea of involvement on some level with the Teşkilat-ı Mahsusa.[23] Nursi led a military regiment in the Van region in 1915 before he was captured in March 1916 by the Russians in Bitlis. He escaped from prison in Kosturma in early 1918, arriving back in Istanbul in June of that year via Warsaw, Vienna, and possibly Berlin.[24]

By the end of the war Nursi was a recognised authority alongside the other major Muslim scholars of the period. He was appointed by the CUP government to the Darü'l-Hikmeti'l-İslamiye which was tasked after the war with responding to the presumed Anglican Church request about Islam. Nursi adopted a strong anti-colonial stance, withdrawing from political life in Istanbul until in 1922 he finally acceded to Ankara's requests to join the rival political authority.[25] He immediately understood the Anglican affair in the context of British attempts to win over Istanbul Muslims and break the back of any resistance. Though Nursi later stated in *Risale-i Nur* that he had refused any involvement from the outset, he provided a riposte of sorts in a section of his 1920 pamphlet *Rumuz* (Signs) titled 'Yüksekten Bakmak İsteyen Dessas bir Papasa Cevap' (Response to a Haughty Scheming Priest).[26] 'A man tries to kill you, throwing you to the ground and putting his foot on your throat. Then he asks you contemptuously about your religion. The way to silence him is to go quiet in anger then spit in his face [*cevab-ı müskit küsmekle sükût edip yüzüne tükürmektir*]', he wrote.[27] He then offered four terse answers to Boutwood's questions:

1. What is the religion of Muḥammad? The Qurʾan. 2. What did it give to thought and life? The unicity of God and guidance. 3. What are its solutions to the trouble

psychiatric tests over his perceived impudence; Şahiner, *Bilinmeyen Taraflarıyla*, 91–103; Vahide, *Islam in Modern Turkey*, 43–4.

[23] Vahide, *Islam in Modern Turkey*, 104–5, 111–29.

[24] Ibid., 131. Nursi cites his ties to Enver and imprisonment in *Mektubat* (Istanbul: Yeni Asya, 1997), appendix to eleventh letter, 76–7.

[25] Şahiner, *Bilinmeyen Taraflarıyla*, 258.

[26] Bediüzzaman (Said Nursi), *Rumuz* (Istanbul: Evkaf-ı İslamiye Matbaası, 1920), 23; see also references to this in *Mektubat*, 405 (29:6) and *Lem'alar*, 180 (21:3).

[27] Nursi, *Rumuz*, 23.

of the times? Preventing usury and the necessity of alms giving [*zekat*]. 4. What does it say about this war turmoil [*şu zelzele*]? That man will be judged by his efforts, as will those who amass wealth [*laysa li-l-insān illā mā saʿā wa-lladhīna yaknizūn al-dhahab*].[28]

Nursi was laying the groundwork here for what became the central element of his discourse after the war as an opponent of the British occupation and then of the Kemalist regime: challenging atheism through an inward turn to spirituality, ritual, and Qurʾan as the miraculous font of faith (both he and Quṭb were in search there of 'signs', as their book titles indicate).[29]

Though honoured with a parliamentary welcome in November 1922, Nursi grew disillusioned with the lack of piety shown by most delegates, particularly over the ritual prayers, so he distributed a statement in January 1923 that marked the beginning of the breakdown in his relations with Atatürk. The duty of parliamentarians was to preserve religious rites, not to allow Europe-enamoured imitators (*Avrupa meftunu frenk mukallidleri*) to do the West's job of breaking down Islamic culture, Nursi wrote.[30] Like Akif, he rejected offers from Mustafa Kemal to co-operate further, including a post as general preacher of the Eastern Provinces.[31] It was at this time that Nursi made the critical decision to switch to Turkish from Arabic in order to reach a mass public. Nursi said it was during the publication of *Ḥabāb Min ʿUmmān al-Qurʾān al-Karīm* (A Bubble from the Ocean of the Qurʾan) in 1923 that he came to this point.[32] He wrote in a preamble that he realised he would have to use Turkish given the magnitude of the task of countering the spread of atheist thought (*dinsizlik fikri*).[33] In spring of 1923 Nursi quit Ankara for Van, but following the Shaykh Said rebellion he was jailed in 1926, the beginning of long years of

[28] Ibid., 24. The last question abbreviates Boutwood's query about the political and spiritual forces shaping the world for good or bad; the first part of the response cites Qurʾan 53:39 and the second part Qurʾan 9:34.

[29] For further evidence of this Qurʾanic turn, see his article 'Kur'an-ı Azimüşşa'nın Hakimiyet-i Mutlakası,' *SR*, 6 May 1920. A list of his forty published articles from 1908 to 1920 are in Ceylan, *Gerçeğin Aynasında*, 286–90.

[30] Şahiner, *Bilinmeyen Taraflarıyla*, 262. For full text see 260–9.

[31] Vahide, *Islam in Modern Turkey*, 171.

[32] *Ḥabāb* is part of a collection of Arabic treatises composed in the period 1921–3 and published as *al-Mathnawī al-ʿArabī al-Nūrī* in 1955. *Ḥabāb* was rewritten in Turkish in 1934 around the single theme of causation under the title *Tabiat Risalesi* and included in the *Lem'alar* collection of the *Risale-i Nur* compendium as well as *al-Mathnawī*'s Turkish imprint, *Mesnevi-i Nuriye* (1957).

[33] Nursi, 'Tabiat Risalesi,' in *Lem'alar*, 183.

detention and trial which only ended in 1956. During those years he devoted himself to the re-formulation of much of his work and ideas in Turkish under the generic title *Risale-i Nur*, a compendium of loose Qur'anic commentary, theological reflection, and personal history, using the name Said Nursi, with its play on the Turkish *nur* (divine light), rather than the Said-i Kürdi, Bediüzzaman Said Molla, Bediüzzaman Said, or simply Bediüzzaman by which he was known until 1923. Handwritten in Ottoman and in later years transliterated into Latin script, the texts were dictated to scribes who would copy them for silent distribution to study groups around the country, such that these writings themselves became the focus of government suppression. Like Akif's refusal to deliver a Turkish Qur'an from Egyptian exile, the *Risale* was a vast act of resistance to the Kemalist regime and its project to de-centre religion. Nursi's final act was a return to the overtly political: to support the Democrat Party in the 1950s by directing his followers to give it their vote, while overseeing the translation of his Arabic works to Turkish and printing them in the Latin script.[34]

Nursi's thought is highly personalised, branded with his stamp like a consumer product. He saw himself as a cypher whose material – words taken down by others, written text shifting from Arabic to Turkish – emanated Qur'anic truths through the vessel of his person. There is something in this of Akif's notion of himself as an artist through whom God does his work, and both recall the prophetic function of revealing the speech of another. Nursi's views on creed, law, shari'a, state, and Sufi metaphysics were largely formed before his years of internal exile and expressed first in the collection of Arabic writings he published in the period 1918–23 (later gathered in the *Mathnawī*), which form something of an Urtext for the *Risale*. Thoroughly trained in the common corpus of Islamic tradition, he was more naturally drawn to the Sufi masters concerned with techniques of arrival at knowledge of God. In *Mektubat* (Letters) he praised the path of Jīlānī, Shaykh Naqshband, and Sirhindī as a means to achieve the truths of faith (*haḳā'iḳ-i imaniye*) and attain paradise but suggested that in troubled times a quicker route to the secrets of the Qur'an was his *Sözler* (Words) collection.[35] God has provided *Sözler* as 'spiritual flashes from the miracle of the Qur'an, an antidote to errant atheism [*i'caz-ı Kur'an'ın manevi lum'atından olan malum sözler,*

[34] Vahide, *Islam in Modern Turkey*, 322–3.
[35] Nursi, *Mektubat*, fifth letter, 26–7. This book was composed between 1928 and 1932 but published in 1958; *Sözler*, composed in the same period, was published in 1957.

şu dalalet zındıkasına bir tiryak hasiyeti]', he wrote.[36] Elsewhere he was fairly typical of his time in placing limits on Sufi metaphysics: the testimonies of Ibn ʿArabī in *al-Futūḥāt al-Makkiyya* or al-Jīlī in *al-Insān al-Kāmil* to attaining knowledge of God (*velayet*, *şuhud*) should be accepted as they are, but the truths of faith are more properly arrived at through Qurʾan and sunna.[37] Nursi reprimanded Sabri for his criticisms of Ibn ʿArabī, who he said is not expected to be an exemplary guide in everything he wrote (*her kitabında mühdī ve mürşid*),[38] but warned that nevertheless Ibn ʿArabī's theosophy could be misunderstood as merging God and His creation into one.[39]

Nursi wanted to centre the believer in the Qurʾan as the response to the challenge of positivist philosophies and veneration of the individual,[40] but merging legalistic and Sufi approaches to the text. This combination reflected the Ottoman state tradition that honoured the Sufi orders and their thought culture alongside the İlmiye and its requirements.[41] Muslims should follow the prescribed observances (*ʿibādāt*) to assert personal strength vis-à-vis the materialist menace but must understand the individual's place. Nursi often referred to the individual in the third person as *al-nafs* (the self) or '*anā*' (the 'I'), suggesting a possible familiarity with Iqbāl's writing on *khūdī*.[42] He wrote in *Dhayl li-l-Qaṭra* (Addendum to The Droplet), a part of the *Mathnawī*, that this modern self seeks to establish a sense of its own divinity (*dāʾirat rubūbiyyat nafsihā*) and deny God through empirical arguments. 'Know! O "I", you have learned [*iʿlam! Ya 'anā' qad ʿalimta*] that of the thousands of possibilities only a certain part is in your hands; so build on that weak voluntary element [*al-juzʾ al-ikhtiyārī*] what it can bear', he wrote.[43] In a notable passage, Nursi explained that for thirty years he had been 'struggling against two false

[36] Ibid., 27.

[37] Ibid., eighteenth letter, 82–8.

[38] Nursi, *Lem'alar*, twenty-eighth Lem'a, 285–6. Şerif Mardin's description of Nursi as 'repelled' by Sabri's view seems overstated; Mardin, *Religion and Social Change*, 143.

[39] Nursi, *Lem'alar*, twenty-eighth Lem'a, 284–5.

[40] Nursi, 'Kur'an-ı Azimü'ş-Şa'nın Hakimiyet-i Mutlakası,' *SR*, 6 May 1920, 18/463: 242–3.

[41] Mardin, *Religion and Social Change*, 184.

[42] Jibrān Khalīl Jibrān's *The Prophet* talked of self-knowledge but was published in 1923. Freud's seminal study on the human psyche was also published in 1923, as *Das Ich und das Es* (The Ego and the Id, or lit. 'the I and the It').

[43] Nursi, *Dhayl li-l-Qaṭra*, in *Qaṭra, Ḥabāb, Ḥabba, Zahra, Dhurra, Shamma* (Istanbul: Necmeddin İstikbal Matbaası, 1923), 11. The inverted commas around *anā* are in the original text. Also, in *al-Mathnawī al-ʿArabī al-Nūrī*, ed. Iḥsān Qāsim al-Ṣāliḥī (Istanbul: Sözler, 1994), 170.

gods' (*mujādala maʿa ṭāghūtayn*): subjective understandings of the individual (*anā*) that make him independent of God and materialist understandings that transform nature into Nature, an entity in its own right rather than a creation of God.[44] He explained that via his Arabic texts he had succeeded in destroying these idols so that the veil of this imagined Nature was ripped away to reveal the fact of God's work and natural law (*al-sharīʿa al-fiṭriyya*) and the individual (*anā*) was revealed as existing in the shadow of God (*huwa*).[45]

Although Nursi largely avoided the formal discussions of *kalām*, he was firmly within the Māturīdī tradition regarding predestination, the particular will (*cüz-i ihtiyari*),[46] and major sin not being considered proof of false faith.[47] Men have become obsessed with causality and natural causes (*esbab-perest*, *tabiat-perest*) in their wont to establish actions as independent of God's power,[48] he said, but he did not rethink his position as Sabri did.[49] While ʿAbduh and Akif stressed human agency to exhort Muslims to engage in the building of their nations, Nursi urged action to affirm belief in God: he saw no need to imply received creed was at fault in order to make that point. As for law, he rejected the modernist/Salafi call to rework the methodological and institutional culture of *fiqh*: on core issues he said there is no need for new legal thinking (*ijtihād*), which more often than not has destructive intent,[50] and the multiplicity of schools is appropriate to the different conditions of different communities.[51] In foregoing the familiar genres of writing Nursi created a modernism framed in the language of Anatolian Sufism but which in fact transferred the charisma of the Sufi shaykh into a supra-*tarikat* text in that, like the ʿulamaʾ

[44] Nursi, *Ḥabba min Nawātāt Thamra min Thamarāt Jinān al-Qurʾān*, in *Qaṭra*, 4.

[45] Ibid., 4. There is some confusion over the grammar of this passage, particularly the last sentence. The editor of *al-Mathnawī* has altered some elements as if they were printing errors or grammatical mistakes on Nursi's part; 221. Turkish and English translations airbrush the difficulties aside since the broad meaning is clear; see Abdülmecid Nursî, trans., *Mesnevi-i Nuriye* (Istanbul: Şahdamar Yayınları, 2014), 107; and Huseyin Akarsu, trans., *al-Mathnawi al-Nuri: Seedbed of the Light* (Somerset, NJ: Light, 2007), 197–8.

[46] Nursi, 'Kader Risalesi' (twenty-sixth Söz), in *Sözler* (Ankara: Diyanet Vakfı, 2016), 567–603.

[47] Nursi, *Lem'alar*, thirteenth Lem'a, 78–9.

[48] Nursi, 'Tabiat Risalesi,' 193–4.

[49] His position was Māturīdī but could appear otherwise in that he was addressing a public he feared was under the spell of positivist voluntarism; Colin Turner, *The Qurʾan Revealed* (Berlin: Gerlach Press, 2013), 95–6.

[50] Nursi, *Ḥabāb min ʿUmmān al-Qurʾān al-Ḥakīm*, in *al-Mathnawī* (ed. al-Ṣāliḥī) 182.

[51] Nursi, 'İctihad Risalesi' (twenty-seventh Söz), in *Sözler*, 600–2.

renouncing school affiliation, he never identified with any particular order.[52] Nursi's approach to the state was also different from that of his contemporaries: while his aim was to prevent the Kemalist republic from breaking the hold of faith outside its metropolitan centres, he did not pathologise the state as the focus of his attention in the manner of Sabri, al-Bannā, Quṭb, Mawdūdī, and many others. His legacy was claimed by movements such as that of Fethüllah Gülen (b. 1941) whose methodology was more infiltration of state institutions and the discourse of civic rights than open political contestation and theorising about the nature, Islamic or otherwise, of the modern state.

TURKISH ISLAMISM FROM 1950

The literature on Nursi is immense, giving the impression that the Turkish Islamic movement emerged almost singlehandedly from his oeuvre. This has been tempting to accept because Nursi remained in Turkey and produced his material in first Arabic, then Ottoman Turkish, and then modern Turkish. Nursi's supporters tell the story of an envoy, Ahmet Ramazan Ağabey, sent by Nursi to Cairo in 1951 to give copies of *Risale-i Nur* to al-Azhar and to pass a message to the Muslim Brotherhood through Saʿīd Ramaḍān, a son-in-law of Ḥasan al-Bannā. During the trip Ağabey also sought out Sabri and Kevseri and years later offered recollections of his meeting with Sabri in particular. In one account Sabri tears up on receiving Nursi's messenger, telling him, 'he resisted, he stayed in the country' (*o direndi, memlekette kaldı*),[53] although earlier published versions do not mention this detail which serves to perpetuate the narrative of Turkish Islam's survival as the work of Said Nursi.[54] In a separate account of a visit to Istanbul in 1953 by Sabri's student Ali Özek, it is Nursi who is highly reverential of Sabri, telling Özek it is because of the work of Sabri that he has managed to amass some half a million followers.[55] However, Vahide tells us: 'Of all the Islamists of the previous era, Nursi stands out as

[52] This point is made by Mardin, *Religion and Social Change*, 230.

[53] Ömer Özcan, 'Osmanlının son Şeyhülislam'ı Mustafa Sabri Efendi'nin Said Nursi pişmanlığı,' *Risale Haber*, 12 March 2017; www.risalehaber.com/osmanlinin-son-seyhulislami-mustafa-sabri-efendinin-said-nursi-pismanligi-296674h.htm (accessed 30 December 2018).

[54] Necmeddin Şahiner, *Son Şahitler Bediüzzaman Said Nursi'yi Anlatıyor* (Istanbul: Yeni Asya, 1994), 195–6. Nursi cites the mission in *Risale-i Nur* 27, aka *Emirdağ Lahikası* (Istanbul: Yeni Asya, 2018), 390–1 (2:275).

[55] Yıldırım, *Medrese'den Üniversite'ye*, 117.

unique in carrying forward into the Republican period the great debate between Westernism and Islam, and presenting the case of Islam and the Qur'an in a way that was to be enthusiastically taken up by large numbers of people.'[56] Ibrahim Abu-Rabiʿ writes that Nursi and his followers were the only group to defend intellectually the bond between Turkish nation and Muslim *umma*.[57] And Şerif Mardin argues it was Nursi who was fundamental in facilitating Turkey's reception of modernity through an Islamic paradigm.[58] How justified are these views?

Two major trends regarding religion can be observed in the evolving republic: on the one hand, the continued strength of Islam as a social phenomenon, a way of viewing the world, a form of organisation, and a daily practice; on the other, Islam articulated in an innovative manner as a political force, in other words what I have called its ideologisation. This re-Islamisation, as it is often termed, was made possible by İsmet İnönü's decision to end the one-party state after the Second World War and loosen restrictions on public observance of faith. This was a multi-faceted process involving the efforts of numerous religious figures with diverse claims to authority located in historical Sufi networks (while the *tarikat*s remained banned) as well as the re-introduction of forms of religious education in primary, secondary, and tertiary educational institutions and the rapid growth of an Islamic print media. The Democrat Party, which won a landslide victory in the first multiparty elections in 1950, played heavily on themes of popular religious culture, attracting the support of not only the Nurcu movement but shaykhs within various Naqshbandī chains. A new level of politicisation kicked in with the National Order Party (Milli Nizam Partisi), established by Erbakan in 1970 and reformed as the National Salvation Party (Milli Selamet Partisi, MSP) in 1972. There were many other actors in this process. The poet Necip Fazıl Kısakürek (1904–83) promoted the idea of an Islamic 'Great East' (*Büyük Doğu*) that would revive the caliphate and overturn the secular republic with a journal of that name published intermittently from 1943. His was a conservative nationalism that was at first supportive of Erbakan's National Vision but became critical of Erbakan's concessions to the Left after the MSP joined government in 1974 and accused him of mimicking the Great

56 Vahide, *Islam in Modern Turkey*, 192.

57 Ibrahim Abu-Rabiʿ, ed., *Spiritual Dimensions of Bediuzzaman Said Nursi's Risale-i Nur* (Albany: State University of New York Press, 2008), ix.

58 Mardin, *Religion and Social Change*, 229.

East thesis.[59] The Nurcu movement also had a conflicted relationship with Erbakan: the Gülenists supported the 1980 coup and the early neoliberal policies of Turgut Özal that Erbakan opposed.[60]

As an engineering student from Konya, Erbakan was urged to enter the political sphere by Mehmed Zahid Kotku (1897–1980), the leader of the Gümüşhanevi chain of the Khālidī Naqshbandī (Nakşibendi-Halidi) based at the İskenderpaşa mosque in Istanbul.[61] They shared a conviction about the importance of an independent industrial economy: Kotku chose him to lead the project after Erbakan sent him an essay on post-war industrialisation in Germany, where he was studying,[62] and Erbakan often talked later of his debt to Kotku in the 'industrialisation struggle' (*sanayileşme mücadelesi*).[63] The Nakşibendi-Halidis under Kotku's guidance were inheritors of an anti-colonialism linked to their politicised nature as allies of the state and the İlmiye in the nineteenth century.[64] So while religious awareness was an area in which Nursi was fundamental, and the Nursi groups inspired by his work were motivated by the idea of reconciling

59 Umut Uzer, 'The Genealogy of Turkish Nationalism: From Civic and Ethnic to Conservative Nationalism in Turkey,' in *Symbiotic Antagonisms: Competing Nationalisms in Turkey*, ed. Ayşe Kadıoğlu and Emin Fuat Keyman (Salt Lake City: University of Utah Press, 2011), 129.

60 Hakan Yavuz, *Islamic Political Identity in Turkey* (Oxford; Oxford University Press, 2003), 16, 170.

61 On the Khālidī Naqshbandiyya in modern Turkey see Hakan Yavuz, 'The Matrix of Modern Turkish Islamic Movements: The Naqshbandī Sufi Order,' in *Naqshbandis in Western and Central Asia: Change and Continuity*, ed. Elisabeth Özdalga (Istanbul: Svenska Forskningsinstitutet, 1999): 129–46; Birol Yeşilada, 'The Refah Party Phenomenon in Turkey,' in *Comparative Political Parties and Party Elites: Essays in Honor of Samuel J. Eldersveld*, ed. Birol Yeşilada (Ann Arbor: University of Michigan Press, 1999), 123–50; Sencer Ayata, 'Traditional Sufi Orders on the Periphery: Kadiri and Nakşibendi Islam in Konya and Trabzon,' in *Islam in Modern Turkey*, ed. Richard Tapper (London: Tauris, 1991), 223–53; Hamid Algar, 'The Naqshibendi Order in Republican Turkey,' *Islamic World Report*, 1/3 (1996): 51–67; Şerif Mardin, 'The Nakşibendi Order in Turkish History,' in Tapper, *Islam*, 121–42; Svante E. Cornell, 'The Naqshbandi-Khalidi Order and Political Islam in Turkey,' Hudson Institute, 3 September 2015; www.hudson.org/research/11601-the-naqshbandi-khalidi-order-and-political-Islām-in-turkey (accessed 15 August 2019).

62 Hasan Bitmez, Saadet Party assistant to the chairman for foreign affairs and former official at the International Islamic Federation of Student Organisations; interview with author, Gebze, 23 August 2018.

63 Necmettin Erbakan, *Davam: Ne Yaptıysam Allah Rızası İçin Yaptım* (Ankara: Milli Gazete, 2014), 9.

64 Butrus Abu-Manneh notes Gümüşhanevi's quietism vis-à-vis other Khalidiyya branches. He considers Erbakan to be a continuation of this quietism, which seems an odd conclusion considering Erbakan launched a political movement (Abu-Manneh, 'Shaykh Ahmed Ziyaʾüddin el-Gümüşhanevi,' 116–17).

faith with modern science, political mobilisation was led by adepts of the İskenderpaşa-based Halidi line who were well placed to innovate an Islamic electoral politics. If the leading groups of the period of transition from empire to republic – Young Turks, CUP, Kemalists – can be considered a new military-bureaucratic class,[65] the conservative Anatolians who moved into political life and the bureaucracy from the 1950s with increasing force were equally a class that came to rival the secular republicans of the military, the judiciary, the presidency, and other key institutions of state.[66] The dynamic of Anatolian hinterland versus republican centre of power spoke to a historical feature of the country's political geography. Ernest Gellner once argued that in the Turkish context political power did not run inexorably from the periphery to the centre, rather Ottoman ruling elites governed through an idea of the state as 'a gift from the tribe'.[67] In the same vein the Islamic movements flourished because of the state's failure to reconfigure hinterland religion through its modernisation policies. Indeed, Erbakan's movement adopted a political structure suited to this circumstance. Its youth arm (Millî Gençlik Vakfı) was structured as a series of independently run groups organising their own activities in the provinces without a unified education curriculum.[68] This atomistic approach was adopted by the İbda group, a Necip Fazıl-inspired student movement that broke with Erbakan in the 1970s and later developed a paramilitary arm. İbda adopted a strategy of forming small, autonomous cells around the country which could act on their own initiative, and in this spirit of fragmentation it also published a multitude of magazines spreading its message in different formats and platforms, making it more difficult for the state to shut it down.[69]

Erbakan's movement established links with the Muslim Brotherhood at an early stage. The Brotherhood's long experience, its tribulations during the Nasserist period, and its revival in the 1970s were a source of inspiration for the Islamic *Kulturkampf* in Turkey. The ideas of Sayyid Quṭb and

[65] Berktay argues they formed a new class: Lecture on Ottoman and Turkish History, EDEP İhtisas Merkezi, Ibn Haldun University, 10 July 2017. For class analysis of empire and republic see Halil Berktay and Suraiya Faroqhi, ed., *New Approaches to State and Peasant in Ottoman History* (London: Cass, 1992).

[66] David Shankland, *Islam and Society in Turkey* (Huntingdon: Eothen, 1999).

[67] Ernest Gellner, 'The Turkish Option in Comparative Perspective,' in *Rethinking Modernity and National Identity in Turkey*, ed. Sibel Bozdoğan and Reşat Kasaba (Seattle: University of Washington Press, 1997), 233–44.

[68] Bitmez, interview.

[69] Ruşen Çakır, *Ayet ve Slogan: Türkiye'de İslami Oluşumlar* (Istanbul: Metis Yayınları, 1991), 170.

Ḥasan al-Bannā transferred to Turkey with the rise in Islamic publishing from the late 1940s. Contacts between the two movements were instituted between Erbakan and Mahdī ʿĀkif (1928–2017), then an advisor to the World Assembly of Muslim Youth (WAMY) in Riyadh, after ʿĀkif's release in July 1974 from twenty years in prison. ʿĀkif was a senior figure of the group's old guard, close to al-Bannā after he joined in 1943 and close to Quṭb in prison, and he was among those who read *Maʿālim fī al-Ṭarīq* before its publication.[70] He became an important figure in the Brotherhood's international organisation after it was formally founded in 1982,[71] serving as director of the Islamic Centre in Munich until 1987. Erbakan and ʿĀkif wanted to focus on transnational Muslim youth, so initiated summer camps in Cyprus, Malta, and Turkey in co-ordination with the already existing International Islamic Federation of Student Organisations (IIFSO).[72] A committee of Brotherhood chapters visited Erbakan in Turkey in 1976, including Ibrāhīm al-Miṣrī from the Islamic Group in Lebanon, Kamāl al-Hilbāwī, who was then chairman of WAMY and later the Brotherhood's spokesman in London, and Muṣṭafā Ṭaḥḥān (1938–2019), a member of the Brotherhood's Lebanese chapter who in later years encouraged Erbakan to publish more and translated him into Arabic.[73] Also involved was Khurshīd Aḥmad, Mawdūdī's close confidante in the Jamāʿat-i Islāmī of Pakistan, and later the Malaysian Islamic Party, when a formal council for co-ordination between these Islamic movements was estabished in 1988.[74] An agreement was made among these groups that the Egyptian Brotherhood would not try to recruit or operate in Turkey or Pakistan because equivalent movements already existed.[75] The first camp was held in North Cyprus in 1977 when Rauf Denktash, then president of the newly established Turkish Federated State of Cyprus, gave them the use of eight sea-front villas.[76] The first and only camp in Turkey was brought to an end in Konya in 1980 during the military coup, when some 300 activists including ʿĀkif were deported.[77]

[70] Victor Willi, *The Fourth Ordeal: A History of the Society of the Muslim Brothers in Egypt, 1973–2013* (Cambridge: Cambridge University Press, 2021), 109–10.
[71] Ibid., 110.
[72] Bitmez, interview.
[73] Ibid.
[74] Kamāl al-Hilbāwī; interview, London, 6 September 2018.
[75] Bitmez, al-Hilbāwī, interviews.
[76] Al-Hilbāwī, interview.
[77] Munīr, interview.

Differences emerged between the Turkish and Egyptian organisations over strategy: Erbakan argued the Brotherhood should apply itself to the open public arena as a political party and the Brotherhood urged Erbakan to concentrate on being a societal movement united by the discipline of education.[78] The Brotherhood's leader during this period, ʿUmar al-Tilmisānī, took the organisation into electoral politics in 1984, but resistance to open political engagement persisted among its ruling clique after al-Tilmisānī's death in 1986, with drastic consequences when it formed a short-lived government in 2012.[79] By the 1980s the Turkish cohort at al-Azhar had grown to around 3,000.[80] Erbakan's movement was never a chapter of the Egyptian organisation, formally imbedded in its structure and receiving instructions on policy from Cairo. Despite that, Erbakan would sometimes refer to the Egyptian *murshid* (leader) as his own *mürşit* (for example, during a trip to Cairo in 1993), but he only spoke in this manner as a mark of respect to the Brotherhood as the foundational organisation.[81] The close links extended to intermarriage: Brotherhood activist in Germany Ibrāhīm al-Zayāt (b. 1968) married a niece of Erbakan, and Ḥasan al-Bannā's son Sayf al-Islām (1934–2016) married a Turkish student who was introduced to him by Ali Yakub Cenkçiler.[82]

Sabri and Kevseri's Turkish students played a key role in spreading word of the Brotherhood and translating their works when they returned to Turkey in the mid-1950s. Quṭb became an important figure because of the work of Emin Saraç, Ali Yakub, and others.[83] *Al-ʿAdāla al-Ijtimāʿiyya* was first published in translation in 1962 by Cağaloğlu publishing house in Arabic and translated by Yaşar Tunagür, a member of the World Muslim League and vice director of the government's Diyanet adminstration.[84] Dedicating the book to 'our enlightened youth' (*münevver gençliğimiz*) its translators noted that it had been chosen by the American Council for Learned Societies in 1953 as the first in a series of Arabic translations to

78 Ibid.
79 Willi, *Fourth Ordeal, passim.*
80 Ibid.
81 Ibid.
82 Düzdağ, *Hatıralar*, 1:311–12; interview with Sayf al-Islām's widow Berat el-Banna; Istanbul, 20 August 2018.
83 Ashraf ʿAbd al-Ghaffār, a former Muslim Brotherhood Guidance Council member who left Egypt in December 2013, said Saraç and Cenkçiler were arrested in the 1954 crackdown (ʿAbd al-Ghaffār; interview, Istanbul, 17 August 2018). There is no confirmation of this. Cenkçiler's memoir says he returned to Turkey in 1957.
84 Hakan Köni, 'Saudi Influence on Islamic Institutions in Turkey Beginning in the 1970s,' *Middle East Journal*, 66/1 (2012): 105.

English.[85] At the time Quṭb was understood to be an intellectual critiquing socialism through Islamic discourse – an early trace of the 'Turkish-Islamic synthesis' (Türk-İslam sentezi) adopted by the military regime in 1980[86] – which made him popular in both nationalist and religious circles, but opinions began to change after Saraç's translation and İsmail Hakkı Şengüler and Bekir Karlığa's translation of *Fī Ẓilāl al-Qurʾān* (*Fizılal-il-Kur'an: Kur'an'ın Gölgesinde*) in 1968. *Maʿālim fī al-Ṭarīq* was published almost immediately as *Beklenen Lider İçin Yoldaki İşaretler* (Signs on the Path for the Awaited Leader, 1966) by *Hilal* magazine, one of the leading Islamic journals of the period whose publishing house was at the forefront of publishing translated Egyptian and Pakistani material for a Turkish audience.[87] Ali Yakub was the lead translator of *Jāhiliyyat al-Qarn al-ʿIshrīn* (The Jāhiliyya of the Twentieth Century, 1964) by Quṭb's brother Muḥammad, published by Cağaloğlu as *20. Asrın Cahiliyeti* in two volumes (1967, 1971). Largely a summation of Sayyid Quṭb's ideas, it argued that *jāhiliyya* expresses the psychological mindset of modern society that rejects Islam as a way of life and as a politico-juridical system. Mustafa Runyun (1917–88), a student of Sabri and Kevseri during twelve years in Egypt, returned in 1950 to take the post of preacher in Istanbul's Hacıbayram mosque. He published a series of eighteen booklets in 1967 under the collective title *Dinî Hikâyeler* (Religious Tales), translations of stories of the prophets for children published in 1947 by Quṭb and Egyptian novelist ʿAbd al-Ḥamīd Jūda al-Saḥḥār (1913–74).

Runyun's preaching during the period of Democrat Party government was typical of the Islamic discourse couched in nationalist language of the period – stressing the prescribed prayers, building mosques, holding the Ramaḍān fast, making pilgrimage, active work, refusing bribes, avoiding alcohol, and acknowledging the Turkish nation's (*Türk milleti*) glory realised historically through Islam.[88] Runyun also had a platform to address the listeners of state-owned Ankara Radio and his radio talks were

[85] Yaşar Tunagür and Adnan Mansur, trans., 'Foreword,' Seyyid Kutub, *İslamda Sosyal Adalet* (Istanbul: Cağaloğlu Yayınevi, 1962).

[86] İsmail Kara suggests the government was acting covertly to encourage the translations to counter the Left; *Cumhuriyet Türkiyesi'nde Bir Mesele Olarak İslâm*, 2 vols. (İstanbul: Dergâh, 2019), 2:521–2.

[87] Published by Salih Özcan, a former student of Nursi who helped established the Saudi-backed Islamic bank in Turkey and served as National Salvation Party parliamentarian (Köni, 'Saudi Influence,' 104).

[88] Mustafa Runyun, *Hacıbayram Minberinden Hutbelerim* (Ankara: Diyanet, 1956).

printed in booklets, some of which he published on his own account.[89] This Islamic revival manifested itself primarily through the religious print media that appeared from around 1945; at least ten papers were established between 1945 and 1949 and at least sixteen more in the period 1950–2, including the journals *Büyük Doğu* (1943–75), a vehicle for Necip Fazıl, the revived *Sebilürreşad* (1948–66), which heavily promoted Akif, and *Hilal* (1958–91), which was more open to the international Islamist trend.[90] The main aim of these publications was to establish the acceptability of discussing religion in public space and cast off the charge of reactionism (*irtica*), and they reflected the broad concern with the question of Islam and the state that had dominated political debate since the late nineteenth century, contra the civil society discourse prevalent from the 1990s.

Hilal provides a register of the concerns of the time. It covered a wide range of international Muslim issues, with articles about or by writers in Turkey or abroad, but two figures dominated among them, rarely passing unmentioned for long in its issues: Akif and Nursi. The first issue carried on its cover Akif's well-known line from *Çanakkale Şehidlerine* (To the Gallipoli Martyrs) which likened Ottoman soldiers sacrificing their lives in battle to suns setting for the sake of the crescent moon (*bir hilal uğruna, ya Rab ne güneşler batıyor*).[91] Akif and Nursi's images often featured on the cover[92] and most issues carried some material from Nursi's *Risale*. Describing a literary salon in Erzurum in 1963 in which Kemalist literary critic Nurullah Ataç attacked Akif as worthless for Turkish national poetry, *Hilal* defended him as the era's 'greatest and most deep-thinking poet of Muslim Turkism' (*müslüman Türklüğün en büyük ve mütefekkir şairidir*) and, in implicit criticism of Gökalp, the intellectual with the most effective ideas on national culture (*ulusal kültür diye uydurulan millî hars*).[93] His Indian counterpart Iqbāl also featured prominently through translations and articles, and Ali Ulvi Kurucu, the student of Sabri and Kevseri who had moved to Medina, often supplied poetry and articles. By contrast, Sabri,

[89] Runyun, *Dinî ve Ahlakî Konuşmalar* (Ankara: Diyanet, 1955); Runyun, *Dinî ve Ahlakî Müsahabelerim*, 3. vols. (Ankara: Ayyıldız Matbaası, 1957/58).

[90] Gavin Brockett, *How Happy to Call Oneself a Turk: Provincial Newspapers and the Negotiation of a Muslim National Identity* (Austin.: University of Texas Press, 2011), 124–5.

[91] *Hilal*, 1/1 (November 1958), cover.

[92] For Akif, *Hilal*, 1/12 (January 1960); on the occasion of Nursi's death, *Hilal*, 1/14 (April–May 1960).

[93] Semaheddin Cem, 'Akifimiz,' *Hilal*, 5/56, March 1966, 23–4.

the radical opponent of the republic who died in Egypt, was honoured only briefly in the early issues, with excerpts of *al-Qawl al-Faṣl*, his tract on Islam and the modern state, running in issue three and four.[94] Early issues presented Nasser in flattering terms, publishing a translation of the preface to a book on Islam he had written, in which he concluded: 'As long as I live, with all my power, determination and faith I will work to make the Islamic call an undeniable truth.'[95]

Material by Quṭb began appearing from 1963[96] – one article published shortly after his release in December 1964 described him as 'the true Muslim' (*hakikî Müslüman*) for choosing jail to win God's favour[97] – and the first material on al-Bannā was published in 1965.[98] The tone shifted significantly with the beginning of Quṭb's trial. 'What the Egyptian dictator Nasser is doing to Muslims is unprecedented in history, his massacres and tortures outdo the pharaohs', its editorial commentary said.[99] Another article said Muslims had to consider one way or another what their response would be: 'If the hand holding a sword over the head of any Muslim anywhere is not broken today then tomorrow it will come down on your head. Justice will have its revenge. So, let's not stand and imagine justice, let's make it happen.'[100] The following issues featured material in translation by Quṭb, al-Bannā, Mawdūdī, Nadwī, and ʿAbd al-Qādir ʿAwda, a Brotherhood judge who was executed in 1954, and with Quṭb's death in August 1966 two issues ran translations of *Maʿālim fī al-Ṭarīq*, 'the work that provoked the death penalty', until *Hilal*'s full book version was confiscated and its translator arrested.[101] But *Hilal* issued a rush of Quṭb's other works in translation as books and excerpts in the following years.[102]

94 Mustafa Sabri, 'Gaybe İnananları inanmıyanlardan ayıran kesin söz,' *Hilal*, 1/3 (January 1959), 21; 1/4 (February 1959), 19.

95 Cemal Abdülnasır, 'İslam Daveti,' *Hilal*, 1/7 (May 1959), 9–10.

96 Seyyid Kutub, 'Habil ve Kabil,' *Hilal*, 4/38 (April 1963): 20–1; idem, 'İslam Kumandanlığını Yapacaktır,' *Hilal*, 5/53 (July 1965), 5; idem, 'Kur'an Yolunun Esası,' *Hilal*, 5/54 (August 1965), 27–8; Mühibbizade, 'Seyyid Kutub Kimdir?' *Hilal*, 5/54 (August 1965), 20–1.

97 İsmail Kazdal, 'Hakikî Müslüman,' *Hilal*, 5/49 (February 1965), 7.

98 Mühibbizade (Nihat Armağan), 'Şeyh Ḥasan-El Banna Kimdir?' *Hilal*, 5/53 (July 1965), 20–1.

99 Editorial comment, 'Hilal'den Size,' *Hilal*, 5/56 (March 1966), 1.

100 Idem, 'Mısır'da Olup Bitenler,' *Hilal*, 5/56 (March 1966), 2.

101 Hamza Türkmen, 'Seyyid Kutub Anlaşılabildi mi?' *Haksöz Okulu*, August 1995; www.haksozhaber.net/okul/seyyid-kutub-anlasilabildi-mi-1019yy.htm (accessed 26 August 2021).

102 Kara counts thirty-nine Islamist translated books in total published by *Hilal* between 1957 and 1980, by Quṭb, Mawdūdī, Nadwī, ʿAwda, and Syrian Brotherhood ideologue Saʿīd Ḥawwā (1935–89). The translators included Turkish Azhar students in the 1950s,

These early publications did not use the term *İslamcı/İslamcılık* to describe the Islamic movement and its adherents. These remained largely terms of analysis,[103] and devout intellectuals who rose to prominence in the period when Erbakan's Welfare Party went from strength to strength did not like the term.[104] If we were to attempt to define the point at which Islam becomes Islamism, the definition would focus on two stages: first, the point at which the constituent parts of the Islamic tradition, in its recognisable genres of talking, writing, and thinking about *kalām*, *fiqh*, *falsafa*, *taṣawwuf*, et al., fragment and disconnect to reform in new discursive arrangements belonging to the public sphere, and second, the deployment of these new formulas in the political arena, with all that implies in terms of organisation, seeking public office, contestation in electoral processes, and engaging mass media. The second stage is only attained through the first, and the first alone is sufficient to talk of Islam rendered as ideology. If the first stage is enough to qualify as 'Islamism' then we are obliged to talk of Said Nursi as much as of Sayyid Quṭb as an Islamist. If the second stage of political contestation was a requirement, then the Muslim Brotherhood would only qualify as Islamist from 1942 when al-Bannā first tried to run for office or 1984 when the Brotherhood took part en masse in parliamentary elections. With this broad definition, Akif would count as an Islamist, Kevseri most likely would not, unless we considered his use of print media as enough of a qualifying factor on its own, while Sabri would stand in the middle ground: acting politically as the Ottoman parliamentarian, as sheikh ül-Islam, and as a writer in Egypt, though in defence of the old order in as much as that was possible.[105]

In Turkey and Egypt official institutions such as Diyanet and al-Azhar held to their traditional positions on theological questions and upheld the juridical methodologies they had always followed, within the new boundaries first established in the mid to late nineteenth century concerning

Ali Arslan Aydın, Mustafa Mutlu, and Abdülkadir Şener. The full list of books can be found in Kara, *Cumhuriyet Türkiyesi'nde*, 2:525–6.

[103] Runyun used *İslamlik* in 1957 for Islam; Runyun, *Dini ve Ahlaki Mūsāhabelerim* (Ankara: Ayyıldız matbaası, 1957), 1:9, 36. Erişirgil describes Akif as *islamcı* in his 1958 biography *İslamcı bir Şairin Romanı*; Tarık Zafer Tunaya's *İslamcılık Cereyanı* (The Islamist Trend, 1962) is one of the first analyses of the Ottoman/republican movement to use the term.

[104] Michael Meeker, 'The New Muslim Intellectuals in the Republic of Turkey,' in Tapper, *Islam in Modern Turkey*, 189.

[105] See William Shepard's typology; 'Islam and Ideology: Towards a Typology,' *IJMES*, 19/3 (1987): 307–35.

issuance of fatwas, fields of shariʿa law application, educational curricula, etc. However, these new boundaries meant they wielded diminished authority,[106] and this may have further impacted the reception and spread of iconoclastic thinking in both societies. While on the one hand Nursi adopted a supra-*tarikat* approach, Hayreddin Karaman (b. 1934) advanced a form of *lā-madhhabiyya*, not as a Salafi in the manner of al-Albānī or al-Maʿṣūmī, but as a modernist reformer in the style of ʿAbduh. A graduate of the Imam-Hatip schools which were allowed to open in the 1950s, Karaman wrote his thesis at the Istanbul Higher Islamic Institute on *ijtihād* in the early Islamic period. He later became a professor at the same institute when it was transformed into a theology faculty. Karaman advanced his view of *ijtihād* over *taqlīd* and *talfīq* between the schools,[107] in *Dört Risale* (Four Treatises, 1971), *İslam Hukukunda İctihad* (Ijtihād in Islamic Law, 1975), and the journal *Nesil* (1976–80).[108] The Gülen movement also embraced supra-*madhhab* themes but as a form of inclusive pluralism, embracing all without privileging one group over another.[109] New institutions such as the Ankara Divinity School, established in 1949 to promote a deconstructive historicist approach to religion, began to move away in the 1990s from terms such as reformist because of the general collapse in standing of Muslim modernism in the latter decades of the twentieth century, which, as we have seen, Sabri had done his best to induce.[110]

As for al-Albānī's more radical attempt to produce a pre-*madhhab fiqh*, it made its way into Turkey from the 1990s through self-described Salafi preachers who had studied in Saudi Arabia such as Abdullah Yolcu (b. 1958). Through his own material and translations of al-Albānī and leading Saudi scholars, Yolcu used the Guraba publishing house that he established in Istanbul in 1992 to propagate the contemporary ideology of

106 Masooda Bano, 'Introduction,' in *Modern Islamic Authority and Social Change. Volume 1, Evolving Debates in Muslim Majority Countries,* ed. Bano (Edinburgh: Edinburgh University Press, 2018).

107 Karaman translated Riḍā's 'Muḥāwarāt al-Muṣliḥ wa-l-Muqallid' series as *İslam'da Birlik ve Fıkıh Mezhepleri* (1974).

108 Michelangelo Guida, 'The New Islamists' Understanding of Democracy in Turkey: The Examples of Ali Bulaç and Hayreddin Karaman,' *Turkish Studies*, 11/3 (2010): 359–60.

109 Hilmi Demir, 'FETÖ: Mezhepler Üstü Din Öğretimi ve Alevi Açılımı,' *Türkiye Gazetesi*, 1 June 2018; www.turkiyegazetesi.com.tr/yazarlar/hilmi-demir/602515.aspx (accessed 13 January 2019).

110 See Recep Şentürk, 'Islamic Reformist Discourses and Intellectuals in Turkey,' in *Reformist Voices of Islam: Mediating Islam and Modernity*, ed. Shireen Hunter (Armonk, NY: M. E. Sharpe, 2009), 227–46.

Salafism, with particular emphasis on popular practices and the theology of faith proven through action but tailored towards a Turkish audience. Previously, Salafi had been understood according to the creedal division outlined by ʿAbduh and which İsmail Hakkı articulated in his book of modernist theology *Yeni İlm-i Kelam* (1920). Thus, according to an article in *Nesil* published in 1977, Selefiyye was the rejection of rationalist approaches to scripture, but nothing to do with rejecting the legal *madhhab*.[111] This purely creed-based definition was upheld by Diyanet in its catechism first published in 1999 and still in print.[112] Reflecting his al-Albānī influence, Yolcu introduced not only a reinvigorated critique of Sufism[113] but the open assault on the Ḥanafī-Māturīdī system that Kevseri had feared. It is too early to ascertain if transnational Salafism has had a significant impact on belief and practice,[114] but in the face of these trends nationalist writers have indulged a fetishisation of Ḥanafī-Māturīdism as the expression of a non-Arab, liberal Turkish Islam.[115] The Turkish Islamist movement, on the other hand, has held close to classic Ottoman Māturīdism: Erbakan would often make mention of the concept of the particular will (*irade-i cüzʾiye*) in his public disquisitions and writings on creation and human responsibility.[116]

CONCLUDING REMARKS

The question of influence relates to the notion of canonicity in Turkish Islam, a category that has been defined largely around the figure of Said Nursi and the Gümüşhanevi Naqshbandiyya. Turkish Islam has been no

[111] Bekir Topaloğlu, 'Selefiye,' *Nesil*, 1/7 (April 1977): 3–7. The article named as Salafis Ibn Taymiyya, Ibn al-Qayyim, and al-Shawkānī, and in contemporary Turkey Nursi student Ahmed Husrev Altınbaşak (1899–1977), a student of Nursi, mosque imam Celaleddin Ökten (1882–1961), and İsmail Hakkı himself.

[112] Diyanet İşleri Başkanlığı, *İlmihal 1: İman ve İbadetler* (Istanbul: Diyanet, 1999), 23. In 2015 Diyanet amended the definition to include movements since the 1980s; idem, *Daiş'in Temel Felsefesi ve Dini Referansları Raporu* (Ankara: Diyanet, 2015), 8.

[113] On the anti-Sufism of Ercümend Özkan, see Alberto Fabio Ambrosio, 'Mapping Modern Turkish Sufism and Anti-Sufism,' in Ridgeon, *Sufis and Salafis*, 59–70.

[114] Hilmi Demir sees signs of a shift; 'Nakşibendilik Selefileşiyor mu?' *21. Yüzyıl*, No. 70 (January 2014).

[115] Mehmet Zeki İşcan analyses the phenomenon in 'Türk Basınında Matüridi ve Matüridilik,' *Marmara University İlahiyat Fakültesi Vakfı Yayınları*, 261 (2012): 478–92.

[116] Erbakan, *Davam*, 23. On Turkish scholars among contemporary intellectuals calling for a new theological approach see Wielandt, 'Main Trends of Islamic Theological Thought,' 749–53.

less constructed along national lines than literature and other fields in which textual authority is established through the vector of national identity.[117] We see how easy it has been for nationalist thought to shut Sabri and Kevseri out of Islamic history in Turkey, and how much easier it has been to embrace a figure like Akif who penned a national anthem and staged a tragi-heroic return home to die. Here their works in the widest sense, including the acts of their life as well as their writings, take on meanings detached from intent and action. The field of hermeneutics has shown how after words are committed to writing the text acquires an autonomy beyond the control of its originator.[118] Some have wanted to read Akif as a solely Turkish thinker, Kevseri as an Arab *ʿālim* or anti-Arab Ottoman, Sabri as a cantankerous rejectionist of Kemalism. Yet they are more than these functional descriptions in that they came to represent a crucial bridge between the Late Ottoman and republican periods in Turkish Islamic thought and can be easily injected into the broader narrative of Islamic intellectual history from which they have been largely erased via disciplinary conventions that define writers and historical fields along ethnic, linguistic, and national lines. Sabri and Kevseri left deep traces in the arena of Islamic discourse in Arabic with a refutation of modernism and Salafism that remains powerful today. These thinkers form a missing link in our understanding of Late Ottoman religious thought, including its extensions outside the Turkish republic, and the role of that thought in the modern Islamic history of Turkey and Egypt, including the Muslim Brotherhood. In their writings they were among the last major Muslim thinkers of their generation to grapple with new modes of thinking and doing Islam produced by the matrix of processes around the European scientific revolution and the Enlightenment.

It is also true that in engaging with the positivist and materialist trends that were the most recent iteration of European thought, like their peers the Ottoman exiles were often given to a reductive or blinkered view of Western intellectual history.[119] Since they were recent and ongoing phenomena Sabri can perhaps be forgiven for missing contemporary trends such as the rise of analytic philosophy and the mid-twentieth turn away

[117] Jauss, *Toward an Aesthetic of Reception*, 51.

[118] Paul Ricoeur (trans. David Pellauer), *Hermeneutics* (Cambridge: Polity Press, 2016), 135.

[119] Gadamer notes that modern European philosophy for long imagined there had been a continuity in the Western philosophical tradition despite the fragmentation caused by the reception of Greek concepts in Latin, the reception of those Latin concepts in modern languages, and the emergence of a new historical consciousness (Gadamer, *Truth and Method*, xxiii).

from positivism in its various forms as a political and social philosophy, though they no doubt would have cheered him.[120] Among the reformers (ʿAbduh, Akif, Iqbāl) the European caricature of Islam as a fatalistic religion induced a desire for theological reassessment to stress human agency and the search for a Martin Luther, against which the traditionalists (Sabri, Kevseri) had a visceral reaction. It also fed the trend towards dismissing Sufism as unproductive intellection and indulgent devotion. Yet had any of them delved further back than the nineteenth century or closely read theorists such as Max Weber, they would have realised that the Calvinists at the heart of the Protestant Reformation in fact believed in the very predestination from which some were striving so hard to distance themselves. In his 1904 study of Protestantism and capitalism, Weber argued that it was the Calvinist belief that those slated for salvation must demonstrate their elect status through unemotional pious works and systematic ethical conduct that was the guiding force behind the work ethic at the centre of European modernity. But in the pages of Weber there was also to be found a form of vindication of the modernists' denigration of Sufi asceticism, in that Weber saw this work ethic as another repurposing of pre-modern piety, such as that seen in the life of the monastery. With this ascetic spirit informing capitalist society, now the idea of duty in one's calling inhabited modern lives 'like the ghost of dead religious beliefs', Weber wrote.[121]

But the fundamental question they wrestled with – what could be salvaged from the Islamic tradition in the hope of moulding the new Western structures claiming universality into future forms to their advantage? – speaks to their significance as thinkers. The modern transformations in Islamic thought were such that they could not ultimately have imagined a return to a de-colonised pre-modernity. And while they did not live to experience post-colonial Nasserism, they most likely would have considered it as displaying more intense forms of the coloniality they had critiqued in Kemalist Turkey and liberal Egypt. Their sympathies tended towards the Islamist movements with their statist politicisation of religion and ambition to create an alternative modernity. The Salafis on the other

[120] Cottingham, *Philosophy of Religion*, 35–9; John Gray, *Seven Types of Atheism* (London: Penguin, 2019), 9–23; Stephen Toulmin, *Return to Reason* (Cambridge: Harvard University Press, 2001).

[121] Max Weber, *The Protestant Ethic and the Spirit of Capitalism* (London: Routledge, 2001), 124. Weber was not translated into English until 1930. Gökalp's previously cited 'İslamiyet ve Asri Medeniyet' articles published in 1917 indicate possible familiarity with his ideas in its discussion of religious and non-religious government in Christian history, though Gökalp was hardly averse to citing his European sources.

hand stood a few degrees distant from the notion of response to modernity in that they claimed to preserve a system of knowledge that was not only pre-modern but, in some respects, pre- or proto-Islamic in its determination to discount most of classical period. It was too early for the Ottoman thinkers to address the generation of Muslim philosophers who came to public prominence from the 1960s with analyses of Islam and Arab identity and history informed by an array of post-structuralist approaches decentring the notion of fixed knowledge and placing problematised religion at the centre of their analysis of political, social, and economic degradation in Muslim societies today.[122] These last Ottomans would likely have seen this embrace of Western knowledge and its universalist claims as a bridge too far, and for Sabri and Kevseri at least a vindication of their warning against enabling the iconoclastic trends they had identified in Islamic intellectual culture, not least that of ʿAbduh modernism.[123]

Indeed, the findings of this study suggest that the model for understanding the fate of the centuries-long tradition of Ottoman imperial Islam and the place of Turkey in the landscape of modern Islamic thought needs to be reconsidered. This model posits that with the drastic re-shaping of the Ottoman İlmiye in the 1920s into a diminished, tightly controlled system shorn of the Sufi, educational, and legal institutions that gave Muslim culture its distinctive epistemic character, the republican revival of public religion in various forms from the 1950s was uniquely Turkish in character and thus the category 'Turkish Islam' shared little in common with the Islamic world. In other words, what İsmail Kara has called 'the great rupture' (*büyük kopukluk*) sought by Mustafa Kemal was real, deep, and lasting. This theory led Kara to argue that movements like the Muslim Brotherhood and Jamāʿat-i Islāmī had limited impact in Turkey, also because of colonial histories in each of their local contexts that produced their own post-colonial radicalisations.[124] It is now possible to put forward another model. First, the ideological transformation of the Islamic

[122] For example, Mohammed Arkoun, 'Rethinking Islam Today,' *The Annals of the American Academy of Political and Social Science*, 588/1 (2003): 18–39; Mohammed ʿAbed al-Jabri (trans. Aziz Abbassi), *Arab-Islamic Philosophy: A Contemporary Critique* (Austin: University of Texas, 1999); Abdallah Laroui, *Islam et histoire: essai d'épistémologie* (Paris: A. Michel, 1999); also, Talal Asad's discussion of the poet Adonis' view of the 'power of tradition' in Arab culture; *Formations of the Secular*, 54–6.

[123] Sedgwick, *Muhammad Abduh*, 120–1; the philosophers were in part a product of ʿAbduh-Afghānī thought.

[124] Kara, *Cumhuriyet Türkiyesi'nde*, 501–45.

tradition into a political programme and new style of living was well underway in the Late Ottoman period. Second, the greatest minds of that era took those innovations with them into their Egyptian exile and developed them further. Third, this new thinking was passed on to (1) Egyptian ʿulamaʾ, devout intellectuals, and political activists who had begun to think in similar terms about Islam and modern society in light of the Turkish republic's repudiation of religious faith and its institutions, on the one hand, and the continuing struggle against colonialism, on the other and (2) to the growing body of Turkish students who, in awe of Sabri, Kevseri, Akif, al-Bannā, and Quṭb, made pilgrimage to Cairo as a historic centre of Islamic learning continuing to attract the best minds and process ideas. Finally, this shared Egyptian-Turkish intellectual production in Egypt, which was contemporaneous with the work of Mawdūdī in India and Pakistan, spread not only throughout the Islamic sphere but was fed back to Turkey, where it was especially impactful in inspiring the political movement launched by Erbakan, although the fact that the Egyptian and Arab writers had formed their ideas on a basis of intimate familiarity with the Ottoman legacy was largely obscured.

Turkish Islam, in its cosmopolitan and rural settings, has its specificities like any other but it has been too easily essentialised in the scholarly literature through tropes such as that of irenic Nurcus, who typically function as a counterweight to insurrectionary Muslim Brothers.[125] This image is easily dismissed. Since the 1990s the Muslim Brotherhood has been riven by dispute between on the one hand an old guard who shared prison with Quṭb and on the other younger figures favouring political participation on a post-Islamist basis, yet it is the old guard who in recent times steadfastly rejected the call to arms, even after the violence of a military coup.[126] At the same time, in Turkey the inheritors of Egyptian Islamist thought are those who pioneered political participation, while it is the Gülenists claiming Nursi's mantle who stood accused (rightly or wrongly) of sedition and violence. In the shaping of Islamic thought and politics in modern Turkey, just as consequential as the shuttering of Islamic institutions over three decades was the Late Ottoman tradition of political contestation and open public debate, which the Kemalist regime was obliged to re-instate after the Second World War. It was the revival of this legacy that created a regulated public sphere in which political forces

[125] Kara does this in relating a story of Muslim Brotherhood leader Muṣṭafā Mashhūr's meeting with Nurcus during a 1996 visit to Istanbul; *Cumhuriyet Türkiyesi'nde*, 536.
[126] Willi, *The Fourth Ordeal*, 305–87.

including the Islamist among them could jostle for position, however troubled its trajectory has been. Indeed, the notion of a sharp rupture in global Islamic thought itself between the era of empires and that of nation-states appears to have been overstated by scholarship in that some of the key arguments of modern Islamism were informed by the crisis attending the end of the Ottoman polity, whose key Muslim actors left to tell their story. Their mission was to preserve whatever continuities were possible in managing the disruption of Islamic knowledge.

Appendices

Appendix 1: Sabri's Letter to the Vatican, 1925

Roma 14 Mai 1925

Emminence,

Depuis la grande guerre, les peuples, surtout ceux de l'Orient, sous la poussée des lois économiques, ou sous l'impulsion des aspirations nationalistes, cherchent une nouvelle orientation, pour créer une nouvelle ordre sociale.

La conséquence de cetté orientation, a eu pour résultat la chute des manarchies, et en même temps malheureusement la destruction de la religion.

Sous la direction habile des nouveaux apôtres, des meneurs, des loges maçoniques, le Khalifat, un des remparts les plus importants du conservatisme, de la modération et de paix en Orient est renversé.

Inutile de rappeler ici l'étendu, l'importance géographique, économique du monde musulman ainsi que le nombre des croyants.

Ce monde porte sur son seine des chrétiens, des institutions religieuses, des églises, des écoles dépendant en grande partie de Saint Siège.

A Son Emminence

Le Cardinal GASPARRI

etc. etc. etc.

Saint Siége

21620

6

FIGURE A1.1 Sabri's letter to the Vatican, 1925.

Città del Vaticano, Archivio Storico della Segreteria di Stato – Sezione per i Rapporti con gli Stati, fondo Congregazione degli Affari Ecclesiastici Straordinari, Pio XI, Turchia, Pos. 43, Fascicolo 55, ff. 6^r, 6^v e 7^r.

D'aprés nos informations dignes de foi, nous croyons savoir que des nouvelles aventures attendent ces pays, surtout au Proche Orient, non seulement au préjudice de l'élément musulman, mais aussi à celles de l'élément chrétien.

Le fanatisme du bas peuple des deux partis, peut-être exploité au premier signal, que ceux-ci recevront des centres intéressés de pêcher dans l'eau trouble.

Le Khalifat, puissance modératrice du monde musulman n'existe plus pour empêcher les nouveaux malheurs et barrer chemin à ces nouvelles idées destructrices de l'ordre sociale.

De l'autre côté la grande rivalité d'intêrets qui sévit entre les grandes puissances mandataires our possesseurs ou voisines des contrées ou pays musulmans, les rend aveugles et il n'y a aucune espoir d'aide, de collaboration, de la part de celles-ci, pour apaiser les nouvelles passions, les nouvelles apirations venant de l'Est vers l'Occident.

Or pour empêcher tous ces malheurs, dans la mesure du possible, un comité de patriotes Turcs et des emminents personnalités du monde musulman s'est constitué pour restaurer le Khalifat en Turquie et de donner à l'Islam son chef spirituel et temporel, et par ce moyen, tâcher de refouler les ondes dangeureuses de l'Asie vers leurs sources.

Ce comité commencera à prêcher par l'entremise de ses émissaires, ses publications, sa propagande aux musulmans du monde ses vrais intérêts, l'obeissance et la loyanté envers les gouvernements dont ils dépendent, la fraternité envers les chrétiens en géléral, et pourvoira en même temps aux moyent de restaurer le Khalifat.

FIGURE A1.1 (*cont.*)

Le Coran ne dit-il pas que le peuple du Christ est le plus proche de l'Islam, puisque ce peuple a ses évêques, ses religieux qui lui prêchent le bon chemin et dans le même livre le Bon Dieu nous reppelle qu'il a donné aux coeurs des chrétiens la clémence et la bonté.

Nous croyons que la Saint Siége a tout interêt de collaborer avec nous, dans la voie, qu'elle lui est convenable, soit pour empêcher des nouveaux mâlheurs dans les pays melangés des adeptes des deux religions, soit pour protéger ses églises et ses institutions contre de nouveaux changements et ainsi préserver sa propre position contre les mêmes courants qui pourront, le cas échéant, venir un jour lui donner un choc irréparable.

D'ailleurs aujourd'hui dans le monde il n'y a plus la lutte entre musulmans et chrétiens mais il y a plutôt la lutte entre les religions et l'irreligion.

Pour les raisons et les buts ci-haut exposés et encouragé par la promesse qu'une proposition écrite dans ce sens sera étudiée avec bienveillance, j'ose de demander à Votre Emminence, jusqu'à quel point je pourrai compter sur l'aide morale et matérielle de Saint Siége dans la voie apaisante dont ce comité, que j'ai l'honneur de présider afait le noble but.

Veuillez agréer, Emminance, l'assurance, de ma haute considération.

Signée:Moustafa Sabri
ancien Cheik-Ul-Islam de Turquie.

7

FIGURE A1.1 (*cont.*)

Appendix 2: Chronological List of Kevseri's Articles (by Original Publication Date)

Cited in this study:

'Ḥawla Kalima Tuʿza ilā al-Suyūṭī Ghalaṭan [On Words Falsely Attributed to al-Suyūṭī],' *al-Islām*, 5/32, 9 October 1936 (*Maqālāt*, 307–11).

'Al-Hijra al-Nabawiyya [The Prophet's Hijra],' *al-Islām*, 6/1, 19 March 1937 (*Maqālāt*, 383–6).

'Al-Lāmadhhabiyya Qanṭarat al-Lādīniyya [Anti-Madhhabism, the Bridge to Secularism],' *al-Islām*, 6/40, 24 December 1937 (*Maqālāt*, 129–36).

'Taḥdhīr al-Umma min Duʿāt al-Wathaniyya [Warning the Nation about Advocates of Paganism],' *al-Islām*, 8/19, 3 June 1939 (*Maqālāt*, 277–82).

'Al-Azhar Qubayla ʿĪdihi al-Alfī [al-Azhar on the Eve of its 1000th anniversary],' *al-Islām*, 10/30, 22 August 1941 (*Maqālāt*, 478–9).

'*Al-Risāla* wa-l-Azhar [*al-Risāla* and al-Azhar],' *al-Islām*, 11/18, 22 May 1942 (*Maqālāt*, 317–21).

'Manshaʾ Ilzām Ahl al-Dhimma bi-Shuʿār Khāṣṣ wa-Ḥukm Talabbus al-Muslim bihi ʿInd al-Fuqahāʾ [Origin of Requiring Protected Subjects to Self-Identify Through Attire and the Jurists' Ruling on Muslims Wearing the Same],' *al-Islām*, 11/23, 26 June 1942 (*Maqālāt*, 219–27).

'Muḥādatha Qadīma Ḥawla al-Waqf al-Ahlī [An Old Conversation about Family Waqfs],' *al-Islām*, 11/29, 7 August 1942 (*Maqālāt*, 190–6).

'Maẓhar Jadīd fī al-Azhar al-Ḥadīth - 2: al-ʿAqīda al-Mutawāritha wa-l-Fiqh al-Mutawārith [A New Look for the Modern al-Ahzar – 2: Inherited Belief and Inherited Law],' *al-Islām*, 11/41, 6 November 1942 (*Maqālāt*, 247–9).

'Maẓhar Jadīd fī al-Azhar al-Ḥadīth - 6: Naẓar al-Marʾ ilā Sharʿ Allāh Miʿyāru Dīnihi [A New Look for the Modern al-Azhar – 6: One's View of God's Law is the Measure of One's Religion],' *al-Islām*, 11/46, 12 November 1942 (*Maqālāt*, 233–8).

'Iḥyāʾ ʿUlūm al-Sunna fī al-Azhar [Reviving Sunni Sciences in al-Azhar],' *al-Sharq al-ʿArabī*, 1/43, 16 May 1947 (*Maqālāt*, 481–90).

'Kashf al-Ruʾūs wa-Libs al-Naʿāl fī al-Ṣalāh [Uncovering the Head and Wearing Sandals During Prayer],' *al-Sharq al-ʿArabī*, 1/45, 30 May 1947 (*Maqālāt*, 165–80).

Other:

'Al-Ishfāq ʿalā Aḥkām al-Ṭalāq [Concern about the Divorce Laws],' *al-Islām*, 5/32, 30 October 1936 (not in *Maqālāt*).

'Sharʿ Allāh fī Naẓar al-Muslimīn [God's Law in the View of Muslims],' *al-Islām*, 6/25, 3 September 1937 (*Maqālāt*, 96–101).

'Mūṣānnafāt al-Imām Abi Jaʿfar al-Ṭaḥāwī [The Compilations of Imām Abū Jaʿfar al-Ṭaḥāwī],' *al-Islām*, 6/34, 5 November 1937 (*Maqālāt*, 408–13).

'Al-Dīn al-Islāmī wa-l-Taʿaṣṣub al-Madhhabī [Islam and Partisanship re the Legal Schools],' *al-Islām*, 6/40, 24 December 1937 (not in *Maqālāt*).

'Ḥawla al-Lāmadhhabiyya wa-Duʿātihā fī Miṣr [On Anti-Madhhabism and its Advocates in Egypt],' *al-Islām*, 6/42, 7 January 1938 (not in *Maqālāt*).

'Al-Hijra al-Nabawiyya, Fataḥat ʿAhd Jadīd Fayyāḍ [The Prophet's Hijra Opened a Bounteous New Era],' *al-Islām*, 7/3, 18 March 1938 (*Maqālāt*, 376–8).

'Tarjamat Kātib Chalabī, Muʾallif *Kashf al-Ẓunūn ʿan Asāmī Kutub wa-l-Funūn* [Kâtip Çelebi, Author of The Removal of Doubt over the Names of Books and the Arts],' *al-Islām*, 7/4, 25 March 1938 (*Maqālāt*, 414–18).

'Mawlid Khātim Rusul Allāh, ʿalayhi Azkā al-Ṣalawāt [The Birthday of the Seal of the Prophets, May the Purest of Prayers Be Upon Him],' *al-Islām*, 7/11, 13 May 1938 (not in *Maqālāt*).

'Fatḥ al-Mulhim fī Sharḥ *Ṣaḥīḥ Muslim* [Unlocking the Inspirational in Explication of Muslim's *Ṣaḥīḥ*],' *al-Islām*, 7/32, 7 October 1938 (not in *Maqālāt*).

'Ṭaraf Min Anbā' al-'Ilm wa-l-'Ulamā' - 1 [Some News of Islamic Knowdedge and the 'Ulama'],' *al-Islām*, 8/41, 8 December 1939 (*Maqālāt*, 440–4).

'Kulayma Ḥawla al-Maḥārīb [A Short Word on Pulpits],' *al-Islām*, 9/6, 15 March 1940 (*Maqālāt*, 142–7).

'Ḥawla Mas'alat al-Miḥrāb: Intihāk Ḥurmat al-Ḥaqīqa wa-l-Tārīkh Musāyaratan li-l-Hawā [On the Issue of Pulpits: Violating the Sanctity of Facts and History on the Basis of Personal Opinion],' *al-Islām*, 9/7, 22 March 1940 (*Maqālāt*, 148–52).

'Al-Dīn wa-l-Fiqh [Religion and Law],' *al-Islām*, 10/4, 21 February 1941 (*Maqālāt*, 92–5).

'Īdāḥ Lā Budd minhu bi-Munāsabat Maqāl li-Azharī [A Necessary Clarification on the Occasion of an Azharī's Article],' *al-Islām*, 10/33, 12 September 1941 (*Maqālāt*, 479–80).

'A-Naskh al-Aḥkām min Ḥaqq al-Imām?!! Kamā Yadda'īhi "'Ālim Fāḍil' fī *al-Risāla* [Does an Imam Have the Right to Abrogate Laws, as a Respected Scholar Claims in *al-Risāla*?],' *al-Islām*, 11/36, 25 September 1942 (*Maqālāt*, 102–8).

'Maẓhar Jadīd fī al-Azhar al-Ḥadīth–7: Athar al-'Urf wa-l-Maṣlaḥa fī al-Aḥkām [A New Look for the Modern al-Azhar – 7: Signs of Custom and Public Interest in Laws],' *al-Islām*, 11/47, 18 December 1942 (*Maqālāt*, 239–42).

'Kalima Ḥawla al-Aḥādīth al-Ḍa'īfa [A Word on Weak Hadiths],' *al-Islām*, 15/48, 15 November 1946 (not in *Maqālāt*).

'Al-Isrā' wa-l-Mi'rāj [The Night Journey and Ascension],' *al-Islām*, 16/29, 13 June 1947 (*Maqālāt*, 370–3).

'Min 'Ibar al-Tārīkh [From the Lessons of History],' *al-Sharq al-'Arabī*, 2/5, 11 July 1947 (not in *Maqālāt*).

'Ḥawla Ḥadīth al-Tajdīd [On the Discussion About Renewal],' *al-Islām*, 16/41, 12 September 1947 (*Maqālāt*, 117–19).

'Ḥajj Bayt Allāh al-Ḥirām [Pilgrimage to Mecca],' *al-Islām*, 16/44, 3 October 1947 (*Maqālāt*, 186–9).

'Usṭurat Qatl Murtadda Sharra Qatla fī 'Ahd al-Ṣiddīq [The Story of an Apostate Woman's Most Horrible Murder in the Era of Abu Bakr],' *al-Islām*, 18/36, 8 July 1949 (*Maqālāt*, 65–70).

Appendix 3: Ottoman Letter Written by Kevseri, 1952, to His Brother in Düzce

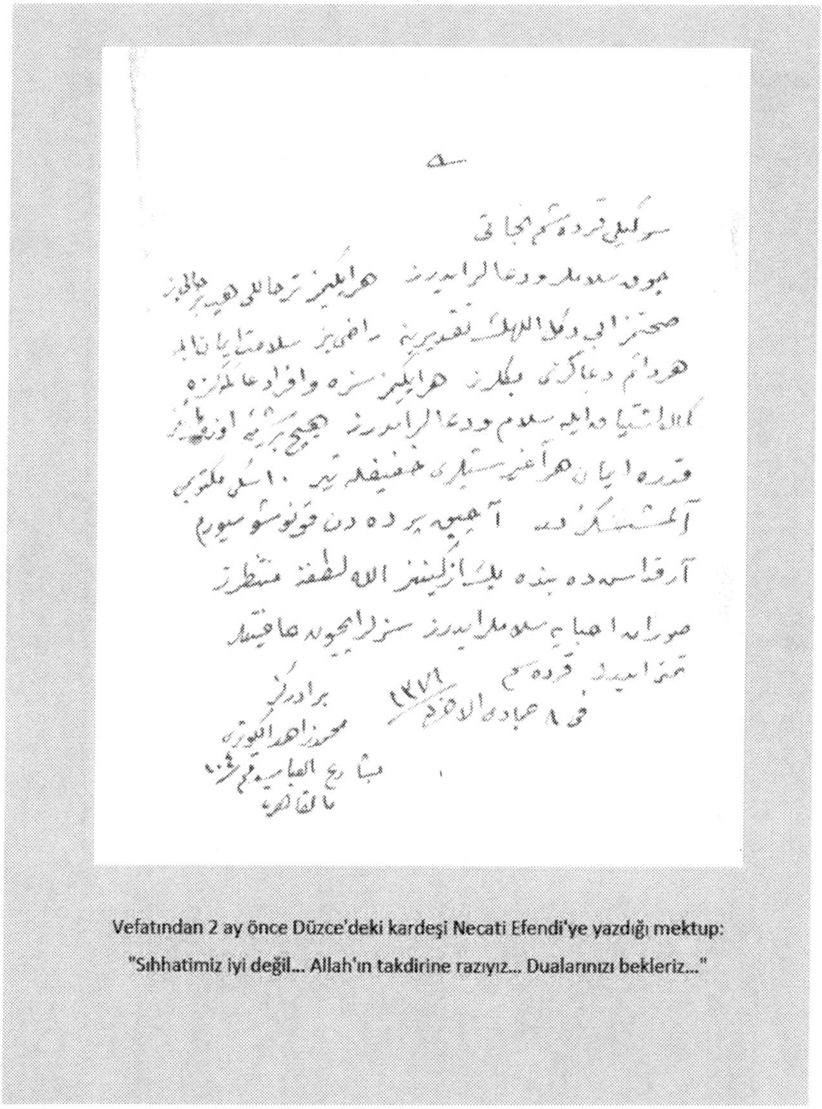

FIGURE A3.1 Ottoman letter written by Kevseri, 1952, to his brother in Düzce. Courtesy of Rıhle Kitap

Appendix 4: Ottoman Letter Written by Akif, 1932, Discussing Plans to Print *Gölgeler*

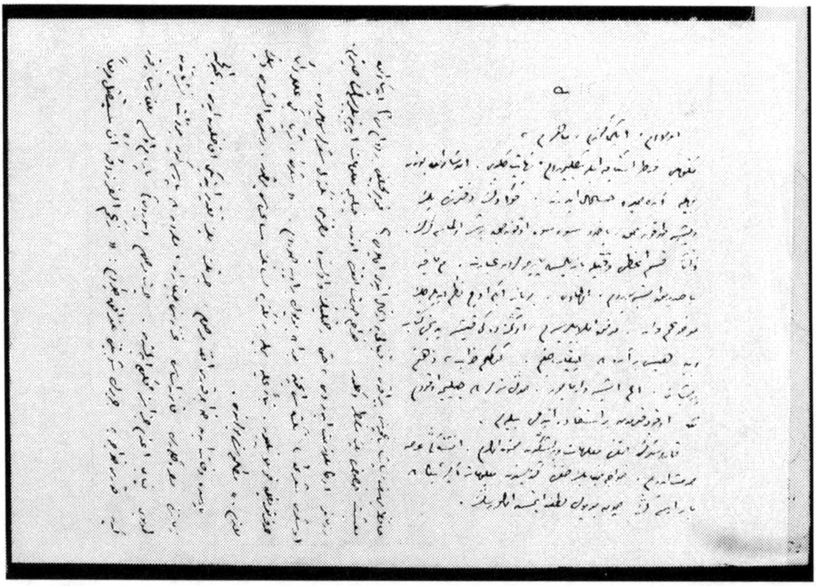

FIGURE A4.1 Ottoman letter written by Akif, 1932, discussing plans to print *Gölgeler*.
Courtesy of Türkiye Yazma Eserler Kurumu Başkanlığı, Süleymaniye Library, microfilm collection, no. 2568, pages 35–6

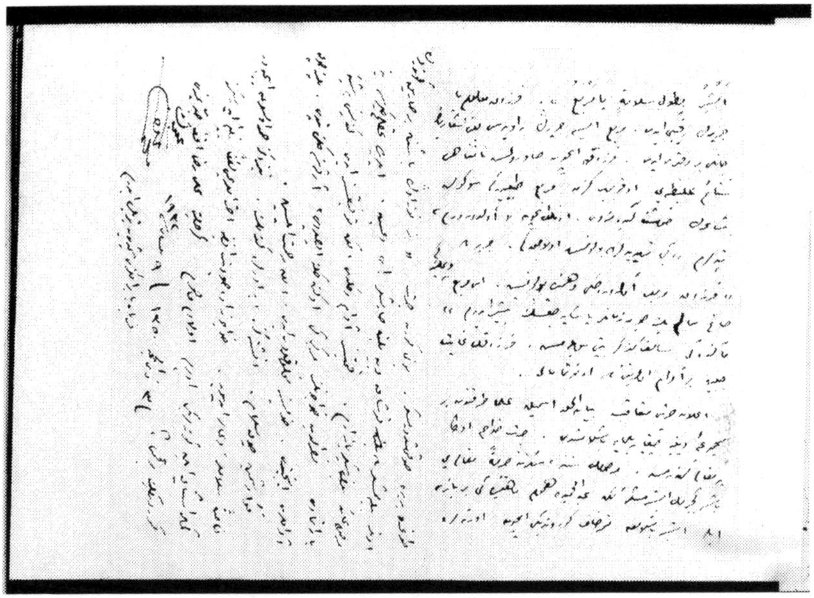

FIGURE A4.1 (*cont.*)

Bibliography

PRIMARY SOURCES

Mehmed Akif

Abdulkadiroğlu, Abdulkerim and Nuran Abdulkadiroğlu, eds. *Mehmed Âkif Ersoy'un Makaleleri: Sırat-ı Müstakim ve Sebilü'r-Reşad Mecmuaları'nda Çıkan*. Ankara: Kültür Bakanlığı, 1990.

Mehmed Akif'in Kur'an-ı Kerim'i Tefsiri Mev'iza ve Hutbeleri. Ankara: Diyanet, 1992.

Akif, Mehmed. *Hanotonun Hücumuna Karşı Şeyh Muhammed Abdunun İslamı Müdafaası*. Istanbul: Tevsi-i Tıbaat Matbaası, 1913.

Safahat. Ed. M. Ertuğrul Düzdağ. Istanbul: Çağrı, 2015.

Ersoy, Mehmet Akif. *Safahat*. Ed. Yakup Çelik. Istanbul: Akçağ, 2013.

Günaydın, Yusuf Turan. *Kavâid-i Edebiyye*. Istanbul: Büyüyenay Yayınları, 2016.

Mehmet Akif Ersoy: Mektuplar. Istanbul: Atlas, 2016.

Özalp, Ömer Hakan. *Firaklı Nâmeler Âkif'in Gurbet Mektupları*. Istanbul: Timaş Yayınları, 2011.

Sa'di (Akif). 'Mebahis-i İlm-i Servet: Say ve Amel.' *Maarif*, 7/187 (27 June 1895), 261–3.

Şengüler, İsmail Hakkı. *Mehmed Akif Kulliyatı*, 10 vols. Istanbul: Hikmet Neşriyat, 1992.

Sırat-ı Müstakim/Sebilürreşad journal (*SM*, *SR*; 1908–25):

Sırâtımüstakīm - Sebîlürreşâd Külliyâtı Neşri, ed. M. Ertuğrul Düzdağ (in Latin script). Istanbul: Bağcılar Belediye Başkanlığı, 2012.

Arabic script text accessible online at İslâm Araştırmaları Merkezi (İSAM); http://ktp.isam.org.tr/?url=makaleosm/findrecords.php.

Süleymaniye Library, Archive no. 2568, 'Mektuplar: Mehmet Akif Ersoy' (Letters to Mahir Iz).

Mustafa Sabri

Beyanülhak newspaper (BH; 1908–12). Arabic script text accessible online at İslâm Araştırmaları Merkezi (İSAM); http://ktp.isam.org.tr/?url=makaleosm/findrecords.php.

Sabri, Mustafa. *Dinî Müceddidler, Yahud 'Türkiye İçin Necat ve İğtila Yolları'nda bir Rehber*. Istanbul: Âsitâne Kitabevi, nda [1922].

'Gaybe İnananları inanmıyanlardan ayıran kesin söz.' *Hilal*, 1/3 (January 1959), 21; 1/4 (February 1959), 19.

Hilafetin İlgasının Arka Planı. Trans. Oktay Yılmaz. Istanbul: Insan, 1998.

Letter to Cardinal Pietro Gasparri, 14 May 1925. 'Espulsione del Califfo,' Turchia, No. 43 P.O., in Archivio Storico, Segretaria di Stato, Vatican City.

Mas'alat Tarjamat al-Qur'ān. Cairo: al-Maktaba al-Salafiyya, 1932.

Mawqif al-Bashar Taḥta Sulṭān al-Qadar. Cairo: al-Maktaba al-Salafiyya, 1933.

Mawqif al-'Aql wa-l-'Ilm wa-l-'Ālam min Rabb al-'Ālamīn wa-Rusulihi, 4 vols. Beirut: Dār Iḥyā' al-Kutub al-'Arabiyya, 1981 [1949].

Meseleler Hakkında Cevaplar. Istanbul: Sebil, 1995.

Al-Nakīr 'alā Munkirī al-Ni'ma min al-Dīn wa-l-Khilāfa wa-l-Umma. Beirut: Dār al-Qādirī, 1924.

Yarın newspaper (1927–30). IRCICA Kütüphanesi, Istanbul.

Yeni İslam Müctehidlerinin Kıymet-i İlmiyesi. Istanbul: Âsitâne Kitabevi, nda [1916].

Zahid Kevseri

al-Kawtharī, Zāhid. *al-Asmā' wa-l-Ṣifāt li-l-Imām al-Bayhaqī*. Ed. al-Kawtharī. Cairo: al-Maktaba al-Azhariyya li-l-Turāth, 2000 [1939].

Bayān Zaghl al-'Ilm wa-l-Ṭalab. Cairo: al-Azhariyya li-l-Turāth, 2010 [Damascus, 1928]

Fiqh Ahl al-'Irāq wa-Ḥadīthuhum. Ed. 'Abd al-Fattāḥ Abū Ghudda. Cairo: al-Maktaba al-Azhariyya li-l-Turāth, 2002 [1970].

Al-Ḥāwī fī Sīrat al-Imām Abī Ja'far al-Ṭaḥāwī. Cairo: al-Azhariyya li-l-Turāth, 1999 [1949].

Al-Ikhtilāf fi-l-Lafẓ wa-l-Radd 'alā al-Jahmiyya wa-l-Mushabbiha li-Ibn Quṭayba. Ed. al-Kawtharī. Cairo: al-Maktaba al-Azhariyya, 2001 [1930].

Irghām al-Murīd. Cairo: al-Azhariyya, 2000 [1910].

Al-Ishfāq 'alā Aḥkām al-Ṭalāq. Cairo: al-Azhariyya li-l-Turāth, 1994 [1936].

Al-Istibṣār fī al-Taḥadduth 'an al-Jabr wa-l-Ikhtiyār. Cairo: al-Azhariyya, 2005 [1951].

Maqālāt al-Kawtharī. Ed. Yūsuf Banūrī. Cairo: Al-Tawfikia Bookshop, 2000 [1953].

Muqaddimāt al-Imām al-Kawtharī. Damascus: Dār al-Thurayyā, 1997.

Al-Muqaddimāt al-Khams wa-l-'Ishrūn. Cairo: al-Sa'āda, 1949.

Naẓra 'Ābira fī Mazā'im man Yunkir Nuzūl 'Īsā 'alayhi al-Salām Qabla al-Ākhira. Cairo: Dār al-Khalīl, 1987.

Al-Nukat al-Ṭarīfa fī al-Taḥadduth 'an Rudūd Ibn Abī al-Shayba 'alā Abi Ḥanīfa. Cairo: al-Maktaba al-Azhariyya li-l-Turāth, 2000 [1946].

Ṣafʿāt al-Burhān ʿalā Ṣafaḥāt al-ʿUdwān. Cairo: al-Azhariyya li-l-Turāth, 2005 [Damascus, 1929].
Al-Sayf al-Ṣaqīl fī al-Radd ʿalā Ibn Zufayl. Cairo: al-Maktaba al-Azhariyya li-l-Turāth, 2003 [1937].
Al-Taḥrīr al-Wajīz fīmā Yabtaghīh al-Mustajīz. Aleppo: al-Matbūʿāt al-Islāmiyya, 1992 [1941].
'Taʿlīqunā ʿalā Ibn Fahd fī Dhuyūl Tadhkirat al-Ḥuffāẓ'. In *Ṣafʿāt al-Burhān ʿalā Ṣafaḥāt al- ʿUdwān*, 52–6. Cairo: al-Azhariyya li-l-Turāth, 2005.
Taʾnīb al-Khaṭīb ʿalā Mā Sāqahu fī Tarjamat Abī Ḥanīfa min al-Akādhīb. Publisher unknown, 1990 [1941].
al-Tarḥīb bi-Naqd al-Khaṭīb. In *Taʾnīb al-Khaṭīb*, al-Kawtharī, 370–418.
Al-Sarḥān, Saʿūd, ed. *Rasāʾil al-Imām Muḥammad Zāhid al-Kawtharī ilā al-ʿAllāma Muḥammad Yūsuf al-Banūrī*. Amman: Dār al-Fatḥ, 2013.

Other

ʿAbduh, Muḥammad. *Al-Aʿmāl al-Kāmila*, 5 vols. Ed. Muḥammad ʿImāra. Cairo: Dār al-Shurūq, 1993.
Al-Islām bayn al-ʿIlm wa-l-Madaniyya. Cairo: Dār al-Hilāl, 1960.
Al-Islām wa-l-Naṣrāniyya fī al-ʿIlm wa-l-Madaniyya. Beirut: Dār al-Ḥadātha, 1988 [1905].
'Al-Ittiḥād fī al-Naṣrāniyya wa-l-Islām.' *Al-Manār*, 5/15 (4 September 1902): 405.
Risālat al-Tawḥīd. 1st edn. Ed. Maḥmūd Abū Rayya. Cairo: Dār al-Maʿārif, 2003 [1897].
Risālat al-Tawḥīd. Ed. Rashīd Riḍā. Cairo: al-Manār, 1942.
Risālat al-Tawḥīd. Ed. Muḥammad ʿImāra. Cairo: Dār al-Shurūq, 1994.
Risālat al-Wāridāt. Ed. Rashīd Riḍā. Cairo: al-Manār, 1925
'Taassub.' *Sırat-ı Müstakim*, 10 Eylül 1325, 3/55 (23 September 1909): 33–7.
ʿAbduh, Muḥammad and Gabriel Hanotaux. *Al-Islām wa-l-Radd ʿalā Muntaqidīhi*. Cairo: Maṭbaʿat al-Tawfīq al-Adabiyya, 1924.
Abū Zayd, Bakr. *Barāʾat Ahl al-Sunna min al-Waqīʿa fī ʿUlamāʾ al-Islām*. Riyadh: Ministry of Information, 1987.
Al-Afghānī, Jamāl al-Dīn. *Al-Radd ʿalā al-Dahriyyīn*. Translated by Muḥammad ʿAbduh. Cairo: Maṭbaʿat al-Jamāliyya, 1915.
Al-Afghānī, Jamāl al-Dīn and Muḥammad ʿAbduh. *Al-Taʿlīqāt ʿalā Sharḥ al-ʿAqāʾid al-ʿAḍudiyya*. Cairo: Maktabat al-Shurūq al-Dawliyya, 2002.
Al-ʿUrwa al-Wuthqā. Cairo: Hindāwī, 2014.
Al-Albānī, Nāṣir al-Dīn. *Jilbāb al-Marʾa al-Muslima fī al-Kitāb wa-l-Sunna*. Damascus: Dār al-Salām, 1991.
Maqālāt al-Albānī: Tunshar Majmūʿatan li-Awwal Marra. Ed. Nūr al-Dīn Ṭālib. Riyadh: Dār Aṭlas, 2000.
Mukhtaṣar al-ʿUluww li-l-ʿAliyy al-Ghaffār, Taʾlīf al-Ḥāfiẓ Shams al-Dīn al-Dhahabī. Beirut: al-Maktab al-Islāmī, 1981.
'Preface to al-Tankīl.' In *al-Kawtharī wa-Taʿaddīhi ʿalā al-Turāth wa-Bayān Ḥālihi fī Muʾallafātihi wa-Muʿallaqātihi*, by Muḥammad Bahjat al-Bayṭār et al., 142–4. Cairo: Dār al-Ḥaramayn, 1999.

'Ṣawt al-'Arab Tas'al wa-l-Muḥaddith Nāṣir al-Dīn al-Albānī Yujīb.' *Ṣawt al-'Arab*, 28 April 1960; www.ahlalhdeeth.com/vb/showthread.php?t=256132.
Ṣifāt Ṣalāt al-Nabī min al-Takbīr ilā al-Taslīm Ka-annaka Tarāhu. Riyadh: Maktabat al-Ma'ārif li-l-Nashr wa-l-Tawzī', 1996 [1961].
'Silsilat al-Aḥādīth al-Ḍa'īfa: 3.' *Al-Tamaddun al-Islāmī*, 21 (1954): 657–64.
Wujūb al-Akhdh bi-Ḥadīth al-Āḥād fī al-'Aqīda wa-l-Radd 'alā Shibh al-Mukhālifīn. Damascus: al-Maktab al-Islāmī, 1974.
Al-'Aqqad, 'Abbas. *'Abqariyyat Muḥammad*. Beirut: al-Maktaba al-'Aṣriyya, 1942.
Akçura, Yūsuf. *Üç Tarz-ı Siyaset*. Ankara: Türk Tarih Kurumu Basımevi, 1976.
Amin, Aḥmad. 'Muḥammad ibn 'Abd al-Wahhāb – 1.' *Al-Thaqāfa*, 30 November 1943, no. 257.
'Muḥammad ibn 'Abd al-Wahhāb – 2.' *Al-Thaqāfa*, 7 December 1943, no. 258.
Anṭūn, Faraḥ. *Ibn Rushd wa-Falsafatuhu*. Alexandria: al-Jāmi'a, 1903.
Asım, Mustafa. 'Dindarlık ve Dinsizlik.' *Beyanülhak*, 15 Şubat 1325 (28 February 1909), 2/49: 1038–40.
Aytaç, Kemal. *Gazi M. Kemal Atatürk, Eğitim Politikası Üzerine Konuşmalar*. Ankara: Türk İnkilap Tarihi Enstitüsü, 1984.
Al-Bannā, Ḥasan. *Majmū'at Rasā'il al-Imām al-Shahīd Ḥasan al-Bannā*. Beirut: Dār al-Andalus, 1965.
Mudhakkirāt al-Da'wā wa-l-Dā'iya. Kuwait: Maktabat Āfāq, 2012 [1950].
Al-Bayṭār, Muḥammad Bahjat et al. *Al-Kawtharī wa-Ta'addīhi 'alā al-Turāth wa-Bayān Ḥālihi fī Mu'allafātihi wa-Mu'allaqātihi*. Cairo: Dār al-Ḥaramayn, 1999 [1940].
Bigiev, Musa Jarullah. *Rahmet-i İlahiye Bürhanları. In İlâhî Adalet*, ed. Ömer Özalp, 253–342. Istanbul: Pınar Yayınları, 1996.
Al-Da'wā, journal of Muslim Brotherhood; 1976–81.
Faraj, 'Abd al-Salām. *Jihād, al-Farīḍa al-Ghā'iba*. Amman: npa, 1982.
Gökalp, Ziya. 'İslamiyet ve Asri Medeniyet.' In *İslam Mecmuası*, 26 Kanunusani 1332 (8 February 1917), 5/51 and 1 Mart 1333 (1 March 1917), 5/52.
Makaleler II. Ankara: Kültür Bakanlığı, 1981.
Makaleler VII. Ankara: Kültür Bakanlığı, 1982.
Türkçülüğün Esasları. Istanbul: Kültür Bakanlığı, 1976 [1923].
Türkleşmek, İslamlaşmak, Muasırlaşmak. Istanbul: Yeni Mecmua, 1918.
Halim, Said. *İslamlaşmak*. Trans. Mehmed Akif. Istanbul: Dar ül-Hilafe, 1918.
Les institutions politiques dans la société musulmane. Rome: Editrice Italia, 1921.
'The Reform of Muslim Society.' *Islamic Culture: The Hyderabad Quarterly Review*, 1 (1927): 111–35.
Hanotaux, Gabriel. *L'Europe et l'Islam*. Cairo: J. Politis, 1905.
Haykal, Muḥammad Ḥusayn. *Ḥayāt Muḥammad*. Cairo: Dār al-Ma'ārif, 2001 [1935].
Hilal journal (Turkey), 1958 to 1966. Accessible online at: http://katalog.idp.org.tr/dergiler/77/hilal.
Ibn Taymiyya. *Al-Fatāwā al-Kubrā*, vol. 5. Cairo: Dār al-Kutub al-Ḥadītha, 1966.
Kitāb al-Īmān. Beirut: al-Maktab al-Islāmī, 1996.
Majmū' Fatāwā Ibn Taymiyya, vol. 33. Medina: Majma' al-Malik Fahd, 1995.

Majmū'at al-Rasā'il wa-l-Masā'il. Ed. Rashīd Riḍā. Beirut: Dār Iḥyā' al-Turāth al-'Arabī, 1972.

Iqbāl, Muḥammad. *Javid-Nama*. Trans. A. J. Arberry. Ajman, UAE: Islamic Books, 2000.

Payām-i Mashriq: Dar Javāb-i Dīvān-i Shā'ir-i Almānavī Go'eṭe. 12th ed. Lahore: Jāvīd Iqbāl, 1969.

Payām-i Mashriq: Risālat al-Mashriq. Trans. 'Abd al-Wahhāb 'Azzām. Lahore: Iqbāl Academy Pakistan, 1981.

The Moonbeams Over the East: A Translation of Poems from Allama Iqbal's Payām-i-Mashriq. Trans. Syed Abbas Ali Jaffery. Karachi: Royal Book Co., 1996.

The Secrets of the Self (Asrár-i Khudí): A Philosophical Poem. Trans. Reynold Nicholson. Lahore: Sh. Muhammed Ashraf, 1920.

The Reconstruction of Religious Thought in Islam. London: Oxford University Press, 1934.

İzmirli, İsmail Hakkı. *El-Cevabü's-Sedid fî Beyan-ı Dinü'l-Tevhid*. Ankara: Tedkikat ve Telifat-ı İslamiye Heyeti, 1923.

Yeni İlmi Kelam. Ankara: Ankara Okulu, 2013.

Yeni İlm-i Kelam. Istanbul: Evkaf-i İslamiye Matbaası, 1920.

Jāwīsh, 'Abd al-'Azīz. *Ajwibatī fī al-Islām 'an As'ilat al-Kanīsa al-Anglīkāniyya*. Istanbul: Evkaf-ı İslamiye Matbaası, 1923.

Anglikan Kilisesine Cevap. Trans. Mehmed Akif. Istanbul: Evkaf-i İslamiye Matbaası, 1339 [1923].

Āthār al-Khamr fī Naẓar Arqā al-Umam al-Masīḥiyya bi-Amīrqa wa-Ghayrihā. Istanbul: Evkaf-i İslamiye Matbaası, 1923.

Al-Islām Dīn al-Fiṭra wa-l-Ḥurriyya. Cairo: Dār al-Hilāl, 1905.

Kutub, Seyyid. 'Habil ve Kabil.' *Hilal*, 4/38 (April 1963): 20–1.

İslamda Sosyal Adalet. Trans. Yaşar Tunagür and Adnan Mansur. Istanbul: Cağaloğlu Yayınevi, 1962.

'İslam Kumandanlığını Yapacaktır.' *Hilal*, 5/53 (July 1965), 5.

'Kur'an Yolunun Esası.' *Hilal*, 5/54 (August 1965), 27–8.

Al-Marṣafī, Shaykh Ḥusayn. *Risālat al-Kalim al-Thamān*. Beirut: Dār al-Ṭalī'a, 1982.

Mawdūdī, Abū al-A'lā. *Islām aur Jāhiliyyat*. Pathankot: Maktaba-i Jamā'at-i Islāmī, 1941.

Islām kā Naẓariyya-i Siyāsī. Pathankot: Maktaba-i Jamā'at-i Islāmī, 1939.

Al-Muṣṭalaḥāt al-Arba'a fī al-Qur'ān: al-Ilāh, al-Rabb, al-'Ibāda, al-Dīn. Trans. Muḥammad Kāẓim Sabbāq. Kuwait: Dār al-Qalam, 1971 [1955].

Naẓariyyat al-Islām al-Siyāsiyya. Trans. Muḥammad 'Āṣim al-Ḥaddād. Damascus: Dār al-Fikr, 1967.

The Islamic Law and Constitution. Trans. Khurshīd Aḥmad. Karachi: Jamaat-e-Islami Publications, 1955.

Mithat, Ahmet. *Sevda-yı Sa'y ü Amel*. Istanbul: Kitap Dünyası, 2016.

Mu'allimī, 'Abd al-Raḥmān ibn Yaḥyā. *Al-Tankīl bi-mā fī Ta'nīb al-Kawtharī min Abāṭīl*. Ed. Nāṣir al-Dīn al-Albānī, Zuhayr Shāwīsh, 'Abd al-Razzāq Ḥamza. Beirut: al-Maktab al-Islāmī, 1986 [1965].

Mubārak, Zakī. 'Asmaʿūnī Sīḥat al-Ḥaqq.' *Al-Risāla*, 27 February 1939, 7/295: 387–9.
Nahid, Haşim. *Türkiye İçin: Necat ve İğtila Yolları*. Istanbul: Ikbal Kitaphanesi, 1912.
Naim, Ahmed. *İslam'da Dava-ı Kavmiyet*. Darülhilaafe: Sebilürreşad Kütüphanesi, 1914.
Nursi, Said. *Emirdağ Lahikası*. Istanbul: Yeni Asya, 2018.
Qaṭra, Ḥabāb, Ḥabba, Zahra, Dhurra, Shamma. Istanbul: Necmeddin İstikbal Matbaası, 1923.
'Kur'an-ı Azimü'ş-Şa'nın Hakimiyet-i Mutlakası.' *Sebilürreşad*, 6 May 1920, 18/463: 242–3.
Lem'alar. Istanbul: Sözler, 2012.
Al-Mathnawī al-ʿArabī al-Nūrī (Kulliyyāt Rasā'il al-Nūr – 6). Ed. Iḥsān Qāsim al-Ṣāliḥī. Istanbul: Sözler, 1994.
al-Mathnawi al-Nuri: Seedbed of the Light. Trans. Huseyin Akarsu. Somerset, NJ: Light, 2007.
Mektubat. Istanbul: Yeni Asya, 1997 [1958].
Mesnevi-i Nuriye. Trans. Abdülmecid Nursî. Istanbul: Şahdamar Yayınları, 2014 [1957].
Rumuz. Istanbul: Evkaf-ı İslamiye Matbaası, 1920.
Sözler. Ankara: Diyanet Vakfı, 2016 [1957].
Öztürk, Kazım. *Türk Parlamento Tarihi, TBMM – I. Dönem, 1919–1923*, vol. 2 (Ankara: TBMM Vakfı, 1994).
Türk Parlamento Tarihi, TBMM – II. Dönem, 1923–1927, vol. 1 (Ankara: TBMM Vakfı, 1994).
Al-Qaṣīmī, ʿAbd Allāh. *Hādhihi Hiya al-Aghlāl*. Cologne: Al-Kamel Verlag, 2000 [1946].
Quṭb, Sayyid. *Al-ʿAdāla al-Ijtimāʿiyya fī al-Islām*. Cairo: Dār Iḥyāʾ al-Kutub al-ʿArabiyya, 1954.
Fī Ẓilāl al-Qurʾān, 6 vols. Cairo: Dār al-Shurūq, 1992 [1952–9].
Hādhā al-Dīn. Cairo: Dār al-Shurūq, 2001 [1962].
Al-Islām wa-Mushkilat al-Ḥaḍāra. Cairo: Dār al-Shurūq, 1992 [1962].
Khaṣāʾiṣ al-Taṣawwur al-Islāmī wa-Muqawwimātuhu. Cairo: Dār al-Shurūq, 2002 [1962].
Limādhā Aʿdamūnī? London: Saudi Research and Publishing Company, 1980 [1966].
Maʿālim fī al-Ṭarīq. Cairo: Dār al-Shurūq, 1979 [1964].
Maʿrakat al-Islām wa-l-Raʾsmāliyya. Cairo: Dār al-Shurūq, 1993 [1951].
Maʿrakatunā maʿa al-Yahūd. Cairo: Dār al-Shurūq, 1993.
Al-Mustaqbal li-Hādhā al-Dīn. Cairo: Dār al-Shurūq, 1993 [1965].
Review of ʿAbd Allāh al-Qaṣīmī's Hādhihi Hiya al-Aghlāl. In *al-Shawāhid wa-l-Nuṣūṣ min Kitāb al-Aghlāl*, ed. Muḥammad ʿAbd al-Razzāq Ḥamza, mm-ss. Riyadh: Maṭbaʿat al-Imām, 1948.
Şevketi, Eşref Efendizade. *Say ve Sermaye Mücadelatının Dinen Suret-i Halli*. Istanbul: Matbaa-ı Osmaniye, 1923.
The Islamic Review journal. Woking Muslim Mission and Literary Trust, volumes 6–12 (1918–24).

Türkiye Büyük Millet Meclisi Zabıt Ceridesi, devre 1 (1920–3), devre 2 (1924–7). Online access at: www.tbmm.gov.tr/siteharita.htm.
Wajdī, Muḥammad Farīd. 'Al-Dīn fī Muʿtarak al-Shukūk.' *al-Risāla*, 15 January 1945, 13/602: 57–9.
'Mā Hiya al-Nubuwwa wa-Mā Hiya al-Risāla wa-l-Adilla al-ʿIlmiyya fī Imkān al-Waḥy.' *Majallat al-Azhar*, 10/2 (1939): 90–8.
'Mā Rabaḥahu al-Dīn min al-ʿIlm fī al-Zamān al-Ākhar.' *al-Risāla*, 6 January 1947, 15/705: 12–13.
Al-Marʾa al-Muslima. Cairo: al-Taraqqī, 1901.
'Muḥammad Ṣallā Allāh ʿalayhi wa-Sallam fī Taqdīr Quḍāt al-Raʾy fī Urubbā.' *Majallat al-Azhar*, 8/5 (1937): 358–61.
Müslüman Kadını. Trans. Mehmed Akif. Istanbul: Sırat-ı Müstakim, 1325 [1909].
'Al-Sīra al-Muḥammadiyya Taḥta Ḍawʾ al-ʿIlm wa-l-Falsafa.' *Majallat al-Azhar*, 11/7 (1940): 385–90.
'Al-Sīra al-Muḥammadiyya Taḥta Ḍawʾ al-ʿIlm wa-l-Falsafa: Muqaddima.' *Majallat al-Azhar*, 10/1 (1939): 12–17.
Al-Ẓawāhirī, Ayman. *Fursān fī Rāyat al-Nabī*. Amman: Minbar al-Tawḥīd wa-l-Jihād, 2001.

SECONDARY LITERATURE

Biographical Sources on Akif, Sabri, and Kevseri

Abū Zahra, Muḥammad. 'Al-Imām al-Kawtharī.' In *Maqālāt al-Kawtharī*, al-Kawtharī, 13–19.
Akbulut, Ahmet. 'Şeyhulislam Mustafa Sabri ve Görüşleri (1869–1954).' *İslami Araştırmalar*, 6/1 (1992): 32–43.
Āl Rashīd, Muḥammad ibn ʿAbd Allāh. 'Al-Imām al-Kawtharī wa-Ishāmātuhu fī ʿIlm al-Riwāya wa-l-Isnād.' In *Uluslararası Düzceli M. Zâhid Kevserî Sempozyumu Bildirileri*, 85–59. Düzce/Sakarya: Sakarya Üniversitesi İlahiyat Fakültesi/Düzce Belediye Başkanlıgı, 2007.
'Introduction.' In *Rasāʾil al-Imām*, ed. Saud Al-Sarhan, 9–18.
Altıntaş, Ramazan. 'Kevseri'nin Ta'lik Yöntemine Bir Bakış: Cüveyni'nin El-Akidetü'n-Nizamiyye Adlı Eseri Örneği.' In *Uluslararası Düzceli M. Zâhid Kevserî*, 541–5.
ʿAwwāma, Muḥammad. 'Manhaj al-Imām M. Zāhid al-Kawtharī fī Naqd al-Rijāl.' In *Uluslararası Düzceli M. Zâhid Kevserî*, 271–313.
Ayas, Nevzad. 'Mehmed Akif, Zihniyeti ve Düşünce Hayatı.' In *Mehmed Âkif: Hayatı Eserleri ve Yetmiş Muharririn Yazıları*, ed. Eşref Edib, 489–541. Istanbul: Beyan, 2011.
Aydın, Ömer. 'Mehmed Zahid Kevseri ile Mustafa Sabri Efendi'nin Kader Konusundaki Tartışması.' In *Uluslararası Düzceli M. Zâhid Kevserî*, 637–47.
ʿAzzām, ʿAbd al-Wahhāb. 'Shāʿir al-Islām Muḥammad ʿĀkif.' *Al-Risāla*, 1 February 1937, 5/187: 181–2.

Al-Bakrī, Ḥamza. *Introduction in al-Kawtharī, Ḥusn al-Taqāḍī fī Sīrat al-Imām Abī Yūsuf al-Qaḍī, 2 vols.* Amman: Dār al-Fatḥ, 2017.

Al-Bayyūmī, Muḥammad Rajab. 'Muḥammad Zāhid al-Kawtharī, Rāwiyat al-ʿAṣr wa-Amīn al-Turāth al-Islāmī.' In *Muqaddimāt al-Imām al-Kawtharī*, Zāhid al-Kawtharī, 19–34.

Bein, Amit. 'ʿUlama' and Political Activism in the Late Ottoman Empire: The Political Career of Şeyhülislâm Mustafa Sabri Efendi.' In *Guardians of Faith in Modern Times: ʿulama' in the Middle East*, ed. Meir Hatina, 67–90. Series: Social, Economic and Political Studies of the Middle East and Asia, Volume: 105. Leiden/Boston: Brill, 2009.

Beşir, Muhammed Beşir. *Farklı Yönleriyle Mustafa Sabri Efendi.* Istanbul: Tahlil, 2013.

Bilmen, Ömer Nasuhi. 'Mehmed Akif: Hayatı ve Eserleri.' In *Mehmed Âkif*, ed. Edib, 811–19.

Boyacıoğlu, Ramazan. 'II. Meşrûtiyet Döneminde Beyânü'l-Hak Dergisindeki Bazı Görüş ve Düşünceler Üzerine.' *Cumhuriyet Üniversitesi İlahiyat Fakültesi Dergisi*, vol. 3, December 1999: 27–50.

Cenkçiler, Ali Yakub. *Hatıra Kitabı.* Istanbul: Darulhadis, 2005.

Coşkun, Akif. *İstanbul'dan Mısır'a Bir İslam Alimi: Zahidü'l-Kevseri.* Istanbul: Işık, 2013.

Coşkun, Muharrem. *Kod Adı: İrtica – 906, Mehmed Akif Ersoy.* Istanbul: Gaziosmanpaşa Belediyesi, 2014.

Cundioğlu, Dücane. *Bir Kur'an Şâiri: Mehmed Akif ve Kur'an Meâli.* Istanbul: Birun, 2000.

Doğrul, Ömer Rıza. 'Mehmed Akif: Şahsi ve Aile Hayatı.' In *Mehmed Âkif*, ed. Edib, 430–61.

Düzdağ, M. Ertuğrul, ed. 'Mehmed Âkif Ersoy: Hayatı ve Eserleri.' In *Safahat*, Mehmet Âkif Ersoy. Ankara: Kültür Bakanlığı, 1989.

Mehmed Âkif: Mısır Hayatı ve Kur'ân Meâli. Istanbul: Şule, 2011.

Üstad Ali Ulvi Kurucu Hatıralar, 5 vols. Istanbul: Kaynak, 2007.

Edib, Eşref, ed. *Mehmed Âkif: Hayatı Eserleri ve Yetmiş Muharririn Yazıları.* Istanbul: Beyan, 2011.

Erdeha, Kamil. *Yüzellilikler yahud Milli Mücadelenin Muhasebesi.* Istanbul: Tekin, 1998.

Erişirgil, Emin. *İslamcı bir Şairin Romanı Mehmet Âkif.* Istanbul: Atlas, 2017.

Ersoy, Emin Âkif. *Babam Mehmet Âkif: İstiklal Harbi Hatıraları.* Istanbul: Kurtuba, 2017.

Fahmī, ʿAbd al-Salām ʿAbd al-ʿAzīz. *Shāʿir al-Islām Muḥammad ʿĀkif.* Mecca: al-Ṭālib al-Jāmiʿī, 1984.

Al-Ghūj, Iyād Aḥmad. 'Al-Imām al-Kawtharī wa-Sijillātuhu al-ʿIlmiyya fī al-Ṣuḥuf wa-l-Majallāt maʿ al-Kashf ʿAmmā Lam Yujmaʿ min Maqālātihi.' In *Uluslararası Düzceli M. Zâhid Kevserî*, 63–84.

Habib, İsmail. 'Şahsiyeti, Evsaf-ı Mümeyyizesi.' In *Mehmed Âkif*, ed. Edib, 379–85.

Hamdi, Aksekili Ahmet. 'Âkif'e ait Bazı Hâtirat.' In *Mehmed Âkif*, ed. Edib, 547–52.

Ḥusayn, Muḥammad. *Al-Ittijāhāt al-Waṭaniyya fī al-Adab al-Muʿāṣir*. Cairo: al-Adab, 1954.
Al-Ḥusaynī, Isḥāq Mūsā. *Al-Ikhwān al-Muslimūn: Kubrā al-Ḥarakāt al-Dīniyya al-Ḥadītha*. Beirut: Dār Beirut, 1952.
İz, Mahir. *Yılların İzi*. Istanbul: Kitabevi, 1990.
Jaydal, Ammar. 'Mujmal Āthār wa-Ārāʾ Zāhid al-Kawtharī.' In *Uluslararası Düzceli M. Zâhid Kevserî*, 35–58.
Kaḥḥāla, ʿUmar Riḍā. *Muʿjam al-Muʾallifīn: Tarājim Muṣannifī al-Kutub al-ʿArabiyya*, vol. 10. Damascus: al-Taraqqī, 1961.
Karabela, Mehmet Kadri. *One of the Last Ottoman Şeyhülislams, Mustafa Sabri Efendi (1869–1954): His Life, Works and Intellectual Contributions*. MA Thesis, McGill University, August 2003.
Khayrī, Aḥmad. 'Al-Imām al-Kawtharī.' In *Maqālāt al-Kawtharī*, 491–547. Cairo: Al-Tawfikia Bookshop, 2000.
Kuntay, Midhat Cemal. *Mehmet Akif: Hayatı-Seciyesi-Sanatı*. Istanbul: Oğlak, 2015 [1939].
Kutay, Cemal. *Necid Çöllerinde Mehmet Akif*. Istanbul: Posta Kutusu, 1978 [1963].
Makhlūf, Mājida. 'Al-Kawtharī fī Miṣr, 1928–1952.' In *Uluslararası Düzceli M. Zâhid Kevserî*, 23–31.
Nihal, Şukufe. 'Bana Göre Mehmed Akif.' In *Mehmed Âkif*, ed. Edib, 744–5.
Özafşar, Mehmet Emin. 'Muhammed Zahid el-Kevseri Hayatı.' In *Muhammed Zâhid El-Kevserî: Hayatı-Eserleri-Tesirleri*, ed. Necdet Yılmaz, 29–54. Istanbul: Seha, 1996.
Özcanoğlu, Muzaffer. 'M. Zâhid el-Kevserî ile Yaşadığım Kırık Anılarım.' In *Uluslararası Düzceli M. Zâhid Kevserî Sempozyumu Bildirileri*, 755–64.
Al-Qawsī, Mufarriḥ ibn Sulaymān. *Muṣṭafā Ṣabrī: al-Mufakkir al-Islāmī wa-l-ʿĀlim al-ʿĀlamī wa-Shaykh al-Islām fī al-Dawla al-ʿUthmāniyya Sābiqan*. Damascus: Dār al-Qalam, 2006.
Sabit, Halim, Mehmed Âkif. 'İslamçılığı ve Milliyetçiliği.' In *Mehmed Âkif*, ed. Edib, 541–7.
Sarıkoyuncu, Ali. 'Şeyhülislam Mustafa Sabri'nin Millî Mücadele ve Atatürk İnkilapları Karşıtı Tutum ve Davranışları,' *Atatürk Araştırma Merkezi Dergisi*, 39 (1997): 787–812.
Süha, Ali. 'Laik şair, din şairi.' In *Mehmed Âkif*, ed. Edib, 753–4.
Şimşir, Bilal. *İngiliz Belgelerinde Atatürk, 1919–1938*, vols. 1–3. Ankara: Türk Tarih Kurumu Basımevi, 1973.
Uluslararası Düzceli M. Zâhid Kevserî Sempozyumu Bildirileri. Düzce/Sakarya: Sakarya Üniversitesi İlahiyat Fakültesi/ Düzce Belediyesi, 2007.
Uzun, Mustafa İsmet, ed. *Mehmed Akif Ersoy*. Ankara: Kültür ve Turizm Bakanlığı, 2011.
Yavuz, Yusuf Şevki. 'Mustafa Sabri Efendi.' *Islam Ansiklopedisi*, vol. 31 (2006): 350–3.
Yazar, Mehmed Behcet. 'Mehmed Âkif: Lisanı, Nazmı, Şiiri, Sanatı.' In *Mehmed Âkif*, ed. Edib, 461–88.
Yılmaz, Necdet, ed. *Muhammed Zâhid El-Kevserî: Hayatı-Eserleri-Tesirleri*. Istanbul: Seha, 1996.

GENERAL

ʿAbbāsī, Muḥammad ʿĪd. *Bidʿat al-Taʿaṣṣub al-Madhhabī wa-Āthāruhā al-Khaṭīra fī Jumūd al-Fikr wa-Inḥiṭāṭ al-Muslimīn*. Amman: al-Maktaba al-Islāmiyya, 1986 [1970].

ʿAbd al-Majīd, Aḥmad. *Al-Ikhwān wa-ʿAbd al-Nāṣir: al-Qiṣṣa al-Kāmila li-Tanẓīm 1965*. Cairo: al-Zahrāʾ li-l-Iʿlām al-ʿArabī, 1991.

Abdel-Malek, Anouar. *Egypt: Military Society.* Trans. Charles Lam Markmann. New York: Random House, 1968.

Abdülnasır, Cemal. 'İslam Daveti.' *Hilal*, 1/7 (May 1959), 9–10.

Abrahamov, Binyamin. 'Al-Dārimī, Abū Saʿīd.' In *Encyclopaedia of Islam 3* ed. Kate Fleet, Gudrun Krämer, Denis Matringe, John Nawas, Everett Rowson, http://dx.doi.org/10.1163/1573-3912_ei3_COM_23880. Leiden/Boston: Brill, 2016. [henceforth *EI3*],

Abou El Fadl, Khaled. *Reasoning with God: Reclaiming Shariʿah in the Modern Age*. Lanham: Rowman & Littlefield, 2014.

The Great Theft: Wrestling Islam from the Extremists. New York: Harper San Francisco, 2005.

Abū Dāwūd. 'Kitāb al-Malāḥim.' In *Sunan Abī Dāwūd*, vol. 5, ed. Shuʿayb al-Arnāʾūṭ. Damascus: al-Risāla al-ʿĀlamiyya, 2009.

Abū al-Futūḥ, ʿAbd al-Munʿim. *Shāhid ʿalā Tārīkh al-Ḥaraka al-Islāmiyya fī Miṣr 1970–1984*. Cairo: Dār al-Shurūq, 2012.

Abu-Manneh, Butrus. 'Salafiyya and the Rise of the Khalidiyya in Baghdad in the Early Nineteenth Century.' *Die Welt des Islams*, 43/3 (2003): 349–72.

'Shaykh Ahmed Ziyāʾüddīn el-Gümüşhanevi and the Ziyāʾī-Khālidī suborder.' In *Shiʿa Islam, Sects and Sufism*, ed. Frederick De Jong, 105–17. Utrecht: M.Th. Houtsma Stichting, 1992.

'Sultan Abdülhamid II and Shaikh Abulhuda Al-Sayyadi.' *Middle Eastern Studies*, 15/2 (May 1979): 131–53.

'The Sultan and the Bureaucracy: The Anti-Tanzimat Concepts of Grand Vizier Mahmud Nedim Paşa.' *IJMES*, 22/3 (1990): 257–74.

'Two Concepts of State in the Tanzimat Period: The Hatt-ı Şerif of Gülhane and the Hatt-ı Hümayun.' *Turkish Historical Review* 6 (2015): 117–37.

Abu Rabiʿ, Ibrahim. *Intellectual Origins of Islamic Resurgence in the Modern Arab World.* Albany: State University of New York Press, 1996.

'Sayyid Quṭb: From Religious Realism to Radical Social Criticism.' *Islamic Quarterly*, 28/2 (1984): 103–27.

Spiritual Dimensions of Bediuzzaman Said Nursi's Risale-i Nur, editor. Albany: State University of New York Press, 2008.

Abū Zayd, Naṣr. 'The Dilemma of the Literary Approach to the Qurʾan.' *Alif: Journal of Comparative Poetics*, 23 (2003): 8–47.

Adams, Charles. *Islam and Modernism in Egypt: A Study of the Modern Reform Movement Inaugurated by Muḥammad ʿAbduh*. London: Oxford University Press/H. Milford, 1933.

'Mawdudi and the Islamic State.' In *Voices of Resurgent Islam*, ed. John Esposito, 99–133. New York: Oxford University Press, 1983.

Al-ʿAdawī, Ibrāhīm Aḥmad. *Rashīd Riḍā, al-Imām al-Mujtahid*. Cairo: al-Muʾassasa al-Miṣriyya al-ʿĀmma, 1964.

ʿAfīfī, Abū al-ʿAlāʾ, ed. *Fuṣūṣ al-Ḥikam li-Muḥyī al-Dīn Ibn ʿArabī*. Beirut: Dār al-Kitāb al-Arabī, 1980.

Agamben, Giorgio. *Homo Sacer: Sovereign Power and Bare Life*. Stanford: Stanford University Press, 1998.

Aḥmad, ʿAzīz. *Islamic Modernism in India and Pakistan, 1857–1964*. London: Oxford University Press, 1967.

Ahmad, Feroz. 'Feroz Ahmad replies.' *The American Historical Review*, **102**/4 (1997): 1302–3.

'Military and Politics in Turkey.' In *Turkey's Engagement with Modernity: Conflict and Change in the Twentieth Century*, ed. Celia Kerslake, Kerem Öktem, Philip Robins, 92–116. London: Palgrave Macmillan, 2010.

'Review of *Muslims in Modern Turkey: Kemalism, Modernism and the Revolt of the Islamic Intellectuals* by Sena Karasipahi,' *Journal of Islamic Studies*, **22**/1 (2011): 89–91.

The Turkish Experiment in Democracy 1950–1975. London: Hurst, 1977.

Ahmad, Irfan. 'Genealogy of the Islamic State: Reflections on Maududi's Political Thought and Islamism.' *Journal of the Royal Anthropological Institute*, **15**/ 2009: 145–62.

Aḥmad, Rifʿat Sayyid. *Al-Nabī al-Muṣallaḥ 1: al-Rāfiḍūn*. London: Riad El-Rayyes, 1991.

Ahmed, Shahab. *What Is Islam?: The Importance of Being Islamic*. Princeton: Princeton University Press, 2016.

Al-ʿAjmī, Muḥammad ibn Nāṣir. *Al-Rasāʾil al-Mutabādila bayn Jamāl al-Dīn al-Qāsimī wa-Maḥmūd Shukrī al-Ālūsī*. Beirut: al-Bashāʾir, 2001.

Akman, Zekeriya. 'Anglikan Kilisesi'nin Meşihat Kurumuna Soruları ve Bunlara Verilen Cevaplar.' *Hikmet Yurdu*, **6**/11 (January–June 2013): 357–77.

Osmanlı Devleti'nin Son Döneminde Bir Üst Kurul, Dâru'l-Hikmeti'l İslâmiye. Ankara: DİB Yayınları, 2009.

Al-Atawneh, Muhammad. *Wahhābī Islam Facing theChallenges of Modernity: Dār al-Iftā in the Modern Saudi State*. Series: Studies in Islamic Law and Society. Leiden/Boston: Brill, 2010.

Al-Azmeh, Aziz. *Islams and Modernities*. London: Verso, 1993.

Albayrak, Sadık. *Şeriat Yolunda Yürüyenler ve Sürünenler*. Istanbul: Medrese, 1979.

Son Devir Osmanlı Uleması: Ilmiye Ricalinin Teracim-i Ahvali, vol. 4. Istanbul: Medrese, 1981.

Ali, Syed Ameer. *The Spirit of Islam, or The Life and Teachings of Mohammed*. Calcutta: S. K. Lahiri, 1902.

ʿAli, Hāshimī Muḥammad. *Al-Shaykh ʿAbd al-Fattāḥ Abū Ghudda Kamā ʿAraftuhu*. Beirut: al-Bashāʾir al-Islāmiyya, 2004.

Altunsu, Abdülkadir. *Osmanlı Şeyhülislamları*. Ankara: Ayyıldız, 1972.

Al-Ālūsī, Shihāb al-Dīn. *Gharāʾib al-Ightirāb wa-Nuzhat al-Albāb*. Baghdad: Shahbandar Press, 1909/10.

Ambrosio, Alberto Fabio. 'Mapping Modern Turkish Sufism and Anti-Sufism.' In *Sufis and Salafis in the Contemporary Age*, ed. Lloyd Ridgeon, 59–70. London: Bloomsbury, 2016.

Amīn, Aḥmad and Zakī Najīb Maḥmūd. *Qiṣṣat al-Falsafa al-Ḥadītha*. Cairo: Dār al-Kutub al-Miṣriyya, 1935.

Amin, Kamaruddin. 'Nāṣiruddīn al-Albānī on Muslim's *Ṣaḥīḥ*: A Critical Study of His Method.' *Islamic Law and Society*, 11/2 (2004): 149–76.

Andrews, Walter G. 'Ottoman Lyrics: Introductory Essay.' In *Ottoman Lyric Poetry: An Anthology*, ed. Walter G. Andrews, Najaat Black, Mehmet Kalpaklı. Seattle: University of Washington Press, 2006.

Anjum, Ovamir. 'Cultural Memory of the Pious Ancestors (*Salaf*) in al-Ghazālī.' *Numen*, 58/2-3 (2011): 344–74.

'Islamic as a Discursive Tradition: Talal Asad and His Interlocutors.' *Comparative Studies of South Asia, Africa and the Middle East*, 27/3 (2007): 656–72.

Anscombe, Frederick. *The Ottoman Gulf: The Creation of Kuwait, Saudi Arabia, and Qatar*. New York: Columbia University Press, 1997.

Arendt, Hannah. *The Human Condition*. London: University of Chicago Press, 1998.

Arkoun, Mohammed. 'Rethinking Islam Today.' *The Annals of the American Academy of Political and Social Science*, 588/1 (2003): 18–39.

Arnaldez, R. 'Ibn Rus̲h̲d.' In *Encyclopaedia of Islam, Second Edition*, ed. P. Bearman, Th. Bianquis, C. E. Bosworth, E. van Donzel, W. P. Heinrichs. Leiden, Netherlands: Brill, 2012; http://dx.doi.org/10.1163/1573-3912_islam_COM_0340.

Arslān, Shakīb. *Sīra Dhātiyya*. al-Mukhtāra: al-Dār al-Taqaddumiyya, 2008.

Asad, Talal. *Formations of the Secular: Christianity, Islam, Modernity*. Stanford: Stanford University Press, 2003.

Genealogies of Religion: Discipline and Reasons of Power in Christianity and Islam. Baltimore: Johns Hopkins University Press, 1993.

'The Idea of an Anthropology of Islam.' *Qui Parle*, 17/2 (Spring/Summer 2009): 5–8.

Asrar, Nisar Ahmed. 'Muhammed İkbal'in Eserlerinde Türkiye ve Türkler.' In *Muhammed İkbal Kitabı Uluslararası Muhammed İkbal Sempozyumu Bildirileri*, 76–80. Istanbul: Istanbul Büyükşehir Belediyesi Kültür İşleri, 1997.

Al-Atharī, Muḥammad Bahjat. *Maḥmūd Shukrī al-Ālūsī wa-Ārā'uhu al-Lughawiyya*. Cairo: al-Kamaliyya Press, 1958.

Ayaşlı, Münevver. *İşittiklerim Gördüklerim Bildiklerim*. Istanbul: Güryay Mat., 1973.

Aybars, Ergün. *İstiklal Mahkemeleri*. Ankara: Bilgi Yayınevi, 1975.

Aydın, Cemil. *The Idea of the Muslim World: A Global Intellectual History*. Cambridge/London: Harvard University Press, 2017.

Ayluçtarhan, Sevda. *Abdullah Cevdet's Translations (1908–1910): The Making of a Westernist Culture Repertoire in a Resistant Ottoman Context*. Saarbrücken: Lap Lambert Academic, 2017.

Aytürk, İlker. 'Script Charisma in Hebrew and Turkish: A Comparative Framework for Explaining Success and Failure of Romanization.' *Journal of World History*, 21/1 (2010): 97–130.

Ayvazoğlu, Beşir. 'Mehmed Akif ve Muhammed İkbal.' In *Muhammed İkbal Kitabı Uluslararası*, 43–56.

ʿAzzām, ʿAbd al-Wahhāb. 'Muqaddimat al-Mutarjim.' In *Payām-i Mashriq: Risālat al-Mashriq*, 1–18.

Baines, John. 'Writing and Its Multiple Disappearances.' In *The Disappearance of Writing Systems: Perspectives on Literacy and Communication*, ed. John Baines, John Bennet, Stephen Houston, 347–62. London: Equinox, 2008.

Bano, Masooda. Introduction. In *Modern Islamic Authority and Social Change. Volume 1, Evolving Debates in Muslim Majority Countries*, ed. Bano. Edinburgh: Edinburgh University Press, 2018.

Bardakçı, Murad. 'Mehmed Âkif devlet tarafından'İrtica-906' diye kodlanmış, ölüm döşeğinde yatarken bile izlenmiş ve Safahat'ı da imha edilmişti,' *Habertürk*, 19 November 2018; www.haberturk.com/yazarlar/murat-bardakci/2225662-mehmed-akif-devlet-tarafindan-irtica-906-diye-kodlanmis-olum-doseginde-yatarken-bile-izlenmis-ve-safahati-da-imha-edilmisti (accessed 12 August 2019).

Baudelaire, Charles. *The Painter of Modern Life and Other Essays*, 2nd ed. Trans. Jonathan Mayne. London: Phaidon, 1995 [1863].

Bayly, Christopher. *The Birth of the Modern World, 1780–1914: Global Connections and Comparisons*. Oxford: Blackwell, 2004.

Bein, Amit. *Ottoman Ulema, Turkish Republic: Agents of Change and Guardians of Tradition*. Stanford: Stanford University Press, 2011.

Berkes, Niyazi. .*The Development of Secularism in Turkey*. Montreal: McGill University Press, 1964.

Türk Düsününde Batı Sorunu. Ankara: Bilgi Yayınevi, 1975.

Berktay, Halil and Suraiya Faroqhi, eds. *New Approaches to State and Peasant in Ottoman History*. London: Cass, 1992.

Bilgili, Ismail. 'Bekir Sami Paşa Nakşbendî Halidî Zaviyesinin Konya Islah-i Medâris-i İslamiye Medresesine Dönüşümü Bağlamında Nakşbendîliğin İlmi Ḥayāta Tesiri.' In *Uluslararası Bahaeddin Nakşibend ve Nakşibendilik Sempozyumu*, 312–40. Istanbul: Hüdayi Vakfı, 2016.

Binder, Leonard. *Islamic Liberalism: A Critique of Development Ideologies*. Chicago: University of Chicago Press, 1988.

Bori, Caterina. 'Al-Dhahabī.' In *EI3*, http://dx.doi.org/10.1163/1573-3912_ei3_COM_25995.

Bostan, M. Hanefi. 'Said Halim Paşa ve Fikirleri.' 21. *Yüzyılda Eğitim ve Toplum*, 8/22 (2019): 53–90.

Blunt, Wilfrid Scawen. *The Future of Islam*. Richmond: Curzon, 2001.

Brandenburg, Ulrich. 'The Multiple Publics of a Transnational Activist: Abdürreşid İbrahim, Pan-Asianism, and the Creation of Islam in Japan.' *Die Welt des Islams*, **58** (2018): 143–72.

Brockett, Gavin. *How Happy to Call Oneself a Turk: Provincial Newspapers and the Negotiation of a Muslim National Identity*. Austin: University of Texas Press, 2011.

Brown, Jonathan. 'Did the Prophet Say It or Not? The Literal, Historical, and Effective Truth of Ḥadīths in Early Sunnism.' *Journal of the American Oriental Society*, **129**/2 (2009): 259–85.

Hadith: Muhammad's Legacy in the Medieval and Modern World. Oxford: Oneworld, 2009.

The Canonization of al-Bukhārī and Muslim: The Formation and Function of the Sunnī Ḥadīth Canon. Series: Islamic History and Civilization, Volume: 69. Leiden: Brill, 2007.

Bruckmayr, Philipp. 'The Particular Will (*al-irādat al-juz'iyya*): Excavations Regarding a Latecomer in Kalām Terminology on Human Agency and Its Position in Naqshbandī Discourse.' *European Journal of Turkish Studies*, **13**/ 2011: 1–23 (December 2012) [online only].

Bsheer, Rosie. 'A Counter-Revolutionary State: Popular Movements and the Making of Saudi Arabia.' *Past and Present*, **239**/1 (2018): 233–77.

Bulaç, Ali. *İslam Dünyasında Düşünce Sorunları*. Istanbul: Burhan Yayınları, 1983.

Al-Būṭī, Sa'īd Ramaḍān. *Kubrā al-Yaqīniyyāt al-Kawniyya: Wujūd al-Khāliq wa-Waẓīfat al-Makhlūq*. Damascus: Dār al-Fikr, 1997.

Al-Lāmadhhabiyya: Akhṭar Bid'a Tuhaddid al-Sharī'a al-Islāmiyya. 2nd ed. Damascus: 1970.

Calder, Norman. 'The Limits of Islamic Orthodoxy.' In *Intellectual Traditions in Islam*, ed. Farhad Daftary, 66–86. London: I. B. Tauris/Institute of Ismaili Studies, 2000.

Calvert, John. *Sayyid Quṭb and the Origins of Radical Islamism*. London: Hurst, 2010.

Carré, Olivier. 'Eléments de la 'aqîda de Sayyid Quṭb dans 'Fî zilâl al-qur'ân'.' *Studia Islamica*, **91** (2000): 165–97.

Mysticism and Politics: A Critical Reading of Fī Ẓilāl al-Qur'ān by Sayyid Quṭb (1906–1966). Series: Social, Economic and Political Studies of the Middle East and Asia, Volume: 85. Leiden: Brill, 2003.

Carrel, Alexis. *Man, The Unknown*. Trans. Charles. E. Rosenberg. New York/ London: Harper and Bros, 1939 [1935].

Caspar, Robert. 'Un aspect de la pensée musulmane moderne: le renouveau du mo'tazilisme.' *Melanges de l'Institut Dominicain d'Etudes Orientales du Caire*, **4** (1957): 141–202.

Çelik, Zeynep. *Europe Knows Nothing about the Orient: A Critical Discourse from the East, 1872–1932*. Istanbul: Koç University Press, 2021.

Cem, Semaheddin. 'Akifimiz.' *Hilal*, **5**/56, March 1966, 23–4.

Cevdet, Abdullah. *Tarih-i İslamiyet*, 2 vols. Istanbul: Matbaa-i İctihad, 1909. Translation of *Essai sur l'histoire de l'Islamisme, Reinhart Dozy*. Paris: Maisonneuve, 1879.

Ceylan, Nurettin. *Gerçeğin Aynasında Bediüzzaman*. Istanbul: Nesil, 2016.

Chakrabarty, Dipesh. 'The Muddle of Modernity.' *American Historical Review*, **116**/3 (June 2011): 663–75.

Chekuri, Christopher. 'Writing Politics Back into History.' *History and Theory*, **46** (October 2007): 384–95.

Choueiri, Youssef. *Islamic Fundamentalism: The Story of Islamist Movements*. London/New York: Continuum, 2010.

Christmann, Andreas. 'Islamic Scholar and Religious Leader: A portrait of Shaykh Muḥammad Sa'īd Ramaḍān al-Būṭī.' *Islam and Christian-Muslim Relations*, **9**/ 2 (1998): 149–69.

Cole, Juan. 'Printing in Urban Islam.' In *Modernity & Culture: From the Mediterranean to the Indian Ocean*, ed. Leila Fawaz, Christopher Bayly, Robert Ilbert, 344–64. New York: Columbia University Press, 2002.

'Rashid Rida on the Baha'i Faith: A Utilitarian Theory of the Spread of Religions.' *Arab Studies Quarterly*, 5/3 (1983): 276–91.

Commins, David. 'Claiming the Pious Ancestors.' In *Tarihte ve Günümüzde Selefilik*, ed. Ahmet Kavas, 431–48. Istanbul: Ensar Neşriyat, 2014.

'From Wahhabi to Salafi.' In *Saudi Arabia in Transition: Insights on Social, Political, Economic and Religious Change*, ed. Bernard Haykel, Thomas Hegghammer, Stéphane Lacroix, 151–66. Cambridge: Cambridge University Press, 2015.

Islamic Reform: Politics and Social Change in Late Ottoman Syria. New York: Oxford University Press, 1990.

Coppens, Pieter. 'Did Modernity End Polyvalence? Some Observations on Tolerance for Ambiguity in Sunni tafsīr.' *Journal of Qur'anic Studies*, 23/1 (2021): 36–70.

Cornell, Svante E. 'The Naqshbandi-Khalidi Order and Political Islam in Turkey,' Hudson Institute, 3 September 2015; www.hudson.org/research/11601-the-naqshbandi-khalidi-order-and-political-Islām-in-turkey.

Cornell, Vincent J. 'Muḥammad 'Abduh: A Sufi-Inspired Modernist?' In *Tradition and Modernity: Christian and Muslim Perspectives*, ed. David Marshall, 105–14. Washington: Georgetown University Press, 2013.

Cottingham, John. *Philosophy of Religion: Towards a More Humane Approach*. New York: Cambridge University Press, 2014.

Coury, Ralph. *The Making of an Egyptian Arab Nationalist: The Early Years of Azzam Pasha, 1893–1936*. Reading, UK: Ithaca Press, 1998.

Cromer, Earl of (Evelyn Baring). *Modern Egypt*. 2 vols. London: Macmillan, 1908.

Crone, Patricia. *Pre-Industrial Societies: Anatomy of the Pre-Modern World*. Oxford: Basil Blackwell, 1989.

Crone, Patricia and Martin Hinds. *God's Caliph: Religious Authority in the First Centuries of Islam*. Cambridge: Cambridge University Press, 2003.

Cundioğlu, Dücane. *Türkçe İbadet 1*. Istanbul: Kitabevi, 1999.

Çağatay, Neşet. 'Allama Muḥammad İqbal and Mehmet Akif Ersoy.' *İslam İlimleri Enstitüsü Dergisi*, 4 (1980): 61–6.

Çakır, Ruşen. *Ayet ve Slogan: Türkiye'de İslami Oluşumlar*. Istanbul: Metis Yayınları, 1991.

Çalış, Halim. 'Mustafa Sabri Efendi ve Kant Felsefesine Yaptığı Eleştiriler.' *Yeni Ümit*, 54 (2001): 58–62.

Çelik, İsa. 'Çagdaş İki İslam Şairi: Muhammed İkbal ve Mehmed Akif,' *Atatürk Üniversitesi İlahiyat Fakültesi Dergisi*, 22 (Erzurum, 2004): 151–92.

Al-Dawīsh, Aḥmad ibn 'Abd al-Rāziq. *Fatāwā al-Lajna al-Dā'ima li-l-Buḥūth al-'Ilmiyya wa-l-Da'wā wa-l-Irshād*, vol. 2. Riyadh: Dār al-Mu'ayyad, 2003.

Demir, Hilmi. 'FETÖ: Mezhepler Üstü Din Öğretimi ve Alevi Açılımı.' *Türkiye Gazetesi*, 1 June 2018; www.turkiyegazetesi.com.tr/yazarlar/hilmi-demir/602515.aspx.

'Nakşibendilik Selefileşiyor mu?' *21. Yüzyıl*, No. 70 (January 2014); www.21yyte.org/tr/arastirma/teostrateji-arastirmalarimerkezi/2014/09/17/7764/naksibendilik-selefilesiyor-mu (accessed 3 May 2015).

Demir, Hilmi and Muzaffer Tan. *Ehl-i Sünnetin Reislerinden İmam-ı Matüridi.* Istanbul: Büyük Resim, 2017.

Deringil, Selim. *The Well-Protected Domains: Ideology and the Legitimation of Power in the Ottoman Empire, 1876–1909.* London: I. B. Tauris, 1998.

Al-Dhahabī, Shams al-Dīn. *Muʿjam al-Shuyūkh al-Kabīr*, vol. 2. Ṭāʾif: Maktabat al-Ṣiddīq, 1987.

Dhanani, Alnoor. 'Al-Mawāqif fī ʿilm al-kalām by ʿAḍud al-Dīn al-Ījī (d. 1355), and Its Commentaries.' In *The Oxford Handbook of Islamic Philosophy*, ed. Khaled El-Rouayheb and Sabine Schmidtke, 375–98. New York: Oxford University Press, 2016.

Al-Dijwī, Yūsuf. 'Kalima fī al-Salafiyya al-Ḥāḍira.' In *Qatʿ al-ʿUrūq al-Wardiyya min Ṣāḥib 'al-Burūq al-Najdiyya'*, by Aḥmad al-Ghumārī. 25–33. Leiden: Dār al-Muṣṭafā, 2007.

Diyanet İşleri Başkanlığı. *Daiş'in Temel Felsefesi ve Dini Referansları Raporu.* Ankara: Diyanet, 2015.

İlmihal 1: İman ve İbadetler. Istanbul: Diyanet, 1999.

Douglas, Fedwa Malti. 'Controversy and its Effects in the Biographical Tradition of Al-Khaṭīb Al-Baghdādī.' *Studia Islamica*, **46** (1977): 115–31.

Dozy, Reinhart. *Essai sur l'histoire de l'Islamisme*. Paris: Maisonneuve, 1879.

Dressler, Markus. 'Rereading Ziya Gökalp: Secularism and Reform of the Islamic State in the Late Young Turk Period.' *IJMES*, **47**/3 (2015): 511–31.

Eich, Thomas. 'Abū l-Hudā al-Ṣayyādī.' In *EI3*, http://dx.doi.org/10.1163/1573-3912_ei3_SIM_0028.

Eisenstadt, S. N. 'Multiple Modernities.' *Daedalus*, **129**/1 (Winter 2000): 1–29.

Ellison, Grace. *Turkey To-Day.* London: Hutchinson, 1928.

El-Rouayheb, Khaled. 'From Ibn Ḥajar al-Haytamī (d. 1566) to Khayr al-Dīn al-Ālūsī (d. 1899): Changing Views of Ibn Taymiyya Among non-Ḥanbalī Sunni Scholars.' In *Ibn Taymiyya and His Times*, ed. Yossef Rapoport and Shahab Ahmed, 269–318. Karachi: Oxford University Press, 2010.

Islamic Intellectual History in the Seventeenth Century: Scholarly Currents in the Ottoman Empire and the Maghreb. Cambridge: Cambridge University Press, 2015.

El Shakry, Omnia. '"History Without Documents": The Vexed Archives of Decolonization in the Middle East.' *American Historical Review*, **120**/3 (2015): 920–34.

'The Vexed Archives of Decolonization in the Middle East.' *American Historical Review*, **120** (2015): 920–34.

El Shamsy, Ahmed. *Rediscovering the Islamic Classics: How Editors and Print Culture Transformed an Intellectual Tradition.* Princeton: Princeton University Press, 2020.

The Canonization of Islamic Law: A Social and Intellectual History. New York: Cambridge University Press, 2013.

El-Zein, Abdul Hamid. 'Beyond Ideology and Theology: The Search for the Anthropology of Islam.' *Annual Review of Anthropology* **6** (1977): 227–54.

Engelhardt, Edouard. *La Turquie et le tanzimat, ou Histoire des reformes dans l'Empire ottoman depuis 1826 jusqu'a nos jours*. Paris: Cotillon, 1882.

Eraslan, Sadık. *Meşihat-i İslâmiyye ve Ceride-i İlmiyye: Osmanlılarda Fetva Makamı ve Yayın Organı*. Ankara: DİB Yayınları, 2009.

Erbakan, Necmettin. *Davam: Ne Yaptıysam Allah Rızası İçin Yaptım*. Ankara: Milli Gazete, 2014.

Erişirgil, Emin. *Bir Fikir Adamının Romanı: Ziya Gökalp*. Istanbul: Remzi Kitabevi, 1984.

Erol, Ertan. 'Safahat'ta Emek ve Gayret Kavramları Üzerine,' *Uluslararası Sosyal Araştırmalar Dergisi*, 5/21 (Spring 2012): 106–16.

Ersanlı, Buşra. 'The Ottoman Empire in the Historiography of the Kemalist Era: A Theory of Fatal Decline.' In *The Ottomans and the Balkans: A Discussion of Historiography*, ed. Fikret Adanir, Suraiya Faroqhi, 15–54. Series: The Ottoman Empire and its Heritage, Volume: 25. Leiden: Brill, 2002.

Escovitz, J. H. 'He was the Muḥammad ʿAbduh of Syria: A Study of Tahir Al-Jazaʾiri and his Influence.' *IJMES*, 18/3 (1986): 293–310.

Euben, Roxanne, ed. *Enemy in the Mirror: Islamic Fundamentalism and the Limits of Modern Rationalism*. Princeton: Princeton University Press, 1999.

Princeton Readings in Islamist Thought: Texts and Contexts from al-Bannā to Bin Laden. Princeton: Princeton University Press, 2009.

Al-Fahad, Abdulaziz. 'From Exclusivism to Accommodation: Doctrinal and Legal Evolution of Wahhabism.' *New York University Law Review*, 79 (2004): 485–519.

Fahmy, Khaled. *In Quest of Justice: Islamic Law and Forensic Medicine in Modern Egypt*. Oakland: University of California Press, 2018.

Fakhry, Majid. *Islamic Philosophy, Theology and Mysticism: A Short Introduction*. Oxford: Oneworld, 1997.

Fanon, Frantz. *The Wretched of the Earth*. Trans. Constance Farrington. London: Penguin, 2001.

Finlayson, James Gordon. 'Bare Life and Politics in Agamben's Reading of Aristotle.' *The Review of Politics*, 72 (2010), 97–126.

Foer, Franklin. 'Moral Hazard,' *New Republic*, 18 November 2002.

Fortna, Benjamin. *Learning to Read in the Late Ottoman Empire and the Early Turkish Republic*. Basingstoke: Palgrave Macmillan, 2011.

The Circassian: A Life of Esref Bey, Late Ottoman Insurgent and Special Agent. London: Hurst, 2016.

Foucault, Michel. *'Society Must Be Defended': Lectures at the Collège de France, 1975–76*. New York: Picador, 2003.

The Archaeology of Knowledge. London: Routledge, 2002.

'The Birth of Biopolitics.' In *Ethics: Subjectivity and Truth*, vol. 1, ed. Foucault and Paul Rabinow, 73–80. New York: The New Press, 1997.

'Why Study Power? The Question of the Subject.' In *Michel Foucault: Beyond Structuralism and Hermeneutics*, ed. Hubert L. Dreyfus, Paul Rabinow, 208–15. Chicago: University of Chicago Press, 1983.

Freeden, Michael. *Ideology: A Very Short Introduction.* Oxford: Oxford University Press, 2003.

Friedmann, Yohanan. *Shaykh Aḥmad Sirhindī: An Outline of His Thought and a Study of His Image in the Eyes of Posterity.* New Delhi/Oxford: Oxford University Press.

Gadamer, Hans-Georg. *Truth and Method.* Trans. Joel Weinsheimer, Donald J. Marshall. London: Bloomsbury Academic, 2013.

Gardet, Louis. 'Signification du 'renouveau Muʿtazilite' dans la pensee musulmane contemporaine.' In *Islamic Philosophy and the Classical Tradition*, ed. S. M. Stern, A. Hourani, V. Brown, 63–75. Oxford: Cassirer, 1972.

Gaunt, David. *Massacres, Resistance, Protectors: Muslim-Christian Relations in Eastern Anatolia during World War I.* Piscataway, NJ: Gorgias, 2006.

Gauvain, Richard. *Salafi Ritual Purity: In the Presence of God.* London: Routledge, 2013.

Gen, Kasuya. 'The Influence of Al-Manār on Islamism in Turkey: The Case of Mehmed Akif.' In *Intellectuals in the Modern Islamic World: Transmission, Transformation, Communication*, ed. Stéphane Dudoignon, Komatsu Hisao, Kosugi Yasushi, 74–84. London: Routledge, 2016.

Gellner, Ernest. 'The Turkish Option in Comparative Perspective.' In *Rethinking Modernity and National Identity in Turkey*, ed. Sibel Bozdoğan, Reşat Kasaba, 233–44. Seattle: University of Washington Press, 1997.

Gershoni, Israel. 'The Theory of Crisis and the Crisis in a Theory: Intellectual History in Twentieth-Century Middle Eastern Studies.' In *Middle East Historiographies: Narrating the Twentieth Century*, ed. Israel Gershoni, Amy Singer, Hakan Erdem, 131–82. Seattle: University of Washington Press, 2011.

Gershoni, Israel and James P. Jankowski. *Confronting Fascism in Egypt: Dictatorship Versus Democracy in the 1930s.* Stanford: Stanford University Press, 2010.

Redefining the Egyptian Nation, 1930–1945. Cambridge: Cambridge University Press, 1995.

Gesink, Indira Falk. *Islamic Reform and Conservatism: Al-Azhar and the Evolution of Modern Sunni Islam.* London: Tauris Academic Studies, 2010.

Ghazal, Amal. 'Sufism, *Ijtihād* and Modernity: Yūsuf al-Nabhānī in the Age of ʿAbd al-Ḥamīd II.' *Archivum Ottomanicum*, 19 (2001): 239–71.

Ghazaleh, Pascale, ed. *Held in Trust: Waqf in the Islamic World.* Cairo: American University in Cairo Press, 2011.

Al-Ghazālī, Abū Ḥāmid. *Iljām al-ʿAwāmm ʿan ʿIlm al-Kalām.* Ed. Ismail Agha Vakfı. Istanbul: Siraç Yayınevi, 2017.

Tahāfut al-Falāsifa. Ed. Ṣalāḥ al-Dīn al-Hawwārī. Beirut: al-Maktaba al-ʿAṣriyya, 2005.

'Studies in Contemporary Arabic Literature: III.' *Bulletin of the School of Oriental and African Studies*, 5/3 (1929): 445–66.

Al-Ghazālī, Muḥammad. *Al-Sunna al-Nabawiyya bayn Ahl al-Fiqh wa-Ahl al-Ḥadīth.* Cairo: Dār al-Shurūq, 1989.

Gibb, Elias J.W. *A History of Ottoman Poetry, vol. 1.* Ed. Edward G. Browne. Warminister: The E.J.W. Gibb Memorial Trust, 2013.

Gibb, H.A.R. *Modern Trends in Islam*. Chicago: The University of Chicago Press, 1947.
Gimaret, Daniel. *La Doctrine d'al-Ash'arī*. Paris: Cerf, 1990.
Goldstone, Jack. 'The Problem of the "Early Modern" World.' *Journal of Sociology* 46/3 (2005): 249–84.
Goldziher, Ignácz. *Muslim Studies*, vol. 1. London: Allen & Unwin, 1967.
Görlach, Joseph-Simon. 'Western Representations of Fascist Influences on Islamist Thought.' In *Cultural Transfers in Dispute: Representations in Asia, Europe and the Arab World since the Middle Ages*, ed. Jörg Feuchter, Friedhelm Hoffmann, Bee Yun, 149–66. Frankfurt/New York: Campus Verlag, 2011.
Gözaydın, İstar B. 'Diyanet and Politics.' *The Muslim World*, 98/2–3 (April/July 2008): 216–27.
Gözübüyük, Faik. 'Mehmed Akif ve Muhammed İkbal.' *Türk Yurdu*, 50/280, January 1960: 49–51.
Gray, John. *Seven Types of Atheism*. London: Penguin, 2019.
Griffel, Frank. 'What do We Mean by "Salafī"? Connecting Muḥammad 'Abduh with Egypt's Nūr Party in Islam's Contemporary Intellectual History.' *Die Welt des Islams*, 55 (2015): 186–220.
Guizot, François. *Histoire générale de la civilisation en Europe*. Paris: Victor Masson Libraire, 1851.
Gürpınar, Doğan. *Ottoman/Turkish Visions of the Nation, 1860–1950*. Basingstoke: Palgrave Macmillan, 2013.
Gran, Peter. 'Ḥasan al-'Aṭṭār.' In *Essays in Arabic Literary Biography: 1350–1850*, ed. Roger Allen, Terri DeYoung, 56–68. Wiesbaden: Harrassowitz, 2009.
Green, E.H.H. *Ideologies of Conservatism: Conservative Political Ideas in the Twentieth Century*. Oxford: Oxford University Press, 2002.
Guida, Michelangelo. 'The Life and Political Ideas of Grand Vezir Said Halim Pasha.' *İslâm Araştırmaları Dergisi*, 18 (2007): 101–18.
'The New Islamists' Understanding of Democracy in Turkey: The Examples of Ali Bulaç and Hayreddin Karaman.' *Turkish Studies*, 11/3 (2010): 347–70.
Günaltay, Şemsettin. *Zulmetten Nura*. Istanbul: Tevsi-i Tıbaat Matbaası, 1913.
Gündoğdu, Abdullah. *Ümmetten Millete: Ahmet Ağaoğlu'nun Sırat-ı Müstakim ve Sebilürreşad Dergilerindeki Yazıları Üzerine bir İnceleme*. Istanbul: IQ Kültür Sanat Yayıncılık, 2007.
Gündüz, Irfan. *Osmanlılarda Devlet-Tekke Münasebetleri*. Ankara: Seha Neşriyat, 1984.
Haddad, Yvonne. 'The Qur'anic Justification for an Islamic Revolution: The View of Sayyid Quṭb.' *Middle East Journal*, 37/1 (Winter 1983): 14–29.
Hādī, 'Iṣām Mūsā. *Al-Da'wā al-Salafiyya: Ahdāfuhā wa-Mawqifuhā min al-Mukhālifīn Lahā*. Amman: 2013.
Haim, Sylvia. 'Blunt and Kawakibi.' *Oriente Moderno*, 35/3 (1955): 132–43.
Haj, Samira. *Reconfiguring Islamic Tradition: Reform, Rationality, and Modernity*. Stanford: Stanford University Press, 2009.
Al-Ḥakīm, Su'ād. *Al-Mu'jam al-Ṣūfī: al-Ḥikma fī Ḥudūd al-Kalima*. Beirut: Dandara li-l-Ṭibā'a wa-l-Nashr, 1981.
Hallaq, Wael. *An Introduction to Islamic Law*. Cambridge: Cambridge University Press, 2009.

Reforming Modernity: Ethics and the New Human in the Philosophy of Addurrahman Taha. New York: Columbia University Press, 2019.

Sharīʿa: Theory, Practice, Transformations. Cambridge: Cambridge University Press, 2009.

The Impossible State: Islam, Politics and Modernity's Predicament. New York: Columbia University Press, 2014.

Halverson, Jeffry. *Theology and Creed in Sunni Islam: The Muslim Brotherhood, Ashʿarīsm, and Political Sunnism*. New York: Palgrave Macmillan, 2010.

Hamdeh, Emad. 'Qurʾān and Sunna or the Madhhabs?: A Salafi Polemic Against Islamic Legal Tradition.' *Islamic Law and Society*, **24** (2017): 211–53.

Hamilton, David. *The First Transplant Surgeon: The Flawed Genius of Nobel Prize Winner, Alexis Carrel*. Singapore: World Scientific, 2017.

Ḥanafī, Ḥasan. 'Al-Salafiyya wa-l-ʿAlmāniyya.' In *Tarihte ve Günümüzde Selefilik*, ed. Kavas, 135–56.

Hanioğlu, M. Şükrü. *A Brief History of the Late Ottoman Empire*. Princeton: Princeton University Press, 2008.

Atatürk: An Intellectual Biography. Princeton: Princeton University Press, 2017.

'Garbcılar: Their Attitudes toward Religion and Their Impact on the Official Ideology of the Turkish Republic.' *Studia Islamica*, **86** (1997): 133–58.

The Young Turks in Opposition. New York: Oxford University Press, 1995.

'To the Editor.' *American Historical Review*, **102**/4 (1997): 1301–2.

Hanna, Nelly. *Artisan Entrepreneurs in Cairo and Early-Modern Capitalism (1600–1800)*. Syracuse, NY: Syracuse University Press, 2011.

Hansu, Hüseyin. 'Notes on the Term Mutawātir and Its Reception in Ḥadīth Criticism.' *Islamic Law and Society*, **16**/3–4 (2009): 383–408.

Hartung, Jan-Peter. *A System of Life: Mawdudi and the Ideologisation of Islam*. London: Hurst, 2014.

Haykel, Bernard. 'On the Nature of Salafi Thought and Action.' In *Global Salafism*, ed. Roel Meijer, 33–58. London: Hurst, 2009.

Revival and Reform in Islam: The Legacy of Muḥammad al-Shawkānī. Cambridge: Cambridge University Press, 2003.

Hegel, G. W. F. *The Philosophy of History*. Mineola, NY: Dover Publications, 1956.

Heine, Peter. 'Sâlih ash-Sharîf at-Tûnisî, a North African Nationalist in Berlin During the First World War.' *Revue de l'Occident musulman et de la Méditerranée*, **33**/1 (1982): 89–95.

Hilal. 'Hilal'den Size.' *Hilal*, 5/56 (March 1966), 1.

'Mısır'da Olup Bitenler.' *Hilal*, 5/56 (March 1966), 2.

Hildebrandt, Thomas. 'Waren Ǧamāl ad-Dīn al-Afġānī und Muḥammad ʿAbduh Neo-Muʿtaziliten?' *Welt des Islams*, **42**/2 (2002): 207–62.

Hinnebusch, Raymond. *The International Politics of the Middle East*. 1st and 2nd ed. Manchester: Manchester University Press, 2003/2015.

Hisao, Komatsu. 'Muslim Intellectuals and Japan: A Pan-Islamist Mediator, Abdurreshid Ibrāhīm.' In *Intellectuals in the Modern Islamic World: Transmission, Transformation, Communication*, ed. Stéphane Dudoignon, Komatsu Hisao, Kosugi Yasushi, 273–88. London: Routledge, 2016.

Holbrook. Victoria. *The Unreadable Shores of Love: Turkish Modernity and Mystic Romance*. Austin: University of Texas Press, 2004.

Holyoake, George. *English Secularism: A Confession of Belief*. Chicago: Open Court, 1896.

Hoover, Jon. 'Ḥashwiyya.' In *EI3*, http://dx.doi.org/10.1163/1573-3912_ei3_COM_30377.

Hourani, Albert. *Arabic Thought in the Liberal Age 1798–1939*. Cambridge: Cambridge University Press, 1983.

Houston, Stephen, ed. *The Shape of Script: How and Why Writing Systems Change*. Santa Fe, NM: School for Advanced Research Press, 2012.

Al-Huḍaybī, Ḥasan. *Duʿāh Lā Quḍāh*. Cairo: Dār al-Ṭibāʿa wa-l-Nashr al-Islāmiyya, 1977.

Al-Ḥuzaymī, Nāṣir. *Ayyām maʿa Juhaymān: Kuntu maʿ al-Jamāʿa al-Salafiyya al-Muḥtasiba*. Beirut: Arab Network for Research and Publishing, 2011.

Ibn Rushd. *Tahāfut al-Tahāfut*. Beirut: al-Maktaba al-ʿAṣriyya, 2005.

Ibrāhīm, Ahmed Fekry. 'Rethinking the Taqlīd-Ijtihād Dichotomy: A Conceptual-Historical Approach.' *Journal of the American Oriental Society*, **136**/2 (2016): 285–303.

İhsanoğlu, Ekmeleddin. 'Teâlî-i İslâm Cemiyeti,' İslâm Ansiklopedisi (Istanbul: Türkiye Diyanet Vakfı, 2001), 207–8; online database: https://islamansiklopedisi.org.tr/arama/.

The Turks in Egypt and their Cultural Legacy. Trans. Humphrey Davies. Cairo: American University in Cairo Press, 2012.

ʿIllaysh, Muḥammad. *Hidāyat al-Murīd li-ʿAqīdat Ahl al-Tawḥīd*. Bayda, Libya: Muḥammad al-Sanūsī University, 1968 [1888].

İnal, Mahmud Kemal. *Osmanlı Devrinde Son Sadrazamlar*, vol. 4. Istanbul: Dergah Yayınları, 1982.

İnalcık, Halil. *The Ottoman Empire: The Classical Age, 1300–1600*. London: Weidenfeld & Nicolson, 1973.

İşcan, Mehmet Zeki. 'Türk Basınında Matüridi ve Matüridilik.' *Marmara University İlahiyat Fakültesi Vakfı Yayınları*, **261** (2012): 478–92.

Işık, Hüseyin Hilmi. *Dinde Reformcular*. Istanbul: Işık Kitabevi, 1976.

The Religion Reformers in Islam. Istanbul: Ikhlas Publications, 1978.

Işımer, Yalçın. 'Atatürküm ve Türkçem.' *Gülhane Tıp Akademisi 1999–2000 Eğitim-Öğretim Yılı Açılış Töreni* (Ankara: GATA, 27 September 1999), 65–72.

İz, Fahir. 'Mehmet Akif: A Biography.' *Erdem*, **4**/11 (May 1988): 311–37.

Izutsu, Toshihiko. *Ethico-Religious Concepts in the Qurʾān*. Montreal: McGill-Queen's University Press, 2002.

The Concept of Belief in Islamic Theology. Kuala Lumpur: Islamic Book Trust, 2006.

Al-Jabri, Mohammed ʿAbed. *Arab-Islamic Philosophy: A Contemporary Critique*. Trans. Aziz Abbassi. Austin: University of Texas, 1999.

Jauss, Hans Robert. *Toward an Aesthetic of Reception*. Trans. Timothy Bahti. Minneapolis: University of Minnesota Press, 1982.

Jomier, Jacques. *Le Commentaire Coranique du Manar: Tendances Modernes d'Exégèse Coranique en Égypte*. Paris: G. P. Maisaneuve, 1954.

Al-Jundī, Anwar. *ʿAbd al-ʿAzīz Jāwīsh min Ruwwād al-Tarbiya wa-l-Ṣiḥāfa wa-l-Ijtimāʿ*. Cairo: al-Muʾassasa al-Miṣriyya al-ʿĀmma, 1965.

al-Imām al-Marāghī. Cairo: Dār al-Maʿārif, 1952.
Al-Kawākibī, ʿAbd al-Raḥmān. *Umm al-Qurā*. Beirut: Dār al-Rāʾid al-ʿArabī, 1982 [1900].
Kafadar, Cemal. 'The Question of Ottoman Decline.' *Harvard Middle Eastern and Islamic Review*, 4/ 1–2 (1997–8): 30–75.
Kanlıdere, Ahmet. *Reform within Islam: The Tajdid Movement Among the Kazan Tatars, 1809–1917*. Istanbul: Eren, 1997.
Kant, Immanuel. 'Was ist Aufklärung?' (1784); www.projekt-gutenberg.org/kant/aufklae/aufkl001.html.
Kara, Ismail. *Cumhuriyet Türkiyesi'nde Bir Mesele Olarak İslâm*, vol. 2. İstanbul: Dergâh, 2019.
İslâmcıların Siyasî Görüşleri. Istanbul: Mecidiyeköy, 1994.
Türkiye'de İslâmcılık Düşüncesi, 3 vols. Istanbul: Risale, 1986.
Karaca, Yusuf. 'Akif ve İkbal,' *İslami Edebiyat*, 3 (January–March 1990): 28–30.
Karakaş, Berrin. 'Sadece Muhafazakârlardan Oluşan bir Cemiyet Yaşanmaz Olurdu.' *Radikal*, 4 May 2012.
Karay, Refik Halit. *Minelbab İlelmihrab: 1918 Mütarekesi Devrinde Olan Biten İşlere ve Gelip Geçen İnsanlara Dair Bildiklerim*. Istanbul: İnkilâp, 1992.
Kaviraj, Sudipto. 'An Outline of a Revisionist Theory of Modernity.' *European Journal of Sociology*, 46/3 (2005): 497–526.
Kayalı, Ḥasan. 'Islam in the Thought and Politics of Two Late Ottoman Intellectuals: Mehmed Akif and Said Halim.' *Archivum Ottomanicum*, 19 (2001): 307–33.
Kazdal, İsmail. 'Hakikî Müslüman.' *Hilal*, 5/49 (February 1965), 7.
Keddie, Nikki. 'Al-Sayyid Jamal al-Din 'al-Afghani'.' In *Pioneers of Islamic Revival*, ed. Ali Rahnema. London: Zed, 1994.
Kedourie, Elie. *Afghani and ʿAbduh: An Essay on Religious Unbelief and Political Activism in Modern Islam*. London: Cass, 1966.
Kemal, Namık. *Renan Müdafaanamesi*. Istanbul: Mahmut Bey Matbaası, 1910.
'Say.' In *Kıraat-ı Edebiye*, 3 vols. Ed. Celal Sahir Erozan, Mehmed Fuad Köprülü, 51–8. Istanbul: Karabet Matbaası, 1912.
Kendall, Elisabeth. 'Between Politics and Literature: Journals in Alexandria and Istanbul at the end of the Nineteenth Century.' In *Modernity & Culture*, ed. Fawaz, Bayly, Ilbert, 330–43.
Kepel, Gilles. *Muslim Extremism in Egypt: The Prophet and the Pharaoh*. Trans. Jon Rothschild. Berkeley: University of California Press, 1993.
Kerr, Malcolm. *Islamic Reform: The Political and Legal Theories of Muḥammad ʿAbduh and Rashīd Riḍā*. Berkeley: University of California Press, 1966.
Kersten, Carool. *Cosmopolitans and Heretics: New Muslim Intellectuals and the Study of Islam*. London: Hurst, 2011.
'Critical Islam: Muslims and their Religion in a Post-Islamist World.' *Singapore Middle East Papers*, VI (2015): 107–24.
Khalid, Adeeb. *The Politics of Muslim Cultural Reform: Jadīdism in Central Asia*. Berkeley: University of California Press, 1998.
Khalid, Detlev. 'Some Aspects of Neo-Muʿtazilism.' *Islamic Studies*, 8/4 (1969): 319–47.

Khan, Aḥmad. 'Islamic Tradition in an Age of Print: Editing, Printing and Publishing the Classical Heritage.' In *Reclaiming Islamic Tradition: Modern Interpretations of the Classical Heritage*, ed. Elisabeth Kendall, Aḥmad Khan, 52–99. Edinburgh: Edinburgh University Press, 2016.

Al-Khaṭīb, Muḥibb al-Dīn. 'Ḥarakat al-Nashr wa-l-Taʾlīf: Dhuyūl Tadhkirat al-Ḥuffāẓ li-l-Dhahabī,' *al-Zahrāʾ*, Dhū al-Qaʿda 1347 (May 1928), 5/5: 364.

'Al-Wahhābiyya.' *Al-Zahrāʾ*, Ṣafar 1345 (February 1926) 2/2: 81–99.

''Udwān ʿalā ʿUlamāʾ al-Islām Yajib An Yakūn Lahu Ḥadd Yaqif ʿIndahu.' In *Ṣafʿāt al-Burhān*, al-Kawtharī, 57–62. Cairo: al-Azhariyya li-l-Turāth, 2005.

Kinross, Patrick Balfour. *Atatürk: The Rebirth of a Nation*. London: Weidenfeld & Nicolson, 1990 [1964].

Al-Khālidī, ʿAbd al-Fattāḥ. *Sayyid Quṭb: Min al-Mīlād ilā al-Istishhād*. Damascus: Dār al-Qalam, 2007.

Khalil, Mohammad Ḥasan. *Islam and The Fate of Others: The Salvation Question*. Oxford: Oxford University Press, 2012.

Kieser, Hans-Lukas. 'Europe's Seminal Proto-Fascist? Historically Approaching Ziya Gökalp, Mentor of Turkish Nationalism.' *Die Welt des Islams*, **61**/4 (2021): 411–47.

Kister, M. J. '"Do not Assimilate Yourselves …" Lā tashabbahū …' *Jerusalem Studies in Arabic and Islam*, **12** (1989): 321–70.

Köni, Hakan. 'Saudi Influence on Islamic Institutions in Turkey Beginning in the 1970s.' *Middle East Journal*, **66**/1 (2012): 97–110.

Knysh, Alexander. *Ibn ʿArabī in the Later Islamic Tradition: The Making of a Polemical Image in Medieval Islam*. Albany: State University of New York Press.

Koselleck, Reinhart. *Futures Past: On the Semantics of Historical Time*. Cambridge, MA: MIT, 1985.

Kramer, Hans Martin. 'Pan-Asianism's Religious Undercurrents: The Reception of Islam and Translation of the Qur'ān in Twentieth-Century Japan.' *The Journal of Asian Studies*, **73**/3 (August 2014): 619–40.

Kuran, Timur. *The Long Divergence: How Islamic Law Held Back the Middle East*. Princeton: Princeton University Press, 2010.

Kurucu, Ali Ulvi. *Gecelerin Gündüzü: Nurlu Belde Medine'den Yazılar*. Istanbul: Marifet, 1990.

Kurzman, Charles, ed. *Modernist Islam, 1840–1940: A Sourcebook*. New York: Oxford University Press, 2002.

Kushner, David. 'The Place of the Ulema in the Ottoman Empire During the Age of Reform (1839–1918).' *Turcica*, **19** (1987): 51–74.

The Rise of Turkish Nationalism, 1876–1908. London: Cass, 1977.

Kutay, Cemal. *Çağımızda bir Asr-ı Saadet Müslümanı Bediüzzaman Said Nursî*. Istanbul: Yeni Asya, 1980.

Lacroix, Stephane. 'Between Revolution and Apoliticism: Nasir al-Din al-Albānī and his Impact on the Shaping of Contemporary Salafism.' In *Global Salafism: Islam's New Religious Movement*, ed. Roel Meijer, 59–82. London: Hurst, 2009.

Ḥākimiyya.' In *EI3*, http://dx.doi.org/10.1163/1573-3912_ei3_COM_30217.

Landau, Jacob. *The Politics of Pan-Islam: Ideology and Organization*. Oxford: Clarendon Press, 1990.
Landau-Tasseron, Ella. 'The "Cyclical Reform": A Study of the *mujaddid* Tradition,' *Studia Islamica*, **70** (1989): 79–117.
Laoust, Henri. 'Le réformisme orthodoxe des "Salafiya" et les caractères généraux de son orientation actuelle.' *Revue des études islamiques*, **2** (1932): 175–224.
Lauzière, Henri. 'The Construction of Salafiyya: Reconsidering Salafism from the Perspective of Conceptual History.' *IJMES*, **42**/3 (2010): 369–89.
The Making of Salafism: Islamic Reform in the Twentieth Century. New York: Columbia University Press, 2016.
'What We Mean versus What They Meant by "Salafi": A Reply to Frank Griffel.' *Die Welt des Islams*, **56**/1 (2016): 89–96.
Le Bon, Gustave. *La civilisation des Arabes*. Paris: Firmin-Didot, 1884.
Lefèvre, Raphaël. *Ashes of Hama: The Muslim Brotherhood in Syria*. London: Hurst, 2013.
Lewis, Bernard. 'Some Reflections on the Decline of the Ottoman Empire.' *Studia Islamica*, **9** (1958): 111–27.
The Emergence of Modern Turkey. London: Oxford University Press, 1961.
'The Mongols, the Turks and the Muslim Polity.' *Transactions of the Royal Historical Society*, **18** (1968): 49–68.
Lewis, Geoffrey. *The Turkish Language Reform: A Catastrophic Success*. Oxford: Oxford University Press, 1999.
Loimeier, Roman. 'Is There Something like "Protestant Islam?"' *Die Welt des Islams*, **45**/2 (2005): 216–54.
Lucas, Scott C. 'The Legal Principles of Muḥammad b. Ismāʿīl Al-Bukhārī and their Relationship to Classical Salafi Islam.' *Islamic Law and Society*, **13**/3 (2006): 289–324.
'Where are the Legal Ḥadīth? A Study of the Muṣannaf of Ibn Abī Shayba.' *Islamic Law and Society*, **25**/3 (2008): 283–314.
Lüdke, Tilman. '(Not) Using Political Islam: The German Empire and its Failed Propaganda Campaign in the Near and Middle East, 1914–1918 and Beyond.' In *Jihad and Islam in World War I*, ed. Eric Zürcher, 71–94. Leiden: Leiden University Press, 2016.
MacIntyre, Alasdair. *After Virtue: A Study in Moral Theory*. London: Bloomsbury, 2013.
Madelung, Wilferd. 'The Origins of the Controversy Concerning the Creation of the Koran.' In *Orientalia Hispanica sive studia F. M. Pareja octogenario dicata*, ed. J. M. Barral, 504–25. Leiden: E. J. Brill, 1974.
'The Spread of Māturīdism and the Turks.' In *Actas IV: Congresso de Estudos Arabes e Islamicos, Coimbra-Lisboa 1968*, 109–68. Leiden: Brill, 1971.
Maḥfūẓ, Ḥāfiẓ and Nabīla Isḥāq. *Iqbāl wa-l-Azhar*. Cairo: Dār al-Bayān, 1999.
Majallat al-Majmaʿ al-Fiqhī al-Islāmī. 'Bi-Shaʾn al-Khilāf al-Fiqhī bayn al-Madhāhib wa-l-Taʿaṣṣub al-Madhhabī.' Year 4, 2nd ed. (Mecca: World Muslim League, 2005), 383–6.
Makdisi, George. 'Law and Traditionalism in the Institutions of Learning of Medieval Islam.' In *Theology and Law in Islam*, ed. Gustave Grunebaum, 75–88. Wiesbaden: Harrassowitz, 1971.

Al-Maqdisī, Abū Muḥammad. *Al-Kawāshif al-Jaliyya fī Kufr al-Dawla al-Saʿūdiyya*. Amman: Minbar al-Tawḥīd wa-l-Jihād, 1989.

Millat Ibrāhīm wa-Daʿwā al-Anbiyāʾ wa-l-Mursalīn. Amman: npa, 1984.

Mardin, Ebü'l-Ula. *Huzur Dersleri*, 3 vols. Istanbul: Ismail Akgün, 1966.

Mardin, Şerif. *Religion and Social Change in Modern Turkey: The Case of Bediüzzaman Said Nursi*. Albany: State University of New York Press, 1989.

The Genesis of Young Ottoman Thought: A Study in the Modernization of Turkish Political Ideas. Princeton: Princeton University Press, 1962.

Massad, Joseph. *Islam in Liberalism*. Chicago: University of Chicago Press, 2015.

Al-Maʿṣūmī, Muḥammad Sulṭān. *Hal al-Muslim Mulzām bi-Ittibāʿ Madhhab Muʿayyan min al-Madhāhib al-Arbaʿa? Ed. Salīm ibn ʿĪd al-Hilālī*. Riyadh: Markaz al-Dirāsat al-Manhajiyya al-Salafiyya, 1984.

Matar, Nabil. 'Confronting Decline in Early Modern Arabic Thought.' *Journal of Early Modern History*, 9/1 (2005): 51–78.

Matthiesen, Toby. 'Saudi Arabia and the Cold War.' In *Salman's Legacy: The Dilemmas of a New Era in Saudi Arabia*, ed. Madawi Al-Rasheed, 217–33. London: Hurst, 2018.

Meeker, Michael. 'The New Muslim Intellectuals in the Republic of Turkey.' In *Islam in Modern Turkey*, ed. Richard Tapper, 189–219. London: I. B. Tauris, 1991.

Melchert, Christopher. 'Al-Barbahārī.' In *EI3*, http://dx.doi.org/10.1163/1573-3912_ei3_COM_22944.

'Muḥammad Nāṣir al-Dīn al-Albānī and Traditional Hadith Criticism.' In *Reclaiming Islamic Tradition: Modern Interpretations of the Classical Heritage*, ed. Elisabeth Kendall, Aḥmad Khan, 43–51. Edinburgh: Edinburgh University Press, 2016.

'The Adversaries of Aḥmad Ibn Ḥanbal.' *Arabica*, 44/2 (April 1997): 233–53.

The Formation of the Sunni Schools of Law, 9th–10th Centuries C.E. Series: Studies in Islamic Law and Society, Vol. 4. Leiden: Brill, 1997.

'The Relation of Ibn Taymiyya and Ibn Qayyim al-Jawziyya to the Ḥanbalī School of Law.' In *Islamic Theology, Philosophy and Law: Debating Ibn Taymiyya and Ibn Qayyim al-Jawziyya*, ed. Alina Kokoschka, Birgit Krawietz, Georges Tamer, 146–61. Berlin: De Gruyter, 2013.

Meloy, John Lash. 'Ibn Fahd.' In *EI3*, http://dx.doi.org/10.1163/1573-3912_ei3_COM_30441.

Mertoğlu, Suat. 'Ahmed Muhiddin: Hayatı, Eserleri, Düşüncesi.' In *Modern Türklükte Kültür Hareketi, by Ahmed Muhiddin and* ed. Suat Mertoğlu, 3–46. Istanbul: Küre, 2004.

Messick, Brinkley. *The Calligraphic State: Textual Domination and History in a Muslim Society*. Berkeley: University of California Press, 1993.

Méténier, Edouard. 'Al-Ālūsī family.' In *EI3*, http://dx.doi.org/10.1163/1573-3912_ei3_COM_22713.

Michot, Yahya. *Against Smoking: An Ottoman Manifesto*. Oxford: Interface Publications, 2010.

Mignolo, Walter and Catherine Walsh. *On Decoloniality: Concepts, Analytics, Praxis*. Durham: Duke University Press, 2018.

Mignon, Laurent. 'Lost in Transliteration: A Few Remarks on the Armeno-Turkish Novel and Turkish Literary Historiography.' In *Between Religion and Language: Turkish-speaking Christians, Jews and Greek-speaking Muslims and Catholics in the Ottoman Empire*, ed. Evangelia Balta, Mehmet Sönmez, 111–23. Istanbul: Eren 2011.

'Of Moors, Jews and Gentiles.' *Journal of Turkish Studies*, 35/1 (June 2011): 65–83.

'Sömürge Sonrası Edebiyat ve Tanzimat Sonrası Edebiyat Üzerine Notlar.' In *Elifbâlar Sevdası*, Laurent Mignon, 77–89. Ankara: Hece Yayınları, 2003.

'The Literati and the Letters: A Few Words on the Turkish Alphabet Reform.' *Journal of the Royal Asiatic Society*, 20/1 (2010): 11–24.

Minault, Gail. 'Sayyid Aḥmad Dehlavi and the 'Delhi Renaissance'.' In *Delhi through the Ages: Essays in Urban History, Culture, and Society*, ed. Robert E. Frykenberg, 287–98. Delhi: Oxford University Press, 1986.

Mitchell, Timothy. *Colonising Egypt*. Berkeley: University of California Press, 1991.

Moran, Berna. *Türk Romanına Eleştirel bir Bakış: Ahmet Mithat'tan, A. H. Tanpınar'a*. İstanbul: İletişim Yayınları, 1983.

Mouline, Nabil. *The Clerics of Islam: Religious Authority and Political Power in Saudi Arabia*. New Haven: Yale University Press, 2014.

Moustafa, Ahmed and Stefan Sperl. *The Cosmic Script: Sacred Geometry and the Science of Arabic Penmanship*. London: Thames & Hudson, 2014.

Mühibbizade. 'Seyyid Kutub Kimdir?' *Hilal*, 5/54 (August 1965), 20–1.

Muhiddin, Ahmed. *Modern Türklükte Kültür Hareketi*. Ed. Suat Mertoğlu. Istanbul: Küre, 2004.

Musallam, Adnan. 'Sayyid Quṭb and Social Justice, 1945–1948.' *Journal of Islamic Studies*, 4/1 (1993): 52–70.

Mustansir, Mir. *Iqbal*. New Delhi: Oxford University Press, 2006.

Nadwī, Abū al-Ḥasan. *Mādhā Khasira al-ʿĀlam bi-Inḥiṭāṭ al-Muslimīn*. Cairo: Maktabat al-Īmān, 1994.

Mudhakkirāt Sāʾiḥ fī al-Sharq al-ʿArabī. Beirut: Muʾassasat al-Risāla, 1975.

Nafi, Basheer. 'Abu al-Thanaʾ al-Alusi: An Alim, Ottoman Mufti, and Exegete of the Qurʾan.' *IJMES*, 34/3 (2002): 465–94.

'A Teacher of Ibn ʿAbd al-Wahhāb: Muḥammad Ḥayāt al-Sindī and the Revival of Aṣḥab al-Ḥadīth's Methodology.' *Islamic Law and Society*, 13 (2006): 208–41.

Naim, Mustafa. 'Luterlik Yapmak Istiyorlar.' *Medrese İtikadları*, 2 Ağustos 1329 (15 August 1913), issue 13: 103–4.

Nasr, Vali. *Mawdudi and the Making of Islamic Revivalism*. New York: Oxford University Press, 1996.

Nawas, John. 'A Reexamination of Three Current Explanations for al-Maʾmun's Introduction of the *Miḥna*.' *IJMES*, 26/4 (1994): 615–29.

Neep, Daniel. '"What Have the Ottomans Ever Done for Us?" Why History Matters for Politics in the Arab Middle East.' *International Affairs*, 17 September 2021, https://doi.org/10.1093/ia/iiab145.

Nettler, Ronald. *Past Trials and Present Tribulations: A Muslim Fundamentalist's View of the Jews*. Oxford: Pergamon, 1987.

Nietzsche, Friedrich. *The Untimely Meditations (Thoughts Out of Season Parts I and II)*. Trans. Anthony M. Ludovici, Adrian Collins. Lawrence, KS: Digireads.com, 2009.

Al-Nīsābūrī, Muslim ibn al-Ḥajjāj. *Al-Jāmiʿ al-Ṣaḥīḥ (Ṣaḥīḥ Muslim)*. Beirut: al-Jīl, 2009.

Nuri, Celal. *Türk İnkılabı*. Istanbul: Sühulet Kütüphanesi, 1926.

Ochsenwald, William. *Religion, Society, and the State in Arabia: The Hijaz Under Ottoman Control, 1840–1908*. Columbus: Ohio State University Press, 1984.

O'Hanlon, Rosalind. 'Contested Conjunctures: Brahman Communities and "Early Modernity" in India.' *American Historical Review*, **118**/3 (2013): 765–87.

Olidort, Jacob. *In Defense of Tradition: Muḥammad Nāṣir Al-Dīn Al-Albānī and the Salafī Method*. PhD thesis, Princeton University, 2015.

Önder, Mehmet. 'İkbal'in Yaşamı ve Mevlana Hayranlığı.' *Pakistan Postası*, **24**/1 (January 1976): 5–6, 14.

'Mehmet Akif ve Muhammed İkbal.' *Milli Kültür*, **57** (May 1987), 51–3.

Özcan, Ömer. 'Osmanlının son Şeyhülislam'ı Mustafa Sabri Efendi'nin Said Nursi pişmanlığı.' *Risale Haber*, 12 March 2017; www.risalehaber.com/osmanlinin-son-seyhulislami-mustafa-sabri-efendinin-said-nursi-pismanligi-296674h.htm.

Özdalga, Elisabeth. 'The Hidden Arab: A Critical Reading of the Notion of "Turkish Islam".' *Middle Eastern Studies*, **42**/4 (July 2006): 551–70.

Özervarlı, M. Sait. 'Alternative Approaches to Modernization in the Late Ottoman Period: Izmirli Ismail Hakkı's Religious Thought against Materialist Scientism.' *IJMES*, **39**/1 (2007): 77–102.

'Reading Durkheim Through Ottoman Lenses: Interpretations of Customary Law, Religion, and Society by the School of Gökalp.' *Modern Intellectual History*, **14**/2 (2017): 393–419.

Özgür, Iren. *Islamic Schools in Modern Turkey: Faith, Politics, and Education*. Cambridge: Cambridge University Press, 2012.

Pall, Zoltan. *Lebanese Salafis Between the Gulf and Europe*. Amsterdam: Amsterdam University Press, 2013.

Pierret, Thomas. *Religion and State in Syria: The Sunni ʿulamaʾ from Coup to Revolution*. Cambridge: Cambridge University Press, 2013.

Quijano, Aníbal. 'Coloniality and Modernity/Rationality.' *In Cultural Studies*, **21**/2–3 (2007): 168–78.

Pollock, Sheldon. 'Pretextures of Time.' *History and Theory*, **46** (October 2007): 366–83.

Radtke, Bernd. 'Between Projection and Suppression: Some Considerations Concerning the Study of Sufism.' In *Shiʿa Islam, Sects and Sufism*, ed. Frederick De Jong, 70–82.

Rahman, Fazlur. *Islam and Modernity: Transformation of an Intellectual Tradition*. Chicago: University of Chicago Press, 1982.

Rāʾif, Aḥmad. *Al-Bawwāba al-Sawdāʾ: Ṣafaḥāt min Tārīkh al-Ikhwān al-Muslimīn*. Cairo: al-Zahrāʾ li-l-Iʿlām al-ʿArabī, 1985.

Ramadan, Tariq. *Aux Sources du Renouveau Musulman*. Paris: Bayard Editions/Centurion, 1998.

Rao, Velcheru Narayana and David Shulman. *Textures of Time: Writing History in South India*, 1600–1800. Delhi: Permanent Black, 2001.

Redissi, Hamidi. 'The Refutation of Wahhabism in Arabic Sources, 1745–1932.' In *Kingdom Without Borders: Saudi Arabia's Political, Religious and Media Frontiers*, ed. Madawi Al-Rasheed, 157–81. London: Hurst, 2008.

Reid, D. M. *The Odyssey of Faraḥ Anṭūn: A Syrian Christian's Quest for Secularism*. Minneapolis: Bibliotheca Islamica, 1975.

Reinhart, Kevin. 'Civilization and its Discussants: Medeniyet and the Turkish Conversion to Modernism.' In *Converting Cultures: Religion, Ideology, and Transformations of Modernity*, ed. Dennis Washburn, A. Kevin Reinhart, 267–79. Series: Social Sciences in Asia, Vol. 14. Leiden: Brill, 2007.

Renan, Ernest. *L'Islam et la science; avec la réponse d'Afghâni*. Montpellier: Archange Minotaure, 2003.

Ricoeur, Paul. *Hermeneutics*. Trans. David Pellauer. Cambridge: Polity, 2016.

Riḍā, Rashid. 'Al-Ḥikma al-Sharʿiyya fī Muḥākamat al-Qādiriyya wa-l-Rifāʿiyya.' *Al-Manār*, 1/28 (7 October 1898): 524–34.

'Bāb al-Suʾāl wa-l-Fatwā.' *Al-Manār*, 6/17 (20 November 1903): 823–31.

'Riḥlat Ṣāḥib *al-Manār* fī Sūriyya – 3.' *Al-Manār*, 11/12 (22 January 1909): 936–53.

Tārīkh al-Ustādh al-Imām al-Shaykh Muḥammad ʿAbduh, 3 vols. Cairo: Dār al-Faḍīla, 2006.

Robinson, Glenn. 'Jihadi Information Strategy: Sources, Opportunities, and Vulnerabilities.' In *Information Strategy and Warfare: A Guide to Theory and Practice*, ed. John Arquilla, Douglas A. Borer, 86–112. London: Routledge, 2007.

Rock-Singer, Aaron. 'Prayer and the Islamic Revival: A Timely Challenge.' *IJMES*, 48/2 (2016): 293–312.

Ross, Danielle. 'Caught in the Middle: Reform and Youth Rebellion in Russia's Madrasas, 1900–10.' *Kritika: Explorations in Russian and Eurasian History*, 16/1 (2015): 57–89.

Rudolph, Ulrich. *Al-Māturīdī and the Development of Sunnī Theology in Samarqand*. Series: Islamic History and Civilization, Vol. 100. Trans. Rodrigo Adem. Leiden: Brill, 2015.

Runyun, Mustafa. *Dinî ve Ahlakî Konuşmalar*. Ankara: Diyanet, 1955.

Dinî ve Ahlakî Müsahabelerim, vols 1–3. Ankara: Ayyıldız Matbaası, 1957/58.

Hacıbayram Minberinden Hutbelerim. Ankara: Diyanet, 1956.

Rustow, Dankwart. 'The Army and the Founding of the Turkish Republic.' In *Men of Order: Authoritarian Modernization under Atatürk and Reza Shah*, ed. Touraj Atabaki, Eric Zürcher, 164–208. London: I. B. Tauris, 2004.

Sabaseviciute, Giedre. 'Sayyid Quṭb and the Crisis of Culture in Late 1940s Egypt.' *IJMES*, 50/1 (2018): 85–101.

Sābiq, Al-Sayyid. *Fiqh al-Sunna*. Jeddah: Dār al-Qibla al-Thaqāfiyya al-Islāmiyya, 1945.

Safi, Polat. 'History in the Trench: The Ottoman Special Organization – Teşkilat-ı Mahsusa Literature.' *Middle Eastern Studies*, 48/1 (2012): 89–106.

Şahiner, Necmeddin. *Bilinmeyen Taraflarıyla Bediüzzaman Said Nursi*. Istanbul: Nesil, 1999.

Son Şahitler Bediüzzaman Said Nursi'yi Anlatıyor. Istanbul: Yeni Asya, 1994.
Sahota, G.S. 'Uncanny Affinities: A Translation of Iqbal's Preface to Payam-e Mashriq.' *Postcolonial Studies*, 15/4 (2012): 437–52.
Said, Edward. *Covering Islam: How the Media and the Experts Determine How We See the Rest of the World*. London: Routledge & Kegan Paul, 1981.
Orientalism. New York: Vintage, 1994.
Al-Salafī, Abū ʿAbd Allāh Shakīb, ed. *Aqwāl Ahl al-ʿIlm fī Muḥammad al-Ghazālī al-Saqqā*. Riyadh: Saḥāb al-Salafiyya, nda.
Saleh, Walid. 'Preliminary Remarks on the Historiography of *tafsīr* in Arabic: A History of the Book Approach.' *Journal of Qur'anic Studies*, 12 (2010): 6–40.
Salvatore, Armando. *Islam and the Political Discourse of Modernity*. Reading: Ithaca Press, 1997.
Al-Samʿānī, ʿAbd al-Karīm. *Kitāb al-Ansāb*, vol. 7. Hayderabad: Dāʾirat al-Maʿārif al-ʿUthmāniyya, 1976.
Sami, Şemsettin. *Qamus-i Türki*. Istanbul: Çağrı Yayınları, 1996.
Schacht, Joseph. 'New Sources for the History of Muḥammadan Theology.' *Studia Islamica*, 1 (1953): 23–42.
Scharbrodt, Oliver. 'The Salafiyya and Sufism: Muḥammad ʿAbduh and His Risālat al-Wāridāt (Treatise on Mystical Inspirations).' *Bulletin of the School of Oriental and African Studies*, 70/1 (2007): 89–115.
Schimmel, Annemarie. *Gabriel's Wing: A Study into the Religious Ideas of Sir Muḥammad Iqbal*. Numen Book Series, Vol. 6. Leiden: Brill, 1963.
'Önsöz.' In *Cavidname*, by Muhammed İkbal and trans. Annemarie Schmimel, 11–61. Istanbul: Kırkambar, 2010.
Schmitt, Carl. *Political Theology: Four Chapters on the Concept of Sovereignty*. Chicago: University of Chicago Press, 2005 [1922].
The Crisis of Parliamentary Democracy. Trans. Ellen Kennedy. Cambridge: MIT, 1985.
Schulze, Reinhard. *A Modern History of the Islamic World*. London/New York: I. B. Tauris, 2000.
'Was ist die Islamische Aufklärung?' *Die Welt des Islams*, 36/3 (1996): 276–325.
Sedgwick, Mark. *Muhammad Abduh*. Oxford: Oneworld, 2009.
Selek, Sabahattin. *Milli Mücadele*, 2 vols. Istanbul: Burçak Yayınevi, 1966.
Shākir, Aḥmad Muḥammad, ed. *Sharḥ al-Ṭaḥāwīyya fī al-ʿAqīda al-Salafiyya*. Cairo: Dār al-Turāth, 1954.
Shankland, David. *Islam and Society in Turkey*. Huntingdon: Eothen, 1999.
Sheikh, Saeed. *Studies in Iqbal's Thought and Art: Select Articles from the Quarterly 'Iqbal'*. Lahore: Bazm-i Iqbal, 1972.
Shepard, William. 'Islam and Ideology: Towards a Typology.' *IJMES*, 19/3 (1987): 307–35.
'Islam as a "System" in the Later Writings of Sayyid Quṭb.' *Middle Eastern Studies*, 25/1 (1989): 31–50.
Sayyid Quṭb and Islamic Activism: A Translation and Critical Analysis of Social Justice in Islam. Series: Social, Economic and Political Studies of the Middle East and Asia, Vol. 54. Leiden: Brill, 1996.

Sherrill, Charles. *A Year's Embassy to Mustafa Kemal*. New York/London: Charles Scribner, 1934.

Sirry, Mun'im. 'Jamāl al-Dīn al-Qāsimī and the Salafi Approach to Sufism.' *Die Welt des Islams*, 51/1 (2011): 75–108.

Sivan, Emmanuel. *Radical Islam: Medieval Theology and Modern Politics*. New Haven/London: Yale University Press, 1990.

Skovgaard-Petersen, Jakob. *Defining Islam for the Egyptian State: Muftis and Fatwas of the Dār al-Iftā*. Series: Social, Economic and Political Studies of the Middle East and Asia, Vol. 59. Leiden: Brill, 1997.

Smith, Wilfred Cantwell. *Islam in Modern History*. Princeton: Princeton University Press, 1957.

The Meaning and End of Religion. Minneapolis: Fortress Press, 1991 [1962].

Soames, Scott. 'Justice Scalia's Philosophy of Interpretation: From Textualism to Deferentialism.' In *Justice Scalia: Rhetoric and the Rule of Law*, ed. Brian G. Slocum, Francis J. Mootz III, 21–34. Chicago: University of Chicago Press, 2019.

Stoddard, Philip. *The Ottoman Government and the Arabs, 1911 to 1918: A Preliminary Study of the Teskilat-ı Mahsusa*. PhD thesis, Princeton University, 1963.

Szurek, Emmanuel. 'The Linguist and the Politician. The Türk Dil Kurumu and the Field of Power in the Single-party Period.' In *Order and Compromise: Government Practices in Turkey from the Late Ottoman Empire to the Early 21st Century*, ed. Marc Aymes, Benjamin Gourisse, Élise Massicard, 68–96. Series: Social, Economic and Political Studies of the Middle East and Asia, Vol. 113. Leiden: Brill, 2015.

Şentürk, Recep, ed. *Direnen Meal: Akif'in Kur'an Meali'nin Tarihi ve Tahlili*. Istanbul: Mahya, 2016.

'Islamic Reformist Discourses and Intellectuals in Turkey.' In *Reformist Voices of Islam: Mediating Islam and Modernity*, ed. Shireen Hunter, 227–46. Armonk, NY: M. E. Sharpe, 2009.

Şeyhun, Ahmet. *Said Halim Pasha: Ottoman Statesman and Islamist Thinker (1865–1921)*. Istanbul: Isis, 2003.

Ṭāhā, ʿAbd al-Raḥmān. *Buʾs al-Dahrāniyya: al-Naqd al-Iʾtimānī li-Faṣl al-Akhlāq ʿan al-Dīn*. Beirut: Arab Network for Research and Publishing, 2014.

Suʾāl al-Akhlāq: Musāhama fī al-Naqd al-Akhlāqī li-l-Ḥadātha al-Gharbiyya. Casablanca: al-Markaz al-Thaqāfī al-ʿArabī, 2000.

Al-Ṭāhir, Aḥmad Muḥammad. *Jamāʿat Anṣār al-Sunna al-Muḥammadiyya*. Riyadh: Dār al-Faḍīla, 2004.

Al-Ṭahṭāwī, Aḥmad Rāfiʿ. *Tanbīh wa-l-Īqāz li-Mā fī Dhuyūl Tadhkirat al-Ḥuffāẓ*. Damascus: al-Qudsī, 1929.

Tammām, Ḥusām. *Tasalluf al-Ikhwān: Taʾākul al-Uṭrūḥa al-Ikhwāniyya wa-Ṣuʿūd al-Salafiyya fī Jamāʿat al-Ikhwān al-Muslimīn*. Alexandria, Egypt: Bibliotheca Alexandrina/Future Studies Unit, 2010.

Tarlan, Ali Nihat. *İkbal'den Şiirler: Şarktan Haber ve Zebur-u Acem*. Istanbul: Türkiye İş Bankası Kültür Yayınları, 1971.

Taylor, Richard C. 'Averroes on the Ontology of the Human Soul.' *The Muslim World*, **102**/3–4 (2012): 580–96.
Ter-Matevosyan, Vahram. 'Turkish Experience with Totalitarianism and Fascism: Tracing the Intellectual Origins.' *Iran and the Caucasus*, **19**/4 (2015): 387–401.
Terzioğlu, Derin. 'Ibn Taymiyya, al-Siyāsa al-Sharʿiyya, and the Early Modern Ottomans.' In *Historicizing Sunni Islam in the Ottoman Empire, c. 1450–c. 1750*, ed. T. Krstić and D. Terzioğlu, 101–54. Boston: Brill, 2020.
Tezcan, Baki. *The Second Ottoman Empire: Political and Social Transformations in the Early Modern World*. Cambridge: Cambridge University Press, 2010.
Al-Tilmisānī, ʿUmar. *Dhikrāyāt Lā Mudhakkirāt*. Cairo: Dār al-Iʿtiṣām, 1985.
Tınaz, Kerem. *An Imperial Ideology and its Legacy: Ottomanism in a Comparative Perspective, 1894–1928*. DPhil thesis, University of Oxford, 2018.
Topal, Alp Eren. 'Against Influence: Ziya Gökalp in Context and Tradition.' *Journal of Islamic Studies*, **28**/3 (2017): 283–310.
Toth, James. *Sayyid Quṭb: The Life and Legacy of a Radical Islamic Intellectual*. New York: Oxford University Press, 2013.
Toulmin, Stephen. *Return to Reason*. Cambridge: Harvard University Press, 2001.
Tunagür, Yaşar and ʿAdnān Manṣūr, trans. Foreword to *İslam'da Sosyal Adalet*, by Seyyid Kutub. Istanbul: Cağaloğlu Yayınevi, 1962.
Tunaya, Tarık Zafer. *Türkiye'de Siyasal Partiler*, vol. 2. Istanbul: Hürriyet Vakfı Yayınları, 1986.
Türkgeldi, Ali Fuat. *Görüp İşittiklerim*. Ankara: Türk Tarih Kurumu, 1951.
Turnaoğlu, Banu. 'Ideological struggle during the formative years of the Turkish Republic.' *Middle Eastern Studies*, 52/4 (2016): 677–93.
Turner, Colin. *The Qurʾan Revealed: A Critical Analysis of Said Nursi's Epistles of Light*. Berlin: Gerlach, 2013.
Ullah, Haroon K. *Vying for Allah's Vote: Understanding Islamic Parties, Political Violence, and Extremism in Pakistan*. Washington DC: Georgetown University Press, 2014.
Al-ʿUmar, ʿAbd al-Karīm. *Mudhakkirāt al-Ḥājj Muḥammad Amīn al-Ḥusaynī*. Damascus: Ahālī, 1999.
Umm al-Qurā (Mecca newspaper). 'Fī al-Maʾdaba al-Kubrā,' 16 May 1929, no. 229, pp.1 and 3.
Üngör, Uğur Ümit. *The Making of Modern Turkey: Nation and State in Eastern Anatolia, 1913–1950*. Oxford: Oxford University Press, 2011.
Uzer, Umut. 'The Genealogy of Turkish Nationalism: From Civic and Ethnic to Conservative Nationalism in Turkey.' In *Symbiotic Antagonisms: Competing Nationalisms in Turkey*, ed. Ayşe Kadıoğlu, Emin Fuat Keyman, 103–32. Salt Lake City: University of Utah Press, 2011.
Vahide, Şükran. *Islam in Modern Turkey: An Intellectual Biography of Bediuzzaman Said Nursi*. Ed. Ibrāhīm Abu-Rabiʿ. Albany: State University of New York Press, 2005.
Von Grunebaum, Gustave. *Islam: Essays in the Nature and Growth of a Cultural Tradition*. London: Routledge & Kegan Paul, 1955.

Wallerstein, Immanuel. 'The Rise and Future Demise of the World Capitalist System: Concepts for Comparative Analysis.' *Comparative Studies in Society and History*, **16**/4 (1974), 387–415.

Weber, Max. 'Science as a Vocation.' In *From Max Weber: Essays in Sociology*, ed. H. H. Gerth, Wright Mills. London: Routledge, 2013.

The Protestant Ethic and the Spirit of Capitalism. London: Routledge, 2001 [1904].

Weismann, Itzchak. 'Abū l-Hudā l-Ṣayyādī and the Rise of Islamic Fundamentalism.' *Arabica*, **54**/4 (October 2007): 586–92.

'Modernity from Within: Islamic Fundamentalism and Sufism,' in *Sufis and Salafis in the Contemporary Age*, ed. Lloyd Ridgeon, 9–32.

Taste of Modernity: Sufism, Salafiya, and Arabism in Late Ottoman Damascus. Islamic History and Civilization, Vol. 34. Leiden: Brill, 2001.

'The Invention of a Populist Islamic Leader: Badr al-Dīn al-Ḥasanī, the Religious Educational Movement and the Great Syrian Revolt.' *Arabica*, **52**/1 (2005): 109–39.

Whittingham, Martin. *Al-Ghazālī and the Qur'ān: One Book, Many Meanings*. London: Routledge, 2007.

Wielandt, Rotraud. 'Main Trends of Islamic Theological Thought from the Late Nineteenth Century to Present Times.' In *The Oxford Handbook of Islamic Theology*, ed. Sabine Schmidtke, 707–64. Oxford: Oxford University Press, 2016.

Wiktorowicz, Quintan. 'Anatomy of the Salafi Movement.' *Studies in Conflict and Terrorism*, **29**/3 (2006): 207–39.

Wild, Stefan. 'Islamic Enlightenment and the Paradox of Averroes.' *Die Welt des Islams*, **36**/3 (1996): 379–90.

'Muslim und Madhab: Ein Brief von Tokio nach Mekka und seine Folgen in Damaskus.' In *Die Islamische Welt zwischen Mittelalter und Neuzeit: Festschrift für Hans Robert Roemer zum 65. Geburtstag*, ed. Hans Robert Roemer, Ulrich Haarmann, Peter Bachmann, 674–89. Beirut: Wiesbaden, 1979.

Willi, Victor. *The Fourth Ordeal: A History of the Society of the Muslim Brothers in Egypt, 1973–2013*. Cambridge: Cambridge University Press, 2021.

Wilson, Brett. *Translating the Qur'an in an Age of Nationalism: Print Culture and Modern Islam in Turkey*. Oxford: Oxford University Press, 2014.

Wisnovsky, Robert. 'Avicenna's Islamic Reception.' In *Interpreting Avicenna: Critical Essays*, ed. Peter Adamson, 190–213. Cambridge: Cambridge University Press.

Woodside, Alexander. *Lost Modernities: China, Vietnam, Korea, and the Hazards of World History*. Cambridge, MA: Harvard University Press, 2006.

Al-Yassini, Ayman. *Religion and State in the Kingdom of Saudi Arabia*. Boulder, CO: Westview, 1985.

Yavuz, Hakan. *Islamic Political Identity in Turkey*. Oxford; Oxford University Press, 2003.

Yeşilada, Birol. 'The Refah Party Phenomenon in Turkey.' In *Comparative Political Parties and Party Elites: Essays in Honor of Samuel J. Eldersveld*, ed. Birol Yeşilada, 123–50. Ann Arbor: University of Michigan Press, 1999.

Yıldırım, Ramazan. *Medrese'den Üniversite'ye Ali Özek*. Istanbul: Düşün Yayıncılık, 2012.

Yılmaz, Arif. 'Mehmet Akif Ersoy'un Şiirlerinde Halk Dilinin Kullanımı.' *Mustafa Kemal University Journal of Social Sciences Institute*, 6/11 (2009): 189–210.

Yılmaz, Hale. 'Learning to Read (Again): The Social Experiences of Turkey's 1928 Alphabet Reform.' *IJMES*, 43/4 (2011): 677–97.

Zaman, Muḥammad Qasim. *Modern Islamic Thought in a Radical Age: Religious Authority and Internal Criticism*. Cambridge: Cambridge University Press, 2012.

'The Sovereignty of God in Modern Islamic Thought.' *Journal of the Royal Asiatic Society*, 25/3 (July 2015), 389–418.

Zeghal, Malika. *Islamism in Morocco: Religion, Authoritarianism, and Electoral Politics*. Princeton: Markus Wiener, 2008.

Zilfi, Madeline. *The Politics of Piety: The Ottoman Ulema in the Post-Classical Age (1600–1800)*. Minneapolis: Bibliotheca Islamica, 1988.

Zollner, Barbara. 'Prison Talk: The Muslim Brotherhood's Internal Struggle during Gamal Abdel Nasser's Persecution, 1954 to 1971.' *IJMES*, 39/3 (2007): 411–33.

Zysow, Aron. *The Economy of Certainty: An Introduction to the Typology of Islamic Legal Theory*. Atlanta: Lockwood, 2013.

DOCUMENT ARCHIVES

Arnold Toynbee Papers, Bodleian Modern Papers, Weston Library, Oxford; files MS. 13967/50/1–2, MS. 13967/51–8, MS. 13967/77.

Arthur Boutwood Papers, Corpus Christi College Library, Cambridge, UK.

Istanbul Müftülük, Shariʿa Records and Meşihat Archive; files 2/1786/1 and 2/1787/1.

Lambeth Palace Library, Church of England; MS. 1617, 1618, 1620 and Douglas 10, 15, 17, 24, 67, 70, 73.

The National Archives of the United Kingdom, London; Charity Commission files CHAR 6/34–9 and Foreign Office file FO 371/4158.

WEBSITES

ʿAbd al-Wahhāb ʿAzzām, biography: https://archive.islamonline.net/?p=9053.

Al-Albānī, lecture, 27 August 1960: www.4shared.com/file/75693629/8f9c2cdd/albani-1960.html?dirPwdVerified=4f3514e1.

Feyzullah Efendi, biography: https://feyzullahefendi.wordpress.com.

Ḥamza Türkmen, article on Sayyid Quṭb, 'Seyyid Kutub Anlaşılabildi mi?' Haksöz Okulu website, August 1995; www.haksozhaber.net/okul/seyyid-kutub-anlasilabildi-mi-1019yy.htm.

İsmail Kara, interview, October 2017, *The Maydan*: www.themaydan.com/2017/10/islam-islamism-turkey-conversation-ismail-kara.

Jonathan Brown, article, 7 March 2018, *Yaqeen*: 'The Fate of Non-Muslims: Perspectives on Salvation Outside of Islam,' https://yaqeeninstitute.org/en/jonathan-brown/the-fate-of-non-muslims-perspectives-on-salvation-outside-of-islam.

Kevseri, letter, 5 March 1952: https://www.facebook.com/arslan.hamdi2016/posts/10155424320453953.

M. A. Sherif, article, undated, *Salaam*. 'Review: A System of Life, Mawdudi and the Ideologisation of Islam,' www.salaam.co.uk/a-system-of-life-mawdudi-and-the-ideologisation-of-islam.

Mark Sedgwick, blog on Muḥammad ʿAbduh, 18 April 2012: http://Abduhinfo.blogspot.com/2012/04/solution-to-problem-of-why-Muḥammad.html.

Mehmed Akif, article on his nationalism: 'Mehmet Akif Ersoy nədən millətçiliyi deyil, ümmətçiliyi seçdi?' Modern.az, 10 February 2015; http://modern.az/articles/72035/1/#gsc.tab=0.

Said Salih Kaymakci, on Wael Hallaq's *The Impossible State*, 18 December 2016: www.themaydan.com/2016/12/book-review-wael-hallaqs-impossible-state-said-salih-kaymakci.

Shaykh Khiḍr, biography: 'Sheikh Muḥammad Al-Khiḍr Ḥusayn, un Grand Imâm d'Al-Azhar,' islamophile.org, 16 May 2000, http://islamophile.org/spip/Sheikh-Muhammad-Al-Khidr-Husayn,376.html

T24, '"PayitahtAbdülhamid" dizisinde Mehmet Akif Ersoy'a "Mason" göndermesi,' 13 October 2020: https://t24.com.tr/video/payitaht-abdulhamid-dizisinde-mehmet-akif-ersoy-a-mason-gondermesi,33217Ḥusayn,376.html.

Walid Saleh, lecture: 'The Politics of Qurʾanic Hermeneutics: Royalties on Interpretation,' 6 July 2009, www.international.ucla.edu/cnes/podcasts/article.asp?parentid=110233.

INTERVIEWS

Ashraf ʿAbd al-Ghaffār. Istanbul, 17 August 2018.

Berat el-Banna. Istanbul, 20 August 2018.

Hasan Bitmez. Gebze, 23 August 2018.

Ibrāhīm Munīr. London, 20 January 2019.

Kamāl al-Hilbāwī. London, 6 September 2018.

Khurshīd Aḥmad. Leicester, 23 February 2019.

LECTURES

Andréas Stauder, Materiality and Reading (ancient/modern) of Ancient Egyptian Texts, Queen's College, University of Oxford, 31 May 2017.

Halil Berktay, Overview of Ottoman and Turkish History, EDEP İhtisas Merkezi, Ibn Haldun University, 10 July 2017.

Index

ʿAbd al-Rāziq, ʿAlī 78, 204
ʿAbduh, Muḥammad 77
  Akif 106, 128, 196
  Anṭūn debate 94–106
  Ashʿari criticism 91
  created Qurʾan 144–5
  early works 88
  Kevseri 131–45
  Risālat al-Tawḥīd 15, 60, 88–9, 101–2, 141, 143, 158
  Sabri 81–106
  Salafism 160
  Transvaal fatwa 139
Abū Ghudda, ʿAbd al-Fattāḥ 67, 154, 166
Abū Zayd, Bakr 166
Abū Zayd, Naṣr 212
al-Afghānī, Jamāl al-Dīn 10, 28
Agamben, Giorgio 211
Aḥmadiyya 87, 130, 142
Akçura, Yūsuf 21, 58, 197
Akif, Mehmed 27–38
  ʿAbduh, view of 106, 128, 196
  al-Afghānī, view of 196
  Arabic 74–5
  death 27
  early life 27
  Egypt 36, 64–6
  Germany and Najd trip 33, 119
  Gölgeler confiscated 69
  Hanotaux, Gabriel 106–10
  modernist theology in poetry 126, 130
  Qurʾan 24–5
  Reinhart Dozy 190
  Safahat 29–32, 35, 37, 69, 74, 126, 191
  sermons 35, 192, 198
  Turkish nationalism 189–200
  Turkish scholarship 57–64
AKP 60–1
al-Albānī, Nāṣir al-Dīn 56, 63, 162–73, 239
al-Ālūsī, Maḥmūd Shukrī 157–8
Anglican Church 35, 111–18, 248–9
Anṭūn, Faraḥ 94–106, 134, 157, 206
Arabism 136, 160
Arendt, Hannah 210–11
Arkoun, Mohammed 212–13
Armenian genocide 195–6
Asad, Talal 214–15
Ashʿarism 171
Atatürk, Mustafa Kemal
  Akif 35, 37, 65–6, 191, 194
  Anglican Church 111, 114–17
  Iqbal 124
  Kevseri 70
  Nursi 248
  Quṭb 228
  Sabri 42–3, 65–6
Al-Azhar 45, 53, 59, 64, 67, 78–9, 87, 111, 131, 141–2, 148–9, 161, 168, 171–2, 204–5, 215, 242, 253, 258, 262, 275
ʿAzzām, ʿAbd al-Wahhāb 60, 67, 118–21, 124
al-Bannā, Ḥasan 47, 67–8, 162, 172, 218, 235, 244, 253, 257–8
al-Bannā, Sayf al-Islām Ḥasan 258

Banūrī, Yūsuf 53–4, 56, 72, 142
Bayṭār, Muḥammad Bahjat 56, 160
Beyanülhak 3, 20, 82, 84
al-Baghdādī, al-Khaṭīb 56, 143
Bigiev, Mūsā Jārullāh 68, 82–4, 93
Biography 26–7
Boutwood, Arthur 112–13
Bruckmayr, Philipp 91
buṭlān al-tasalsul 101
al-Būṭī, Sa'īd Ramaḍān 168, 170, 177, 244

Carrel, Alexis 229, 233–4
Cemiyet-i Müderrisin 42
Cenkçiler, Ali Yakub 42 (footnote 18), 47 (footnote 111), 258–9
Cevdet, Abdullah 13 (footnote 51), 64, 190
Christ's resurrection 141
Circassian 33, 49, 62, 134–5, 191
Communism 114–15, 222, 229
CUP 13, 19, 31, 34, 40–3, 50–1, 64, 84, 86, 92, 109, 111, 115, 140, 191, 196, 199, 201, 203, 209, 248, 256
al-Dārimī, 'Uthmān ibn Sa'īd 134, 148

Decline, theory of 9–14
  Salafi view of 14–18
dinsizlik 137, 245, 249
Diyanet 24, 118, 258, 262, 264

Edib, Eşref 28, 33, 36, 58
Egypt
  Akif 35–7, 64–5
  Ibn Taymiyya publishing 144–5
  Iqbāl 119–20
  Kevseri 52–6, 66–7
  liberal age modernism 77–81
  place of exile 64–5, 68
  Quṭb 216–39
  Sabri 43, 45, 65–6, 204–12
Enlightenment 4, 7, 12, 15–16, 29, 81, 87, 97, 99–101, 116, 131, 208, 210, 234, 240, 243, 245, 265
Enver 32–3, 111
Erbakan, Necmettin 60, 198, 254–6, 258, 262, 264, 268

Fanon, Frantz 231
Fascism 234, 244
Fatalism 20, 47, 57, 93, 109, 266
Fikret, Tevfik 38
al-Fiqī, Muḥammad Ḥāmid 146, 149, 161
Foucault, Michel 176, 206, 210–11
Free Officers 1

al-Ghazālī 81, 94, 96, 156, 168, 176, 247
al-Ghazālī, Muḥammad 168
Gibb E. J. W. 10
Gibb, Hamilton 78, 80
Gökalp, Ziya 10, 20–3, 34, 38, 58, 74, 81, 121, 126, 137, 191, 197–8, 202, 241, 260
Guizot, Francois 5, 10, 13, 107
Gülenists 255, 268
Gümüşhanevi 50, 159, 255, 264

ḥākimiyya 226–8, 231, 236–7
Hakkı, İsmail 20, 113, 116–17, 259, 264
Halim, Abbas 36–7
Halim, Said 23, 34, 36, 116, 121, 126, 195, 199, 242, 244–5
Hallaq, Wael 207–9, 216
Ḥanafī, Ḥasan 212
Ḥanafism 48, 51, 55
Ḥanbalism 156, 167
Hanotaux, Gabriel 29, 99, 106–10
Haykel, Bernard 16, 175–6
Hegel 5, 102, 123
Hourani, Albert 80, 99–100
al-Huḍaybī, Ḥasan 237, 239
Ḥusayn, Sharīf 32, 44
Ḥusayn, Ṭāhā 72, 78–9, 217
Ḥusaynī, Amīn 68
al-Ḥusaynī, Isḥāq Mūsā 62

Ibn 'Arabī 14, 28, 30, 83, 106, 129, 241, 251
ibn Bāz, 'Abd al-'Azīz 166
Ibn Rushd 94–6, 101, 128
Ibn Sīnā 95–6, 128, 144
Ibn Taymiyya 14, 20, 55, 63, 89, 104, 132–3, 135–6, 138, 145–6, 148–9, 151, 154, 156–8, 160–2, 164, 177, 231–2
İbrahim, Abdürreşid 170, 170 (footnote 218), 191
İhsan Efendi 25, 66
īmān 48, 132, 146, 150, 218, 231, 245
ijtihād 81, 104, 136, 152, 156, 161, 171, 207, 227, 241, 252
Iqbāl, Muḥammad 118–30
irjā' 149, 173
Işık, Hüseyin Hilmi 178 (footnote 260)
İskenderpaşa mosque 255
İslam Mecmuası 20
Islamisation 23, 169, 189, 245, 254
Islamist, as a term 21, 59, 239, 242, 262

al-Jābirī, Muḥammad ʿĀbid 212
jāhiliyya 222–4, 228–30, 235, 259
Japan 109, 191–2
Jāwīsh, ʿAbd al-ʿAzīz 33, 111, 115–18, 196
al-Jazāʾirī, Ṭāhir 160
al-jihāt 133, 148, 160
jumūd 13, 28, 135, 206, 211

Kadızadelis 9, 18
Kant 102, 104
Karaman, Hayreddin 263
Kemal, Namık 10–11, 28
Kevseri, Zahid
  ʿAbduh 131–45
  al-Albānī 153–4, 162
  Arabic 69–70
  during war 52
  early life 48–57
  Egypt 52–6, 65–6
  Syria 65
  Turkish scholarship 61–3
  waqf 210, 215
Khalaf Allāh, Muḥammad Aḥmad 217
Khān, Sayyid Aḥmad 13
al-Khaṭīb, Muḥibb al-Dīn 56, 132, 146, 160, 162, 172
Kısakürek, Necip Fazıl 254, 256, 260
Köprülü, Fuat 118
Kotku, Mehmed Zahid 255
kufr 83, 147
Kurucu, Ali Ulvi 68, 71, 218, 260

lā-dīniyya 137, 202
lā-madhhabiyya 54, 136–7, 139, 167, 169–71, 177, 243, 245
Language reforms 69–76, 121
Laroui, Abdallah 212
Lausanne, Treaty of 36, 115
Le Bon, Gustave 12
Lenin 114, 232

Maimonides 148 (footnote 97)
al-Manār 28, 84, 89, 99, 138, 162
al-Maqdisī, Abū Muḥammad 168, 233 (footnote 252)
al-Marāghī, Muṣṭafā 45, 78
Massad, Joseph 5
al-Maʿṣūmī, Muḥammad Sulṭān 169–70
Māturīdism 20, 39, 55–6, 87–8, 90–2, 142, 144–55, 175, 237, 243, 245, 252, 264
Mawdūdī, Abū al-Aʿlā 3, 24, 178, 218, 222–8, 232, 238, 244, 261, 268
Midhat, Ahmed 29, 31, 33, 109
miracles 79, 97–8, 101–2, 113, 116, 145, 160
Modernity, theories of 7–8
al-Muʿallimī, ʿAbd al-Raḥmān 56
Muhiddin, Ahmed 20, 240, 242
Muslim Brotherhood 47, 62, 67, 80, 162, 164, 166, 173, 221, 245, 253, 256, 262, 265, 267–8
Muṣṭafā, Shukrī 237–8
Muʿtazilism 88, 91, 143, 147

al-Nabhānī, Yūsuf 160
Nadwī, Abū al-Ḥasan 218, 222, 233, 261
nahḍa 9, 175
Naim, Ahmed 21, 28, 66, 117
Naqshbandism 29–30, 50, 54–5, 91, 159, 247, 250, 254, 264
Naṣīf, Muḥammad 56, 132, 149, 161
Nasser xii, 78, 173, 224, 238, 244, 261
National Forces (Kuva-ı Milliye) 42–3, 115, 193, 195–6
national struggle (*millî mücadele*) 200–4
National Vision (Millî Görüş) 198, 254
Nazif, Süleyman 84, 195
Nietzsche 122–3
Nursi, Said 2, 24, 114, 226, 246–53, 255, 260

Orientalism 8–9, 11–12, 18, 54, 93, 118–19, 121, 161, 178, 190, 214, 225
qidam al-ʿālam 104

particular will 252, 264
positivism 2, 10, 17, 23–4, 48, 76, 137, 220, 226, 228, 266
the Prophet, genius of 46, 102, 105
Protestantism 10, 93, 97, 266

al-qaḍāʾ wa-l-qadar 79 (footnote 6), 89
al-Qaṣīmī, ʿAbd Allāh 78, 216
al-Qāsimī, Jamāl al-Dīn 157–8, 160, 163
Qurʾan
  burning 25
  created 79, 142, 144–5, 245
  translation 24, 37, 46, 58–9, 73, 87, 93
Quṭb, Sayyid 216–22
  Maʿālim fī al-Ṭarīq 224, 229–30, 235
  Sabri 216–22
  Turkish translation 250

Ramaḍān, Saʿīd 253
Reformation 5, 7, 20, 93, 93 (Luther), 266
Renan, Ernest 11, 94, 96–7, 99, 103, 107, 135

Riḍā, Rashīd 56, 58, 79, 87, 111, 135, 138, 146, 157, 160, 162
Risale-i Nur 248, 250, 253
Runyun, Mustafa 59 (footnote 171), 259 (footnote 101)

Sābiq, al-Sayyid 172 (footnote 235), 172
Sabri, İbrahim 25, 46
Sabri, Mustafa
  ʿAbduh 81–93
  Arabic 73
  Arabs vs. Turks 73
  early life 38–48
  during war 42
  Egypt 44, 46, 48, 65, 204–12
  Greece 35, 45
  Grand Mufti 139, 166
  Nursi 247–8
  Quṭb 216–22
  Turkish scholarship 57, 61, 63
  Vatican 44
  independence war 203, 205, 231, 243
Salafism 56, 63, 131, 134, 136–7, 155, 160–1, 164–5, 167–8, 171–3, 175–6, 178, 233, 246, 264–5
  decline 14–18
  modern scholarship 173–8
  origins 155–62
Said, Edward 4
Sandals in prayer 139–40
Saraç, Emin 40 (footnote 70), 42 (footenote 82), 258
Saudi Arabia 154, 162–73
al-Ṣayyādī, Abū al-Hudā 159, 163
Scawen Blunt, Wilfred 6
Schmitt, Carl 209–11, 232, 235–6, 246
Sebilürreşad 20, 23, 31, 34–6, 58, 65, 82, 115, 125, 130, 260, 278
Sencer, Eşref Kuşçubaşı 33–4, 53, 68, 195
Sèvres, Treaty of 35, 192, 194
Şevketi, Eşref Efendizade 112, 114
Shaltūt, Maḥmūd 45
Sharīʿatī, ʿAlī 233
al-Sharīf, Ṣālih 33, 163, 199
al-Shawkānī, Muḥammad 14, 16, 151 (foonote 114), 156, 164, 172 (foonote 235)
Sırat-ı Müstakim 20, 28, 30, 81, 86, 190
Smith, Wilfred Cantwell 4, 165, 245
Sufism 20, 29–30, 47–9, 54, 79–81, 95, 109, 117, 127, 130, 161–2, 172, 174–5, 231, 243, 252, 264, 266
Sultan Abdülhamid 19, 40, 60, 159, 209
Sultan Vahideddin (Mehmed VI) 42
Syria 65, 67, 73, 131

takfīr 136, 151, 161, 173, 231, 235–7, 239, 243
tajdīd 7, 9, 16, 39, 78, 131
tajsīm 55, 132, 135, 148, 165
taqlīd 16, 28, 39, 104, 136, 156, 161, 207
Targan, Şerif Muhiddin 70, 126
Teşkilat-ı Mahsusa 32–3, 195, 248
al-Tilmisānī, ʿUmar 239, 258
Toynbee, Arnold 114
turāthiyyūn 213
Turkey
  Early republican ideology 2, 6, 23, 46, 121, 198, 204, 212, 224, 242, 246
  Iqbāl 120, 123
  Islam and post-war democratisation 65, 246–53
  Nationalism 2–3, 10, 38, 61, 71, 87, 193, 197–8, 241
  Nursi 246–53
  Students in Cairo 52, 64–8, 73, 245, 253, 268
  Trajectory of Islamic thought 253–64
Türk Yurdu 20–1

al-ʿUrwa al-Wuthqā 28, 88, 90, 139 (footnote 43), 196

Wahhabism 16, 78, 160, 162–3, 166–7
Wajdī, Muḥammad Farīd 29, 46, 60, 62, 65, 78, 80, 86–7, 105–7
waḥdat al-wujūd 30, 106, 138
wājib al-wujūd 95, 101, 106
waqf 51, 140, 172, 210, 215
Walīullāh, Shāh 14, 16
Weber, Max 243, 266

Yarın 45, 66, 84
Yolcu, Abdullah 263–4
Young Turks 13, 256

Other titles in the series

Agents of the Hidden Imam: Forging Twelver Shi'ism, 850–950 CE, Edmund Hayes
*Revealed Sciences: The Natural Sciences in Islam in Seventeenth-Century Morocco*Justin K. Stearns
Agricultural Innovation in the Early Islamic World: The Diffusion of Crops and Farming Techniques, 700–1100, Andrew M. Watson
Muslim Tradition: Studies in Chronology, Provenance and Authorship of Early Hadith, G. H. A. Juynboll
Social History of Timbuktu: The Role of Muslim Scholars and Notables 1400–1900, Elias N. Saad
Sex and Society in Islam: Birth Control before the Nineteenth Century, B. F. Musallam
Towns and Townsmen of Ottoman Anatolia: Trade, Crafts and Food Production in an Urban Setting 1520–1650, Suraiya Faroqhi
Unlawful Gain and Legitimate Profit in Islamic Law: Riba, Gharar and Islamic Banking, Nabil A. Saleh
Men of Modest Substance: House Owners and House Property in Seventeenth-Century Ankara and Kayseri, Suraiya Faroqhi
Roman, Provincial and Islamic Law: The Origins of the Islamic Patronate, Patricia Crone
Economic Life in Ottoman Jerusalem, Amnon Cohen
Mannerism in Arabic Poetry: A Structural Analysis of Selected Texts (3rd Century AH/9th Century AD – 5th Century AH/11th Century AD), Stefan Sperl
The Rise and Rule of Tamerlane, Beatrice Forbes Manz
Popular Culture in Medieval Cairo, Boaz Shoshan
Early Philosophical Shiism: The Ismaili Neoplatonism of Abu Ya'qub Al-Sijistani, Paul E. Walker
Indian Merchants and Eurasian Trade, 1600–1750, Stephen Frederic Dale
Palestinian Peasants and Ottoman Officials: Rural Administration around Sixteenth-Century Jerusalem, Amy Singer
Arabic Historical Thought in the Classical Period, Tarif Khalidi
Mongols and Mamluks: The Mamluk-Ilkhanid War, 1260–1281, Reuven Amitai-Preiss
Knowledge and Social Practice in Medieval Damascus, 1190–1350, Michael Chamberlain
The Politics of Households in Ottoman Egypt: The Rise of the Qazdağlis, Jane Hathaway
Hierarchy and Egalitarianism in Islamic Thought, Louise Marlow
Commodity and Exchange in the Mongol Empire: A Cultural History of Islamic Textiles, Thomas T. Allsen
State and Provincial Society in the Ottoman Empire: Mosul, 1540–1834, Dina Rizk Khoury
The Mamluks in Egyptian Politics and Society, Thomas Philipp and Ulrich Haarmann (eds.)
The Delhi Sultanate: A Political and Military History, Peter Jackson

European and Islamic Trade in the Early Ottoman State: The Merchants of Genoa and Turkey, Kate Fleet
The Ottoman City between East and West: Aleppo, Izmir, and Istanbul, Edhem Eldem, Daniel Goffman, and Bruce Masters
The Politics of Trade in Safavid Iran: Silk for Silver, 1600–1730, Rudolph P. Matthee
The Idea of Idolatry and the Emergence of Islam: From Polemic to History, G. R. Hawting
A Monetary History of the Ottoman Empire, Şevket Pamuk
Classical Arabic Biography: The Heirs of the Prophets in the Age of Al-Ma'mun, Michael Cooperson
Empire and Elites after the Muslim Conquest: The Transformation of Northern Mesopotamia, Chase F. Robinson
Poverty and Charity in Medieval Islam: Mamluk Egypt, 1250–1517, Adam Sabra
Culture and Conquest in Mongol Eurasia, Thomas T. Allsen
Christians and Jews in the Ottoman Arab World: The Roots of Sectarianism, Bruce Masters
Arabic Administration in Norman Sicily: The Royal Diwan, Jeremy Johns
Law, Society and Culture in the Maghrib, 1300–1500, David S. Powers
Revival and Reform in Islam: The Legacy of Muhammad al-Shawkani, Bernard Haykel
Tolerance and Coercion in Islam: Interfaith Relations in the Muslim Tradition, Yohanan Friedmann
Guns for the Sultan: Military Power and the Weapons Industry in the Ottoman Empire, Gábor Ágoston
Marriage, Money and Divorce in Medieval Islamic Society, Yossef Rapoport
The Empire of the Qara Khitai in Eurasian History: Between China and the Islamic World, Michal Biran
Domesticity and Power in the Early Mughal World, Ruby Lal
Power, Politics and Religion in Timurid Iran, Beatrice Forbes Manz
Postal Systems in the Pre-Modern Islamic World, Adam J. Silverstein
Kingship and Ideology in the Islamic and Mongol Worlds, Anne F. Broadbridge
Justice, Punishment and the Medieval Muslim Imagination, Christian Lange
The Shiites of Lebanon under Ottoman Rule, 1516–1788, Stefan Winter
Women and Slavery in the Late Ottoman Empire, Madeline Zilfi
The Second Ottoman Empire: Political and Social Transformation in the Early Modern World, Baki Tezcan
The Legendary Biographies of Tamerlane: Islam and Heroic Apocrypha in Central Asia, Ron Sela
Non-Muslims in the Early Islamic Empire: From Surrender to Coexistence, Milka Levy-Rubin
The Origins of the Shi'a: Identity, Ritual, and Sacred Space in Eighth-Century Kufa, Najam Haider
Politics, Law, and Community in Islamic Thought: The Taymiyyan Moment, Ovamir Anjum
The Power of Oratory in the Medieval Muslim World, Linda G. Jones

Animals in the Qur'an, Sarra Tlili
The Logic of Law Making in Islam: Women and Prayer in the Legal Tradition, Behnam Sadeghi
Empire and Power in the Reign of Süleyman: Narrating the Sixteenth-Century Ottoman World, Kaya Şahin
Law and Piety in Medieval Islam, Megan H. Reid
Women and the Transmission of Religious Knowledge in Islam, Asma Sayeed
The New Muslims of Post-Conquest Iran: Tradition, Memory, and Conversion, Sarah Bowen Savant
The Mamluk City in the Middle East: History, Culture, and the Urban Landscape, Nimrod Luz
Disability in the Ottoman Arab World, 1500–1800, Sara Scalenghe
The Holy City of Medina: Sacred Space in Early Islamic Arabia, Harry Munt
Muslim Midwives: The Craft of Birthing in the Premodern Middle East, Avner Giladi
Doubt in Islamic Law: A History of Legal Maxims, Interpretation, and Islamic Criminal Law, Intisar A. Rabb
The Second Formation of Islamic Law: The Hanafi School in the Early Modern Ottoman Empire, Guy Burak
Sexual Violation in Islamic Law: Substance, Evidence, and Procedure, Hina Azam
Gender Hierarchy in the Qur'an: Medieval Interpretations, Modern Responses, Karen Bauer
Intellectual Networks in Timurid Iran: Sharaf al-Din 'Ali Yazdi and the Islamicate Republic of Letters, Ilker Evrim Binbaş
Authority and Identity in Medieval Islamic Historiography: Persian Histories from the Peripheries, Mimi Hanaoka
The Economics of Ottoman Justice: Settlement and Trial in the Sharia Courts, Top of Form, Metin Coşgel and Boğaç Ergene
The Mystics of al-Andalus: Ibn Barrajan and Islamic Thought in the Twelfth Century, Yousef Casewit
Muhammad's Heirs: The Rise of Muslim Scholarly Communities, 622–950, Jonathan E. Brockopp
The First of the Modern Ottomans: The Intellectual History of Ahmed Vasif, Ethan Menchinger
Non-Muslim Provinces under Early Islam: Islamic Rule and Iranian Legitimacy in Armenia and Caucasian Albania, Alison Vacca
Women and the Making of the Mongol Empire, Anne F. Broadbridge
Slavery and Empire in Central Asia, Jeff Eden
Christianity in Fifteenth-Century Iraq, Thomas A. Carlson
Child Custody in Islamic Law: Theory and Practice in Egypt Since the Sixteenth Century, Ahmed Fekry Ibrahim
Ibadi Muslims of North Africa: Manuscripts, Mobilization and the Making of a Written Tradition, Paul M. Love Jr
Islamic Law of the Sea: Freedom of Navigation and Passage Rights in Islamic Thought, Hassan S. Khalilieh

Law and Politics under the Abassids: An Intellectual Portrait of al-Juwayni, Sohaira Z. M. Siddiqui
Friends of the Emir: Non-Muslim State Officials in Premodern Islamic Thought, Luke B. Yarbrough
The Crisis of Kingship in Late Medieval Islam: Persian Emigres and the Making of Ottoman Sovereignty, Christopher Markiewicz
Collective Liability in Islam: The ʿĀqila and Blood Money Payments, Nurit Tsafrir
Arabic Poetics: Aesthetic Experience in Classical Arabic Literature, Lara Harb
The Sufi Saint of Jam: History, Religion and Politics of a Sunni Shrine in Shi'i Iran, Shivan Mahendrarajah
Opposing the Imām: The Legacy of the Nawāṣib in Islamic Literature, Nebil Husayn
Agents of the Hidden Imam: Forging Twelver Shiʿism, 850–950 CE, Edmund Hayes
Islamic Law in Circulation: Shāfiʿī Texts across the Indian Ocean and the Mediterranean, Mahmood Kooria